HELLENISTIC ASTROLOGY

The Study of Fate and Fortune

———— ✸ ————

CHRIS BRENNAN

Amor Fati Publications | Denver, Colorado

© 2017 by Chris Brennan
All rights reserved
First edition, published February 10, 2017.

ISBN-13: 978-0-9985889-0-2 (paper)
ISBN-10: 0-9985889-0-3 (paper)

Publisher's Cataloging-in-Publication data

Names: Brennan, Christopher W., author.
Title: Hellenistic astrology : the study of fate and fortune / Chris Brennan.
Description: Includes bibliographical references and index. | Denver, CO: Amor Fati Publications, 2017.
Identifiers: ISBN 978-0-9985889-0-2 | LCCN 2017901117
Subjects: LCSH Astrology--History. | Hellenism. | Philosophy, Ancient. | BISAC BODY, MIND & SPIRIT / Astrology / General
Classification: LCC BF1671 .B74 2017 | DDC 133.5/09/01--dc23

This book has been typeset in Arno Pro 12/15 pt.

Printed on acid-free paper.

For Katie, Vickie, and Billy.

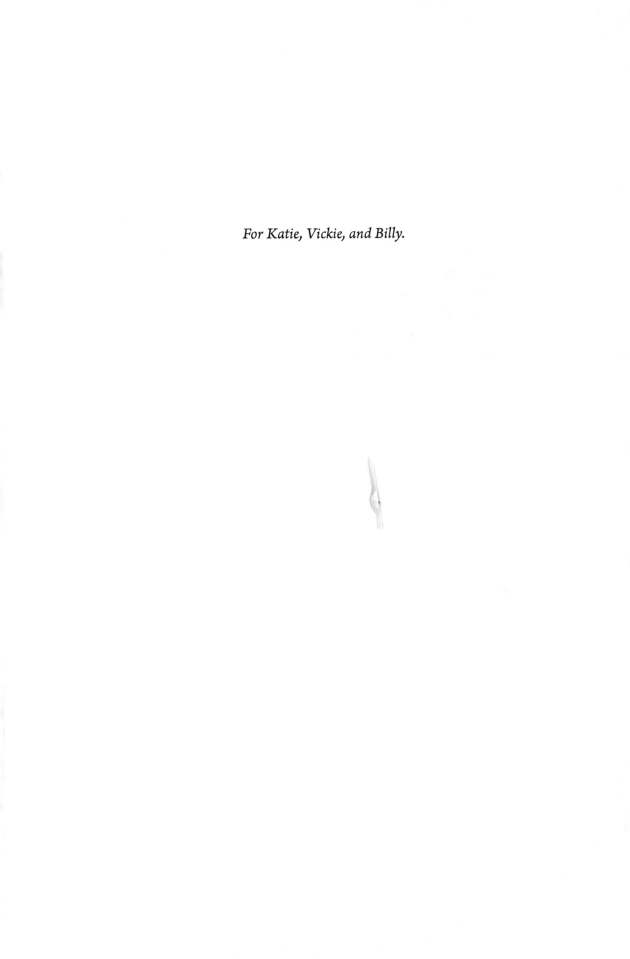

Those who engage in the prediction of the future and the truth, having acquired a soul that is free and not enslaved, do not think highly of fortune, and do not devote themselves to hope, nor are they afraid of death, but instead they live their lives undaunted by disturbance by training their souls to be confident, and neither rejoice excessively in the case of good, nor become depressed in the case of bad, but instead are content with whatever is present. Those who do not desire the impossible are capable of bearing that which is preordained through their own self-mastery; and being estranged from all pleasure or praise, they become established as soldiers of fate.

—Vettius Valens
c. 175 CE

TABLE OF CONTENTS

LIST OF FIGURES AND TABLES

FIGURES

TABLES

Details for Charts 1–120 are located in Appendix: Chart Data on page 595.

FOREWORD

———— ✹ ————

It is with great pleasure that I welcome the publication of *Hellenistic Astrology: The Study of Fate and Fortune* by Chris Brennan. This book presents a comprehensive overview of the original doctrines of Western horoscopic astrology and is a stunning and remarkable achievement for his first work.

I met Chris when he entered Kepler College, fresh out of high school, just nineteen years old. Before long, all of the faculty members recognized the brilliant and incisive mind within this shy and quiet young man. He had a fiery passion for learning astrology, and his flame consumed all we had to teach, integrating the known, but also questioning the given, and ever pushing into the yet-uncharted horizons of the discipline.

However, his first love was not Hellenistic astrology. I smile remembering his conviction that modern psychological astrology was "where it was at," and how he couldn't wait to begin studying it further. He tried organizing his classmates to protest the requirement that they had to take a prerequisite class because that antiquated old-school astrology was "just a waste of time." But the curriculum prevailed, and when he entered my Hellenistic classroom in the winter of 2004, it was as if he suddenly and unexpectedly rediscovered the place where he knew he had always belonged.

From that moment, the shooting star flew across the heavens with lightning speed. He quickly took in the entire course as well as the following one, and then, while still enrolled at Kepler College, he moved across the country to live for several years at the headquarters of Project Hindsight. There he inhaled Hellenistic astrology and classical philosophy daily, surrounded by and participating in the coterie of thinkers who came to visit, discuss, and study with Robert Schmidt and Ellen Black. I have watched Chris read the primary sources over and over; track the transmission of doctrines through the various authors and cultures; note and compare who said what, when, and where; study ancient Greek on his own; pursue endless footnotes; keep abreast of the new scholarship; test the techniques and concepts; come up with his own ideas; and question everything until he himself had made sense of the material.

Over the past decade, Chris and I have spent countless hours in conversation discussing, reconstructing, and translating the texts. During this time, I have encouraged his progress and witnessed his growing expertise. Much of our study has been collaborative as I also have been writing a book, *Ancient Astrology: A Practitioners Guide,* a step-by-step workbook for the application of Hellenistic techniques to one's own chart. These two books will be companion pieces with some overlaps and some differences, but our hopes are that together they will provide both the theoretical and practical tools for the study of Hellenistic astrology.

In the ensuing years, Chris has introduced many hundreds of astrologers around the world to Hellenistic astrology through his online course, articles, podcasts, lectures, and websites. Building upon the seminal works of Robert Schmidt and James Holden, who during the last twenty years have produced English translations of most of the original texts of western astrology, Chris Brennan's book advances our understanding by synthesizing and integrating the history, philosophy, and techniques of Hellenistic astrology in one place and in a way that is accessible to the contemporary astrologer.

Hellenistic Astrology: The Study of Fate and Fortune carries the wisdom of the past forward into the future, providing a solid foundation to support an ever-deepening understanding of our discipline. Chris Brennan has gifted us with an invaluable contribution that will enhance and expand the astrology of the twenty-first century.

Demetra George, M.A. (Classics)
Recipient of 2002 UAC Regulus Award for
Theory and Understanding in Astrology
November 2016

ACKNOWLEDGMENTS

———————— ✸ ————————

I started working on this book ten years ago, using a reasonably auspicious election on September 11, 2006 at 6:12 a.m. in Cumberland, Maryland, USA. I have a lot of people to thank who have helped at different stages of the process.

First I want to thank my mother, Vickie, and my sister, Katie, for their support and encouragement over the years after I decided to pursue an education and eventually a career as an astrologer, starting while I was still in high school. It was only through their help that I was able to attend Kepler College shortly after I turned nineteen, and if I did not have the good fortune to have such a supportive family then I know that I would not have made it this far. In dedicating this book to them I fulfill a promise I made to Katie in one of the last conversations that I had with her, shortly before she passed away in October of 2007.

I would also like to thank the many astrologers who were involved in putting together the degree program for Kepler College, which was offered for about a decade in the Seattle area starting in the year 2000. The program sparked my interest in the history of astrology, showed me the value of studying different traditions of astrology, and taught me how to think critically. I arrived at Kepler wanting to study modern psychological astrology, but when I got to the second year of the program they said that I had to spend a semester taking an introductory course on Hellenistic and Indian astrology, which was co-taught by Demetra George and Dennis Harness. I actually protested this at first, as I had no interest in studying older traditions of astrology, because I assumed that they were outdated and obsolete, and thus that there was nothing to be gained from them. Fortunately, the Kepler faculty told me I had no choice because the psychological track was not ready yet, so I begrudgingly took the course. Very quickly I realized that my presumptions about the older traditions had been wrong, and that there was much there of value. By early 2005 I had dedicated myself to the study of Hellenistic astrology.

I owe much to my friend and mentor Demetra George, whom I first studied Hellenistic astrology with, and who has been a constant source of support and guidance as we have continued to explore this tradition together over the past decade. I also want to express my appreciation for my friend Benjamin Dykes, whose work on traditional astrology over the past decade has been an inspiration, and whom I have benefited much from collaborating with, especially in our work together on the planetary joys. Together Ben and Demetra and I have had many successful and productive periods of collaboration in reviving traditional astrology in recent years, especially with some of the work that was done on reconstructing the aspect doctrine of Antiochus and the conditions of bonification and maltreatment, which I will present later in this volume. Demetra and Ben are my two closest collaborators, and there are many crucial ways in which this book would be vastly different and inferior if I did not know them.

I would like to thank Bill Johnston for inviting me out to live at Project Hindsight in Cumberland, Maryland in the summer of 2005, and for seeing my potential as an up-and-coming student of Hellenistic astrology. I am indebted to the late Robert Victor Gross for partially sponsoring me during my time at Project Hindsight, and for sharing his library with me. I'm also grateful to the late Alan White for his support during my time in Cumberland, as well as his no-nonsense approach to talking about and promoting Hellenistic astrology, which I benefited from when one of his lectures led to it being taught at Kepler. Thank you to Curtis Manwaring for designing the Delphic Oracle software program and giving me access to it while I was at Hindsight, as it helped to accelerate my studies of the timing techniques, and I used it to calculate many of the time-lord periods that appear later in this work. Thanks also to my close friends Nick Dagan Best and Meredith Garstin; I will always look back on the time that the three of us spent at Hindsight reading Valens out loud together, testing the techniques, and discussing astrology as one of the best times of my life. To Meredith I owe particular thanks for her help in making diagrams over the years, several of which appear in this book.

Most of all I would like to thank the central figures of Project Hindsight, Robert Schmidt and his wife Ellen Black, for graciously hosting me for two years in their home, providing me with ample opportunity for research, and for the immensely important work that they have done in reviving Hellenistic astrology. To Robert I owe the greatest debt of gratitude for the many mornings he spent on the back porch of Project Hindsight talking to me, answering my questions, taking the time to help me with my own research projects, and for sharing portions of his vast knowledge with me. Without his tireless work and research over the past twenty-five years, this book would not have been possible, nor would the revival of Hellenistic astrology for that matter. While we have since gone our separate ways, and do not always see eye to eye in our views on Hellenistic astrology, I have an immense amount of respect and gratitude for the work that he has done.

I would like to thank my editor, Aaron Cheak, whose extensive work and valuable feedback on the manuscript of this book over the past year has improved it far beyond what I could have accomplished on my own. I would also like to single out Levente László to give thanks for his many comments and corrections on the final version of the manuscript. There were also a number of other friends and students who gave helpful feedback or worked with me on research projects that contributed to the book over the years, whom I will name alphabetically: Anthony Capoccia, Ricardo Carmona, John Cole, Austin Coppock, Tania Daniels, Adam Elenbaas, Andrea Gehrz, Eduardo Gramaglia, Robert Hand, Daniel Larkin, Charles Obert, Lars Panaro, Tom Pommerel, Maria Mateus, Kenneth Miller, Michael Douglas Neely, Scott Silverman, and Patrick Watson. Any errors or deficiencies that remain in the book are my own.

Thank you to Shannon García for lending her exceptional design skills in order to do the typesetting and layout of the book, and for assisting me to finalize the arrangement of the diagrams, chart examples, and especially the index. I'm very grateful to Paula Belluomini for her brilliant work in designing the book cover, as well as for helping me to create the final versions of many of the diagrams. Thank you to Kenneth Hirst for designing the Astro font that I used to depict the planets and zodiacal signs in the diagrams and chart examples, as well as for his permission to use it here. Thanks also to Radoje Pejović for his help in illustrating parts of the central figure on the cover. The cover is partially inspired by the image of the Goddess Fortuna and the wheel of fortune that appeared on the cover of the sheet music for Carl Orff's *Carmina Burana*.

I will be eternally grateful to my partner Leisa Schaim for her support and patience as I have periodically spent long periods of time researching and writing this book at different points over what is nearly a decade now that we have known each other. The past year of writing a completely new draft of the book from scratch in order to adopt a more consistent tone has been particularly intense, and I doubt that I could have done it without the environment of love and mutual support that the two of us have created together over the past several years. She also lent her Virgo Moon to this project, and as a result saved us all from many, many typos.

Thanks to all of the students and clients whom I have worked with over the past decade, as the feedback you have provided about the techniques and concepts presented in this book have proved to be invaluable.

Finally, I want to thank all of the astrologers, scribes, philologists, translators, and other people who have transmitted and preserved the texts of the astrological tradition over the past few dozen centuries. They are the reason why we have any ancient texts to analyze at all, and the overview of Hellenistic astrology presented in this book would not be possible without their labors.

Chris Brennan
November 2016

Introduction

More than two thousand years have passed since Hellenistic astrology first began to be practiced in the ancient world. The origins of this system are mysterious, although we know that it emerged in the Hellenistic period sometime after the conquests of Alexander the Great, and that it reached the height of its popularity during the time of the Roman Empire. It is the type of astrology that was in use in the Mediterranean region when the gospels of the New Testament were written in the first century CE, and like Christianity, it has had an enduring impact on western culture over the past two millennia. Hellenistic astrology represents the origins and foundations of western astrology, since most of the basic techniques and precepts that astrologers still take for granted today can be traced back to this period. The purpose of this book, then, is to provide an overview of the original tradition of western astrology.

Since the time of the Roman Empire, astrology has passed through many different cultures and languages. In some ways, there are many similarities between Hellenistic astrology and modern astrology. In particular, the fourfold system of interpreting astrological charts that incorporates the planets, signs of the zodiac, aspects, and the twelve houses first made its appearance in the Hellenistic era around the first century BCE, and this approach still very much characterizes the core of western astrology today. As we will see, many of the meanings and qualities that modern astrologers ascribe to different components in astrological charts were first defined by astrologers who lived around the first century of the common era. The advantage of looking back into the origins of some of these concepts is that it can help astrologers to understand where these techniques came from, how they were first developed, and in some instances, how they can be used more effectively today.

Despite these similarities, Hellenistic astrology is in many important respects quite different from the type of mainstream modern astrology that is practiced today. Some of these differences have to do with the transmission of astrology over the past two thousand years, and the changes that would occur each time the system was translated from one language to another. Each time astrology was transmitted, it changed, and some new concepts were added, while others were lost. Translation is an imperfect art, and it was made even more complicated prior to modern times by the fact that books had to be copied by hand, and sometimes only a few texts from earlier traditions would be available in any era. Part of the purpose of the modern revival of Hellenistic astrology is to bypass the past several hundred years of the accumulated astrological tradition and look back directly at the earliest versions of western astrology through an analysis of the surviving textual tradition. Often what one finds is that instead of the system appearing to be less complex or less refined, it is the opposite; we discover many important and powerful techniques that were lost in transmission over the centuries. While this does not negate some of the important developments that have taken place in the more recent astrological traditions, it does force us to abandon the assumption that contemporary astrology is the result of a linear development of the subject that has culminated in the form that it is in today. A recurring theme among astrologers who have taken part in the revival of Hellenistic astrology over the past two decades is the realization that some things were lost in the transmission that we didn't even know were missing, and in some instances, these are techniques that can do things that we didn't even think were possible.

The purpose of this book is to provide an overview of the history, philosophy, and techniques of Hellenistic astrology. Since this is one of the first works of its kind in modern times, I felt the need to attempt to write something that could provide a broad foundation for future studies. While the size and scope of this book may convey the pretense that it is a fully comprehensive work on the subject, in reality it is only an introduction to a vast field; there are many facets of the tradition that I will either have to omit entirely or only give the briefest of treatments. It is thus a starting point for future studies, and it is meant to initiate the reader into the subject so that they can independently engage some of the earliest source texts of the tradition. By providing a guide that will help orient and contextualize readings, my hope is to spur further interest in the study of the subject in general, and to make some of the research that has already been done up to this point more accessible.

My primary intended audience is astrologers who are interested in learning about the practice of Hellenistic astrology, although I hope that those who specialize in the study of ancient history or philosophy will find something of value here as well. One of the tensions that I had when writing the practical sections of this book was between the desire to write a purely historical survey of how Hellenistic astrology was practiced back then, versus the desire to write an instructional manual on how some of the techniques can be used by contemporary astrologers today, based on my experience in using them over the past decade. It is always a potential liability when a practitioner writes a work that deals with topics ordinarily studied in an academic historical context; however, I believe that my perspective as a practicing astrologer can also be an asset in some instances because it allows me to engage the material with an earnestness that might be lacking if I did not think that the material had any practical value or validity. I have attempted to balance the tensions between my role as a historian and my role as an astrologer as much as possible, and while I may alternate between emphasizing historical or practical concerns at different points, I have tried to be very careful about noting when I am speaking about certain techniques from the perspective of my own experience. In most instances in the practical sections, my goal is simply to demonstrate how many of the techniques work when you apply them in contemporary practice as the ancient texts instruct, and I think in most instances my faithfulness to the textual tradition will be evident. Ultimately, my primary goal as an astrologer is to revive a tradition of astrology that has been dead for centuries and reconnect contemporary astrologers with it; indeed, the extent to which a person can understand and practice an authentic form of Hellenistic astrology in modern times will be the primary litmus test for the success of this book.

Having said that, one point that I should acknowledge from the outset is that reviving the practice of Hellenistic astrology requires quite a lot of reconstruction. Only a relatively small number of ancient astrological texts have survived into modern times, and many of these are damaged or fragmentary. No single text outlines everything, and they often use technical terms that are not clearly defined, and only rarely demonstrated. Sometimes we can compare how different authors use the same term or technique, and then develop a better understanding of it based on the areas where they agree, while other times these comparisons highlight disparities in the tradition where different authors will use the same concept in different ways. There is a remarkable level of both coherency and diversity in the surviving texts, and for this reason I will alternate between referring to Hellenistic astrology as a system and as a tradition. This is because in some instances, we are reconstructing a lost system that many different astrologers shared in common, while in other cases we are simply documenting the different ways that a long tradition of astrology was practiced by a diverse group of people over several centuries. It is important to recognize both the areas of consistency as well as the areas of diversity, and not to overemphasize one or the other.

This is why some understanding of the historical backdrop of the tradition is necessary in order to recover the techniques, because it provides crucial information about who was using which methods, and there is a long process of textual analysis that must be undertaken before any conclusions can be drawn about the practice. Fortunately, the groundwork for many of these studies was laid by philologists and other academic historians over the past century. It is only in the past twenty years or so that some people in the astrological community have started to explore this material. What distinguishes this book is that it is one of the first studies on the subject written for a general audience of astrologers in modern times. While part of our goal is to revive the practice of Hellenistic astrology, it must be acknowledged that we have an incomplete picture, and as such whatever we create will partially be shaped by the limited number of texts that we have at our disposal, as well as by our interpretations of those texts. In some instances, those who research Hellenistic astrology and attempt to reconstruct its practice will come to different conclusions about what the original texts said or meant, and sometimes this will result in variant approaches to Hellenistic astrology in modern times. This is a natural part of the process of the transmission and revival of the older traditions, and it is a process that many other generations of astrologers have gone through previously, over the past several thousand years. While we may not be able to perfectly recreate what the practice of Hellenistic astrology once was, we can certainly come close. As long as we try to do so with the utmost care and consideration, we will be successful in genuinely reconnecting the ancient traditions with the modern ones, even if only in part. My goal here is to present, to the best of my understanding, both (1) a narrative that describes what Hellenistic astrology was, where it came from, and how it was practiced; and (2) a demonstration of how it can be used again today.

This book assumes that the reader already has some basic familiarity with modern astrology, although since part of the purpose is to explore the fundamentals of western astrology, my hope is that it could also act as a reasonably useful introduction to the subject of astrology as a whole. Part of the excitement surrounding Hellenistic astrology over the past twenty years has been the instances where it either represents a radical departure from modern astrology, or where it gives insight into the origins and conceptual motivation underlying techniques that astrologers have long taken for granted. There are many techniques that astrologers use today, and yet they don't really know where they came from, how they were developed, or what the original conceptual motivation was for why certain things mean what they are supposed to mean. In Hellenistic astrology we find the answers to many of these questions, although sometimes in the process it requires a radical revisioning of how one practices astrology. Sometimes this involves unlearning concepts that one has previously learned and taken for granted as a contemporary practitioner of astrology. While this can be a difficult or disorienting process for some astrologers, the benefit is that it can result in a vastly improved ability to interpret astrological charts. Of course, for those who read this book without any presumptions about what astrology is or how it works, some of these points may not be as striking; however, you will be in the enviable position of having a clean slate to work from without having to unlearn various premises that others take for granted. Either way, our approach here will be to go straight to the heart of the original foundations of all of the major concepts in the earliest traditions of western astrology.

Another one of the challenges in reviving Hellenistic astrology in modern times is that there are many different technical terms in Greek and Latin that we don't have equivalents for in modern astrology. This sometimes necessitates the introduction of new terms in English to use in contemporary discussions about those ancient techniques. In other instances, there may already be a term that is used in modern astrology that is related to an ancient concept, and we have a choice between using the modern term or coming up with a brand new one. This has been an area of uncertainty over the past few decades, with some translators opting to introduce a completely new technical vocabulary for nearly every concept in Hellenistic astrology, in order to fully convey all of the subtleties and nuances of the original language; however, this sometimes occurs at the expense of the readability for modern audiences. Other translators have simply adopted modern terminology whenever possible in order to make the ancient texts easier to understand, although in some instances this has obscured the original meaning underlying the texts, when the modern terms do not accurately convey the original concepts. I have tried to adopt a middle ground approach between these two extremes by introducing new technical terms when necessary, but using modern equivalents when I feel that the meaning is sufficiently close. My general rule of thumb is that unless introducing a new term would make a notable improvement in the understanding of the concept, it is not necessary to reinvent the wheel.

That being said, from the perspective of a modern astrologer, there are still going to be a lot of new technical terms that one will have to learn in studying Hellenistic astrology, and there are a number of extended discussions about why I have proposed or chosen one word or another in order to represent certain concepts. Since part of the purpose of this book is to bring Hellenistic astrology into the mainstream of contemporary astrological practice, I have attempted to balance word choices that convey the meaning of the original Greek term with those that sound familiar (rather than foreign) to practicing astrologers. A lot of very thoughtful work on issues surrounding the terminology in Hellenistic astrology has already been carried out by Robert Schmidt, and in many instances I have adopted translation conventions that he first introduced. However, in some areas I have disagreed with Schmidt's conventions and introduced my own, and while I have some concern about having multiple terms floating around for the same concept, I trust that this is something the astrological community will eventually resolve on its own as these techniques become commonplace in contemporary practice.

Part of the thesis of this book is that, at its core, Hellenistic astrology was originally designed as a complex system that uses celestial phenomena in order to study an individual's fate. This includes information not just about a person's character or psyche, but also about the concrete external circumstances and events that take place during the course of their life. What is fascinating about this is not only that someone in the ancient world would attempt to do something as incredible as design a system for studying fate, but that they were successful, and that the system actually works. The first few chapters of this book deal with the history surrounding how the system was developed, the time period in which it was practiced, and the astrologers who are our primary sources for recovering it. This is followed by a chapter on some philosophical issues that are relevant to the practice of ancient astrology, including a discussion about the role of fate and its conceptualization in ancient astrological practice. I then give an extended overview of the basic concepts of astrology, focusing on the fourfold system of planets, signs, aspects, and houses. This section is capped off by a long and somewhat complicated essay on the origins of the different approaches to house division, which is necessary due to some ongoing debates about the subject in modern times. Afterwards we move into a discussion about intermediate techniques for interpreting birth charts and synthesizing different placements, which allow us to articulate some of the most distinctive features of an individual's life. Finally, towards the end of the book, we will discuss some basic and advanced timing techniques—known in the Hellenistic tradition as time-lord systems—for determining when events that are indicated in the birth chart will occur in a person's life.

In the technical chapters, I present a number of example charts in order to demonstrate how the different techniques work in practice. I've tried to use a blend of contemporary charts belonging to eminent individuals as well as personal charts from my own private files. While there are pros and cons for using either category, my approach here is in keeping with the Hellenistic practice of including both notable and non-notable nativities in the instructional manuals. To that end, I have tried to pattern my presentation of the example charts after the way they are presented in some of the ancient manuals, especially that of the second-century astrologer Vettius Valens and the instructional texts that he wrote for his students. The purpose of this is to demonstrate not just how the techniques work, but also to partially recreate how they are presented in the ancient instructional manuals, thus providing another preparatory step towards reading the texts on their own. While this can sometimes seem cumbersome compared to modern approaches, my hope is that it will help to create a more authentic and immersive experience.

One of the most striking realizations that people have when they begin to study the textbooks of the ancient astrologers is that life is still surprisingly similar now to how it was back then. Many of the core concerns that people have about their lives today are fundamentally the same, and this is part of the reason why a system that was created more than two thousand years ago for studying the lives of individuals can still be useful now. In point of fact, there is something about the system of astrology created during the Hellenistic period that was so compelling in its ability to clearly articulate the fundamental facets of human life, that parts of it have survived for two millennia. Although only part of this system made it into modern times, it is now possible to revive the rest of it and thus reunite the ancient and modern traditions. By looking back into the past, we can create a better astrology for the future.

CHAPTER 1
EARLY ASTROLOGY IN MESOPOTAMIA AND EGYPT

Mesopotamian Astrology

The origins of western astrology can be traced back about 4,000 years to ancient Mesopotamia, a geographical area that roughly coincides with what is now modern-day Iraq.[1] Around this time, people began recording observations about correlations between celestial movements and earthly events. These observations were usually recorded as simple celestial omens in the form of conditional statements that followed the formula "if *x*, then *y*." A hypothetical celestial omen might read: "if there is an eclipse, then the king will die."[2] In contemporary discussions, the first part of the statement is referred to as the *protasis*, while the second part is called the *apodosis*. The Mesopotamian astrologers began recording hundreds of these types of omens on tiny clay tablets, using the wedge-shaped script called cuneiform. Many of the earliest surviving omens that were collected are lunar eclipse omens that date to the Old

---

[1] While the term "Babylonian" is sometimes used interchangeably in some astrological and academic texts to refer to the people who lived in Mesopotamia, or to refer to the traditions of astrology that originated in that region (e.g. "Babylonian astrology"), this can be misleading since several different cultures and empires were in control of this area during the period under consideration. Between the third and first millennium BCE the area was incorporated into the Sumerian, Akkadian, Babylonian, Assyrian, Neo-Assyrian, Neo-Babylonian, Achaemenid, Seleucid, and Parthian empires. For the sake of simplicity, I will use the generic term "Mesopotamian" here to refer to this astrological tradition, while occasionally specifying specific cultures when certain innovations are mentioned.

[2] For examples of actual eclipse omens see Rochberg-Halton, *Aspects of Babylonian Celestial Divination*. On p. 94 one omen reads "If an eclipse occurs on the 14th of Du'ūzu and begins and clears in the south: A great king will die."

Babylonian period (2000–1600 BCE).[3] Eventually, large libraries of celestial omens were amassed, and the astrologers began standardizing their collections by creating compilations, the most popular of which was known as the *Enūma Anu Enlil*.[4]

Despite the formulaic nature of the astrological omens, the astrologers themselves did not necessarily think that there was a direct causal connection between celestial and earthly events. Instead, the celestial omens acted as signs or indications of the future that were sent by the gods, and not as causes of the events that they correlated with.[5] The stars in particular were seen as a sort of "heavenly writing" that was inscribed across the sky. Naturally, as Rochberg points out, "the notion of the stars as a heavenly script implies their capacity to be read and interpreted."[6] Thus, in the earliest Babylonian strata of the astrological tradition, astrology was seen to be a type of language. For many Mesopotamian cultures, it became one of the languages through which the gods communicated their intentions to humankind.[7]

At this time, the type of astrology that was practiced in Mesopotamia was limited to what modern astrologers refer to as "mundane astrology," which is a branch of astrology that deals with large groups of people such as cities and nations. The astrological omens were interpreted as messages that pertained to the state as a whole, or sometimes to the king as the earthly representative of the state. This connection with national affairs made astrology a state-supported activity, and eventually groups of astrologers would come to operate under the patronage of the king. Astrology and astronomy were intertwined at this time, and astrologers assumed both the duties of observers as well as interpreters of the stars.

One of the most well-documented high points for Mesopotamian, state-supported astrology appears to have occurred in the seventh century BCE

---

[3] Koch-Westenholz, *Mesopotamian Astrology*, p. 36. Pingree (*From Astral Omens*, p. 12) says that while evidence that celestial omens were being recorded only begins to appear in the first half of the second millennium BCE, they were probably already being recorded earlier in the late third millennium, although no hard evidence has been found yet.

[4] For an overview of the *Enūma Anu Enlil* and its contents see Hunger and Pingree, *Astral Sciences in Mesopotamia*, pp. 12–22.

[5] Discussed in Rochberg, *The Heavenly Writing*, esp. p. 58ff.

[6] Rochberg, *The Heavenly Writing*, p. 1.

[7] Pingree summarizes this by saying that "the importance of these celestial omens in Mesopotamian royal courts from the last few centuries of the 2nd millennium B.C. till the Achaemenid period depended on their being regarded as the principle means for the gods to signal their intentions to the king." Pingree, *From Astral Omens*, p. 18. Earlier (on p. 11) Pingree characterizes celestial omens as a "relatively late development," since other forms of divination had been introduced earlier.

under the Neo-Assyrian Empire.[8] By this point there were at least ten different "colleges" of astrologers located in different cities around Mesopotamia.[9] These colleges of astrologers consisted of an elite class of literate scholars who served the kings directly by regularly sending them letters and reports regarding their astronomical observations and astrological predictions. We know the most about the Neo-Assyrian period because of the survival of these letters and reports between the astrologers and the kings Esarhaddon and Ashurbanipal, whose dynasty occupied Babylon from 721–609 BCE.[10]

One of the side effects of the development of astrology was that it provided the Mesopotamians with an impetus to develop a more complex mathematical astronomy. Originally astrology was based entirely on observable phenomena such as an eclipse of the Sun, or a halo around the Moon, partially because the Mesopotamians lacked the ability to calculate where the planets would be in the future or where they had been in the past. However, centuries of observing the skies eventually led to the identification of some celestial movements as cyclical and periodic, just like the monthly cycle of the Moon or the yearly cycle of the Sun. This led to the development of complex mathematical models for determining the positions of the planets in astronomy, which in turn allowed for the development of more complicated astrological techniques and doctrines.[11]

In the eighth century BCE, the Mesopotamian astrologer-astronomers began a scientific program of meticulously observing the visible planets and recording their locations on a daily basis.[12] These records are generally referred to today as the *Astronomical Diaries*, or simply as the *Diaries*.[13] They would eventually be used as a sort of reference bank for astrologers in the following centuries.

Several important developments occurred in the history of astrology over the next few centuries. First, there was the ascent of the Achaemenid Persian Empire in the sixth century BCE, which at its height spanned from the Mediterranean across the Middle East, as far as the westernmost portions of India. The astronomical programs that were initiated during earlier civilizations such as the *Diaries* continued, although some decentralization of astrology seems to have occurred during this time, perhaps indicating that the astrologers

---

[8] The majority of our surviving sources for Mesopotamian astrology date to this time period according to Rochberg-Halton, "New Evidence for the History of Astrology," p. 116.

[9] Pingree, *From Astral Omens*, p. 16.

[10] For translations of the reports see Hunger, *Astrological Reports to Assyrian Kings*; for the letters see Parpola, *Letters from Assyrian Scholars to the Kings Esarhaddon and Assurbanipal*.

[11] The issue of whether or not astrology was the impetus for the development of more complex astronomical methods is dealt with in Rochberg, *The Heavenly Writing*, p. 160ff.

[12] For the dating see Pingree and Hunger, *Astral Sciences in Mesopotamia*, p. 139ff.

[13] For a translation of the *Diaries* see Sachs and Hunger, *Astronomical Diaries*.

did not enjoy the same level of support under the Persian kings that they had under the previous rulers.

By the fifth century BCE, the zodiac became standardized to consist of twelve signs that were exactly thirty degrees in length each.[14] Prior to this time, the zodiac was uneven because the zodiacal constellations that fall on the ecliptic have different sizes, with some being very large (e.g. Virgo) and others being relatively small (e.g. Cancer). While the Mesopotamians do not appear to have associated many of the qualities with the zodiacal signs that later became common, such as gender, element, or planetary rulership, this standardization of the spaces occupied by the signs in the fifth century was an important step because it was a necessary precursor for the later introduction of those concepts.

The fifth century was also a pivotal turning point because the concept of natal astrology appears to have been introduced around this time. The earliest surviving birth charts date to the year 410 BCE.[15] At the present time there are a total of twenty-eight known birth charts that survived from the Mesopotamian tradition.[16] None of these charts are particularly elaborate; they primarily list which sign of the zodiac each of the seven traditional planets were located in on the day of the native's birth, and there is very little technical or interpretive information accompanying them. What these charts make clear, though, is that by this time astrologers had taken the earlier idea that celestial phenomena could provide omens for the state as a whole, and began applying this concept to individuals by looking at the alignment of the planets on the day that they were born.

The development of natal astrology was connected to and complemented by the introduction of the ancient equivalent of ephemerides around the same time frame.[17] Astrologers no longer had to personally observe the sky in order to know where the planets were on a certain date; instead they could look up in these prepared texts where the planets were in the past, or where they would be in the future. This is crucial for the practice of natal astrology because it would then allow astrologers to calculate a person's birth chart simply by knowing the date they were born. While the observational components of astrology continued in some form for many centuries, it was at this point that astrology

---

[14] The earliest direct evidence for the standardized twelve-sign zodiac comes from the *Diaries*, according to Rochberg, *The Heavenly Writing*, p. 130. Cf. Brack-Bernsen and Hunger, "The Babylonian Zodiac."

[15] Rochberg, *Babylonian Horoscopes*, p. 3.

[16] All twenty-eight of the extant Mesopotamian birth charts are collected in Rochberg, *Babylonian Horoscopes*.

[17] Rochberg discusses the development and use of "almanacs" and "ephemerides" in the Mesopotamian tradition in *The Heavenly Writing*, pp. 153–163.

and astronomy slowly began to diverge, since astrologers acquired the ability to do much of their work without directly witnessing the stars themselves.

After the fifth century BCE, we know that astrology in Mesopotamia continued to become more advanced, and a number of new technical concepts were introduced, although our understanding of the full scope of astrological practice during this period is limited due to a lack of surviving sources. As in modern times, most astrological consultations probably would have been conducted verbally, and thus the surviving Mesopotamian birth charts provide us with very little information about how they were interpreted. Nonetheless, we do know that by this time the astrologers had begun distinguishing between two groups of planets that were thought to provide positive or negative indications, which anticipated the later Hellenistic distinction between "benefic" and "malefic" planets.[18] We also know that they started grouping the twelve signs of the zodiac into four sets of three, which seems to be a precursor to the later Hellenistic concept of grouping the signs into "triplicities" or "triangles," although at this stage they do not seem to have associated the signs with the four elements of Greek philosophy (fire, earth, air, water).[19]

There are also some glimpses of interpretive principles surrounding the signs of the zodiac and the planets in natal astrology, preserved in fragmentary form from what must have been a late Mesopotamian manual on the subject, referred to by scholars as TCL 6 14.[20] Some of the delineations associated with the planets are particularly interesting:

> If a child is born when the moon has come forth, (then his life? will be) bright, excellent, regular, and long. [...]
>
> If a child is born when Jupiter has come forth, (then his life? will be) regular, well; he will become rich, he will grow old, (his) day(s) will be long.
>
> If a child is born when Venus has come forth, (then his life? will be) exceptionally(?) calm; wherever he may go, it will be favorable; (his) days will be long.
>
> If a child is born when Mars has come forth, (then) ......, hot(?) temper(?). [...]

---

[18] Rochberg-Halton, "Benefic and Malefic Planets in Babylonian Astrology."

[19] Rochberg-Halton, "Elements of the Babylonian Contribution," pp. 60–62.

[20] Translated in Sachs, "Babylonian Horoscopes," pp. 65–70. There are similar delineations on a tablet translated in Rochberg-Halton, "TCL 6 13: Mixed Traditions in Late Babylonian Astrology," which she says comes from the Mesopotamian city of Uruk during the Seleucid/Hellenistic period (c. 334–63 BCE).

> If a child is born when Saturn has come forth, (then his life? will be) dark, obscure, sick, and constrained.[21]

Campion points out that these delineations represent some of the earliest statements connecting a person's psychological disposition with the alignment of the planets on the day of their birth, and he notes that several of the characteristics are consistent with ones mentioned by later Hellenistic astrologers such as Ptolemy.[22] Later on, the same text gives some delineations that involve two planets at the same time:

> If a child is born when Venus comes forth and Jupiter (had?) set, his wife will be stronger than he.
> If a child is born when Venus comes forth and Saturn (had?) set, his oldest son will die.
> If a child is born when Venus comes forth and Mars (had?) set, he will capture his personal enemy.[23]

The text goes on to list other combinations of planets or fixed stars rising before it breaks off at the end.

What we are left with, then, is an astrology that was still relatively basic, at least compared to some of the later traditions, but which was growing more complex as time went on. The primary contributions the Mesopotamians made to the later astrological traditions were the introduction of the zodiac, the invention of natal astrology, and the development of a complex mathematical astronomy that was capable of determining the positions of the planets in the past and future.

A tradition of astrology was also developing in ancient Egypt during the same period in which the Mesopotamian tradition was forming. Although initially developed independently, the two traditions would eventually begin to coalesce sometime around the middle of the first millennium BCE.

Egyptian Astrology

The ancient Egyptians used a calendar that had twelve months of thirty days each, with five additional days added at the end of every year. Essentially it was an idealized 360-day calendar. Each thirty-day month was divided into thirds, and each of these ten-day periods was associated with a specific fixed star or

---

[21] Sachs, "Babylonian Horoscopes," p. 68. I omitted the delineations for the Sun and Mercury, which are either missing or fragmentary.

[22] Campion, "More on the Transmission of the Babylonian Zodiac," p. 199ff.

[23] Sachs, "Babylonian Horoscopes," p. 69.

cluster of fixed stars. These fixed star groupings or asterisms later came to be known as "decans," from the Greek word *deka*, which means "ten." In total there were thirty-six decans. Each decan had a name, as well as certain deities associated with it.

The decans first appear on coffin lids around the time of the Middle Kingdom in Egypt, circa 2100 BCE.[24] There is some debate in the academic community about when they first came to be used in an astrological context, partially because there is some disagreement about what exactly constitutes "astrology." In the beginning the decans may have only been used for calendrical and timekeeping purposes, and their primary function was to measure or mark the different hours of the night in order for priests to time different religious rituals. However, we know that at least by the fourth century BCE, the decans were being ascribed astrological significance, as can be seen from a shrine that has been recently recovered called the Naos of the Decades. A naos is a large stone structure that is designed to sit inside the holiest part of a temple. The Naos of the Decades is one such shrine, and what makes it unique is that it is engraved with each of the thirty-six decans, along with descriptions about the protective astrological power that each was thought to possess.[25]

The Egyptians were particularly focused on the rising and culmination of the stars associated with the decans. In early texts, the decans were said to mark or designate which hour of the night it was when they would rise over the eastern horizon, while in later texts the decans marked the hour of the night when they culminated overhead in the sky.[26] This focus on the diurnal rotation, where the stars and planets rise, culminate, and set each day, is often thought to imply that the Egyptian use of the decans acted as a precursor to the later Hellenistic doctrine of the twelve "places" (Greek: *topoi*), which are referred to as the twelve "houses" in modern astrology.[27]

The important point here is that while the Mesopotamians were primarily focused on the ecliptic and the movement of the planets through the signs of the zodiac, the Egyptians were focused on the diurnal rotation and the movement of the stars through the regions of the sky that would later become associated with the twelve houses.

---

[24] Neugebauer, *The Exact Sciences*, p. 82, 88. Bomhard, *The Egyptian Calendar*, p. 65.

[25] See Bomhard, *The Naos of the Decades*.

[26] Greenbaum and Ross, "The Role of Egypt," p. 155.

[27] The role of the Egyptian decans in motivating the later development of the doctrine of the twelve "houses" is argued the most thoroughly and persuasively in Greenbaum and Ross, "The Role of Egypt in the Development of the Horoscope." For earlier versions of the same argument see Pingree, *Yavanajātaka*, vol. 2, p. 219; Tester, *A History of Western Astrology*, pp. 25–26; Schmidt in the preface to his translation of Ptolemy, *Tetrabiblos*, Book III, pp. viii–ix.

Figure 1.1 - Zodiac of Dendera, from an Egyptian Temple c. First Century BCE

By the second half of the first millennium BCE, some parts of Mesopotamian astrology were transmitted to Egypt. Around 500 BCE, a text on mundane astrology containing astrological eclipse omens from Mesopotamia was translated into the Egyptian language and altered to fit the geographical setting of Egypt.[28] Sometime around the third century BCE, the twelve-sign zodiac was imported from Mesopotamia into Egypt.[29] After this, the zodiac begins appearing in depictions on the ceilings of Egyptian temples and tombs, with the oldest dating to approximately 200 BCE.[30] Some of these Egyptian representations of the

---

[28] See Parker, *A Vienna Demotic Papyrus on Eclipse- and Lunar-Omina.*

[29] Neugebauer, "Demotic Horoscopes," pp. 121–3. Neugebauer and Parker, *Egyptian Astronomical Texts*, vol. 3, p. 203.

[30] Clagett, *Ancient Egyptian Science*, vol. 2, p. 126. For a list of known Egyptian zodiacs see Neugebauer and Parker, *Egyptian Astronomical Texts*, vol. 3, p. 204f.

zodiac incorporated the decans, which subsequently started to become ten-degree divisions of each of the signs of the zodiac, rather than a separate or independent system on their own.

This seems to represent a stage in the history of astrology in which omens from Mesopotamia were being transmitted to Egypt and adapted for use there. The decans and the zodiac naturally would have been used side by side by whoever was practicing astrology in Egypt during this time. This set the stage for the melding of the Mesopotamian and Egyptian astrological traditions in the period shortly before the appearance of Hellenistic astrology.

CHAPTER 2
ORIGINS OF HELLENISTIC ASTROLOGY

❁

The Hellenistic Period

In 334 BCE, a young Macedonian king named Alexander led an army of Macedonians and Greeks out of southern Europe and into Asia Minor (modern-day Turkey), beginning a war with the Achaemenid Persian Empire. The Persian Empire had controlled much of the Middle East and parts of the Mediterranean for the previous two centuries, although Alexander's armies quickly won a series of decisive victories that left the Persian forces in disarray. Within ten years of launching his campaign, Alexander and his armies had defeated the Persian Empire and conquered a large swath of land that spanned from southeast Europe down through Egypt, across the Middle East through Mesopotamia and Persia, and as far as the northwesternmost portions of India. In 323 BCE, Alexander ended his military campaign, and subsequently died a sudden death under mysterious circumstances in Babylon, right in the heart of Mesopotamia.

The death of Alexander is often used by historians to mark the beginning of the "Hellenistic period." This period lasted for approximately three centuries, until Rome became the dominant superpower in the Mediterranean in the first century BCE. The Hellenistic period is usually characterized by the spread of Greek culture, philosophy, and science across the ancient world, as well as a blending or syncretism of Greek and other cultures over the next few centuries. In a relatively short span of time, a large part of the known world was under the control of people who spoke Greek, and from that point forward, Greek became a common language that was used across the ancient world.

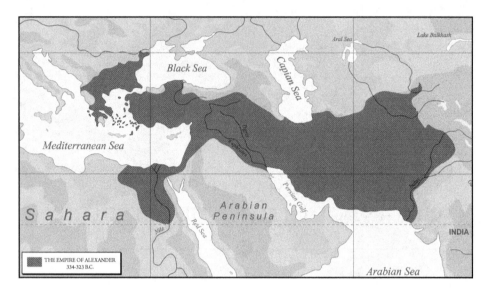

Figure 2.1 - Conquests of Alexander the Great

Alexandria

One of the most important historical developments in the Hellenistic period was the founding of the city of Alexandria in Egypt by Alexander the Great during the early part of his military campaign, sometime shortly after 332 BCE. Because Alexander died suddenly at the end of his campaign, he didn't appoint a successor, and this led to a controversy amongst his generals about who would have control over the new empire. The generals subsequently went to war with each other, and began dividing up different sections of the lands that their armies had conquered under Alexander. A general named Ptolemy took control of Egypt, and eventually established himself there as king. This inaugurated the Ptolemaic dynasty in Egypt, which lasted for nearly 300 years, until the death of Cleopatra VII and the subsequent annexation of Egypt by Rome in 30 BCE.

During the reign of Ptolemy I Soter and his son, Ptolemy II Philadelphus, Alexandria began to flourish as the financial, cultural, and intellectual hub of the ancient world. James Holden explains that after the city of Alexandria was founded

the new city rapidly became an important cultural and commercial center. Its population consisted of three main groups: Greeks, Egyptians, and Jews. Thus, the cultural, religious and (what passed for) scientific traditions of the Greeks, Egyptians, and Babylonians were intermingled in one place.[1]

---

[1] Holden, *A History of Horoscopic Astrology*, p. 11.

The city became a major center for scientific and literary research in the ancient world as a result of the state-supported library and research facilities that were built there. The famous Library of Alexandria acquired thousands of texts from various places in the ancient world, quickly becoming the largest library the world had ever seen.[2] The library and the facilities associated with it became a sort of institute for intellectuals, and the Ptolemies sponsored different types of scholarly and scientific activities with their royal patronage.[3]

Alexandria became the most important focal point in the development and practice of Hellenistic astrology. This happened not just because its rulers were patrons of the arts and sciences, which consequently fostered a rich environment for research and intellectual exchanges of all kinds, but also because there were direct lines of transmission from areas in the ancient world where individuals were actively involved in the translation and adaptation of the Mesopotamian astral sciences into the Greek language.

Berossus and the Transmission of Astrology

Partially due to its natural harbors, Alexandria also became a major naval power in the ancient world. The Ptolemies controlled a number of islands in the Mediterranean, including at one point an important Greek island in the Aegean Sea named Kos.

Sometime around the first quarter of the third century BCE, probably during the 280s, a Mesopotamian astrologer and historian named Berossus is said to have emigrated to the west and founded a school for astrology on the Greek island of Kos.[4] Kos had long been known as one of the main centers for medicine in the ancient world, and it was the home of a major healing temple associated with the cult of Asclepius.

The Roman writer Vitruvius (first century CE) relates the following legend

---

[2] For a good overview of the library see Erskine, "Culture and Power in Ptolemaic Egypt." For a more conservative estimate of the number of books the library held see Bagnall, "Alexandria: Library of Dreams," pp. 351–356.

[3] Erskine, "Culture and Power in Ptolemaic Egypt," p. 40.

[4] On the dating of Berossus see Verbrugghe and Wickersham, *Berossos and Manetho*, pp. 13–15. See the following passage from Vitruvius for the legend about Berossus' emigration to Kos. Pingree followed Jacoby in distinguishing between a historian named Berossus and an astrologer, who Pingree dubbed pseudo-Berossus, dating the former to 290–280 BCE and the latter to the late second or early first century BCE. See Pingree, *From Astral Omens*, p. 24. However, Verbrugghe and Wickersham make a compelling case for rejecting such a distinction between two different authors, pointing out that there is nothing inherently contradictory about Berossus' works in the surviving sources, and indeed in some sources he is clearly given credit as being the author of both works on astrology/astronomy as well as history.

surrounding the transmission of Mesopotamian astrology to the Hellenistic world and the role that Berossus was said to have played:

> For the rest, as to astrology, the effects produced on the human course of life by the twelve signs, the five planets, the sun and moon, we must give way to the calculations of the Chaldaeans [i.e. Mesopotamians], because the casting of nativities is special to them so that they can explain the past and the future from astronomical calculations. Those who have sprung from the Chaldaean nation have handed on their discoveries about matters in which they have approved themselves of great skill and subtlety. And first, Berossus settled in the island of Kos as a citizen and opened up a school there. Then Antipater took up the pursuit, and further, Athenodorus, who left a method of casting nativities, not from the time of birth but from that of conception.[5]

Vitruvius's story about Berossus settling in Kos and setting up a school for astrology there is complemented by another early author, the Jewish historian Josephus (first century CE), who reports that Berossus took an active role in translating Mesopotamian works on astronomy, astrology, and philosophy into Greek:

> Berossus ... was a Chaldean by birth, but known in educated Greek circles, because he translated into Greek works on the astronomy and the philosophy of the Chaldeans.[6]

These sources seem to suggest that Berossus may have played a role in the transmission of Mesopotamian astrology to the west sometime around the third century BCE, which was during the early part of the Hellenistic period. The general narrative amongst later authors seems to have been that he set up a school for astrology on the island of Kos, and then subsequently gained a reputation for himself in the ancient world as an astrologer as well as historian. In the first century CE, Pliny the Elder even goes so far as to say that a statue of Berossus was erected in Athens, and that it had a golden tongue due to the accuracy of his astrological predictions.[7] Vitruvius also mentions two of Berossus's students by

---

[5] Vitruvius, *On Architecture*, 9, 6: 2, trans. Granger, p. 245, modified.

[6] Josephus, *Against Apion*, 1: 129, quoted in Verbrugghe and Wickersham, *Berossos and Manetho*, T4, p. 37, slightly modified.

[7] Pliny, *Natural History*, 7, 37: 123. Pingree considered this story about the gilded tongue to be spurious, although we don't really know for sure either way. See Pingree, *From Astral Omens to Astrology*, p. 24.

name, Antipater and Athenodorus, apparently indicating that he had successors who carried on his teachings and even expanded upon some of the astrological practices that he taught at his school.[8]

Kos was a part of a confederation of islands in the Aegean Sea that came under the control of the Ptolemaic kings of Egypt sometime around the year 290 BCE.[9] This dating is interesting because it coincides with the dating of Berossus, who is thought to have written his *History of Babylonia* around the year 290 BCE.[10] If Berossus moved to Kos and set up his school around or after the publication of his *History*, then he would have arrived there and begun teaching at a time when there was a direct link between Kos and Alexandria. It seems reasonable to assume that both texts and students from Berossus's school eventually made their way to Alexandria, where, as Peter Green notes, "a liberal immigration policy, coupled with lavish patronage of scholarship and the arts through the royally funded Museum and Library, produced an exceptionally varied and intelligent corps of foreign residents."[11] As the historian Frederick Cramer pointed out:

> Even if Berossus was neither the first nor the only Babylonian to reveal the details of his priestly knowledge of horoscopal astrology to his Greek contemporaries, his name was the first one associated with such a trend.[12]

In other words, regardless of whether the specific legends about Berossus are true, we do know that Mesopotamian astrology was transmitted to the west during this period, and there is evidence that some of the earliest Greek texts on mundane astrology were partially based on translations of earlier texts from the Mesopotamian tradition.[13]

The Emergence of Hellenistic Astrology

Traces of a new and more complicated system of astrology begin to appear in historical sources by the first century BCE. At this time we find some of the

---

[8] Verbrugghe and Wickersham caution that Athenodorus' name is somewhat garbled in the manuscripts, and so it is not clear if this is an accurate restoration of the original name that was given here. Verbrugghe and Wickersham, *Berossos and Manetho*, p. 35, n. 2. The Vitruvius manuscripts write "Achinapolus." At the very least we do know that Berossus had at least two students who carried on his work.

[9] Shipley, *The Greek World After Alexander*, p. 202.

[10] Verbrugghe and Wickersham, *Berossos and Manetho*, p. 13.

[11] Green, *The Hellenistic Age*, p. 49.

[12] Cramer, *Astrology in Roman Law and Politics*, p. 14.

[13] See Williams, "Some Details on the Transmission of Astral Omens in Antiquity," for a discussion of some astrological omens from the *Enūma Anu Enlil* that show up in early Greek works on mundane astrology associated with Petosiris.

first surviving birth charts that were written in the Greek language, and they incorporate a number of new technical concepts that we have no record of in the earlier traditions. There is also a noticeable increase in discussions about astrology in literary sources at this time, which seems to indicate that it had started to take a more prominent role in Greek and Roman culture, as well as in other Mediterranean cultures in general.

The earliest surviving technical manuals on this new type of astrology date to the early first century CE, although they cite texts that would have been written slightly earlier, probably in the late second or early first century BCE. The new astrological system contained in these texts seems to represent a synthesis of the older Mesopotamian and Egyptian astrological traditions, although there is also a noticeable introduction of many new techniques and concepts. It is at this point that the fourfold system of astrology familiar to modern western astrologers became fully established, incorporating: (1) the planets, (2) the signs of the zodiac, (3) the concept of aspects, and (4) the doctrine of the twelve houses. This system is known today as Hellenistic astrology.

Defining "Hellenistic" Astrology

Hellenistic astrology appears to have originated in Egypt during the late Hellenistic period, around the late second or early first century BCE. However, it continued to be practiced for several centuries throughout the Mediterranean region as part of a continuous tradition that largely coincided with rise and fall of the Roman Empire. In fact, virtually all of our surviving sources for the practice of Hellenistic astrology come from astrologers who lived in different parts of the Roman Empire between the first century CE and the seventh century CE. Thus, Hellenistic astrology could legitimately be referred to as "Roman astrology," although adopting this designation would force us to neglect some of the important cultural connotations implied by having its origins in Hellenistic Egypt.

Similarly, Hellenistic astrology is sometimes referred to as "Greek astrology," since the majority of the surviving texts were written in Greek; but using this as our primary designation is also problematic because it leaves out some important information about the diverse cultural composition of the astrologers who developed and practiced the subject over the centuries. Greek had become the common language used all around the Mediterranean, and it was the primary language for scientific texts in the Roman Empire, similar to the way that English is used in many scientific publications today.[14] It is therefore important to recognize that just because an ancient author wrote in Greek, it

---

[14] Heilen makes this point in "Problems in Translating Ancient Greek Astrological Texts," p. 299.

did not necessarily mean that they were ethnically Greek. Additionally, while it is true that the majority of the surviving astrological texts from this time were written in Greek, there are also other relevant texts from this period that were written in other languages, albeit more sparsely, such as Latin, Demotic, Coptic, Aramaic, and Syriac. Thus the phrase "Greek astrology" does not adequately encompass the full range of this tradition.

As we have seen, historians usually define the "Hellenistic period" as an era that begins with the death of Alexander the Great in 323 BCE, and ends with the death of Cleopatra VII and the Roman conquest of Ptolemaic Egypt in 30 BCE.[15] In the Greek language the word *Hellēn* means "Greek," and in historical discussions the term "Hellenism" is used to define the lasting influence that Greek culture had on other cultures in terms of language, customs, art, philosophy, religion, and science. This dissemination of Greek culture began with the campaigns of Alexander and the subsequent Hellenistic empires, which resulted in the founding of many Greek cities all over the Mediterranean and the emigration of large groups of Greeks across the ancient world.

From the first century BCE, this process continued on into the Roman Empire due to the Roman assimilation or adoption of Greek cultural traits. This was part of the general process known as "Hellenization" in which different cities and cultures would actively or passively synthesize Greek culture with their own native customs and traditions. This resulted in people who were not ethnically Greek adopting the Greek language, and then expressing themselves through their written works in Greek, which in turn fed back into the broader cultural trends and influenced what it meant to be Greek in the first place.

It is this synthesis or syncretism of Greek and other cultures that occurred in the late Hellenistic period that produced what we call Hellenistic astrology, and this diversity is what provides it with a large part of its characteristic nature. Many elements of Hellenistic astrology remained more or less consistent in the tradition through to Late Antiquity and into the early Middle Ages.

Thus, while it is not a perfect descriptor, for the purposes of this book it seems that the most appropriate designation is Hellenistic astrology, which is defined here as a tradition of Greco-Roman horoscopic astrology that was practiced in the Mediterranean region from approximately the first century BCE until the seventh century CE. Horoscopic astrology refers to any tradition of astrology that utilizes the Ascendant and things derived from it such as the twelve houses, from the Greek word that was used to refer to the Ascendant and the first house, *hōroskopos* ("hour-marker"). Since Hellenistic astrology was the

---

[15] Bugh, *The Cambridge Companion to the Hellenistic World*, p. 2; Erskine, *A Companion to the Hellenistic World*, p. 2; Green, *The Hellenistic Age*, p. xv.

first tradition that utilized the Ascendant and the twelve houses, it is the first tradition of horoscopic astrology.[16]

Obscure Origins of Hellenistic Astrology

The origins of Hellenistic astrology are somewhat obscure due to an absence of written evidence, both in the two or three centuries leading up to its appearance, as well as during the first century or so in which we know it was being practiced. Part of the issue may be that while the Library of Alexandria had flourished under the patronage of the kings in the earlier Ptolemaic period, from 48 BCE onward the library lost some of its support and prominence, as well as some of its books due to fires and other disasters.[17] The lack of surviving written evidence from the Hellenistic era is not a phenomenon limited to astrology; historians often note that one of the challenges of studying the Hellenistic period in general is a lack of surviving sources, especially in terms of the written texts of some of the major historians and philosophers of that time.[18] In the introduction to *The Cambridge History of Hellenistic Philosophy*, the editors' assessment of what survives of the philosophical corpus from this period applies equally to the situation with the astrological texts: "few texts from the [Hellenistic] period survive in their entirety; and the fragments and testimonies to which we are now reduced derive for the most part from jejune epitomators or hostile commentators."[19] For any astrological texts written prior to the first century CE, the situation is similarly dismal, although we are in somewhat better shape for texts written after that. We are thus left to piece together the origins of Hellenistic astrology based on what later astrologers from the first century CE onward said about the sources they were drawing on.

---

[16] There is some debate over the designation "horoscopic astrology" in the astrological and academic communities due to the two or three different meanings of the term "horoscope" in modern times, as discussed in Greenbaum and Ross, "The Role of Egypt," p. 146ff. Here I use a stricter definition of the designation "horoscopic astrology" to refer only to those traditions that utilize both the Ascendant and the twelve houses, although later I will also use the term "horoscope" more generally to refer to any sort of astrological "chart," regardless of whether it contains the Ascendant and houses. This distinction is mainly important because while the earlier Mesopotamian birth charts might be referred to generally as "horoscopes," they would not be classified as a form of "horoscopic astrology," since they do not appear to utilize the Ascendant or houses.

[17] For a recent discussion: Hatzimichali, "Ashes to Ashes? The Library of Alexandria after 48 BC."

[18] As noted in Erskine, *A Companion to the Hellenistic World*, p. 3f.

[19] Algra, *The Cambridge History of Hellenistic Philosophy*, p. xi. Historians of Hellenistic philosophy find themselves in a similar position when it comes to studying the early Stoics, because none of the works of the early founders of Stoicism survived into the present day, and scholars have had to reconstruct the doctrines of the founders of Stoicism largely based on statements that later philosophers made about their views.

We have some sense of the timing of the emergence of Hellenistic astrology because the last surviving cuneiform birth chart from the Mesopotamian tradition dates to 69 BCE, right around the same time that the first extant Greek birth charts begin to appear in the mid- to late first century BCE.[20] This almost gives the impression of one astrological tradition displacing or giving way to another around the same time. However, no complete technical manuals on astrology have survived from prior to the first century CE, and so we are left somewhat in the dark about what late Mesopotamian astrology looked like, and with only glimpses of what the earliest versions of Hellenistic astrology consisted of.

Early Greek and Roman Exposure to Astrology

Discussions about astrology in Greek and Latin are sparse prior to the Hellenistic period, with only a few scattered references or allusions.[21] Generally, the evidence seems to indicate a growing awareness of Mesopotamian astrology and astronomy from about 400 BCE onward. Cicero cites Eudoxus of Cnidus (c. 365–340 BCE) as having said "no reliance whatever is to be placed in Chaldean astrologers when they profess to forecast a man's future from the position of the stars on the day of his birth."[22] Eudoxus was a student of Plato, and this shows that the concept of natal astrology was starting to become familiar to the Greeks already by the first half of the fourth century BCE. This makes sense, since as we saw earlier, some of the oldest Mesopotamian birth charts date to 410 BCE.

References to astrology begin to pick up around the time of Alexander the Great. The philosopher Theophrastus, Aristotle's successor, reportedly said that the Mesopotamian astrologers of his day were capable of predicting "lifestyles and deaths in the lives of individuals."[23] Alexander himself was said to have come into contact with and been the subject of predictions by the astrologers in Mesopotamia after he conquered the city of Babylon. One account by the historian Diodorus Siculus (first century BCE) has the astrologers warning Alexander of his impending death in Babylon:

---

[20] For the cuneiform chart see Rochberg, *Babylonian Horoscopes*, text 27, pp. 137–140. For the Greek charts see the section below on that topic.

[21] For a collection of most of the Greek evidence, see Waterfield, "The Evidence for Astrology in Classical Greece," although several of the pieces of evidence he cites seem like a bit of a stretch. For a more sober account, see Pingree, *From Astral Omens to Astrology*, pp. 21–29. For a broader account of the early literary references in Greek and Latin, see Cramer, *Astrology in Roman Law and Politics*, pp. 1–80. For a more recent account of the rise of astrology in Roman society, see Green, *Disclosure and Discretion*, p. 65ff.

[22] Cicero, *On Divination*, 2: 88, trans. Falconer, pp. 469–71.

[23] Proclus, *Commentary on Plato's Timaeus*, 4, 151f., trans. Baltzly, vol. 5, p. 256.

> While he was still three hundred furlongs from the city, the scholars called Chaldaeans, who have gained a great reputation in astrology (*astrologia*) and are accustomed to predict future events by a method based on age-long observations, chose from their number the eldest and most experienced. By the configuration of the stars they had learned of the coming death of the king in Babylon, and they instructed their representatives to report to the king the danger which threatened.[24]

It is difficult to determine the veracity of stories like this one, although it seems likely that Alexander and his army would have come into close contact with astrologers around this time, as they became first an occupying force, and subsequently the undisputed rulers of Mesopotamia. From this point forward, the references to astrology in Greek and Latin sources begin to increase in frequency, although the practice of astrology is often viewed as a distinctly foreign concept, largely practiced by Mesopotamians, albeit increasingly in different parts of the Mediterranean. In the year 139 BCE, a Roman edict expelled all astrologers from Italy, evidently for the first time in history.[25] The edict was recorded by Valerius Maximus (c. 31 CE):

> Cn. Cornelius Hispalus, praetor with responsibility for foreigners in the consulship of M. Popilius Laenas and L. Calpurnius, by an edict ordered astrologers (*Chaldaei*) to leave Rome and Italy within ten days because by means of a fallacious interpretation of the stars they threw unstable and shallow minds into a darkness profitable to them through their lies. The same praetor forced the Jews, who had tried to infect Roman customs by the worship of Jupiter Sabazius, to return to their own homes.[26]

This edict gives the impression that even by the mid-second century BCE, astrology was still seen as something practiced by foreigners from Mesopotamia, at least from a Roman perspective. This ceased to be the case only a short while later, when an explosion of discussion about astrology began to occur in Mediterranean culture beginning in the first century BCE. Coincidentally, it is around this time that some of the earliest technical manuals on astrology written in Greek and Latin begin to appear.

---

[24] Diodorus Siculus, *Library of History*, 17: 112, trans. Oldfather, p. 449. For a discussion of this passage and other parallel accounts see Cramer, *Astrology in Roman Law*, p. 10.

[25] Cramer, *Astrology in Roman Law*, p. 58.

[26] Valerius Maximus, *Memorable Deeds and Sayings*, 1, 3: 3, trans. Wardle, p. 39.

Earliest Datable Technical Manuals

The earliest reliably datable technical manuals on Hellenistic astrology that have survived are by the astrologers Thrasyllus and Manilius. Thrasyllus' Greek astrological text was entitled *The Tablet* (*Pinax*), and has only survived via a summary.[27] But since we know that he died in the year 36 CE, we know that he probably wrote it sometime around the early first century CE. In this work he cites earlier astrological texts attributed to three legendary figures named Hermes Trismegistus, Nechepso, and Petosiris, which must have been written prior to Thrasyllus, probably around the late second or early first century BCE.

Manilius wrote an instructional poem on astrology in Latin known as the *Astronomica*.[28] The precise dating of Manilius is debated, but he is generally thought to have written either towards the end of the reign of the Roman Emperor Augustus, or during the early part of the reign of Tiberius. Since Augustus died in the year 14 CE, it is probably safe to assume that Manilius wrote his *Astronomica* within a decade or so of that year. Manilius is also thought to allude to earlier authors such as Hermes, Nechepso, and Petosiris, although this is obscured somewhat due to the use of poetic allusions rather than explicit references.

Fragments of the texts attributed to Hermes, Nechepso, and Petosiris survive, but they are incomplete and difficult to date; all we know for sure is that they must have been written prior to Thrasyllus and Manilius. Thus, our earliest surviving treatises on Hellenistic astrology were written in the early first century CE in Greek and Latin, but drew on texts that were written in Greek a century or so earlier which no longer survive in their entirety.

Earliest Datable Charts

In addition to the instructional astrological texts, there are also a number of surviving horoscopes or astrological charts that can be dated to this period.[29] These surviving horoscopes are usually divided into two categories: the first involves charts that are used within the context of the instructional books as examples, which are sometimes referred to as "literary horoscopes"; the second are isolated horoscopes that survived on their own, typically written on small pieces of papyrus.

---

[27] See Thrasyllus, *Summary*.

[28] See Manilius, *Astronomica*.

[29] Just about all of the surviving horoscopes written in Greek have been collected together in three separate works: Neugebauer and Van Hoesen, *Greek Horoscopes*; Baccani, *Oroscopi greci*; Jones, *Astronomical Papyri from Oxyrhynchus*. There are also a handful of horoscopes written in Demotic Egyptian, surveyed in Ross, *A Survey of Demotic Astrological Texts*. Heilen recently published a very useful and up-to-date survey of all known horoscopes from antiquity in *Hadriani Genitura*, pp. 204–333.

The oldest literary horoscopes in Greek date to 72 and 43 BCE, although they are both from an astrologer who lived in the mid-first century CE, Balbillus, and thus they may have been cast many years after the native's birth. [30] The next oldest literary chart appears in the work of the late first century astrologer, Dorotheus of Sidon, which dates to March 29, 7 BCE.[31] The oldest non-literary charts written in Greek all date to the last decade of the first century BCE, with the first being dated to August 14, 10 BCE.[32] These are the earliest Greek astrological charts that we know of, and thus provide an important piece of evidence for determining when astrology started to be practiced by those who spoke Greek.

The famous lion "horoscope" of Mount Nemrud in Turkey is sometimes said to be one of the earliest Greek horoscopes.[33] It is a large stone engraving of a lion with four stars on it, and each of the stars has the Greek name of a planet written next to it (Mars, Mercury, Jupiter, and possibly the Moon). The planetary positions engraved on the relief are generally thought to reflect a planetary alignment on a specific date around the first century BCE, and to commemorate a political event associated with the royal dynasty of Commagene, which erected the monument. However, the dating of the monument has recently become somewhat contentious, with proposed dates as early as 109 BCE and 62 BCE, or as late as 49 BCE.[34] It is also not clear whether it can accurately be classified as evidence of horoscopic astrology in Greek, since the chart does not contain an Ascendant, houses, or any other factors usually associated with Hellenistic astrology.[35] If it does in fact reflect an actual alignment of planets at some point in time, it seems to mark the inception of an event rather than the birth of a person. Except for the fact that it was written in Greek, there is nothing else about the monument that gives us any indication as to whether it was influenced by Mesopotamian or Hellenistic tradition. Thus, for our purposes it is not necessary

---

[30] Balbillus used the charts as examples in order to demonstrate the length of life technique. A Greek paraphrase of Balbillus' delineation of this chart appears in CCAG 8, part 4, pp. 236–237. Neugebauer and Van Hoesen date and discuss this chart in *Greek Horoscopes*, pp. 76–78: No. L -71 and No. L -42. Schmidt translated the delineation in *Sages*, pp. 68–71. Neugebauer didn't think that the older chart would have been cast prior to 22 BCE, since the date of the death of the native was already known. If it is true that Balbillus was the son of Thrasyllus, then Heilen is probably correct in speculating that these charts came from his father's personal files. See Heilen, *Hadriani Genitura*, p. 214.

[31] This horoscope appears in Dorotheus, *Carmen*, 1, 24: 15–16. Pingree dates it on p. viii of the preface. Cf. Heilen, *Hadriani Genitura*, p. 216.

[32] Neugebauer and Van Hoesen, *Greek Horoscopes*, p. 16. Cf. Heilen, *Hadriani Genitura*, p. 216.

[33] Neugebauer and Van Hoesen, *Greek Horoscopes*, pp. 14–16.

[34] Belmonte and González-García, "Nemrud Dag," esp. p. 1663.

[35] As Campion puts it, "it is not actually clear why this monument should be regarded as a Greek horoscope other than that Commagene was now in the Hellenistic world." *A History of Western Astrology*, vol. 1, p. 180.

to use it as a critical piece of evidence in terms of dating, but simply to note that it may fall within the same general time frame as the emergence of some of the other early Greek horoscopes.

There are also some early horoscopes written in Demotic (a late Egyptian script), with the first dating to May 4, 38 BCE.[36] The rest date to the early first century CE or later.[37] The fact that some of these charts were found in collections written by Egyptian priests connected with specific temples has been taken to indicate that astrology became one of the forms of divination that was practiced by the priesthood in Egypt.[38]

Reliably datable charts from Latin sources are surprisingly infrequent in classical antiquity, and the ones that do exist do not begin to appear until after the first century CE.[39] It should be noted that Holden identified and attempted to date two possible charts in Latin that appear in Firmicus Maternus, which he dated to 139 and 96 BCE.[40] He speculated that the 139 BCE chart may have been the horoscope of Sulla, an association which Hübner later explored and endorsed.[41] If true, this chart would be the oldest of any Greek or Latin charts known to have survived. However, we should probably be cautious about using these charts for the purposes of dating the emergence of Hellenistic astrology, because Firmicus is relatively late in the tradition (fourth century CE), and the chart itself may have been rectified by whatever source he got it from. It appears in a section of his book that contains many other hypothetical and rectified chart examples for figures like Homer, Paris of Troy, and Plato. Moreover, Hübner points out that while the position of Saturn given in the chart matches Sulla's known year of birth (138 BCE), the positions of the other planets are only correct for the preceding year (139 BCE), which Heilen and Hübner speculate may have been an accidental or deliberate conflation of positions obtained from

---

[36] Neugebauer and Parker, "Two Demotic Horoscopes." Cf. Heilen, *Hadriani Genitura*, p. 316.

[37] Heilen, *Hadriani Genitura*, p. 316f.

[38] Jones, "The Place of Astronomy in Roman Egypt," p. 39ff. This inference has been confirmed in recent years due to the discovery of a number of Demotic instructional manuals on astrology that came from a temple in the Egyptian city of Tebtunis, although much of this material has not been published yet. See Winkler, "On the Astrological Papyri from the Tebtunis Temple Library," and more recently Quack, "On the Concomitancy of the Seemingly Incommensurable," and Winkler, "Some Astrologers and Their Handbooks in Demotic Egyptian," esp. pp. 269–278.

[39] For the Latin charts see Heilen, *Hadriani Genitura*, p. 326–330, although note that he includes a number of hypothetical charts that may have been rectified at a much later date.

[40] Holden, *A History of Horoscopic Astrology*, pp. 76–77. There was a typographical error in the original 1996 publication that said 138 BCE, which Holden later corrected to 139 BCE in later editions of the book. For the charts see Firmicus, *Mathesis*, 6, 31: 1, 55.

[41] Hübner, "Sulla's horoscope? (Firm., Math. 6,31,1)."

the ephemeris.[42] This may indicate that the horoscope was calculated many years later. Thus, the only reliable horoscopes in Latin, that we know were actually cast within the native's lifetime, are from after the first century CE.

In summary, horoscopes from the Hellenistic tradition do not begin to appear on the historical timeline from our vantage point until the mid to late first century BCE. From there the number of horoscopes increase dramatically, eventually peaking in the second and third centuries CE, roughly coinciding with the height of the Roman Empire.[43]

Ancient Views on the Origins of the Tradition

Ancient discussions about the origins of astrology often revolved around debates over which culture deserved credit for first having developed the subject, usually with credit going either to the Mesopotamians or to the Egyptians. Some of these debates seem to have their origins in claims made by representatives of each of these cultures, although the issue was compounded by the circulation of astrological pseudepigrapha in the early Hellenistic tradition that purported to be written by ancient Egyptian, Persian, Greek, or Jewish sages. This complicated the narratives about which culture was truly responsible for astrology in antiquity, because some of the texts attributed to these figures then became quite popular and widely circulated in the Hellenistic astrological tradition.

Mesopotamia or Egypt?

Ancient authors had some general awareness of the Mesopotamian and Egyptian origins of astrology, although there seem to have been debates about which culture deserved credit for having first developed the subject. Some authors credited the Mesopotamians as the originators, while others gave credit to the Egyptians, and a third group simply credited both.

During the Hellenistic period the term "Chaldean" (*Chaldaios*) came to be widely used to refer to astrologers or to the astrological profession in general. The word was originally used as a designation for a geographical area in Mesopotamia or an ethnic group that originated there.[44] Later it came to be used to refer to a class of priests from Mesopotamia who were thought to specialize in divination and astrology; eventually, from the first century CE onward, it largely became a generic term used to refer to all astrologers. To give an example, in the

---

[42] Hübner, "Sulla's horoscope," p. 18.

[43] Jones has some useful graphs which list the frequency of the surviving horoscopes by century in *Astronomical Papyri from Oxyrhynchus*, pp. 6–7.

[44] For most of this discussion, see Rochberg, *New Evidence for the History of Astrology*, p. 115.

second century CE, Sextus Empiricus uses the term during the course of his critique of astrology:

> the casting of nativities, which the Chaldeans adorn with more high-sounding titles, describing themselves as "mathematicians" (*mathēmatikoi*) and "astrologers" (*astrologoi*).[45]

Also in the second century, Aulus Gellius similarly refers to "those who call themselves 'Chaldeans' (*Chaldaei*) or 'nativity-casters' (*genethliaci*)."[46] The widespread use of the term Chaldean to refer to astrologers carried with it implications that the roots of astrology could be traced back to Mesopotamia, or that it was something that was at least originally associated with Mesopotamian priests. To a lesser extent there were probably similar connotations underlying the use of the term *magi* in the *Gospel of Matthew* (first century CE), which was used in the Christian nativity story to refer to a group of astrologers from the east (i.e. Mesopotamia or Persia) who traveled to see Jesus when he was born, after having witnessed some sort of astrological alignment that they interpreted as signifying his coming.[47]

At the other end of the spectrum, in his treatment of the history of Egypt, the mid-first century BCE historian Diodorus Siculus (fl. c. 60–30 BCE) initially associates the knowledge of astrology, divination, and the prediction of the future with Egyptian priests.[48] He says that the Egyptians claimed to have first developed astrology:

> The Thebans [of Egypt] say that they are the earliest of all men and the first people among whom philosophy and the exact science of the stars (*astrologia*) were discovered, since their country enables them to observe more distinctly than others the rising and settings of the stars.[49]

Diogenes Laertius makes a similar remark about the Egyptians around the third century CE, saying that they "claimed to have invented geometry, astrology (*astrologia*), and arithmetic."[50] There was some fluidity between the terms astrology and astronomy during this period, which sometimes makes it unclear

---

[45] Sextus Empiricus, *Against the Professors*, 5: 2, trans. Bury, p. 323.

[46] Aulus Gellius, *Attic Nights*, 14: 1, trans. Rolfe, vol. 3, p. 3, modified.

[47] *Matthew*, 2: 1–16. For extensive coverage of the different theories surrounding this topic see *The Star of Bethlehem and the Magi*, ed. Barthel and van Kooten.

[48] Diodorus Siculus, *Library of History*, 1, 73: 4.

[49] Diodorus Siculus, *Library of History*, 1, 50: 1, trans. Oldfather, pp. 175–77.

[50] Diogenes Laertius, *Lives of Eminent Philosophers*, 1: 11, trans. Hicks, vol. 1, p. 13.

which is being referred to, and this is usually interpreted to mean that the division between the two was not as strict then as it is today.[51] Nonetheless, the general point seems to have been that the Egyptians took credit for the development of both.

Later in the text, Diodorus expands on his earlier point, and says that the Egyptians claimed that the Mesopotamians actually learned astrology from the Egyptians, rather than the other way around:

> For the positions and arrangements of the stars as well as their motions have always been the subject of careful observation among the Egyptians, if anywhere in the world; they have preserved to this day the records concerning each of these stars over an incredible number of years, this subject of study having been zealously preserved among them from ancient times, and they have also observed with the utmost avidity the motions and orbits and stoppings of the planets, as well as the influences of each one on the generation of all living things — the good or the evil effects, namely, of which they are the cause. [...] And according to them the Chaldaeans of Babylon, being colonists from Egypt, enjoy the fame which they have for their astrology because they learned that science from the priests of Egypt.[52]

Later when he deals with the history of Mesopotamia, Diodorus discusses the Chaldeans, who he views as Babylonian priests that have experience with astrology and divination.[53] He goes on to discuss their expertise in astrology, and says that the astrologers from that area also make great claims about the antiquity of their tradition:

---

[51] While this especially is true in earlier periods, particularly in Mesopotamia, this point is sometimes overstated in some contemporary discussions to make it seem as if there was little to no distinction between astronomy and astrology throughout the Greco-Roman period. This partially seems like it was simply a linguistic issue in Greek and Latin texts due to a lack of standardization about which term to use for astrology and astronomy, perhaps partially deriving from earlier periods where the distinction was blurrier, but that does not necessarily mean that there was absolutely no distinction between the two in the west in classical antiquity. Baigent points out that the hostility of some early Greek astronomers such as Eudoxus towards astrology when it first started to be imported to the west implies that there was already more of a division between astronomy and astrology among the Greeks than there had been in the earlier Mesopotamian tradition (*From the Omens of Babylon*, p. 178). While it is true that sometimes we see individuals such as Ptolemy practicing astronomy and astrology side by side, not every classical astronomer necessarily believed in or practiced astrology, and not every astrologer was necessarily highly skilled in the complex theory and practice of mathematical astronomy.

[52] Diodorus Siculus, *Library of History*, 1, 81: 4–6, trans. Oldfather, pp. 277–279.

[53] Diodorus Siculus, *Library of History*, 2, 24: 2.

This point, however, a man may fittingly maintain, that the Chaldaeans have of all men the greatest grasp of astrology, and that they have bestowed the greatest diligence upon the study of it. But as to the number of years which, according to their statements, the order of the Chaldaeans has spent on the story of the bodies of the universe, a man can scarcely believe them; for they reckon that, down to Alexander's crossing over into Asia, it has been four hundred and seventy-three thousand years, since they began in early times to make their observations of the stars.[54]

In the latter part of the first century CE, Pliny the Elder reported some similarly far-fetched number of years being attributed to the Mesopotamian astral sciences, this time with one of the claims potentially coming from Berossus himself:

On the other side, Epigenes, an authority of the first rank, teaches that the Babylonians had astronomical observations for 730,000 years inscribed on baked bricks; and those who give the shortest period, Berossus and Critodemus, make it 490,000 years.[55]

Other authors seem to attempt to deal with the competing claims coming from each of these traditions by simply recognizing both. For example, in the early fourth century CE, the philosopher Iamblichus simply remarks that "theories about celestial bodies are referred by some to the Egyptians and Chaldeans in common."[56] Similarly, the late first century astrologer, Dorotheus of Sidon, says that he travelled widely in Egypt and Mesopotamia, and collected information from some of the foremost astrological authorities in those two areas in order to compose his treatise on astrology.[57] While it is not clear if this statement from Dorotheus is true or if it is just being used for rhetorical purposes, it does imply that the Hellenistic astrologers were conscious of the long traditions of astrology that they had inherited from Mesopotamia and Egypt, and in some instances they sought to synthesize them in what was essentially a new hybrid approach.

Legendary Founders and Pseudepigrapha
Some of the most popular astrological texts of the early Hellenistic tradition were written under pseudonyms, where the author would intentionally attribute

---

[54] Diodorus Siculus, *Library of History*, 2, 31: 8–9, trans. Oldfather, pp. 455–457.
[55] Pliny, *Natural History*, 7, 193, trans. Rackham, p. 637, modified.
[56] Iamblichus, *On the Pythagorean Way of Life*, 158, trans. Dillon and Hershbell, p. 175.
[57] Dorotheus, *Carmen*, 1, 1: 1–5. Cf. 5, 1: 1–4.

the text to a legendary, mythical, or religious figure from the past.[58] This was a common practice in the ancient world, especially for texts dealing with what we might classify today as "occult" matters, such as astrology, alchemy, or magic, although it also happened with philosophical, religious, and medical texts as well. The genre of falsely ascribed texts is generally referred to as "pseudepigrapha."

The exploration of this practice is important in the astrological tradition because many of the earliest and most authoritative or influential texts from the Hellenistic period were pseudepigrapha. Some were ascribed to mythical figures, such as Hermes Trismegistus or Asclepius, while others were ascribed to historical or religious figures, such as Nechepso, Petosiris, Abraham, and Zoroaster.

The exact reasons why the authors of these astrological texts ascribed them to legendary figures rather than acknowledging authorship of them are unknown, although various speculations have been put forward by modern scholars. Some assume that the purpose was to make the texts seem more authoritative, and thus to give them more value on the intellectual market, resulting in better circulation of the ideas and doctrines.[59] Beck argues that the purpose of attaching names like Zoroaster to certain texts was because it "conferred the desired authority of a remote and revelational wisdom."[60] Along similar lines, Bouché-Leclercq said that pseudepigrapha and related works were the natural result of all faiths that seek proof in tradition, and simply invent what they do not find.[61]

On the other hand, it might be tempting to assume that some of the ascriptions to religious or cultural figures like Abraham or Zoroaster might imply some sort of cultural connection between those figures and the actual authors of the texts. For example, perhaps the author who ascribed his astrological text to the patriarch of the Jewish faith, Abraham, was himself Jewish. Or maybe the author of the text attributed to Zoroaster had ethnic roots in Persia or followed the Zoroastrian faith.[62]

Unfortunately it is hard to say for sure. In some instances it has been argued that these cultural ascriptions had more to do with the allure of foreign wisdom and exotic-sounding names, since the texts themselves often contain little to

---

[58] Discussed extensively in Pérez Jiménez, "Pseudepígrafos de la astrología griega."

[59] Rudolf, "Propaganda for Astrology in Aramaic Literature," p. 125. Cramer speculated that the astrologer who wrote under the name Petosiris could have adopted the name of an ancient high priest in order to "boost the sales of his new book." Cramer, *Astrology in Roman Law*, p. 17.

[60] Beck, "Thus Spake Not Zarathustra," p. 493.

[61] Bouché-Leclercq, *L'Astrologie grecque*, p. 3, fn. 1.

[62] For example, Quack argues that some of the texts ascribed to Zoroaster may have been written by members of the Persian community that lived in Egypt for centuries after the Achaemenid period. Quack, "Les Mages Égyptianisés," p. 282.

nothing that could be associated with the specific religious or cultural traditions that the names were meant evoke.[63] The famous classicist Arnaldo Momigliano put it somewhat more bluntly:

> If we have to resort to a generalization about the fortunes of Oriental thought in the Hellenistic world and in its Roman prolongation, we must say that the mass of writings claiming to be translations from Oriental languages were mainly forgeries by writers in Greek. What circulated in Greek under the names of Zoroaster, Hystaspes, Thoth [i.e. Hermes], and even Abraham was quite simply faked, though no doubt some of the writings contained a modicum of "Oriental" thoughts combined with Greek ideas.[64]

However, within the context of some of the Hermetic pseudepigrapha, Garth Fowden argued for a softer view, which is worth quoting at length here:

> it is perhaps unlikely that pseudepigrapha of this sort were cold-bloodedly or indiscriminately 'attributed' to just any ancient or mythical figure in order to increase their authority or circulation – though this might be alleged by a hostile critic, as when Porphyry maintained that the gnostic 'book of Zoroaster' was 'entirely spurious and modern, made up by the sectarians to convey the impression that the doctrines which they had chosen to hold in honour were those of the ancient Zoroaster.' Rather one should suppose, in the Hermetic tradition as among the Pythagoreans and Orphics, some sense of a continuity of inspiration, of which each text added to the genre was seen as a new manifestation which could fairly, if not with pedantic precision, be ascribed to the eponymous founder. As Iamblichus put it, since Hermes was the source of all knowledge, it was only natural that the ancient Egyptian priests should render him homage by attributing their writings to him. So we need not imagine that a spiritual teacher who was in the habit of circulating his compositions under the name of Hermes will have felt that he was perpetuating a deception, or that he needed to dissemble what he was doing as potentially scandalous. And indeed his work will have gained weight, in the eyes of his followers, precisely because it was not merely the product of an autonomous authorial act, but reflected

---

[63] Beck discusses this in the context of the Zoroastrian pseudepigrapha in "Thus Spake Not Zarathustra," pp. 491–493, although the point is true for what little survives from the text ascribed to Abraham as well.

[64] Momigliano, "The Fault of the Greeks," p. 17.

the sedimentary intellectual culture of his own and earlier times – in short, because it did *not* strive after originality.[65]

This view may be more tenable within the context of the pseudepigrapha explicitly associated with the Hermetic tradition, which would include the astrological texts attributed to Hermes, Asclepius, Nechepso, and Petosiris.[66] Where other later pseudepigraphical texts such as those attributed to Zoroaster or Abraham fit in seems more open to question.

Thus, in the early Hellenistic tradition, there was a set of technical manuals on astrology in circulation that were widely cited and viewed as authoritative by later authors. Many of the basic technical doctrines that became widespread in Hellenistic astrology may be traced back to these texts. Unfortunately, the texts themselves no longer survive, and we can only develop an understanding of what they contained based on reports by later authors. This in turn has given rise to a debate about the origins of Hellenistic astrology.

Debate Over the Origins of Hellenistic Astrology

The scarcity of evidence, apparent suddenness of its appearance on the historical timeline, and systematic nature of some of its doctrines has given rise to a debate over the origins of Hellenistic astrology amongst some contemporary astrologers and academics. This debate essentially hinges upon the question of whether the technical doctrines that appear in the early tradition of Hellenistic astrology represent a deliberate invention by one person or a group of people in a relatively short span of time, perhaps over the course of a generation or two, or alternatively whether the techniques were developed gradually over the course of several centuries during the late Mesopotamian or Egyptian traditions, and we simply don't have complete documentation of this development due to the loss of so many texts.

I refer to this as the "gradual development versus sudden invention debate." There are two major points of view in this debate, and each has its own unique strengths and weaknesses. I will first give an overview of some of the main points made by proponents on each side of this debate, and then follow with a third option which I think represents a more plausible middle ground between the two.

---

[65] Fowden, *The Egyptian Hermes*, p. 187.

[66] Barton (*Ancient Astrology*, p. 26) explains that some of the early texts such as those attributed to Nechepso and Petosiris are "usually seen as Hermetic, since it is often said that they gained their knowledge from Hermes."

Sudden Invention Hypothesis

Proponents of the sudden invention hypothesis generally hold the view that somewhere around the late second or early first century BCE, some unknown person or perhaps a group of people deliberately invented Hellenistic astrology as a sort of technical construct. While proponents of this view acknowledge that there were long traditions of astrology in Mesopotamia and Egypt which preceded and contributed specific techniques and doctrines to the Hellenistic tradition, the general view is that someone in the Hellenistic period deliberately synthesized those earlier traditions at a specific point in time, and then introduced or invented a number of new technical, conceptual, and philosophical notions in order to create some of the earliest versions of what we associate with Hellenistic astrology today.[67]

The sudden invention hypothesis partially arises out of the apparent disconnect between the late Mesopotamian and early Hellenistic traditions of astrology. While it is clear that astrology was developing and becoming more complicated in the late Mesopotamian tradition, especially with the introduction of natal astrology and different concepts for reading birth charts, by the time we get to the Hellenistic tradition there seems to be an explosion of new techniques and doctrines. This includes a very elaborate system for natal chart interpretation, which seems to represent a dramatic expansion over what we can see in the earlier traditions. Two of the biggest innovations were the concept of the twelve houses or places, as well as the doctrine of aspects or configurations, neither of which appear in the Mesopotamian tradition.[68] Dozens of other significant technical concepts only appear for the first time in the Hellenistic tradition as well, such the domicile rulership scheme, or the distinction between day and night charts known as sect.

One of the strong points of the sudden invention hypothesis is the fact that many of the later astrological authors seem to be drawing on a similar set of early source texts, which sometimes results in different authors who are separated

---

[67] Recent proponents of the sudden invention hypothesis include Pingree (*From Astral Omens to Astrology*, pp. 26–7), Holden (*A History of Horoscopic Astrology*, p. 12, fn. 2), and especially Schmidt (*The Kepler College Sourcebook*, pp. 7–13). The view can be traced back further, though, and seems to be the dominant trend in most of the academic scholarship over the past century. Barton (*Ancient Astrology*, p. 26) seems to have acknowledged it as the prevailing view circa 1994, saying "because Petosiris and Nechepso are most consistently portrayed as the founders of astrology and cited for particular doctrines, most scholars have agreed that there must have been Hellenistic texts circulating under their names which represented an early synthesis of astrological doctrines."

[68] Pingree (*From Astral Omens*, p. 27) cites these and other concepts as part of what he saw as being invented in the development of Hellenistic astrology.

by centuries repeating the same doctrines and techniques because they are both reading the same source. For example, several different authors cite the same texts attributed to Hermes and Asclepius when discussing the significations of the twelve houses; in the same fashion, different authors use a similar technique for determining the length of life that was derived from the text of Petosiris. It does indeed seem that there was a collection of early texts attributed to Hermes, Nechepso, and Petosiris that were widely read and cited by later authors, and if some of the basic techniques used by later Hellenistic astrologers were first introduced in these texts, then that would constitute a sort of sudden invention.

The notion of some early source texts that established the fundamental concepts of Hellenistic astrology is additionally supported by what seems to be a high degree of coherency in some of the technical doctrines. Many of the techniques seem to be designed in such a way that they integrate or fit together with other techniques, to the extent that it seems like certain parts of Hellenistic astrology were designed with some sort of overarching technical construct or system in mind. The way that the Thema Mundi connects the concepts of sign rulership, planetary gender, sect, and the aspect doctrine is an example of this. Or, to give another example: the way that the planetary joys scheme ties together the significations of the houses with the concept of sect, aspects, triplicity rulers, and the exaltations. Schmidt points out that it is unlikely that some of these techniques and constructs were developed as a result of empirical observations, but instead they appear to have been invented based on specific conceptual or philosophical motivations.[69]

In his 1996 book *A History of Horoscopic Astrology*, James Holden deliberately employed the term "inventors" in order to describe the authors of the earliest texts on Hellenistic astrology:

> The scholars and "scientists" of Alexandria were particularly active in the third and second centuries [BCE]. Among them were the inventors of Western horoscopic astrology. Their real names are unknown, since they chose to issue their books under the names of gods, kings, heroes, or wise men of the past. Their books are lost except for scattered fragments preserved by later authors. However, the essential features of their astrological theories have been transmitted to us through the writings of the later Greek astrologers.[70]

---

[69] Schmidt, *Kepler College Sourcebook*, p. 10.
[70] Holden, *A History of Horoscopic Astrology*, p. 12.

In a footnote to the term "inventors," Holden defended the sudden invention hypothesis:

> One of my valued colleagues objects to the word "inventors." He points out that Greek horoscopic astrology, even in its early second century form, was a new and very complicated system, and he thinks it doubtful that it could have been "invented" by one or more individuals all at once. He would prefer me to say that horoscopic astrology "appeared" at that time. My rejoinder is that Euclid, who lived perhaps a century before the Alexandrian astrologers, wrote the elements of geometry in a comprehensive and nearly perfect form, and if he could do that all at once, there seems to be no reason why some later Alexandrians or perhaps two generations of them could not have created horoscopic astrology.[71]

Thus, from our vantage point, the sudden invention argument explains why this new system of astrology seems to appear somewhat abruptly around the first century BCE.

Gradual Development Argument

Recently there has been a countertrend that has called into question the sudden invention hypothesis, advocating instead what I call the "gradual development argument."[72] Proponents of the gradual development argument generally maintain that (1) there was a great deal of diversity in the techniques and/or philosophies associated with Hellenistic astrology, thus negating the idea that it all could have come from a singular source or set of sources, and (2) because many basic techniques and concepts originated in the earlier Mesopotamian and Egyptian traditions, many other techniques that we only first see in the Hellenistic tradition may have originated earlier, and the apparent suddenness of their introduction is only the result of the loss of so many texts from the last few centuries BCE.

The strength of the gradual development argument lies in the fact that there is ample evidence for continuous traditions of astrology in Mesopotamia and Egypt for hundreds of years prior to the Hellenistic tradition, and it

---

[71] Holden, *A History of Horoscopic Astrology*, p. 12, n. 2.

[72] The primary proponents of the gradual development argument at this point in time are Robert Hand, Nicholas Campion (*A History of Western Astrology*, vol. 1, pp. 203–223), and Greenbaum and Ross ("The Role of Egypt," pp. 146–182). Hand's argument was outlined in a special evening lecture at a Kepler College symposium on April 16, 2005, in Seattle, Washington. The argument has not yet appeared in print, although I attended it in person that evening and took extensive notes from a recording.

is clear that Hellenistic astrology represents a continuation of many of the techniques, concepts, and philosophical notions that were already present in the earlier traditions. We know that astrology was becoming more and more complex in the Mesopotamian tradition in the centuries prior to the advent of Hellenistic astrology, and to some extent the techniques that were developed in the Hellenistic period seem like logical extensions of some of the earlier ideas and concepts.

One of the main issues that gradual development proponents point out is that we have lost so many texts from the last three centuries BCE that it is impossible to be certain about anything from that period. In particular, we do not possess much in the way of astrological handbooks from the late Mesopotamian tradition which would tell us how an astrologer would have interpreted a birth chart. While we do have some birth charts that survived from that period, they do not usually contain very extensive delineations, probably because that information would have been conveyed verbally in person, as it was in the Hellenistic tradition and still is today.

Additionally, while the different texts which comprise the Hellenistic tradition have much in common, there is still quite a bit of diversity between the different techniques (and astrologers) during that period. Whereas sudden invention proponents tend to argue that there was more coherency or consistency in the Hellenistic tradition, especially from a technical standpoint, the gradual development proponents tend to argue that there was more diversity. Campion in particular points out that there was a large spectrum of different philosophical and religious positions taken by advocates of astrology in the ancient world, as well as different religious schools which incorporated astrology into their belief systems in different ways, which he argues is evidence against a singular invention.[73] Greenbaum and Ross emphasize areas of technical diversity.[74] It is this perception of diversity in both the techniques and the philosophy of Hellenistic astrology which leads proponents of this view to argue that Hellenistic astrology must have developed more gradually and organically over an extended period of time.

Thus, according to the gradual development argument, the Hellenistic tradition simply represents the end result of centuries of development and experimentation in the earlier Mesopotamian and Egyptian traditions, and it only appears suddenly on the historical timeline from our vantage point due to the loss of so many texts from that time period.

---

[73] Campion, *A History of Western Astrology*, vol. 1, p. 223.
[74] Greenbaum and Ross, "The Role of Egypt," pp. 149–150.

Pros and Cons of Both Sides

This is an ongoing debate that has yet to be settled, and it may in fact never be fully resolved, but it is important to be aware of it and to contemplate the issue because it can have serious implications for the way that one approaches the study and reconstruction of Hellenistic astrology, as well as the practice of astrology in general.

My personal opinion is that adopting an extreme position on either side of the argument is problematic, because there are good points to be made for both sides, and there is much truth in each. Additionally, it seems as if advocates on both sides have had a tendency to exaggerate their arguments. Proponents of the sudden invention hypothesis tend to overstate the degree of consistency or unity within the Hellenistic tradition, while proponents of the gradual development argument tend to exaggerate the extent of its diversity and incoherency. On the sudden invention side, the insistence that some have had on reconstructing a hypothetical "original" system has led to some radical steps being taken in the reconstruction and interpretation of certain texts, sometimes leading them to infer or invent complex doctrines from a text that may never have contained them. On the other side of the spectrum, the insistence that some gradual development proponents have had on the complete diversity and utter lack of cohesion in the Hellenistic tradition is overstated, and if left unchecked could result in researchers overlooking or ignoring some important conceptual coherencies and connections between different ancient sources that do in fact exist.

In some ways this debate is similar to a debate that comes up amongst historians over whether Aristotle's philosophy was entirely worked out before he began writing and remained consistent throughout his works, or whether his thought grew and changed during the course of his life and could be separated into different stages. Daniel W. Graham outlined the argument as follows:

> The unitarians view Aristotle as having a unified system which it is the interpreter's task to reconstruct, harmonizing apparent conflicts. The developmentalists attempt to trace the growth of Aristotle's thought and see conflicts as evidence of different temporal strata from which the stages of development can be reconstructed. We noted problems for both views: the developmentalists tend to fragment Aristotle's thought, while the unitarians try to reconcile too much.[75]

In terms of the Hellenistic astrological tradition, ultimately the truth of the matter seems to lie somewhere between the two extremes of opinion that

---

[75] Graham, *Aristotle's Two Systems*, pp. 290–1.

have been outlined above. In what follows I would like to outline what I think represents the middle ground between these two positions, and seems to be the most likely scenario for the development of Hellenistic astrology.

The Development of Hellenistic Astrology

It is clear that there was a gradual development of astrology in the Mesopotamian and Egyptian traditions that took place over the course of many centuries, with the doctrines becoming increasingly complex. It is primarily from the Mesopotamians that we receive the concept of natal astrology and the introduction of the zodiac. From the Egyptian tradition we get the decans and the focus on diurnal rotation, with the related concept of planets rising and culminating, which acts as a precursor to the development of the houses or places. It was the fusion of these two different reference systems, the zodiac with its focus on the ecliptic, and the decans with their focus on diurnal rotation, which allowed for the development of Hellenistic astrology.

We know that this fusion already started to take place by at least 200 BCE, when we see the zodiac and the decans starting to appear together in depictions in Egyptian temples and tombs, with the decans becoming ten-degree divisions within the zodiac itself. Mesopotamian texts on mundane astrology were already being translated and adapted to the geographical and political setting of Egypt since 500 BCE, and by 200 BCE or so students of Berossus' school and other practitioners of Mesopotamian astrology would have made their way to Alexandria, importing the concept and practice of natal astrology there.

Somewhere around this point a mysterious text on the decans known as the *Salmeschiniaka* may have been composed. In some of the sources it is cited as an example of the type of astrology practiced by the Egyptian priesthood, and it is mentioned by Porphyry and Iamblichus in connection with an Egyptian priest named Chaeremon who lived in the first century CE.[76] A fragment of this text preserved by Hephaestio of Thebes may provide us with some important insights into what the practice of astrology looked like in Egypt prior to the first century:

And one must also examine the decans, since the first decan of the Hour-Marker deals with birth; the 28th from the Hour-Marker, which

---

[76] For the surviving fragments and testimonia of Chaeremon's work see Van der Horst, *Chaeremon*. For the fragments dealing with the *Salmeschiniaka* see F5 and F9, citing Porphyry, *Letter to Anebo*, 2: 12–13, and Iamblichus, *On the Mysteries*, 8: 4, respectively. In the latter fragment, Iamblichus says that the *Salmeschiniaka* contains "only a very small part of the Hermetic system" (trans. Van der Horst, p. 17).

culminates early, deals with livelihood; the 25th, which culminates at noon, deals with sickness; the [1]9th, which rises late in the east, deals with injury; the 17th, which rises in the west, deals with marriage and wives; the 8th, door of Hades, deals with children, the one in the subterranean [angle] deals with death. These are the places that the ancient Egyptians used in every nativity.[77]

If this fragment is genuinely early, which I think it is, then there are three important points that we can take from it about the state of Egyptian astrology around the second century BCE. First, it shows that the Egyptians were using the rising decan as an Ascendant or Hour-Marker (*hōroskopos*), and then ascribing significations to the other decans depending on where they fell relative to the rising decan. The use of the decans in this way thus acts as a direct conceptual precursor to the later development of the twelve houses or places. Second, this fragment shows that the Egyptians were already using what would correspond to the four angles in the later traditions, which in this context are the rising, culminating, setting, and anti-culminating decans. This means that the use of these four sectors probably arose prior to the development of the doctrine of the twelve houses and the significations that were ascribed to those sectors, thus making the use of the four angles a sort of intermediary stage between the traditions.[78]

Sometime around the early second century BCE, a mathematician and astronomer named Hypsicles of Alexandria wrote a short work titled *On Ascensions* (*Anaphorikos*), in which he showed how to calculate the rising times of the signs of the zodiac.[79] This was important because it was the first work in Greek that made it easy to calculate the rising sign and degree, which later became known as the Ascendant or Hour-Marker, and later astrologers would draw on Hypsicles' work as a source for their calculations for centuries.[80] It is

---

[77] Hephaestio, *Apotelesmatika*, 2, 18: 75–6, trans. Schmidt, p. 66, slightly modified.

[78] I believe that we can find further evidence for this in the electional material of the first century astrologer, Dorotheus of Sidon, whose book on inceptional astrology seems like it draws on a tradition in which most of the rules are only designed to take into account the four angular places. Dorotheus claimed to have drawn on both the Egyptian and Mesopotamian traditions, so it is not clear which tradition these electional rules came from, but nonetheless it seems to confirm a stage in the history of astrology where only the four angles were used. See Dorotheus, *Carmen*, 5, and Hephaestio, *Apotelesmatika*, 3.

[79] Edited in Hypsicles, *Hypsikles: Die Aufgangszeiten der Gestirne*, ed. de Falco and Krause. For a translation and commentary see Montelle, "The *Anaphoricus* of Hypsicles of Alexandria." Montelle tentatively dates Hypsicles' period of activity to c. 190 BCE, while others usually put him as flourishing sometime around the first quarter or first half of the second century.

[80] He is cited explicitly in Valens, *Anthology*, 3, 13: 5. Elsewhere, the values given for the

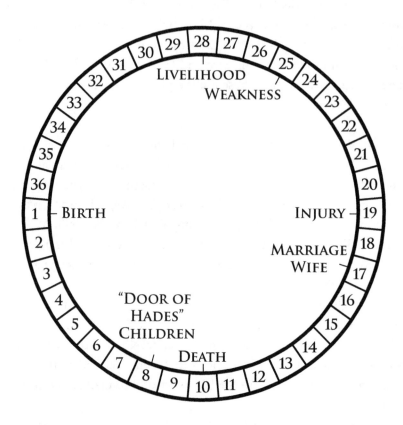

Figure 2.2 - Significations of the Decans from the Salmeschiniaka

also the first surviving Greek source that divides the circle of zodiacal signs into 360 portions or degrees, which is usually thought to indicate that Hypsicles was drawing on Mesopotamian sources, where this had long been a common practice.[81] The publication of this text seems to mark an important turning point in the history of astrology, because not long after Hypsicles' time astrologers regularly started calculating the rising zodiacal sign at the moment of a person's birth, and using this as the basis for calculating the system of twelve "houses" or "places." In this way Hypsicles' work may have acted as a necessary precursor for the development of horoscopic astrology, and this helps us to narrow down the approximate time frame in which it started being practiced.

---

ascensional times of the signs at the end of Paulus, *Introduction*, 2, are the same values given by Hypsicles. Paulus attributes these values to "the Egyptians," which probably means Nechepso and Petosiris.

[81] Evans, *The History and Practice of Ancient Astronomy*, p. 124.

The Hermes, Asclepius, and Nechepso-Petosiris Lineage

It seems that somewhere around the second half of the second century BCE or early part of the first century BCE, a set of incredibly important and influential astrological texts were written in Egypt. These texts were so important that they became mythologized in some of the narratives surrounding the origins of Hellenistic astrology by later astrologers.

At least two of our ancient sources describe the history of Hellenistic astrology by ascribing its creation to a sage named Hermes Trismegistus. According to this legend, Hermes wrote some sort of foundational text which formed the basis of the system, or perhaps its evolution from the system of astrology that was inherited from the Babylonians and the Egyptians. The system was then passed on to another figure named Asclepius, and then to two other key figures named Nechepso and Petosiris, and then to other subsequent expositors. This historical narrative appears attached to an astrological chart delineation dating to the second century CE:

> By examining in many books how it was handed down to us by the wise ancients, that is, by the Chaldeans, and Petosiris and especially the King Nechepso, just as they also based themselves on our lord Hermes together with Asclepius, who is of Imouthos, son of Hephaestus—in accordance with the time given me for the first year of the lord Antonius Caesar.[82]

A similar account is given by the fourth century astrologer Firmicus Maternus:

> We have written in these books all the things which Hermes and Hanubius handed down to Asclepius; which Petosiris and Nechepso explained; which Abraham, Orpheus, and Critodemus wrote, and all the others knowledgeable in this art.[83]

---

[82] Anonymous papyrus fragment from CCAG, 8, 4, p. 95 (Papyrus Paris 19b, col. I, 2–6 = Riess, "Nechepsonis et Petosiridis," test. 6), trans. Schmidt, *Kepler College Sourcebook*, p. 5, slightly modified. For an alternative translation, along with the Greek horoscope that the statement prefaced, see Neugebauer and Van Hoesen, *Greek Horoscopes*, No. 137c, p. 42.

[83] Firmicus, *Mathesis*, 4, proem: 5 (= Riess, "Nechepsonis et Petosiridis," test. 7), trans. Bram, p. 118, modified. The name "Hanubius" was suggested by an early editor as a reading of the otherwise meaningless phrase "einhnus vix" that is given in the manuscripts. Some have speculated that it refers to the Egyptian god Anubis, while others have tried to connect it with the later astrological author named Anubio. Heilen discusses this issue and makes a pretty good case for arguing that it is not a reference to the astrologer Anubio in "Anubio Reconsidered," pp. 140–41. Elsewhere Heilen cites Joachim Quack for suggesting that the text should read "Chmifis," referring to Kneph/Kmeph (Heilen, "Some Metrical Fragments," p. 51).

An anonymous astrologer who wrote a book on the fixed stars in the year 379, usually referred to as Anonymous of 379, was aware of the Mesopotamian origins of the tradition, and he even singles out Berossus for special mention, although he also mentions the Egyptian contribution, of which he seems to view Hermes, Nechepso, and Petosiris as the originators:

> The Babylonians and the Chaldeans, then, were just about the first to discover the knowledge of phenomena, as far as we knew from our progenitors. For Apollonius the Myndion and Artemidorus write accounts... [lacuna]. And Berossus and those following wrote about them [the fixed stars]. And the ancestors of our Egyptians bore them in mind and made predictions concerning them, from whom Hermes first arose and wrote in his cosmic predictions concerning the annual rising of the Sirius, and Nechao and Cerasphorus, and Petosiris and Nechepso, and some others wrote about them in a different zone, and especially Timaeus and Asclation. And those born later, being indebted to these compilers.[84]

In the second century CE the astrologer Manetho also seems to have been familiar with this narrative, as he mentions Hermes, Asclepius, and Petosiris when describing the origins of astrology:

> From the books of the temple sanctuaries, O King Ptolemy, and the hidden steles, which all-wise Hermes devised and inscribed with the appropriate forecasts of the heavenly stars, having found Asclepius as an adviser of prudent wisdom [...] For no one else has acquired the renown of such great wisdom besides Petosiris alone, the man dearest to me by far.[85]

Finally, in the early first century CE, the astrologer Marcus Manilius may have echoed a similar historical narrative, alluding to Hermes, Nechepso, and Petosiris, although this is somewhat obscured due to the fact that he wrote his astrological work in the form of a poem:

> You, God of Cyllene [i.e. Hermes], are the first founder of this great and holy science; through you has man gained a deeper knowledge of the sky— the constellations, the names and courses of the signs, their importance and influences... Moreover, nature proffered her aid and of her own

---

[84] Anonymous of 379, *Fixed Stars*, p. 204: 13–22, trans. Schmidt, p. 10.

[85] Manetho, *Apotelesmatika*, 5: 1–10 (= Riess, "Nechepsonis et Petosiridis," test. 9), trans. Lopilato, p. 263. The Ptolemy that is being addressed here is the king, not the astrologer.

accord opened herself, deigning first to inspire those kings whose minds reached out to heights bordering on heaven, kings who civilized savage peoples beneath the eastern sky, where the stars return to view and soar above the cities of dusky nations. Then priests who all their lives offered sacrifices in temples and were chosen to voice people's prayer secured by their devotion to the sympathy of God; their pure minds were kindled by the very presence of the powerful deity, and the God of heaven brought his servants to a knowledge of heaven and disclosed its secrets to them. These were the men who founded our noble science and were the first by their art to discern the destinies dependent on the wandering stars.[86]

In Greek mythology Hermes was said to have been born on Mount Cyllene, and thus the reference to Cyllene is a reference to Hermes. There is however some dispute about who the kings and priests are. Goold, the translator of this passage, thinks that the kings are Zoroaster and Belus, while the priests are Nechepso and Petosiris.[87] Given the general Hellenistic belief that Nechepso was a king, it seems more likely that Nechepso is the primary authority alluded to with the statement about kings, while it is possible that Petosiris is one of the priests.[88] Thus, Manilius seems to echo the same narrative about the origins of Hellenistic astrology as the other sources, especially in ascribing the creation of the tradition to Hermes.

While these lineages initially appear as if they are simply based on a sort of mythology, it turns out they may actually refer to a set of interrelated texts that were in circulation in the earliest strata of the Hellenistic astrological tradition. One of the earliest datable Greek astrological texts that survives, the summary of The Tablet (Pinax) of Thrasyllus, indicates that Nechepso, Petosiris, and Hermes Trismegistus were the only sources cited. Moreover, he cited them for specific technical doctrines and views, evidently from texts that carried their names. Similarly, another early text that may date to the first century CE, the summary of a book of definitions by Antiochus of Athens, indicates that he also only cited Nechepso, Petosiris, Hermes, and Timaeus as authorities. Again, Antiochus cites these authors not as mythical figures; rather, he attributes specific technical doctrines to each of them.

The reason for this seems to be that there were a set of pseudepigraphical manuals on astrology that were attributed to these authors which contained and potentially introduced some of what became core doctrines in Hellenistic

---

[86] Manilius, *Astronomica*, trans. Goold, 1: 30–52.

[87] Manilius, *Astronomica*, trans. Goold, p. 9, n. a, c.

[88] See the discussion in Volk, *Manilius and his Intellectual Background*, pp. 68–70.

astrology. When I say "core doctrines," what I mean are concepts and techniques that were both important or central in Hellenistic astrology, but also distinct from what was being practiced in the earlier traditions, thus representing the evolution of astrology from the Mesopotamian and Egyptian traditions.

It seems that the text attributed to Hermes may have been the first to introduce the concept of the twelve places, which was known as the *dōdekatopos* ("twelve-place" system) or *dōdekatropos* ("twelve-turning") in antiquity. This involves identifying the rising sign, and then assigning topics to each of the signs in zodiacal order from there, using what modern-day astrologers call the whole sign house system. Thrasyllus cites the Hermes text for a specific set of significations for the twelve places, which seems like a rudimentary form of the meanings that would become common in later authors.[89] Some of these significations match the significations for certain sectors given in the *Salmeschiniaka*, such as assigning livelihood (*bios*) to the culminating sign, while others have been rearranged in minor or sometimes major ways. For example, in the *Salmeschiniaka*, marriage was assigned to the seventeenth decan, which would fall in the sixth whole sign house, but Hermes moves the topic of marriage to the seventh house. The *Salmeschiniaka* associates injury with the area that would coincide with the seventh house, and death with the fourth, whereas Hermes moves injury to the sixth and death to the seventh. Whatever the relationship between the *Salmeschiniaka* and the Hermes text was, it seems as if the Hermes text took the basic idea of assigning topics or areas of life based on where a sector fell in the diurnal rotation, and then created a new and elaborate approach based on a unique set of internal reasoning.

In the Hermes text as cited by Thrasyllus we also find the first references to the names that were associated with each of the places, which became common among later authors; for example, calling the first place the Helm, the fifth Good Fortune, the eleventh Good Spirit, and the twelfth Bad Spirit. These names were connected with an important scheme known as the planetary joys. This is probably the earliest datable indirect reference to the planetary joys scheme, which indicates that the scheme itself may have first been introduced in the Hermes text as well.

At some point after the Hermes text, there was another early pseudepigraphical work that was attributed by its author to Asclepius.[90] Like the Hermes text, this text also seems to have primarily dealt with the significations or meanings of the places. However, its purpose seems to have been to introduce

---

[89] Thrasyllus, *Summary*, p. 101: 16–31.
[90] See the later sections on Asclepius and the *oktatropos* for a full set of citations.

a modified or additional set of significations for just the first eight places, which became known as the *oktatopos* ("eight-topic" system) or *oktatropos* ("eight-turning"). In some instances, the Asclepius text changed the placement of certain significations from the Hermes text, for example by moving death from the seventh place to the eighth place. In other instances, the Asclepius text leaves some of Hermes' significations without modifying them, such as associating the sixth place with injury. Schmidt points out that the Asclepius text is unique in assigning family members to the places, which were largely absent in the Hermes text, thus possibly indicating part of the motivation for this second work that covers just the first eight places.[91] Elsewhere he notes that later lists of the significations of the places represent a conflation or synthesis of the Hermes and Asclepius systems, even though they originally appear to have been introduced separately.[92]

Finally, sometime after the Hermes and Asclepius texts, another set of early texts were written that were attributed to Nechepso and Petosiris. These two authors are usually mentioned together as a pair, although sometimes individual works are attributed to them separately. Whatever their relationship, the works attributed to them undoubtedly became the most influential and widely-cited astrological texts in antiquity. They seem to have covered a wide range of topics, but the most important for our purposes is the doctrine of the Thema Mundi— the birth chart of the world—attributed to them by Firmicus Maternus.[93] The Thema Mundi forms the conceptual rationale for the assignment of the planetary domiciles to the signs of the zodiac, and provides part of the rationale for the qualities of the aspects.

These four texts, then, seem to have introduced many of the most fundamental technical doctrines of Hellenistic astrology, or at least we can only trace these doctrines back as far as these texts. What makes Hellenistic astrology unique from a technical standpoint is that it is the first time that the fourfold system that later became common in western astrology was put into place, which incorporates planets, signs of the zodiac, the twelve houses, and aspects. There are also a number of unique technical doctrines connected with these four parts of the system that appear very early on in the Hellenistic tradition:

---

[91] Schmidt, *Definitions and Foundations*, p. 309.

[92] Schmidt, *Kepler College Sourcebook*, p. 77. For example, in Thrasyllus, *Summary*, p. 101: 3–30, the *oktatropos* is presented first, and then the *dōdekatropos* afterward. But then in later sources such as Valens, *Anthology*, 4, 12: 1–2, the significations from each system are mixed together into a single account.

[93] Firmicus, *Mathesis*, 3, preface: 4.

1. The planets, and the important related concept of sect, which is the distinction between day and night charts.
2. The zodiac, and the domicile and triplicity rulership schemes, along with the four classical elements as applied to the signs.
3. The twelve places, which is connected to the planetary joys scheme, the use of the whole sign house system, and the concept of "lots," which is an alternative method of assigning topics to signs.
4. Aspects, and concepts related to aspects, such as right versus left, overcoming, striking with a ray, etc.

All of the technical concepts listed above form a sort of system, and are unique to the Hellenistic tradition. To the extent that these concepts and techniques were introduced and systemized over the course of perhaps a generation or two, especially within the texts attributed to Hermes, Asclepius, Nechepso, and Petosiris, then this does appear to indicate that Hellenistic astrology partially represents a sudden invention.

To be clear, that does not mean that Hellenistic astrology was invented out of thin air without any precedent or influence from the earlier traditions. It is clear that the earlier Mesopotamian and Egyptian traditions played a major role in contributing a number of earlier techniques and concepts to the core of what would later become Hellenistic astrology. We also must remain open to the possibility that new discoveries may still come to light in the future which could change our understanding of which techniques were being practiced in the earlier astrological traditions.[94] Additionally, we should not expect that the lineage represented by Hermes, Asclepius, Nechepso, and Petosiris was the only source for new astrological doctrines, or that the Hellenistic tradition was completely uniform. For one, even the founders of Hellenistic astrology appear to have disagreed with each other in some instances, as we have seen for example with the Hermes and Asclepius texts, which assign the topic of death to different houses. There were also probably other lines of transmission in terms of the adoption and circulation of Mesopotamian astrology in the west, which may have led to the development of alternative or competing doctrines in the Hellenistic tradition. The concept of antiscia, for example, seems to be based on a similar conceptual premise and serves a similar or overlapping function as

---

[94] This happened recently with the discovery of the so-called Egyptian bounds or terms, which is a concept that was thought to have been unique to the Hellenistic tradition, in an older cuneiform source, thus apparently indicating that the technique ultimately originated in the Mesopotamian tradition. See Jones and Steele, "A New Discovery of a Component of Greek Astrology in Babylonian Tablets: The 'Terms.'"

the doctrine of aspects, and it may represent a competing concept in the early Hellenistic tradition that didn't catch on in quite the same way that the standard doctrine of aspects did. Thus, sometimes the later diversity in the tradition is likely the result of competing doctrines and traditions that were introduced by different astrologers.

Differing Interpretations of Cryptic Source Texts

There are also other potential sources for technical variations in the tradition that derive from the foundational texts themselves. Some of the quotes that later Hellenistic astrologers give from early authors such as Nechepso and Petosiris indicate that their texts were written in a way that was cryptic or enigmatic, which sometimes made it difficult to understand the doctrines contained in these texts. Differing interpretations about what the authors of the earliest source texts were actually saying may have been the source of a number of variations in the technical doctrines of the Hellenistic tradition.

At one point in his work, the second century astrologer, Vettius Valens, bemoans the cryptic nature of the source texts that he was working with; singling out Nechepso in particular, he figuratively throws his hands up in the air and exclaims:

> Whether the ancients, though knowing the workings of prognostication, jealously concealed it because it was a matter for boasting and hard for human nature to understand, or whether, not grasping what nature was articulating and ordaining and giving to men ungrudgingly as a gift because of necessity she had to box it up, they nevertheless wrote in a riddling manner, I cannot say. For, it seems to me that none of the finest elements in the cosmos and none of its numerous and great instances of workmanship is begrudged to mankind by god for opportune use; for the divine would not foreshow if it did not want to provide. However, it being surely the case that those men either so wished it or that they were so unable, even so, in mentioning the chief of them below [i.e. Nechepso], I am astonished that his meaning is so twisted and hard to catch.[95]

Valens is essentially suggesting that the ancients were either purposely going out of their way to make this material obscure because they wanted to keep it for themselves, or they simply didn't know what they were talking about. Evidently Valens favored the former scenario, since he continued trying to unravel and interpret the source texts at his disposal, despite his frustrations with them.

---

[95] Valens, *Anthology*, 7, 4: 1–3, trans. Schmidt, pp. 28–29.

In the fourth century CE, Firmicus Maternus voiced similar complaints about the cryptic nature of Petosiris' writings. At one point in his discussion about a specific technical concept, he remarks: "The tract of Petosiris on this subject seems to me to display a kind of hostile prejudice and an attempt to conceal the concept."[96] This issue of differing interpretations of cryptic passages about specific techniques actually comes up quite explicitly at one point in Valens during a discussion about the calculation for the Lot of Fortune. Valens quotes a difficult passage from Nechepso on the calculation of the Lot of Fortune, and then proceeds to give his opinion on how it should be interpreted, saying that other astrologers have come to different conclusions about it.[97] The passage discusses whether the calculation for the Lot of Fortune should be reversed for day and night charts, and in fact we see other Hellenistic astrologers coming to different conclusions about whether to reverse the calculation.[98] What this seems to demonstrate is that sometimes diversity in the tradition and disagreements about technical concepts were rooted in differing interpretations of a set of early source texts that were written in an enigmatic manner.

Mystery Traditions

A related issue is the apparent existence of mystery traditions within the astrological community, and the possibility that many of the ancient doctrines were kept secret, with some of the astrological schools being kept private or underground.

Valens says that the purpose of his treatise is to initiate (*mustagōgeō*) the reader into astrology, as if it were part of a mystery tradition.[99] Immediately after this statement he makes the reader swear an oath to keep his teachings secret:

> Concerning this book, then, I must before all prescribe an oath for those who happen to encounter it, that they may keep watch over what is written and withhold it in a manner appropriate to the mysteries [...] I adjure them by the sacred circle of the Sun and the irregular courses of the Moon, and by the powers of the remaining stars and the circle of the twelve zodiacal signs, to keep these things secret, and not to impart them to the unlearned or the uninitiated, and to give a portion of honor and remembrance to

---

[96] Firmicus, *Mathesis*, 8, 2: 1, trans. Bram, p. 267 (= Riess, "Nechepsonis et Petosiridis," fr. 16).

[97] Valens, *Anthology*, 3, 11.

[98] Ptolemy for example says that you should not reverse the calculation for the Lot of Fortune depending on whether it is a day or night chart (*Tetrabiblos*, 3, 11: 5), whereas Paulus reverses the calculation (*Introduction*, 23). I will deal with this issue more thoroughly in the later chapter on the lots.

[99] Valens, *Anthology*, 4, 11: 11.

him who introduced them [to this discipline]. May it go well for those who keep this oath, and may the afore-mentioned gods be in accord with their wishes, but may the opposite be the case for those who forswear this oath.[100]

Firmicus Maternus makes the reader swear a similar oath at the beginning of book seven of his *Mathesis*:

> Therefore, following the rule of these men [Orpheus, Plato, Pythagoras, and Porphyry], my dear Mavortius, I beg you to take an oath by God, the Creator of the Universe, who has made and regulated everything under the control of everlasting Necessity, who has shaped the Sun and Moon, who arranged the order and courses of all the stars, who collected the waves of the sea between boundaries of land, who forever kindles the encircling divinity of the heavens, who maintains the earth balanced evenly in the middle of the universe, who has created with his majestic divine skill all men, beasts, birds, and every manner of living thing, who moistens the earth with ever-flowing fountains, who makes constant and ever-changing the breath of the winds, who has created all things out of the four contrasting elements, who initiated the rising and setting of the stars and the movements of the earth, who set up stars as stations for the ascent and descent of souls [...] We beg you to take an oath that these revered doctrines will not be revealed to profane ears but that the entire teaching of divinity will be made known only to those equipped with pure splendor of mind, whom an uncorrupted soul has led to the right path of life, whose loyalty is above reproach, whose hands are free of all crime. Receive, therefore, the detailed account which with the greatest trepidation of spirit we have promised you.[101]

Firmicus again makes similar closing statements at the very end of his work, saying:

> It is for you to remember the sanctity of your oath: guard these books with a pure mind and soul and do not reveal this science to inexperienced ears or sacrilegious minds. The nature of the divine prefers to be hidden in diverse coverings; access to it should not be easy nor its majesty open to all.[102]

---

[100] Valens, *Anthology*, 7, proem: 1–4, trans. Schmidt, pp. 1–2, slightly modified.
[101] Firmicus, *Mathesis*, 7, 1: 2–3, trans. Bram, p. 233.
[102] Firmicus, *Mathesis*, 8, 33: 2, trans. Bram, p. 302.

Valens has three different oath passages in his books, and Komorowska speculated that they were each so formulaic that he might be getting them from another, probably Hermetic, source.[103] I believe that this speculation can be confirmed by comparing Valens' oath with another oath that appears in a Hermetic treatise from the Nag Hammadi library known as the *Discourse on the Eighth and Ninth*:

> I adjure you who will read this holy book, by heaven and earth and fire and water, and seven rulers of substance and the creative spirit in them, and the <un>begotten God and the self-begotten and the begotten, that you guard what Hermes has communicated. God will be at one with those who keep the oath and everyone we have named, but the wrath of each of them will come upon those who violate the oath.[104]

The implications of this parallel are that Valens and others drew on and wrote texts that were part of a Hermetic mystery tradition, and some of the texts that survived were never meant for public consumption. This may be part of the reason why only fragments of the earliest source texts (which we see allusions to in authors like Valens) survived into the present day.

Thus, some of the disparities or areas of divergence in the Hellenistic tradition may be the result of either differing interpretations of what were in some instances rather cryptic source texts, or on the other hand certain texts simply not being widely available to every astrologer, but instead being passed along in mystery schools, from teacher to student, for generations. While this certainly does not account for all of the variations in the later tradition, these two issues must be kept in mind when it comes to the debate about the origins and cohesion of the Hellenistic tradition, where diversity amongst later authors is often used as an argument against the sudden invention hypothesis.

Later Expositors and the Flourishing of the Tradition

The attribution of some of the early foundational texts to Egyptian figures such as Nechepso and Petosiris may have been meant to invoke ideas of an Egyptian lineage or origin of the tradition, although we don't really know who the authors of the texts were. We do know that at least by the middle of the first century BCE, Hellenistic astrology started being practiced more widely and publicly, and became very popular and influential in terms of the culture of its day. At this point there seem to have been a number of early expositors of the tradition

---

[103] Komorowska, *Vettius Valens of Antioch*, p. 238.
[104] Meyer, *The Nag Hammadi Scriptures*, NHC VI, 6: 63, p. 418.

who elaborated upon the basic framework that was introduced in the Hermetic lineage. There was still a tendency for a number of the early expositors to write their works as pseudepigrapha, attributing them to figures such as Timaeus, Orpheus, Abraham, and Zoroaster. It is not clear why these names were chosen, and what relation they had to the earlier texts attributed to Hermes, Asclepius, and Nechepso-Petosiris. They may have been part of the same lineage or school, or they may represent alternative or competing traditions. It is hard to say, since our knowledge of these texts is also fragmentary.

By the late first century BCE, most of the basic doctrines were in place, and Hellenistic astrology emerged onto the world stage. Whatever its origins, from this point forward it became a technical system that was broad enough and malleable enough to be applied to many different areas of study, and it was adopted and used within the context of many different philosophical, religious, and scientific worldviews. Authors would pick and choose what parts of the system to use based on their own technical or philosophical predilections, and new techniques and concepts would be introduced and developed, while existing ones would sometimes be modified or lost. Despite these changes, the core of the fourfold system of planets, signs, aspects, and houses stayed largely intact, and it is this system that would go on to become one of the most enduring legacies of the Hellenistic age.

CHAPTER 3
PRACTICING ASTROLOGY
IN THE ROMAN EMPIRE

The Roman Empire

The Republic of Rome began expanding its power outside of Italy in the third century BCE, roughly coinciding with the start of the Hellenistic period. Eventually by the second and first centuries BCE, it had become the dominant power in the Mediterranean. In the middle of the first century BCE, a Roman general named Julius Caesar seized control of the Republic, and after he was assassinated his adopted son Octavian inherited his power and eventually became the head of the state. A subsequent civil war between Octavian and a rival general named Mark Antony ended famously in 30 BCE when Anthony and his consort Cleopatra VII, who was the queen of Egypt, were defeated in battle and committed suicide. Rome subsequently annexed Egypt, thus ending the 275-year rule of the Ptolemaic dynasty. Octavian then adopted the title of Augustus, and became the first of a series of emperors of Rome, thereby inaugurating the imperial period of the Roman Empire.

The Roman Empire continued to expand over the course of the next century, eventually reaching its height around the second century CE, at which point it controlled the entire area around the Mediterranean. The height of the Roman Empire roughly coincides with what appears to have been the high point of the practice of Hellenistic astrology, with the majority of the surviving horoscopes dating to the second and third centuries CE, and with most of the surviving texts being written by individuals who lived in the Roman Empire between

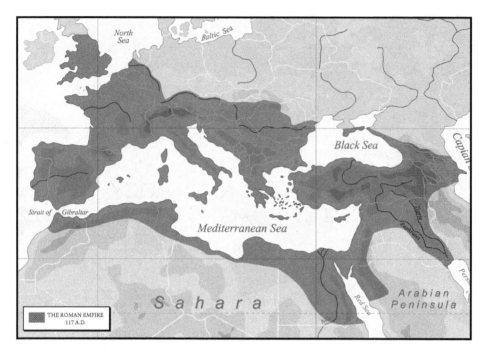

Figure 3.1 - The Roman Empire in the Second Century CE

the first and seventh centuries CE. Thus, while Hellenistic astrology originated in the Hellenistic era, the majority of its history and practice occurred within the Roman Empire, and this is the period that we must look to in order to understand the society that it flourished in.

The Three Branches of Hellenistic Astrology

There are three main branches of Hellenistic astrology. While the core of the technical structure in each of the three branches is very similar, the area of focus and the scope of the application of the techniques varies from branch to branch, depending on what is being studied. While it is often implied, this threefold division is not usually explicitly acknowledged in the Hellenistic astrological texts, although it is useful in categorizing the different applications of astrology that were used in the ancient world.[1] It is also still largely applicable when studying other, later traditions of western astrology.

---

[1] Ptolemy does distinguish between what he calls universal (*katholikon*) astrology and natal astrology (*genethlialogikon*) in *Tetrabiblos*, 2, 1: 2. Elsewhere, Dorotheus spends the first four books of his work on natal astrology, but then in book five he deals entirely with inceptional astrology. Hephaestio deals with introductory concepts and universal astrology in book 1 of his *Apotelesmatika*, natal astrology in book 2, and inceptional astrology in book 3. Thus there was a clear distinction between the three different branches that were used in practice.

Natal Astrology

The first branch of Hellenistic astrology is known as *genethlialogy*, which means the "study of nativities," from the Greek word *genethlios*, which means "pertaining to one's birth." This is the branch of astrology that is more commonly known in modern times as *natal astrology*. Genethlialogy is the practice of studying the positions of the planets at the moment of a person's birth in order to determine information about the nature and course of their life. This usually involves creating a diagram which provides a visual representation of where the planets were when the native was born, otherwise known as a birth "chart" (*thema*) or "nativity" (*genesis*).

Hellenistic astrology appears to have been primarily oriented towards the study of natal astrology, and this shift in focus towards the individual rather than the collective is one of the major differences between Hellenistic astrology and the earlier Mesopotamian and Egyptian traditions. Certainly this should be seen as a continuation of the movement towards a more personalized form of astrology which began in the Mesopotamian tradition in the fifth century BCE, although the Hellenistic approach does appear to represent a considerable elaboration of many of the basic concepts that were developed during the earlier periods. Indeed, the application of astrology to the birth of individuals became the cornerstone of astrological theory and practice in the Hellenistic tradition, and the majority of the techniques in Hellenistic astrology are specifically designed or geared towards natal astrology. Astrologers became so closely associated with the practice that they were sometimes referred to as "nativity-studiers" or "horoscope casters" (*genethlialogoi*).

There were a number of different applications and subsets of natal astrology. One subset is known in modern times as "rectification," which is when an astrologer attempts to deduce when a person was born and what the precise arrangement of their birth chart would have been based on information that is known about the person's life. This is most commonly done in order to determine the time that a person was born, either when the birth time was not recorded, or when it was not recorded with enough precision that is required in order to use certain techniques.

One of the earliest references to rectification as a practice dates to the first century BCE, when the Roman historian Varro consulted an astrologer named Lucius Tarutius Firmanus in order to attempt to determine the birth chart for Romulus, the founder of Rome, resulting in a speculative chart with a specific date and time seven centuries earlier.[2] Tarutius also attempted to determine the chart for Romulus' conception, as well as the inception chart for the founding

---

[2] See the discussion in Heilen, "Ancient Scholars on the Horoscope of Rome."

of Rome, which demonstrates that rectification can sometimes be used more broadly in order to attempt to reconstruct an astrological chart for any event that has occurred in the past. This is based on a process of inferring what placements the chart should have according to the rules of astrology, based on the events and circumstances known to have occurred later on.

Both Valens and Hephaestio include their own conception charts in their works, which likely would have been rectified by using specific techniques.[3] This tradition may go back to Berossus and his students, who were said to have a method for casting charts both for birth and conception.[4] The purpose of conception charts is a bit obscure, although Hephaestio seems to follow Ptolemy in saying that the purpose is to study events that occurred during the gestation period during the formation of the body, even though the chart for the moment of birth is viewed as having more weight in terms of determining the course of the native's life once born.[5]

Universal Astrology
The second branch of the Hellenistic tradition of astrology is known as *universal astrology*, from the Greek term *katholikos*, which means "concerning the whole," "universal," or "general." This branch is more commonly known in modern times as *mundane astrology*. Universal astrology is the application of astrological principles to groups of people such as cities and nations, as well as to natural phenomena such as weather and earthquakes. Conceptually this is essentially the same type of astrology that originated in and was predominant during the Mesopotamian tradition, although in the Hellenistic tradition the techniques became somewhat more elaborate, since they were developed within the context of the new technical framework of Hellenistic astrology, with its added emphasis on aspects and houses.[6]

Universal astrology does not seem to have played as central a role in the Hellenistic tradition as natal astrology did. While many astrologers during the Hellenistic and Roman periods were involved in politics and served as court astrologers to several kings and emperors, they appear to have focused primarily on using the natal charts of political figures in order to make personal predictions, and works on universal astrology appear to be less common than those on natal astrology. It appears that it was during the Persian and

---

[3] Hephaestio says that the time of conception can be known either by observation or by calculation (*Apotelesmatika*, 2, 1: 35), although he does so within the context of a chapter in which he presents specific techniques for rectifying the conception chart.

[4] Vitruvius, *On Architecture*, 9, 6: 2.

[5] Hephaestio, *Apotelesmatika*, 2, 1: 35–38. Compare Ptolemy, *Tetrabiblos*, 3, 2.

[6] One of the primary treatments of universal astrology is book two of Ptolemy's *Tetrabiblos*.

Arabic astrological traditions between the third and ninth centuries CE that some of the more advanced forms of universal, political, and historical astrology were developed.[7]

Inceptional Astrology

The third branch of Hellenistic astrology is known as *inceptional astrology* or *katarchic astrology*, from the Greek word *katarchē*, which means "beginning," "inception," or "commencement." The premise of inceptional astrology is that you can determine information about the quality and future of any event or venture by studying the alignment of the cosmos at the moment that it began. It is essentially the same premise as natal astrology, but instead of casting charts for the birth of individuals, the charts are cast for the inception of events, such as the start of a journey, the founding of a city, or the beginning of a marriage. The main focus is to determine how auspicious the astrological configurations were at the moment the venture began (*katarchē*), and thus what the potential outcome will be (*apotelesma*).[8]

The most popular application of inceptional astrology in the Hellenistic tradition was to use it to proactively choose auspicious moments in order to begin new ventures and undertakings, under the premise that the astrologer could help to ensure a more successful outcome by choosing a set of planetary alignments that were particularly positive. In modern times, the proactive use of astrology to choose auspicious moments in the future is referred to as *electional astrology*, while the retrospective application of astrology towards analyzing events that have occurred already in the past is more commonly referred to as *inceptional astrology*. However, in the Hellenistic tradition, the term *katarchē* was used to refer to both electional as well as inceptional astrology, since both involved looking at the chart for the commencement or inception of the matter.

Because it can be applied to so many different things, several different subsets or applications of astrology developed out of inceptional astrology. One was the use of what later became known as "decumbiture charts," which is when an astrologer casts a chart for the time when a person falls ill and "takes to their bed," in order to use the chart as both a diagnostic tool, as well as to give some idea about the length and severity of the illness.[9] Another application of

---

[7] Pingree thought that "historical astrology" proper, with its focus on the periodic conjunctions of Jupiter and Saturn in the different triplicities, was invented by the Sassanian Persian astrologers sometime between the third and the sixth centuries CE. See Pingree, *From Astral Omens*, pp. 49 & 64.

[8] This will be discussed more thoroughly later in the philosophy chapter.

[9] The Greek term used to refer to this subset of inceptional astrology was *kataklisis*, which means "lying down," "taking to one's bed," or "taking to bed ill." There is a nice summary

inceptional astrology was for what is known in modern times as "consultation charts," which is when an astrologer casts a chart for the beginning of a consultation with a client, in order to determine what is on the client's mind at that time and what the focus of the consultation will be.[10] Dykes refers to this as thought-interpretation.[11]

The Emergence of Interrogational Astrology

At some point in the Hellenistic tradition, a fourth branch or application of astrology began to emerge, which in the later Medieval tradition would eventually become known as *interrogational astrology* or *horary questions*.[12] In this application of astrology an astrologer casts a chart for the moment when a client asks them a single specific question, and the assumption is that the chart cast for the moment of the question will describe both the nature of the inquiry as well as the outcome.

Interrogational astrology was very popular in the Medieval and Renaissance traditions, to the point that it became a full-fledged fourth branch of the tradition. By contrast, references to the practice in the Hellenistic tradition are noticeably rare. They are in fact so rare that some have concluded that interrogational astrology wasn't practiced in the Hellenistic tradition at all, but instead that it emerged later in the Indian, Persian, or Medieval Arabic astrological traditions.[13]

---

of the views of several Hellenistic astrologers on the subject edited in CCAG 1, pp. 122–124. This summary mentions several different authors as having dealt with the subject of decumbitures, including Dorotheus, Hermes, Petosiris, Protagoras of Nicaea, and Julian of Laodicea. A separate fragment appears on CCAG 1, p. 128, outlining a numerological method for decumbitures attributed to Hermes, and alluding to other methods by Petosiris and Pythagoras as well. Both fragments were translated by Schmidt in *Sages*, pp. 12–16. Valens also has a brief treatment of decumbitures in *Anthology*, 9, 5.

[10] For an example see Hephaestio, *Apotelesmatika*, 3, 4: esp. 19–34. Gramaglia translates the title of this chapter as "How someone can know beforehand the inquiries of those wishing to investigate [a matter], from the inception." Hephaestio, *Apotelesmatika*, 3, trans. Gramaglia, p. 39.

[11] Hephaestio, *Apotelesmatika*, 3, trans. Gramaglia, ed. Dykes, pp. 9–17.

[12] In the Medieval tradition it became known as "interrogations" or "questions," from the Arabic word *masā'il*, or in Byzantine Greek *erōtēseis*. In modern times it is often referred to with the shortened phrase "horary astrology," from the longer designation that started being used in the seventeenth century "horary questions."

[13] Pingree argued towards the end of his career that interrogational astrology was invented in the Indian tradition, and then passed to the west later during the Medieval period (*From Astral Omens*, p. 36). Earlier in his career he had taken for granted that interrogational astrology was practiced in the Hellenistic tradition, tracing it back to Dorotheus, although he acknowledged that "interrogations are fairly infrequent before the Byzantine period." Pingree, "Astrology," p. 124. His thinking seems to have changed sometime around the late 80s or early 90s, although he never fully explained why. Much of this is documented in Brennan, "The

The issue largely hinges on whether the scattered references to interrogational astrology in book five of the corrupt Arabic translation of Dorotheus were in the original text, or whether they represent later interpolations in the text from the Persian or Arabic translators once the practice had already become common. I published a paper in 2007 in which I argued that interrogational astrology was not practiced in the Hellenistic tradition, calling into question the reliability of the Arabic version of Dorotheus.[14] This was later shown to be incorrect with the 2013 publication of a translation of book three of Hephaestio of Thebes by Gramaglia and Dykes, where they demonstrated that there is at least one clear reference to interrogational astrology in the text, which seems to confirm that a parallel reference in the Arabic version of Dorotheus is genuine.[15]

What seems to have happened is that interrogational astrology was originally developed as a subset of inceptional astrology, partially in connection with the practice of using "consultation charts" or "thought-interpretation." Inceptional astrology was already an established practice, where one could cast a chart for the beginning of an event in order to find out information about the quality and outcome of whatever was initiated at that time. This was then extended to the practice of casting a chart for the inception of a consultation between an astrologer and their client, with the assumption that the resulting chart would be able to depict what was on the mind of the client at the time. From there some astrologers started using these consultation charts or thought-interpretation charts in order to determine the actual outcome of the thoughts of the client, or in order to answer a specific question that was posed to the astrologer about the situation on the client's mind, and from there interrogational astrology began to develop as its own separate practice.[16] This reconstruction partially relies on the view that determining what is on the client's mind is both conceptually and procedurally distinct from answering a specific question from the client about the outcome of their inquiry.[17]

Katarche of Horary," although I have since come to different conclusions after the publication of Gramaglia and Dykes' translation of book 3 of Hephaestio in 2013.

[14] Brennan, "The Katarche of Horary."

[15] The reference is in Hephaestio, *Apotelesmatika*, 3, 11: 2. This confirmed as genuine the reference in the Arabic Dorotheus, *Carmen*, 5, 17: 1. Hephaestio drew on Dorotheus for this chapter.

[16] This was part of my thesis in Brennan, "The Katarche of Horary," and it later seemed to be confirmed by Benjamin Dykes, who showed how closely "thought-interpretation" was related to interrogational astrology in many early Medieval works. See Dykes, *Works of Sahl and Māshā'allāh*, pp. xxxiv–xxxviii, and especially Hermann of Carinthia, *The Search of the Heart*, trans. Dykes, pp. 2–11; pp. 20–29.

[17] That there was a distinction between thought-interpretation and interrogations in the early tradition is argued persuasively by Dykes in his preface to Hermann of Carinthia, *The*

In Hephaestio, interrogational astrology appears as if it is the last option in a hierarchy of different moments of symbolic importance that the astrologer can cast an inceptional chart for in order to give the client information about their concerns. In chapter 47, which is on runaway slaves, the first instruction is to cast the inception chart for when the slave ran away, from the perspective of the master, in order to see if the slave will return; but then it says that if the time is unknown to instead cast the chart for when the master first learned that the slave had run away.[18] In chapter 11, which is on determining if a person's spouse will return to them after a separation has occurred, it says to cast the inception chart for the moment the separation occurs, or if that is not known, to cast the chart for the time that the client inquires about the matter with the astrologer.[19] In this way we can distinguish three different symbolic moments of importance:

1. The moment that the event actually occurs.
2. The moment that the person involved in the event learns of its occurrence.
3. The moment that the person involved in the event asks the astrologer about the outcome of the event.

From this perspective, it seems as if interrogations may have originally developed as one of the lesser moments of symbolic importance that could be used in order to get insight into the client's problems, but only if other options were unavailable.

Although this example in Dorotheus dates to the first century CE, there is some uncertainty surrounding the development of interrogational astrology after that point. There is a short passage that seems to be on interrogational astrology that is attributed to Hermes Trismegistus, but it is difficult to date since we know that new texts were being attributed to Hermes throughout the Hellenistic and Medieval periods, and there is nothing within the text itself that allows us to narrow the time frame involved.[20] It is only in the late fifth century that we find the first examples of actual charts that seem to have been cast for the moment of a question within the context of interrogational astrology, from a collection attributed to "Palchus."[21] Most of the charts in this collection seem

---

Search of the Heart, trans. Dykes, pp. 2–11.

[18] Hephaestio, *Apotelesmatika,* 3, 47: 51.

[19] Hephaestio, *Apotelesmatika,* 3, 11: 2.

[20] CCAG 8, 1, p. 172–177. Translated by Schmidt in *Sages,* pp. 7–11.

[21] Neugebauer and Van Hoesen, *Greek Horoscopes,* pp. 142–148. For the identity of Palchus, see Pingree, "The Astrological School of John Abramius." In a personal communication Levente László notes that these charts probably come from an astrologer who was employed

to be inception charts for specific events, or possibly consultation charts that are being used to describe the focus of the consultation and thoughts of the client, although one of them seems to be a question from a client in Smyrna who asked about the fate of a ship that had not arrived when expected from Alexandria.[22] The coordinates of the chart indicate that it was cast for the location of the client in what is now modern-day Turkey rather than for Alexandria where the ship would have departed from, and from this the astrologer attempted to predict what happened to the ship. The rules that were used in the interpretation were still very similar to the Hellenistic rules used for judging inceptional or event charts, and it was evidently not until the Medieval tradition that some of the more standard rules for interpreting interrogational charts that involved the rulers of the houses would be developed.

Interrogational astrology may have already started to develop in the Sassanian Persian tradition between the third and seventh centuries. A story survives about the last Parthian king Ardavan V asking his astrological advisor a question about where his maid ran off to with Ardashīr I, who would become the first king of the new Sassanian Persian Empire.[23] Pingree and Panaino take this as an example of interrogational astrology, although it is not clear in the story if the chart was cast for the moment of the question or simply for the time that the two people escaped.[24] If it was the latter, then it would just be a standard instance of using inceptional astrology to study the escape of slaves from the moment of their departure, of which there are several examples in the Hellenistic tradition, and thus it would not necessarily be an example of an interrogation.

Around the same time period, interrogational astrology may have also been developing in the Indian tradition. The late third century CE text known as the *Yavanajātaka* has ten chapters that largely deal with thought-interpretation.[25] Immediately after this section it has a short chapter that briefly deals with how to determine the "fruition" of the client's thoughts, followed by other chapters on finding lost objects, determining whether an illness will result in death, and determining the gender of children that have not yet been born.[26] While it seems that the material on thought-interpretation is more extensive and worked out,

---

by the Eastern Roman emperor Zeno.

[22] Neugebauer and Van Hoesen, *Greek Horoscopes*, pp.144–146 (horoscope no. L 479), based on Cumont's edition in CCAG 1, pp. 103–4, checked against variants in the Vienna manuscript which are listed in CCAG 6, p. 14.

[23] Panaino, "The Two Astrological Reports."

[24] Panaino, "The Two Astrological Reports," p. 183–4; Pingree, *From Astral Omens*, p. 40; reiterated more recently by Panaino in "Cosmologies and Astrology," p. 250.

[25] *Yavanajātaka*, 52–62.

[26] *Yavanajātaka*, 63–66.

it is clear that a nascent branch of interrogational astrology is already starting to develop in this material.

Eventually these three strands from the Hellenistic, Persian, and Indian traditions all coalesced in the Medieval period, and the first complete works on interrogations that survive from the western tradition come from the late eighth and early ninth century astrologers Theophilus of Edessa, Māshā'allāh, and Sahl ibn Bishr.

Surviving Horoscopes or Charts

Taken at face value, one of the surprising features about the surviving corpus of individual horoscopes or charts (*themata*) from the Hellenistic tradition is that virtually all of them are simply lists of calculated planetary positions, with almost nothing in the way of concrete statements or interpretations about what the placements mean. As we have seen, these "original horoscopes," which were usually written on scraps of papyrus, are to be distinguished from the "literary horoscopes" that appear within the context of technical manuals on astrology, since the former usually simply present the raw technical data of a chart, while the latter are usually employed within the context of the astrologer's case studies in order to demonstrate the application of specific astrological techniques. Neugebauer and van Hoesen point out that if the longer literary texts hadn't survived then it would hardly be apparent what the purpose of the bare-bones astronomical positions in the standalone charts was in the first place.[27] This is an important point to keep in mind when it comes to the surviving Mesopotamian horoscopes as well, which are similarly sparse on interpretations, and for which little to no interpretive handbooks survive.

A typical Hellenistic horoscope will simply list the date that a person was born, the hour, the signs of the zodiac that each of the planets and the Ascendant were located in, and occasionally the sign of the Lot of Fortune. Here is a typical example of a chart from the city of Oxyrhynchus in Egypt that dates to the fourth century CE, which was written on a piece of papyrus:[28]

---

[27] Neugebauer and Van Hoesen, *Greek Horoscopes*, p. 162.

[28] This is horoscope no. 4269 in Jones, *Astronomical Papyri from Oxyrhynchus*, vol. 2, pp. 408–410. Jones dated the chart to February 17, 320 CE. In the recalculated chart, Jupiter is right around the border between Leo and Virgo, thus the statement in the horoscope that it is in Leo and Virgo on the same day. The term or phrase at the end of the horoscope, *dieutuchei*, or variations of it, appears somewhat frequently in other surviving horoscopes. For example, see the end of horoscopes No. 81, Nos 138/161, No. 277, and No. 238 in Neugebauer and Van Hoesen, *Greek Horoscopes*. They discuss the term briefly on p. 163. The term also appears in horoscopes 4249, 4264, 4266 (twice), 4268, 4269, and 4295 in Jones, *Astronomical Papyri*.

ἔτους λς' Διοκλητιανοῦ,	Year 36 of Diocletian,
Μεχεὶρ κβ', ὥρ(ᾳ) β' ἡμέραις.	Mecheir 22, hour 2 of day.
ὡρ(οσκόπος) Ἰχθύσι.	Ascendant in Pisces.
Κρόνος Κρίῳ.	Saturn in Aries.
Ζεὺς Λέοντι, αὐθη-	Jupiter in Leo, on the same
μερὶ Παρθένῳ.	day in Virgo.
ἥλιος Ὑδρηχόῳ.	Sun in Aquarius.
Ἄρης Ὑδρηχόῳ.	Mars in Aquarius.
Ἀφροδίτη Ὑδρηχόῳ.	Venus in Aquarius.
Ἑρμῆς Ὑδρηχόῳ.	Mercury in Aquarius.
σελήνη Σκορπίῳ.	Moon in Scorpio.
διευτυχεῖ.	Good luck!

There are also some more elaborate "deluxe horoscopes" that survived, which are contained in Alexander Jones' collection of charts from Oxyrhynchus, but these are really only slightly more elaborate versions of the example above. The more elaborate charts include more specific technical data, such as the position of the planets by degree and minute; which planet rules the sign; the bounds, triplicity, and monomoiria that a planet is located in; the gender, modality, and other characteristics of the zodiacal sign; which decan it is in; what phase relation it has to the Sun; and the location of additional "lots" besides the Lot of Fortune, such as Eros or Necessity. Essentially, these "deluxe horoscopes" encompass most of the data that would be represented visually in modern times in an actual diagram of a chart.

Astrological Consultation Boards

When compared with the very extensive and detailed predictive doctrines contained in the astrological manuals, the almost complete lack of delineation material in the surviving horoscopes leads one to the conclusion that most of the time astrological delineations were likely conveyed orally in antiquity. The surviving scraps of papyrus which contain the basic chart data of the nativity were probably just the starting point, or the precursor to an actual consultation. It was the most basic set of information that was needed in order to actually display a chart so that it could be interpreted. A prospective client would have needed to consult an astrologer who was skilled in the astronomical and mathematical computations necessary to accurately calculate the positions of the planets at the time of their birth; this may have been the reason why one of the more widespread appellations for astrologers was "mathematicians" (*mathēmatikoi*).

When it was time to conduct an actual consultation with a client, it seems that the astrologers would use an astrological consultation board (*pinax*) in order to display the chart.[29] These were similar to modern-day chess boards, except that the astrological boards depicted the twelve signs of the zodiac and sometimes the decans or other subdivisions, and then different stones were placed around the board in order to represent the positions of the planets in the chart. Several of these boards have survived, and some of the more elaborate ones were made out of ivory, gold, and wood. Some of the astrologers may have used different stones as markers for the planets, so that the nature of the stone was the same as the nature of the planet (e.g. gold for the Sun, silver for the Moon).[30] The oldest board that has been discovered was dated to somewhere around the first century BCE.[31]

Charts in the Hellenistic tradition were typically presented as circular, and evidently it was only in the Medieval tradition that square charts became more popular.[32] One of the surviving boards has two concentric zodiacal wheels on it. Evans suggests that this type of board could have been used for synastry, which is when the planetary positions in two natal charts are compared in order to gauge how two people will interact, usually in terms of romantic relationships.[33] It also seems likely that the second zodiacal ring could have additionally been used in order to study transits or time-lord periods, which often involve moving planetary positions forward and then measuring them relative to where the planets were placed in the natal chart.

Astrologers who were unable to afford the more elaborate versions of the horoscope boards may have used simpler methods, such as drawing charts in sand. In the late fourth or early fifth century, Nonnus of Panopolis describes a fictional scene in which a diviner casts a birth chart by covering the surface of a table with dark sand or dust, and then proceeds to inscribe a circle on it, which he then divides into segments.[34]

The term used to refer to the horoscope boards was *pinax*, which means "board," "table," or "tablet." Both Thrasyllus and Critodemus were said to have written astrological texts that were given the title *Pinax*, and it seems plausible that it was in reference to the horoscope boards, since their books were essentially instructional texts on how to use or interpret the placements laid out in one.

---

[29] For the most extensive treatment see Evans, "The Astrologer's Apparatus."
[30] Packman, "Instructions for the Use of Planet Markers on a Horoscope Board."
[31] Forenbaher and Jones, "The Nakovana Zodiac," p. 433.
[32] Thomann, "Square Horoscope Diagrams."
[33] Evans, "The Astrologer's Apparatus," p. 7.
[34] Nonnos, *Dionysiaca*, 6: 15–24.

Telling Time

There were a few different methods of telling time in the ancient world. During the day, sundials were used, while at night water clocks could be used. For astrologers, the most accurate method of telling time was by using a metal device called an astrolabe. The original Greek term for this device, *astrolabos*, means something like "star-reckoner."[35] Astrolabes could be used in order to determine local time, calculate the degree of the Ascendant, and a number of other functions. The astrolabe may have been introduced by Hipparchus already in the second century BCE, and Ptolemy's reference to a "horoscopic instrument" in one of his minor works called *Planisphere* is sometimes taken to indicate it was definitely in use by the second century CE.[36] However, it is not until the fourth century that we know for sure of the existence of a now-lost treatise on how to build an astrolabe, written by Theon of Alexandria; in the sixth century, the first complete surviving text in Greek on the construction and use of an astrolabe is written by John Philoponus.[37] Its first unequivocal mention in a Greek astrological text is by the fourth-century astrologer, Paulus of Alexandria, in a chapter on how to calculate the Ascendant.[38]

Paulus also mentions a water clock indicating the moment that the native is born and draws their first breath, thus providing the degree of the Ascendant.[39] Hephaestio mentions determining the correct degree of the Ascendant at the time of an astrological consultation by using a water clock, an astrolabe, or some other unspecified instrument for telling time.[40] He seems to think that these instruments are accurate enough to determine the exact degree of the Ascendant, and the discussion occurs within the context of a passage about how to interpret the twelfth-part that is rising at the moment of a consultation, which

---

[35] The term is usually translated more literally as "star-taker." In earlier Greek texts, the term tends to be used to refer to the armillary sphere, while in later texts it starts to be used to refer to what we associate with the term today, which is a plane astrolabe.

[36] Neugebauer, "The Early History of the Astrolabe," pp. 240–6. Cf. Neugebauer, *A History of Ancient Mathematical Astronomy*, p. 868ff. More recently Sidoli and Berggren expressed skepticism in their edition of the Arabic text of Ptolemy's *Planisphere* about whether the reference to what their translation of the Arabic calls an "instrument of hours" is actually a plane astrolabe, as Neugebauer thought. See Sidoli and Berggren, "The Arabic version of Ptolemy's *Planisphere* or *Flattening the Surface of the Sphere*," p. 126f.

[37] Neugebauer, *A History of Ancient Mathematical Astronomy*, p. 877f. A new critical edition of Philoponus' text was recently published: John Philoponus, *Ioannes Philoponus, De usu astrolabii eiusque constructione*, ed. Stückelberger.

[38] Neugebauer, *A History of Ancient Mathematical Astronomy*, p. 878, citing Paulus, *Introduction*, 29 (p. 80: 13 and 20 in the Boer edition).

[39] Paulus, *Introduction*, 23, ed. Boer, p. 50: 17–21.

[40] Hephaestio, *Apotelesmatika*, 3, 4: 22.

would require the degree of the Ascendant to be within a specific two and a half degree range.

Use of Glyphs or Symbols

The glyphs or symbols that are commonly used by modern astrologers to represent the planets and signs of the zodiac were not fully established until the Middle Ages. While there is evidence that some of these glyphs may have evolved out of symbols that were used within the Hellenistic tradition, for the most part the Hellenistic astrologers do not appear to have had a standardized system for drawing the glyphs. Instead they tended to write out the full names of the planets and signs of the zodiac as words, or sometimes just used the first letter of the name of the planet as shorthand, with some exceptions.

Neugebauer pointed out that tracing the history and development of the astrological glyphs in Greek and Latin manuscripts is difficult not just due to the checkered transmission of the manuscripts themselves, but also due to the tendency for scholars in the nineteenth and early twentieth century to disregard the symbols and replace them with words in printed editions, or sometimes the reverse.[41] What this means is that many critical editions of astrological texts don't accurately convey the symbols used in the manuscripts, so it is hard to get an idea from them of what symbols were being used, if any. Aside from that, most of the manuscripts that have survived are copies of copies of copies, the oldest of which usually only date back to the Middle Ages; thus, they are not usually the best exemplars of what symbols were being used in the original manuscripts to begin with.[42] Fortunately, some archaeological discoveries over the course of the past century have turned up horoscopes written on papyrus and ostraca (pieces of pottery used to write on), and these give us some direct insight into some of the symbols that were used in the Hellenistic tradition.

In the collection of horoscopes written on papyrus that have been recovered from the waste dumps of the ancient Greco-Roman city of Oxyrhynchus in Egypt, some symbols are used in the later charts from the fourth century onward.[43] Only the symbols for Mercury, Venus, and the Moon have some similarity to the later symbols that became standard. The symbol for the Sun is a circle with a beam or a ray on the top right, which seems standardized across the charts and in some of the later Byzantine Greek texts, although it is not the same symbol featuring a circle with a point in the middle that would be used

---

[41] Neugebauer, "Demotic Horoscopes," pp. 123–124.

[42] For illustrations of some later Medieval symbols from manuscripts see Evans, *The History and Practice of Ancient Astronomy*, p. 104.

[43] Jones, *Astronomical Papyri from Oxyrhynchus*, vol. 1, pp. 61–63.

SIGNS

♈	ARIES	♌	LEO	♐	SAGITTARIUS
♉	TAURUS	♍	VIRGO	♑	CAPRICORN
♊	GEMINI	♎	LIBRA	♒	AQUARIUS
♋	CANCER	♏	SCORPIO	♓	PISCES

PLANETS

☽	MOON	♂	MARS
☉	SUN	♃	JUPITER
☿	MERCURY	♄	SATURN
♀	VENUS	⊗	LOT OF FORTUNE

Table 3.1 - Modern Astrological Symbols

in the later Renaissance and modern astrological traditions. The symbols for Saturn and Jupiter are evidently just the first letter of the Greek words for the names of those planets, K(ronos) and Z(eus). Finally, there is a symbol that is consistently used for the Ascendant, although it is just a monogram where the first two letters in the word for the Ascendant, *hōroskopos*, are merged together, forming an overlapping omega (ω) and rho (ρ) symbol. In terms of the signs of the zodiac, Jones notes that none of the symbols that would become standard in the Medieval tradition show up in the Greek papyri.[44] Instead the names of the signs tend to be written out.

Specific glyphs or symbols are used in some of the Demotic Egyptian horoscopes for both the planets and the signs of the zodiac, and there have been speculations since the early twentieth century that some of these symbols may have motivated some of the later Medieval glyphs.[45] In particular the Demotic

---

[44] Jones, *Astronomical Papyri from Oxyrhynchus*, vol. 1, pp. 62.

[45] For most of this discussion see Ross, *Horoscopic Ostraca from Medînet Mâdi*, pp. 40–44, and Winkler, *Looking at the Future*, pp. 239–240. The connection between the some of the Demotic symbols and the later Medieval astrological glyphs was first established by Spiegelberg in his 1911 paper "Die ägyptische Namen und Zeichen der Tierkreisbilder in demotischer Schrift."

symbol used for Libra has been noted as being very similar to the glyph that would later become standardized for that sign.[46] There are also some similarities in the Demotic glyph for Sagittarius, which is an upward pointing arrow, as well as the glyph for Aquarius, which is three horizontal lines.[47] The other zodiacal symbols are otherwise not terribly similar to their modern counterparts. When it comes to the planets, the symbols for the Sun and Moon are very similar to their modern versions, except the Sun does not have a point in the middle of the circle. Mercury's symbol is also somewhat similar to its modern counterpart. The symbol for Saturn is a square, while the symbol for Mars is a knife. The rest of the symbols for the planets are difficult to describe, and bear no resemblance to the Medieval and modern glyphs.

Elsewhere, Heilen suggests that some of the odd grammatical constructions in later Greek delineation texts may have resulted from the earlier source texts (such as Nechepso and Petosiris) using symbols rather than writing out the words in order to convey configurations like "Saturn trine Mars."[48] This is a tempting hypothesis, although it seems difficult to confirm at this point, since no original fragments of those texts written on papyrus have yet been discovered.

For the sake of simplicity I will use the modern glyphs for the planets and signs of the zodiac in this book, although it is important to keep in mind that charts in the Hellenistic tradition would have looked different.

---

[46] Neugebauer, "Demotic Horoscopes," esp. p. 121ff.
[47] See the illustrations in Ross, *Horoscopic Ostraca from Medînet Mâdi*, pp. 41–2, or Parker, "A Horoscopic Text in Triplicate," pp. 143.
[48] Heilen, "Anubio Reconsidered," p. 143.

CHAPTER 4
THE HELLENISTIC ASTROLOGERS

———————— ⊛ ————————

This chapter contains brief biographical sketches of the lives and works of the Hellenistic astrologers. The purpose is to introduce most of the major surviving sources that we have to draw on in reconstructing the practice of Hellenistic astrology, and to briefly discuss what is known about them.[1] It is important to establish the dating and sequence of each of the astrologers, since sometimes the date in which certain figures lived can have a significant impact on historical arguments related to their writings, or understanding where they fall within the broader context of the astrological tradition as a whole. Some parts of this chapter that focus on dating will only be relevant to specialists, and it is primarily meant to act as a reference section, although for general readers these discussions will still provide a useful look into how the dating of ancient figures is usually established. I will also intersperse some of these discussions about dating with historical anecdotes in order to provide more information about the cultural context of the practice of astrology in classical antiquity. The entries are listed chronologically, from the earliest to the latest.

———————————

[1] For more detailed biographies and bibliographies for most of these astrologers, see the following sources: Pingree, *Yavanajātaka*, vol. 2, pp. 419–451. Holden, *A History of Horoscopic Astrology*, pp. 11–102. *Dictionary of Scientific Biography*, ed. Gillispie. *New Dictionary of Scientific Biography*, ed. Koertge. *Brill's New Pauly*, ed. Cancik and Schneider. *The Encyclopedia of Ancient Natural Scientists*, ed. Keyser and Irby-Massie. Holden, *Biographical Dictionary of Western Astrologers*. *The Encyclopedia of Ancient History*, ed. Bagnall et al. *Handbook of Archaeoastronomy and Ethnoastronomy*, ed. Ruggles. I will also be writing more extensive and up-to-date entries for each of the astrologers on my website, at HellenisticAstrology.com.

Hermes Trismegistus (First Century BCE?)

Hermes Trismegistus is the putative founder of the Hellenistic tradition, at least according to some sources.[2] Sometimes it is not clear if he is listed as the founder of the tradition simply for mythological reasons, or if it is because there was an early set of astrological texts in circulation that were attributed to him. From a mythological standpoint, Hermes Trismegistus is an amalgam of the Greek god Hermes and the Egyptian god Thoth that was created in the Hellenistic period as a result of the cultural fusion that occurred in Egypt after it was conquered by Alexander. Thoth was associated with wisdom, writing, language, funerary rituals, magic, and sacred rites, among other things, and these were similar to many of the attributes that the Greeks associated with the god Hermes, especially with both of them playing the important role of the messenger of the gods.[3] Hermes Trismegistus became a sort of legendary figure that many works on philosophy, astrology, alchemy, magic, and other subjects were attributed to.[4] The fourth-century philosopher, Iamblichus, said that attributing texts to Hermes was a common practice that was meant to indicate some sort of intellectual indebtedness or lineage:

> Hermes, the god who presides over rational discourse, has long been considered, quite rightly, to be the common patron of all priests; he who presides over true knowledge about the gods is one and the same always and everywhere. It is to him that our ancestors in particular dedicated the fruits of their wisdom, attributing all their own writings to Hermes.[5]

The core set of about seventeen philosophical texts attributed to Hermes and other figures associated with him is known as the *Corpus Hermeticum*, and it formed the basis of the philosophy referred to today as Hermeticism.[6] Hermeticism was an eclectic philosophy that incorporated Platonic, Stoic, Gnostic, Egyptian, and Jewish elements.[7] These works also feature astrology

---

[2] See the citations of Firmicus and others above in the section on the emergence of Hellenistic astrology.

[3] Fowden, *The Egyptian Hermes*, pp. 22–24; Jasnow and Zauzich, *Conversations in the House of Life*, pp. 31–37.

[4] The two classic studies on the works of Hermes Trismegistus in the Greco-Roman period are Festugière, *La Révélation d'Hermès Trismégiste*, and Fowden, *The Egyptian Hermes*.

[5] Iamblichus, *On the Mysteries*, 1.2–2.3, trans. Clarke et al, p. 5.

[6] The standard critical edition of the philosophical works is Hermès Trismégiste, *Corpus Hermeticum*, ed. Nock and Festugière. The standard English translation is *Hermetica*, trans. Copenhaver.

[7] Struck, "Hermetic writings." Struck does not mention the Stoic component, although this is rightly emphasized as one of the particularly prominent contributing elements drawn

very prominently at times, as well as related concepts such as the mirroring of microcosm and macrocosm, and issues related to the concept of fate. The philosophical works of the *Corpus Hermeticum* were written in Greek, usually in the form of dialogues involving an enlightened teacher who is passing down revealed wisdom (*gnōsis*) to a student. By the end of the dialogue the student acknowledges or demonstrates that they have received the teaching, and often goes on to become a teacher in their own right, passing down the wisdom to other students in subsequent dialogues.

The Hermetic works on philosophy, sometimes called the "philosophical Hermetica," were complemented by other works ascribed to Hermes and his associates on technical matters like astrology, which are sometimes called the "technical Hermetica."[8] While modern scholars are often quick to point out that this distinction between philosophical and technical Hermetica is a modern convention, it may still be a useful one to keep in mind since it is not always clear what relationship there was between the two. In some instances the astrologers would draw on sources associated with the technical Hermetica while not necessarily subscribing to what might be broadly defined as Hermetic philosophy. The philosophical Hermetica are usually thought to have been composed between the first and third centuries CE, while there is evidence for some of the technical Hermetica related to astrology dating to the first century BCE or earlier, as we will see.[9]

The fact that some astrologers frequently attribute specific astrological doctrines to Hermes Trismegistus gives the impression that there was an important early astrological text or set of texts that contained some core doctrines that were attributed to him. The technical doctrine perhaps most commonly or consistently attributed to Hermes is the doctrine of the twelve "houses" or "places" (*dōdekatropos*), and it appears that one of the earliest texts that contained a list of significations for each of the twelve houses carried his name.[10] This text and its attribution to Hermes is mentioned by Thrasyllus already in the early first

---

from Greek philosophical thought in other sources such as Denzey Lewis, *Introduction to Gnosticism*, p. 211.

[8] See the discussion in Copenhaver, *Hermetica*, p. xxxii–xl.

[9] For the dating of the philosophical Hermetica see Fowden, *The Egyptian Hermes*, p. 11.

[10] Antiochus (CCAG 8, 3, p. 116: 3–12) cited the author Timaeus as having attributed a specific doctrine related to which houses are "advantageous" (*chrēmatistikos*) to Hermes. Dorotheus (*Carmen*, 2, 20) opens a section in his book that gives interpretations of the planets when they are located in the twelve houses by citing a statement that Hermes makes about the topic, perhaps indicating that some of the subsequent delineations were excerpted from an earlier Hermetic text. Rhetorius mentions in passing that Hermes deliberately designated the twelfth place as having to do with childbirth (CCAG 8, 4, p. 131: 4–8). Also see the citation in Thrasyllus, in the next note.

century CE, which indicates that the text on the significations of the houses attributed to Hermes would have been written sometime in the first century BCE or earlier.[11] This would then make it the oldest text that we know of that talks about the twelve houses and their significations, which may then by extension mean that it was the *original* text that introduced the concept of the twelve houses to begin with. If this is true, then the publication of this text would essentially mark the point of departure between the Mesopotamian and Hellenistic astrological traditions. It would also explain why Hermes was sometimes said to be the founder of the astrological tradition, since the publication of this text would mark the birth of horoscopic astrology.

A number of other astrological texts were attributed to Hermes as well, although it is often difficult to date them or determine their relationship, if any, with the early text on the twelve houses. In the second century, Valens preserves some material on the timing technique known as profections that was either attributed to Hermes himself or to a Hermetic school.[12] In the fourth century, Paulus preserves a set of seven lots associated with each of the seven planets that was evidently from a text attributed to Hermes called the *Panaretus*, which means "all-virtuous."[13] There were also other works on earthquakes and medical astrology attributed to Hermes as well.[14]

Finally, in the Middle Ages a compilation of excerpts from different Hellenistic astrologers was translated into Latin and published as the *Liber Hermetis* or "Book of Hermes."[15] Pingree has shown that this work is largely just a compilation of material that has been excerpted from Hellenistic astrologers such as Vettius Valens, Paulus of Alexandria, Firmicus Maternus (or his source), and Rhetorius.[16] The fact that the author drew on later sources like Rhetorius indicates that it wasn't composed until sometime after the sixth or seventh century CE. Nonetheless, it is still useful for checking the works of those authors, and sometimes it seems to preserve material from the earlier sources that some of the later Hellenistic astrologers were drawing on. Pingree points out that

---

[11] CCAG, 8, 3, p. 101: 16–30.

[12] Valens, *Anthology*, 4, 27–29.

[13] Paulus, *Introduction*, 23. The scholia on Paulus' text and the commentary by Olympiodorus inform us that this work was ascribed to Hermes Trismegistus. For the scholia, see Paulus, *Introduction*, ed. Boer, p. 118: 24–26 (scholia 48). For the commentary see Olympiodorus, *Commentary*, ed. Boer, p. 51: 13–15.

[14] For the work on earthquakes see CCAG 7, pp. 167–171. There are several different medical works, but see especially the *Iatromathematika of Hermes Trismegistus to Ammon the Egyptian* edited in Ideler, *Physici et Medici Graeci Minores*, vol. 1, pp. 387–396. For other works see Pingree, *Yavanajātaka*, vol. 2, p. 430.

[15] The most recent critical edition is Feraboli (ed.), *Hermetis Trismegisti de triginta sex decanis*.

[16] Pingree, *Yavanajātaka*, vol. 2, pp. 431–433.

the fixed star positions given in two chapters of the work indicate a date of c. 130–60 BCE.[17] While this does not indicate the date of the composition of the work as a whole, it may help us to narrow down the time frame in which some of the earliest works on Hellenistic astrology were written, perhaps including the original work attributed to Hermes on the twelve houses.[18]

Asclepius (First Century BCE?)

In pre-Hellenistic Greek mythology, Asclepius was a god of healing and medicine. The early Hellenistic period saw the establishment of numerous cults to Asclepius, eventually spreading to and flourishing in Rome, particularly in the early centuries of the Common Era. During the same time period, the cultural synthesis in Egypt that produced Hermes Trismegistus also resulted in the identification of the Greek god Asclepius with a divine figure from Egypt named Imhotep, who was regarded a wise man, seer, and a sort of intermediary between humans and divine beings.[19]

Asclepius plays a particularly important role in the philosophical Hermetica, with several of the discourses in the *Corpus Hermeticum* taking place between Hermes and Asclepius. This established a widely acknowledged student-teacher relationship between the two figures in the Greco-Roman world, whereby Asclepius was seen to have been the receiver of knowledge directly from Hermes, and then later the teacher and transmitter of this knowledge to others.[20]

This appears to be the same role envisioned for Asclepius in some of the technical Hermetica associated with the astrological tradition as well. Firmicus Maternus and another anonymous astrological source both portray Asclepius as being the receiver of astrological doctrines from Hermes, and then say that he went on to transmit the knowledge to later expositors such as Nechepso and

---

[17] Pingree, *Yavanajātaka*, vol. 2, pp. 432.

[18] Pingree (*Yavanajātaka*, vol. 2, p. 431) says that the Greek original of the *Liber Hermetis* was probably compiled around the seventh century, and then the Latin translation that we have would have been produced around the twelfth century or later.

[19] Jasnow and Zauzich, *Conversations in the House of Life*, p. 37.

[20] Books 2, 6, 9 and 14 of the *Corpus Hermeticum* are dialogues in which Hermes instructs Asclepius, while in book 16 Asclepius takes on the role of teacher in a letter addressed to King Ammon. In another text called *The Definitions of Hermes Trismegistus to Asclepius* Hermes is similarly seen to be in the role of instructing Asclepius. Mahé (*The Way of Hermes*, trans. Salaman et al, p. 101) argues that the core of the *Definitions* likely antedates the *Corpus Hermeticum*, perhaps already being available in some form in the first century CE. A recently discovered Demotic Egyptian religious text that was written sometime between the third century BCE and fourth century CE features Thoth and Imhotep as part of a dialogue, and this has raised some questions about whether some of the Hermetic texts may have had a connection with this Egyptian literary genre. See Jasnow and Zauzich, *Conversations in the House of Life*.

Petosiris.[21] At one point, Firmicus explicitly says that Asclepius himself claimed to have his work or doctrines revealed to him by Hermes.[22] Firmicus also gives the name of a specific astrological work attributed to Asclepius that was called *Myriogenesis*, which means *Infinite Nativities*.[23] Firmicus seems to say that the book provided delineations for the Ascendant in each individual minute of each degree of each sign of the zodiac, which seems a bit implausible since there are 21,600 minutes in the zodiac, although this might explain the title *Infinite Nativities*.

In terms of what Asclepius's text actually contributed to the astrological tradition, he is credited, like Hermes, with having written an influential work on the houses or places. In fact, there seems to have been a specific text attributed to him that introduced a unique set of significations for the first eight houses, and this system became known as the *oktatropos*, or "eight-turning." The *oktatropos* is mentioned by Thrasyllus in the early first century CE, indicating that it must have been introduced already by the first century BCE.[24] The anonymous author of the *Michigan Papyrus* says that Asclepius was the author of the *oktatropos*, and Valens seems to agree when he says that Asclepius made a major contribution to the doctrine of the houses.[25]

Since Asclepius is usually listed as chronologically later than Hermes, presumably his text was produced sometime after the original Hermes text, perhaps as a dialogue like in the philosophical Hermetica. Schmidt has noted that later Hellenistic astrologers tended to synthesize the twelve-topic system attributed to Hermes and the eight-topic system attributed to Asclepius, but early authors make it clear that the two systems were originally distinct, or at least were introduced in separate texts attributed to different authors.[26] If this is true, then there are good reasons to regard the text attributed to Asclepius on the *oktatropos* as one of the foundational texts of the Hellenistic tradition.

Nechepso and Petosiris (First Century BCE?)

Nechepso and Petosiris are the two most widely cited and influential authors of the Hellenistic astrological tradition. Even though Hermes and Asclepius are given chronological priority in the lineages outlined by Firmicus Maternus and others, Nechepso and Petosiris are actually mentioned and associated with

---

[21] Firmicus, *Mathesis*, 4, proem: 5; CCAG, 8, 4, p. 95, translated in Neugebauer and van Hoesen, *Greek Horoscopes*, No. 137c, p. 42.

[22] Firmicus, *Mathesis*, 5, 1: 36.

[23] Firmicus, *Mathesis*, 5, 1: 36–38. The title is discussed in Tester, *A History*, p. 137.

[24] CCAG 8, 3, p. 101: 3–9.

[25] *Michigan Papyrus*, col. ix: 20–27 (p. 149); Valens, *Anthology*, 9, 3: 5.

[26] Schmidt, *Kepler College Sourcebook*, p. 77.

specific astrological doctrines far more frequently. Some authors such as Vettius Valens almost seem to treat them as the founders of Hellenistic astrology, which creates some confusion regarding the origins of the tradition. They are both mentioned already in the early first century CE by Thrasyllus, so their texts must have been in circulation already by the first century BCE.[27]

Despite the fact that they were the most influential astrological authors in antiquity, none of the works attributed to Nechepso and Petosiris survived into the present day. All we have of their works is a collection of fragments, quotations, and citations by later authors who drew on their texts and sometimes mentioned doctrines contained in them.[28] The largest number of fragments from Nechepso and Petosiris are preserved by the second century astrologer, Vettius Valens. Valens seems to have thought that Nechepso was actually an Egyptian king who ruled at some point in the distant past, during some sort of golden age for the practice of astrology.[29] He frequently expresses respect for both figures, although at times he also voices his frustration with their cryptic or enigmatic writing style.[30]

In the astrological literature, Nechepso is frequently referred to as "the King" (*basileus*), especially by Valens, who also sometimes calls him "the Compiler" (*sungrapheus*).[31] Together Nechepso and Petosiris are sometimes referred to as "the Egyptians" (*Aiguptoi*) or "the ancients" (*palaioi*). Ptolemy once seems to refer to Petosiris as "the ancient one" (*archaios*) during a discussion of the length of life technique, although this is an inference based on other authors who associate Petosiris with what became the standard technique used to measure the length of a native's life.[32] Their names are often mentioned together and treated as a pair, although occasionally one was cited independently from the other, which makes the relationship between their works somewhat unclear. Heilen points out that there may have been a corpus of different works in circulation under their names, since a few different discrete works from each author are mentioned in the surviving texts, including a thirteenth, fourteenth,

---

[27] For Thrasyllus see CCAG 8, 3, p. 100: 19–20.

[28] The standard collection of fragments is contained in Riess, "Nechepsonis et Petosiridis fragmenta magica." For a more up-to-date list of fragments and testimonia see Heilen, "Some metrical fragments from Nechepsos and Petosiris," which is reproduced in Heilen, *Hadriani Genitura*, pp. 39–52.

[29] Valens, *Anthology*, 6, 1: 7–9. Firmicus similarly calls Nechepso the emperor (*imperator*) of Egypt (*Mathesis*, 4, 22: 2).

[30] Valens, *Anthology*, 7, 4: 1–3.

[31] For the Compiler see Valens, *Anthology*, 2, 37: 37; 2, 41: 15 (contrasting his opinion with Petosiris); 5, 6: 15, etc.

[32] Ptolemy, *Tetrabiblos*, 3, 11: 1. For the attribution of this technique to Nechepso and Petosiris see Pliny, *Natural History*, 7, 49: 160.

and fifteenth book by Nechepso, as well as a separate work that Valens attributes to Petosiris called *Definitions* (*Horoi*).[33]

The fact that Firmicus and others place Nechepso and Petosiris in the lineage of Hermes Trismegistus and Asclepius may imply that the texts attributed to them were written under the typical Hermetic premise of receiving revealed knowledge from the earlier sages directly. This seems to be confirmed by Firmicus' statement that Nechepso and Petosiris received the doctrine of the Thema Mundi from Hermes and Asclepius.[34] Nechepso must have been portrayed in his text as an Egyptian king who lived at some distant point in the past, which is paralleled in the philosophical Hermetica, where one of the texts takes the form of a letter from Asclepius addressed to King Ammon.[35]

Modern scholars have long wondered whether Nechepso was meant to be associated with a specific historical figure from the past, by the author of the pseudepigraphical astrological work who chose to use that name. Recently he has been identified with Necho II of the Twenty-sixth Dynasty, who ruled Egypt briefly starting in 610 BCE.[36] The motivations for this association are still somewhat unclear; Ryholt speculates that it may have had to do with the fact that an eclipse occurred at the time of Necho's accession, although it is not entirely clear why this would provide the impetus for an astrological author who lived several centuries later to attribute a text to him.[37] Ryholt also suggests that the name Petosiris which became so common in the later astrological tradition may be a corruption of the Egyptian name Petesis, who was a well-known sage in the earlier Egyptian literary tradition, who in one later story was said to have taught astrology to Plato.[38] Perhaps more importantly, Ryholt cites an unpublished Demotic astrological manual from the temple library in the ancient Egyptian city of Tebtunis that dates to the first or second century CE, which contains a story that he summarizes as follows:

> It is told how a block of stone fell out of a wall and revealed a papyrus. Only the well-known sage Petesis can decipher the text which turns out to be an astrological treatise written by none other than Imhotep. The text is presented by Petesis to king Nechepsos.[39]

---

[33] Heilen, "Some Metrical Fragments," p. 24. Valens, *Anthology*, 2, 3: 3.
[34] Firmicus, *Mathesis*, 3, proem: 4ff.
[35] *Corpus Hermeticum* 16.
[36] Ryholt, "New Light on the Legendary King Nechepsos of Egypt."
[37] Ryholt, "New Light," p. 69.
[38] Ryholt, "New Light," p. 70.
[39] Ryholt, "New Light," p. 62.

Imhotep is the Egyptian equivalent of Asclepius, and so what this seems to represent is a similar version of the legend that was being told by later Greco-Roman astrological authors such as Firmicus, but it clarifies that the doctrines were indeed envisioned as being handed down from Asclepius to Petosiris and Nechepso. Petesis (or Petese) was known as a sage or priest in the Demotic literary tradition from the fourth century BCE forward, and it then seems likely that Petosiris would have been viewed in a similar way by the Hellenistic astrologers.[40]

The astrological doctrines attributed to or associated with Nechepso and Petosiris by later astrologers are too numerous to list here, although the following highlights may be noted:

1. Their works included coverage of all three branches of Hellenistic astrology, including universal, natal, and inceptional astrology.[41] It also included some subsets of these branches such as medical astrology, and Firmicus informs us that Nechepso used the decans to predict illness and afflictions, as well as to show how to cure illnesses through the counteraction of one decan with another.[42]

2. Firmicus says the Thema Mundi or birth chart of the cosmos came from Nechepso and Petosiris, although he seems to imply that they received it from Hermes and Asclepius.[43]

3. Petosiris seems to have introduced the core technique for determining the length of life that was used by all subsequent authors.[44]

4. The so-called "Egyptian bounds" are sometimes assumed to have been popularized by Nechepso and Petosiris, since they were the Egyptians *par excellence*, perhaps within the context of the length of life technique mentioned above.[45]

5. A system of determining the "advantageous" (*chrēmatistikos*) places was attributed to Nechepso by Antiochus.[46]

---

[40] Heilen ("Some Metrical Fragments," p. 29) points out that the modern references to Petosiris as a priest have previously been based on somewhat questionable assumptions. It seems like the connection between Petosiris and Petesis may confirm the idea that Petosiris was viewed as some sort of sage or priest, however, especially when taken together with the passage in Manilius (*Astronomica*, 1: 40–65) referring to kings and priests of old who first developed astrology, which has often been interpreted as referring to Nechepso and Petosiris.

[41] Heilen, *Hadriani Genitura*, pp. 48–50.

[42] Firmicus, *Mathesis*, 4, 22: 2.

[43] Firmicus, *Mathesis*, 3, proem: 4; 3, 1: 1–2.

[44] See the earlier citation of the passages in Ptolemy and Pliny.

[45] Pingree, *Yavanajātaka*, vol. 2, p. 214.

[46] CCAG 8, 3, p. 116: 11–12.

6. Valens associates some timing methods with Nechepso that involve planetary periods and ascensional times.[47]

7. Nechepso may have written on the time-lord technique known as profections, as Valens gives a method of determining the lord of the profected month from Nechepso.[48]

8. Nechepso and Petosiris both dealt with the Lot of Fortune, and Valens preserves some passages from both related to it.[49]

To give some idea of how widely they were cited, direct references or allusions to Nechepso and Petosiris occur in the texts of the following major Hellenistic astrologers: Thrasyllus, Manilius, Antiochus, Manetho, Ptolemy, Valens, Porphyry, Firmicus, and Hephaestio.[50] Other authors such as Dorotheus and Antigonus were said to have drawn on the works of Nechepso and Petosiris.[51] Heilen suggested that Nechepso and Petosiris wrote what became the standard source text for delineations of basic astrological placements, which was then incorporated into the works of later authors such as Dorotheus, Anubio, Manetho, and Firmicus.[52] Nechepso and Petosiris were unique in that their astrological texts were so widely known that they were also cited by people outside of the astrological community. This includes references by the Roman poet Juvenal in his *Satires*,[53] Pliny in his encyclopedia,[54] the guide to herbal remedies attributed to the physician Thessalus of Tralles,[55] and in the Neoplatonist philosopher Proclus' commentary on Plato's *Republic*.[56]

Heilen cautiously dates Nechepso and Petosiris to the second half of the second century BCE, under the premise that a few of the fragments attributed to them take for granted the astronomical work of Hypsicles, who lived around the first half of the second century, as well as some historical events that are thought to be alluded to in some of the fragments attributed to them.[57] This is generally in accord with the dating that scholars have given the compilation over

---

[47] Valens, *Anthology*, 7, 6.

[48] Valens, *Anthology*, 5, 4: 1f.

[49] Valens, *Anthology*, 2, 3.

[50] For most of these references see Heilen, "Some metrical fragments," pp. 31–34.

[51] Hephaestio, *Apotelesmatika*, 2, 21: 26 (Dorotheus); 2, 18: 21 (Antigonus).

[52] Heilen, "Anubio Reconsidered," p. 136ff.

[53] Juvenal, *Satires*, 6: 580–581.

[54] Pliny, *Natural History*, 2: 88.

[55] *Thessalos von Tralles*, proem, ed. Friedrich. For a translation see Harland, "Journeys in Pursuit of Divine Wisdom," pp. 124–126. See also the discussion in Moyer, *Egypt and the Limits of Hellenism*, pp. 208–273.

[56] Proclus, *Procli Diadochi in Platonis rem publicam*, ed. Kroll, vol. 2, p. 59: 3–60.

[57] Heilen, "Some metrical fragments," pp. 23–24.

the past century, both by older scholars such as Cumont who placed it around 150 BCE, as well as newer scholars such as Pingree who placed the oldest part of the compilation around the late second or early first century BCE.[58]

Timaeus (Late First Century BCE?)

Timaeus is an early author who is cited sporadically by some later astrologers, although very little of his work survives. He is mentioned in connection with some astrological and astronomical doctrines by Pliny the Elder, who died in the year 79 CE, which probably means that the astrological work ascribed to Timaeus was written in the late first century BCE or early first century CE.[59] Antiochus cites him as reporting some doctrines from Hermes on the advantageous places, while Anonymous of 379 lists him as coming after Nechepso and Petosiris.[60] This means that chronologically he lived after the Hermes and Nechepso-Petosiris texts were written. Valens excerpts some material from Timaeus that deals with the topic of parents, and in these sections the technical terms used seem to be older and more distinctive compared to Valens.[61] There is also a brief excerpt that survives from Timaeus that gives some instructions for interpreting inceptional charts for runaway slaves and thieves.[62] In that fragment he is referred to as Timaeus Praxidos.

It is possible that the astrological work attributed to Timaeus may represent another instance of pseudepigrapha, as it could have been intended to look as if it was authored by Timaeus of Locri, who was a prominent character in one of Plato's most famous philosophical dialogues, the *Timaeus*. There was a Middle Platonic philosophical work titled *On the Nature of the World and the Soul* that was written and ascribed to Timaeus of Locri probably sometime around the late first century BCE or first century CE, and it seems suggestive that an astrological work was attributed to a Timaeus during the same period.[63] This would be in keeping with other early works that were ascribed to mythical and legendary figures in this period of the astrological tradition.

---

[58] Cumont, *Astrology and Religion*, p. 76, Pingree, *From Astral Omens*, pp. 25–26.

[59] Pliny, *Natural History*, 2, 6: 38; 5, 10: 55–56; 16, 34: 82. Hübner ("Timaeus") dates him to the first century BCE for similar reasons, while Jones ("Timaios," p. 810) adopts a wider range of 75 BCE–79 CE, using Pliny's death as the *terminus ante quem*.

[60] Antiochus, *Summary*, p. 116: 3–12; Anonymous of 379, *Fixed Stars*, p. 204: 22.

[61] Valens, *Anthology*, 2, 32. I suspect that chapters 33 and 34 are also excerpted, based on the continued use of certain terms.

[62] CCAG 1, pp. 97–99. Translated in Schmidt, *Sages*, pp. 41–44.

[63] For the philosophical work see Timaios of Locri, *On the Nature of the World and the Soul*, trans. Tobin. The late first century BCE or first century CE dating is said to be the consensus on pp. 5–7.

Teucer of Babylon (First Century BCE)

Teucer of Babylon wrote about the significations of the planets, signs of the zodiac, decans, and co-rising stars (*paranatellonta*). There is some uncertainty about his dating. Porphyry may be the first author who mentions him for certain by name, which would mean that he lived prior to the third century BCE.[64] The editors of the *Catalogus Codicum Astrologorum Graecorum* noted that some of the material on the planets and signs that survives from him is similar to the treatment of the significations of the planets contained in Valens and Rhetorius.[65] Early in his career Pingree concluded from this that Teucer was the original source of the material on the planets and signs in both Valens and Rhetorius, which then pushes Teucer's dating back to the first century CE, and probably implies that he was from the city of Babylon in Egypt rather than Mesopotamia.[66] More recently Hübner has argued that Manilius and Firmicus drew on Teucer for some of their material on the fixed stars, which, if true, would push his dating back to the first century BCE.[67] Unfortunately, not much of his work survived into the present time. Rhetorius evidently summarizes some of Teucer's delineations of the decans, although they are somewhat brief.[68]

Thrasyllus (d. 36 CE)

Thrasyllus was the court astrologer to the Roman Emperor Tiberius during the early Roman imperial period.[69] A number of stories about his involvement in

---

[64] Porphyry, *Introduction*, 47. In a private communication Levente László says that this chapter may have been copied into the archetype of the Porphyry manuscripts from Rhetorius 5, 10, and therefore would not be authentic.

[65] The material on the signs is edited in CCAG, 7, pp. 192–213, while the material on the planets is edited in pp. 213–224. Holden notes in his translation of this material that it comes from Rhetorius, who has tampered with it by inserting information from Ptolemy, so it must be used with caution (*Rhetorius the Egyptian*, p. 165).

[66] Pingree, *Yavanajātaka*, p. 442. Neugebauer (*The Exact Sciences in Antiquity*, p. 189), rejected locating Teucer in Egypt rather than Mesopotamia, although more recently Rochberg seems to have accepted it under the premise that Babylon in Mesopotamia would have been a "greatly diminished city" by the first century CE (Rochberg, "Teukros of Egyptian Babylon," p. 778). Levente László points out in a personal communication that Pingree may have changed his mind later in his career, deciding that the treatment of planets is from neither Teucer nor Rhetorius, but instead that it only uses Valens' descriptions and other sources (the relevant sections are published as Appendix II in Valens, *Anthology*, ed. Pingree, pp. 390–392).

[67] Hübner, "Manilio e Teucro di Babilonia;" Hübner, *Manilius, Astronomica, Buch V*, pp. 16–20.

[68] Rhetorius, *Compendium*, 10. Further fragments from Teucer in Rhetorius are found in his description of the signs in CCAG 7, pp. 194–213, although Levente László notes privately that the edition is a conflated text, and only manuscript R is really Rhetorius.

[69] All surviving testimonia and fragments of Thrasyllus' work are collected together (without translation) in Tarrant, *Thrasyllan Platonism*, pp. 215–249.

imperial politics are preserved by the Roman historians Tacitus, Seutonius, and Cassius Dio. The most famous legend involves his first meeting with Tiberius before he became the second Roman emperor.[70] According to one version of the story, after Thrasyllus finished interpreting Tiberius' birth chart for the first time and predicted great things for him, Tiberius then turned the tables and asked Thrasyllus what his own chart said for that day. Apparently Tiberius was in the habit of having the astrologers he consulted with killed immediately after they were done reading his chart, by throwing them off a cliff. After doing some quick calculations Thrasyllus broke out into a cold sweat and exclaimed that he was in imminent danger. At this point, impressed by Thrasyllus' ability to determine the danger he was in simply from looking at his own chart, Tiberius made the astrologer one of his closest advisors.

A second legend about Thrasyllus held that one day while he and Tiberius were still living on the island of Rhodes, they saw a ship approaching in the distance, and Thrasyllus was able to correctly predict that it contained a message from the Emperor recalling Tiberius to Rome, where he would soon become Augustus' successor.[71] The veracity of both of these legends is not certain, and they are sometimes dismissed by historians as fanciful, although both seem to be well within the realm of the standard types of techniques that the Hellenistic astrologers were known to have employed during that time period.[72] From a technical standpoint, Thrasyllus would have used natal astrology both when looking at Tiberius' chart and predicting his future, and then he probably would have calculated his own time-lord periods and transits, which could plausibly have indicated a crisis or critical period on the day of the consultation. The prediction that Thrasyllus made on the day of the arrival of the ship could have been based on his familiarity with Tiberius' natal chart and time-lords that were being activated on that day. Alternatively, the prediction also could have been based on some techniques that were used in inceptional astrology for knowing the content of a letter that has been sent to you and the intentions of the one who sent it based on the chart cast for the time that the message is received.[73]

---

[70] Tacitus, *Annals*, 6: 21.

[71] Cassius Dio, *Roman History*, 55, 11: 1–3.

[72] The primary article that is critical of the Thrasyllus legends is Krappe, "Tiberius and Thrasyllus," who is then followed by Cramer (*Astrology in Roman Law*, p. 94) and others. Krappe treats the Tacitus version of the story as spurious, comparing it to the other versions given by Cassius Dio and Seutonius (*Lives*, Tiberius: 14), which he sees as more plausible. However, it seems clear that Seutonius has simply conflated the two different legends that are meant to be separate incidents in Cassius Dio, and when this is understood there is nothing inconsistent about the accounts given by Tacitus and Dio. For another slightly more sympathetic account see Oliver, "Thrasyllus in Tacitus (Ann. 6.21)."

[73] See the excerpt from Zoroaster in CCAG 2, p. 192–195, trans. Schmidt, *Sages*, pp. 26–29. See

Whatever the truth of the stories was, Thrasyllus' fame as an astrologer became legendary, to the extent that he was even mocked by the Roman poet Juvenal in the late first or early second century, where in book six of his *Satires* he sardonically states that female astrology enthusiasts would refuse to travel if the rules laid down by Thrasyllus indicated that the date was astrologically inauspicious.[74]

There are some fragments on the study of stones attributed to a "Thrasyllus of Mendes," which is a city in northern Egypt, although it is not clear if this Thrasyllus is the same as the astrologer.[75] The same text cites Thrasyllus of Mendes for a work titled *Egyptian Matters* (*Aiguptiakois*).[76] Tarrant points out that Thrasyllus' interests are known to have been wide enough that there isn't necessarily any reason to think that he could not have been the author of works on geography or stones.[77] One note about him that appears as a piece of scholia says that "Thrasyllus professed the knowledge of many arts."[78] If he was in fact the author of this work, then the astrologer's name was originally Thrasyllus of Mendes, and he would have come from Egypt, not too far from Alexandria. Later he appears to have acquired Roman citizenship with the help of Tiberius, and an inscription shows that his full name became Tiberius Claudius Thrasyllus.[79] He is referred to almost universally in later sources simply as Thrasyllus.

Thrasyllus wrote an astrological work known as *The Tablet* (*Pinax*), which was addressed to an unknown figure named Hierocles. Unfortunately, this work did not survive into the present day, although we do possess a later summary of it.[80] In the summary Thrasyllus only cites Nechepso, Petosiris, and Hermes Trismegistus as sources, which makes it an extremely valuable text for insight into what astrology looked like during the early part of the Hellenistic tradition.

Thrasyllus is mentioned once by the second century astrologer, Vettius Valens, within the context of a method for rectifying the Ascendant.[81] Later he was mentioned in the third century by Porphyry on the concept of striking with

---

also Hephaestio, *Apotelesmatika*, 3, 27: 2–5.

[74] Juvenal, *Satires*, 6: 573–579.

[75] This is T11a in Tarrant, *Thrasyllan Platonism*, citing Pseudo-Plutarch, *On Rivers* (*De Fluviis*), 11, 4: 1–5.

[76] T11b in Tarrant, *Thrasyllan Platonism*, citing Pseudo-Plutarch, *On Rivers* (*De Fluviis*), 16, 2: 1–10.

[77] Tarrant, *Thrasyllan Platonism*, p. 7, n. 11.

[78] "Thrasillus multarum artium scientiam professus." T1a in Tarrant, *Thrasyllan Platonism*, citing a scholion next to the reference to Thrasyllus in Juvenal, *Satires*, 6: 573–579.

[79] Tarrant, *Thrasyllan Platonism*, p. 8, n. 15, citing T8, pp. 219–20 of his appendix.

[80] The Greek text was edited in CCAG 8, 3, pp. 99–101. Translations of it are available in Schmidt, *Sages*, pp. 57–60, and Schmidt, *Definitions and Foundations*, pp. 341–347.

[81] Valens, *Anthology*, 9, 11: 10.

a ray (*aktinobolia*), and then again when he is grouped together with Petosiris and other unnamed "elders" (*presbuterōn*) who advocated a system of bounds or terms (*horia*) that were different from the sets advocated by Ptolemy and Apollinarius.[82] Finally, in the fifth century, Hephaestio of Thebes mentioned Thrasyllus twice in his *Apotelesmatika*, citing his opinion that Aries and Libra are not capable of hearing or seeing each other, despite the conventional doctrine that they can since they are both equinoctial signs.[83] It would seem then that his astrological work still had some circulation in the later tradition.

Aside from his work as an astrologer, Thrasyllus also has the reputation of being a semi-important figure in the history of philosophy. According to the third-century biographer, Diogenes Laertius, Thrasyllus is responsible for arranging the works of Plato and Democritus into sets of four, otherwise known as tetralogies.[84] Harold Tarrant explored Thrasyllus' role in arranging the Platonic corpus, arguing that Thrasyllus was an important figure in shaping the way that the texts have been read over the past 2,000 years, in addition to being a significant philosopher in his own right.[85] Porphyry's *Life of Plotinus* quotes a passage from his teacher Longinus in which Thrasyllus is mentioned together with a group of philosophers who wrote on Pythagorean and Platonic philosophical principles.[86] This essentially matches Tarrant's assessment of Thrasyllus as a Platonist with Pythagorean leanings.

The Roman historian Cassius Dio informs us that the Emperor Tiberius died the following spring after the death of Thrasyllus.[87] Since we know from other sources that Tiberius died in the year 37, this puts Thrasyllus' death as having taken place in the year 36 CE.

The historian Tacitus says that Thrasyllus had a son who predicted Nero's reign.[88] Some scholars have inferred that this son was probably the astrologer Balbillus, who served as court astrologer to the Emperors Claudius, Nero, and Vespasian. This connection between Thrasyllus and Balbillus was first argued by Conrad Cichorius in 1922, and subsequently endorsed and explored by Frederick Cramer in his extensive study of astrology in Roman law and politics.[89] Recently scholars such as Tarrant and Beck have taken a more cautious

---

[82] Porphyry, *Introduction*, chapters 24 and 41, respectively.

[83] Hephaestio, *Apotelesmatika*, 2, 11: 57 and 2, 23: 13.

[84] Diogenes Laertius, *Lives of Eminent Philosophers*, 9: 45; 3: 56–61.

[85] Tarrant, *Thrasyllan Platonism*.

[86] Porphyry, *On the Life of Plotinus*, 20.

[87] Cassius Dio, *Roman History*, 58: 27.

[88] Tacitus, *Annals*, 6: 22.

[89] Cichorius, "Der Astrologe Ti. Claudius Balbillus, Sohn des Thrasyllus." Cramer, *Astrology in Roman Law and Politics*, p. 95.

approach, choosing to suspend judgment on whether the two are related.[90]

I tend to side with those who argue that Balbillus probably was Thrasyllus' son, based on Tacitus' statement that he plans to talk about the son later within the context of Nero in particular, and then the subsequent prominence of Balbillus as an astrologer during the reign of Nero. If we take this connection between the two for granted, then Thrasyllus may have been the central figure in a family line of prominent astrologers that stretched from the first century BCE through to the mid-second century CE or later.[91]

Balbillus (First Century CE)

Balbillus is probably the most politically eminent Hellenistic astrologer that we know of. He flourished during the middle of the first century CE, and served as court astrologer to several of the Roman emperors, as well as becoming the prefect or governor of Egypt himself.

As discussed earlier, Balbillus may have been the son of Thrasyllus, and he seems to become active as a court astrologer in Rome after Thrasyllus' death in 36 CE. After the death of the Emperor Tiberius the following year, Balbillus left for Egypt and seems to have lived in Alexandria during the reign of Caligula, from 37–41 CE.[92] He appears to have returned to Rome in 41 CE due to the accession of the Emperor Claudius, during whose reign he enjoyed quite a bit of prosperity in various capacities as a member of the imperial cabinet. During this time he also held a number of posts in his native Egypt, for example as the high priest of the temple of Hermes in Alexandria, overseer of all imperial buildings and sacred sites in Egypt, and perhaps most importantly, as the head of the Museum and Library of Alexandria.[93] The Roman philosopher Seneca referred to Balbillus as "a very distinguished man, exceptionally accomplished in every type of literature."[94]

Unfortunately, little of Balbillus' astrological work survives. A summary of his book titled *Astrological Practices* (*Astrologoumena*), dedicated to an unknown figure named Hermogenes, survives.[95] The summary is exceedingly brief, but the

---

[90] Tarrant, *Thrasyllan Platonism*, p. 10; Beck, "The Mysteries of Mithras," p. 127, n. 60.

[91] Cramer explored the potential lineage of the family in *Astrology in Roman Law*, p. 92ff.

[92] Cramer, *Astrology in Roman Law and Politics*, p. 108.

[93] Cramer, *Astrology in Roman Law and Politics*, pp. 113–114.

[94] Seneca, *Natural Questions*, Book 4A, 2: 13, trans. Corcoran, p. 31. The context of this reference to Balbillus is somewhat humorous, with Seneca relating an odd story that seems to derive directly from Balbillus himself during his time as the prefect of Egypt, in which he witnessed a battle between a group of dolphins and crocodiles at one of the larger mouths of the Nile River. Cramer points out that "The story reads as if based on an oral account of Balbillus." Cramer, *Astrology in Roman Law and Politics*, p. 127, n. 16.

[95] Edited in CCAG, 8, 3, pp. 103–4. For a translation see Schmidt, *Sages*, pp. 66–68.

work seems to have primarily dealt with the length of life technique, as well as a few other topics in passing. A separate excerpt in the CCAG seems to preserve two chart examples from Balbillus, presumably from the same work, which he uses to demonstrate how the length of life technique works.[96] Interestingly, Balbillus used the charts of two people who were born about a century before he was active, and these are the two oldest chart examples in a literary source in Greek, dating to 72 BCE and 43 BCE.[97] Heilen is probably right in speculating that Balbillus may have obtained these charts from the case histories of his father, Thrasyllus.[98]

In terms of his legacy, Roger Beck has suggested that Balbillus may have been the source of some of the astrological doctrine that became integrated into the cult of Mithraism in the Roman Empire, although this is somewhat difficult to substantiate.[99] We do know with more certainty that the emperor Vespasian authorized a festival to be held in the city of Ephesus in honor of Balbillus, which was known as the Balbillea. The first Balbillea was held in the year 85 or 86 CE, and was subsequently celebrated every four years until at least the mid-third century.[100]

Marcus Manilius (Early First Century CE)

Manilius wrote a long instructional poem on astrology in Latin known as the *Astronomica* sometime around the early first century CE.[101] As a result of historical accident, this text is essentially the first major work on Hellenistic astrology to have survived largely intact into the present day, which is ironic given that it contains a number of idiosyncratic doctrines that are unique to Manilius.

The dating of Manilius is somewhat controversial, although he is generally thought to have written the *Astronomica* either sometime towards the end of the reign of the Roman Emperor Augustus, or not long after the ascension of the Emperor Tiberius to the throne.[102] This dating is entirely the result of allusions

---

[96] CCAG 8, 4, pp. 235–238. For a translation see Schmidt, *Sages*, pp. 68–71. For a more detailed analysis of these two charts see Gansten, "Balbillus and the Method of *aphesis*."

[97] Neugebauer and van Hoesen, *Greek Horoscopes*, pp. 76–78.

[98] Heilen, *Hadriani Genitura*, p. 214.

[99] Beck, *The Religion of the Mithras Cult in the Roman Empire*, p. 51. He originally introduced this argument in Beck, "The Mysteries of Mithras."

[100] Brunet, "The Date of the First Balbillea at Ephesos."

[101] The standard translation with facing Latin text is the Loeb edition: Manilius, *Astronomica*, trans. Goold. For the full critical edition with a proper critical apparatus see Manilius, *M. Manilii Astronomica*, ed. Goold.

[102] For a detailed survey and discussion about the dating of Manilius see Volk, *Manilius and his Intellectual Background*, pp. 137ff.

that Manilius makes to the emperor(s) during the course of his five-book poem, and these allusions have long been the subject of debate by historians. A date of circa 14 CE is probably the safest, as this is when Augustus died and Tiberius became Emperor.

Even though Manilius is one of our earliest surviving sources for information about the practice and techniques of Hellenistic astrology, in several areas the approach that he outlines is unusual when compared with other astrologers from that period. This has led to some debates over the reliability of Manilius as a source for understanding the practice of Hellenistic astrology. For example, virtually every astrologer from the first century through the seventh century reports that Venus rejoices in the fifth place and Saturn in the twelfth, but Manilius is the only author who says that Venus rejoices in the tenth and Saturn in the fourth.[103] It is not clear if Manilius is representing an otherwise unknown variant tradition here, or if this variation in the planetary "joys" scheme was introduced by Manilius himself for unknown reasons. Whatever the case, subsequent astrologers over the next several centuries largely seem to have ignored Manilius' version of the joys.

In the surviving manuscripts of the *Astronomica*, it is notable that Manilius fails to address the significations of the planets. While this might simply indicate that something is missing in the manuscripts, in some instances Manilius seems to go out of his way to avoid invoking the planets in situations where they would otherwise normally be used, such as in the assignment of the planets to the decans, for example, which he instead assigns to the signs of the zodiac.[104] Volk refers to this issue as the "puzzle of the planets," and suggests that Manilius may have purposely ignored the planets for philosophical or religious reasons.[105]

As David Pingree points out in his review of Goold's translation of the *Astronomica*, while Manilius' work is partially meant to be instructional, "its principal purpose seems to have been to delight its audience with poetry and to arouse admiration for the poet by its cleverness."[106] In other words, Manilius' purpose may have been more literary or artistic than instructional or scientific. Schmidt is a bit more blunt in his assessment, saying that while Manilius' poem contains "a wealth of astrological material […] much of it seems idiosyncratic" and "it is not clear that Manilius understood very well the astrological tradition he was versifying."[107] It has also been pointed out that Manilius may not have fully understood some of the astronomical concepts he was working with. Evans

---

[103] Manilius, *Astronomica*, 2: 918–938. The doctrine of the planetary joys will be discussed more in a later chapter, along with citations for the astrologers who mention the placements.
[104] Manilius, *Astronomica*, 4: 294–407.
[105] Volk, *Manilius and His Intellectual Background*, p. 48f.
[106] Pingree, "Review of Manilius, *Astronomica*," p. 263.
[107] Schmidt, *Kepler College Sourcebook*, pp. 17–18.

notes that Manilius "gives a list of rising times that follows system A and a list of day lengths that follows system B, without realizing that these are inconsistent with one another."[108]

Today Manilius is known more for the Stoic and deterministic sentiments that he expresses throughout the course of the poem than for his astrological technique. While his work does contain some useful information about the twelve places, the Lot of Fortune, and profections, most of these techniques are fleshed out more clearly and in greater detail by other authors, and so Manilius mainly becomes useful for providing corroborating testimony for certain doctrines.

Antiochus of Athens (First Century CE?)

Antiochus wrote an important book in which he introduced and defined all of the basic technical concepts of Hellenistic astrology; it was known either as the *Introduction* (*Eisagōgika*) or the *Thesaurus* (*Thēsauroi*).[109] This is important because most of the other surviving astrological handbooks teach us how to use various techniques, but they assume that the reader is already familiar with the basic technical terminology (which would have been dealt with in an introductory work). Antiochus' book is additionally important because it was based on early sources, citing only the authors Hermes, Nechepso, Petosiris, and Timaeus.

Unfortunately, the original text of Antiochus no longer survives. Instead, what we have is three later works which preserve some of his definitions. A comparison of the definitions preserved by these three texts show that they all derive from the same source—the lost work of Antiochus—which allows us to attempt to reconstruct the original definitions. Unfortunately there are problems with all three texts, and they often differ from one another in both major and minor ways, making the reconstruction of the original set of definitions challenging. The three surviving primary texts preserving Antiochus' definitions may be summarized as follows:

1. A partial Byzantine *Summary* of Antiochus' work.[110] The grammar is sometimes a bit shaky, and the text breaks off early in book 2, but

---

[108] Evans, *The History and Practice of Ancient Astronomy*, p. 124.

[109] In the past these were thought to be two separate works by Antiochus, although Schmidt is probably right in arguing that they instead appear to be different titles for the same work. Schmidt, *Definitions and Foundations*, p. 21. For the previous view see Pingree, "Antiochus and Rhetorius."

[110] Edited in CCAG 8, 3, pp. 111–119. Referred to henceforth as Antiochus, *Summary*. For a translation see Schmidt, *Definitions and Foundations*.

otherwise it is useful as a control for determining what the original text did or did not say.

2. An *Introduction to the Apotelesmatika of Ptolemy* is attributed to the third-century Neoplatonic philosopher, Porphyry of Tyre, which largely consists of definitions extracted from Antiochus.[111] The text is not complete, and it has some interpolations where the Arabic text of the ninth-century astrologer, Sahl ibn Bishr, has been translated into Greek and inserted into the text in a few places.[112] Otherwise, the grammar of the definitions is clearer and probably closer to the original than what is preserved in the *Summary*.

3. Altered versions of many of Antiochus' definitions have been incorporated into the *Compendium* of Rhetorius.[113] He seems to have rewritten many of the definitions, in some instances to attempt to clarify the ambiguity in certain definitions, while in others in order to update them and bring them more in line with contemporary terminology and usage in the later part of the Hellenistic astrological tradition. As a result of the revisions, Rhetorius' versions of the definitions are often at variance with the ones that appear in the *Summary* and in Porphyry, although in some instances they are still useful for clarifying earlier and later practices.

Schmidt published an attempt to reconstruct the original definitions of Antiochus by comparing all three texts in 2009.[114] Much of his reconstruction seems compelling and sensible, except for his reconstruction of the aspect doctrine, where he may have read between the lines of the text too far and inferred a more elaborate set of doctrines than the text actually called for. This led Demetra George, Benjamin Dykes, and myself to create a new translation of the definitions related to the aspect doctrine from the *Summary*, Porphyry, and Rhetorius, to see if we would come to the same conclusions. This culminated

---

[111] Edited in CCAG 5, 4, pp. 187–228. Henceforth Porphyry, *Introduction*. Hephaestio seems to draw on several of Porphyry's versions of Antiochus' definitions in book 1 of his *Apotelesmatika*, so I have not listed him here as a primary source for the definitions.

[112] Holden points out in the footnotes of his translation of Porphyry, *Introduction*, that chapters 53, 54, and 55 are interpolations from Sahl, *Introduction*, but fails to note that chapters 17, 18, and 19 are interpolations as well. See the entry for Porphyry for citations of the corresponding chapter numbers in Sahl.

[113] Originally edited primarily in CCAG 1, pp. 140–164. This was recently re-edited with an additional manuscript tradition in Caballero Sánchez and Bautista Ruiz, "Una paráfrasis." Pingree and Heilen's forthcoming edition of Rhetorius should provide the definitive edition.

[114] Schmidt, *Definitions and Foundations*.

in a week-long retreat in August of 2010, which resulted in an alternative reconstruction of the original aspect doctrine of Antiochus, which I subsequently presented in a lecture in June of 2011. Most of this reconstruction will be presented in the later chapters of this book on the aspect doctrine and the conditions of bonification and maltreatment.

The dating of Antiochus is unknown because there are no references to specific dates in the text, and there have been some disputes about where to place his work in the tradition. Cumont and Schmidt argue that Antiochus wrote as early as the first century BCE, and have attempted to connect him to Antiochus of Ascalon, the founder of Middle Platonism, who died around 68 BCE.[115] Pingree disagreed with Cumont's argument, instead dating Antiochus to the latter half of the second century CE.[116] There are problems with both of these attempts to date Antiochus.

While Cumont and Schmidt make some reasonable points for dating the astrologer Antiochus towards the earlier end of the possible spectrum rather than later, the attempts to connect him with the Middle Platonist Antiochus of Ascalon seem somewhat weak, even if the suggestion is certainly interesting given the philosopher's stature. One potential counterargument is that while in the astrological texts he is usually simply referred to as "Antiochus," Hephaestio once refers to him as "Antiochus of Athens," and there is no reason to believe that he is talking about a different author.[117] Thus, unless Hephaestio is mistaken about Antiochus' place of origin, he would not be one and the same as Antiochus of Ascalon. While it is true that Antiochus of Ascalon became head

---

[115] This argument was first outlined by Cumont in his article "Antiochus d'Athènes et Porphyre." There he dates Antiochus to sometime between 100 BCE–50 CE (p. 144). In the introduction to his reconstruction of Antiochus' work, Schmidt is initially somewhat dismissive of Cumont's arguments, but then goes on to say that certain aspects of Antiochus' text do have "a decidedly Platonic ring" to them. Schmidt, *Definitions and Foundations*, pp. 19–20. However, in the audio lecture that accompanied the book, Schmidt is much more open about entertaining the association between Antiochus the astrologer and Antiochus the Middle Platonist. Towards the end of the introduction he says: "I believe that Antiochus composed this work during the founding era of Hellenistic astrology, which is somewhere in the late second or early first century before the Christian Era, and that would be the appropriate time for Antiochus of Ascalon to have written such a treatise, if in fact a Platonist would deign to do such a thing" (1, *Introduction*, 13:06–13:30). Later he concludes by saying: "So, I find it perhaps a bit ironic, or at least the possibility a bit ironic, that we do have a surviving writing, or partially surviving writing, by a Middle Platonist named Antiochus of Ascalon, and lo and behold, it may very well be an astrological writing" (1, *Introduction*, 14:41–15:04). For the dating of Antiochus of Ascalon see Hatzimichali, "Antiochus' biography," esp. p. 28, who says that Antiochus was still alive in October of 69 BCE, but died not long after.

[116] Pingree, "Antiochus and Rhetorius."

[117] Hephaestio, *Apotelesmatika*, 2, 1: 5.

of the Platonic Academy at Athens and taught there at one point in his career, the sources for his life consistently refer to him as being from Ascalon.[118]

With respect to Pingree's argument for a late second century CE dating, it seems to be largely based on circumstantial evidence.[119] He points out that Hephaestio says that Antiochus and Apollinarius are largely in agreement with Ptolemy about their approach concerning a specific technical doctrine, although he acknowledges that this is "certainly not definitive proof of their relative chronologies," and noncommittally characterizes the late second century dating as a "guess."[120] Elsewhere he points out that Anonymous of 379 mentions Antiochus together with the second-century astrologers Vettius Valens and Antigonus of Nicaea, although it is worth noting that Anonymous puts Antiochus before Valens and Antigonus in this chronology.[121] Pingree also mentions that Firmicus Maternus cites Ptolemy and Antiochus together in the same paragraph as having dealt with the doctrine of antiscia, which he takes to mean that they both lived in the second century, but he fails to mention that the first-century astrologer Dorotheus of Sidon is also mentioned in the following sentence.[122] Finally, Pingree inexplicably assigns Nechepso, Petosiris, Hermes, and Timaeus to the first century CE only when discussing Antiochus, despite the evidence from sources like Thrasyllus that indicate that the first three of those authors should probably be dated to the first century BCE or earlier.

More recently, Heilen has followed Pingree in dating Antiochus to the late second century, citing chapter 51 from Porphyry's *Introduction* and chapter 15 from Rhetorius' *Compendium*.[123] In these chapters the second-century astrologer Antigonus is mentioned, and since the chapter is nearly identical in Porphyry and Rhetorius, Heilen inferrs that they are both derived from the lost work of Antiochus. This would actually be a much more compelling argument for dating Antiochus to the late second century, since we know that Antigonus wrote his work sometime after 138 CE, and if Antiochus mentioned him in his original work then he would have lived sometime after Antigonus. However, it is not clear that this chapter in Porphyry and Rhetorius does in

---

[118] See the guide to the testimonies for Antiochus of Ascalon in Sedley, *The Philosophy of Antiochus*, pp. 334–46.

[119] His arguments were originally outlined in Pingree, "Antiochus and Rhetorius," and then later reiterated and narrowed in "From Alexandria to Baghdad," p. 7.

[120] Hephaestio, *Apotelesmatika*, 2, 10: 9 & 29. Pingree, "From Alexandria," p. 7, fn. 35.

[121] CCAG 5, 1, p. 205: 14.

[122] Firmicus, *Mathesis*, 2, 29: 2.

[123] Heilen, "The Emperor Hadrian," p. 58, fn. 51. There is an extended discussion in Heilen, *Hadriani Genitura*, pp. 23–27.

fact derive from the lost work of Antiochus. First, there is no clear evidence for it in the *Summary* of Antiochus' work, which is problematic since that is our best control for determining what the author originally wrote. Second, the two chapters in Porphyry and Rhetorius are nearly identical in their wording, which is rare in the other chapters where we know for sure that they both drew on Antiochus, because Rhetorius usually altered and updated the wording of Antiochus' definitions in a way that is usually quite distinctive. Pingree in fact noted that a number of chapters in Rhetorius' *Compendium* were taken directly from Porphyry's *Introduction*, and he seems to have identified this chapter as being one of them.[124] If that is the case, then it means that it may have been Porphyry who cited Antigonus rather than Antiochus citing him, and thus there would be no basis for dating Antiochus after Antigonus.

Instead, Antiochus' exclusive citation of early authors as sources makes him similar to Thrasyllus, and thus seems to imply that the text was written relatively early in the tradition. The latest author he cites in the *Summary* is Timaeus, who Antiochus seems to have cited as an intermediary for material from Hermes on the advantageous places.[125] Timaeus is cited for some astrological and astronomical doctrines by Pliny, who died in the year 79 CE, which probably means that the astrological work ascribed to Timaeus was written in the late first century BCE or early first century CE.[126] Thus, Antiochus probably wrote sometime around the second half of the first century CE, or perhaps in the early second century. This dating is naturally a bit speculative, though, as the first authors that mention him are Porphyry in the late third century, followed by Firmicus Maternus and Anonymous of 379 in the fourth century. Whatever the case, Antiochus' citation of early authors for his definitions makes him an important source for the early Hellenistic tradition.

Critodemus (First Century CE?)

Critodemus was a semi-significant early expositor of the tradition, although unfortunately little of his work has survived. Firmicus, in his list of the early founders of Hellenistic astrology, cites him as one of the writers who came

---

[124] Pingree, "Antiochus and Rhetorius," p. 207, and then again with expanded commentary in "From Alexandria to Baghdad," pp. 7–8. Holden notes that this chapter in Porphyry is "nearly identical" to the one in Rhetorius (Porphyry, *Introduction*, trans. Holden, p. 44, fn. 1). Schmidt omitted it from his reconstruction of the original Antiochus text, saying in the introduction that "there are indeed some chapters in Porphyry that were inserted later from Rhetorius, but these do not concern any material that can be correlated with the Antiochus *Summary*" (*Definitions and Foundations*, pp. 22–3).

[125] CCAG 8, 3, p. 116: 3–12.

[126] Pliny, *Natural History*, 2, 6: 38; 5, 10: 55–56; 16, 34: 82.

after Hermes, Asclepius, Nechepso, and Petosiris, which implies that he lived sometime after those authors but still relatively early in the tradition.[127]

The second-century astrologer Vettius Valens drew on the work of Critodemus quite a bit and seems to have regarded him as an important authority, although he frequently laments his cryptic and theatrical style.[128] In some ways Valens' criticism of Critodemus was similar to his statements about Nechepso and Petosiris, at least as far as his views on the cryptic and often frustrating nature of their works, although he comes off as slightly more restrained in his criticisms of Nechepso and Petosiris than he does Critodemus.

According to Valens, Critodemus wrote a work titled *Vision* (*Horasis*).[129] Hephaestio credits him with another work titled *Tablet* (*Pinax*), and he extracts a section from his work on indications for a short span of life.[130] Critodemus is mentioned along with Berossus by Pliny the Elder as having claimed that the Babylonians had astronomical observations recorded on cuneiform tablets dating back 490,000 years.[131] This indicates that he wrote sometime before Pliny died in 79 CE. At first glance this seems to fit well with Riley's assumption that a chart which appears in book five of Valens' *Anthology* comes directly from Critodemus, since Valens introduces it right after presenting a table from Critodemus' work.[132] The date of the chart itself puts the native as being born in 37 CE, and then encountering some sort of crisis or possibly death in the year 68 CE.[133] Thus, if Riley's speculation about the provenance of this example chart is correct, it would allow us to date the composition of Critodemus work to sometime between 68 and 77 CE.

However, Pingree points out that the enigmatic nature of Critodemus' text, as frequently lamented by Valens, makes the use of example charts in his work doubtful, and instead he puts forward a hypothesis that the group of charts from the first century that Valens was drawing on were probably from a commentator on Critodemus, who would have flourished around 70 CE.[134] Unfortunately it is hard to know for sure. All we can say for certain is that Critodemus lived sometime around the first century CE or slightly earlier.

A brief summary of one of Critodemus' works survives, and it deals with an advanced method of annual profections that is very similar to Valens' treatment

---

[127] Firmicus, *Mathesis*, 4, proem: 5.
[128] Valens complaining about Critodemus' style: *Anthology*, 3, 9: 1–6; 9, 1: 5–7.
[129] Valens, *Anthology*, 3, 9: 3.
[130] Hephaestio, *Apotelesmatika*, 2, 10: 41.
[131] Pliny, *Natural History*, 7, 56: 193.
[132] Valens, *Anthology*, 5, 7: 17ff. Riley, *A Survey of Vettius Valens*, p. 24.
[133] The chart is No. L 37 in Neugebauer and Van Hoesen, *Greek Horoscopes*, pp. 78–79.
[134] Pingree, *Yavanajātaka*, vol. 2, p. 426.

of the same topic in book 4 of the *Anthology*.[135] While Valens does mention Critodemus as having dealt with profections, he doesn't otherwise seem to say that he acquired the profections material from Critodemus, but instead that it was taught to him by a teacher he found in Egypt.[136] Riley suspects that Valens "may have taken more from Critodemus than he explicitly acknowledges," although Valens does mention him frequently and gives him quite a bit of credit already.[137]

Abraham (First Century CE?)

Abraham (written as Abram in the texts) is another early author who is mentioned by Firmicus as being one of the later expositors in the lineage of Hermes, Asclepius, Nechepso, and Petosiris.[138] There he is listed as if he was a contemporary of Critodemus. This seems to be another instance of pseudepigrapha, since Abraham is of course the biblical patriarch of the Jewish religion, although there appears to have been a specific technical manual on astrology with his name on it that was in circulation by the first or second century CE.

The astrological text attributed to Abraham seems to have primarily dealt with the topic of the lots, and to have introduced a complex time-lord technique called zodiacal releasing. Valens cites Abraham as having introduced zodiacal releasing in order to time the different periods in a person's life when they would travel.[139] Zodiacal releasing uses the Lot of Spirit and the Lot of Fortune as starting points in order to calculate the timing periods, and later in the *Anthology* when Valens returns to the topic he says that the Sun is associated with the Lot of Spirit and the Moon with the Lot of Fortune.[140] We have a secondary account of the astrological work attributed to Abraham in Firmicus, who also links him to the doctrine of lots. In his discussion of the Lot of Fortune, Firmicus tells us that "Abraham called it the Place of the Moon," and similarly with respect to the Lot of Spirit, Firmicus tells us that "Abraham called it the Place of the Sun."[141] This parallel between Valens and Firmicus seems to imply that they were both drawing on the same source text, which was a work on the lots attributed to

---

[135] Critodemus summary edited in CCAG 8, 3, p. 102. For a translation see Schmidt, *Sages*, p. 49. Compare with Valens, *Anthology*, 4, 11–24.

[136] Critodemus mentioning profections: Valens, *Anthology*, 3, 9: 4. Valens being taught the advanced method of profections in Egypt: Valens, *Anthology*, 4, 11: 7.

[137] Riley, *A Survey of Vettius Valens*, p. 9.

[138] Firmicus, *Mathesis*, 4, proem: 5.

[139] Valens, *Anthology*, 2, 30: 5–7.

[140] Valens, *Anthology*, 4, 4: 1–2.

[141] Firmicus, *Mathesis*, 4, 17: 5; 4, 18: 1.

Abraham. Later, Firmicus also cites Abraham for an otherwise undocumented scheme for establishing which signs of the zodiac can hear and see each other.[142]

There was a large Jewish community in Alexandria from the Hellenistic era onward, and the attribution of Abraham's name to an early astrological text may imply that the author had some connection with Judaism.[143] By the first century CE, Jewish writers such as Josephus tried to portray the biblical figure of Abraham as the original founder or discoverer of astronomy and possibly astrology, and the astrological text bearing his name could have been written with similar intentions in mind.[144] If the name does imply some sort of cultural connection on the part of the author of the astrological text, then this would be one of the only known Hellenistic astrologers of Jewish ancestry. On the other hand, it seems as if texts were ascribed to religious figures from other faiths as well, such as Zoroaster, and it is not necessarily clear whether the actual authors of these texts were motivated by cultural connections, or perhaps just the allure of foreign wisdom.

Since Valens is the first source that cites Abraham in the second century CE, and Firmicus otherwise lists him as a contemporary of Critodemus, this probably means that the work attributed to him was written around the first century CE, or maybe slightly earlier.

Zoroaster (First Century CE?)

Zoroaster (or Zarathustra) was a Persian prophet who lived prior to the Hellenistic period and founded the religion known as Zoroastrianism. He is another one of the major religious figures that pseudepigraphical texts were ascribed to during the Hellenistic astrological tradition.

Valens cites him for a specific timing technique, saying that he spoke of it in a riddling fashion (*ēnixato*), and that Nechepso and others followed a similar approach.[145] The text Valens was drawing on then would have been written prior to the second century CE, and thus perhaps in the first century CE or earlier. In the fifth century, the philosopher Proclus cites Zoroaster together with Petosiris

---

[142] Firmicus, *Mathesis*, 8, 3: 5.

[143] In talking about Jewish interest in astrology in the Hellenistic period, Charlesworth says "during the last two centuries B.C. astrological ideas, symbols, and beliefs permeated much deeper into many sectors of Jewish culture" and "by the fourth century A.D. abundant archeological evidence in Galilee proves that Jews were attracted by astrological images, signs, and symbols; the prominent symbolic and central use of the zodiacal mosaics indicates that many Jews assimilated astrological beliefs." Charlesworth, "Jewish Interest in Astrology," p. 948.

[144] For Josephus' portrayal of Abraham see Reed, "Abraham as Chaldean Scientist and Father of the Jews."

[145] Valens, *Anthology*, 9, 4: 1–3.

for the doctrine that the sign of the zodiac that the Moon is located in at the time of a native's conception will be the rising sign at the moment of their birth.[146] This doctrine is otherwise only attributed to Petosiris in other authors such as Porphyry and Hephaestio, which may imply that the text Proclus was reading that was attributed to Zoroaster was influenced by Petosiris in this doctrine, thus making it date to either the first century BCE or the first century CE.[147] Unfortunately, the presumed antiquity of Zoroaster in ancient times seems like it often led many authors to assume that he necessarily must have lived prior to other sources they were drawing on, and this can sometimes complicate attempts to construct chronologies involving him.[148] A number of other fragments from different astrological texts ascribed to Zoroaster exist, although they can be difficult to date, and they seem to derive from different authors who lived in different eras.[149]

Bidez and Cumont originally argued that many of the astrological works attributed to Zoroaster may have originated with the Maguseans, which were a group of Zoroastrians who lived in Syria during the Hellenistic period.[150] Pingree took their argument for granted, which led him to conclude that the Maguseans would have been partially responsible for transmitting some forms of Mesopotamian astrology to the west during the Hellenistic period, in addition to Berossus and the Egyptian authors who wrote under the names Hermes, Nechepso, and Petosiris.[151] However, Beck later contested this hypothesis, pointing out that there is little to nothing in the pseudepigrapha attributed to Zoroaster that indicates a Persian or Mesopotamian origin, and that ultimately these fragments are probably the products of Hellenistic learning, and only used

---

[146] Proclus, *Procli Diadochi in Platonis rem publicam*, ed. Kroll, vol. 2, p. 59: 3–6.

[147] Porphyry, *Introduction*, 38; Hephaestio, *Apotelesmatika*, 2, 1: 2.

[148] According to Pliny (*Natural History*, 30: 2), Eudoxus claimed that Zoroaster lived 6000 years before Plato. In the sixth century John Lydus seems to list Zoroaster as coming before Petosiris, although it is not clear if this is because the text of Petosiris cited Zoroaster, or if it is because Lydus assumed that Zoroaster would necessarily have been earlier, based on some of the legends. See John Lydus, *De Ostentis*, proem: 2.

[149] Schmidt translated three brief fragments in *Sages*, pp. 23–29. These were edited in CCAG 8, 3, pp. 120–22; CCAG 2, pp. 192–195; CCAG 5, 3, p. 87. Quack ("Les Mages Égyptianisés," p. 274) notes that Hübner (*Raum, Zeit*, pp. 228–35) pointed out that the third fragment is actually from Theophilus of Edessa, which underlines some attribution issues that come up frequently in the fragments attributed to Zoroaster. For the standard collection of other Zoroaster fragments see *Les Mages Hellénisés*, ed. Bidez and Cumont. Most of these fragments are translated in *Zarathushtra and The Religion of Ancient Iran*, ed. Vasunia. For some important critical analysis of most of the astrological fragments see Quack, "Les Mages Égyptianisés."

[150] *Les Mages Hellénisés*, ed. Bidez and Cumont, esp. pp. 56–84.

[151] Pingree, *Yavanajātaka*, vol. 2, p. 445.

the name Zoroaster in order to confer authority on the texts.[152] In the late third century CE, Porphyry made a point of refuting the antiquity of some religious texts that were supposedly written by Zoroaster in his time:

> I Porphyry have produced numerous refutations of the book of Zoroaster, proving the book to be entirely spurious and recent, a fabrication of those who upheld this heresy to make it seem that the doctrines which they had chosen to acclaim were those of the ancient Zoroaster.[153]

More recently, Quack endorsed Beck's rejection of the Magusean hypothesis of Bidez and Cumont, while pointing out that many of the fragments associated with Zoroaster incorporate elements that imply an Egyptian origin or setting.[154] He suggested that perhaps the authors of the texts attributed to Zoroaster were part of ethnic Persian communities that had been living in Egypt since the Persian conquest prior to the Hellenistic period.[155] Unfortunately it is difficult to infer the motives of authors who chose to write their texts under pseudonyms.

Serapio of Alexandria (First Century CE?)

Serapio of Alexandria was an astrologer who wrote on inceptional astrology and possibly other topics, although only fragments of his work survive. Anonymous of 379 is the first astrological author who mentions him, and he says that Ptolemy was born after Serapio chronologically, which has been assumed to place Serapio sometime prior to the second century CE.[156] Pingree notes that Serapio's use of early terminology and techniques probably places him towards the earlier end of the tradition, and so he may have lived in the late first century BCE or early first century CE.[157] Most of the fragments that survive of Serapio's work deal with different topics in inceptional astrology, and Schmidt notes that he may have been one of the early systemizers of that branch of the tradition.[158]

There is a long list of definitions of basic astrological concepts attributed to Serapio that was edited by Franz Cumont in the CCAG.[159] This list of

---

[152] Beck, "Thus Spake Not Zarathustra."

[153] Porphyry, *Life of Plotinus*, 16, trans. Edwards, *Neoplatonic Saints*, p. 29.

[154] Quack, "Les Mages Égyptianisés."

[155] Quack, "Les Mages Égyptianisés," p. 282.

[156] Cumont first made this argument in CCAG 8, 4, p. 225.

[157] Pingree, *Yavanajātaka*, vol. 2, pp. 440–441.

[158] Schmidt, *Sages*, p. 45. The fragments of Serapio's work are edited in CCAG 1, p. 99–102, and CCAG 5, 1, pp. 179–180. For translations see Schmidt, *Sages*, pp. 44-48.

[159] CCAG 8, 4, p. 225–232. For a translation see Porphyry, *Introduction*, trans. Holden, pp. 59–73; or Serapio, *Definitions*, trans. Gramaglia. Some of the definitions are also translated in Schmidt, *Definitions and Foundations*.

definitions is titled *Derived Names of the Configurations of the Stars* (*Paronomasiai schēmatismōn tōn asterōn*), or *Definitions* for short. This list is apparently a later Byzantine compilation which contains some of Serapio's own definitions, although material from other authors seems to have been added in as well, so it should be used with caution.[160] It is in this text that he is called Serapio of Alexandria. The list is incomplete, with the last page of the manuscript missing.

Anubio (First Century CE?)

Anubio (or Anoubiōn) was the author of an instructional poem on astrology that was written sometime around the first century CE. He is unique because he is the only astrological author who is known to have written a text in verse using elegiac couplets, which is a form of Greek metrical poetry. Instructional texts were sometimes written in verse in the ancient world because this makes them easier to recite and memorize, and we will see that several other Hellenistic astrologers also wrote their texts in verse as well. Unfortunately only a few fragments and excerpts from Anubio's text survive.

Hephaestio of Thebes quoted him in the fifth century on the topic of determining the degree of the Ascendant, using a strange method that involves the domicile lords of the luminaries.[161] Rhetorius cited him in the sixth or seventh century in a chapter on determining the native's occupation.[162]

A long prose paraphrase of some delineations for each of the planets when they are configured to each other is attributed to Anubio.[163] In the early twentieth century the original editors of this text noticed that some of these delineations seem to have been incorporated into book six of Firmicus, and suggested that Anubio was one of his sources.[164] This seemed to have been confirmed later when some new papyrus fragments of Anubio's work were found buried in a rubbish heap near the ancient Greco-Roman city of Oxyrhynchus.[165] The editor of these fragments showed that there were many more parallels in the Latin text of Firmicus, which seemed to imply that he had translated much material from the Greek text of Anubio.[166] However, the editor noted that oftentimes Firmicus

---

[160] As noted in Pingree, *Yavanajātaka*, vol. 2, p. 441.

[161] Hephaestio, *Apotelesmatika*, 2, 2: 11–18.

[162] Rhetorius, *Compendium*, 82.

[163] Originally edited in CCAG 2, pp. 204–212.

[164] CCAG 2, p. 159f.

[165] Originally published with Greek text and translation by Obbink in "Anoubion, Elegiacs," pp. 67–109, and then later in a complete critical edition of all known fragments in Anubio, *Carmen*, ed. Obbink.

[166] Anubio, *Carmen*, ed. Obbink, pp. 23–37.

is more expansive in the delineations he gives, and sometimes there can be major discrepancies between Anubio and Firmicus.[167] Heilen argued that the reason for this is that Firmicus was actually translating the delineations into Latin from a common source text that Anubio also used (Nechepso and Petosiris), rather than drawing the delineations from Anubio directly.[168] Recently a more comprehensive critical edition and French translation of Anubio was published by Paul Schubert, which takes much of this new research into account.[169]

Anubio's dating is problematic, because the first astrologer that explicitly mentions him is Hephaestio in the fifth century. However, the papyrus fragments recovered from Oxyrhynchus are thought to date to the second or third century CE.[170] The dating is usually further narrowed down by the fact that an astrologer named Anubio of Diospolis is mentioned several times in the fictional Christian story known as the *Pseudo-Clementines*, which survives in two versions known as the *Homilies* and the *Recognitions*.[171] Early in the *Homilies*, the gist of the story is that Anubio is an associate of the magician Simon Magus, and they are eventually chased off as sorcerers by an angry crowd.[172] Anubio appears later in the *Homilies* within the context of a discussion about astrology, eventually taking a semi-important role in its conclusion.[173] Bremmer speculates that Anubio must have appeared as a character in the original story that the *Homilies* are based on for the purpose of a debate about astrology with Clement, although it is a debate that is

---

[167] Obbink, "Anoubion, Elegiacs," p. 75; p.80.

[168] Heilen, "Anubio Reconsidered," esp. pp. 129–137.

[169] Anubio, *Anoubion. Poème astrologique*, ed. Schubert.

[170] Obbink in "Anoubion, Elegiacs," p. 68.

[171] Pseudo-Clement of Rome, *Homilies*, 4, 6, edited in *Patrologia Graeca*, ed. Jacques-Paul Migne, vol. 2, 1857, p. 161 = T1 in Anubio, *Carmen*, ed. Obbink, p. 2. In the *Recognitions*, which is an alternate version of the story underlying the Greek *Homilies* for which only a Latin translation exists, Anubio does not appear until the last third of book 10, being specifically cited in chapters 52, 56–59, and 62–63. For the Latin see *Patrologia Graeca*, ed. Jacques-Paul Migne, vol. 1, pp. 1157–1474.

[172] For this see Pseudo-Clement, *Homilies*, 4, 6. Anubio is introduced at this point in the narrative, and then he comes up again later within the context of the same storyline in book 6, chapters 1 and 26, and for the final time in the same context in book 7, ch. 9.

[173] He reappears in the storyline in *Homilies*, 14, 11–12. This book is interesting because it contains a narrative involving astrology and a discussion of the subject, except that the Greek term often used in the second half of the book to refer to the subject of astrology is *genesis*, which usually means "nativity" rather than "astrology." The term is clearly employed to mean "nativity" in chapter 6 when a character mentions the arrangement of someone's birth chart, although later in chapters 11 and 12 it seems to take on a broader meaning as "astrology" or perhaps "natal astrology." Anubio appears for the final time as a prominent character in book 20, being mentioned in chapters 11, 14–17, and 20–21.

built up and then never takes place in the extant versions of the story.[174]

It is not clear whether the Anubio that appears in the *Pseudo-Clementines* was meant to be the same astrologer as the one who wrote the didactic poem under that name. Pingree rejected the association, simply saying that there were no grounds for assuming the identification.[175] Obbink elaborates on possible objections to the association, pointing out that the *Homilies* don't say anything about Anubio having written in verse, and there is likely to have been more than one astrologer in Egypt using that rather common name.[176] However, he still argues that the association between our Anubio and the one that appears in the *Pseudo-Clementines* is likely because

> the fact that only one Anoubion is recorded (and uniquely as an elegiac poet) in the later astrological tradition suggests that the link is more than coincidental, and that the author of the pseudo-Clementine homily appropriated a figure of notoriety in order to lend plausibility and contemporary colour to his account.[177]

The original text underlying the *Pseudo-Clementines* is thought to date to the mid-third century CE.[178] Heilen points out that some of the material in the story associated with Anubio was quoted by Origen, which means that these parts would not have originated any later than 200 CE.[179] Additionally, the fact that Anubio was said to be associated with Simon Magus and a contemporary of the apostle Peter is often taken to suggest a first century CE dating, since it presumes that the audience would have accepted them as contemporaries. Taking all of this together, Heilen concludes that Anubio probably published his work sometime in the second half of the first century CE, or during the early second century at the latest.[180]

If the name given in the *Pseudo-Clementines* is correct, then Obbink presumes that Anubio would have hailed from Diospolis Magna, which is in Egypt.[181] Diospolis Magna was also known as Thebes, and it is where the major fifth-century astrologer Hephaestio also came from.

---

[174] Bremmer, "Foolish Egyptians: Apion and Anoubion in the Pseudo-Clementines."

[175] Pingree, *Yavanajātaka*, vol. 2, p. 422.

[176] Obbink, "Anoubion, Elegiacs", p. 61.

[177] Obbink, "Anoubion, Elegiacs", p. 61.

[178] Kelley, *Knowledge and Religious Authority*, p. 11.

[179] Heilen, "Anubio Reconsidered," p. 139.

[180] Heilen, "Anubio Reconsidered," p. 140.

[181] Obbink, "Anoubion, Elegiacs", p. 60.

Dorotheus of Sidon (Late First Century CE)

Dorotheus wrote an instructional poem on astrology in Greek in the late first century CE. His work had an enormous impact on the later tradition, particularly in the Medieval period, when it became one of the primary source texts for astrologers such as Māshā'allāh and Sahl ibn Bishr.

His work may have been known as the *Pentateuch* ("Five Books"), based on its structure, although in modern times it is usually cited as the *Carmen Astrologicum* ("Poem of Astrology"), based on the generic title its editor gave the critical edition.[182] The first four books deal with natal astrology, and the fifth with inceptional astrology.[183] In general, the first two books deal with topical methods for studying different areas of the native's life, often involving the use of certain triplicity rulers and lots. The third book focuses on the length of life technique, while the fourth book deals with other timing techniques such as profections and transits. His fifth book is the earliest and the longest surviving work on inceptional astrology from the Hellenistic tradition.

The original Greek text of Dorotheus' poem no longer survives in its entirety. The most complete version of the text survives in an Arabic translation that was made around the year 800 by 'Umar ibn al-Farrukhān al-Tabarī, based on an earlier Middle Persian translation of the original Greek text.[184] Unfortunately, the extant Arabic version of Dorotheus' text contains a number of errors, omissions, and interpolations by later authors.[185] Some of the interpolations are innocuous, such as the references to the Indian subdivisions of the zodiac known as *navamshas*, or references to astrologers who lived later than Dorotheus, such as Vettius Valens. Other interpolations are more problematic, as it is not clear how many of the references to interrogational astrology were inserted into several chapters in the fifth book after the fact. Certainly the title of the fifth book in the Arabic translation has been changed, since it says that it is on "questions" (i.e. interrogational astrology), even though the majority of the book is clearly on inceptional astrology. Luckily there are some scattered fragments and quotations from Dorotheus in Greek and Latin preserved by later astrologers such as Hephaestio, and these sometimes allow us to have a control when studying the Arabic translation. In those areas in which no fragments of

---

[182] For Pingree's critical edition and translation of the Arabic see Dorotheus, *Carmen*. See also the forthcoming translation by Benjamin Dykes.

[183] Pingree points out that the first four books primarily focus on the topics associated with the *oktatropos* (Dorotheus, *Carmen*, p. 439).

[184] Translated into English by Pingree in Dorotheus, *Carmen*, pp. 161–322. For the dating see Pingree, *From Astral Omens*, p. 46.

[185] Some of this is discussed in Pingree, *From Astral Omens*, pp. 46–47.

the text exist besides the Arabic translation, which is the case for the majority of the work, we must use the text cautiously, and acknowledge that we are using a contaminated English translation of an Arabic translation of a Persian translation of Dorotheus' original Greek poem.

Dorotheus uses several birth charts as examples in his work, all of which date to between 7 BCE and 44 CE.[186] Since the details of these individuals' lives were already known to Dorotheus, this implies that he probably wrote his work sometime around the late first century CE. Pingree gave him an approximate date of c. 75 CE, which is probably more or less correct.[187]

Even though Dorotheus was writing in the late first century CE, he was already acting as more of a compiler of earlier knowledge and doctrines, or at least that is the way he portrays himself in his prefatory remarks. He says that he traveled widely in Egypt and Mesopotamia, and collected information from some of the foremost astrological authorities in those areas.[188] At one point, Hephaestio seems to indicate that one of Dorotheus' sources was Nechepso, and he also seems to have drawn on a text ascribed to Hermes Trismegistus on the significations of the twelve places as well.[189]

In the Hellenistic tradition, Dorotheus had his greatest influence over Hephaestio of Thebes, who essentially tried to synthesize the systems of Dorotheus and Ptolemy in his fifth-century work, although references to Dorotheus can also be found in other authors such as Firmicus and Rhetorius as well.[190] There are a number of distinct similarities between the approaches of Dorotheus and Vettius Valens, who lived almost a century later, although Valens never mentions Dorotheus as a source. The similarities probably resulted from drawing on the same tradition, and as a pair they are useful for establishing what the mainstream of astrological practice looked like in the first and second centuries CE, especially in comparison to other authors such as Ptolemy. Eventually Dorotheus became a major influence on the early medieval astrological tradition due to the Persian and Arabic translations of his work.

---

[186] The chart that Pingree originally dated to 281 CE and thought was a Persian interpolation was later plausibly re-dated to 44 CE by Holden, which is within Dorotheus' apparent time frame. See Holden, *A History*, p. 35, n. 83. In the Arabic text the chart appears in Dorotheus, *Carmen*, 3, 2.

[187] Pingree, *From Astral Omens*, p. 46.

[188] Dorotheus, *Carmen*, 1, 1: 1–5. Cf. 5, 1: 1–4.

[189] Hephaestio, *Apotelesmatika*, 2, 21: 26; Dorotheus, *Carmen*, 2, 20.

[190] Firmicus mentions Dorotheus in connection with the doctrine of antiscia (*Mathesis*, 2, 29: 2). Rhetorius mentions Dorotheus explicitly several times in his *Compendium*, in connection with the twelfth-parts (ch. 19), the placement of the Lot of Fortune in relation to the predeceasing of the parents (ch. 48), the Lot of Livelihood (ch. 57), and the Lot of Injury (ch. 60).

Manetho (Early Second Century CE)

Another long instructional poem on astrology that survives from the Hellenistic tradition is attributed to Manetho (or Manethōn). The work is titled *Apotelesmatika*, and it is divided into six books.[191] The modern editor of the text considers it to be a compilation that was added to in later eras, with the core of the original text consisting of books 2, 3, and 6, and then books 1, 4, and 5 being written by later authors.[192] The original author included his birth chart in the book, which has been dated to 80 CE, and this has then been taken to imply that the core of the work was originally composed sometime around 120 CE or so, while the other parts were all assembled together in the third century.[193] The first astrologer who cites Manetho is Hephaestio of Thebes in the early fifth century.[194]

This text evidently represents another instance of pseudepigrapha, as the historical personage of Manetho was an Egyptian priest who wrote a history of Egypt in Greek sometime around the third century BCE. Verbrugghe and Wickersham point out that the astrological text deliberately attempts to pass itself off as a work by the historian Manetho, for example in passages where the author addresses "King Ptolemy."[195] Lopilato is of the opinion that the intended association was supposed to be with Ptolemy II Philadelphus, who reigned from 283–246 BCE.[196] This is spurious because the astrological compendium would have been compiled several centuries after Ptolemy II died. As a result of this, some scholars refer to the author of this text as Pseudo-Manetho.

Anonymous Michigan Papyrus (Second Century CE?)

The *Michigan Papyrus* (P. Mich. 149) is a fragmentary astrological manual that was rediscovered, edited, and translated in the early twentieth century.[197] The

---

[191] The standard edition is Manetho, *Apotelesmatika*, ed. and trans. Lopilato.

[192] Lopilato in Manetho, *Apotelesmatika*, p. 10–12.

[193] Lopilato in Manetho, *Apotelesmatika*, p. 12. For the birth chart see Manetho, *Apotelesmatika*, 6: 739–750. The chart was dated in Neugebauer and Van Hoesen, *Greek Horoscopes*, No. L80, p. 82. They dated it to May 28 or 27, 80 CE, about two hours after sunset.

[194] Hephaestio, *Apotelesmatika*, 2, 4: 27; 2, 11: 125.

[195] Verbrugghe and Wickersham, *Berossos and Manetho*, p. 102. For the references to King Ptolemy see Manetho, *Apotelesmatika*, 1: 1–15; 5: 1–11.

[196] Lopilato in Manetho, *Apotelesmatika*, p. 417. Cf. p. 8.

[197] The discovery of the text was announced in 1927 with the publication of an edition of the Greek text with commentary in Robbins, "A New Astrological Treatise: Michigan Papyrus No. 1." Robbins later published a revised version of the Greek text along with an English translation and expanded commentary in "Michigan Papyrus 149: Astrological Treatise," ed. Robbins. There it is referred to as P. Mich. 149. It is the later edition that I refer to in this work with the abbreviation *Michigan Papyrus*.

editor of the text, Frank Egleston Robbins, was also the translator of the Loeb edition of Ptolemy's *Tetrabiblos*. The text was acquired in Egypt in 1920/21, and Robbins dated it to the second century CE for philological reasons, based on the handwriting.[198] The papyrus roll that the text was written on was in extremely bad shape, and much of the text is damaged or missing, although there are several long sections that are in good enough condition that they can be read quite well. Many words and sentences in the text had to be reconstructed based on words that are only partially legible, or based on inferences. The text as we have it seems to be part of an introductory manual on astrology. Many facets of the text seem to represent standard Hellenistic astrological doctrines, although there are also areas that present unique or idiosyncratic doctrines that are not reported elsewhere. The text is mainly useful as an additional piece of corroborating testimony for those doctrines that are mentioned by other authors, as it helps to confirm which techniques and concepts were widely used. The *Michigan Papyrus* is also important because it identifies Asclepius as the author of the *oktatropos*.[199]

Claudius Ptolemy (Middle of the Second Century CE)

Ptolemy was a scientist and polymath who worked in Egypt around the middle of the second century CE. He is most well known for his influential works on astronomy and astrology, although he also wrote on other topics such as optics, geography, and harmonics.

He is primarily known for having written the single most authoritative text on astronomy in classical antiquity, called the *Mathematical Treatise* (*mathēmatikē suntaxis*), or simply *Suntaxis*, which later came to be known as the *Almagest* in the Medieval period.[200] Records of astronomical observations that Ptolemy made in Alexandria dating from 127–141 CE are contained in the work, indicating that the *Almagest* was composed sometime after 141 CE.[201] Recent scholarship has pushed the date of the composition of the *Almagest* later due to an astronomical inscription that has been recognized as being written by Ptolemy in the year 146 or 147 CE.[202] The so-called "Canobic Inscription" is thought to represent an earlier stage in Ptolemy's thinking, prior to the publication of the *Almagest*, which would indicate that he didn't complete the *Almagest* until sometime after the year 150 CE. Since Ptolemy mentions the *Almagest* in the introduction to his

---

[198] Robbins, "A New Astrological Treatise," p. 1.

[199] *Michigan Papyrus*, col. ix: 19–27.

[200] For a translation see Ptolemy, *Ptolemy's Almagest*, trans. Toomer.

[201] Ptolemy, *Ptolemy's Almagest*, trans. Toomer, p. 1. There is a useful list of dated observations that are mentioned in the *Almagest* in Pedersen, *A Survey of the Almagest*, pp. 408–422.

[202] Hamilton, Swerdlow, and Toomer, "The Canobic Inscription."

astrological work, the *Tetrabiblos*, this implies that the *Tetrabiblos* was finished later, perhaps sometime in the 150s or 160s. Thus, Ptolemy probably lived from approximately 100 CE–175 CE.

Ptolemy's astrological work was apparently originally known as the *Apotelesmatika*, which means something like "Inquiry into (Astrological) Outcomes," although it later became known more widely as the *Tetrabiblos* ("Four Books").[203] The first book of the *Tetrabiblos* is on introductory techniques and concepts, as well as philosophical arguments in defense of astrology. The second book deals with universal astrology. Books three and four deal with a set of standard topics in natal astrology.

Ptolemy's *Almagest* marked a major turning point in the history of astronomy, and set a new standard for the way that many astronomical calculations were done for centuries after his death. This included the popularization of a new set of astronomical tables that were derived from the *Almagest*, known as the *Handy Tables*, which allowed astrologers to calculate astrological charts with greater ease and precision. The success of Ptolemy's astronomical works probably resulted in greater circulation and prestige for his astrological work, and the later Greco-Roman astrologers of the third through seventh centuries seem to have held him in high regard. Anonymous of 379 calls him "the divine Ptolemy,"[204] while Hephaestio refers to him as "the truth-loving Ptolemy" (*ho philalēthēs Ptolemaios*).[205] Ptolemy's *Tetrabiblos* was the only Hellenistic astrological text that was continuously transmitted and translated over the centuries since it was originally published. As a result of this, he was often regarded as not just the most important and influential astrologer of antiquity, but also often assumed to be the most representative of what the practice of astrology looked like in the Greco-Roman period.

However, despite the considerable influence that Ptolemy had on later astrologers, his *Tetrabiblos* does not necessarily appear to be fully representative of the mainstream of the Hellenistic astrological tradition. Ptolemy's program seems to have been to reformulate astrology as a natural science, largely along Aristotelian lines, partially to help legitimize it.[206] One of the ways that he did

---

[203] Ptolemy, *Tetrabiblos*, ed. Hübner, pp. xxxvi–xxxix. This edition by Hübner is the standard critical edition. The standard translation is the Loeb edition by Robbins, although Schmidt later produced a preliminary translation of books 1, 3, and 4 that is based on a more authoritative critical edition than the one Robbins compiled on his own.

[204] CCAG 5, 1, p. 204: 9.

[205] Hephaestio, *Apotelesmatika*, 1, proem: 4.

[206] That Ptolemy possibly structured parts of the *Tetrabiblos* in response to earlier skeptical critiques of astrology is discussed in Long, "Astrology: Arguments Pro and Contra." In terms of Ptolemy's incorporation of Aristotelian elements into his cosmology, there is an excellent

this was by reconceptualizing the mechanism underlying astrology as working through some sort of celestial influence from the planets and stars. This was in contrast with earlier views which held that celestial objects were capable of giving signs of future events without necessarily being causes.

Campion argues that it was Ptolemy's causal or naturalistic rationale for astrology that allowed it to survive into the Middle Ages and the Renaissance as a respected science, despite religious opposition.[207] Geoffrey Cornelius makes a similar argument about the importance of Ptolemy's astrological work in the survival of astrology through to modern times, although he argues that this came at the cost of obscuring the earlier theoretical foundations of astrology as being rooted in divination.[208] Holden emphasizes the technical rather than the philosophical departures that Ptolemy made from the rest of the astrological tradition, calling the *Tetrabiblos* an "abridged" and "deviant" version of Hellenistic astrology.[209] To a certain extent, this view represents a strong reactionary movement against Ptolemy that arose in the astrological community in the 1980s and 1990s, partially as a result of the recovery of other Hellenistic astrological sources, and the subsequent realization that Ptolemy's work was not necessarily representative of the mainstream of the Greco-Roman tradition of astrology.[210] As Holden explains, prior to recent times Ptolemy's astrological work "has been wrongly considered by most modern astrologers to be the ultimate sourcebook of astrology," largely because it was the oldest text that stayed in circulation in one form or another over the centuries.[211]

Despite these recent reappraisals of Ptolemy's work, the *Tetrabiblos* is still useful and informative as a source, and his deviations from the tradition should

---

survey of Ptolemy's philosophy in Feke and Jones, "Ptolemy." While they characterize his overall approach as that of an eclectic "Platonic empiricist," they say that he "appropriates the ideas and concerns of the Platonic, Aristotelian, and, to a lesser extent, Stoic traditions" (p. 209). In the same paper, they characterize Ptolemy's cosmology as Aristotelian (p. 203). Anthony Long similarly characterizes Ptolemy as eclectic, although he notes that the Aristotelian tendencies are somewhat more prominent in the areas of Ptolemy's epistemology and empiricism (Long, "Ptolemy on the Criterion," p. 163). Elsewhere, Alexander Jones characterizes the *Tetrabiblos* as "Ptolemy's attempt to set Greek astrology on a more or less Aristotelian physical basis" (Jones 2012, "Ptolemy").

[207] Campion, *A History of Western Astrology*, vol. 1, p. 208ff.

[208] Cornelius, *The Moment of Astrology*.

[209] Holden, *A History of Horoscopic Astrology*, p. 46.

[210] This has also been noted more recently by some academics. Riley discusses some discrepancies between Ptolemy and other astrologers such as Porphyry in "Theoretical and Practical Astrology," p. 246. Heilen characterizes the modern perception that the *Tetrabiblos* is representative of the standard Greek astrological tradition as a "misapprehension," and says that it "is in many respects not true." Heilen, "Ptolemy's Doctrine of the Terms," p. 77.

[211] Holden, *A History*, p. 45.

not be overstated. While sometimes Ptolemy would make major changes or modifications to certain doctrines, more often he would simply emphasize the techniques or rationales that made the most conceptual sense to him, and would underemphasize or omit the ones that he did not agree with.[212] In this way Ptolemy often ends up emphasizing things that were genuine facets of the tradition, but it is important to compare his statements with the works of other authors in order to see what he left out. In this way Ptolemy's work is still extremely useful, even if he may not necessarily be the most representative example of what a typical astrologer looked like in the second century CE. Instead, astrologers such as Dorotheus of Sidon and Vettius Valens appear to be much more useful examples in that regard.

An anonymous commentary on the *Tetrabiblos* was written in Greek at some point later in the tradition, which is sometimes attributed to the fifth-century Neoplatonist philosopher Proclus.[213] Caballero Sánchez says that the commentary would have been written after Porphyry's *Introduction*, since it cites him, and that while it is difficult to establish the latest date that it could have been written, it is unlikely that it would have been written after the sixth century.[214] The *Commentary* contains two chart examples, dated by Pingree to December 22, 175, and July 29, 241 CE.[215] Only the earlier chart cast for 175 CE seems to be correct, though, as the planetary positions that Pingree found for 241 do not accord very well with the chart given in the text.[216]

There is also a paraphrase of the *Tetrabiblos* that was written in Greek sometime in Late Antiquity or in the early Byzantine period.[217] It is also

---

[212] Instances where Ptolemy probably emphasized only part of the original rationale underlying certain concepts occur in his discussions of the arrangement of the domiciles and exaltations, which will be discussed later in the sections on those topics. Instances where he made major changes or modifications to important technical doctrines occur in his treatment of the triplicity rulers and bounds, which will also be discussed later.

[213] The original edition was published in 1559: *In Claudii Ptolemaei quadripartitum*, ed. Wolf. More recently Caballero Sánchez has begun work on a new edition, which he laid a blueprint for in "Historia del texto del Comentario anónimo al Tetrabiblos de Tolomeo," followed by the first installment that covers part of the commentary from book one: "El Comentario anónimo al Tetrabiblos de Tolomeo. Edición crítica y traducción castellana de los escolios metodológicos del libro I (in Ptol. Tetr. 1.1.1-1.3.1)."

[214] Caballero Sánchez, "Historia del texto del Comentario anónimo al Tetrabiblos de Tolomeo," pp. 78–9.

[215] For the charts see Wolf, *In Claudii Ptolemaei*, p. 98 & 112. Neugebauer and Van Hoesen mention Pingree's dating briefly in "Astrological Papyri and Ostraca," p. 66.

[216] The chart for 175 CE is the one given on p. 112 of Wolf, *In Claudii Ptolemaei*. The data is given in the text itself on p. 114.

[217] There is no modern critical edition of the Greek text of the paraphrase. The two printed editions are Melanchthon, *Procli Paraphrasis in quatuor Ptolemaei libros de siderum effectionibus*

attributed to Proclus, and so it is often referred to as the *Proclus Paraphrase*.[218] The purpose of the paraphrase is to make Ptolemy's extremely condensed and complicated writing style easier to understand. It sometimes differs in significant ways from the standard text of the *Tetrabiblos* that has come down to us in the manuscripts, and so it can be useful in some instances in detailed textual studies. Holden notes that prior to the twentieth century most of the translations of the *Tetrabiblos* into English by astrologers were based on the *Proclus Paraphrase* rather than directly from Ptolemy's original text.[219]

Vettius Valens (b. 120 CE – c. 175 CE)

Vettius Valens was an astrologer originally from the Greco-Roman city of Antioch, who lived in the middle of the second century CE. He is the single most important surviving source for studying the Hellenistic astrological tradition.

Valens wrote a series of instructional texts on the practice of astrology that has come down to us in nine books, known collectively as the *Anthology*.[220] Some of the books were evidently written for Valens' students, and twice he addresses an otherwise unknown figure (student?) named Marcus.[221] He cites numerous astrological sources from the past, many of which no longer exist, including frequent citations from the lost works of Nechepso and Petosiris.[222] He also includes over a hundred example charts in his text, which are used to demonstrate the application of the techniques that he discusses.

The writings often have a very personal tone, as the technical material is sometimes interspersed with digressions about Valens' private life, his feelings about some of the sources he was drawing on, and thoughts on the philosophy of astrology. He also frequently contrasts how other astrologers say that certain techniques should be used, compared to the approach that makes more sense or seems more "natural" (*phusikōteron*) to him in terms of his personal practice.

Valens' chronology was first worked out by Otto Neugebauer during the process of writing the book *Greek Horoscopes* with H. B. van Hoesen. In a

---

(Greek text), and Allatios, *Procli Diadochi Paraphrasis in Ptolemaei libros IV* (Greek text with Latin translation).

[218] For two recent discussions about the paraphrase see Heilen, "Ptolemy's Doctrine of the Terms and Its Reception," pp. 62–65, and Ptolemy, *Ptolemy's Tetrabiblos in the Translation of William of Moerbeke*, ed. Vuillemin-Diem and Steel, pp. 56–57.

[219] Holden, *A History*, p. 85. This includes the widely used Ashmand translation.

[220] The standard critical edition is Valens, *Anthology*, ed. Pingree. There is a preliminary translation of books 1–7 by Schmidt, and a complete translation by Riley.

[221] Valens mentions writing the books for his students in *Anthology*, 3, 13: 16. For Marcus see Valens, *Anthology*, 7, 6: 230; 9, 1: 1.

[222] For a full list of sources Valens cites see Riley, *A Survey of Vettius Valens*, pp. 8–11.

1954 paper he concluded that the majority of Valens' work on the *Anthology* took place between 152 and 162 CE, after dating all of the example charts that he used.[223] Some of the individual books of the *Anthology* seem to have originally been published as standalone units, while other books seem to form interrelated groups that cover similar topics and themes. Riley has shown that the composition of some of the books during different parts of Valens' life can be determined by studying some of the chart examples that he uses.[224]

Pingree plausibly suggested that one of the birth charts that Valens uses as a frequent example throughout the *Anthology* is probably his own nativity, although Valens never explicitly acknowledges that this is the case.[225] Other Hellenistic astrologers such as Manetho and Hephaestio also included their birth charts in their compilations, and Paulus of Alexandria may have even used his son's, so this would not necessarily be uncommon. If the chart that Pingree identified as Valens' is really his, then Valens was born on February 8, 120 CE. Like Hephaestio, Valens also includes his own conception chart, which was cast for May 13, 119 CE.

Valens was born in the ancient city of Antioch, which is located in what is now modern-day Antakya, Turkey. The Emperor Marcus Aurelius was born about a year later, so the two were contemporaries. Valens tells a story about how at one point in his life he travelled to Egypt in search of more precise timing techniques, and eventually he settled there and set up a school, evidently in Alexandria.[226] He was involved in a shipwreck when he was thirty-four years old, which would have been around the year 154 CE, and in book seven of the *Anthology* he presents the charts of five other people who were on the same ship.[227] His primary period of activity was in the 150s and 160s; nothing is known of him after the early 170s. This is around the same time that the Antonine Plague broke out across the Roman Empire, and it is possible that Valens was one of the millions of people who succumbed to it at this time.

Antigonus of Nicaea (Late Second Century CE)

Antigonus wrote an instructional manual on astrology which included a number of chart examples sometime around the late second century CE or so.

---

[223] Neugebauer, "The Chronology of Vettius Valens' Anthologiae." Cf. Neugebauer and Van Hoesen, *Greek Horoscopes*, pp. 176–185. Further work on Valens' chronology and the date of the composition of various books of the *Anthology* was done in Riley, *A Survey of Vettius Valens*, and Komorowska, *Vettius Valens of Antioch*.

[224] Riley, *A Survey of Vettius Valens*.

[225] Valens, *Anthology*, ed. Pingree, p. v.

[226] Valens, *Anthology*, 4, 11: 1–10.

[227] Valens, *Anthology*, 7, 6: 127–160. Discussed in Beck, *Ancient Astrology*, pp. 101–11.

It evidently consisted of at least four books, although very little of it survives.[228] Hephaestio of Thebes preserves three long example charts with delineations from Antigonus' work, which accounts for the majority of what we know about his approach.[229] These happen to be the lengthiest surviving examples of delineated natal charts from the entire Hellenistic tradition, and so they are of considerable importance for seeing how some of the techniques were used. Additionally, in the same fragments, Hephaestio says that Antigonus drew on the works of Nechepso and Petosiris as well as the mysterious Egyptian text on the decans known as the *Salmeschiniaka*, so his work may have some additional value for understanding how some of the earliest authors would have interpreted charts. He may not have always completely followed the approaches outlined by the earliest authors, though, as Hephaestio criticizes him at one point for rejecting some techniques outlined by authors such as Petosiris and Antiochus for determining the moment of conception.[230] If it is true that the astrologer Antigonus was identical with the doctor named Antigonus of Nicaea who lived around the same time, which Heilen believes is probably the case, then perhaps he had other, non-astrological reasons for rejecting this doctrine.[231]

In terms of dating, two of the charts that Antigonus uses have been identified as the Emperor Hadrian and his grandnephew Pedanius Fuscus.[232] Both evidently died in the year 138 CE, and since their deaths are mentioned in the delineations, Antigonus must have written sometime after this date. Anonymous of 379 mentions Antigonus in a brief chronology of astrologers that he gives, and he places him just after Vettius Valens, which may imply that either they were contemporaries in the mid-second century or that Antigonus lived sometime after Valens.[233] The first astrologer who mentions Antigonus seems to be Porphyry in his *Introduction* around the late third century CE, followed by Anonymous of 379, which means that his work must have been published

---

[228] There is a reference to the fourth book in Rhetorius (CCAG 8, 1, p. 242: 15–17), which is T5 in Heilen, *Hadriani Genitura*.

[229] All of the surviving fragments and testimonia related to Antigonus were recently published by Heilen in *Hadriani Genitura*. The three example charts are F1–6 in Heilen, which equals Hephaestio, *Apotelesmatika*, 2, 18: 21–76, although Heilen has improved Pingree's main text of Hephaestio by integrating material from Epitome IV. Schmidt provided two translations of these delineations from Pingree's main text of Hephaestio, first in his translation of book 2 of Hephaestio, and then later in *Definitions and Foundations*, pp. 349–369. These are horoscopes No. L 40, L 76, and L 113, IV in Neugebauer and Van Hoesen, *Greek Horoscopes*.

[230] Hephaestio, *Apotelesmatika*, 2, 1: 8 = T3 in Heilen, *Hadriani Genitura*.

[231] Heilen, "Antigonos of Nicaea," p. 464. For a fuller explanation see Heilen, *Hadriani Genitura*, p. 27f.

[232] Heilen, "The Emperor Hadrian in the Horoscopes of Antigonus of Nicaea."

[233] CCAG 5, 1, p. 205: 14 = T2 in Heilen, *Hadriani Genitura*.

a while before that.[234] Based on this I would date him to the second half of the second century CE, or perhaps early third century.

Porphyry of Tyre (Late Third Century CE)

Porphyry of Tyre was a prominent Neoplatonic philosopher who flourished in the late third century CE. He is primarily known as the student of the founder of Neoplatonism, Plotinus, although he was regarded as an important philosopher in his own right in Late Antiquity. He occasionally made references to astrological doctrines in his philosophical works, and there is at least one surviving text on astrology that was attributed to him.

Porphyry is sometimes considered to be the author of an introduction to Ptolemy's *Tetrabiblos*, entitled *Introduction to the Apotelesmatika of Ptolemy* (*Eisagōgē eis tēn Apotelesmatikēn tou Ptolemaiou*).[235] The *Introduction* mainly consists of a series of definitions of basic astrological concepts, which Porphyry says were not all clearly defined by Ptolemy. Most of the definitions were copied verbatim from a lost work of definitions by Antiochus of Athens. The extant version of the *Introduction* appears to be incomplete, and it also contains a few interpolations from a work by the ninth-century astrologer, Sahl ibn Bishr, which have been translated from Arabic into Greek and then placed into the text by a later Byzantine editor.[236]

Porphyry is best known by astrologers in modern times for the system of quadrant house division that bears his name, the so-called "Porphyry House System," which is outlined in chapter 43 of Porphyry's *Introduction*. However, as Holden rightly points out, the same system was already described about a century earlier by Valens, and so it is only an accident of history that Porphyry's name became associated with this system rather than that of Valens.[237]

Porphyry's authorship of the *Introduction* is sometimes doubted, although I take it as genuine both because of his frequent references to and obvious familiarity with astrology in his philosophical works, as well as because later astrologers of the Hellenistic tradition such as Hephaestio and the author of the anonymous commentary on the *Tetrabiblos* seem to have thought that

---

[234] Porphyry, *Introduction*, 51 = F7 in Heilen, *Hadriani Genitura*.

[235] Edited by Emilie Boer and Stefan Weinstock in CCAG 5, 4, pp. 187–228. For a translation see Porphyry, *Introduction*, trans. Holden.

[236] Chapters 17, 18, and 19, as well as 53, 54, and 55 of Porphyry, *Introduction* are interpolations from Sahl, *Introduction*. Porphyry 17 = Sahl 5.5; Porphyry 18 = Sahl 5.6; Porphyry 19 = Sahl 5.7; Porphyry 53 = Sahl 5.14; Porphyry 54 = Sahl 8–9; Porphyry 55 = Sahl 5.3.

[237] Holden, *Biographical Dictionary*, p. 580, citing Valens, *Anthology*, 3, 2.

Porphyry was definitely the author of the text.[238] Porphyry is also known to have authored a commentary on Ptolemy's *Harmonics*, which shows that he was familiar with Ptolemy's work and had an interest in commenting on it.[239] Additionally, in his astrological work, Firmicus refers to him as "our Porphyry" (*noster Porphyrius*), which could indicate that Firmicus considered him to be a fellow astrologer.[240] In terms of dating, the latest author mentioned in the *Introduction* is Antigonus, who would have written sometime in the second half of the second century, or perhaps early third century.[241] The first author who cites Porphyry and drew on the *Introduction* is Hephaestio, who lived in the early fifth century. This places the composition of the *Introduction* sometime between 215 and 415 CE, which fits Porphyry's dating nicely, since the philosopher is known to have been born around 234 and died around 305 CE.[242]

Firmicus Maternus (Middle of the Fourth Century CE)

Firmicus Maternus was a lawyer from Sicily who lived during the time of the Emperor Constantine and his sons in the mid-fourth century CE. He wrote a long textbook on astrology in Latin known as the *Mathesis*.[243] Technically, his full name was Julius Firmicus Maternus, although he is usually simply referred to as Firmicus Maternus. The title of the book derives from a Greek term that means "learning" or "the act of learning." In the Latin of Firmicus' day the word came to mean "knowledge" or "science," and Firmicus frequently refers to astrology within the latter context as "the *mathesis*" or "the *science*."[244] Firmicus' *Mathesis* thus means "The Science (of Astrology)."

---

[238] Porphyry famously discussed the astrological doctrine of the Master of the Nativity in his *Letter to Anebo*, and this technique is outlined in chapter 30 of the *Introduction* to the *Tetrabiblos*. Elsewhere, he cites the views of the astrologers regarding when the soul enters the body in his text *To Gaurus on How Embryos are Ensouled*. Hephaestio mentions him twice in *Apotelesmatika*, 2, 10: 63, and 2, 18: 15. For the reference in the anonymous commentary on the *Tetrabiblos* see *In Claudii Ptolemaei quadripartitum*, ed. Wolf, p. 169. For some other references to astrology in Porphyry's philosophical works see Johnson, *Religion and Identity in Porphyry of Tyre*, pp. 112–121, which also gives a nice treatment of the *Introduction* on pp. 159–164.

[239] Porphyry, *Porphyry's Commentary on Ptolemy's Harmonics*, trans. Baker.

[240] Firmicus, *Mathesis*, 7, 1, 1.

[241] Porphyry, *Introduction*, 51.

[242] Karamanolis, "Porphurios of Tyre," p. 688.

[243] The standard critical edition is still Firmicus Maternus, *Iulii Firmici Materni Matheseos libri VIII*, ed. Kroll, Skutsch, and Ziegler, although a more recent critical edition was published by Monat in 1992–97. For translations, the standard has been the one published by Bram in 1975, although this sometimes omits or abbreviates some delineation material, and it has recently been superseded by the translation by Holden in 2011.

[244] For example, Firmicus, *Mathesis*, 1, 1: 7.

Firmicus' book largely consists of delineation material that has been excerpted from earlier Greek authors and translated into Latin.[245] He has a somewhat bombastic style, and he may have been more of an amateur rather than a professional astrologer compared to someone like Valens, although his work is still useful because he preserves quite a bit of older material that would otherwise have been lost. As a result of all of the interpretive material that his book preserves, the *Mathesis* is the longest surviving astrological text from the Hellenistic tradition. It is also one of only two surviving textbooks on astrology from the Hellenistic tradition that were written in Latin rather than Greek, with the other being Manilius.

Firmicus dedicated the *Mathesis* to a government official and friend of his named Lollianus Mavortius. Mavortius had apparently nursed Firmicus back to health after a difficult winter journey, and during their time together he introduced Firmicus to the subject of astrology.[246] At one point during their time together, Firmicus apparently offered to write a textbook on astrology in Latin for Mavortius based on earlier sources, perhaps due to his ability to read Greek. In the book he says that he came to regret committing himself to what became a very laborious task, although he eventually fulfilled his promise and completed the work.[247]

Later in his life Firmicus appears to have converted to Christianity and wrote a rather extreme attack against the pagan traditions, titled *The Error of the Profane Religions* (*De errore profanarum religionum*).[248] He does not mention astrology in this attack, although it is not entirely clear why.

Although researchers agree that Firmicus lived and wrote towards the middle of the fourth century, there is a debate about which decade of that century he published his astrological work. The debate is of moderate importance since it may have a bearing on Firmicus' relationship to astrology and Christianity.

Firmicus dedicated his Christian polemical text, *The Error*, to the two co-ruling brother emperors, Constantius and Constans. This suggests it must have been completed sometime between 343 and 350 CE, the period in which they were both ruling together.[249] We also know that Firmicus had started work on the *Mathesis* by at least the year 334, as he mentions an eclipse that had recently taken place in book one, and this eclipse has been dated to July 17, 334.[250] Later

---

[245] For example, see Anubio, *Carmen*, ed. Obbink, pp. 23–37 for parallels between delineation material in books two and six of Firmicus and Greek fragments from the lost work of Anubio.

[246] Firmicus, *Mathesis*, 1, proem: 2–5.

[247] Firmicus, *Mathesis*, 1, proem: 6–8

[248] For a translation see Firmicus, *The Error of the Pagan Religions*, trans. Forbes.

[249] Firmicus, *The Error*, trans. Forbes, p. 9.

[250] For the reference to the eclipse see Firmicus, *Mathesis*, 1, 4: 10. For the dating of the

in book one of the *Mathesis*, Firmicus has an invocation to Constantine, whom he treats as if he is still the current emperor, and since Constantine died in 337, this seems to provide us with an end point for Firmicus' work on the *Mathesis*.[251]

Further confirmation of this dating is seen to be provided through the unnamed birth chart that Firmicus uses in order to demonstrate the concept of antiscia in book two of the *Mathesis*.[252] The subject of the chart has been identified as Ceionius Rufius Albinus, who would have been born in the year 303 based on the chart Firmicus provided.[253] Firmicus provides a number of details about the native's life, but the last chronological statement that he makes about him is that he became the Prefect of Rome. Surviving records indicate that Albinus was Prefect from December 30, 335 through March 10, 337, which accords well with the dates derived from book one of the *Mathesis*, and narrows the time frame of publication down to the year 336 or early 337.[254]

The point of dispute involves Firmicus' friend and patron Mavortius, whom Firmicus refers to in the *Mathesis* as "Proconsul and designated Consul Ordinarius."[255] Since it is known that Mavortius didn't actually become consul of Rome until 355, some have assumed that this must have been the year in which Firmicus actually finished writing the *Mathesis*, which would place it after he wrote his attack on paganism.[256]

This dating is problematic for several reasons. On the one hand, it does not fit the other indications given in book one, which place Firmicus as likely having written his *Mathesis* sometime between 336 and 337. Additionally, it does not

---

eclipse see Firmicus, *The Error*, trans. Forbes, p. 4, or Bram, *Mathesis*, p. 1.

[251] Firmicus, *The Error*, trans. Forbes, p. 4

[252] Firmicus, *Mathesis*, 2, 29: 10–20.

[253] The original identification of Albinus was made in Mommsen, "Firmicus Maternus." Neugebauer later calculated the date of the birth based on the planetary positions given by Firmicus as March 14, 303 CE at about 9:00 PM. See Neugebauer, "The Horoscope of Ceionius Rufius Albinus." T. D. Barnes pointed out that the same date was also arrived at over twenty years earlier by the German astrologer Walter Koch, known primarily today for having invented the Koch system of quadrant houses, in Koch, "Ceionius Rufius Albinus." See Barnes, "Two Senators under Constantine," p. 41. In the same paper Barnes also rightly points out that the date of the birth chart could be either March 14 or 15.

[254] Barnes, "Two Senators Under Constantine," p. 42. Barnes' paper provides a very thorough overview of the details and controversies surrounding the identification of Ceionius Rufius Albinus with this chart.

[255] Firmicus, *Mathesis*, 1, proem: 8.

[256] The primary advocate of this dating is Lynn Thorndike, who is followed by James Holden. Thorndike originally outlined his argument in Lynn Thorndike, "A Roman Astrologer as a Historical Source," p. 419, n. 2. He later expanded it in *A History of Magic and Experimental Science*, vol. 1, p. 525ff. For Holden's views see *A History of Horoscopic Astrology*, pp. 66–69, which he expands on a bit in his translation of Firmicus, *Mathesis*, pp. vi–viii.

fit the timeline of Firmicus' other known work, *The Error*, since it seems much more likely that Firmicus wrote the astrological work before the Christian polemic, rather than after.

The majority of scholars have followed the argument first put forward by Theodor Mommsen in 1894, which held that although Mavortius was *designated* as consul in 337, Constantine's death in the same year caused a delay in Mavortius' receiving the full consulship, because Constantine's sons were not required to follow through on their father's appointments.[257] Firmicus dedicated his work to Mavortius at a point when Mavortius had been promised the position, but had not actually started it. As it turned out, there was a delay of almost two decades before he actually took up the office.

Firmicus says that it was when Mavortius was appointed "Governor of the East" (*comes Orientis*) by Constantine that he "lost no time in demanding" that Firmicus finish the book that he had promised him. Since Mavortius was governor of the east from 330–336, presumably this reminder to Firmicus would have occurred around 330, when he assumed the governorship. The *Mathesis* was finally completed and dedicated to Mavortius, then, sometime around 336/7. This is also one of the reasons why Ceionius Rufius Albinus' birth chart would have been used—because he was the current Prefect of Rome at the time that Firmicus finished the book, and obviously someone that both he and Mavortius knew.

Firmicus says that Mavortius had just become the governor of Campania when the two met (when Firmicus first promised to write the book for him). Mavortius was governor of Campania starting in the year 328, so this likely would have been the year in question, when Firmicus first made the promise. Then in 330, two years later, Mavortius becomes governor of the east and reminds Firmicus of his promise. This would have been when the greater part of Firmicus' activity in writing the *Mathesis* occurred, during the seven-year period from 330–337. He finally dedicated it to Mavortius in the year in which he was still Proconsul of Africa and had been designated Consul Ordinarius, which was 337. Ironically, Mavortius' own fortunes changed unexpectedly that very same year, and the death of Constantine caused a delay in his career aspirations for nearly twenty years.

Sometime during the course of the next decade, Firmicus converted to Christianity.[258] He appears to have published his attack on paganism, *The Error*

---

[257] Mommsen, "Firmicus Maternus." For a detailed account of this whole issue see Firmicus, *The Error*, trans. Forbes, pp. 3–5, and also Barnes, "Two Senators Under Constantine."

[258] On Firmicus' conversion see Firmicus, *The Error*, trans. Forbes, pp. 7–8; p. 172, n. 197. The statement that is usually interpreted as Firmicus' only explicit reference to his conversion

of the Profane Religions, around the year 347 or shortly thereafter.[259] This would have been a full ten years after the publication of the *Mathesis*. While Firmicus did not mention astrology in the attack, and so there is some ambiguity over whether he had completely rejected it by that point, it seems certain that he did in fact convert to Christianity during the intervening years because his demeanor in a number of areas had changed markedly.

One example of this is Firmicus' radically different treatment of Porphyry between the two works. In the *Mathesis* he refers to him affectionately as "our Porphyry" (*noster Porphyrius*), but in his Christian polemic, he attacks Porphyry rather viciously.[260] At one point he calls him "Porphyry, the defender of the cults, enemy of God, foe of the truth, teacher of the arts of wickedness."[261] Clearly Firmicus had a change of heart, and it seems likely to me that Firmicus became more hostile towards Porphyry after his conversion to Christianity as a result of Porphyry's famous fifteen-book attack, *Against the Christians*.[262] This provides some interesting insight into the social climate of astrology during

---

occurs in *The Error*, 8: 4, although it is not terribly overt.

[259] This is based on an allusion that Firmicus makes to Persian military defeats that would have occurred either in the year 346 or 348. See Firmicus, *The Error*, trans. Forbes, p. 9. For the allusion in Firmicus see *The Error*, 29: 3. Pingree appears to agree with this dating, putting the publication of *The Error* in 347 precisely. See Pingree, *Yavanajātaka*, vol. 2, p. 428.

[260] Firmicus, *Mathesis*, 7, 1: 1. Pingree suggested that this statement might have been an indication that Firmicus studied under Porphyry earlier in his life. Pingree, *Yavanajātaka*, vol. 2, p. 438. Holden is apparently in agreement, using this assumption as part of his rationale for the purposes of dating. Holden, *A History of Horoscopic Astrology*, p. 66, n. 158. This assumption that Firmicus' statement indicates a student-teacher relationship between the two seems like a bit of a stretch, though, as Firmicus' reference to "our Porphyry" could have been meant in a number of different ways. For example, Firmicus' noted Neoplatonic leanings in the *Mathesis* may have put him in the position of having identified himself as being part of the same philosophical school or milieu as Porphyry. Thus the "our Porphyry" could signify general affinity with the Neoplatonists. On the other hand, given some of Porphyry's astrological leanings, it just as easily could have been the identification of him as an astrologer, or at least as someone sympathetic to astrology. Moreover, he uses the same phrase to refer to a few different people throughout the course of his book. While it is true that he uses it for Mavortius, who was a contemporary, he also refers to "our Fronto" (*Mathesis*, 2, pref: 2) at one point, and "our Navigius" (*Mathesis*, 2, pref: 4). If Bram is right in identifying these two names as corrupted references to Fonteius Capito and Nigidius Figulus (Firmicus, *Mathesis*, trans. Bram, p. 305; pp. 323–4), both of whom flourished and were involved in the practice of astrology in the first century BCE, then this demonstrates that Firmicus employed the term *noster* without necessarily meaning that he had a direct relationship with the individuals named. For Fonteius, see Weinstock, "C. Fonteius Capito and the 'Libri Tagetici.'"

[261] Firmicus, *The Error*, 13: 4, trans. Forbes, p. 72. Forbes discusses Firmicus's stance on Porphyry briefly on pp. 26–27.

[262] See Porphyry, *Porphyry Against the Christians*, trans. Berchman.

the rise of Christianity in the fourth century, and how quickly views began to change, sometimes even within a single lifetime.

Paulus of Alexandria (fl. c. 378 CE)

In the late fourth century, an astrologer named Paul of Alexandria wrote an astrological text known as the *Introduction*, which he dedicated to his son, whose name was Cronamon.[263] He is usually referred to with the Latinized form of his name, Paulus Alexandrinus, although I will use a mixed form here and call him Paulus of Alexandria.

The version of the *Introduction* that we have is apparently a second edition of the work. In the proem, Paulus says that his son pointed out that the calculations for the ascensional times of the signs were wrong, so Paulus wrote a second edition of the work in order to incorporate the ascensional times according to Ptolemy, or so he says in the beginning of the work.[264] However, Holden points out that Paulus doesn't seem to have actually incorporated the rising times of Ptolemy in the second chapter of the *Introduction* where he addresses the subject, so perhaps only parts of the second edition survived.[265]

Almost nothing is known about Paulus's life, although we know the date of the composition of his work because in chapter 20, within the context of a discussion about determining the planetary ruler of the day, Paulus demonstrates the technique by calculating what the lord of the day is "on the present day" (*epi tēs sēmeron hēmeras*).[266] Apparently he was writing that chapter of his book on Wednesday, February 14, 378 CE.[267]

Holden discovered a previously unknown birth chart embedded in Paulus' work, and he speculates that it is likely that of his son, Cronamon.[268] In chapter 23 on the lots, Paulus demonstrates how to calculate the Lots of Fortune, Spirit, and Eros by giving an example with exact positions for the Sun, Moon, Venus, and Ascendant. Later in chapter 31, his chapter on annual profections, Paulus again uses the same example chart with Leo rising in order to demonstrate the technique, but he also gives us the positions of Mercury, Jupiter, and Saturn. With this information, Holden was able to determine that the native was born on March 19, 353 CE, at about 2:00 p.m., presumably in Alexandria, Egypt.

When using this chart as an example in order to demonstrate how to use

---

[263] For the Greek text see Paulus, *Pauli Alexandrini Elementa Apotelesmatica*, ed. Boer. There are currently three English translations, by Schmidt, Greenbaum, and Holden.

[264] Paulus, *Introduction*, 1.

[265] Holden, *A History of Horoscopic Astrology*, p. 79.

[266] Paulus, *Introduction*, ed. Boer, p. 41: 3–4.

[267] Pingree, "Paul of Alexandria," p. 419.

[268] Holden, "The Horoscope of Cronamon."

annual profections, Paulus analyzes the twenty-fifth year in the native's life, which would have occurred in the year 378 CE, thus falling precisely within the previously established time period for when Paulus composed his work. Since the native is identified as being a twenty-five-year-old male, it seems very plausible that Holden is correct in speculating that this is the birth chart of Paulus's son.

Anonymous of 379

In the year 379 CE an unknown astrologer wrote a treatise on the fixed stars in the city of Rome.[269] He is generally referred to as Anonymous of 379. His text is important because it provides us with one of the earliest and longest sets of delineations in Greek for how the fixed stars are used and interpreted within the context of natal astrology.

Early in the text, Anonymous says that he is writing during the consulship of Olybrius and Ausonius.[270] This is evidently in reference to Quintus Clodius Hermogenianus Olybrius and Decimius Magnus Ausonius, who are known to have shared the consulship in Rome in the year 379 CE.[271] Later in the text, Anonymous says that he is not including the delineations for the fixed star Canopus because he is in Rome, and the star doesn't rise at that latitude.[272]

Franz Cumont suggested that Anonymous of 379 may be the astrologer Paulus of Alexandria, who is known to have written his *Introduction* only a year earlier in 378 CE.[273] Pingree later rejected this hypothesis, although he did not explain why.[274] Presumably it was based on unspecified linguistic or philological grounds. In his translation of Anonymous of 379, Schmidt notes that the writing style is more straightforward than Paulus's.[275]

The main source that Anonymous mentions throughout his work is Ptolemy, whom he seems to have great admiration for, at one point calling him "the divine Ptolemy" (*tou theiotatou Ptolemaiou*). Anonymous refers to his predecessors frequently, and at one point, during a brief digression, he gives a sort of historical overview of astrology and the study of fixed stars.[276] During this digression he mentions the following astrologers in order: the Babylonians and the Chaldeans, Berossus, the Egyptians, Hermes, Nechao and Cerasphorus, Petosiris and

---

[269] Edited in CCAG, 5, 1, pp. 194–212. For a translation see Anonymous of 379, *The Treatise on the Bright Fixed Stars*, trans. Schmidt.

[270] CCAG 5, 1, p. 198: 3–6.

[271] Bagnall, *Consuls of the Later Roman Empire*, pp. 292–3.

[272] CCAG 5, 1, p. 204: 4–8.

[273] CCAG 5, 1: 194, 199.

[274] Pingree, *Yavanajātaka*, vol. 2, p. 438.

[275] Anonymous of 379, *Fixed Stars*, trans. Schmidt, p. viii.

[276] CCAG 5, 1: 204–205.

Nechepso, Timaeus, Asclation, Antiochus, Valens, Antigonus, Heraiscos, Serapio, and Ptolemy. Anonymous also mentions the astronomers Meton, Apollinarius, Euctemon, Dositheus, Callipus, Philippus, Phocis, and Hipparchus.

Anonymous' stated goal was to outline the astrological meaning of thirty bright fixed stars of the first and second magnitude, although only twenty-nine are referred to in the extant text. Each star represents a "mixture" or "combination" (*krasis*) of the nature of two planets. For example, Spica is said to be a mixture of Venus and Mercury.[277] He then provides delineations for each star when it becomes prominent in a nativity, either by being close to the degree of an angle, or by being closely conjunct the Moon. Many of the interpretations are altered based on where certain planets are in the chart.

Portions of the text are known to have been used by Theophilus of Edessa in the eighth century, and through Theophilus it eventually influenced the work of Abū Ma'shar in the ninth century.[278]

Maximus (Fourth Century CE?)

An astrologer named Maximus wrote a treatise on inceptional astrology in Greek verse titled *On Inceptions* (*Peri Katarchōn*) at some point between the second and fifth centuries CE.[279] He evidently incorporated material from Dorotheus, which places him after the first century CE, and then was used by the author Nonnus in his *Dionysiaca* in the fifth century.[280] The tenth-century Byzantine encyclopedia known as the *Suda* says that Maximus was a teacher to the Roman Emperor Julian, who ruled from 361–363 CE, although this is usually treated with either uncertainty or outright skepticism by contemporary historians.[281]

Hephaestio of Thebes (Early Fifth Century)

Hephaestio of Thebes wrote a three-book compilation of earlier astrological doctrines titled *Apotelesmatika* in the early fifth century CE.[282] He primarily draws on Ptolemy and Dorotheus, although he also cites a number of other authors at various points in his work, such as Thrasyllus, Antiochus of Athens,

---

[277] CCAG 5, 1, p. 198: 12–25.

[278] Anonymous of 379, *Fixed Stars*, trans. Schmidt, pp. vii–viii; CCAG 5, 1: p. 169, n. 1; 194–195.

[279] For the critical edition see *Maximus et Ammonis carminum de actionum auspiciis reliquiae*, ed. Ludwich. The text has not been translated yet.

[280] Hübner, "Maximus."

[281] Jones ("Maximus," p. 536) points out that it isn't clear what this is based on in the *Suda*, while Hübner (*op. cit.*) considers the association to be "highly unlikely."

[282] The standard critical edition is Hephaestio of Thebes, *Hephaestionis Thebani apotelesmaticorum libri tres*, ed. Pingree. Books 1 and 2 were translated into English by Schmidt, while book 3 was recently translated by Gramaglia and Dykes.

Anubio, Manetho, Antigonus of Nicaea, Apollinarius, and Porphyry. In books 1 and 2 he seems to favor Ptolemy mainly, although in book 3, where he deals with inceptional astrology, he draws primarily on Dorotheus, excerpting and paraphrasing many long passages from the fifth book of his didactic Greek poem. Since Dorotheus' text only survives in a corrupt Arabic translation of a Persian translation, the fragments of Dorotheus that Hephaestio preserves in Greek are very important for establishing what Dorotheus originally said.

Hephaestio introduces his own birth data at one point within the context of a discussion about determining the precise degree of the Ascendant, saying "I was born on the 30th of Athyr during the day, with the Sun occupying approximately 4 degrees of Sagittarius."[283] The same birth data is mentioned in the previous chapter, without attribution, in a discussion on determining the conception chart of a native.[284] Based on this, Pingree concluded that Hephaestio was conceived on February 20, 380 CE and born on November 26, 380 CE.[285] The fixed star placements that Hephaestio gives in his work date to sometime around the year 390 CE, and thus Pingree thinks that he wrote his work in Egypt sometime around 415 CE.[286]

Hypatia and Female Practitioners of Astrology

Women did not typically receive the same education as men in the Greco-Roman world, and partially as a result of this, all of the astrologers we know of by name from the Hellenistic tradition were men. We do know that women consulted with astrologers, because the astrological handbooks of authors like Valens and Firmicus are full of references to how certain configurations should be interpreted in the charts of females. Often the delineations in Valens are framed as if they are being applied to the charts of males as the default, but then there will be a digression and Valens will either say that the same is true in the charts of females, or he will give a modified approach to use in the charts of women.[287] The modified approach often comes up in issues related to relationships and marriage, where in the charts of men Venus was said to signify marriage, whereas in the charts of women Mars was said to signify the marriage partner.[288]

Probably the earliest evidence for female practitioners of astrology occurs in the Roman poet Juvenal (c. 100 CE) in his *Satires*. There he mocks female

---

[283] Hephaestio, *Apotelesmatika*, 2, 2: 23, trans. Schmidt, p. 11.

[284] Hephaestio, *Apotelesmatika*, 2, 1: 32–34.

[285] Pingree, "Classical and Byzantine Astrology in Sassanian Persia," p. 229.

[286] Pingree, *Yavanajātaka*, vol. 2, p. 429.

[287] For example, Valens says that annual profections can also be applied to the charts of women in *Anthology*, 4, 25: 17.

[288] Valens, *Anthology*, 2, 38: 57. Cf. Firmicus, *Mathesis*, 2, 14: 4.

clients of astrologers who eventually begin practicing the subject on their own:

> Be sure to keep out of the way of that type, too; you will see her carrying round in her hands, like a ball of scented amber, a well-thumbed ephemeris. She no longer consults, but rather she herself is consulted. When her husband is leaving for camp or home, she will not go too, if Thrasyllus and his calculations detain her. When she decides to travel a mile, a suitable hour is produced from her book.[289]

While the purpose of this passage is satirical, it probably points to an underlying reality in which, by the first century CE, some of the women who regularly consulted with astrologers, probably especially in the upper classes, would eventually gain enough familiarity with the subject to begin using it on their own, and perhaps even see clients.

The first woman we know of by name who would have probably had some training in astrology was the philosopher Hypatia of Alexandria, who lived in the late fourth and early fifth century.[290] She was the daughter of the mathematician and astronomer Theon of Alexandria, who is known to have written commentaries on Ptolemy's astronomical works, the *Almagest* and *Handy Tables*, and possibly an early work on the use and construction of an astrolabe.[291] Bernard notes that a significant portion of the audience that Theon composed his commentaries for were astrologers or students of astrology, who needed help understanding how to use Ptolemy's astronomical works in order to calculate astrological charts, and the sources suggest that Hypatia herself would

---

[289] Juvenal, *Satires*, 6: 573–578. The majority of this translation is taken from Juvenal, *The Satires*, trans. Rudd, p. 57, although I have changed his translation of the Latin term *ephemeridas*, which he translates as "almanac," to say "ephemeris." I also changed his translation of Thrasyllus' "sums," from the Latin *numeris*, to refer to Thrasyllus' "calculations," which conveys the sense more clearly, and is in line with the Loeb translation.

[290] For her life and work see Dzielska, *Hypatia of Alexandria*; Deakin, *Hypatia of Alexandria*. One of the books of Valens' *Anthology* has a line at the end saying that it was dedicated or addressed to an otherwise unknown figure named Daphne (Valens, *Anthology*, ed. Pingree, p. 281: 19–20), although it is not clear whether this is a student or perhaps just a family member. It is also odd since in the preceding paragraph Valens closes book 7 by addressing someone named Marcus, which gives the impression that the book was actually dedicated to him.

[291] See Bernard, "The Alexandrian School," for an excellent treatment of the works and thought of Theon and Hypatia. For Theon's work on the astrolabe see Neugebauer, *A History of Ancient Mathematical Astronomy*, p. 877f, although Bernard notes elsewhere that Neugebauer's argument for Theon having written a treatise on the astrolabe has been questioned by some scholars since the evidence is somewhat meager (Bernard, "Theon of Alexandria," pp. 793–4).

have "at least had some astrological training."[292] Like her father, she is known to have had an interest in astronomy, and she evidently worked together with him on a commentary on Ptolemy's *Almagest*.[293] As an adult, Hypatia gained a reputation as a teacher of philosophy and mathematics, and she had a number of students who held her in high regard.

Unfortunately, by this time in history a major division had developed between Christianity and paganism, and astrology had become less permissible amongst many Christians due to its perceived association with earlier pagan culture. This may have some bearing on the reason why Hypatia was murdered by a Christian mob in the year 415. The motivations are a bit unclear, and it seems that it may have been primarily for political reasons, although one later hostile Christian source says that she was involved in evil practices involving "magic" and "astrolabes."[294] Bernard says it seems plausible that "some Christians in Alexandria believed (or were led to believe) that she used her competence in mathematics and astrology (both related to magic in popular opinion) to influence Orestus," who was a political figure and probable student of Hypatia, and to lead him away from his Christian faith.[295] The suggestion is that Hypatia's background in astronomy and potentially astrology could have been a pretext to rally up the mob against her.

We cannot say for sure whether Hypatia was a practicing astrologer, or even what her views on astrology were, since almost nothing of her work survives. However, we can say that since she was someone who was interested in and had some training in astronomy, that she also likely would have had at least some training in astrology as well. This would make her the first female figure that we know of by name to have had that sort of training, although undoubtedly there would have been other female astrologers before her whose names have been lost.

Julian of Laodicea (fl. c. 500 CE)

Julian of Laodicea was an astrologer who is thought to have flourished sometime around the year 500 CE, based on an astronomical observation he made in the year 497, as well as fixed star longitudes he used in one of his works.[296] Although some chapters of his work have been edited and published in the CCAG, the rest is still only available in manuscripts.[297] Several of the chapters of Julian's

---

[292] Bernard, "The Alexandrian School," p. 435.

[293] Bernard, "The Alexandrian School," p. 419.

[294] For the Christian source see John of Nikiu, *The Chronicle of John, Bishop of Nikiu*, trans. Charles, 84: 87–103.

[295] Bernard, "The Alexandrian School," pp. 419–420.

[296] Pingree, *Yavanajātaka*, vol. 2, p. 435.

[297] For a full list of his works and where they can be found see Pingree, ibid.

work that have been published so far are on inceptional astrology, and in one important excerpt he cites a number of rules from Petosiris.[298]

Olympiodorus (Middle of the Sixth Century CE)

Olympiodorus was a Neoplatonic philosopher who taught at a school in Alexandria in the sixth century. What survives are primarily transcripts of his lectures. He is sometimes referred to as Olympiodorus the Younger (*Olumpiodōros ho Neōteros*), since there was an older philosopher named Olympiodorus who also taught in Alexandria in the fifth century, often referred to as Olympiodorus the Elder.

There is a commentary on the *Introduction* of Paulus of Alexandria that is generally believed to be based on a series of lectures that Olympiodorus gave between May and July of 564 CE.[299] Previously this commentary was attributed to a late fifth-century author named Heliodorus, and while it is now generally attributed to Olympiodorus instead, it may still incorporate some earlier material from Heliodorus.[300]

Olympiodorus' commentary is useful because it clarifies a few statements made in the text of Paulus, and it also provides us with a glimpse of what astrology was like towards the very end of the Hellenistic tradition.[301]

Rhetorius of Egypt (Early Sixth or Seventh Century)

Rhetorius is the last major astrologer of the Hellenistic tradition. He wrote a large *Compendium* of astrological material in the sixth or seventh century CE.[302] He drew on or cited a large variety of earlier sources, including Hermes, Dorotheus, Anubio, Valens, Ptolemy, Antigonus, and others.

Pingree dated Rhetorius to the early seventh century, just before the conquest of Egypt by the Islamic empire, based on a chart contained in his work which he dated to February 24, 601 CE.[303] However, Holden challenged

---

[298] CCAG, 1, p. 138. For a translation see Schmidt, *Sages*, p. 19.

[299] This was first established in Westerink, "Ein astrologisches Kolleg aus dem Jahre 564." Pingree found the argument to be rather convincing in his entry on Heliodorus in *Yavanajātaka*, vol. 2, pp. 428–429.

[300] Pingree, "The Teaching of the Almagest in Late Antiquity," p. 86.

[301] The standard critical edition is Olympiodorus, *Heliodori, ut dicitur, In Paulum Alexandrinum commentarium*, ed. Boer. There is an English translation by Greenbaum.

[302] The structure of Rhetorius' *Compendium* was first established in Pingree, "Antiochus and Rhetorius." Chapters 1–53 are edited in CCAG 1, pp. 140–64. Chapters 54–98, 104, and 113–17 are edited in CCAG 8, 4: pp. 115–224. The rest will appear in Pingree and Heilen's forthcoming edition of Rhetorius. For an English translation, see Rhetorius the Egyptian, *Astrological Compendium*, trans. Holden.

[303] Pingree, "Classical and Byzantine Astrology," p. 232.

Pingree's dating by arguing that this example is a hypothetical chart with arbitrary positions rather than an actual datable nativity, because neither the position of the Ascendant nor any facts about the native's life are given in that chapter of Rhetorius' text.[304] Holden points out that the majority of the internal evidence within Rhetorius' *Compendium* indicates an early sixth century dating, such as the two other birth charts that date to the second half of the fifth century, or the fixed star positions being set for a date around 504 CE. He says that when the legitimacy of the seventh-century chart is called into question, it makes the earlier dating the only tenable conclusion.

While Holden appears to have more evidence in favor of his argument for a sixth century dating of Rhetorius, it is not necessarily clear that the seventh-century chart is hypothetical, and thus the dating of Rhetorius must still be left as an unresolved issue. In either event, Rhetorius would still be the last major astrologer of the tradition, especially since Olympiodorus' text is just a commentary, and it does not add as much to our overall understanding of the later tradition as Rhetorius does.

A recurring issue with Rhetorius is that there are a number of notable differences in the way that he practices certain facets of astrology when compared with earlier authors, but it is not always clear whether he is just being more overt about doing something that was already implicit earlier in the tradition, or if these differences represent changes and innovations that occurred by the very end of the Hellenistic tradition. We will explore some of these differences later, especially in the sections dealing with the reconstruction of the aspect doctrine and the conditions of bonification and maltreatment.

---

[304] Rhetorius, *Compendium*, trans. Holden, p. 158. Bezza made a similar argument in "L'astrologia greca dopo Tolemeo: Retorio," esp. p. 184.

CHAPTER 5
DECLINE AND TRANSMISSION

Decline of the Roman Empire and Astrology

The Roman Empire started to decline by the third century, facing an increasing number of external military threats, as well as internal instability in the political sphere. The decline of the Roman Empire coincided with a decline in the practice of Hellenistic astrology, both due to a loss of learning and literacy in the wake of the decay of the state, and also due to changing intellectual, social, and religious trends that resulted from the rise in popularity of Christianity. From a social perspective, although some astrological motifs appear in the New Testament, such as the story about the magi interpreting the Star of Bethlehem as signifying the birth of Jesus, after the first century CE mainstream Christianity became increasingly hostile towards astrology.[1]

The main point of contention seems to have been the belief that many astrologers held that the lives of individuals are predetermined to some extent based on their birth charts, with different astrologers holding a spectrum of views as to the extent to which things were fated. This brought astrology into conflict with Christian thinkers who associated fatalism with astrology, which they sought to reject for theological reasons.[2] After the first century, a number of Christian theologians and church fathers wrote sharp polemics against astrology and fate, since the two subjects were seen as intertwined. The fourth-century church father John Chrysostom said "in truth, no doctrine is so depraved and

---

[1] For Christian attitudes toward astrology see Hegedus, *Early Christianity and Ancient Astrology*, and Denzey Lewis, *Cosmology and Fate*. There is also a nice treatment of how Christians dealt with the Star of Bethlehem issue in the first four centuries CE in Denzey, "A New Star on the Horizon."

[2] Discussed in Hegedus, *Early Christianity and Ancient Astrology*, p. 23; 113–115.

bordering on incurable madness as the doctrine of fate and astrology."[3] While there were some Gnostic Christian sects that incorporated astrology into their belief systems, many of them were marginalized and eventually stamped out as orthodox Christianity became more clearly defined.[4]

A major turning point came in the year 313 when the Emperor Constantine legalized Christianity in the Roman Empire. This would ultimately have negative consequences for the practice of astrology, because while Roman rulers had unsuccessfully attempted to impose bans on astrology over the centuries for political reasons, the changing theological climate would prove much more effective in curbing the acceptance of astrology among the general populace. Hegedus explains that "Christian opponents of astrology were primarily motivated by the conviction that astrology posed a significant threat to Christianity."[5]

Stricter edicts outlawing the practice of astrology were issued in 357, 409, and 425 CE, at first requiring astrologers to burn their books or face exile, and then later banishing them altogether.[6] Some of the worst persecutions of astrologers subsequently occurred under the Emperor Justinian in the sixth century. Justinian sought to purge the empire of heresy, of which astrology was regarded as one of the prime examples. The sixth century historian Procopius of Caesarea provides us with an eyewitness account:

> they also turned viciously against the astrologers as well. That was why the authorities in charge of cases of theft took to maltreating them; there was no other reason for it. After flogging many of them on the back, they paraded them on camels through the entire city in disgrace, though they were old men and otherwise completely respectable citizens, having nothing other to charge them with than that they wanted to be experts regarding the stars in a place such as this.[7]

Ultimately this was a much different intellectual climate than the one in which Hellenistic astrology had originally emerged and flourished. While earlier

---

[3] Quoted in Barton, *Ancient Astrology*, p. 77, citing John Chrysostom, *On Fate and Providence*, edited in Migne, *Patrologia Graeca*, 50.756, 58–757, 8.

[4] For a discussion of one Gnostic Christian sect known as the Peratics that incorporated some astrological themes into their theology see DeConick, "From the Bowels of Hell to Draco: The Mysteries of the Peratics."

[5] Hegedus, *Early Christianity and Ancient Astrology*, p. 23.

[6] Tester, *A History*, p. 95. For the edict of 357 see Sandwell, "Outlawing 'Magic' or Outlawing 'Religion'?," p. 114ff.

[7] Prokopios, *The Secret History*, 11: 37, trans. Kaldellis, p. 55.

emperors as far back as the first century had occasionally imposed bans on astrology for political reasons, these bans were often of a temporary character, and do not appear to have been terribly effective at stemming the tide of the practice of astrology. The new combination of both political and religious injunctions against astrology proved to be much more effective. In some ways the determinism of the astrologers, which enjoyed much more popularity when Stoicism was a more dominant philosophy in the Roman Empire, had now become a liability and a relic of the past.

There were also changes in the empire itself that led to the decline of astrology. In the fourth century, the capital of the empire was moved from Rome to Constantinople (modern-day Istanbul, Turkey), taking the seat of power away from Italy. By the end of the fourth century, the Roman Empire had been split in half, creating an Eastern Roman Empire ruled from Constantinople, and a Western Roman Empire ruled from Rome. The Western Roman Empire entered a steep decline at this point. The city of Rome was sacked by a Germanic tribe known as the Visigoths in the year 410, and then the last Western Roman Emperor, Romulus Augustus, was deposed in the year 476. This led to the onset of the Middle Ages in Europe, as the Western Roman Empire became only a shadow of its former self. According to historian Nicholas Campion:

> it is clear that astrology virtually disappeared in Western Europe because of the collapse in literacy, especially knowledge of Greek, as Germanic culture, with its rural rather than urban focus, combined with war and invasion, gradually undermined Roman culture from Britain to north Africa, taking in France, Italy and Spain, through the fifth and sixth centuries. The disappearance of Roman culture was most extreme in the north – in Britain – and far more gradual around the Mediterranean, but even in Italy the ravages of looting armies extracted a huge cost. The incoming Germanic tribes had their lunar months, lucky days, star lore and constellation stories, but horoscopic astrology, with its literary base and mathematical complexities, was not part of their culture.[8]

Meanwhile the Eastern Roman Empire, which is usually called the Byzantine Empire from about the fifth century forward, continued to thrive and flourish. This side of the empire maintained control over Egypt through the early seventh century, which is important since Egypt had been the focal point for the practice of Hellenistic astrology since its inception. While this did stave off the disappearance of astrology in Egypt for several centuries, the practice

---

[8] Campion, *A History of Western Astrology*, vol. 1, pp. 287–288.

of astrology still continued to decline and was pushed underground in the Byzantine Empire in general. The Emperor Justinian closed the philosophical schools in Athens by banning the teaching of "pagan" philosophy in the year 529 CE. The philosophical school in Alexandria appears to have stayed active despite this, but it was small and somewhat isolated since the population of Egypt in late antiquity had largely become Christian. In the summer of 564, the Neoplatonic philosopher Olympiodorus the Younger gave a series of lectures on astrology which formed a commentary on the work of the fourth-century astrologer, Paulus of Alexandria. Around the same time, the astrologer Rhetorius of Egypt compiled the last great work on Hellenistic astrology in the early sixth or seventh century.

Egypt stayed under the control of the Byzantine Empire well into the seventh century, and thus the Greek language continued to be used and understood there, but some major political changes took place towards the end of that period. First, the Sassanian Persian Empire invaded Egypt in the year 619, and their forces occupied the country for about a decade. The Byzantine Empire regained control of Egypt in 629, but then in 639 the armies of the rapidly expanding Islamic Empire invaded Egypt and captured Alexandria in 642. This marked the end of seven centuries of Roman control over Egypt, which had begun in the year 30 BCE with Octavian's annexation. At this point it was not simply a change in intellectual or theological tides that was causing astrology to fall out of favor; a new culture with a new language and theology was now in control of what was essentially the homeland of Hellenistic astrology. For all intents and purposes, this marked the end of the Hellenistic astrological tradition.

Transmission to Other Cultures

Starting as early as the second century CE, texts on Hellenistic astrology began to be transmitted to other cultures outside of the Roman Empire; they were subsequently translated, adapted to suit their host cultures, and then expanded due to the introduction of additional techniques. The three most significant transmissions of Hellenistic astrology were to India, Persia, and eventually to the medieval Islamic Empire.

Transmission to India

Trade between the Roman Empire and India increased after the first century BCE, when sailors learned how to use the monsoon winds in order to make a direct trip between Egypt and the western shores of India.[9] Groups of Greeks

---

[9] For a discussion about trade between Rome/Egypt and India see McLaughlin, *Rome and the Distant East*, pp. 23–60, and Young, *Rome's Eastern Trade*, pp. 27–32.

and Romans settled in India, with some of them adopting the language and customs of the local population. It was under these circumstances that a Greek text on Hellenistic astrology was transmitted to India sometime around the second century CE, where it was translated into Sanskrit. This text, known as the *Yavanajātaka*, is thought to have played a major role in shaping the traditions of astrology that subsequently developed in India over the past two thousand years.

The primary researcher who pioneered work in this area was David Pingree. For his doctoral dissertation, Pingree edited, translated, and wrote a commentary on the *Yavanajātaka*.[10] The main purpose of his dissertation was to compare the astrological doctrines contained in the *Yavanajātaka* with those of various astrologers from the Hellenistic tradition. Pingree argued that many of the techniques of the Indian tradition of horoscopic astrology were largely derived from Hellenistic astrology, and that the *Yavanajātaka* was the principal source of this transmission.[11] This was done by showing that the *Yavanajātaka* was the earliest Indian text of its kind on natal astrology, and that it formed the basis of many later traditions of astrology in India. He argued that the *Yavanajātaka*, which means "Horoscopy of the Greeks," was actually a Sanskrit translation of a Greek astrological text that was probably written in the first century CE in Alexandria, Egypt, and that the vast majority of doctrines contained in the text could be traced back either directly or indirectly to western sources.

According to Pingree, the Greek original of the *Yavanajātaka* was translated into Sanskrit in the year 149 or 150 CE by a Greek in the Indian city of Ujjain known as Yavaneśvara, who had adopted Indian social and religious customs.[12] The text was then turned into an instructional poem in the year 269 or 270 CE by another Indianized Greek known as Sphujidhvaja, and it is this versified version of the text that survived into the present time. The *Yavanajātaka* then subsequently influenced many later Indian astrologers, as Pingree demonstrated in his commentary through comparisons with other Sanskrit texts.

The astrology that was imported into India from Egypt was merged with the indigenous forms of astrology that had already been developed there, which included the twenty-seven or twenty-eight sign lunar "zodiac" known as the nakshatras. There were also probably some preexisting forms of astral omens

---

[10] Pingree published his critical edition of the *Yavanajātaka* as a two-volume set in 1978. The first volume contains the Sanskrit text itself along with a critical apparatus and brief introduction; the second volume contains his English translation along with his commentary. See Pingree, *Yavanajātaka*.

[11] For an overview see Pingree, *From Astral Omens*, pp. 31–38.

[12] Pingree, *Yavanajātaka.*, vol. 1, pp. 3–5; Pingree, *From Astral Omens*, p. 34.

in India that were derived from earlier Mesopotamian sources.[13] The Indians subsequently made this form of astrology their own, and it has flourished there for nearly two thousand years, with many new developments and innovations that are unique to the Indian tradition.

As Pingree pointed out, the strongest evidence that Indian astrology was influenced by the Hellenistic tradition is that many of the technical terms in the early Indian tradition, and even today, are simply transliterations of Greek terms into Sanskrit.[14] In Greek, these words have a range of concrete and abstract meanings, but in Sanskrit the words just become technical terms that have little or no meaning outside of their usage in astrology. That is to say, most of these transliterated terms don't actually mean anything in Sanskrit outside of their technical usage, but in Greek the terms have actual semantic connections with other words outside astrology, thus showing their origin in the Greek language. For example, in the *Yavanajātaka*, the Greek word for an angular house or place, *kentron,* is transliterated as *kendra* in Sanskrit. The Greek term for a succedent house, *epanaphora,* becomes *panaphara* in Sanskrit. The Greek term for a cadent place, *apoklima,* simply becomes *apoklima.*[15] In other instances, the Greek term for a void of course Moon, *kenodromia,* becomes *kemadruma* in Sanskrit.[16] The term for an applying aspect, *sunaphe,* becomes *sunapha.*[17] The ten-degree segments of the ecliptic known as decans or *dekanos* in Greek become *drekanas.*[18]

In the vast majority of cases, the actual technical application of the astrological concepts that are described by these transliterated Sanskrit terms are still very similar, if not identical, to the Hellenistic application of the same concepts. While many technical modifications and adaptations had already been made to the Indian system by the time of the composition of the versified version of the *Yavanajātaka* by Sphujidhvaja, the overwhelming emphasis of this early Indian astrological tradition is still remarkably similar to what was being practiced in the early Hellenistic tradition of astrology. As a result of this, the *Yavanajātaka* can be a useful source for understanding some facets of the practice of Hellenistic astrology, although it must be used with caution.

---

[13] Pingree, *From Astral Omens,* pp. 31–33.

[14] See Pingree, *From Astral Omens to Astrology,* pp. 34–35, for a concise summary of this argument. For a more detailed treatment of the terms used in the Indian texts and their derivation from Greek words, see Pingree's extensive commentary in *Yavanajātaka,* vol. 2, pp. 195–415.

[15] Pingree, *Yavanajātaka,* 1: 53.

[16] Pingree, *Yavanajātaka,* 10: 2.

[17] Pingree, *Yavanajātaka,* 10: 1.

[18] Pingree, *Yavanajātaka,* 3: 1.

Despite many of the similarities, there are also some noticeable differences between the doctrines contained in the *Yavanajātaka* and those that we have documentation of in the Hellenistic sources. Some of these differences simply result from the fact that some elements of the indigenous forms of astrology such as the nakshatras were synthesized with the Hellenistic techniques, thus creating something reminiscent of but not necessarily the same as the original traditions that fed into it. In other instances, some of the differences may result from mistakes or errors in the textual transmission of the source text underlying the *Yavanajātaka* itself. For example, Pingree showed how the difference between the exaltation degrees in the Hellenistic and Indian sources could be explained by a single number dropping out of the manuscript of the original Greek text, so that Jupiter being exalted at "15" degrees of Cancer in the Hellenistic tradition becomes "5" degrees of Cancer in the Indian tradition.[19] In other areas, such as the aspect doctrine, there are major differences between the traditions, and it is not clear where these variations came from. They may simply represent developments in the Indian tradition that had already taken place prior to the arrival of the *Yavanajātaka*.

Pingree's work on the *Yavanajātaka* has recently come under criticism by a scholar named Bill M. Mak, who has questioned the basis of Pingree's dating of the text, as well as some other details surrounding its characterization.[20] While Mak acknowledges that the presence of Greek loanwords indicates some Hellenistic influence on the Indian tradition, he argues that the extent to which indigenous Indian concepts such as *karma*, *Āyurveda*, and references to Hindu deities have been integrated into the text should not be overlooked, as it implies that a more thorough and unique synthesis of the traditions had taken place by the time the extant text was composed. He also rejects Pingree's reading of the last chapter, which makes Yavaneśvara and Sphujidhvaja two separate individuals, instead arguing that the *Yavanajātaka* represents an original text that was composed by a single individual sometime between the first and seventh centuries CE, and not necessarily based on an original Greek prose text. Nonetheless, he still characterizes the *Yavanajātaka* as an amalgamation of Greek and Indian astrological doctrines, thus acknowledging that some sort of transmission took place, although the details surrounding it may not be as clear or as clean as it originally seemed, and there is much additional research that needs to be done.

---

[19] Pingree, *Yavanajātaka*, vol. 2, pp. 220–221. Pingree says that this may have been the case for the exaltation of the Sun as well, which is said to be exalted at 10° Aries in the *Yavanajātaka*, rather than the 19° Aries of the Hellenistic tradition.

[20] Mak, "The Date and Nature of Sphujidhvaja's *Yavanajātaka* reconsidered," and Mak, "The Last Chapter of Sphujidhvaja's *Yavanajātaka* critically edited with notes."

Interestingly, as a result of this transmission, Indian astrology today is often much more similar to the early forms of Hellenistic astrology than modern western astrology is to Hellenistic astrology. The reason for this is that the astrological tradition in India has been relatively continuous for the past two thousand years, and they have had a relatively long and unbroken tradition since the second century CE, with only a moderate amount of change due to the influx of other traditions and the development of new doctrines. On the other hand, in the west there have been several major transmissions of astrology from one language to another, and one culture to another, as well as a long period between the seventeenth and nineteenth centuries when the practice of astrology largely died out altogether. Each time western astrology was transmitted to another language or to a new culture it was changed in some way. As a result of this, there are a number of things that western astrologers can learn from the Indian tradition as we recover and revive the practice of Hellenistic astrology.

Transmission to Persia
In the third century CE, a new empire emerged in Persia, which is usually called the Sassanian Empire by historians. The Persian kings Ardashīr I and his son Shāpūr I reigned in succession from 222 through 267 CE. According to the tenth century Arab bibliographer, Ibn al-Nadīm, the Sassanian Empire began sending envoys to India, China, and Rome to collect scientific texts around this time.[21] It was during this period that the work of the Hellenistic astrologer, Dorotheus of Sidon, was transmitted, as well as some portions of the *Anthology* of Vettius Valens. Both were subsequently translated from Greek into the Middle Persian language, Pahlavi.[22]

A natal chart dating to the year 381 CE seems to have been inserted into what survives of the third book of Dorotheus at some point after he wrote it in the first century CE.[23] According to al-Nadīm, the text of Dorotheus was edited or expanded during the reign of the Persian king Khusro Anūshirwān, who ruled from 531–578 CE.[24] Pingree believed that it was during this period, in the sixth century, that a program of textual revision took place, which resulted in a number of alterations and interpolations in the Persian translations of both Dorotheus and Valens.[25]

These texts of Dorotheus, Valens, and a few others formed the basis of the

---

[21] Dodge, *The Fihrist of al-Nadim*, p. 575.
[22] Pingree, "Classical and Byzantine Astrology;" Pingree, *From Astral Omens*, p. 47.
[23] Dorotheus, *Carmen*, 3, 1: 27–65.
[24] Dodge, *The Fihrist of al-Nadim*, p. 575; Pingree, *From Astral Omens*, p. 50.
[25] Pingree, *From Astral Omens*, p. 49.

practice of astrology in Persia, which evidently flourished during the Sassanian period, although little of this tradition survives due to the destruction of texts that occurred during the initial rise of the Islamic Empire in the seventh century.

Transmission to the Islamic Empire

The Islamic calendar begins in the year 622 with the flight of Muhammad from Mecca to Medina, and the subsequent establishment of his political and religious authority there. After this point the Islamic Empire began expanding rapidly, first across the Arabian Peninsula, and then across the entire Middle East. Eventually, by the mid-seventh century, the Islamic Empire gained control over lands ranging as far east as northern India, to as far west as north Africa and most of the Iberian Peninsula (modern-day Spain and Portugal).

It appears that it wasn't until about the middle of the eighth century that astrology began to flourish in the Islamic Empire. This took place after the accession of a dynasty of rulers known as the Abbasids, which inaugurated a period of Islamic history known as the Abbasid Caliphate. The Abbasids were very open towards learning and scholarship, and had a particular interest in astrology.[26] In the mid-eighth century, they wished to move the capital of the Empire from Damascus to Baghdad; they convened a group of astrologers and asked them to select an auspicious electional chart for the founding of the new capital, which they did.[27]

Once Baghdad was established in 762 it became the new Alexandria, and a program of translating scientific texts from other cultures began.[28] Some of the earliest texts that were translated into Arabic were astrological texts.[29] Dorotheus was translated into Arabic twice, first around the year 775, and then again around 800, although both times the translation was based on the Pahlavi (Middle Persian) version and not upon the original Greek text.[30] The Pahlavi version of portions of Valens' *Anthology* was translated into Arabic in the late eighth or early ninth century.[31] Rhetorius' *Compendium* was also probably translated into Arabic around this time as well, as Pingree argued that it was obtained by Theophilus of Edessa between 765 and 770, and then passed to his colleague in the Abbasid court in Baghdad, the astrologer Māshā'allāh.[32]

---

[26] Discussed in Gutas, *Greek Thought, Arabic Culture*, pp. 108–110.

[27] Holden, *A History of Horoscopic Astrology*, pp. 103–4; Gutas, *Greek Thought, Arabic Culture*, p. 33.

[28] For a detailed discussion see Gutas, *Greek Thought, Arabic Culture*.

[29] Pingree, *From Astral Omens*, p. 41.

[30] Pingree, "Māshā'allāh's (?) Arabic Translation of Dorotheus."

[31] King, "A Hellenistic Astrological Table," p. 667.

[32] Pingree, "From Alexandria to Baghdād to Byzantium."

Ptolemy's *Tetrabiblos* was also translated into Arabic, and it became the subject of several commentaries and paraphrases starting in the eighth and ninth centuries.[33] At the same time, other texts from Persia and India were translated into Arabic, resulting in a new synthesis of the different astrological traditions. The locus of activity centered around Baghdad, and the primary language of most astrological texts shifted from Greek to Arabic.

Later Transmission and Traditions

While astrology flourished under the Islamic Empire in the eighth and ninth centuries, its popularity in the Arabic-speaking world appears to have declined after the tenth century due to shifting theological and political trends.[34] After a long lull, there was eventually a resurgence of interest in astrology in the Byzantine Empire from the tenth and eleventh centuries forward.[35] The majority of the Greek texts on Hellenistic astrology that survived into modern times were preserved in Constantinople and other Byzantine cities in the centuries after the decline of Rome, where Greek continued to be the common language. Although many texts were copied and preserved, there does not appear to have been much innovation in the astrological doctrines during this time; instead, some of the main changes that took place were the result of medieval Arabic astrological works that were translated into Greek by the Byzantine astrologers and compilers.[36]

In the twelfth century, the Second Crusade had the unintended side effect of reintroducing astrology to Europe when the Northern European Crusaders began conquering Muslim lands in Spain, discovering huge libraries of Arabic scientific texts there. Scholars from all around Europe began flocking to Spain and translating texts from Arabic into Latin. Many Arabic astrological texts from the Early Medieval Period (eighth and ninth centuries) were translated

---

[33] Saliba, *A History of Arabic Astronomy*, p. 67; Heilen, "Ptolemy's Doctrine of the Terms," p. 68.

[34] Saliba notes that "as soon as the religious texts began to be standardized and codified, from the tenth century onward, there were systematic religious attacks on astrology" in the Islamic world. Saliba, *A History of Arabic Astronomy*, p. 56. This period also saw the decline of Abbasid power.

[35] There may have also been a brief resurgence around the year 775 due to a student of Theophilus named Stephanus moving from Baghdad to Constantinople and bringing a number of texts with him (Pingree, *From Astral Omens*, pp. 64–65), although Pingree's identification of Stephanus has been disputed. See Papathanassiou, "Stephanus of Athens," and Papathanassiou, "Stephanos of Alexandria." For the resurgence of interest in astrology in the Byzantine empire from the tenth century forward see Pingree, *From Astral Omens*, p. 66ff.

[36] For a discussion of some of the Arabic texts that were translated see Pingree, *From Astral Omens*, pp. 63–77; Burnett, "Astrological Translations in Byzantium." For a general treatment of astrology in the Byzantine Empire see Magdalino, *L'Orthodoxie des astrologues*.

at this time, and by the end of the twelfth century, the knowledge and practice of astrology had been fully revived in Europe after a hiatus of several centuries.

The astrology that was reintroduced into Europe at this time was the type that was developed in the eighth and ninth centuries, based on a synthesis of elements from the earlier Hellenistic, Persian, and Indian traditions. This was not a revival of Hellenistic astrology itself, but instead a revival of the modified version of astrology that had developed in the subsequent period.

This revival of astrology took place within the context of an overall reawakening of science and learning in Europe from the twelfth century onward. Universities were established in Europe during this time, and chairs for astrology were created. Astrology was heavily integrated into medicine, and many doctors had some background in astrology for use as a diagnostic tool. After the invention of the printing press in the late fifteenth century, many of the Latin translations of Arabic astrological texts produced in the twelfth century were published and became more widely circulated. The fall of Constantinople to the Ottoman Empire in 1453 led to an influx of many previously unknown Greek texts into Europe, as scholars fled the dying Byzantine Empire. This helped to ensure the widespread practice and acceptance of astrology during the Renaissance, which is a period that is partially characterized by the "rebirth" of classical wisdom. Some Hellenistic astrological texts such as Ptolemy and Manilius became available during this time, but for the most part the type of astrology that was practiced in Europe by the fifteenth and sixteenth centuries was based on the medieval synthesis that had occurred in the eighth and twelfth centuries.

By the seventeenth century, the practice and perception of astrology started to decline in Europe due to a variety of social, political, and scientific reasons.[37] In particular, the cosmology that Ptolemy had outlined in his astronomical and astrological works in the second century was suddenly disproven through a relatively quick succession of astronomical discoveries by figures such as Copernicus, Kepler, and Galileo. The last great flourishing of astrology occurred in England with William Lilly and his contemporaries. Lilly published the first English-language textbook on astrology in 1647.[38] This was not enough to prevent the decline of astrology, however, and by the end of the century the subject had fallen into disfavor and obscurity.

After a low point in the eighteenth and nineteenth centuries, astrology started to be revived again in the west in the late nineteenth and early twentieth centuries. The first half of the twentieth century saw the birth of what we know as

---

[37] There is an excellent treatment of the decline of astrology in the early modern period in Rutkin, "Astrology," which includes citations for much of the literature on the topic.

[38] Campion, *A History*, vol. 2, p. 151.

modern astrology. Figures such as Alan Leo in early twentieth-century England were successful in both popularizing astrology and simplifying the techniques. At the same time, due to his involvement in the Theosophical Society, the subject became associated with the burgeoning New Age movement. From the 1930s onward, astrologers such as Dane Rudhyar made efforts to reconceptualize astrology within the context of depth psychology and character analysis, which were largely successful, gaining popularity from the 1960s through to the 1980s. At this point, western astrology became focused primarily on character analysis and psychological introspection; there was an emphasis on innovation and creativity, the introduction of many new techniques and celestial bodies, and in some instances, a deliberate attempt to reject some of the few remaining techniques and concepts that had survived from the earlier traditions.[39]

The Rediscovery of Hellenistic Astrology

The rediscovery and revival of Hellenistic astrology in the astrological community today is the result of two separate but related factors. The first is the work carried out in the academic community over the course of the past century by philologists, classicists, and historians who recovered, edited, and published many of the surviving texts of the ancient astrological traditions. The second is a more recent movement in the astrological community that has only taken place in the past two or three decades to revive the practice of the ancient traditions of astrology.

The Recovery by the Academic Community

Large numbers of astrological manuscripts still sleep in the libraries.
                                        –Bouché-Leclercq, writing in 1899.[40]

The groundwork for the revival of Hellenistic astrology was laid over the course of the past century by scholars working within the academic community who focused a large part of their work on the investigation of the history of astrology. The most important efforts in this area, at least for the purposes of our present study, were initiated by a group of scholars in Europe towards the end of the nineteenth century. They undertook to collect and catalogue all of the existing

---

[39] For a more detailed treatment of the history of astrology from the twelfth century through to modern times see Campion, *A History of Western Astrology*, vol. 2, and Holden, *A History of Horoscopic Astrology*, pp. 134ff.

[40] Bouché-Leclercq, *L'Astrologie grecque*, trans. Lester Ness, pp. vii–viii: "Quantité de manuscrits astrologiques dorment encore dans les bibliothèques."

manuscripts on astrology that were written in Greek during the Hellenistic, Roman, and Byzantine periods. This project, which was initially led by a Belgian scholar named Franz Cumont, took over fifty years to complete. It entailed scouring all of the major European libraries for ancient texts and manuscripts that had been copied and preserved over the centuries since their original composition. This project resulted in the publication of a massive twelve-volume compendium called the *Catalogus Codicum Astrologorum Graecorum* (Catalogue of the Codices of the Greek Astrologers), more commonly known by its acronym: the CCAG.[41]

This massive compendium, published in twelve volumes between 1898 and 1953, is primarily a catalog of all of the existing Greek astrological manuscripts in library holdings around Europe. The CCAG also contains many extended excerpts and fragments from hundreds of the texts that were found during the course of compiling the catalog. Each of these excerpts was carefully sifted through, examined, and edited by diligent philologists in order to produce critical editions of many of the most significant surviving Greek astrological texts from antiquity.[42]

Producing a "critical edition" of a text is a time-consuming process which involves gathering together all of the extant manuscripts and printed editions of the text, and then comparing the differences and variations in the manuscript tradition, with the final result being the reconstruction of the archetype of the original manuscript, or at least something as close to the original as possible. However, these critical editions are not translations of the original works, but instead edited and printed editions of the texts themselves in their original language, with the introduction and footnotes by the editors usually written in Latin, which was the standard scholarly language that anyone studying the history of science or classics would be expected to know. Thus, although much of this massive compendium of astrological material has been available in print since the beginning of the twentieth century, it lay neglected, unknown, and largely unused by the astrological community for the majority of the century. This was partially due to the challenges involved in studying the ancient texts in their original languages, but also due to lack of interest in older forms of astrology in general.

The CCAG project began at a time when astrology was just coming out

---

[41] *Catalogus Codicum Astrologorum Graecorum*, ed. Cumont et al.

[42] Frederick Cramer gave an excellent overview of the twelve volumes of the CCAG in his review, which appeared upon its completion in 1954. This was also the same year that his masterful work, *Astrology in Roman Law and Politics*, was published, and also, sadly, the year of his untimely death. See Cramer, "Review of Catalogus Codicum Astrologorum Graecorum."

of its decline during the seventeenth and eighteenth centuries. Prior to the revival of astrology in the twentieth century it was only kept alive in the west in the form of popular almanacs, and few serious astrological texts were written in this period. For all intents and purposes, astrology as a serious subject of study had nearly died out as a result of disuse and disrepute. It was under these cultural circumstances that the editors of the CCAG began compiling their compendium. They were studying the traditions and transmission of an obsolete system with the expectation that it would shed some light on the religious beliefs of the ancient peoples who practiced it, as well as their cultural customs, their scientific methods, and other such concerns. In 1913, the historian Lynn Thorndike attempted to demonstrate how astrological texts were relevant to modern historians, and how they could be used to shed light on the cultures in which they were written. Thorndike intended to show

> that an astrological treatise may also give us a picture of past society and thus contribute to the content of history. The point is that in trying to predict the future the astrologers really depict their own civilization. Their scope is as broad as are human life and human interests.[43]

He then attempted to provide an analysis of life in the Roman Empire in the fourth century by tallying up and comparing all of the references to different types of occupations and states of being that are mentioned in the work of the astrologer Firmicus Maternus.[44] A similar approach was enthusiastically taken up by Franz Cumont in his 1936 work *L'Égypte des astrologues* (The Egypt of the Astrologers), in which he attempted to sketch out a picture of the social circumstances in Hellenistic and Roman Egypt based on statements made by the astrologers in their delineations.[45]

Thus, for the most part, these scholars were not interested in the actual astrological content of the texts themselves, because they did not consider the texts to be of any inherent practical value or to hold any veracity in the techniques

---

[43] Thorndike, "A Roman Astrologer as a Historical Source," p. 416.

[44] Thorndike points out that this approach can be problematic because it is not always clear whether or not a specific author is actually adapting the general astrological principles and applying them to present societal conditions, of if they are simply copying the delineations of much earlier authors that are not necessarily representative of the culture in which the current author is writing. He says that this needs to be judged on a case-by-case basis based on internal evidence, and concludes that Firmicus himself was not a "mere copyist." Given our current understanding of the degree to which Firmicus did in fact draw directly on earlier authors in much of his delineation material, which is a bit different than Thorndike's take on Firmicus, one wonders to what extent his statistical conclusions in this paper are still valid.

[45] See Cumont, *L'Égypte des astrologues*.

that they preserved. This approach is summed up quite succinctly by Bouché-Leclercq's famous statement in the preface to his 1899 book *L'Astrologie Grecque* (Greek Astrology): "one does not waste his time who studies how others have wasted theirs."[46]

At times the editors of the astrological texts and other scholars who work in the field go so far as to express their disgust with the astrological content of the texts. In some cases it seems like they are simply paying lip service to the academic community by punctuating their reports on the technical content of the texts with statements expressing their expected distaste for it, in order to somehow distance themselves from it and thus maintain credibility in the eyes of their incredulous peers.[47] The need for academics to justify their historical research of ancient occult or divinatory practices seems to have lessened with recent generations of scholars to some extent, although the aims of their studies are still often very different than those of practicing astrologers.

Some scholars have also actively defended the study of astrology in academia. One prominent example is Otto Neugebauer in his brief but infamous 1951 article titled *The Study of Wretched Subjects*, in which he sarcastically responded to a critic, defending the efforts of the scholars who were involved in the compilation of the CCAG:

> They all labored to recover countless wretched collections of astrological treatises from European libraries, and they succeeded in giving us an

---

[46] Bouché-Leclercq, *L'Astrologie grecque*, p. ix: "On voudra bien ne pas prendre pour un paradoxe ma conclusion : à savoir, qu'on ne perd pas son temps en recherchant à quoi d'autres ont perdu le leur." I have used Lester Ness' translation of this sentence from his forthcoming English translation of *L'Astrologie grecque*.

[47] For the more extreme, yet prominent example of the first type of astrology/astrologer-bashing that sometimes occurs in scholarly works of this type, see Bouché-Leclercq, *L'Astrologie grecque*. Bouché-Leclercq seems to have fancied himself as something as a comedian as well as a scholar, peppering his commentary on the technical concepts with cute little quips, such as this statement after discussing the theory underlying the exaltations (Greek: *hupsōma*): "Human reason was not in its *hupsōma*!" (*L'Astrologie grecque*, p. 192, n. 1, trans. Ness). Swerdlow fondly calls *L'Astrologie grecque* "the most amusing book ever written on astrology" (*Ancient Astronomy and Celestial Divination*, ed. Swerdlow, p. 13). For a more recent example of this tendency towards disparaging astrology in academic texts that are supposed to be discussing how it was used in ancient times, see Beck, *A Brief History of Ancient Astrology*. One reviewer of Beck's book, Katharina Volk, noted that Beck came off as sounding "a tad defensive" at times, which seems like a bit of an understatement, although perhaps not when compared to Bouché-Leclercq. See Volk, "Review of *A Brief History of Ancient Astrology* by Roger Beck." Daryn Lehoux put it more bluntly in his review, saying "This would be a very good book if only Beck would stop reminding us that he thinks astrology is silly." See Lehoux, "Review of *A Brief History of Ancient Astrology* by Roger Beck."

insight into the daily life, religion and superstition, and astronomical methods and cosmogonic ideas of generations of men who had to live without the higher blessings of our own scientific era.[48]

He concludes with a statement that the goal of these scholars is simply "the recovery and study of texts as they are, regardless of our own tastes and prejudices."[49] This was the general philosophy underlying the recovery of the texts of the ancient astrological traditions by those in the academic community over the course of the past century. Numerous critical editions and works on astrological scholarship were published by scholars such as Franz Cumont, Franz Boll, A. E. Housman, Frank Egleston Robbins, Emilie Boer, Stefan Weinstock, Otto Neugebauer, G. P. Goold, David Pingree, Wolfgang Hübner, and many others. Collectively, these academics have made great strides in reconstructing the history of ancient astrology.[50]

It is interesting to note that these two parallel movements, the study of the history of astrology by academics, and the revival of the actual practice of astrology by astrologers, were occurring almost simultaneously, although neither of these movements seem to have crossed paths or influenced one another to any great extent during the majority of the twentieth century. For the most part, the astrological community remained unaware of and uninterested in the industrious activities of the scholars and the great advancements that were occurring in the understanding of the history and origins of astrology, while the academics seldom took notice of the practice of astrology in the modern world or consulted with astrologers in order to discuss their findings. Thus, until very recently, the astrological community has remained largely ignorant of the great flourishing of astrological scholarship that has occurred over the course of the past century, along with the important historical, theoretical, and practical implications that it has on their own field.

The Revival of Traditional Astrology

Modern astrology, as it was practiced during much of the twentieth century—and as it is practiced even today by the majority of western astrologers in the early twenty-first century—is not necessarily the result of a linear development and refinement of the subject over the centuries which culminated in the form that it is in today. This is one of the great myths surrounding modern astrological practice. Rather, modern western astrology is largely the result of a handful of

---

[48] Neugebauer, "The Study of Wretched Subjects," p. 111.

[49] Ibid.

[50] See the bibliography at the end of this book for works by some of these authors.

influential astrologers who inherited a few fragments of the astrological tradition and then created a new system around it which was then infused with their own religious, ethical, and theoretical speculations. Although recognizable in some of its basic technical principles, in many ways this system is quite different than the various traditions of astrology that were practiced in the past, both technically and in its conceptual and philosophical approach.

This discrepancy between the modern and ancient traditions of astrology became apparent to some western astrologers starting in the 1980s, who began to investigate and publish works on the older traditions of astrology.[51] In the United States, this initial line of inquiry first came forth with the publication of Robert Zoller's *The Lost Key to Prediction: The Arabic Parts in Astrology* (1980), which was primarily based on his reading of the thirteenth-century astrologer Guido Bonatti.[52] In 1982, the American Federation of Astrologers published George Noonan's book, *Classical Scientific Astrology*, which was largely based on Medieval and Renaissance techniques. That same year, the astrologer, linguist, and historian of astrology, James Herschel Holden, published a paper in the first American Federation of Astrologers *Journal of Research* titled "Ancient House Division." In this paper, Holden, who read Greek and Latin, was the first astrologer in modern times to point out that the original method of house division in the Hellenistic tradition was whole sign houses, or the "sign-house" system as he called it.[53] Later in the same decade, Holden published an English translation of Abū 'Ali al-Khayyāt's *Book of Nativities*, a ninth century astrological text from the Arabic tradition which had been translated into Latin in the Middle Ages.[54] In the United Kingdom, the traditional revival began with the renewal of interest in the practice of interrogational astrology, as well as the rediscovery and reprinting of the earliest English language manual on astrology, William Lilly's mid-seventeenth century work, *Christian Astrology*.[55]

In the United States, a group of astrologers met at the 1992 United Astrology Conference in Washington D.C. and formulated a plan to start a translation project for ancient astrological texts. The translation project became known as Project Hindsight, and it was primarily led by Robert Schmidt, Robert Hand, and Robert Zoller. The three began producing translations of

---

[51] For a partial overview of the recent history of this movement, see Campion, "The Traditional Revival in Modern Astrology: A Preliminary History."

[52] Zoller, *The Lost Key to Prediction: The Arabic Parts in Astrology*. In subsequent printings the book was retitled *The Arabic Parts in Astrology: A Lost Key to Prediction*.

[53] Holden, "Ancient House Division."

[54] Abū 'Ali al-Khayyāt, *The Judgement of Nativities*, trans. Holden.

[55] Discussed in Campion, "The Traditional Revival," as well by Geoffrey Cornelius in the forward to the 2005 reprint of Appleby, *Horary Astrology*.

Greek and Latin texts which were sold to astrologers on a subscription basis. Schmidt's primary focus was translations of the Greek texts, Zoller focused on translating the Latin texts, while Hand edited and made contributions to both series. There was much excitement in the astrological community during the early phases of Project Hindsight in the mid-1990s, and the effort was completely funded by the astrological community through sales of translations, seminars, and donations.

A core group of about thirty-two translations of Greek and Latin astrological texts from the Hellenistic and Medieval period were produced between 1993 and 1998. The first Hellenistic text published was a translation of the *Introduction* of Paulus of Alexandria. Other translations of astrologers such as Vettius Valens, Claudius Ptolemy, Anonymous of 379, Hephaestio of Thebes, Rhetorius of Egypt, and others followed over the next few years. However, these were only intended to be preliminary translations, which would later be revised and published in a final series once the translators had a better grasp on the subject matter, since many of the concepts and techniques were very foreign from a modern perspective. The translator and editor of each volume both wrote an introduction to the text, and provided commentary in the footnotes, which documented the development of their thinking on the subject matter as they learned more during the process of producing each translation.

Unfortunately, Project Hindsight fragmented during the course of the 1990s. Zoller left in 1994 due to creative differences, and pursued his own translations of the medieval texts outside of the project. Hand and Schmidt worked together productively for several years, but in 1998, Hand left the project and formed the Archive for the Retrieval of Historic Astrological Texts (ARHAT), which published translations of Hellenistic and medieval astrological texts. Although Project Hindsight continued under Robert Schmidt, now focusing exclusively on the Greek material, Schmidt's output slowed considerably after Hand left. In 1999, Schmidt published a partial translation of the Greek version of Abū Ma'shar's treatise *On Solar Revolutions*, and in 2001 a preliminary translation of book seven of Valens' *Anthology* appeared. Meanwhile, Hand commissioned Dorian Gieseler Greenbaum to do a new translation of Paulus of Alexandria's *Introduction* along with Olympiodorus' *Commentary*, which she completed and published through ARHAT in 2001.

In May of 2001, an associate of Project Hindsight named Alan White gave an impromptu lecture on Hellenistic astrology at the Northwest Astrological Conference in Seattle; it generated such interest that it eventually led to the subject being integrated into the curriculum of Kepler College, a newly opened school for astrological studies. During the winter of 2001–2002, the astrologer

Demetra George studied with White and Schmidt in person and developed a course on Hellenistic astrology. She began teaching it at Kepler in 2002 using a sourcebook of translations of Hellenistic texts that had been prepared by Schmidt. Thus, for the first time in centuries, astrologers were being instructed in Hellenistic astrology based on some of the earliest surviving texts of the tradition. The present author was one of the students who was fortunate enough to take the course starting in late 2004; in the summer of 2005 I moved to Maryland to study at Project Hindsight for two years.

In 2009, Schmidt released the first volume of his planned thirty-volume final translation series of Hellenistic texts, which included all of the fragments of the lost work of definitions by Antiochus of Athens, together with his attempt to reconstruct the original doctrines underlying the text. No further volumes of the translation series have appeared since. In the meantime, the astrologer and historian James Holden had been working on a series of translations of Greek and Latin astrological texts since the 1950s, and in the decade before he passed away in 2013, these texts were published through the American Federation of Astrologers. This series included translations of Rhetorius, Porphyry, Serapio, Paulus, and Firmicus Maternus. In 2010, a classics scholar named Mark Riley unexpectedly released a full translation of Valens' *Anthology* online, marking the first time that the entire text had been translated into English. More recently, in 2013, Eduardo Gramaglia and Benjamin Dykes produced a translation of the third book of Hephaestio of Thebes' *Apotelesmatika*, which contains some of the earliest material on inceptional astrology. These translations were complemented by earlier translations of other astrological texts by academics over the years, such as Robbins' translation of Ptolemy in 1940, Bram's translation of Firmicus in 1975, Pingree's translation of the Arabic version of Dorotheus in 1976, and Goold's translation of Manilius in 1977.

Additionally, while this account mainly focuses on developments in the English-speaking world, it should be noted that other important work and translations have been carried out in other languages in recent decades, especially in Italy with astrologers and scholars such as Giuseppe Bezza and some of his associates. For example, Bezza published a commentary on Ptolemy in 1990, an anthology of Hellenistic and medieval works titled *Arcana Mundi* in 1995, and a translation of Paulus of Alexandria in 2000, to name a few contributions.

As a result of these efforts, the majority of the most important texts from the Hellenistic astrological tradition are now available again for astrologers to study in modern languages. This allows us to revive and reconstruct as fully as possible the earliest doctrines of western astrology, and in the past ten years Hellenistic astrology has come to be practiced once again by contemporary astrologers.

CHAPTER 6
PHILOSOPHICAL ISSUES
IN HELLENISTIC ASTROLOGY

———————————— ✸ ————————————

Hellenistic astrology was developed and practiced during a very diverse period in which a number of different philosophical and religious schools flourished. A full treatment of the many ways in which these different schools interacted with or incorporated astrology into their approaches is beyond the scope of this book.[1] Instead I will highlight some specific philosophical issues and debates that became relevant to astrologers during the Greco-Roman period, since many of these issues continue to be relevant to astrologers today. I will begin by looking at the nature of divination before looking at issues such as fate and causality.

Astrology, Divination, and Signs

In the earlier Mesopotamian tradition, astrology was originally conceptualized as a form of divination. In fact, astrology was just one of many different forms of divination in the ancient world. Broadly speaking, divination is the interpretation of natural phenomena as conveying symbolically significant information about events in the past, present, or future. Typically, it is understood as the attempt to ascertain information from the divine, and especially to predict the future, by analyzing the arrangement of randomly determined objects at the moment of the inquiry.[2]

---

[1] For an excellent overview see Lawrence, "Hellenistic Astrology."

[2] Hankinson paraphrases Cicero (*On Divination*, 2: 13–15; 26) in saying that "the Stoics defined divination as the foretelling of events that come about by chance." Hankinson, "Stoicism, Science and Divination," p. 153. In the same article he quotes Sextus Empiricus (*Against the Physicists*, 1: 132) as defining divination as "the science which observes and

Within this context, the Mesopotamian astrologers appear to have originally viewed the planets and stars as being capable of sending messages to humankind from the gods about events that would occur, but these planets and stars were not necessarily seen as the cause of those events. Just as a clock is capable of indicating that it is nine in the morning without actually being the cause or reason that it is nine in the morning, the planets were similarly thought to be capable of giving signs for future events without necessarily being the reason that those events occur. As Rochberg explains in her discussion of astrological omens in Mesopotamian tradition:

> The relationship between *x* the phenomenon and *y* the predicted event has given rise to much discussion, the consensus being that the relationship is not causal, but more of the order of simple association or correlation. The omen statement would be interpreted therefore, not as *x* causes *y*, but rather, if *x*, (expect also) *y*.[3]

The Mesopotamian view that celestial phenomena could act as signs of future events was eventually passed on to the Hellenistic tradition. While the interpretations became more complex due to the explosion of new techniques that were introduced, the general principle was still the same: astronomical alignments were interpreted as having symbolic importance in a person's life. For example, the Midheaven or tenth house in a chart became associated with one's occupation and reputation because it coincides with the highest and most visible part of the sky. This is opposite to the fourth house, which represents one's home, living situation, and private life, since the fourth house coincides with the part of the chart that is under the earth and thus in the most hidden part of the cosmos from the perspective of the observer. Hence the part of the chart that is the most visible or prominent becomes symbolically associated with the native's public life, while the part of the chart that is the most hidden becomes associated with one's private life. Or, to draw a specific example from the Hellenistic texts, Rhetorius tells us that when one of the planets that represents marriage is hidden under the beams of the Sun in a person's chart, the native's marriage will take place in secret.[4] Thus, because the planet that represents marriage in the chart was visibly obscured and could not be seen with the naked eye at the moment of the native's birth, it was symbolically

---

interprets the signs given by the gods to men..." (p. 139) See also Struck, "A World Full of Signs."

[3] Rochberg, *The Heavenly Writing*, p. 58.
[4] Rhetorius, *Compendium*, 48 (CCAG 1, p. 161: 28–29).

thought to indicate that there is something about the native's marriage that will be obscured or hidden as well. This type of symbolic reasoning lies at the heart of many of the interpretive techniques in Hellenistic astrology, and in this way the system partially represents a particularly elaborate approach to divination.[5]

Divination from Origins

Part of the conceptual premise underlying the approach to astrological divination that seems to have been formalized in the Hellenistic period was the notion that the alignment of the planets at the moment that something begins will describe both its quality and its future. This idea had already been developed in the Mesopotamian tradition by the fifth century BCE with the introduction of natal astrology and the concept of the birth chart, but in the Hellenistic tradition it was expanded to include many other types of beginnings under the general heading of inceptional astrology.

The technical term that was used to refer to this type of astrology was *katarchē*, which means "inception," "beginning," or "commencement." The general premise underlying different texts on inceptional astrology is that if one knows the moment that something began, then one can predict its outcome. In this same context, we also find another extremely important technical term frequently used in the astrological texts: the term *apotelesma*, which means "outcome," "result," or "completion."[6] Astrologers would sometimes use this term to refer to the predicted outcome of a specific astrological omen, whether it was a placement in a person's birth chart or an indication in an inceptional chart. The term became so closely connected with astrology that some astrologers such as Manetho, Ptolemy, and Hephaestio titled their astrological works *Apotelesmatika*, which means something like "Inquiry into Outcomes."

Taken together, these two terms reveal an important underlying principle implicit in astrological practice: the alignment of the cosmos at the inception (*katarchē*) of something is connected to its outcome (*apotelesma*).[7] While the connection between these two terms is the most explicit within the context of inceptional astrology, at one point Ptolemy refers to the birth of an individual

---

[5] See Cornelius, *The Moment of Astrology*, for more about the divinatory nature of astrology in general.

[6] Robbins points out that while the manuscript tradition of Ptolemy's *Tetrabiblos* sometimes calls the work the *Apotelesmatika*, in some manuscripts it is called *Sumperasmatika*, from the word *sumperasma*, which means "finishing," "end," or "conclusion." This probably confirms that the word "outcome" is the correct translation of *apotelesma*. Ptolemy, *Tetrabiblos*, trans. Robbins, p. xi.

[7] This connection between *katarchē* and *apotelesma* was first pointed out by Schmidt in the preface to *Sages*, pp. xxvi–xxxii.

as a *katarchē*, which implies that even the moment of birth was viewed as a sort of inception as well.[8]

In this way, the "if *x* then *y*" formula that was implicit in the earlier Mesopotamian tradition of astrological omens became formalized into the basic conceptual premise underlying the practice of Hellenistic astrology: the potentiality of anything can be studied by examining its symbolic moment of origin. Thus, Hellenistic astrology was partially developed as a type of divination that took its omens from the alignment of the cosmos at the moment of the symbolic inception of whatever it was the astrologer wanted to study.

An Astrology of Causes

At some point during the Hellenistic period, a new conceptualization of astrology emerged, in which some astrologers began to view the planets as being the causes of future events, either directly or indirectly. Although the history underlying this development is difficult to ascertain, we know that this conceptualization reached its most elaborate and influential form in the work of the second-century astrologer, Claudius Ptolemy.

In Ptolemy's work, the planets were seen as capable of influencing events and people on Earth because they were viewed as being productive of different elemental powers in the sublunar realm, drawing on Aristotle's four primary qualities of hot, cold, wet, and dry.[9] It was through the effects of these general qualities that all of the individual significations of the planets eventually manifested in the world.[10] For example, Mars was understood as exerting a power that manifested in an exceedingly hot and dry quality in the sublunar world, and this was thought to result in specific effects in humans, such as anger or brashness, especially when Mars was having a prominent influence on the natal chart. On the other hand, the power of Saturn was conceptualized as being

---

[8] Ptolemy, *Tetrabiblos*, 3, 2: 3.

[9] The powers of the planets are given in Ptolemy, *Tetrabiblos*, 1, 4. I will outline each of the qualities that Ptolemy gives for the planets later in the chapter on the signs of the zodiac. There is a detailed analysis of the philosophy and cosmology underlying Ptolemy's astrology in Feke, "Ptolemy in Philosophical Context," pp. 153–173. See esp. pp. 161–2 for the planets.

[10] Feke makes an important point that even though Ptolemy conceptualized the planets as having these effects in the sublunar world, that did not necessarily mean that the planet itself was thought to be composed of those elements: "These powers, however, are not the essential characteristics of the planets, as aethereal bodies. Rather, they are the effects caused by the planets which are experienced in the sublunary realm. Ptolemy distinguishes between the underlying nature of a planet and its power in *Tetrabiblos* 1.2." Feke, "Ptolemy in Philosophical Context," p. 161. This is a subtle but important distinction in terms of Ptolemy's overall cosmology, and we will see how it was conceptualized more clearly later on in a quote from Iamblichus in the section on Ptolemy's basic natures of the planets.

excessively cold and dry, and thus became associated with qualities such as sluggishness and depression. In each case, the specific significations associated with each of the planets are byproducts of the general influence of the planets on the environment and temperament of the native. So, for example, if someone was born at a time in which Mars was prominent in the sky, Ptolemy might say that this person would be inclined towards aggression or impetuousness due to the fiery effect of Mars on his temperament. If Saturn was activated by transit later in a person's life, they might experience a period of ill health or depression due to the excessively cooling influence of Saturn.

In Ptolemy's model, astrology is essentially an extension of physics, because it involves studying the effects or influences of the planets upon the lives of individuals, and in this context the term *apotelesma* takes on the meaning of an astrological "effect" which emanates from the planets, rather than just an "outcome" that is indicated. Part of Ptolemy's goal here appears to have been to reconceptualize astrology as a natural science rather than a form of divination, and thus to put it on a more sound footing according to the scientific perspective of his day. There is some evidence that parts of Ptolemy's work were written in response to specific critiques of astrology that had been penned by earlier skeptics such as Cicero, and thus part of Ptolemy's program may have been to counter some of those criticisms by presenting a more natural take on astrology.[11]

It is unclear to what extent Ptolemy was either innovating or drawing on an earlier tradition that already conceptualized astrology in this way. In some instances where we have the ability to compare how Ptolemy explains the rationale for certain astrological doctrines versus how some earlier astrologers explained the same doctrines, we can see that he had a tendency to emphasize the naturalistic rationale for basic concepts and to ignore or downplay other more symbolic rationales. For example, Ptolemy explains the doctrine of sect, which divides the planets into diurnal and nocturnal factions, as being determined by the qualities of heat or moisture associated with each of the planets.[12] However, according to Porphyry's *Introduction*, the rationale for the assignment of the planets to each sect has to do with the fact that the daytime planets do not set under the beams of the Sun very frequently, while the nocturnal planets disappear or become obscured by the beams of the Sun more regularly.[13] Elsewhere, Ptolemy explains the rationale for the assignment of the

---

[11] See Long, "Astrology: Arguments Pro and Contra," for a discussion of some of the parallels between Ptolemy's work and earlier skeptical critiques of astrology.

[12] Ptolemy, *Tetrabiblos*, 1, 7. The doctrine of sect will be discussed in more detail later in the chapter on the planets.

[13] Porphyry, *Introduction*, 4, drawing on an earlier lost work by Antiochus.

planets to their signs of exaltation largely by invoking the different levels of heat and moisture associated with each of the seasons that coincide with those zodiacal signs.[14] But again, in Porphyry's *Introduction*, the primary rationale that is given for the assignment of the exaltations is a more symbolic one, where each of the diurnal planets is exalted in a sign that is configured by trine to one of its domiciles, while each of the nocturnal planets is exalted in a sign that is configured by sextile to one of its domiciles.[15] As we will see, both symbolic and natural rationales were probably taken into account simultaneously when some of these techniques were first formulated, but Ptolemy chose to emphasize the natural explanations when presenting them in his work.

In the Greek philosophical tradition, a general theory of celestial influence was formulated by Aristotle, who in the fourth century BCE outlined a model of the cosmos where the rotations of the planetary spheres were seen as the ultimate source of all motion or change on Earth.[16] This doctrine seems to have been elaborated on by subsequent philosophers over the next few centuries, especially by followers of Aristotle, who became known as Peripatetics. In particular, the pseudo-Aristotelian treatise called *De Mundo* (On the Cosmos) seems to represent a stage that took place in the Peripatetic school sometime between the third and first centuries BCE, during which some of the general views that Aristotle expressed about the celestial spheres transmitting change to the sublunar sphere became more concrete doctrines about the planets having the power to order, regulate, and influence things on Earth.[17]

By the first century CE, it seems that some authors had started to associate certain qualities of heat and moisture with the planets. For example, Pliny the Elder (mid-first century CE) maintained that certain planets were hot, cold, or

---

[14] Ptolemy, *Tetrabiblos*, 1, 20.

[15] Porphyry, *Introduction*, 6, also drawing on Antiochus.

[16] For a good overview of Aristotle's views on celestial influences see Freudenthal, "The Astrologization of the Aristotelian Cosmos," esp. p. 240.

[17] For a translation of *De Mundo* see *The Complete Works of Aristotle*, ed. Barnes, vol. 1, pp. 626–640. This work has traditionally been included in the works of Aristotle since it is attributed to him, although it is usually viewed as a piece of pseudepigrapha. The dating is uncertain, with some dating it as early as the late fourth century BCE, and others dating it to the late first century BCE or early first century CE. Different views on the dating are discussed briefly in Bos, "Supplementary Notes on the 'De mundo,'" p. 313, fn. 2. There seems to be general agreement that it was written sometime around the Hellenistic period. For a good discussion of how Aristotle's views on celestial influence were modified by later Peripatetics see Freudenthal, "The Astrologization of the Aristotelian Cosmos." While Freudenthal focuses mainly on the second century CE Peripatetic Alexander of Aphrodisias, some of his arguments about what he calls the "astrologization of the Aristotelian cosmos" are also applicable to *De Mundo*.

somewhere in between. He says that "Saturn is of a cold and frozen nature," while Mars, "owing to the proximity of the sun" has a "fiery glow." Jupiter, "being situated between them combines the influence of each and is rendered healthy."[18] Also in the first century CE, Dorotheus of Sidon seems to blend symbolic and naturalistic conceptualizations when he describes the combined qualities of Mars and Saturn:

> when Saturn is in conjunction with Mars the Warlike, he makes the (otherwise angry) character gentile. For indeed the impetuous Mars, always vehement and swift, sets unreflecting and inconsiderate speed into rapid motion, because he is hot; Saturn, instead, is slow; but when both are mixed, the mortal (who is being born) will be midway between them and therefore the best.[19]

These references to the planets being hot or cold in the century before Ptolemy confirm that his model was not created entirely from scratch. However, he does seem to have taken the causal or naturalistic conceptualization of astrology much further than some of his predecessors. This is an important point since there has been a tendency amongst academics to take Ptolemy's views as being more representative of the mainstream of the Hellenistic tradition than they probably were, especially when compared to other astrologers such as Vettius Valens or Dorotheus of Sidon. As a result of this, Ptolemy's notions of celestial causation are usually viewed as being paradigmatic or definitive for astrology in the Greco-Roman period.[20] David Pingree went so far as to argue that ideas of planetary causation were the primary distinguishing factor between the Hellenistic and earlier Mesopotamian astrological traditions:

---

[18] Pliny, *Natural History*, 2, 6: 34–35, trans. Rackham, p. 191.

[19] Dorotheus, *Carmen*, ed. Pingree, pp. 368: 25–30–p. 369: 1–3, trans. Heilen, "Ancient Scholars on the Horoscope of Rome," p. 56.

[20] Pingree took for granted that the material on universal astrology in Hephaestio *Apotelesmatika*, 1, 23, that talks about the planets exerting certain influences was from Petosiris, and thus marked the beginning of the causal conceptualization of astrology right at the start of the Hellenistic tradition, around the late second or early first century BCE. See Pingree, *From Astral Omens*, p. 26. However, we should be careful about drawing firm conclusions from this passage, because it is not clear how much of it represents Hephaestio's own views or interjections. Hephaestio lived in the fifth century CE, at a point when Ptolemy's modified Aristotelian causal conceptualization of astrology had already become widely adopted, and Hephaestio himself drew heavily on Ptolemy throughout his work. As a result of this we cannot be certain whether these references to the planets transmitting their effects to earth in this chapter represent the views of Hephaestio or his sources, whom he calls "the ancient Egyptian wise men."

these types of astrology depend on the notion that the planets, in their eternal rotations about the earth, transmit motion (change) to the four elements and to the assemblages of elements, animate and inanimate, in the sublunar world. This theory is completely different than that of celestial omens, in which the gods, whose physical manifestations are the constellations and planets, send messages concerning their intentions regarding kings and countries by means of celestial phenomena.[21]

In this way Pingree's very definition of "astrology" hinges upon celestial causation, and he prefers to refer to the Mesopotamian tradition as having dealt with "celestial omens" rather than "astrology" proper.[22] At one point he went so far as to chastise another scholar for failing to recognize this distinction in the manner that he did in a review of their book:

> The chapter on astrology is written without any hint of an awareness of the philosophical (and "scientific") distinctions that need to be made between astral divination—in which the gods proclaim their intentions through omens, in part at least in the hope that humans will propitiate them with sacrifice, ritual, and prayer so that they will be pleased to alter those intentions—and astrology as the Greeks who invented it in about 100 B.C. conceived of it: a purely mechanical working out of the complicated machinery of celestial motions and their natural influences on the sublunar world, a process with which humans are powerless to interfere.[23]

There are, however, two problems with Pingree's view. The first is that the sign-based conceptualization of astrology did not die out immediately with the end of the Mesopotamian tradition in the first century BCE. In fact, there is evidence that it persisted well into the Hellenistic tradition. For example, in the first century CE, the Roman philosopher Seneca acknowledged both conceptualizations of astrology while making some brief critiques of its usefulness from a Stoic perspective:

> They [the stars] either actuate or signalize all that comes about in the universe. If every event is brought about by them, how is mere familiarity with a process which is unchangeable going to be of any help? If they are pointers to events, what difference does it make to be aware in advance of

---

[21] Pingree, *From Astral Omens*, pp. 21–22.
[22] Cf. Pingree, "Astrology."
[23] Pingree, "Review of Tamsyn S. Barton, *Power and Knowledge*," p. 331.

things you cannot escape? They are going to happen whether you know about them or not.[24]

This reference to two different conceptualizations implies that there was a debate about the mechanism underlying astrology in the mid-first century CE. The technical system that different astrologers were using was essentially the same, but they had differing views about why or how the system worked. There is thus no reason to restrict the definition of astrology to just the causal view, even if notions of celestial causation did represent a unique development in the Hellenistic tradition.

The second issue with Pingree's definition of astrology is that even though Ptolemy's causal conceptualization of astrology did become the dominant viewpoint after the publication of his *Tetrabiblos* in the mid-second century CE, a debate about signs versus causes continued for centuries both inside and outside of the astrological community. The most famous example of this debate appears in the work of the third century philosopher Plotinus, in particular his tracts *On Fate*, and *On Whether the Stars are Causes*.[25] In *On Fate*, Plotinus, who is generally regarded as the founder of Neoplatonism, wrote an impassioned argument against the causal conceptualization of astrology. He didn't argue against the efficacy of astrology, but rather against the view that planets cause events rather than simply signify them. At one point he makes an analogy between astrology and ornithomancy (divination by watching the flight of birds):

> We must rather say that the movement of the stars is for the preservation of the universe, but that they perform in addition another service; this is that those who know how to read this sort of writing can, by looking at them as if they were letters, read the future from their patterns, discovering what is signified by the systematic use of analogy—for instance, if one said that when the bird flies high it signifies some high heroic deeds.[26]

The causal conceptualization of astrology is mocked by Plotinus because the idea that the planets literally cause the predicted events to occur is equivalent to saying that the birds themselves cause the predicted events to happen:

---

[24] Seneca, *Letters From a Stoic*, trans. Campbell, letter LXXXVIII, p.155.

[25] Plotinus, *Ennead*, III, 1, and *Ennead*, II, 6, respectively. For a detailed treatment of Plotinus' attitude towards astrology see Adamson, "Plotinus on Astrology." For discussions of this specific issue in Plotinus' writings see Dillon, "Plotinus on Whether the Stars Are Causes," and Lawrence, "Who Thought the Stars are Causes?"

[26] Plotinus, *Ennead*, III, 1. 6: 18–24, trans. Armstrong.

But if, because, looking at the position of the stars they announce what has happened to particular people, they adduce this as evidence that the happenings were caused by the stars, then in the same way birds would be the causes of what they indicate, and so would everything at which the soothsayers look when they foretell.[27]

That Plotinus felt the need to directly address this issue at least twice in his works is probably indicative of the level of success that Ptolemy's naturalistic (re)formulation of astrology enjoyed in the century after his death. However, even after Plotinus, the issue was not put to rest, and there is evidence that it continued to be debated after his time. In the fourth century an author named Sallustius makes a brief remark about how the causal conceptualization of astrology doesn't make sense in terms of some of the things that astrologers say that they can do:

The mentioning in horoscopes of good birth or evil birth of ancestors shows that the stars do not cause all things, but do no more than indicate some. How indeed could events before the moment of birth be produced by the conjunction of the heavenly bodies at that moment?[28]

His general point is that since the birth chart is supposed to be able to describe some circumstances that occur before the moment of birth, such as the societal status of the parents, it doesn't make sense to say that those things are somehow caused by the planets at the moment of birth itself, but instead they are only signified. Later, in the fifth century, the astrologer Hephaestio of Thebes opened his textbook with an allusion to the two different conceptualizations of astrology:

Our aim here, O most excellent of friends Athanasios, is, God willing, to set forth this handbook as something that can be quite easily followed; it contains some commentary and an essay that has come to us about what was said by the ancients concerning the stars, whether signifying or causing or even in some other fashion encircling and turning everything here under the Moon with their figures relative to each other and to the earth.[29]

Eventually, in the medieval tradition, the causal conceptualization of astrology came to be the dominant view, although other practices that were still more clearly

---

[27] Plotinus, *Ennead*, III, 1. 5: 34–38, trans. Armstrong.

[28] Sallustius, *Concerning the Gods and the Universe*, 9, trans. Nock, p. 19.

[29] Hephaestio, *Apotelesmatika*, 1, proem: 1, trans. Schmidt, p. 1.

rooted in the sign-based approach, such as interrogational astrology, continued to flourish. Interestingly, some scholars such as Campion argue that Ptolemy's causal conceptualization of astrology allowed the practice to survive during later centuries once it was revived in the medieval period, because it established it as a natural science rather than a form of divination, and thus it was able to avoid a certain level of religious opposition that it encountered otherwise.[30]

The Study of Fate

Aside from the differing views as to the mechanism underlying astrology, astrologers also held different opinions about the degree to which our lives and events in the world were viewed as predetermined or fated to occur.

Astrology was first developed in the Mesopotamian tradition prior to the development of a complex mathematical astronomy. That is to say, the fundamental astrological premise that there is a correlation between celestial and earthly events was developed at a time when astronomy was largely restricted to phenomena that could be directly observed with the naked eye. Observable astronomical phenomena include things such as eclipses, halos around the Moon, and comets. Interest in astrology eventually spurred the development of more complex forms of astronomy, which led to the discovery that most planetary cycles are fixed, predetermined, and predictable. This transition from an observational astronomy which had little predictive capabilities to a mathematical astronomy which had the ability to predict planetary positions far into the past and future may have also caused a shift from viewing the workings of the planets and stars as capricious and indeterminate to a more deterministic view. The original Mesopotamian notion that celestial bodies and their movements were somehow related to or correlated with terrestrial events was still the core astrological hypothesis, but the realization that the movements of these celestial bodies were fixed and predetermined naturally led to the realization that the terrestrial events that they were thought to correlate with may be predetermined as well.

Hellenistic astrology was developed shortly after the philosophy of Stoicism emerged as one of the dominant philosophical schools in the ancient world. The Stoic school was founded around the year 300 BCE by Zeno of Citium, and eventually achieved mainstream popularity in the last few centuries BCE and first two centuries CE, which coincided with the high point in the practice of Hellenistic astrology. One of the fundamental principles of Stoicism is that every event that occurs in the world is predetermined as a result of a providential ordering of events in accordance with a divine plan.[31] The Stoics defined "fate"

---

[30] Campion, *A History of Western Astrology*, vol. 1, p. 208ff.
[31] Bobzien, *Determinism and Freedom in Stoic Philosophy*, esp. pp. 28–33.

(*heimarmenē*) as the rational principle which orders and connects all events that take place in the universe, ensuring that everything happens for a reason.[32] Since everything was seen as predetermined according to divine reason, the Stoic ideal was to accept your own personal fate no matter what it is, and to treat all events as having the same essential value.

The popularity of Stoicism in the Hellenistic period provides an important piece of cultural context for understanding the rise in popularity of astrology in the Greco-Roman world around the same period. At a time when the astronomical models were becoming more exact and natal astrology was becoming more popular after its invention in the fifth century BCE, it is significant that there was a major philosophical school that promoted the idea that everything was predetermined, and that the best thing that one could do is accept and embrace their fate. In the first century CE, Pliny the Elder said that "there is nobody who is not eager to learn his destiny (*futura*), or who does not believe that the truest account of it is that gained by watching the skies."[33] Similarly, in the early second century, the Roman historian Tacitus remarked within the context of a discussion about astrology and fate that "most men do not doubt that what will happen to them is predestined from birth."[34] Naturally, the question that arises from a personal standpoint in relation to Stoic determinism is: "what is my fate?" or "what events must I accept?" This is probably where part of the emphasis on and popularity of natal astrology in the Hellenistic tradition derives from, as it became both a means of and a system for determining one's fate.

The enlightened Stoic sage was supposed to be able to accept any events that occur in their life as they happen with complete tranquility, having developed the emotional equilibrium to not become extremely depressed in the case of negative events, nor overjoyed in the case of positive ones. But for someone who has not achieved the enlightenment of a sage, astrology seems to have become the means by which one could get a glimpse into the future in order to know what events were in store for them in different parts of their life; in this way they

---

[32] For Stoic definitions of fate see Long and Sedley, *The Hellenistic Philosophers*, vol. 1, pp. 333–340. In particular, see the report of Chrysippus' views by Stobaeus in 55M (p. 337), which says: "Chrysippus calls the substance of fate a power of breath [or "spirit" (*pneuma*)], carrying out the orderly government of the all. [...] in other works, he expresses a variety of views: 'Fate is the rationale of the world,' or 'the rationale of providence's acts of government in the world,' or 'the rationale in accordance with which past events have happened, present events are happening, and future events will happen.' And as a substitute for 'rationale' he uses 'truth,' 'explanation,' 'nature,' 'necessity,' and further terms, taking these to apply to the same substance from different points of view."

[33] Pliny, *Natural History*, 30: 2, trans. Jones, p. 279.

[34] Quoted in Lehoux, "Tomorrow's News Today," p. 113, from Tacitus, *Annals*, 6: 22.

could prepare themselves ahead of time so as to not be caught off guard. This is one of the only explicit philosophical principles that is repeatedly given for the practice of astrology by a number of different Hellenistic astrologers, to the extent that it seems to be the one thing that everyone agreed on when trying to articulate the purpose of astrology. For example, Valens says:

> For God, in his desire that man should foreknow the future, brought this science into the world, a science through which anyone can know his fate in order to bear the good with great contentment and the bad with great steadfastness. [...] Accordingly then, the initiates of this art, those wishing to have knowledge of the future, will be helped because they will not be burdened with vain hopes, will not expend grievous midnight toil, will not vainly love the impossible, nor in a like manner will they be carried away by their eagerness to attain what they may expect because of some momentary good fortune. A suddenly appearing good often grieves men as if it were an evil; a suddenly appearing evil causes the greatest misery to those who have not trained their minds in advance.[35]

Later he expressed similar sentiments more strongly:

> Those who engage in the prediction of the future and the truth, having acquired a soul that is free and not enslaved, do not think highly of fortune, and do not devote themselves to hope, nor are they afraid of death, but instead they live their lives undaunted by disturbance by training their souls to be confident, and neither rejoice excessively in the case of good, nor become depressed in the case of bad, but instead are content with whatever is present. Those who do not desire the impossible are capable of bearing that which is preordained through their own self-mastery; and being estranged from all pleasure or praise, they become established as soldiers of fate.[36]

Firmicus also expresses a similar attitude:

> This study will most successfully bring us to the point where our souls will despise everything which is considered evil or good in human affairs. For when we learn of the approach of difficulties, we despise the threat of

---

[35] Valens, *Anthology*, 5, 2: 11–14, trans. Riley, p. 96.
[36] Valens, *Anthology*, 5, 6: 9.

evils because we have learned from our doctrine about things to come. We do not shrink from dangers once foretold. By recollection of its majesty, our souls have formed themselves to withstand these things; we are not overcome by bad fortune nor elated by promise of high office. Thus fortified by stable reason we cannot be oppressed by ill fortune nor overjoyed at the expectation of good.[37]

Even Ptolemy expresses a similar sentiment at one point as part of his general statements about the purpose of astrology, even though he otherwise does not adopt an entirely Stoic or deterministic philosophical approach in his astrological work:

For, first of all, it is necessary to consider that even for events that will necessarily result, the unexpected is apt to cause delirious confusion and mad joy, while foreknowing habituates and trains the soul to attend to distant events as though they were present, and prepares it to accept each of the arriving events with peace and tranquility.[38]

This sentiment is repeated in other authors as well, and it is so formulaic that it seems as if it may have been outlined in one of the influential foundational astrological texts that were written towards the beginning of the Hellenistic tradition. In fact, the third-century alchemist Zosimos of Panopolis cites some views outlined in a couple of texts attributed to Hermes Trismegistus and Zoroaster that are strikingly reminiscent of some of the philosophical statements made by Valens and others:

Hermes and Zoroaster say that philosophers as a class are superior to fate because they neither rejoice in her good fortune, for they are master over pleasures, nor are they thrown by the evils she sends, as they always lead an inner life, nor do they accept the fair gifts she offers, since they look to an end of ills.[39]

Alternatively, it is possible that the idea of knowing one's fate in order to accept events in the future had become commonplace due to the popularity of Stoicism, and it was simply something that was taken for granted as part of the culture of

---

[37] Firmicus, *Mathesis*, 8, 1: 8–9, trans. Bram, p. 267.
[38] Ptolemy, *Tetrabiblos*, 1, 3: 5, trans. Schmidt, pp. 9–10.
[39] Zosimos, *On the Letter Omega*, 5, trans. Jackson, p. 23.

the time.[40] In either event, astrology became known as a system, if not *the* system, that could be used in order to study one's fate. The astrologers themselves were clear that this was what they were doing with astrology. For example, Manilius speaks of our ability to use astrology to "learn the laws of fate" (*legem perdiscere fati*),[41] while Firmicus constantly uses different variations of a phrase in order to say that the role of the astrologer, or the role of astrology, is "studying the fate of men" (*tractantem fata hominum*) or "explaining the fates of men" (*explicandis fatis hominum*).[42] Valens once refers to astrologers as "soldiers of fate" (*stratiōtai tes heimarmenēs*), and elsewhere says that a good astrologer is "a guide to life, a good advisor and an unerring prophet of fate (*prophētēs heimarmenēs*)."[43]

In some philosophical and religious traditions from the Hellenistic period onward, the planets became closely associated with fate.[44] Denzey Lewis recently summarized this by saying that "by the second century of the Common Era, many philosophers considered *heimarmenē* indistinguishable from the power of the celestial bodies."[45] This is especially true in Hermetic philosophical texts, such as the first book of the *Corpus Hermeticum*, which describes the creation of the cosmos and the role of the seven planets, saying that they "encompass the sensible world in circles, and their government is called fate."[46] Another Hermetic text states that "the stars are the instrument of fate; it is in accordance with fate that they bring all things to pass for the world of nature and for men."[47]

By the second and third centuries CE, philosophical and theological arguments against the concept of fate became arguments against astrology, and arguments against astrology became intertwined with arguments against fate, so that the two came to be seen as almost interchangeable.[48] For example, the

---

[40] This view about the purpose of astrology is also expressed in other sources such as Lucian, *On Astrology*, 29, and Nonnos, *Dionysiaca*, 6: 55–57.

[41] Manilius, *Astronomica*, 2: 149.

[42] Firmicus, *Mathesis*, 2, 29: 20; 3, 14: 10.

[43] Valens, *Anthology*, 5, 6: 9; 9, 6: 10, trans. Riley, p. 156.

[44] For an overview of this topic along with some background in its development in the Greek and especially Platonic philosophical tradition see Lawrence, "The Young Gods." See also Denzey Lewis, *Cosmology and Fate*, which talks about the religious context of early Christian and Gnostic discussions.

[45] Denzey Lewis, *Cosmology and Fate*, p. 122, transliteration modified.

[46] *Corpus Hermeticum*, 1: 9, trans. Copenhaver, *Hermetica*, p. 2.

[47] *Corpus Hermeticum*, vol. 3, excerpt XII: 2 (from Stobaeus), trans. Scott, *Hermetica*, vol. 1, p. 435, modified.

[48] Some of the Christian arguments against fate and astrology are discussed briefly in Hegedus, *Early Christianity and Ancient Astrology*, pp. 113–115. For a more extensive treatment of anti-fatalism arguments in connection with astrology see Amand, *Fatalisme et liberté dans l'antiquité grecque*, esp. pp. 191–569 for a detailed treatment of the later Christian polemics.

fourth-century Christian bishop Gregory of Nyssa wrote a letter around the year 378 CE titled *Against Fate* (*kata heimarmenēs*), and it is almost entirely focused on a disputation of astrology.[49] At one point in the letter Gregory cites the views of a proponent of astrology that he was debating, who reportedly said that "fate determines a person's life at the hour of birth by the formation of stars, and this order remains constant throughout life."[50] In the Greco-Roman world astrology became, for all intents and purposes, the study of fate.

Astrological Determinism

While there seems to have been a general agreement that the purpose of astrology was to study a person's fate, not all astrologers agreed on the extent to which things were fully predetermined. The basic premise of astrology in general, and natal astrology in particular, implies that there are some things that are fated or predetermined in a person's life from the moment of birth, but the extent to which things are predetermined and unalterable became a point of debate in the astrological tradition. Different astrologers held different views, which created a spectrum of positions.

On one end of the spectrum were those who held that all things are predetermined from the moment of birth, and that there is nothing that a person can do to change their fate, since it is not just the external events and circumstances in their lives that are predetermined, but also the person's internal motivations, character, and choices as well. In Stoic philosophy, this was articulated as the doctrine of internal and external fate.[51] This view represents the most deterministic end of the spectrum, and the most famous example of this line of thought in astrology is in book four of Manilius:

> Fate rules the world, all things stand fixed by its immutable laws, and the long ages are assigned a predestined course of events. At birth our death is sealed and our end is consequent upon our beginning. Fate is the source of riches and kingdoms and the more frequent poverty; by fate are men at birth given their skills and characters, their merits and defects, their losses and gains. None can renounce what is bestowed or possess what is

---

[49] For a translation see McCambley, "*Against Fate* by Gregory of Nyssa."

[50] McCambley, "*Against Fate* by Gregory of Nyssa," p. 328.

[51] This is most famously explained in Chryssipus' cylinder analogy, which is discussed in Bobzien, *Determinism and Freedom*, p. 258ff. Bobzien explains (p. 260) that in one of the sources that cites the story "the analogy is introduced as having the function of illustrating Chrysippus' point that external influences do not necessitate actions but that fate works through the agent's nature."

denied; no man by prayer may seize fortune if it demur, or escape if it draw nigh: each one must bear his appointed lot.[52]

Along similar lines, Manetho, in poetic verse, says that

> No one is able to alter the nativity of men which accompanies from their infancy and forthwith is wound about the threads of the Fates with their unbreakable strings and iron spindles.[53]

Similarly deterministic statements are made at different points by Valens and Firmicus, some of which were quoted earlier. There is a marked tendency for many of the Hellenistic astrologers to be on the more deterministic end of the spectrum, although it is not always clear what the views of every astrologer was. Since most of what survives are technical manuals, we are left to reconstruct much of the philosophy of the astrologers from brief digressions interspersed throughout the texts.

On the other end of the spectrum were those astrologers who held the view that things were only partially predetermined, or that fate was sometimes negotiable or could be mitigated under certain circumstances. Rochberg points out that the presence of apotropaic or propitiation rituals for dispelling or assuaging bad omens in the Mesopotamian astrological tradition is strong evidence that the astrologers of that period were not completely deterministic in their worldview.[54] Similar beliefs continued into the Hellenistic tradition, where they show up the most prominently in the magical and medical texts. In some of the texts that deal with astrological medicine, indications for illness are given together with remedies that can be used in order to treat or counteract certain conditions.[55] Ptolemy uses a medical analogy to explain that while it is true that someone could die if they become sick and do not do anything to treat it, if they seek treatment then the illness can sometimes be mitigated or cured, and the influences of the planets work in a similar way.[56] Similarly, in the surviving corpus of Greek magical texts, at one point there is a reference

---

[52] Manilius, *Astronomica*, 4: 14–22, trans. Goold, pp. 223–5.

[53] Manetho, *Apotelesmatika*, 1: 200, trans. Lopilato, p. 194.

[54] Rochberg, "Heaven and Earth: Divine-Human Relations in Mesopotamian Celestial Divination," p. 182.

[55] See in particular pseudo-Galen's *De Decubitu* (On Decumbiture), which is edited in *Claudii Galeni Omnia Opera*, ed. Kühn, 19.529–73. This text and others that are related to it are discussed in Wilson and George, "Anonymi, *De Decubitu*: Contexts of Rationality."

[56] This is part of his central argument in Ptolemy, *Tetrabiblos*, 1, 3.

to a spell that is supposed to be used to free oneself from the fate indicated by the birth chart: "Protect me from all my own astrological destiny; destroy my foul fate; apportion good things for me in my horoscope."[57] At one point the early fourth century philosopher, Iamblichus, criticized those who believed that the identification of the overall ruler of the birth chart (the Master of the Nativity) could be used to free oneself from fate by appealing to the native's guardian spirit, which implies that there were some who thought that fate could be changed through magic or ritual.[58]

There appears to have been some tensions between proponents of the fully deterministic strand of astrology and those who advocated a less deterministic approach in which fate could be altered through the use of magic, as evinced by Zosimos' citation of the views of Hermes and Zoroaster again:

> Now Zoroaster boastfully affirms that by the knowledge of all things supernatural and by the Magian science of the efficacious use of corporeal speech one averts all the evils of fate, both those of individual and those of universal application. Hermes, however, in his book *On the Inner Life*, condemns even the Magian science, saying that the spiritual man, one who has come to know himself, need not rectify anything through the use of magic, not even if it is considered a good thing, nor must he use force upon necessity, but rather allow necessity to work in accordance with her own nature and decree. He must proceed through that one search to understand himself, and, when he has come to know God, he must hold fast to the ineffable Triad and leave fate to work what she will upon the clay that belongs to her, that is, the body.[59]

In terms of the astrologers, Ptolemy stands out as rejecting the hard-line deterministic view of astrology quite strongly, saying that:

> one need not believe that every single thing accrues to man pursuant to a cause above as if it were ordained for each individual from the beginning by some inescapable and divine ordinance and resulted of necessity, there being not a single other cause able to counteract it in the least.[60]

---

[57] PGM XIII: 633–35, in *The Greek Magical Papyri in Translation*, ed. Betz, p. 187.

[58] Iamblichus, *On the Mysteries*, 9: 3. Porphyry evidently argued that this was possible, and it is his statements that Iamblichus is arguing against here.

[59] Zosimos, *On the Letter Omega*, 7, trans. Jackson, p. 25.

[60] Ptolemy, *Tetrabiblos*, 1, 3: 5, trans. Schmidt, p. 10.

Although Ptolemy's thoughts here are wrapped up in his own quasi-Aristotelian cosmological views about the origin of certain causes and the chain of command that certain influences go though, his fundamental point is that celestial influences, once they filter down to the sublunar realm, are not always immutable. While he admits that there are certain things on a global scale that cannot be avoided, he argues that on a smaller, more local level, there are certain things that can be done to mitigate astrological influences if a person goes out of their way to do so. However, if a person does not go out of their way to mitigate these more mutable influences, then they will certainly result in the astrologically expected manner:

> it is clear that both in general and in particular, for all the occurrences that happen with a first cause which is irresistible and greater than every counteracting cause, it is necessary that these always and in every way result. But for all occurrences which are not so, those that meet with counteracting causes can be easily reversed, while those that do not find them available do indeed follow their primary natures, yet through ignorance and by no means through the necessity of a powerful [fate].[61]

Firmicus appears to criticize this type of moderate or conditional determinism advocated by Ptolemy or others who followed similar lines of thought, saying that "it makes no sense for one to admit the necessity of fate and afterwards to deny it. It is a very faulty argument which rebuts in the later part of the discussion what it had admitted in the earlier."[62]

Elsewhere, the practice of inceptional astrology in the Hellenistic tradition may imply that some astrologers viewed fate as conditional or malleable in some ways. For example, the fifth book of Dorotheus gives rules for beginning different types of ventures under the premise that the alignment of the planets at the moment that an action is initiated would indicate the outcome. It is tempting to see this as being connected to philosophical views of fate that were held by the Middle Platonists and Neoplatonists, who believed that fate acted as a law that was conditional, so that the choice to act was free, but once an action had been taken, the outcome was predetermined.[63] Many of the rules given by Dorotheus for inceptional astrology imply that they are supposed to be used in order to select specific times in order to begin undertakings under the premise that this can help

---

[61] Ptolemy, *Tetrabiblos*, 1, 3: 8, trans. Schmidt, p. 25.

[62] Firmicus, *Mathesis*, 1, 8: 7, trans. Bram, p. 27.

[63] This conceptualization of fate is defined in Alcinous, *The Handbook of Platonism*, 26. For a general discussion of this idea see Sharples, "The Stoic Background to the Middle Platonist Discussion of Fate," and Dillon, *The Middle Platonists*, pp. 294–8.

to ensure a more favorable outcome than what might happen otherwise. Within the context of a general critique of astrology, Augustine specifically criticizes the idea that one could use this type of astrology in order to alter one's fate:

> Now who could tolerate the assumption that in choosing lucky days people manufacture new destinies by their own acts? [...] Can a man by the choice of a day change the destiny already decreed for him?[64]

In sum, there were a spectrum of different beliefs about the extent to which things were fated or predetermined, and while the basic premise of astrology assumed that at least some things could be seen about a person's life ahead of time, the specifics of how far this went were sometimes a matter of debate.

Four Philosophical Positions

These two debates—the question of whether the planets and stars act as signs or causes; and whether events in the world are completely or partially predetermined—resulted in the establishment of four fundamental philosophical positions that were adopted by astrologers in the ancient world.[65] This is illustrated by the Venn diagram below, where on the vertical axis we have the spectrum of whether the planets and other factors used in astrology acted as signs or causes, and on the horizontal axis we have the spectrum of whether everything that occurs in the world was viewed as completely predetermined or only partially predetermined. The points of intersection define the four fundamental philosophical positions adopted by astrologers during this period, and many of them can be placed in one of these categories.

For example, Ptolemy would fall in the overlapping area between causal astrology and partial determinism, because he conceptualized astrology as working as a result of the planets influencing or causing events on earth, but he also said that some of these planetary influences could be counteracted and changed, and thus things were not completely predetermined. This may be contrasted with Firmicus, who also held the view that the planets caused events on earth and in the lives of individuals, but unlike Ptolemy, he viewed everything as being completely predetermined and that fate was unalterable.

The third and fourth philosophical positions involve those who saw the planets as signs or omens of future events rather than causes. Valens, for example,

---

[64] Augustine, *City of God*, 5, 7, trans. McCracken, Green et al, vol. 2, p. 159.

[65] While he doesn't adopt the same fourfold scheme that I'm using here, there is an excellent discussion about the intersection between astrological views on fate, free will, determinism, and the mechanism underlying astrology in Lehoux, "Tomorrow's News Today."

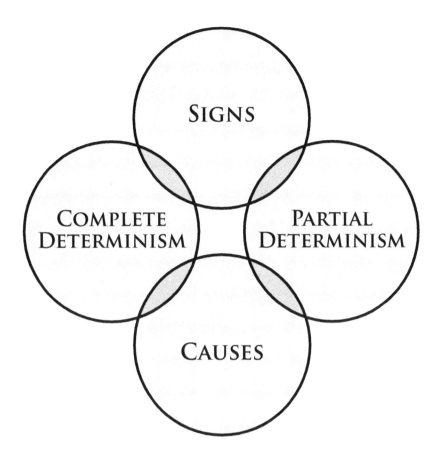

Figure 6.1 - The Four Philosophical Positions

frequently refers to the planets signifying or acting as signs for certain things, and he uses a number of techniques that seem to have been derived from purely symbolic rather than natural considerations. At the same time, he also appears to advocate a more deterministic philosophy, saying that it is not possible to alter one's fate through actions or prayers.[66] This may be contrasted with Dorotheus, who also uses a number of symbolic techniques such as "lots," but whose use of inceptional astrology may imply that he viewed fate as malleable or negotiable, and thus not fully deterministic.

These four fundamental philosophical positions about astrology were first established in the Hellenistic tradition, and they have more or less stayed constant over the past two thousand years. Contemplating the issues related

---

[66] Valens, *Anthology*, 5, 6 in general, esp. sentence 10 for the statement about prayer. Although Komorowska notes that "Valens seems undecided whether stars exercise actual influence on the world or are just intermediaries between humanity and the divine." Komorowska, "Philosophical Foundation of Vettius Valens' Astrological Creed," p. 333.

to these positions is important because it has significant ramifications for how astrology is conceptualized and practiced, both in the way that astrologers view their own lives through the lens of astrology, and also in terms of how the subject is presented when astrologers interpret the charts of clients or try to explain what it is that they do.

Chapter 7
Planets

———————— ✸ ————————

The Seven Wandering Stars

Hellenistic astrology was developed around the five visible planets: Mercury, Venus, Mars, Jupiter, and Saturn, as well as the luminaries, the Sun and the Moon. These seven bodies were often treated as a group, and generally referred to together as the seven "planets" or "wandering stars" (*planētes asteres*). This terminology arose from the fact that if you look at the night sky over a long period of time, you will notice that while most of the stars stay fixed relative to one another, there are some that move slowly, and seem to wander about, passing by other stars in the process. Thus, the planets become known as the wandering stars, while the rest become known as the fixed stars.

Something that makes the seven traditional celestial bodies unique even today is that they are all visible to the naked eye. That is to say, you can go outside on a reasonably clear night and look up at the sky and see the planets without the aid of a telescope or binoculars. In some instances they will make particularly dramatic alignments with each other or with other celestial bodies, and they will stand out even more in the night sky. This point is important in terms of the contemporary practice of astrology and its ever-increasing list of celestial bodies, because the ability to *see* the traditional planets with the naked eye acts as a distinction, and puts them in a class of their own. In most forms of divination in the ancient world, the visible appearance of an ominous phenomenon was extremely important in terms of interpreting its significance for the observer or the situation in relation to which the omen was being studied. Therefore, while it may initially seem odd from a modern perspective to have a system that is entirely predicated on a model where there are only seven planets, the distinction is arguably still relevant and important today.

Names of the Planets

In most of the Greek texts, the planets are usually referred to by the names of the gods that they were thought to be associated with:

Hēlios	Sun
Selēnē	Moon
Hermēs	Mercury
Aphroditē	Venus
Arēs	Mars
Zeus	Jupiter
Kronos	Saturn

The Greeks first assigned the names of the gods to the planets around the fourth century BCE, apparently in imitation of the earlier Mesopotamian attributions, by finding gods in the Greek pantheon who had similar characteristics to the Mesopotamian gods associated with those planets.[1] The complete set of assignments first appear in the *Epinomis*, which is usually thought to have been written by Plato's student Philip of Opus in the fourth century BCE.[2] An alternative set of names for the planets also existed in Greek that are more descriptive of their visual appearance:

Hēlios	Sun
Selēnē	Moon
Stilbōn	The Twinkling One (Mercury)
Phōsphoros	Light-Bringer (Venus)
Pyroeis	The Fiery One (Mars)
Phaethōn	The Radiant One (Jupiter)
Phainōn	The Shining One (Saturn)

These names were used prior to the assignment of the names of the gods to the

---

[1] Campion, *A History of Western Astrology*, vol. 1, p. 153.

[2] Although note that already in the *Timaeus*, Plato refers to Mercury as the star that is "said to be sacred to Hermes." Plato, *Timaeus*, 38d, trans. Waterfield, p. 27. The standard edition and commentary of the *Epinomis* is Tarán, *Academica: Plato, Philip of Opus, and the pseudo-Platonic Epinomis*. For a translation see Plato, *Charmides, Alcibiades 1 & 2, Hipparchus, The Lovers, Theages, Minos, Epinomis*, trans. Lamb.

planets in the fourth century BCE, and they continued to be used sporadically later in the Hellenistic tradition, usually in a poetic context in verse texts.

Significations According to Valens

Our best source for the significations of the planets is Valens, whose *Anthology* begins with a long chapter on the meanings of each of the planets. These significations may be partially derived from a lost work by Teucer of Babylon, who is presumed to have lived around the first century BCE.[3] Rhetorius preserves a similar list that contains many of Teucer's significations; however, it cannot be fully relied on to preserve the early tradition because it seems to contain some interpolations from Rhetorius himself. Thus, Valens is our best source for the early Hellenistic tradition.

In what follows I will provide an English translation of Valens' chapter on the significations of the planets, with some commentary in the footnotes. I primarily used Liddell-Scott-Jones (*A Greek-English Lexicon*, LSJ) and the Bauer-Danker (*A Greek-English Lexicon of the New Testament and Other Early Christian Literature*, BDAG) to study the Greek word for every signification that Valens gives in this chapter.[4] When the meaning of the word seems clear or unambiguous, I only provide a single translation in the body of the text, while in instances when the meaning is ambiguous I list alternative translations in a footnote.

In addition to using the lexicons, I also researched many of the individual terms that Valens uses in order to develop a better understanding of the cultural context in which they were being employed. I found that this sort of research helped immensely to provide a deeper level of understanding into why Valens associated certain significations with certain planets. This became especially important when he discusses certain professions. Much of what I found in these excursions is reported in the footnotes, although there is still a lot more work to be done in this area.

I also compared several of the existing translations of this chapter of Valens in order to see how other translators had rendered certain words or phrases.[5] In

---

[3] For more information see the entry on Teucer earlier in the astrologers chapter.

[4] Unfortunately the publication of Montanari, *The Brill Dictionary of Ancient Greek*, came too late for me to be able to make extensive use of it in this book.

[5] The different translations of Valens that I compared were: Valens, *Vettius Valens d'Antioche*, trans. Bara; Valens, *The Anthology, Book 1*, trans. Schmidt (1993); Schmidt, *The Kepler College Sourcebook* (2005), pp. 42–45; Valens, *Anthology, Book 1*, trans. Holden (unpublished); Beck, *A Brief History of Ancient Astrology*, pp. 74–76; Valens, *Anthologies*, trans. Riley. Beck largely seems to have followed Bara's translation, although he omits any words where the meaning is unclear.

some areas they were in agreement, although there was also a lot of disagreement among the translators at many points. Much of the disagreement simply reflects the fact that parts of this text are very difficult to understand, as Valens employs a lot of unique terminology, as well as some phrases that are not entirely clear. Sometimes I sided with one group of translators over another, or followed one translator's interpretation of the text rather than the others. In each instance, I have made every effort to give credit where it was due. I felt that each translator had a unique perspective on the text, and through comparing each of these perspectives, I was able to develop a more well-rounded understanding of what Valens was trying to convey. I also think that this process of comparing different translations provides a useful demonstration for the reader of some of the issues that translators are faced with when attempting to render ancient texts into modern languages.[6] Sometimes the choice of one word or another in a translation is simply a judgment call, although it can have a significant impact on the meaning and interpretation of a passage.

The Sun - *Hēlios*

The all-seeing Sun, consisting of fiery and intelligent light, the instrument of perception of the soul, in a nativity signifies kingship, authority,[7] mind,[8] intelligence, form, motion, height of fortune, dealings with the gods,[9] judgment, being engaged in public affairs, action,[10] leadership of crowds, father, master, friendship, notable figures,[11] being honored by portraits, statues, and crowns of office, high-priests of the fatherland, ... places.[12] Of the parts of the body, the

---

[6] For a broader discussion of some of these issues see Heilen, "Problems in translating ancient Greek astrological texts."

[7] *Hēgemonian*, "leadership," "hegemony," or "supremacy." Those who are at the top of a command structure.

[8] *Nous* is a complicated word that usually refers to the "mind" or "intellect," although it can also refer to one's sense of perception or understanding (percipience), as well as one's way of thinking or attitude.

[9] Beck infers that the "dealings" with the gods occur through oracles.

[10] *Praxis* is also often mentioned as a signification of the tenth place, and in the astrological texts is often tied up with one's career or occupation, since the term can also refer to one's "deeds" or "doings." Compare English "what do you *do*?" when inquiring about someone's profession.

[11] *Endoxa prosōpa* literally means something like "famous faces" or "notable personages," with underlying notions of esteem and honor. In other words, highly reputable people, or perhaps even "celebrities."

[12] There is a lacuna here after "high-priests of the fatherland," and the text then resumes with the stray statement "of places" (*topōn*, in the genitive plural). According to Pingree, Wendland suggests that the missing word before *topōn* was *prostasias*, which would mean that the missing signification in Valens was something like "leaders of places" or perhaps "management of places."

Sun rules the head; of the sense organs: the right eye;[13] of the torso:[14] it rules the heart, the life-breath or sensory movement, and the nerves.[15] Of substances, it rules gold. Of crops, it rules wheat and barley. He is of the diurnal sect, the color lemon-yellow, and bitter in taste.[16]

The Moon - *Selēnē*

The Moon is born from the reflection of the solar light and, possessing a counterfeit light, signifies in a nativity man's physical life,[17] the body, the mother, conception, <form>,[18] appearance,[19] goddess, living together or lawful marriage, nurse,[20] older sibling,[21] housekeeping, the queen, mistress of the house, possessions, fortune, city, gathering of the masses,[22] gains, expenditures,

---

[13] Porphyry (*Introduction*, 45) specifies that the Sun rules the right eye in males and the left eye in females. Neither Valens nor Teucer/Rhetorius mention this scheme, so it is not clear if it was universally accepted. It may be that it was accepted, but that Valens and Teucer's lists of significations were simply written with males as the default.

[14] *Pleurōn*. Alternatively, "the sides" or "the ribs."

[15] I am following a cue from Riley in breaking up this segment on the parts of the body in a way that is different than how the other translators have interpreted it, which changes the meaning significantly. It involves reading the significations given not as a string of different significations, but instead as more compartmentalized. It is hard to be sure if this interpretation is correct or not, but I think that it brings the list of significations that Valens gives for the Sun into line with other authors such as Porphyry. The only area where I departed from Riley is in the last three significations, which I think should probably be three separate significations on their own, rather than just a general category that only refers to the nerves. Porphyry (*Introduction*, 45), following Antiochus, separates the movement of the life-breath and the perceptive soul into different but related significations. In Greco-Roman medical and philosophical texts, the heart and nerves were thought to be integral to the circulation of the life-breath or spirit (*pneuma*) in the body. All of that said, this is how my translation would read if I was to follow the approach used by the other translators: "Of the parts of the body, he rules the head, the sense organs, the right eye, the flanks, the heart, life-breath or sensory movement, and the nerves."

[16] *Drimus*, "sharp" in taste.

[17] *Zōēn*.

[18] There is a short one-word lacuna here in the manuscript, although the editors have suggested adding *morphēn*, based on a comparison with the Teucer excerpt in Rhetorius where *morphēn* is right before the following word *prosōpon*.

[19] *Prosōpon* literally refers to one's "face" or "countenance," although more broadly it can also refer to external appearances or how one looks to others. This is the same word used to refer to the technical concept of a decan.

[20] *Trophon*, more generally, "care-giver," "nourisher," or "nurturer."

[21] *Adelphon meizona*. Schmidt says "older sister" here, and Holden has a footnote expressing surprise that Valens' text says "older brother" or "older sibling" rather than his expectation of "older sister" based on other texts. For example, Rhetorius (*Compendium*, 107) says that the Moon signifies older sisters and Venus younger sisters. Perhaps Valens takes it for granted that the older sibling signified by the Moon would be female?

[22] Note that one of the significations of the Sun was "leadership of crowds" (*prostasian*

home,[23] boats, travel,[24] wanderings (since it does not hold straight due to the Crab).[25] Of the parts of the body, she rules the left eye,[26] the stomach, breasts, the breath,[27] the spleen, membranes,[28] and marrow (from which it produces dropsy). Of substances, she rules silver and glass. She is of the nocturnal sect, light green in color, and salty in taste.

Saturn / *Kronos*, the "Shining One" (*Phainōn*)

The star of Saturn makes those born under him petty,[29] malicious,[30] having many anxieties, those who bring themselves down,[31] solitary, deceitful, those who conceal their deceit,[32] austere,[33] downcast, those who have a

---

ochlikēn). The contrast here seems to be between the Moon gathering the crowds or the masses and then the Sun leading them.

[23] *Oikian*, more generally one's "dwelling place," with some of the underlying connotations such as household or family.

[24] *Xeniteias*, "living abroad" (according to the LSJ lexicon), however Ptolemy (*Tetrabiblos*, 4, 8) seems to use the term explicitly to mean "foreign travel.".

[25] Presumably this parenthetical remark by Valens refers to the fact that the Moon's domicile is Cancer ("the Crab"), and thus in some way like a crab, the Moon signifies people or situations that are unable to go directly towards their intended goal or destination, but instead walk sideways or approach things in an indirect manner.

[26] According to Porphyry (*Introduction*, 45) the Moon rules the left eye for men but the right eye for women.

[27] *Phusēs*, following Bara and Riley. The root term means something like "to blow" or "to puff up." Schmidt thinks it means "the bladder," although one of Saturn's significations later on is also the bladder, which would seem contradictory.

[28] The term is often used to refer to the membrane that encloses the brain (the dura mater).

[29] *Mikrologous* refers to a person who is overly focused on or quibbling about minor or unimportant things.

[30] *Baskanous* can also mean "slanderous," "envious," or "malignant."

[31] *Heautous katarriptontas*, literally "those who throw themselves down." On the one hand this could mean something like "those who bring themselves into disrepute," which is Schmidt's interpretation; on the other hand, it could also mean something more along the lines of "those who are self-deprecating" or who "put themselves down," which Bara, Beck, and Riley all favor.

[32] Following Schmidt. Alternatively "those who attempt to conceal their treachery."

[33] *Austērous* more generally means "harsh" or "severe," but in reference to people it can mean "rigorous," "strict," or "exacting."

feigned appearance,[34] squalid,[35] clothed in black, importunate,[36] sullen, miserable,[37] given to seafaring, practicing waterside trades. And he causes depressions,[38]sluggishness,[39]inaction,[40]obstacles in undertakings,[41] long-lasting punishments,[42] subversion of matters,[43] secrets,[44] restraints,[45] imprisonment,[46] sorrows,[47] accusations, tears, being orphaned,[48] captivity, exposures.[49] He

---

[34] *Hupokrinomenēn tēn horasin echontas*, following Schmidt. Beck translates as "dissemblers," which is accurate, although an obscure English term. The term *hupokrinomenēn* can refer to actors who "play a part" or "pretend." The phrase seems to imply some sense of deliberateness, like the native willfully "puts on a false appearance" like a piece of clothing or a costume.

[35] *Auchmērous* means "dry" or "parched," although it has a secondary meaning of "dirty" or "squalid," which is how Holden, Riley, and Schmidt translate it. In some Greek texts it can refer to those who are "miserable," "dark," or "gloomy." Bara translates the term as "sad" (*tristes*). All of these meanings are probably relevant.

[36] That is to say, those who are overly persistent or demanding in their requests.

[37] *Kakopatheis*, "suffering."

[38] *Tapeinotētas* generally means "lowness" of position. From this, other notions are derived such as being of "low estate," "abasement," "lowness of spirits," "dejection," "baseness," "vileness," "meanness," etc. Beck thinks that it means "humiliation" in this instance, while Bara thinks it means something like "pettiness." Riley says "humblings." All of these concepts are probably relevant, although because of the terms' relation to the word that is used for the astrological concept of a planet's "depression," as opposed to its "exaltation," I agree with Schmidt here in translating the term as "depressions."

[39] *Nōchelias*, "laziness."

[40] *Apraxias*, in other words, not taking action or not acting, as opposed to taking action. The term also has other meanings such as "leisure," "want of success," or perhaps "futilities." Beck has "inactivity," while Riley thinks it specifically means "unemployment," presumably since Valens sometimes uses the word *praxis* to refer to one's career.

[41] *Enkopas tōn prassomenōn*, alternatively "hindrances" (Holden, Beck) or "interruptions" (Schmidt).

[42] *Poluchronious dikas*. Beck and Riley focus on the primary meaning of the term *dikas*, which has to do with lawsuits, trials, or litigation in general, thus translating this as "long drawn out litigation" or "interminable lawsuits." Schmidt instead emphasizes what results from the trial, such as a punishment or penalty, which is probably more appropriate in this instance.

[43] *Anaskeuas pragmatōn*, in the sense of pulling something down or holding something back. Bara and Beck think that the phrase simply means "reversals," while Schmidt thinks it means "dismantlings of things."

[44] *Krubas*, literally, to "hide," "conceal," or "keep secret."

[45] *Sunochas* more broadly means "holding together" or "contraction," leading Schmidt to translate it as "constrictions." From these are derived more concrete meanings such as "detention," "oppression," (Beck) and "imprisonment" (Riley), but it also has more metaphorical meanings arising from feeling restrained or restricted, such as "anxieties" (Holden), "distress," and "anguish." I decided to go with "restraints" here due to the literal and metaphorical meaning in English, and then to use the next signification for imprisonment.

[46] *Desma* more literally means "bonds" or "chains," like the shackles or handcuffs of a prisoner.

[47] *Penthē*, alternatively "grief" or "mourning."

[48] Or "bereavement."

[49] *Ektheseis* refers to the Greco-Roman practice of rejecting a newborn baby within the

makes farmers and gardeners because he rules the soil.[50] He also produces hired workers of property,[51] tax collectors, and violent actions.[52] He produces those who acquire great reputation, notable rank, guardianships, the administration of that which belongs to others, and fathers of other people's children. Of substances, he rules lead, wood, and stone. Of parts of the body, he rules the legs, the knees, the tendons, the watery parts of the body,[53] phlegm, the bladder, the kidneys, and the inner parts that are hidden. Of illnesses,[54] he is indicative of those that arise from coldness and moisture, such as dropsy, pain in the tendons, gout, cough, dysentery, tumors,[55] convulsions. Of disorders,[56] it indicates spirit possession,[57] unnatural lusts,[58] depravity.[59] He makes those who are unmarried and widowed, orphans, and childlessness. He brings about violent deaths by

---

first week of life when it is unwanted, and leaving the child in a public place, most often to die, although sometimes to be picked up and raised by someone else. In antiquity, exposure was sometimes the fate of a child who was born handicapped, deformed, or as a result of infidelity or rape. For a detailed treatment of this see the chapter titled "Infant Exposure and Infanticide" in *The Oxford Handbook of Childhood and Education in the Classical World*, ed. Grubbs and Parkin, p. 83f.

[50] *Gēs*, literally "earth," perhaps "dirt."

[51] Beck says more concisely "contractors."

[52] *Biaious praxeis*, possibly "compulsory actions." The word *biaios* primarily means "violent," and all of the translators have rendered this signification as something like "violent actions," although Schmidt notes that it has a secondary meaning of actions that are "forced" or "constrained." It is interesting that the preceding signification is tax collectors, as paying taxes might be seen as a sort of compulsory action as well, in the sense that it is something that you can be forced or compelled to do even if you don't want to.

[53] *Ichōrōn*, following Bara. Riley says that this is the "lymph," while Schmidt says "blood-serum."

[54] *Sinōn*, "injuries." Literally "hurts."

[55] *Kēlōn*, possibly "ruptures" or "hernias" (Bara, Riley).

[56] *Pathōn*, disorders of the soul or mind. Hellenistic philosophers tended to characterize *pathos* as a disease of the soul. Alternatively, "sufferings," "passions," "conditions," or "states."

[57] *Daimonismou*, demonic possession.

[58] *Kinaidias*, from the Latin *cinaedus*, which means "he who practices unnatural lust" or those with "unnatural vices," which seems to mean sodomy, or more specifically being a "catamite," which is the younger, passive partner in a pederastic relationship between two males, or in some instances a male prostitute. Riley translated the term simply as "homosexuality," although other scholars that have written on the figure of the *kinaidos* in Roman society argue that the term does not simply refer to homosexuality, but instead is used to refer those who were seen as social deviants as a result of frequently transgressing gender norms. See Williams, *Roman Homosexuality*, p. 209f. Since in some contexts this may also apply to females, "gender deviance" might be a good alternative translation for this signification. For a brief discussion on some of the themes surrounding sexuality in the astrological texts, see Barton, *Ancient Astrology*, p. 163f.

[59] *Akatharsias* generally refers to things that are "unclean," "dirty" or "impure," although it can also be applied to things that are "immoral" or "vile," especially in a sexual context, according to the BDAG lexicon.

water, or by strangulation,[60] or through imprisonment,[61] or from dysentery. And he causes falls on one's face.[62] He is the star of Nemesis, and of the diurnal sect. He is dark brown in color,[63] and astringent in taste.[64]

Jupiter / *Zeus*, the "Radiant One" (*Phaethōn*)

The star of Jupiter signifies the begetting of children, child-birth, desire, love, alliances,[65] knowledge,[66] friendship with great men, abundance,[67] payments,[68] large gifts, an abundance of profits,[69] justice,[70] authorities, governments,[71]

---

[60] *Anchonēs*, or alternatively by "hanging."

[61] *Desmōn* literally means "bonds" or "chains."

[62] Or perhaps more generally, falls upon the front of one's body, or falling forward. Later Valens contrasts this with Mars, which signifies falling backwards. In assigning planets to parts of the body, the *Michigan Papyrus* says that "of the neck, the forward part belongs to Saturn and the back to Mars," which perhaps is related to Valens' statement here. *Michigan Papyrus*, col. vi: 39–40, trans. Robbins, pp. 110–11.

[63] *Kastorizōn*. There has been some confusion surrounding this color association. The Greek word that Valens uses here literally means "castor-like." The problem, as Bara points out (p. 29, n. 8), is that it is not entirely clear whether Valens is referring to the animal, which is a dark-brown colored beaver, or to the plant, which is yellowish. This word is apparently unique to Valens. In his book of remedies, Thessalus of Tralles recommends the use of *castoreum* (*kastorion*) in his chapter on Saturn. See *Thessalos von Tralles*, ed. Friedrich, 2, 3, p. 215: 11. Irby-Massie and Keyser point out that this would have referred to "beaver musk," which was "widely used" at the time. Irby-Massie and Keyser, *Greek Science of the Hellenistic Era*, p. 101. If correct, then Valens' mention of Saturn's color as being "castor-like" would also likely mean that he was referring to the animal, and thus it would literally mean "beaver-like," or perhaps simply "dark brown." The fact that Valens refers to Saturn later in the *Anthology* (6, 3: 5) in a chapter on the colors of the planets as "dark" (*melana*) leads me to believe that this is indeed the correct interpretation. The same color is given for Saturn in Porphyry, *Introduction*, 46. Presumably this is because they both drew on Teucer of Babylon, although this is not clear since Saturn's color is curiously omitted in the Teucer text preserved by Rhetorius.

[64] For example, "sour."

[65] *Sustaseis*, "unions." The BDAG says "a group with common interests, gathering, union, association."

[66] The Greek word is *gnōsis*, from which we derive the term "gnostic."

[67] *Euporias*. More broadly the term means "ease" of doing something. It can also mean "advantages," "wealth," and "solutions of doubts or difficulties." Riley says "prosperity," which is also apt.

[68] *Opsōnia* has a range of meanings that all relate to the notion of being paid money for something, usually for services rendered. The primary lexical entry in the LSJ says "salary." Within this context it can also mean "pay," "allowance," "scholarship," "wages," "fee," etc.

[69] *Karpōn euphorias*, possibly "abundant crops," "fruits," or "produce." The Greek term literally means "fruit," but it can also be used more generally to refer to "returns" or "profits." The "fruit of one's labors," so to speak. It seems like Valens could be speaking either literally or metaphorically here, although I lean towards the latter.

[70] *Dikaiosunēn*, or "righteousness."

[71] *Politeias*, in agreement with Schmidt. Bara and Beck lean more towards the lexical entry

honors, heads of holy places,[72] arbitration of disputes, trusts,[73] inheritances, brotherhood, fellowship,[74] adoption, confirmation of good things, relief from bad things,[75] release from bonds,[76] freedom, entrustments,[77] wealth, stewardship.[78] Of the parts of the body, he is lord of the outer thighs, the feet (for which reason it also produces running in athletic contests). Internally, it is the lord of semen, the womb, the liver, parts on the right side of the body.[79] Of substances, he rules tin. He is of the diurnal sect, grey and mostly white in color, and sweet in taste.

Mars / *Arēs*, the "Fiery One" (*Pyroeis*)

The star of Mars signifies violence,[80] wars,[81] robbery, screams,[82] insolence,[83] adultery, taking away of one's possessions, banishment, exile, estrangement from one's parents, captivity, the rape of women,[84] abortions, sexual

---

"citizenship" and take the term to mean "participation in public affairs" (Bara) or "political participation" (Beck). Riley translates it as "officeholding."

[72] *Prostasias hierōn*, or "heads of temples." Beck gives a more general translation of "important religious positions."

[73] *Pisteis.* This word has a range of meanings that have to do with faith, belief, or trust in something. The term also has other meanings such as "confidence," "honesty," and "assurance." Bara and Beck both take the commercial sense of the term and translate it as "credit," while Schmidt translates it as "fidelity."

[74] *Koinōnian*, possibly "charities."

[75] Or "escape," "deliverance," and "release" from bad things.

[76] Being set free after having been tied up, restrained, or imprisoned in some way.

[77] *Parakatathēkēn.* The LSJ says "deposit of money or property entrusted to one's care."

[78] *Oikonomias.* The LSJ says "management of a household or family, husbandry, thrift."

[79] At the end of this sentence is another word, *odontōn*, which means "teeth." Pingree bracketed it as not belonging there, and other translators have subsequently omitted it.

[80] *Bias.* Or perhaps more broadly "acts of force."

[81] *Polemous.* More broadly it can also mean "battles" or "fights."

[82] Possibly "shouts," "shrieks," or "cries."

[83] *Hubreis*, in agreement with Schmidt. Holden translates this as "assault," while Bara and Beck translate the term simply as "excess," although this only seems to be part of the underlying meaning of the word. The term seems to mean "excessive acts" of violence, aggression or perhaps arrogance. In Classical Greece "it appears that it was felt to involve a kind of arrogant attitude accompanying excessively violent acts meant to bring shame or dishonor to a victim." Cole, "Greek Sanctions Against Sexual Assault," p. 98. A large part of the emphasis of the term is the intent to humiliate the victim on the part of the perpetrator.

[84] *Phthoras gunaikōn.* It actually says "ruination" (Schmidt), "corruption", or perhaps "seduction" (Bara) of women, although this may be a sort of euphemism for rape, which is Beck's interpretation. Later in the *Anthology* 5, 6: 96, Valens uses an example of a native who had Mars activated as a time-lord in the place of slaves along with Venus and the Moon, and in that year he apparently got himself into trouble in a foreign country after "ruining a young female servant" (*phtheiras paidiskēn*). Unfortunately this example doesn't really help to clarify the issue, as it seems that either interpretation is possible. Cole notes that there was no specific

intercourse, marriages,[85] loss of good things, lies, hopeless situations,[86] violent thefts, robbery,[87] plundering,[88] separations of friends,[89] anger,[90] fighting, verbal abuse,[91] hatred, lawsuits.[92] He also brings about violent murders, wounds,[93] and bloodshed; attacks of fevers, ulcers, skin eruptions,[94] inflammations; imprisonment, torture;[95] masculinity, perjury,[96] deception,[97] those who have much experience in wrongdoing;[98] and those who work with fire or iron, those

---

term for rape in ancient Greek, although there were several phrases that could be used to refer to the act indirectly under certain circumstances. She goes on to say that in some instances this occurs when the noun, in this case "corruption," is used together with an objective genitive that means "girls" or "women," which is true in this instance. The term used here would fall into the general category outlined by Cole for terms that are used in such a way that "the violence of the act is defined by its effect on the victim." Cole, "Greek Sanctions Against Sexual Assault," p. 98. It is worth noting that this Greek term is related to a term that is sometimes used to refer to the malefics in general, *phthoropoios*, which means "destruction-maker" or "destroyer."

[85] *Gamous* is the general Greek term for "marriages" or "weddings." Initially it seems out of place here, although later in the *Anthology*, Valens says that while Venus is a general significator of marriage for men, Mars is a general significator of marriage for women (*Anthology*, 2, 38: 57).

[86] *Kenas elpidas*, perhaps "hoping in vain."

[87] *Lēsteias*, or "piracy."

[88] *Sulēseis*. Riley has "looting."

[89] *Diakopas philōn*, literally "breaches of friends." It may simply mean "disputes between friends" (Bara) or "quarrels among friends" (Riley), or the full-fledged severance of ties between parties. Holden thinks it means "lovers' quarrels."

[90] *Orgēn*, or "wrath."

[91] *Loidopian*, following Riley. Alternatively, "insults" (Beck) or "cursing" (Holden).

[92] *Dikas*. Schmidt, Beck, and Bara all essentially translate as "lawsuits." Holden opts for the other sense of the word in translating as "punishment," which is one of the possible outcomes of the lawsuit. The notion of exacting "vengeance" through a judgment rendered follows along the same lines of thought.

[93] *Tomas*, following Holden. Literally "cuts." Beck thinks it means "mutilations," while Riley has "slashings."

[94] Pustules, blisters, etc.

[95] *Basanous*. Also possibly "torments" or "agony."

[96] *Epiorkian*. Swearing "a false oath" or "false swearing."

[97] *Planēn* is a term that means "cause to wander," and it is the same word that we get the term "planet" from, which means "wanderers" or "wandering stars." This notion of "wandering" or "straying" leads to other meanings such as "to lead astray," "mislead" or "deceive." I believe that this is the meaning that Valens had in mind, especially since the signification of "perjury" immediately precedes this one. The difference between Mars' style of deception and Saturn's seems to be that Saturn tries to passively hide or keep things secret, whereas Mars is more about active misdirection. To keep a "secret" is different than to actively "mislead" while under oath. Beck has "error," while Schmidt and Riley both say "wandering."

[98] *Presbeias epi kakois*. This is a difficult phrase that appears to have given every translator some trouble. Holden and Schmidt seem to be the closest to understanding the correct meaning, translating the phrase either literally as "seniority in bad things" (Holden) or more loosely as "excelling at villainy" (Schmidt). Aaron Cheak suggests "seasoned criminals."

who work with their hands,[99] and masons.[100] He brings about leaders and military service[101] and high-ranking officers, soldiers, sovereignty;[102] hunting, chasing, falling from heights or from four-footed animals, poor vision, apoplexy.[103] Of parts of the body he rules over the head, the buttocks, and the genitals. Internally, he rules the blood, the seminal passages, bile, the excretion of feces, the back portion of the individual, walking backwards,[104] and falling on one's back.[105] He also rules that which is hard and abrupt.[106] Of substances, he rules iron, and the regalia of clothing as a result of the Ram,[107] and wine and legumes. It is of the nocturnal sect, the color red, and pungent in taste.

Venus / *Aphroditē*, the "Light-Bringer" (*Phōsphoros*)

Venus is desire and love, and signifies mother and nurse.[108] She makes

---

[99] *Cheirotechnas*, or "handicraftsmen," "artisans," or "manufacturers."

[100] *Sklērourgous*, literally "those who work with hard materials." The LSJ says that this word may specifically refer to "one of a corps of masons in the Roman army."

[101] *Strateias*, or "military campaigns." How to interpret this cluster of military significations is a bit difficult, and the translators all seem to render them differently.

[102] *Hēgemoneias*, following Holden. Schmidt has "supremacy."

[103] *Apoplēxias*, internal bleeding from a hemorrhage or stroke.

[104] *Anapodismou*, following Schmidt, who points out that this is also the term astrologers use to refer to the retrograde motion of a planet.

[105] *Huptiasmou*, following Schmidt, because then it connects with Saturn's signification of falling on one's face. The lexical entry has something more along the lines of "lying on one's back."

[106] *Apotomon*, literally "cut off." Schmidt has "hard and severe."

[107] *Kosmou, himatiōn dia ton Krion*. The zodiacal sign Aries, which is called the Ram in Greek. The connection with clothing is presumably due to the associations between rams and wool. There are some grammatical issues with the Greek of this sentence, since Pingree put a comma between *kosmos* and *himatiōn* to separate them (the previous editor, Kroll, did not), but Riley and Holden agree that these two words are part of the same clause. Riley says "decoration of clothing," while Holden says "ornament of clothing." Schmidt says "iron and order, clothes because of Aries," although in his footnotes he points out that *kosmos* may metaphorically refer to "the honor or credit that one wears as an ornament," and that the clothes may refer to armor. I have taken this a step further in assuming that *kosmos* here refers to military regalia, which is a type of decoration or ornamentation. It may also be worth pointing out that Roman soldiers tended to wear red tunics that were made out of wool.

[108] *Trophon*. The term can also mean more generally one who "rears," "feeds" or "nourishes" the native. It was also listed as one of the significations of the Moon.

priesthoods,[109] public benefactors,[110] wearing of golden ornaments,[111] the wearing of crowns,[112] merriment,[113] friendships, companionship, the acquisition of additional property, purchasing of ornaments,[114] reconciliations for the good,[115] marriages, refined arts,[116] pleasant sounds, music-making, sweet singing, beauty of form,[117] painting, mixing of colors and embroidery, purple-dyeing[118] and

---

[109] *Hierōsunas.* Alternatively, "sacred offices" or "priestly rites."

[110] *Gumnasiarchias.* The word refers to a specific public official known as the *gumnasiarch*, a role that has a long and varied history in Greek, Hellenistic, and Roman cultures. The term *gumnasiarch* specifically refers to the "leader," "head" or "supervisor" of the gymnasium, which was a sort of cultural center in Greek cities. In the Hellenistic period the gymnasium became not just an athletic center, but also a center for the education of young people in the city, as well as a sort of country club for the affluent where one could take a bath, get a massage, or enjoy some refreshments. The *gumnasiarch* was a wealthy private citizen who paid for these civic amenities out of their own pocket when they assumed the public role as Head of the Gymnasium (*gumnasiarch*). The position came with not only a significant level of prestige for the individual, but also a good deal of praise from the city and its citizens for the *gymnasiarch*'s generosity. The emphasis here seems to be that this was a wealthy individual who shared their wealth in a way that directly benefited the community, thus my more general rendering of this signification as "public benefactors." For more information on the role of the *gymnasiarch* in Greco-Roman society, see Parsons, *City of the Sharp-Nosed Fish,* esp. p. 49.

[111] One of the entries in the LSJ indicates that this may be some sort of priestly title.

[112] *Stemmatēphorias.* Or "wreaths."

[113] *Euphrosunas.* Alternatively, "mirth," "good cheer," "glad thoughts," "festivities," etc.

[114] *Agorasmous.* Or "decorations."

[115] *Sunallagas epi to agathon,* following Schmidt and Beck. Others focus on the mercantile aspect of the term *sunallagē,* and translate the phrase as "dealings that turn out well" (Riley) or "agreements on favorable terms" (Holden).

[116] *Technas katharious.* The translators all render this signification differently. The phrase literally means something like "clean skills." Schmidt thinks it means "purification arts." Holden thinks it means something more like "employment in arts or crafts that one can work at without getting dirty." The term definitely has these primary meanings of "cleanliness" or "purity," but it also has other underlying connotations of "elegance" or "refinement," which leads Beck to translate it as "refined arts and crafts." Riley says "pure trades."

[117] *Eumorphias,* sometimes used to refer to someone having a beautiful outward appearance or body, but it was also sometimes used within the context of divination to refer to the "symmetrical" arrangement of the entrails. Within that context the "symmetry" or "good form" of the entrails was seen as a positive omen. The term might be translated more generally as "good form" or "beauty."

[118] There was a specific type of purple dye that was extracted from sea snails in the ancient world called Tyrian Purple. The dye was highly valued and very expensive, and it came to be associated with nobility and royalty. It was worn on the robes of the Ptolemaic kings and the Roman emperors, from which it gained the designation "imperial purple." Valens uses the imagery of attaining "the purple" at different places in the *Anthology* as an allusion to becoming royalty.

perfume making, both the inventors and also the masters of these (professions),[119] artistic or commercial works involving emeralds and precious stones, ivory-working. And those who spin gold thread, decorate with gold, haircutters, those who are fond of cleanliness and play,[120] she brings to pass within its own bounds or degrees of the zodiacal signs. And she grants the office of market overseer,[121] measures, weights, trades, shops, giving, receiving,[122] laughter, rejoicing, order,[123] aquatic animals.[124] And she gives assistance from royal women or relatives[125] and secures a remarkable reputation, when (Venus) cooperates in such matters.[126] Of parts of the body, she rules the neck,[127] face, lips, nose[128] and the front parts from the foot to the head, the parts of intercourse;[129] of the internal parts of the body, it rules the lungs. And Venus is also the nourishing of another who is capable

---

[119] Holden thinks that this refers to the people who do the actual designing and crafting in these areas, as well as those who oversee or direct the production. This may be right, although the first term that Valens uses for those who do the hands-on work seems kind of strange. The term is *propatoras*, which literally means something like "forefathers" or "first founder."

[120] *Philopaignious.* Following Schmidt. Or perhaps "fond of toys" according to LSJ, which Holden and Riley follow.

[121] *Agoranomias.* Alternately, "market clerk," "market supervisor," or "market inspector." This was a public official who supervised the *agora*, or public marketplace in a city. It was their duty to keep order in the marketplace, which involved regulating the price of food and goods, as well as inspecting weights and measures. Note the next two significations that Valens gives after this: "measures" and "weights."

[122] Or "gifts" and "receipts," which is how Schmidt renders it. Riley says "the giving and receiving <of gifts>."

[123] *Kosmon.* Or alternatively, "ornament," "decoration," or "dress." Note that this was also given as a signification for Mars, where it seemed to make more sense as "ornament," although here it is not as clear.

[124] *Thēras ex hugrōn.* The translators disagree over the interpretation of this phrase. It either means something like "hunting" things that live in water, or it means animals that live in the water or in the sea. Schmidt and Riley go with the former, saying "water-chases" (Schmidt) or "hunting in moist places" (Riley), while the others say "water animals" (Holden) or "aquatic animals" (Bara and Beck). Holden has an explanatory note pointing out that the Greek goddess Aphrodite was born from the sea, and that Venus is exalted in the sign of the Fishes (Pisces).

[125] Female relatives seem to be implied here rather than just relatives in general.

[126] The latter part of this sentence is a bit uncertain. Holden thinks that a word may be missing. Riley and Holden interpret the sentence as saying that Venus provides "high rank" or "exceptional fame" when the planet is connected with those matters in the birth chart, perhaps for example by being connected to the tenth place. My translation follows that interpretation.

[127] *Trachēlou.* This term also refers to the throat.

[128] Literally, the "organ of smell" or the "sense of smell."

[129] *Sunousias moriōn*, following Riley. Beck has "the union of the sexual organs."

of receiving, and of pleasure.[130] Of substances, she rules precious stones[131] and multi-colored adornments;[132] of produce, she rules the olive. She is of the nocturnal sect, the color white, and very oily in taste.[133]

Mercury / *Hermēs*, the "Twinkling One" (*Stilbōn*)

The star of Mercury signifies education, writings,[134] disputation,[135] speech,[136] brotherhood,[137] interpretation,[138] the office of Herald,[139] numbers, calculations,[140] geometry, commerce, youth, play,[141] theft,[142] community,[143]

---

[130] Riley renders this sentence a little differently, saying "It is a recipient of support from others and of pleasure."

[131] *Lithōn polutimōn*, or "very costly stones."

[132] Riley says "fancy jewelry."

[133] Holden says that while the Greek word means "very greasy," since Venus generally rules nice things "the reference must be to smooth, rich-tasting food."

[134] *Grammata*, or "letters."

[135] *Elenchon*, or "argumentation."

[136] *Logon (logos)*. The term *logos* is one of the most ambiguous words in the Greek language, and it has a wide range of different meanings. In this context it could also mean "logic" (Beck), "reasoning" (Riley), "language," "discourse," etc. There is some sense in which all of these are probably correct in a way, although I follow Schmidt and Holden in rendering the term as "speech." This comes with the caveat that this should not be thought of only as the mechanical act of speaking itself, but as "the understanding of the speaker which is conveyed through speech and shared with the listener." For more on this conceptualization of *logos* see the essay "Speech, its Strength and its Weaknesses" in Klein, *Lectures and Essays*, pp. 361–374.

[137] *Adelphotēta*, in the sense of a family of like-minded individuals. For example, the term is used in the New Testament to refer to a "fellowship of believers."

[138] *Hermēneian*. Alternately, "explanation," "expression," or "translation."

[139] *Kērukeian*. Holden renders the term more generally as just "being a herald," while Riley and Beck both translate it as "embassies." A *kērux* was a messenger who conveyed announcements and proclamations to the public from high-ranking officials. In mythology, Hermes was the herald or messenger of the gods. The office mentioned here by Valens was basically the "town crier," although they possessed other duties and obligations as well. Interestingly, heralds often carried a staff, and this is where the caduceus became associated with Mercury.

[140] *Psēphon*. This term literally refers to a type of small stone or pebble, although the stone was used for various things that involved calculating or counting numbers. The notion of calculation or counting seems to be primary, although because of this the term also came to be associated with "voting" as well.

[141] *Paignia*. Alternatively "sports" or "games."

[142] *Klopēn*. Can also refer to secret acts that involve stealth, fraud, or surprise. Although this connection is nowhere stated explicitly, this signification seems reminiscent of the myth of the infant god Hermes stealing Apollo's cattle under the cover of night.

[143] *Koinotēta*, or "sharing in common," and that which has a "common" or "universal quality," according to the LSJ. Riley says "association."

messages,[144] service, profit,[145] discoveries,[146] following,[147] contest,[148] wrestling, declamation,[149] sealing,[150] sending   messages,[151] weighing,[152] suspense,[153] testing,[154] hearing, versatility.[155] He is the bestower of critical thinking and judgment,[156] lord of brothers and of younger children, and author of all things pertaining to the market and the craft of banking. Properly speaking, he makes

---

[144] *Angellian*. Riley translates this more generally as "communication." The word can also mean "news," "announcements," or "proclamations."

[145] *Kerdos*, or more generally "gain."

[146] *Heuremata*, or "inventions."

[147] *Akolouthian*, or "attendance." This seems to be in the sense of following someone or being an attendant to someone rather than leading, in the same way that Mercury follows after or is an attendant to the Sun. This leads to other meanings associated with this term such as "conformity" and "obedience," the latter of which Riley opts for in his translation. Holden says "escort."

[148] *Athlēsin*. Usually in an athletic sense, which leads Riley to translate this as "sport" and Holden as "athletics."

[149] *Phōnaskian*. A type of vehement oratory or rhetorical display.

[150] *Sphagizesthai* has the sense of putting a seal or mark on a letter in order to assure the recipient of its authenticity. This was necessary sometimes for important business such as sending legal documents. For a brief discussion see Parsons, *City of the Sharp-Nosed Fish*, p. 126. This signification goes along with the following one, which has to do with sending a message or letter. Associated with the present term are also more metaphorical notions that have to do with "confirming" or "certifying" something by putting the "stamp of approval" on it. Riley has "certification," while Holden has "signing."

[151] *Epistellein*, or "sending letters."

[152] *Histanai*, in the sense of weighing one thing against another.

[153] *Kremasthai*, literally, being "hung up" or "suspended." It can also have a metaphorical meaning of "to be in suspense." Schmidt has "being suspended." Riley thinks this and the previous signification form a pair that mean "weighing and measuring."

[154] *Dokimazein*. This word may instead mean "approving" or "sanctioning" something after having tested it. It is tempting to interpret it that way here because then it would be the third in a series of related significations that would go something like: (1) weighing, (2) being in suspense, (3) being approved after having been scrutinized. Riley seems to think that this has to do with the "testing of coinage" in particular, while Schmidt translates it as "scrutinizing."

[155] *Poikileuesthai*. The term means something like "many colored," which leads to metaphors having to do with diversity, variety, and complexity.

[156] *Dianoias kai phronēseōs*. These are important philosophical terms that have a long history. The translators all largely disagree on how to render them. Schmidt translates them as "intellect and practical wisdom." Beck says "critical thinking and judgment." Holden says "thought and wisdom." Riley says "forethought and intelligence."

temple builders, modelers, sculptors, doctors, teachers,[157] lawyers, orators,[158] philosophers, architects, musicians, diviners, sacrificers, augurs,[159] dream interpreters, braiders, weavers, those who are methodical,[160] and those who are in charge of managing wars or strategic actions, and those who utilize paradoxes and craftiness in calculations or false reasoning,[161] those who are

---

[157] *Grammatikous*, or "grammarians." This word is a bit ambiguous, as it can either refer to a type of "teacher," especially one who focuses on grammar and literature, or it can refer to a "scholar," especially one who focuses on textual analysis and criticism. Schmidt translates the term as "writers," Riley as "secretaries," and Holden says "scribes," although he has a footnote expressing uncertainty and saying that it could mean other things like "specialists in grammar" or "grammar-school teachers." Bara and Beck have "teachers of grammar," which I think is closer to the correct interpretation here. In Greco-Roman Egypt, a *grammatikos* was a relatively well-paid teacher, educator, or tutor, sometimes publicly employed by the city. Today this would be the equivalent of a high school or secondary school teacher, focusing on the teaching of grammar and the classic works of literature such as Homer. Some private correspondences from a public teacher of literature named Lollianos survive from Oxyrhynchus, and they are discussed briefly in Parsons, *City of the Sharp-Nosed Fish*, pp. 73–75, with additional information about the *grammatikoi* and their social status on pp. 137–143. Learning under a "grammarian" was the second in three stages of traditional Greek education (Riggs, *The Oxford Handbook of Roman Egypt*, pp. 528–532). It is worth noting that the third and final stage involved studying under an orator (*rhētōr*), which Valens mentions as another signification of Mercury only two words later. I believe that this helps to confirm that the present signification primarily refers to the specific role of the grammarian as part of the teaching profession.

[158] *Rhētoras*, or "public speakers." In the earlier periods, this would simply refer to an "orator," which is how most translators have interpreted this word, although in the later periods a *rhētōr* was a specific teaching position – a "teacher of rhetoric." A *rhētōr* was ranked above a *grammatikos* in their pay scale and the age of the students they worked with, representing the third and last phase in education. Since this is the second signification that Valens gives after *grammatikos*, it seems to affirm that it is referring to a type of teacher rather than just a public speaker or orator, although those meanings should be kept in mind as well since they were the specific focus of this type of teacher.

[159] Augury is a type of divination that involves interpreting the flight and movement of birds as having symbolic significance.

[160] *Methodikous*. Or "those who are systematic."

[161] *Epicheirountas ta paradoxa kai methodika dia psēphōn ē paralogismōn*. This sentence gave all of the translators a hard time, and they all translate it differently. Holden suggests that there may be an issue with the Greek text, and the final word *paralogismōn* should perhaps be two separate words, *para logismōn*. Riley seems to have also thought that this was the case, and he translated the sentence as "those undertaking any unusual, systematic work in accounting or with reasoning." This seems plausible, although it seems a bit redundant since Valens already talked about those who are "methodical" earlier in the text. The alternative translation that I have in the body of the text here follows the same interpretation as Bara and Beck, who say "those who use paradox and craftiness in calculations and false arguments." The keyword here either way is "tricky." The sentence either refers to people who attempt to unravel "tricky problems," or it refers to what we might call "tricky people."

strong performers[162] or mime-actors,[163] making their livelihood from display, while still wandering and roaming and unstable;[164] and those with knowledge of the heavens or those who seek to become knowledgeable,[165] undertaking the marvelous work with pleasure and contentment, for the sake of the honor and benefit it brings.[166] For this star holds the power of many pursuits, granting occupations in accordance with the variations of the zodiacal signs or the interweavings of the different configurations of the stars; for some it gives knowledge, while for others, brokerage;[167] service for some, while it procures trade or teaching for others; and for some agriculture or temple-keeping[168]

---

[162] *Ischuropaiktas.* Following Schmidt. Holden thinks that this and the following signification do not make sense and that the manuscript has become corrupted. He uses the literal translation of "strong players," although he says that this is meaningless. Riley thinks it means "weight lifters." Bara appears to think it means something like stage magicians or illusionists (*les prestidigitateurs*). Beck has no idea and skips this signification.

[163] *Mimōdous.* In the ancient world mime was a genre of stage performance that involved imitative movements and gestures, usually in the form of dramatic character sketches. Some mimes were spoken, while others were sung. So, this is sort of like a stage actor in a musical. The lexical entry for this word in the LSJ says mime-singer, which is essentially how Schmidt renders it, although Holden says that he disagrees with the conjecture of the original editor of Valens' manuscript here, Kroll, and thinks the Greek should instead say "choir-singers."

[164] I have interpreted this sentence as if it is the performers who are earning their living from display while wandering around, although the last three significations may be part of a separate set that just refer in general to those who wander, roam, and are unstable. Of the other translators, Schmidt probably best renders this alternative interpretation, although he gives it a more negative slant, saying "and furthermore through deception and wandering and confusion…" Beck just says "vagrancy, and unsettled conditions."

[165] Astrologers and students of astrology.

[166] The translators have all rendered this sentence about the experience and motivation for studying astrology differently. Most of them have a slightly negative slant on it, partially arising from relying on the LSJ entry for the otherwise largely undocumented word *endoxokopountas,* which is interpreted there as "covet fame." I don't think that Valens would frame the motivation for studying astrology as simply being for the purpose of getting famous and wealthy, as he shows quite a bit of reverence for the subject in other parts of the Anthology. As a result of that I've focused on the more general meanings of *endoxos* and *ōphelia* here as relating to "honor" and "benefit." I followed Bara and Beck primarily in terms of how they worked out some of the tricky grammar in this sentence.

[167] *Propōlēn.* The word refers to someone who "negotiates a sale," or who "buys for another." Schmidt says "a negotiator," which also makes sense. Valens is contrasting the side of Mercury that has to do with knowledge in the first signification and the mercantile side in the second signification.

[168] *Neōkorias.* The term literally means something like "temple-sweeper," although the role and purpose associated with the designation changed over time, so that the Hellenistic and Roman office of the *neōkoros* is usually rendered as "temple-guardian" or "temple-warden." It was generally a type of temple official who was distinct from the priests and priestesses, but still complementary to them in some way. They generally seem to have had the duty of taking care of the temple and its property. In a detailed paper titled "Neokoroi in the Greek World,"

or public <office>;[169] moreover, for some it grants the ability to exercise authority or leasing rentals or labor contracting or rhythmic performance[170] or managing public services or even body-guarding[171] or wearing the linen robes of the gods[172] or bestowing the pomp of powerful men. It brings about all the irregularities in our fortunes and many distractions from our goals,[173] and even more so when this star is upon signs or degrees ruled by malefics, in which case things may even take a turn for the worse. Of the parts of the body, it rules the hands, the shoulders, the fingers, the joints, the belly, the hearing,[174] the

---

Marijana Ricl discusses some of the themes associated with this position, which helps to clarify why Mercury was associated with it. She says that *neōkoroi* were "considered as attendants of a deity or a priest," (p. 13) which makes sense since one of Mercury's basic significations is "following" or "attendance" (*akolouthian*), and Mercury is commonly said to be one of the attendants of the Sun. Elsewhere Ricl says that "their basic responsibility was to reside at or near the sanctuary at all times," (p. 14) which again makes sense from an astronomical standpoint since Mercury is often noted as the planet that never gets too far away from the Sun. Later Ricl lists the duties associated with the office of the *neōkoros*: "The activities they performed there fall under the following headings: 1. financial management (income and expenditure); 2. policing activities for the protection of the sacred property and the inviolability of the shrine; 3. administrative and secretarial duties; 4. organization of external manifestations of the cult" (pp. 14–15). These clearly tie in with a number of Mercury's other significations, and in some instances help to clarify some of the symbolism that Valens associates with Mercury.

[169] This is a restoration by Kroll, the first editor of the text. The Greek manuscript just says "public," which doesn't quite make sense, so he suggested the general term *archas* had been omitted, which means "office" or "magistracy" in this context. It may be worth noting that the preceding signification, which was the role of the *neōkoros* or "temple-keeper," was an office that was sometimes determined by a public vote or lottery. It is possible that either (1) this signification then is meant to go together with the previous one to specify a publicly elected temple-keeper, or that (2) some of Mercury's previous significations having to do with calculating or tallying things are extended here symbolically to other offices that are subject to a public vote.

[170] *Epideixin* [*ē*] *rhuthmikēn*, following Riley, and assuming that the combining of these two words into the same clause by the editors was correct. This may refer to musical performances, or perhaps he is describing the ancient equivalent of a modern music conductor. Evidently this type of conducting was known as *cheironomy*, and it involved the use of hand movements. Perhaps not surprisingly, we learn towards the end of this list of significations that Mercury rules the hands. This also seems to make sense because then it fits into the string of significations in this sentence that have to do with having authority over or directing someone.

[171] *Doruphorias*, literally, "spear-bearing." Acting as a guard or protector over someone. This combines earlier notions of being an attendant and the idea of having authority over someone. This is also the same term used for a technical astrological concept known as "spear-bearing" (*doruphoria*).

[172] Holden points out that this refers to priestly robes.

[173] Largely following Schmidt, who says "It will make all the irregularities in our fortunes and frequently sidetrack us from our goals." Riley interprets it a bit differently, saying "As for the end result—Mercury will make everything capricious in outcome and quite disturbed."

[174] *Akoēs*, or perhaps just "the ears."

windpipe,[175] the intestines,[176] the tongue. Of substances, it is lord of copper[177] and all coinage, giving, taking: for the god is common.

Benefics and Malefics

As we can see from Valens' list of significations, each planet has a large range of different meanings. Some of these meanings are derived from properties that are thought to be intrinsic or natural qualities unique to the planet, while others arise as a result of the placement and condition of the planet in a given chart. In what follows, we will discuss some different qualities and properties associated with each of the planets, as well as some different considerations for determining planetary condition, which can modify the expression of a planet's significations in different ways.

One of the most fundamental distinctions in Hellenistic astrology is the classification of the planets into two categories, known as "benefic" and "malefic." Benefic and malefic are usually seen as intrinsic qualities that are natural to certain planets, although sometimes different planets can be said to attain such status functionally in a chart due to other conditions. The second-century CE skeptic, Sextus Empiricus, gives a concise overview:

> as to the stars, they say that some of them are "beneficent," some "maleficent," and some "common"; thus Jupiter and Venus are beneficent, but Mars and Saturn maleficent, while Mercury is "common" since it is beneficent when with beneficent stars, but maleficent when with maleficent. But others believe that the same stars are at one time beneficent and at another maleficent according to their varying positions; for either by reason of the sign, or by reason of the configurations of the other stars, the maleficent star is not entirely maleficent, nor is the beneficent entirely beneficent.[178]

---

[175] *Artērias.* There is some disagreement here. In earlier Greek authors, *artēria* meant "windpipe" or trachea, which is how Holden and Schmidt translate it, but in later authors it came to mean something closer to the modern meaning of "arteries," which is how Bara and Beck translate the term. I tend to think that the windpipe would make more sense here given Mercury's connection with speaking and oratory, although the "arteries" could still be relevant to the extent that they were thought to transmit or convey something from one part of the body to another.

[176] *Enterōn,* or possibly the "guts" (Schmidt) or "bowels" (Holden).

[177] *Chalkou.* There is an issue here, as this could mean either "copper," or its alloys "bronze" or "brass." Bara, Riley, and Schmidt translate it as "copper," Beck translates it as "bronze," and Holden translates it as "brass." Roman coins of this nature were originally primarily copper, but as time went on they tended to shift towards the alloys. The fundamental meaning here should still be copper, though.

[178] Sextus Empiricus, *Against the Professors,* 5: 29–30, trans. Bury, pp. 335–7.

As a general classification, Venus and Jupiter are said to be the two benefic planets, while Mars and Saturn are the two malefic planets. Mercury is said to be common or neutral, and capable of acting as a functional benefic or malefic depending on whether it is more closely associated with benefic or malefic planets in a given chart. The Sun and Moon are typically said to be neutral, although in certain conditions they can have functional qualities that are more positive or negative for certain things. We will return to the Sun, Moon, and Mercury later, but for now our focus will be placed on the planets that are naturally said to be benefics and malefics.

The term "benefic" is derived from the Greek word *agathopoios*, which means "good-maker," while the term "malefic" is derived from the Greek term *kakopoios*, which means "bad-maker." The malefics are also sometimes called *phthoropoios*, which means "destroyer" or "destruction-maker." At the most basic level, the distinction between benefic and malefic planets exists in order to set up a binary system with a basic set of contrasts between opposing qualities, especially with respect to the subjective human experience of positive or negative events. The Stoic Chrysippus helps to establish why such a distinction would be necessary:

> There is absolutely nothing more foolish than those who think that there could have been goods without the coexistence of evils. For since goods are opposite to evils, the two must necessarily exist in opposition to each other and supported by a kind of opposed interdependence. And there is no such opposite without its matching opposite. For how could there be perception of justice if there were no injustices? What else is justice, if not the removal of injustice? Likewise, what appreciation of courage could there be except through the contrast with cowardice? Of moderation, if not from immoderation? How, again, could there be prudence if there were not imprudence opposed to it? Why do the fools not similarly wish that there were truth without there being falsity? For goods and evils, fortune and misfortune, pain and pleasure, exist in just the same way: they are joined to each other head to head, as Plato said. Remove one and you remove both.[179]

In Hellenistic astrology, the benefic/malefic distinction serves a similar purpose, and while this is not the only area in which contrasts are used in order to establish significations, as we will see later, it is one of the most fundamental.

---

[179] Quoted in Aulus Gellius, *Attic Nights*, 7.1.1–13, from *The Hellenistic Philosophers*, trans. Long and Sedley, vol. 1, 54Q, p. 329.

The basic principle is that if there is an event or circumstance that should be signified by something in a chart, then there must be something that also represents the opposite. Typically when discussing events or circumstances that human beings find preferable or unpreferable, especially if there are moral or qualitative undertones, this falls under the general domain of the benefics and malefics.

The observation that in the night sky, Venus and Jupiter appear as bright white stars, while Mars appears dark and red, and Saturn dark and brown, was probably at the core of this distinction originally. Thus it sets up an observable contrast between two groups of planets, with one set appearing brighter and the other set appearing darker. This then elicits a light/dark analogy, which is then extended into the realm of other contrasts or polarities between light and dark, such as good and bad, positive and negative, virtue and vice, constructive and destructive, and so on.

Here are some basic contrasts that we can see already in Valens' list of significations that are connected with the benefic/malefic distinction:

> VENUS signifies love while MARS signifies hatred.
> JUPITER signifies freedom, while SATURN signifies imprisonment.
> VENUS signifies the acquisition of additional property while MARS signifies the taking away of one's possessions.
> JUPITER signifies wisdom, while SATURN signifies ignorance.
> JUPITER signifies the begetting of children and childbirth, while MARS signifies abortion and SATURN signifies childlessness.
> VENUS signifies marriage, while SATURN signifies those who are unmarried or widowed.
> VENUS signifies friendship and JUPITER alliances, while MARS signifies separations of friends and war.

Many other such contrasts could be drawn. The point is that this distinction allows us to begin to establish the significations of the planets by setting up binary pairs that are capable of representing both that which is signified and its opposite.

The distinction between benefic and malefic planets was inherited from the earlier Mesopotamian tradition.[180] This makes it one of the most fundamental early concepts that many of the other techniques were developed around or predicated on.

---

[180] Rochberg, "Benefic and Malefic Planets in Babylonian Astrology."

Special Roles of the Benefics and Malefics

The benefics and malefics also play special roles in the chart, because they were conceptualized as having the ability to influence other planets in positive or negative ways, thus conveying some of their benefic or malefic tendencies on those other planets. This ability to influence other planets sometimes occurs simply as a result of proximity or affiliation with the benefics or malefics in the chart, although it can also occur through a special set of rules known as conditions of bonification and maltreatment.

From a practical standpoint, one of the important underlying principles here is the notion that each planet in the chart wants to signify the things that it is naturally associated with. These significations are then affirmed or denied, as well as modified for better or worse, based on the condition of the planet in the chart, and this is where the benefics and malefics come in. Generally speaking, benefics have the special power to affirm, stabilize, or improve the significations of other planets in the chart. Conversely, the malefics have the power to negate, destabilize, or corrupt the significations of other planets in the chart. Another way to look at this is that the benefics have the special power to say "yes" to things in the chart, while the malefics have the special power to say "no" to things.

For example, Venus naturally wants to signify the topic of marriage in the chart. Therefore, the condition of Venus in the chart will indicate, among other things, whether the native is likely to get married at some point in their life. If Venus is connected with Jupiter, then Jupiter will be able to affirm the significations of Venus and say "yes" to them, meaning that the person will get married at some point in their life. Conversely, if Venus is unfavorably connected with Mars or Saturn in the chart then the malefics would have the special power to negate or say "no" to the topic of marriage, meaning that the person could potentially never find a partner or get married.

In addition to affirming or denying the topics that other planets want to signify in a chart, the benefics and malefics also have the power to alter the quality of the expression of the significations of other planets, for better or worse. Within this context the benefics have the tendency to improve the quality of things, while the malefics have the ability to corrupt or degrade the quality of a planet's significations. For example, if benefics are associated with the parts of the chart that signify friends, then the native may find that their friends are generally good people who play a positive role in the native's life; conversely, if malefics are associated with the regions that signify friends, then the native's friends may end up being detrimental people who play a negative role in the native's life. There are many different ways that this can work out depending on the specific placements involved, but the general point is that the benefics and malefics can not only affirm or deny what other planets want to signify, they can also alter the quality of the significations as well, for better or worse. The special powers of the benefics and malefics and the specific rules for determining what relationships they have with other planets in the chart will be discussed later in the section on the conditions of bonification and maltreatment.

Benefic and Malefic as a Spectrum

Most of the discussion about the benefic/malefic distinction is couched in terms of the extreme ends of a spectrum. However, that is not to say that the benefic planets were always thought to indicate purely positive situations, or that the malefic planets were always thought to provide purely negative significations. These were seen as natural tendencies that the planets were inclined towards; however, under certain circumstances the benefics were thought to be capable of indicating negative or challenging things, while the malefics were thought to be capable of indicating positive or constructive things. Whether a planet will express significations on the more positive or negative end of the spectrum largely depends on its condition in a given chart, and there are some considerations that specifically alter how a planet functions in terms of the benefic/malefic spectrum. The concept of "sect" (*hairesis*) is of primary importance in determining whether a planet is functioning in a more positive or negative manner in a chart, and will be discussed later in this chapter, although there are also other relevant modifying factors that are related to a planet's position in the chart according to sign, aspect, and house.

Valens discusses this point explicitly a few times in the *Anthology*, and early in the first book he outlines the specific interpretive principle that is associated with it:

> The benefic stars which are appropriately and favorably situated bring about their proper effects according to their own nature and the nature of their sign, with the aspects and conjunctions of each star being blended. If however they are unfavorably situated, they are indicative of reversals. In the same way even the malefic stars, when they are operative (*chrēmatistikos*) in appropriate places in their own sect, are bestowers of good and indicative of the greatest positions and success; when they are inoperative (*achrēmatistikos*), they bring about disasters and accusations.[181]

The general principle here is that when the planets are well-situated in a chart, their positive significations tend to manifest more readily. The benefics become

---

[181] Valens, *Anthology*, 1, 1: 44–45, trans. Riley, p. 2, slightly modified.

even more benefic, while the malefics tend to have their more constructive significations accentuated and their negative ones diminished. However, if the planets are poorly-situated, then even benefics can signify impediments or reversals, while the malefics can have their negative significations exacerbated and may become more harmful.

This is an overarching idea that we will see demonstrated repeatedly once we start looking at some of the different considerations for planetary condition, but for now it is important to understand that the benefic/malefic distinction sets up an idealized spectrum with positive and negative poles. The benefics and malefics have a tendency to have their significations fall more on one end of the spectrum than the other, although they also have a range of significations in the middle and opposite end of the spectrum that can manifest under certain conditions. Like many things in Hellenistic astrology, it is first important to establish the extremes of the spectrum before fleshing out the nuances that lie in between.

Mercury, the Sun, and the Moon

Mercury often plays a vacillating role in Hellenistic astrology. It can go in either direction, adopting a certain position based on its condition in a given chart. That is to say, Mercury is thought to be intrinsically neutral, although it is highly impressionable and in most cases tends to adapt to whatever it is most closely associated with or in proximity to in a given chart. Within the context of the benefic/malefic distinction, Mercury is often said to adopt the role of a benefic in a chart when it is closely associated with one of them. This can occur in different ways, for example by being placed in close proximity to a benefic in the same sign of the zodiac, or by being configured to them through one of the recognized aspects, or being ruled by one as a result of being located in the domicile of a benefic. Conversely, it will adopt the role of a malefic when closely associated with the malefics in a chart. This impressionable tendency of Mercury to adopt a given role depending on which planets it is more closely associated with is something that is encountered a number of times in the Hellenistic system, as we will see in later chapters.

There is some disagreement by the different Hellenistic authors about the classification of the Sun and Moon in terms of benefic/malefic status. Some sources consider both luminaries to be benefic in nature, while other sources consider them to be neutral. For example, Rhetorius lists the Sun and Moon as benefic.[182] Hephaestio follows Ptolemy in listing the Moon as a benefic, while

---

[182] Rhetorius, *Compendium*, 2.

Mercury and the Sun are said to be moderate or neutral (*mesoi*).[183] From a practical standpoint, it is probably best to treat these three planets as essentially neutral for most purposes.

Sect

One of the most fundamental concepts in Hellenistic astrology is the distinction between day and night charts, which is known as "sect." From a practical standpoint, sect is a qualitative distinction that primarily alters the way that the benefics and malefics function in a given chart. It becomes a large part of the reason why the benefics are not always seen as functioning in fully positive ways, as well as why malefics are not always viewed as entirely negative. Sect is the primary criterion that the Hellenistic astrologers would use in order to determine where each planet falls on the benefic/malefic spectrum in a given chart. Despite its importance in the Hellenistic tradition, sect is one of the major concepts that did not survive into modern astrology, and it is only in the past two decades that it has started to come into use again in the astrological tradition.

Sect of the Planets

According to this concept, the planets are divided into two teams, factions, or "sects," from the Greek word *hairesis*. There is a day or diurnal team of planets which is led by the Sun, and a night or nocturnal team of planets which is led by the Moon. As leaders of their respective sects, each luminary is sometimes referred to as the "sect light." The remaining planets are then divided between the two teams, with one benefic and one malefic being assigned to each. Jupiter and Saturn are assigned to the diurnal sect, while Venus and Mars are assigned to the nocturnal sect.

Mercury is neutral, and is usually said to be capable of joining either team depending on which one he is most closely associated with in a given chart. According to Ptolemy and Porphyry, Mercury joins the diurnal sect when he is a morning star, by rising before the Sun on the day of the native's birth, while he joins the nocturnal sect when he is an evening star, by setting after the Sun on the day of the native's birth.[184] However, there may have been disagreements about how to determine the sect of Mercury in a given chart, since Valens seems to use a different rule for Mercury, saying that it will join the sect of whatever planet

---

[183] Hephaestio, *Apotelesmatika*, 1, 2: 9.

[184] Ptolemy, *Tetrabiblos*, 1, 7: 1; Porphyry, *Introduction*, 4. It is not clear if Porphyry is accurately conveying the views of Antiochus here, or if he is instead following Ptolemy. The parallel passage in Antiochus, *Summary*, 1 (CCAG 8, 3, p. 112: 12–13), almost makes it sound as if Antiochus thought that Mercury adopts the sect of whatever planet it is most closely configured with in a given chart.

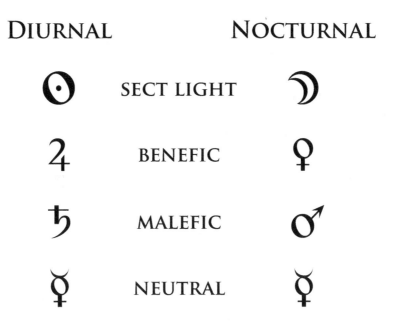

Figure 7.1 - Sect of the Planets

rules the bounds or terms (*horia*) that it falls in, which is a concept that we will discuss later.[185] Elsewhere, the *Michigan Papyrus* says that "Mercury belongs to the Moon by night and to the Sun by day."[186] Practically speaking, Mercury's condition does not seem to make a major difference, as sect is primarily used as a modifying factor for the benefic and malefic planets, although this may be an area that requires more research.

Determining Day versus Night
One of the first considerations in any Hellenistic chart interpretation is to determine the overall sect of the chart by ascertaining whether the person was born during the day or at night. If a person was born during the day, then we would say that they have a diurnal chart, while if they were born at night we would say that they have a nocturnal chart.

---

[185] Valens, *Anthology*, 3, 5: 2. Rhetorius (*Compendium*, 2) says that Mercury is neutral with respect to sect.

[186] *Michigan Papyrus*, col. viii: 19, trans. Robbins, p. 112.

The texts generally do not specify exactly when a chart becomes diurnal or nocturnal, but a good rule to follow is that it becomes a day chart as soon as the Sun reaches and then rises above the exact degree of the Ascendant, since the Ascendant represents the eastern horizon where the Sun rises each morning. Conversely, it becomes a night chart when the Sun sets and then sinks below the exact degree of the Descendant, since the Descendant represents the western horizon where the Sun sets each evening. Thus, if the Sun is in the top half of the chart, anywhere above the exact degrees of the Ascendant-Descendant axis, then it is a day chart, whereas if the Sun is in the bottom half of the chart, anywhere below the exact degrees of the Ascendant-Descendant axis, then it is a night chart.

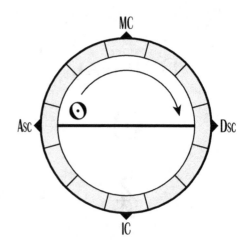

Figure 7.2 - Day Chart

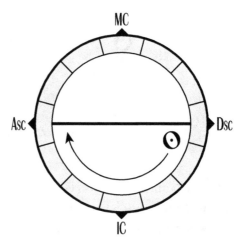

Figure 7.3 - Night Chart

Due to the nature of twilight, there is still some ambiguity and debate over the precise moment that a chart switches between diurnal and nocturnal. Just as the sky starts getting bright before the Sun reaches the exact degree of the Ascendant in the morning, it is also still bright for a certain period after the Sun has sunk below the degree of the Descendant in the evening. Thus, there may be some span of degrees below the horizon where the Sun either starts or ceases to be operative in making it daytime, although the precise establishment of this range for practical purposes is still a matter of ongoing research.

Sect as a Qualitative Factor

Sect is primarily a qualitative factor that alters the benefic or malefic character of a planet in a chart, rather than a quantitative factor that alters how strong or prominent a planet is.

Each planet prefers to be in a chart that matches its own sect, and when this is the case, the Hellenistic astrologers would sometimes use terms that describe the planets as being happier or "rejoicing" (*chairein*). When a planet finds itself in a chart that matches its preferred sect it is said to be "of the sect" or "belonging to the sect" (*tēs haireseōs*). For example, when the diurnal planet Jupiter finds itself in a day chart, it would be "of the sect." Benefic planets become more benefic when they are of the sect, such as when Jupiter is in a day chart or Venus is in a night chart. Their positive significations come to the forefront and are emphasized. Malefic planets become less malefic when they are of the sect, such as when Saturn is in a day chart or Mars is in a night chart. Their negative significations are suppressed, and their more positive or constructive significations are brought out.

On the other hand, the planets can be characterized as unhappy or can even become angry when they are in a chart that does not match their preferred sect. When a planet finds itself in a chart that is the opposite of its preferred sect, it is said to be "contrary to the sect" (*para tēn hairesin*). At one point Valens frames this contrast in terms of whether the planet has a "familiar or foreign relation to the sect."[187] Benefics become less benefic when they are contrary to the sect, such as when Jupiter is in a night chart or Venus is in a day chart. Their positive significations are suppressed, and while still moderately positive, they are not as inclined towards doing good as they otherwise would be. Malefics become even more malefic when they are contrary to the sect, such as when Saturn is in a night chart or Mars is in a day chart. The negative significations of the malefics become exacerbated, and they act in a manner that is more problematic and potentially destructive.

This distinction sets up a spectrum for the benefics and malefics that changes depending on whether they are placed in a day or night chart. In a day chart the most positive end of the benefic spectrum is represented by Jupiter, while the most negative end of the malefic spectrum is represented by Mars; Venus and Saturn fall towards the middle or more moderate part of the spectrum. Conversely, in a night chart, the most positive end of the benefic spectrum is represented by Venus, while the most negative end of the malefic spectrum is represented by Saturn; Jupiter and Mars fall in the middle or moderate segment of the spectrum.

Firmicus Maternus delineates the planets differently depending on the sect of the chart. His interpretation of Saturn in the eighth house provides a clear example of this:

---

[187] Valens, *Anthology*, 7, 2: 2.

DAY CHART

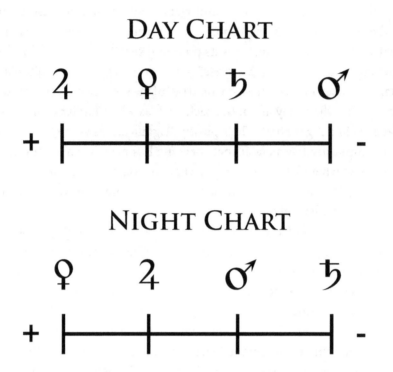

NIGHT CHART

Figure 7.4 - Sect as a Spectrum

Saturn in the eighth house, if by day, allots an increase in income over a period of time. If he is in the domicile or terms of Mars, he indicates for some an inheritance from the death of strangers. But if he is in this place by night the inheritance will be lost.[188]

Note that the interpretation of Saturn in the eighth by day is quite positive, since Saturn is a diurnal planet that prefers to be in day charts, but in a night chart the predicted outcome becomes distinctly negative, because then Saturn is contrary to the sect. We find a similar modification of the interpretation of Jupiter in the tenth house in Firmicus based on the sect of the chart:

Jupiter in the tenth house (that is, the MC) by day makes heads of public businesses, leaders of important states, men on whom great honors are conferred by the people, anxious to be conspicuous for popularity. They always enjoy a good living. Some carry on the affairs of great men

---

[188] Firmicus, *Mathesis*, 3, 2: 16–17, trans. Bram, p. 77.

and emperors; others receive rewards and prizes throughout their lives. [...] But if Jupiter is in the tenth house by night, he makes the natives honorable in character but easily cheated, and their inheritance is often quickly wasted.[189]

Here Firmicus' interpretation of Jupiter in the tenth in a day chart is extremely positive, but then when it switches to a night chart there are still some moderately positive things, but ultimately the delineation becomes more pessimistic. This principle is similarly applied to the rest of the benefics and malefics, depending on whether they are located in a day or night chart, and it is one of the interpretive principles that all of the Hellenistic astrologers seem to have applied quite consistently.

Identifying the Most Positive and Negative Planet

From a practical standpoint, one of the most useful things about sect as a technique is that it makes it easy to quickly identify the most positive and negative planets in a chart. Generally speaking, the most positive planet in a day chart is Jupiter, while the most positive planet in a night chart is Venus. Conversely, the most negative planet in a night chart is Saturn, and the most negative planet in a day chart is Mars. There are mitigating factors that can alter the status and function of these planets in a chart, but for the most part, this rule often holds true despite other factors.

Behind this rule is the notion that the planets that belong to the sect of a given chart tend to work in favor of the native, while planets that are contrary to the sect tend to work against the native's interests. This is a principle that we will see demonstrated more vividly once we start looking at example charts.

Rejoicing Conditions

There are two additional sect-related conditions which are said to allow the planets to "rejoice" (*chairein*).

The first rejoicing condition is by position relative to the horizon.[190] According to this rule, diurnal planets are said to rejoice when they are above the horizon during the day, or below the horizon at night. In other words, the Sun, Jupiter, and Saturn prefer to be in the top half of the chart, above the degrees of the Ascendant-Descendant axis, in day charts, but in night charts they prefer to be in the bottom half of the chart, below the degrees of the Ascendant-Descendant axis. Conversely, the nocturnal planets are said to rejoice when they

---

[189] Firmicus, *Mathesis*, 3, 3: 18–19, trans. Bram, pp. 81–82.
[190] Valens, *Anthology*, 3, 5:2.

are above the horizon at night, or below the horizon during the day. Specifically, the Moon, Venus, and Mars prefer to be in the top half of the chart at night, but in the bottom half of the chart during the day.

The second sect-related rejoicing condition is according to zodiacal sign. However, because there was disagreement about this rejoicing condition in the Hellenistic tradition, there are at least three different variants:

1. In the first variant the masculine signs are associated with the diurnal sect and the feminine signs with the nocturnal sect. According to this variant the diurnal planets rejoice when they are in masculine signs, and the nocturnal planets rejoice when they are in feminine signs. This variant became the most popular in the later Hellenistic tradition, perhaps due to the influence of Ptolemy, who advocated this approach.[191]

2. In the second variant the zodiac is divided into two hemispheres along the Cancer-Leo axis. The signs Leo through Capricorn are then thought to be diurnal, while the signs Aquarius through Cancer are thought to be nocturnal.

3. In the third variant the sect of the signs is determined based on the sect of the domicile lord of the sign. So for example, Taurus becomes a nocturnal sign because it is ruled by the nocturnal planet Venus. Aquarius becomes a diurnal sign because it is ruled by the diurnal planet Saturn; and so on.

Ultimately, the rejoicing conditions, especially rejoicing by sign, do not appear to have been as important or to have received as much emphasis in the Hellenistic tradition as the primary consideration, which is simply whether it is a day or night chart, and which planets belong to the overall sect of the chart versus which are contrary to the sect.

In the Medieval tradition, the two rejoicing conditions were elevated in their level of importance to be on par with the primary consideration, and I suspect that this may have contributed to the decline in the use of sect as a technique as time went on.[192] This was connected with the Medieval doctrine of *hayyiz* (or *hayz*), in which a planet was given one point for each of the three sect conditions, and if a planet was well-placed according to all three then it was thought to be best. The problem with this scheme is that it treats all three

---

[191] Ptolemy, *Tetrabiblos*, 1, 7: 1–2.

[192] For an overview of the development of the concept of sect from the Hellenistic to the Medieval tradition see Bezza, "The Development of an Astrological Term."

conditions equally, when in fact the primary and most important condition is simply whether the planet belongs to the same sect as the chart in general. This loss of clarity about the correct application of sect led to a decline in its usage by the seventeenth century; by the twentieth century it had completely disappeared from the tradition. Thus, while experimentation should be done with the rejoicing conditions, from the perspective of Hellenistic astrology, the most important emphasis is placed on the primary condition.

Masculine and Feminine

The planets are also commonly distinguished based on gender, with some being conceptualized as masculine, and others being conceptualized as feminine. At its most fundamental level, this distinction probably originated in a differentiation between the Sun and Moon and the symbolic significance that was attributed to the fact that one emits light and the other receives or reflects light, which is then extended to certain qualities that were traditionally associated with the two genders. Olympiodorus outlines this view succinctly in one of his philosophical works from the sixth century CE:

> And further they say that the Sun is male and the Moon female, since it belongs to the male to give and to the female to receive. So since the Sun gives the light and the Moon receives it, for this reason they give him a male name and her a female.[193]

After this basic set of binary positions had been established, the rest of the planets were then assigned a gender as well. This distinction results in a division that is similar to sect, although the breakdown is slightly different, which implies that it is based on a separate set of criteria. The most common set of gender assignments that we find in the surviving sources is the one outlined by Ptolemy:

MASCULINE:	Sun, Jupiter, Saturn, Mars
FEMININE:	Moon, Venus
NEUTRAL:	Mercury

Ptolemy's assignments are followed by Hephaestio and others.[194] Most authors tend to treat Mercury as gender neutral, and capable of being masculine or feminine depending on its condition in the chart. Ptolemy and those who follow

---

[193] Olympiodorus, *Commentary on Plato's Gorgias*, 47.4, trans. Jackson et al, p. 299.

[194] Ptolemy, *Tetrabiblos*, 1, 6: 1; Hephaestio, *Apotelesmatika*, 1, 2: 10; Rhetorius, *Compendium*, 1.

him say that Mercury is masculine when it is a morning star, and feminine when it is an evening star.[195] Rhetorius seems to be unique in listing Mercury as a masculine planet.[196]

The standard set of gender assignments are problematic because they create an inconsistency with sect when it comes to Mars. According to sect, Mars is considered to be a nocturnal planet, but according to the gender assignments it is thought to be masculine. This creates a conflict with some of the rejoicing conditions since nocturnal planets are usually said to rejoice in feminine signs or when they are evening stars, while masculine planets are said to rejoice when they are in masculine signs or are morning stars.[197] One way that this discrepancy could have arisen is if the standard set of gender assignments outlined by Ptolemy were originally derived from the names of the gods that are associated with the planets in the Greek pantheon, which would have predated the schematization of other concepts such as sect that came about later. In Greek mythology, Helios, Zeus, Kronos, Ares, and Hermes are all male divinities, while Selene and Aphrodite are female divinities. Ptolemy attempts to rationalize the gender assignments by saying that the Moon and Venus are feminine because they have an excess of the wet essence, while the Sun, Saturn, Jupiter, and Mars are masculine because they are more characterized by the qualities of dryness.[198] However, it is not clear that all astrologers followed this rationalization.

While Ptolemy's views became more accepted as the tradition progressed, it seems notable that early authors such as Antiochus, Thrasyllus, and Porphyry do not specify the gender of the planets, but instead only mention gender in connection with the signs of the zodiac or their status as morning or evening stars. This raises some questions about whether gender was something that was always thought to be an intrinsic property of the planets, or if it was something that some astrologers viewed as variable depending on factors such as the sign a planet was placed in, especially since each planet was said to have a masculine and a feminine domicile – and thus a masculine or feminine expression.

Additionally, Dorotheus may have had a slightly different scheme for the gender assignments in which he made Saturn feminine.[199] This reference only occurs in one line in the corrupt Arabic translation of Dorotheus, so it is

---

[195] Ptolemy, *Tetrabiblos*, 1, 6.

[196] Rhetorius, *Compendium*, 1.

[197] For a discussion of this issue see Schmidt, *Definitions and Foundations*, pp. 98–101.

[198] Ptolemy, *Tetrabiblos*, 1, 6.

[199] Dorotheus, *Carmen*, 1, 10: 18. Noted by Pingree, *Yavanajātaka.*, vol. 2, p. 246. Thank you to Charles Obert for drawing my attention to and making a case for the potential veracity of this reference to Saturn as feminine in Dorotheus.

possible that it is simply an error in the received text, although it would create a remarkably symmetrical scheme:

| MASCULINE: | Sun, Jupiter, Mars |
| FEMININE: | Moon, Venus, Saturn |

Unfortunately it is difficult to determine whether this represents a genuine alternative tradition, as most of the later tradition tended to follow Ptolemy in making Saturn masculine, which was probably an easier association to make in Greco-Roman culture since the god Kronos was a male divinity.[200] Additionally, later in Dorotheus when he discusses siblings, he says that Saturn and the Sun indicate older brothers, while the Moon signifies older sisters and Venus younger ones, and this may imply that the earlier reference to Saturn as feminine was an error in the text.[201] This would not be the only error in the received text of the Arabic version of Dorotheus, so we should probably be careful about taking it for granted as a legitimate variant tradition.[202] Nonetheless, the reference to Saturn as feminine is suggestive due to the symmetry involved, and we will see similar attempts by astrologers to create symmetries like this in other areas of Hellenistic astrology, so it may warrant further research.

The only potential parallel that I am aware of in other possibly contemporaneous sources is that in the Jewish mystical doctrine known as the Tree of Life, some later astrologers associated the planet Saturn with the sphere called Binah, which was evidently thought to be feminine. This is a tempting parallel, especially since the text that the Tree of Life comes from, the *Sefer Yetzirah*, is thought to be based on material that may be traced back as far as the first few centuries of the common era.[203] This could make it roughly

---

[200] Exceptions to this include the *Yavanajātaka*, 1: 115, where Saturn is said to be neutral like Mercury, and capable of being masculine or feminine depending on its condition in the chart. In the early Medieval tradition Theophilus of Edessa makes the statement at one point that Saturn, Venus, and the Moon foster the births of females, while the Sun, Jupiter, and Mars the birth of males. See Theophilus, *On Various Inceptions*, 5: 5 (forthcoming translation by Gramaglia and Dykes). This may result from Theophilus having access to the Persian/Arabic translation of Dorotheus, though, which would not necessarily make it a completely independent piece of testimony.

[201] Dorotheus, *Carmen*, 1, 21: 10.

[202] An instance of an error in the Arabic text occurs in Dorotheus, *Carmen*, 1, 6: 4, which says that "Saturn harms one who is born by day and Mars one who is born at night" (trans. Pingree, p. 165). This is clearly a mistake because it is the reverse of the standard Hellenistic doctrine based on sect, which holds that Saturn is more harmful in night charts while Mars is more harmful by day. That it is simply an error is demonstrated by the fact that the rule is stated correctly elsewhere in the book, such as in *Carmen*, 1, 7: 23–4, and 1, 26: 29.

[203] The *Sefer Yetzirah* was probably composed in the third century CE according to Dan,

contemporaneous with Dorotheus. Unfortunately, it is not clear how early the traditional planetary associations in the Tree of Life were established, and it is possible that they only became common in the Middle Ages. This point is uncertain since the oldest surviving texts and commentaries on the *Sefer Yetzirah* only date to the tenth century, even though these are thought to be based on an earlier tradition.[204] Thus, while the parallel is interesting, it is not clear whether any firm conclusions can be drawn from it.

It should be noted that gender was not necessarily something that was viewed as completely static in the Hellenistic astrological tradition, as there were other considerations that could alter the gender expression of a planet in a given chart. We will return to the issue of gender and its practical application when we discuss the treatment of morning stars versus evening stars, as well as the assignment of gender to the signs of the zodiac.

Under the Beams

When a planet gets too close to the Sun it cannot be seen with the naked eye, and when this occurs the planet was said to set "under the beams" or "under the rays" (*hupaugos*) of the Sun. The exact range in which a planet becomes visible or invisible based on its proximity to the Sun varies depending on the planet involved, as well as other astronomical and atmospheric factors. However, the Hellenistic astrologers usually used a standardized range of fifteen degrees on either side of the Sun for a planet to be considered "under the beams."[205] Thus, according to the Hellenistic tradition, any planet within fifteen degrees of a conjunction with the Sun is said to be under the beams.

When a planet is under the beams, its light is completely overwhelmed and obscured as a result of its proximity to the Sun. Planets that are under the beams are often interpreted as if there is something that is hidden, obscured, or secret with respect to the planet's role in the chart. This principle is summarized in one excerpt derived from Dorotheus, in which planets under the beams are said to "cover and conceal," while planets that are not under the beams "make the matters

---

"Three Phases in the History of the Sefer Yezira," or during the second or third centuries CE according to Unterman, *The Kabbalistic Tradition*, p. xxix. One source is cited for a first century date in Swartz, "Ancient Jewish Mysticism," p. 42.

[204] The standard critical edition is *Sefer Yesira*, ed. and trans. Hayman.

[205] The fifteen-degree range is mentioned in Antiochus, *Summary*, 15 (CCAG 8, 3, p. 115: 1–3); Porphyry, *Introduction*, 2; Rhetorius, *Compendium*, 2; Serapio, *Definitions*, p. 227: 11–14. It evidently goes back to the astronomical work of Autolykos of Pitane c. 320 BCE, in his work *On Risings and Settings*. This is discussed briefly in Evans, *The History and Practice of Ancient Astronomy*, p. 193.

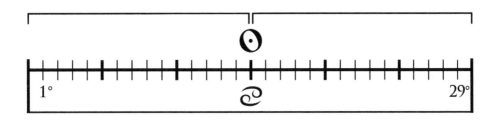

Figure 7.5 - Under the Beams Range

manifest."[206] Here and elsewhere a word that means "setting" or "sinking" (*dutikos*) is used to refer to planets that are under the beams, whereas a term that means "rising" or "arising" (*anatolikos*) is used to refer to planets that are not under the beams. Similarly, in another excerpt, being under the beams is associated with "concealment" (*kruphia*), while planets that are not under the beams are associated with "visibility" and with that which "does not escape detection."[207]

This becomes a concrete interpretive principle when looking at planets that are associated with specific topics or roles in the chart. For example, Rhetorius says that when the planet that signifies marriage is under the beams, the native will get married in secret.[208] Elsewhere, in the Dorotheus excerpts, within the context of inceptional astrology, it says that "the Moon being under the beams is convenient for thieves and runaways, because of her hiddenness."[209]

More broadly, being under the beams is interpreted as a negative indication in a chart, unless there is some significant ameliorating factor that offsets the placement. Paulus says that planets that are under the beams become "impotent" (*adranēs*) and "ineffectual" (*apraktos*), especially when they are within nine degrees of the Sun.[210] In another Dorotheus excerpt he seems to combine the idea of weakness and obscurity when he provides a delineation for what happens when the planet that signifies the native's occupation is under the beams:

> The star which gives the occupation (*praxis*), when under the beams, makes subordinates and people under command, who receive orders from others, [and] obscure and disreputable people who work for a wage.[211]

---

[206] Dorotheus, *Excerpts*, V: 1, trans. Gramaglia.

[207] Dorotheus, *Excerpts*, XXVII, trans. Gramaglia.

[208] Rhetorius, *Compendium*, 48. The ruler of the Lot of Marriage.

[209] Dorotheus, *Excerpts*, LXVIII, trans. Gramaglia, p. 156, slightly modified.

[210] Paulus, *Introduction*, 14, ed. Boer, p. 29: 19–22.

[211] Dorotheus, *Excerpts*, VII, trans. Gramaglia, modified.

Valens speaks more generally about planets setting under the beams of the Sun bringing about "obstacles and pains in one's accomplishments," and that "often they hold out rank and great hopes only to turn them to the worse."[212]

Elsewhere, within a medical context, planets that are under the beams are sometimes associated with things that are internal, whereas planets that are not under the beams are interpreted as indicating things that are external. For example, when a planet that indicates injury to the body is under the beams, this is said to indicate internal injuries or ailments, whereas planets that are not under the beams indicate external injuries.[213] Valens talks about planets that set under the beams of the Sun as sometimes indicating "bodily crises, illnesses, and afflictions of the hidden parts."[214] Thus, the concept of that which is hidden is extended to that which is internal.

Heliacal Rising and Setting

When a planet that is under the beams moves away from the Sun far enough that it passes outside of the fifteen-degree range, it is said to "rise" or "emerge" (*anatolē*), because the planet is literally rising out from under the beams of the Sun and becoming visible again (from our perspective). This is known in contemporary astronomical terms as a heliacal rising. According to the *Michigan Papyrus*, "when the Sun runs 15° away from the stars, the stars rise and exercise especial power upon nativities."[215] Planets that make a heliacal rising within seven days of the native's birth were thought to be particularly prominent and powerful in a chart, almost as if an exclamation point was placed next to the planet. This specific range of seven days is mentioned sporadically throughout the literature. For example, in the Dorotheus excerpts we find a statement that

> If the star which is the cause of wealth is under the rays, but is about to rise within seven days, it will bestow secret wealth, ignored by the many.[216]

Hephaestio makes a similar statement, probably drawing on Dorotheus, saying that if a benefic is configured to the region in the chart that signifies the native's livelihood, and it is under the beams but about to emerge within seven days of the birth, then it will provide wealth and riches.[217]

---

[212] Valens, *Anthology*, 4, 14: 6, trans. Riley, p. 82.
[213] Ptolemy states this as a general principle in *Tetrabiblos*, 3, 13: 6.
[214] Valens, *Anthology*, 4, 14: 6, trans. Riley, p. 82.
[215] *Michigan Papyrus*, col. x: 25–28, trans. Robbins, p. 113, modified.
[216] Dorotheus, *Excerpts*, IV, trans. Gramaglia.
[217] Hephaestio, *Apotelesmatika*, 2, 18: 17.

On the other hand, planets that set under the beams of the Sun by moving into the fifteen-degree range are generally interpreted as becoming weakened or obscured, and going from good circumstances to bad. Manetho succinctly summarizes both rising and setting under the beams as follows:

All the stars rejoice when they are at their rising, just as each is exalted in its own rulerships. Being on the rise, as it were unto their youth, being quite powerful, they accomplish all things for men. But when they are in their setting, as it were slower with advancing years, and falling under the fierce rays, they are wretched and feeble, losing their own strength.[218]

Elsewhere, Hephaestio quotes Dorotheus for the statement that when the ruler of a lot is under the beams or about to set under the beams, whatever is signified by the lot will "dry up," "waste away," or "wither" (*marainetai*).[219] This seems to imply a broader interpretive principle in which the rays of the Sun were seen as detrimental to the planets because they are hot and scorching. To make an analogy, it is like a person who is stuck in the middle of a desert with no shade while the Sun is directly overhead, draining the life from them and causing sunstroke due to the intensity of the heat. This metaphor then brings us to our next interpretive principle.

Chariot as a Mitigating Factor

One of the themes that we see come up repeatedly in different parts of Hellenistic astrology is the existence of mitigating factors that can alter or counteract specific chart placements, for better or worse. Valens mentions this principle in passing when talking about the benefics and malefics:

even if a benefic is able to do something, a malefic in conjunction or aspect will hinder the good. If either malefics alone or benefics alone are in conjunction or in configuration, with no aspect of the other, then the results will be definite.[220]

Here Valens is talking about the benefics and malefics having the power to mitigate each other, but there are also mitigating factors that apply to other conditions as well, such as being under the beams. Antiochus is followed by

---

[218] Manetho, *Apotelesmatika*, 2: 403–409, trans. Lopilato, pp. 216–217.
[219] Hephaestio, *Apotelesmatika*, 2, 18: 18.
[220] Valens, *Anthology*, 5, 2: 12, trans. Riley, p. 96.

Porphyry and Rhetorius in saying that a planet is not hindered by being under the beams as long as it is located in its own zodiacal domicile, exaltation, or bounds.[221] The astrologers referred to this condition as a planet being in its "chariot" (*lampēnē*), and the LSJ lexicon says that this word is sometimes used in a non-astrological context to refer to a type of covered chariot that was used in the Greco-Roman period. This seems to be meant to evoke the image of a person who is riding in a covered chariot, which protects them from the harsh rays of the Sun. This then acts as a mitigating factor that must be taken into account when studying planets that are under the beams, since Antiochus says that a planet can still be "strong" or "powerful" (*dunatos*) even when it is under the beams, as long as it is in its chariot.

In the Heart of the Sun
Towards the end of the Hellenistic tradition, Rhetorius makes what appears to be a personal observation that planets that are within one degree of the Sun do not seem to be harmed as a result of being under the beams. He refers to this condition as being "in the heart" (*enkardios*) of the Sun. He says:

> None of the ancients have made mention of this phase, but, since we have found [it] by experience, we have added it to the list, because even Ptolemy spoke of conjunction as a phase but didn't mention its force.[222]

It is not clear if this personal statement is being made by Rhetorius or someone he was drawing on, and this is complicated by the fact that Porphyry says something brief about the conjunction with the Sun being when it is within one degree, although he does not refer to this as being "in the heart."[223] All we can say is that the concept of being in the heart of the Sun does not appear in any earlier Hellenistic authors that have survived, and it is thus not clear if it was considered to be a significant ameliorating factor outside of Rhetorius.

This condition was adopted by some of the later medieval astrologers, who treated it as a strengthening condition for the planet. Early medieval astrologers such as Sahl ibn Bishr define the condition in the same way as Rhetorius,

---

[221] Antiochus, *Summary*, 14; Porphyry, *Introduction*, 25; Rhetorius, *Compendium*, 43. Porphyry differs from Antiochus and Rhetorius in adding triplicity as a fourth placement. Cf. Serapio, *Definitions*, p. 227: 6–7, who only mentions exaltation as a condition for a planet being in its chariot. For translations and discussion of the passages see Schmidt, *Definitions and Foundations*, pp. 224–5.

[222] Rhetorius, *Compendium*, 1, trans. Holden, p. 4.

[223] Porphyry, *Introduction*, 2.

saying that it occurs when a planet is within one degree of the Sun.[224] Later medieval astrologers such as al-Qabīsī and Abū Maʿshar narrowed the range to within sixteen minutes of a conjunction with the Sun.[225] This became known as *cazimi* in the later Medieval tradition, from Arabic *kasmimi*, which means "as if in the heart," which is a straightforward rendering of Rhetorius' Greek term for the concept.

Morning Star versus Evening Star

Some of the previous considerations that have been covered so far deal with the relationship between a planet and the Sun, otherwise known as the solar phase cycle. Another important concept that is related to the solar phase cycle is the distinction between morning stars versus evening stars.

A planet is said to be a "morning" (*heōia*) star or a "morning riser" (*heōias anatolēs*) when it rises over the horizon before the Sun on the day of the native's birth.[226] Conversely, a planet is said to be an "evening" (*hesperia*) star or an "evening riser" (*hesperias anatolēs*) when it sets under the horizon after the Sun on the day of the native's birth. In Latin, Firmicus refers to these phases as *matutine* and *verspertine*, which means "of the morning" or "of the evening," respectively.[227]

Morning stars always precede the Sun, being earlier in degrees or in the order of the signs, which is counterclockwise, while evening stars always follow after the Sun in terms of the order of the degrees or signs, up to the opposition. For example, today the Sun is at 8° Leo, the Moon is at 11° Cancer, and Venus is at 23° Leo, Mercury at 1° Virgo, and Jupiter at 22° Virgo. Since the Moon is earlier in the order of signs and degrees than the Sun, it rose over the horizon before the Sun today, and therefore it is a morning star or morning riser. Conversely, Venus, Mercury, and Jupiter are all later than the Sun in the order of signs and degrees, and therefore they will only become visible after the Sun sets in the evening, and thus they are evening stars or evening risers.

One critical detail that must be understood here is that for a planet to be seen, it must be more than fifteen degrees away from the Sun before it can properly be said to be a "morning riser" or "evening riser." This is specifically

---

[224] Sahl, *Introduction*, 5.14.

[225] al-Qabīsī, *Introduction*, 3, 7, Abū Maʿshar, *Abbreviation*, 2, 17–21, both trans. Dykes, *Introductions to Traditional Astrology*, pp. 95–97.

[226] Antiochus, *Summary*, 15; Porphyry, *Introduction*, 2, Paulus, *Introduction*, 14. Cf. Schmidt, *Definitions and Foundations*, pp. 229–237.

[227] Firmicus, *Mathesis*, 2, 8.

mentioned by Rhetorius.[228] So, it is not enough for the planet to just be earlier or later than the Sun in zodiacal order; it also needs to be far enough away from the Sun to be capable of making a visible heliacal rising, and therefore to not be under the beams. In the example above, Venus has only recently moved fifteen degrees away from the Sun, and therefore it is making a heliacal rising and has become an evening star or evening riser.

From an interpretive standpoint, morning stars were thought to become more masculine, active, and to produce the things they signify sooner or earlier in the life of the native rather than later.[229] Evening stars were thought to be more feminine, passive, and to produce the things they signify later in the life of the native or with some delay. We will discuss the practical application of this concept and some of the things that it is related to later when we deal with the gender of the signs of the zodiac.[230]

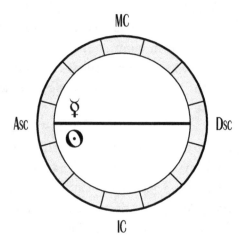

Figure 7.6 - Morning Star

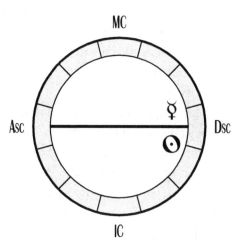

Figure 7.7 - Evening Star

Planetary Speed, Retrogrades, and Stations

There is an interpretive distinction that was employed sometimes in the texts when a planet is moving faster or slower than its usual speed. A planet's typical speed is measured by its average daily motion, which is the average distance that

---

[228] Rhetorius, *Compendium*, 1.

[229] Ptolemy, *Tetrabiblos*, 1, 7; Paulus, *Introduction*, 14.

[230] For a more detailed treatment of the solar phase cycle and some of the ambiguities surrounding the terminology involved see Denningmann, "The Ambiguous Terms ἑῴα and ἑσπερία ἀνατολή, and ἑῴα and ἑσπερία δύσις." I would also recommend consulting Demetra George's forthcoming book on Hellenistic astrology, where she will provide a more extensive and detailed treatment of the solar phase cycle than I have the space for in the present volume.

a planet will travel along the zodiac in a twenty-four-hour period (measured in degrees of longitude on the ecliptic). When a planet is moving faster than its average daily motion it is said to be "additive" (*prosthetikos*), and it was thought to produce what it signifies faster or earlier in the native's life. Conversely, when a planet is moving slower than its average daily motion it was said to be "subtractive" (*aphairetikos*), which was thought to indicate that the planet will produce what it signifies with some delay or sluggishness.

Sometimes the terms additive and subtractive were used instead to describe planets that are direct in motion versus those that are retrograde and thus moving backward in motion along the ecliptic, and it is not always clear which meaning is intended by some authors. The specific word that is usually used to refer to a retrograde planet is *anapodismos*, which literally means "walking backward," or sometimes *hupopodizontes*, which means "retracing their steps."[231] Retrograde and stationary planets are not mentioned very frequently in the surviving texts, and there is some ambiguity about how they were interpreted. In some instances stations are treated as having the power to temporarily intensify the significations of the planet.[232] However, in many other instances it seems that retrograde planets were thought to indicate delays in the manifestation of the planet's significations. Paulus groups retrograde planets together with planets that are under the beams or declining, saying that they are more "impotent" (*adranēs*), "ineffectual" (*apraktos*), and "insignificant" (*anepiphantos*).[233]

Valens makes some brief statements about stationary and retrograde planets within the context of discussing the timing technique called annual profections, saying that when planets are stationing retrograde "they delay expectations, actions, profits, and enterprises."[234] He goes on to say that when planets are in the retrograde phase they are "weakened" (*asthenes*) and "restrained" or "hindered" (*empodistikos*), giving only "appearances" (*fantasias*) and "hopes" (*elpidas*), which he seems to imply are only illusory.[235] Finally, when a planet stations direct it "removes the hindrances and restores and leads to the stability and rectification of life."[236] While these statements in Valens take place within the context of a discussion about profections and transits, they provide some valuable insight into how astrologers would have interpreted this specific astronomical cycle from a symbolic standpoint.

---

[231] For *hupopodizontes* see Paulus, *Introduction*, 14, ed. Boer, p. 29: 4.
[232] Such as in a fragment doubtfully attributed to Petosiris in CCAG, 6, p. 62: 9–17.
[233] Paulus, *Introduction*, 14, ed. Boer, p. 29: 3–5.
[234] Valens, *Anthology*, 4, 14: 4, trans. Riley, p. 82.
[235] Valens, *Anthology*, 4, 14: 5.
[236] Valens, *Anthology*, 4, 14: 6, trans. Schmidt, p. 38.

Ascending and Descending Nodes

The Moon's nodes are moving points on the zodiac where the path of the Moon crosses the path of the ecliptic. Despite their prominence in modern astrology, the nodes are not discussed very frequently in Hellenistic astrology, although we have enough references to develop a basic understanding of their usage by different authors. What modern astrologers refer to as the North Node of the Moon was typically called "Ascending Node" (*anabibazōn*) by the Hellenistic astrologers, since this is the point on the ecliptic where the Moon passes into northward latitude. Conversely, the South Node is called "Descending Node" (*katabibazōn*), because this is the point where the Moon passes into southern latitude. The word "node" itself is from the Greek *sundesmos*, which just means "bond" or "fastening," since it represents the points where the ecliptic and the path of the Moon meet and are bound together. In the texts the nodes are also sometimes referred to as the "eclipsing places" (*ekleiptikōn topōn*), because when a New Moon or Full Moon takes place near the nodes it will result in a solar or lunar eclipse, since the nodes themselves are the points of intersection between what is essentially the path of the Sun and Moon.[237]

Since the nodes coincide with the points on the ecliptic where the luminaries are eclipsed, there were often a number of negative connotations associated with them, especially when the Sun or Moon are in close proximity to or connected with them in certain ways. Antiochus specifically mentions it as difficult for the Moon to be around the nodes because this is where eclipses take place.[238] Valens says that the nodes are "powerful" (*dunastikos*), and he strongly advises against using inception charts (i.e. elections) when the Moon is conjunct, square, or opposing the Ascending Node, especially by degree.[239] He says that new ventures that begin when the Moon is passing over the eclipsing places will not be brought to completion or will be "incomplete" (*ateles*), "inconstant" (*eumetanoētos*), and "subject to punishment" (*epizēminos*).[240] He goes on an uncharacteristically long and pessimistic rant in this same chapter about the Moon being configured to the nodes by hard aspect and how problematic it is in inception charts, evidently based on his personal experiences, saying:

> beware of starting anything: do not sail, do not marry, do not have meetings, do not begin anything, do not plant, do not introduce; in short, do not do anything. What has been started will be judged insecure or

---

[237] Valens, *Anthology*, 5, 2: 21.
[238] Antiochus, *Summary*, 3 (CCAG 8, 3, p. 113: 5–8).
[239] Valens, *Anthology*, 5, 2: 10; 5, 2: 19–20.
[240] Valens, *Anthology*, 5, 2: 21.

prone to come to a bad end; it will be something regrettable, incomplete, subject to penalties, grievous, and not lasting. If someone seems to have begun the development of some business in these days, the business will go bankrupt, will be troublesome, subject to penalties, easily ruined, and a stumbling block. Not even benefics which happen to be in these places do anything entirely good. Therefore, even without <consulting> a natal chart, if anyone guards against the current transits of the moon through the ascending node, he will not make a mistake.[241]

Valens goes on to say that while he has long been aware of this general rule, sometimes he would still have to initiate certain activities at times when the Moon was with the nodes or aspecting them by square or opposition, and each time he observed that things went awry and were subject to delays and problems.[242] Hephaestio similarly says that in inceptions, the nodes indicate things that are incomplete, defective, and subject to reversals.[243] Elsewhere he says that "the Moon becomes bad when on the Nodes or in her southern latitude."[244] In a chapter of the *Liber Hermetis* that was evidently excerpted from Rhetorius, it says at one point that the nodes signify "wanderings" (*errores*) and "disturbances" (*turbationem*) in the life of the native.[245] The same text says that when the nodes are together with either of the luminaries that it indicates harm to the parents.[246]

Valens is unique amongst the astrologers in saying that the Ascending Node breaks down the power of the zodiacal sign and the ruler of the sign that it is located in.[247] He goes on to say that this is also true of the transiting node, and that whatever sign it is moving through in a given year will have its power broken down, so that the power of the ruler will be completely sapped until the node leaves that sign. Unfortunately, this doctrine is not reported by any other authors as far as I am aware, so it is unclear whether others viewed the nodes in the same way.

The nodes are only mentioned sporadically by the earlier authors, and they rarely appear in example charts or surviving horoscopes, but by the time of Rhetorius they appear to have become quite well-integrated into the tradition, although they may have developed different associations than their

---

[241] Valens, *Anthology*, 5, 2: 19–20, trans. Riley, p. 96.

[242] Valens, *Anthology*, 5, 2: 22–27.

[243] Hephaestio, *Apotelesmatika*, 3, 4: 11.

[244] Hephaestio, *Apotelesmatika*, 3, 28: 4, trans. Gramaglia, p. 92.

[245] *Liber Hermetis*, 16: 10.

[246] *Liber Hermetis*, 16: 20. Cf. Rhetorius, *Compendium*, 80 (CCAG 8, 4, p. 205: 9–11).

[247] Valens, *Anthology*, 5, 2: 15–18.

previous ones. In Rhetorius' work, the Ascending Node is generally treated as being good when it is together with the benefics but bad when it is with the malefics, whereas conversely the Descending Node is treated as being bad with the benefics but good with the malefics.[248] Although it does not appear to be stated explicitly in Rhetorius, it is tempting to see the later Medieval rationale as part of the conceptual justification for this, which held that the Ascending Node has the nature of increasing or magnifying, while the Descending Node has the nature of decreasing or diminishing. The ninth-century astrologer Abū Ma'shar explicitly attributed this conceptualization to "some of the early writers."[249] The general idea then is that the Ascending Node is good with the benefics because it increases their inherent tendency towards beneficence, whereas it is bad with the malefics because it exacerbates their inherent tendency towards maleficence. Conversely, the Descending Node was seen as bad with the benefics because it decreases or subtracts from their naturally positive qualities, whereas it is good with the malefics because it diminishes or suppresses their natural tendency towards negativity.

Unfortunately, it is not entirely clear how much this approach represents a later development in the astrological tradition by Rhetorius' time, or whether he is actually preserving older material that just isn't very well-represented in the surviving corpus of texts from the early Hellenistic tradition. There is a brief but suggestive passage in Valens when he mentions the nodes in the first book of the *Anthology*; he says that it is important to see if the benefics are configured with the nodes, especially the Ascending Node, because if they are, the native will be "prosperous and effective."[250] He goes on to say that even if the native's chart does not indicate eminence, the configuration of the benefics to the Ascending Node will indicate that "the native will ascend and rise to a high rank," seemingly emphasizing notions of ascending and rising. However, he goes on to say that when the malefics are configured with the (Ascending?) Node, it indicates loss and accusations. Although this approach is reminiscent of Rhetorius', it is not clear if this interpretive principle applies to both nodes in the same way, or if it is inverted, as in Rhetorius. Valens simply says to look at whether the benefics are configured to the nodes, "especially" (*malista*) the

---

[248] This approach is primarily outlined in Rhetorius, *Compendium*, 57 (CCAG 8, 4, pp. 126ff), which includes delineations of the nodes in each of the twelve places when they are present with the benefics and malefics. It is also referenced briefly in *Liber Hermetis*, 16: 19–21, which is derived from Rhetorius, *Compendium*, 54 (CCAG 8, 4, p. 123: 7–11). Cf. Rhetorius, *Compendium*, 61, trans. Holden, p. 115. The rule is stated explicitly in Rhetorius, *Compendium*, 80 (CCAG 8, 4, p. 205: 13–14).

[249] Abū Ma'shar, *The Abbreviation*, 4: 19, trans. Burnett, p. 33.

[250] Valens, *Anthology*, 1, 15: 10, trans. Riley, p. 13.

Ascending Node; it is not clear if he had the sharp distinction employed by later authors such as Rhetorius.

Elsewhere there is a similarly brief although much more suggestive passage in Hephaestio that preserves some material from Dorotheus on inception charts for buying and selling goods that may support the later usage in Rhetorius. Hephaestio summarizes the principles as follows:

> When the Moon is full, additive in longitude and latitude, on the ascending Node, the buyer in the market will pay a higher price; but when she is waning, subtractive in numbers, and on the descending Node, the buyer will pay a smaller price.[251]

Hephaestio then goes on to quote Dorotheus from the original verse text:

> *When Selēnē passes by the up-leading Node,*
> *if, full of light, she also increases her course in numbers,*
> *[for] whatever you buy, you will give more than what you need to give.*
> *But going on the down-leading paths, on which she decreases,*
> *going towards less, easy will the purchase be.*[252]

The "up-leading Node" here is clearly the Ascending Node, while Gramaglia says that the "down-leading paths" probably refers to "decreasing in latitude toward or around the south Node."[253] Thus, this appears to be a pretty explicit reference going back to the first century CE that indicates an early conceptualization of the Ascending Node being associated with the quality of increasing and the Descending Node being associated with the quality of decreasing. Rhetorius may have still extended the concept or elaborated on it further than some of his predecessors, since he seems to mention the nodes more frequently than most Hellenistic astrologers, but this shows that he was in fact drawing in part on an already established tradition surrounding the nodes. However, this may have been only one way in which the nodes were conceptualized, which in some ways may have represented an alternative take based on the symbolic significance of the Moon's increase and decrease in latitude. The other view developed interpretations out of the associations that the nodes had with eclipses, which were viewed as an ominous and unsettling phenomenon.

---

[251] Hephaestio, *Apotelesmatika*, 3, 16: 11, trans. Gramaglia, p. 81.
[252] Hephaestio, *Apotelesmatika*, 3, 16: 13, trans. Gramaglia, p. 81.
[253] Hephaestio, *Apotelesmatika*, 3, trans. Gramaglia, p. 81, fn. 284.

CHAPTER 8
SIGNS OF THE ZODIAC

The *Zōidia*

Each of the seven traditional "planets" can be observed to wander through the sky, moving past different fixed stars and constellations in the process. If you pay attention over a long enough period of time, you will notice, as ancient sky-watchers did, that the planets move along a relatively narrow path through the sky and only pass through certain constellations. The path that the planets move through in the sky is known as the "ecliptic," which forms a circle or band that wraps all the way around the earth. By the fifth century BCE, the Mesopotamians began dividing the ecliptic circle into twelve equal segments of thirty degrees each, which later became known in the Hellenistic period as the "zodiac," from the Greek word *zōidion*.

It is somewhat difficult to translate the term *zōidion* (plural *zōidia*) into English because in Greek it has two distinct meanings. According to the LSJ lexicon, it is derived from the word *zōion*, which is sometimes used in non-astrological texts to refer to a "living being" or an "animal," while elsewhere it can also be used in an artistic context to refer to an "image," "figure," or "picture" of something. Part of the dual meaning may arise from the fact that the constellations that were originally associated with the zodiacal signs were thought to depict images of living beings, such as the Ram, the Bull, the Twins, the Crab, the Lion, and so on.[1] Matters are additionally complicated by grammatical ambiguities: the astrological term *zōidion* is either a diminutive

---

[1] Pliny may allude to this when he refers to "the circle called the zodiac being marked out into the likeness of twelve animals…" Pliny, *Natural History*, 2, 3: 9, trans. Rackham, p. 177.

of the term *zōion*, which means that the thing described should be smaller or lesser ("a lesser living being" or "a small image"), or it may represent a locative case suffix, which would indicate that the sign is a place in which something is located ("the place of a living being" or "the place of an image").[2]

Unfortunately, there is no English word that can fully encapsulate the different meanings underlying the term *zōidion*. Schmidt wrestled with this issue starting with his translation of Paulus of Alexandria in 1993, and left the term transliterated as *zōidion* for years until he could find a reasonable translation.[3] He was followed by Greenbaum, who similarly left it transliterated in her 2001 translation of Paulus.[4] The conventional designation of referring to the *zōidia* as "signs" was rejected, based on the premise that while the Latin root, *signum*, originally conveyed the meaning of "image," that the English term "sign" had drifted far enough away from this meaning that it no longer conveyed an accurate sense of the original Greek word.[5] In 2009, Schmidt settled on the convention of translating *zōidion* as "image," so that his subsequent translations refer to "the image of the Ram" or "the image of the Water-Pourer," and so on.[6]

For the purpose of this book I will retain the traditional convention of referring to the *zōidia* as the "signs" of the zodiac. I think that this designation is sufficient because of the abstract way that the *zōidia* came to be used: as a collection of intelligible qualities that could be perceived with the mind, and not necessarily always as visible images that could be seen with the eyes.[7] While sometimes it is true that the actual images connected with the constellations informed the interpretation of certain *zōidia*, for some astrologers who used the tropical zodiac, such as Ptolemy, the *zōidia* became not so much images of things but instead abstract divisions of the ecliptic that were thought to be associated with certain qualities. This is probably why astrologers such as Ptolemy would sometimes use a synonym, referring to signs of the zodiac as "twelfth-parts" (*dōdekatēmoria*), thus denoting each of the "signs" as an abstract division of the ecliptic into twelve equal parts.[8] Each of these divisions were thought to be associated with certain qualities, and as a result of this they were thought to

---

[2] The potential for *zōidion* to be a locative suffix was first noted by Schmidt in his translation of Valens, *The Anthology, Book I*, pp. xvi–xix. Cf. Paulus, *Introduction*, trans. Greenbaum, p. ix.

[3] As discussed in the preface of Paulus, *Introductory Matters*, trans. Schmidt, pp. ix–xi.

[4] Paulus, *Introduction*, trans. Greenbaum, p. ix.

[5] Paulus, *Introductory Matters*, trans. Schmidt, p. x.

[6] Discussed in Schmidt, *Definitions and Foundations*, pp. 93–94.

[7] That some astrologers conceptualized and defended the zodiac in this way is stated explicitly by Origen in his critique of the zodiac, which will be quoted below in the section on the tropical versus sidereal zodiac.

[8] e.g. Ptolemy, *Tetrabiblos*, 1, 14: 1. Cf. Thrasyllus, *Summary*, p. 101: 17, citing Hermes Trismegistus.

be capable of giving signs or portents for specific things. To the extent that the modern meaning of the term "sign" refers to something that indicates or signals, thus invoking a range of specific meanings based on the appearance of an image or a symbol, the word is not so different from the application of the concept in Greco-Roman astrology as to warrant the introduction of a completely new convention in contemporary practice. As the Roman polymath Varro said in the first century BCE when discussing the etymology of the Latin words for signs and constellations:

> The same things are called both "signs" and "constellations." [They are called] "Signs" because they signify something, like Libra [signifies] the equinox.[9]

Thus, while the reader should keep in mind some of the other original meanings underlying the term *zōidion*, especially when reading translations, for the purposes of this book I will maintain the modern convention of referring to the *zōidia* as "signs" of the zodiac.

Qualities of the Signs

While the zodiac has its origins in the Mesopotamian tradition, most of the qualities that later astrologers came to associate with the signs seem to have originally been developed in the Hellenistic tradition. The primary role that the signs of the zodiac play in Hellenistic astrology is that they modify the manner in which the significations of the planets manifest in the chart. They do this through four primary qualities:

1. Planetary rulership
2. Gender
3. Triplicity or element
4. Quadruplicity

There are also a number of other miscellaneous qualities associated with the signs that are based on things like the appearance of the constellations, although many of these seem like secondary considerations that often play a subordinate role to the main qualities, and they often seem like they are meant to be used

---

[9] Varro, *On the Latin Language*, 7: 14: "Signa dicuntur eadem et sidera. Signa quod aliquid significent, ut libra aequinoctium..." On Varro's association with the astrologer Lucius Tarutius Firmanus see Heilen, "Ancient Scholars on the Horoscope of Rome." Heilen notes (p. 50) that one of Varro's lost works was a book on astronomy/astrology.

within the context of specific techniques rather than as general interpretive principles.[10] We will deal with these secondary qualities later after first presenting the four primary qualities of the signs.

One important and potentially surprising point here is that unlike in modern astrology, there does not appear to be any systematic borrowing or interchangeability between the significations of the signs of the zodiac and the significations of the twelve houses or places. So, the first house is not equivalent to Aries, and there is generally no borrowing from the significations of the houses in order to derive significations from the signs, or vice versa. This is an important point to understand since it requires us to be careful when trying to reconstruct the practice of Hellenistic astrology, so that we do not anachronistically project modern rationalizations backwards in time, which could potentially obfuscate the conceptual origins of early western astrology rather than help to clarify them. Instead we have to try to get to the logic underlying the original system, and thus develop an understanding of the signs and houses on their own terms. This is a good approach to take as a matter of general practice, but it becomes especially important when dealing with the signs and houses given how much certain conceptualizations have changed in relation to them over the past two thousand years.

Tropical versus Sidereal Zodiacs

Ancient astronomers noticed that the Sun, Moon, and five visible planets regularly wander through a very specific path in the sky. Because the planets never deviate from this path, which we call the ecliptic, there are certain constellations on that path that the planets repeatedly move through. This is how the *constellational zodiac* was first developed. It included every constellation that the planets moved through, and it excluded constellations that they didn't move through. One important point is that each of these constellations are of unequal size. Some are relatively small, such as Cancer, while others are relatively large, such as Virgo. Some of the constellations even overlap a little, such as Aquarius and Pisces.

Eventually, by the fifth century BCE, astrologer-astronomers in Mesopotamia standardized the zodiac so that it contained twelve signs of exactly thirty degrees each. This is what is referred to as the *sidereal zodiac* (from Latin *sidereus*, "of the stars or constellations"). Its reference point is the constellations, even though the constellations themselves vary in size. Accordingly, the sidereal zodiac is an idealized or symbolic division of the constellations into twelve equal segments or "signs," even though it is not perfectly aligned with the constellations themselves.

---

[10] Ptolemy makes a statement to this effect in *Tetrabiblos*, 1, 13: 5.

When Hellenistic astrology was developed a few centuries later, the seasons were roughly aligned with the sidereal zodiac. The beginning of the seasons coincided with the beginning of what modern astrologers call the cardinal signs—Aries, Cancer, Libra, and Capricorn. The middle of the seasons coincided with the fixed signs—Taurus, Leo, Scorpio, and Aquarius. The end of the seasons coincided with the mutable signs—Gemini, Virgo, Sagittarius, and Pisces. Symbolic associations were made between the nature of different parts of the seasons and certain types of actions, circumstances, or qualities that share a formal similarity. That is to say, the alignment of the seasons began to inform the interpretation of the zodiacal signs. At some point this became the basis for a third division of the ecliptic into twelve segments or "signs," which became known as the *tropical zodiac*. The tropical zodiac is measured relative to the seasons, which begin at the precise degree of the equinoxes and the solstices. The starting point is the vernal equinox, which coincides with the first day of spring in the northern hemisphere, and this then becomes the beginning of the sign Aries. After that, the other signs are measured out in thirty-degree increments from there, with the summer solstice coinciding with the first degree of Cancer, the fall equinox marking the beginning of Libra, and finally the winter solstice designating the beginning of Capricorn.

Ultimately this leaves us with three zodiacs:

1. Constellational Zodiac: based on the uneven constellations that lie in the path of the Sun, Moon, and planets (a.k.a. the ecliptic).
2. Sidereal Zodiac: the idealized division of the ecliptic into 12 signs of 30 degrees each that is roughly aligned with the constellations.
3. Tropical Zodiac: the idealized division of the ecliptic into 12 signs of 30 degrees each that is aligned with the equinoxes and solstices.

The tropical and sidereal zodiacs were roughly aligned during the early Hellenistic tradition, and the early astrologers seem to have drawn on elements of both in order to develop the meanings of the individual zodiacal signs. For example, the rationale for the quadruplicities or modalities is clearly more strongly tied in with the tropical zodiac due to its connection with the seasons. In that scheme the cardinal signs are associated with initiating new activities because they coincide with the beginning of the seasons, the fixed signs are associated with stability because they fall in the middle of the seasons, and the mutable signs are associated with transition because they correspond to the end of the seasons.[11]

---

[11] This is roughly the rationale outlined by Ptolemy in *Tetrabiblos*, 1, 12. Cf. Dorotheus, *Carmen*, 5, 3–4.

However, sometimes some of the zodiacal qualities are mentioned within the context of specific fixed stars that occupy the constellations, which is clearly a sidereal consideration. For example, at one point in a discussion about natal indications for injury and illness, Valens says that when Taurus is connected with this topic in a natal chart it can indicate injury to the eyes or blindness, because of its connection with the fixed star cluster known as the Pleiades.[12]

The fact that the Hellenistic astrologers drew elements from both the tropical and sidereal zodiacs when developing the qualities associated with the signs became problematic for later astrologers because the two zodiacs eventually started drifting apart due to the phenomenon known as the precession of the equinoxes. Precession arises from the fact that Earth's axis of rotation wobbles very slowly over the course of roughly 26,000 years.[13] This results in the tropical and sidereal zodiacs gradually drifting apart at a rate of about one degree every 72 years, so that at the present point in time in the early twenty-first century the two zodiacs differ by about 24 degrees. This has led to a debate amongst astrologers in modern times about whether to use the tropical or sidereal zodiac as the primary reference system for calculating astrological charts.

The Greek astronomer Hipparchus discovered precession in the second century BCE, and he adopted the tropical zodiac as a reference system for the purpose of doing astronomical calculations.[14] However, the Hellenistic astrologers of the first few centuries CE largely continued to use older calculations for determining planetary placements that resulted in sidereal positions, sometimes using algorithms derived from Mesopotamian sources.[15] Jones points out that these astrologers may not necessarily have conceptualized this frame of reference as primarily sidereal, and that the phenomenon of precession seems to have been either largely unknown or in some instances rejected as a theory for several centuries.[16]

---

[12] Valens, *Anthology*, 2, 37: 8.

[13] For a good discussion of precession see Evans, *The History and Practice*, p. 245ff.

[14] On Hipparchus' discovery of precession see Evans, *The History and Practice*, p. 246ff. Toomer says that Hipparchus would have discovered precession towards the end of his career, c. 127 BCE (Toomer, "Hipparchus"). On Hipparchus' adoption of the tropical zodiac see Neugebauer, *A History of Ancient Mathematical Astronomy*, p. 278, who cites a passage in Hipparchus' commentary on Aratus where he explicitly says that the solstices and equinoxes should mark the beginnings of the signs, in contrast with other authors such as Eudoxus who place them later. For this passage see Manitius, *Hipparchi in Arati et Eudoxi*, 1, 5: 11 (p. 48: 5–7). Holden notes that Hipparchus published solar and lunar tables that gave positions within the context of the tropical zodiac (*A History of Horoscopic Astrology*, p. 17).

[15] Discussed extensively in Jones, "Ancient Rejection and Adoption of Ptolemy's Frame of Reference for Longitudes." Cf. Holden, "The Classical Zodiac."

[16] Jones, "Ancient Rejection," p. 29.

Ptolemy seems to have been the first astrologer who fully recognized and confirmed Hipparchus' discovery about precession in the second century CE. Ptolemy is also the first major astrologer we know of who unambiguously adopted the tropical zodiac as his preferred reference system for zodiacal measurements. When he explains this in the *Almagest*, he establishes that he is going to continue using the conventional names for the twelve tropical signs of the zodiac even though these names were originally derived from the constellations:

> We shall use the names of the signs of the zodiac for the twelve [30°] divisions of the ecliptic, according to the system in which the divisions begin at the solsticial and equinoctial points. We call the first division, beginning at the spring equinox and going towards the rear with respect to the motion of the universe, 'Aries', the second 'Taurus', and so on for the rest, in the traditional order of the 12 signs.[17]

Ptolemy also uses the spring equinox as the first degree of Aries in his astrological work, the *Tetrabiblos*, and there he seems to have believed that many of the primary qualities associated with the zodiacal signs were originally derived from a tropical rather than sidereal framework. One of his primary statements about this is worth quoting at length:

> But it is indeed reasonable to start the twelfth-parts and the boundaries from the tropical and equipartite points—that we will not omit, as it happens to be worth dwelling over. This is both because the writers in a certain fashion make this clear, and especially because we see from the previous demonstrations that the natures and powers and [planetary] affiliations of the twelfth-parts and boundaries derive their cause from the tropical and equipartite origins and not from any other starting points. For, if other starting points are assumed, we will either be forced no longer to use the natures of the zodiacal signs in prognostication, or else, if we use them, we will be forced to make mistakes because of the overlappings and separations of the intervals that secure the powers in them.[18]

---

[17] Ptolemy, *Almagest*, 2, 7, trans. Toomer, p. 90.
[18] Ptolemy, *Tetrabiblos*, 1, 22: 2–3, trans. Schmidt, p. 45, slightly modified. Ptolemy also says that the spring equinox marks the starting point of Aries in *Tetrabiblos*, 1, 10: 2. Other examples of Ptolemy using seasonal/tropical arguments to rationalize the properties underlying the signs include the discussion of the quadriplicities in *Tetrabiblos*, 1, 12, as well as his rationale for the domicile rulership scheme in *Tetrabiblos*, 1, 18.

This statement is important because not only is Ptolemy saying that most of the traditional qualities associated with the signs seem to be derived from seasonal considerations that make more sense to him within the context of the tropical zodiac, but he is also saying that he understands this to be the implicit intention in some of the earlier (foundational?) astrological authors as well. The question then becomes whether or not this is true, and if some of the earlier texts emphasized interpretations of the zodiacal signs that would make more sense within a tropical rather than sidereal framework.[19]

A brief piece of testimonia from Thrasyllus seems to present conflicting evidence, as the summary of his work reports that he said that "the tropics are not made at the first degree of the sign, as some maintain, but at the eighth degree."[20] This statement is interesting because it may imply that Thrasyllus was deliberately rejecting the tropical zodiac already in the early first century CE, or alternatively it may simply mean that he was still following the earlier Mesopotamian sources which assumed that the equinoxes and solstices stayed fixed at eight degrees of the cardinal signs.[21] Either way, it also raises the question: who are the unnamed others that he is dismissing? Is he referring to Hipparchus and his astronomical tables? Or were there specific astrologers advocating a tropical approach already by the time of Thrasyllus (early first century CE)? Whatever the case, Ptolemy's argument does not initially seem to have gained many supporters, and the sidereal zodiac continued to be used as the primary reference system from what we can tell according to most of the surviving horoscopes through the fourth century, until around 350 CE when there was a shift and Ptolemy's tropical values and tables became more widely adopted.[22]

---

[19] Pingree notes that the quadruplicities can be traced "back in the West to the treatise of Nechepso-Petosiris" (*Yavanajātaka*, vol. 2, p. 216). If this is true, then these may be the earlier writers that Ptolemy had in mind when he made this statement. Valens does in fact cite Petosiris once for a delineation on the topic of children in which the double-bodied or mutable signs are mentioned (*Anthology*, 2, 39: 4–5).

[20] CCAG, 8, 3, p. 99: 6–7, trans. Schmidt, *Definitions and Foundations*, p. 341, modified.

[21] The 8° norm is from the Mesopotamian solar theory known as "System B," as discussed in Neugebauer, *A History of Ancient Mathematical Astronomy*, pp. 594–98, citing several other astrologers and Roman sources who continued to mention or use the norm for several centuries. There is an important discussion about the use of this norm among later astrologers such as Valens in Jones, "Ancient Rejection." Jones notes that Valens does not appear to have been aware of precession, and says that while the placements he uses "are effectively sidereal," by assigning fixed longitudes to the equinoxes and solstices this essentially makes it so that "according to the internal logic of the system the frame of reference is tropical" (p. 23). Thus, there may be a disconnect or at least some ambiguity between the intent and the practice of the astrologers when it comes to the use of the sidereal or tropical zodiac in the Hellenistic tradition, and this should be taken into account in future discussions about this topic.

[22] Jones, "Ancient Rejection," pp. 34–35.

This resulted in the tropical zodiac becoming the dominant reference system in the west during the late Hellenistic tradition and then into the Medieval period, all the way through to modern times.

Ptolemy's influence on the adoption of the tropical zodiac amongst western astrologers in later centuries is a subject of dispute, because it is not clear if he was simply formalizing the adoption of something that had been intended since the beginning of the Hellenistic tradition, or if his adoption of the tropical zodiac represented a complete departure from an earlier tradition that had both practically as well as conceptually intended to use the sidereal zodiac as the primary frame of reference since the beginning. Some modern western astrologers who are proponents of the sidereal zodiac have argued that it was an unfortunate departure, pointing to the earlier Mesopotamian tradition, in which the zodiac ostensibly originated as sidereal.[23] These arguments generally do not take into account the fact that most of the zodiacal qualities that astrologers associate with the signs only seem to have been developed later during the Hellenistic tradition, when the two zodiacs were roughly aligned. This is important, since it cannot be taken for granted that all of the properties that are associated with the signs were derived from the appearance or mythology associated with the constellations, as we will see later in this chapter.

Another argument in favor of the sidereal zodiac is that it has been the primary reference system used in India for almost two thousand years. This is perhaps because after the transmission of Hellenistic astrology to India via the *Yavanajātaka* or some other text, they didn't have the equivalent of a Ptolemy who explicitly defined the zodiac along tropical lines. As a counterpoint, however, the Indian tradition has a much stronger reason to be more grounded in the sidereal framework because of their use of the twenty-seven sign lunar zodiac known as the *nakshatras*, which is explicitly predicated on a set of specific fixed stars. This may have given the Indian astrologers more grounds for sticking with the sidereal framework because the indigenous form of astrology that first developed there was more closely tied in with a system that necessitated the use of the fixed stars, and many of the techniques that were imported from the Greco-Roman tradition were merged with this system.

Whatever Ptolemy's influence was, he was evidently not the only astrologer who went out of his way to make conceptual arguments for the tropical zodiac in the Hellenistic tradition. One of the earliest critiques of astrology that draws on

---

[23] Most recently argued in Bowser, *An Introduction to Western Sidereal Astrology*, drawing on the work of the founder of modern western sidereal astrology, Cyril Fagan. Fagan's historical arguments are probably articulated in their most mature form in his later book *Astrological Origins*.

precession was by a Christian theologian from Alexandria named Origen (third century CE), who mentions some astrologers who attempted to distinguish between the sidereal signs and what he calls the "intelligible" signs of the zodiac:

> There is a well-known theorem which proves that the zodiac, like the planets, moves from west to east at the rate of one degree in a hundred years, and that this movement in the lapse of so long a time changes the local relation of the signs; so that, on the one hand, there is the "intelligible" (*noētos*) sign, and on the other, as it were, the visible "formation" (*morphōmata*) of it; and events, they say, are discovered not from the formation, but from the intelligible sign; though it cannot possibly be apprehended.[24]

This statement seems to confirm the existence, in the century after Ptolemy, of astrologers who defended the tropical zodiac on the grounds that it had some sort of intrinsic value that could be grasped with the mind, even if it could not be observed as easily with the senses. It is unclear whether this represents the results of Ptolemy's efforts to promote the tropical zodiac, or alternatively, if it indicates that there was already a separate tradition independent of Ptolemy that conceptualized the zodiac as tropical.

For the purposes of this book I will be using the tropical zodiac for two primary reasons: First, from a conceptual standpoint, it seems that some of the most important meanings of the zodiacal signs were originally derived from considerations that make more sense within a seasonal or tropical context, which I will discuss more during the course of this chapter. Second, and perhaps more importantly, I have not been able to get the primary time-lord systems I present in the final chapters of this book to work as impressively with the sidereal zodiac as I have with the tropical zodiac. This combination of theoretical and practical considerations has led me to conclude that the tropical zodiac is more appropriate for the primary purposes of what we will be using it for here within the context of Hellenistic astrology. However, I remain open to the idea of finding a way to reconcile the tropical and sidereal zodiacs at some point in the future. Additionally, despite my personal views and preferences, I encourage the reader to explore the zodiac issue from both a conceptual and practical standpoint, and to arrive at your own conclusions.

Names of the Signs

Each of the twelve signs of the zodiac was given a name, which was originally

---

[24] Origen, *Philocalia*, 23: 18, trans. Lewis, p. 192, modified. For a discussion of this passage see Hegedus, *Early Christianity and Ancient Astrology*, pp. 31–33.

derived from the constellation associated with that particular sign. Manetho provides a nice overview of the traditional order and names of the signs, describing them in terms of some of the iconography associated with their constellations:

> The Zodiac which of all the quick-moving circles in the heavens is the most illustrious and visible, well-furnished with twelve images (*eidōloisi*), moves through the ether. About it, all-gleaming with stars, is situated the Ram, and (then) the Bull, and the Twins is next to it. After them, the Crab and the Lion and (then) the Maiden, bearing ears of corn in her hands, longing for the race of former men, and the Claws whose name the holy men changed, and they called it the Scales because it stretches on each side, like the scales of a balance which is weighted down. And the Scorpion is next, and next the mighty Archer, and then the Goat-Horned One after which are the Water-Bearer and the Fishes.[25]

Libra was originally called the Claws in the early Greek astronomical tradition, because it was thought to represent part of the claws of the adjacent constellation, the Scorpion, but it became the Scales at some point after Libra and Scorpio started being differentiated. Occasionally you will still see some Hellenistic astrologers refer to Libra as the Claws as an archaic or poetic epithet.

In Greek, the typical names of the signs are as follows:

ARIES	*Krios*	The Ram
TAURUS	*Tauros*	The Bull
GEMINI	*Didumoi*	The Twins
CANCER	*Karkinos*	The Crab
LEO	*Leōn*	The Lion
VIRGO	*Parthenos*	The Maiden
LIBRA	*Zugos*	The Scales
SCORPIO	*Skorpios*	The Scorpion
SAGITTARIUS	*Toxotēs*	The Archer
CAPRICORN	*Aigokerōs*	The Goat-Horned One
AQUARIUS	*Hvdrochoos*	The Water-Pourer
PISCES	*Ichthues*	The Fishes

The English words for the signs of the zodiac are largely derived from the Latin translations of the Greek terms. For example, *aries* means "ram" in Latin, *taurus* means "bull," *gemini* means "twins," and so on.

---

[25] Manetho, *Apotelesmatika*, 2: 129–140, trans. Lopilato, pp. 206–7, modified.

For the purposes of this book I will continue to use the contemporary English terms for the signs of the zodiac, although we should be aware that some translators use the terms literally in their texts. When translated literally, Greek texts will read "if Hermes is in the Bull," or "if Aphrodite is in the Lion," and so forth.

Masculine and Feminine Signs

One of the simplest and most straightforward classifications of the signs is their division into two groups, with each being assigned a gender, masculine or feminine. The odd signs starting from the first sign, Aries, are said to be masculine, while the even signs starting with Taurus are said to be feminine.[26] The resulting breakdown looks like this:

MASCULINE: Aries, Gemini, Leo,
                    Libra, Sagittarius, Aquarius

FEMININE: Taurus, Cancer, Virgo,
                    Scorpio, Capricorn, Pisces

This doctrine was widely accepted by every major Hellenistic astrologer whose work survives.[27] In discussing this doctrine, Sextus Empiricus notes that the Pythagoreans have a similar belief, in which they associate odd numbers with the masculine and even numbers with the feminine. He assumes that the Pythagoreans were following the astrologers with this association:

> And by them [the astrologers], I suppose, the Pythagoreans were moved to call the monad "male," and the dyad "female," and the triad again "male," and the rest of the even and odd numbers according to the same rule.[28]

Sextus is probably correct in positing a connection between the Pythagorean theory and the astrological doctrine, although the Pythagorean tradition surrounding numbers is probably older than the assignment of gender to the signs of the zodiac. For example, already in the fourth century BCE, Aristotle says in the *Metaphysics* that the Pythagoreans associated odd numbers with the

---

[26] That the gender assignments are assigned by equating odd and even with masculine and feminine is made explicit in Paulus, *Introduction*, 2, ed. Boer, p. 8: 7–12.

[27] It is explicitly defined in authors such as Antiochus, *Summary*, 2; Porphyry, *Introduction*, 40; Rhetorius, *Compendium*, 1. In other authors it is often used as an interpretive principle that is taken for granted without needing to define it.

[28] Sextus Empiricus, *Against the Professors*, 5: 8, trans. Bury, p. 327.

masculine and even numbers with the feminine.[29] Thus, the astrologers who began applying this doctrine to the signs of the zodiac at some point in the Hellenistic period likely got the idea from the Pythagoreans, rather than the other way around.[30]

As an interpretive principle in Hellenistic astrology, these assignments are often invoked in delineations that involve identifying gender in some way. For example, Sextus reports that masculine and feminine signs were thought to "possess a nature which aids in the birth of males or females."[31] In Valens' treatment of siblings he tells us that the gender of the sign that contains the planetary significators for siblings will help to indicate the gender of the native's siblings:

> Venus and the Moon domiciled in the third place from the Ascendant, the Place of Brothers, grants sisters, especially if the sign is feminine. If the Sun, Jupiter, and Mercury are in a masculine sign <in the third place>, they grant brothers.[32]

Dorotheus has a similar treatment for determining the gender of the native's siblings.[33] Elsewhere, in Valens' chapter on determining which of the native's parents will die first, he presents a method that uses a mathematical computation, and if the resulting position falls in a masculine sign then it means that the native's father will die before their mother, whereas if it falls in a feminine sign it means that the mother will die first.[34] In a chapter on the birth of twins, Firmicus invokes the gender of the signs as one consideration for determining whether males or females will be born:

> But whether they will be born of the masculine gender or the feminine one, we determine in this fashion. For if, with the Sun and the Moon and the Ascendant posited in masculine signs, there is testimony from masculine stars, that is from Jupiter, Saturn, and Mars, males will be born. But if Venus alone has made the same [testimony], posited in feminine signs, twins of the feminine gender [will be born].[35]

---

[29] Aristotle, *Metaphysics*, 986a 20–25.

[30] Pingree takes this as a given in *Yavanajātaka*, vol. 2, p. 207.

[31] Sextus Empiricus, *Against the Professors*, 5: 7, trans. Bury, p. 325.

[32] Valens, *Anthology*, 2, 40: 4, trans. Riley, p. 54, modified.

[33] Dorotheus, *Carmen*, 1, 21: 1–4.

[34] Valens, *Anthology*, 2, 31: 6–7. There is another technique that is predicated on the gender of the signs attributed to Anubio in Hephaestio, *Apotelesmatika*, 2, 5: 5.

[35] Firmicus, *Mathesis*, 7, 3: 5, trans. Holden, p. 421, modified.

These examples demonstrate the sometimes very literal interpretations that were derived from the placement of different factors in a chart. In this instance, part of the function of the signs is that they allow you to distinguish between males and females in the life of the native in a concrete way, as a result of the numerological symbolism that is ascribed to the signs.

This literal use of the gender assignments was not the only application of the concept, since it also appears occasionally as a more nuanced descriptive factor in some sources. Sometimes the gender of the signs is interpreted more broadly, so that masculine signs are conceptualized as being active, while feminine signs are conceptualized as being passive. For example, Anubio says that the masculine signs are taken as being "authoritative" (*exousia*) and "commanding" or "leading" (*hēgemonias*), whereas the feminine signs pertain to "subordination" (*hupotagē*).[36] In the *Yavanajātaka*, these signs are described as "hard" and "soft."[37] In this way the technique is partially tied in with traditional gender roles, but it also attempts to make simple distinctions between principles that involve active or passive elements.

Gender assignments are also invoked sometimes in discussions about character, sexuality, and sexual orientation. Traditional gender roles in the Greco-Roman world generally held that it was best for men to be masculine and women to be feminine, although the astrologers seem to have had some interest in identifying where individuals would fall on a gender spectrum, which sometimes includes those who might have a tendency to transgress traditional gender norms. Ptolemy seems to have the most elaborate model for this, in which he establishes gender and sexual orientation as a spectrum, almost like an ancient equivalent to the Kinsey scale. He treats sexual orientation primarily in his chapters on marriage and on ailments of the soul, emphasizing the placements of the Sun, Moon, Mars, and Venus.[38] At the beginning of the discussion Ptolemy says that he is going to focus on "excesses or deficiencies of what is natural for the male and female sex," and this includes both men and women transgressing gender norms, but also what happens when each gender becomes unbalanced by becoming excessively masculine or excessively feminine.[39] Each of the four planetary placements analyzed can become more masculinized or feminized by being placed in a masculine or feminine sign, or by becoming a morning star or an evening star.

---

[36] Anubio, *Carmen*, ed. Obbink, T8: 55–57.

[37] *Yavanajātaka*, vol. 2, 1: 30, trans. Pingree, p. 3.

[38] Ptolemy, *Tetrabiblos*, 4, 5 and 3, 15. The chapter in 3, 15 should be read together with 3, 14, which is on the quality of the soul.

[39] Ptolemy, *Tetrabiblos*, 3, 15: 7, trans. Schmidt, p. 66.

For Ptolemy the ideal situation seems to be for the Sun to be in a masculine sign and the Moon in a feminine sign in a person's birth chart, which are the matching gender assignments for those planets, and therefore the native will then be balanced and behave in a way that is seen as appropriate or proper for the native's gender.[40] However, if both luminaries are in masculine signs in a chart, then for men it will make them overly masculine and thus excessive in what comes naturally to them, whereas for women it will make them excessive in what is seen as unnatural, and therefore they will become more masculine than feminine. If this situation is further compounded by Mars and/or Venus also being in masculine placements (i.e. masculine signs, or morning stars), then he says that men will become insatiable with regards to sex and adulterous, whereas women with this placement will become lesbians. Conversely, he says if the luminaries are both in feminine signs, then it results in excessively feminine women and effeminate men. If Venus is also feminized (i.e. in a feminine sign or becoming an evening star), then the women become so passive and open in sexual matters that they get into problematic situations, while the men become more passive and easily manipulated as well. If Mars is also feminized, then the natives are more overt about their sexuality and promiscuousness. One of the overall points for Ptolemy is that anything that is excessive is seen as bad, and this seems to be the main conceptual motivation underlying the delineations here.[41]

Valens seems to have had a similar approach in mind, especially in terms of morning rising stars being masculinized, and evening rising stars being feminized. In his delineation of Venus sextile Saturn he makes the following distinction:

> If both are at morning rising in the East, they masculinize women, so that the women not only act like men in their daily life, but they even do the work of men when lying with other women. If these stars are evening stars, they feminize men: sometimes men serve as women when lying with men, but often they lose their sex organs.[42]

All of these interpretive principles related to gender are wrapped up in the broader context of Greco-Roman gender and social norms, and while a full

---

[40] This is the implicit premise underlying Ptolemy, *Tetrabiblos*, 3, 15: 7–12. It is also stated more explicitly by other authors, especially Manetho, *Apotelesmatika*, 3: 363–396; 4: 508–526; 5: 209–216.

[41] This is also his explicit rationale for why the benefic planets are positive and the malefic planets are negative, because the benefics are seen as moderate or temperate, whereas the malefics are seen as tending towards extremes or excessive states. See Ptolemy, *Tetrabiblos*, 1, 5.

[42] Valens, *Anthology*, 2, 17: 68, trans. Riley, p. 33.

discussion of the applicability of these distinctions within a modern context is outside of the scope of this book, this should at least provide a starting point for understanding some of the different ways that gender was used as a conceptual distinction in ancient astrology.

The Thema Mundi

One of the most important conceptual constructs at the center of the Hellenistic tradition is the mythical horoscope for the birth of the world, known as the Thema Mundi. The phrase "Thema Mundi" is a Latin translation of the Greek phrase *kosmou genesis*, and both simply mean "Nativity of the Cosmos" or "Birth Chart of the World." Firmicus explains that the Thema Mundi was used as a teaching tool in Hellenistic astrology to help explain the motivation or rationale for different concepts, such as the domicile rulership scheme and the qualities of the different configurations or aspects.[43]

Composition and Rationale

There are a few different versions of the Thema Mundi, but the original one seems to have had Cancer rising, with the Moon in Cancer, Sun in Leo, Mercury in Virgo, Venus in Libra, Mars in Scorpio, Jupiter in Sagittarius, and Saturn in Capricorn.[44] Some later variants give specific degrees for each of the planets; Firmicus says that they were all at fifteen degrees of their respective signs, although this may just represent an attempt to clarify something that was left ambiguous or unspecified in the early source texts.[45]

---

[43] Firmicus, *Mathesis*, 3, 1: 8–15.

[44] This is the version outlined in book 2 of the Antiochus *Summary* (CCAG, 8, 3, p. 119: 1–4), as well as Macrobius, *Commentary on the Dream of Scipio*, 1, 21: 23–25. Most of the other variants are collected together in Rafaelli, *L'oroscopo del mundo*, pp. 141–146.

[45] Firmicus, *Mathesis*, 3, 1: 1. Paulus (*Introduction*, 37) has most of the planets at 15° of the same signs, except he puts the Sun at 19° Aries, Mercury at 7° Virgo, and Venus at 3° Libra. The placement of the Sun in Aries is odd, and seems to be a conflation with the exaltation scheme, where 19° Aries is the very degree of the Sun's exaltation. It is also odd because Paulus says that the birth of the cosmos took place in the eleventh hour of the night, which should place the Sun below the horizon. Boer notes in the critical apparatus for this passage of Paulus (p. 99) that one of the lesser manuscript traditions says that the Sun was in Leo, although this was evidently not represented in enough manuscripts that she thought it ultimately derived from the original version of Paulus. Bezza followed the alternative manuscript tradition and put the Sun in Leo in his translation of Paulus (Paolo d'Alessandria, *Introduzione all'astrologia*, trans. Bezza, p. 163), partially justifying it by pointing out that if the Sun was at 15° Leo as in Firmicus then Mercury and Venus would be close to their traditional degrees of maximum elongation (the furthest they can get from the Sun before stationing retrograde). These ranges are given earlier in Paulus, *Introduction*, 15, where he says that Mercury makes its first station when it is 22° from the Sun, and Venus at 48°. I suspect then that Bezza was correct in

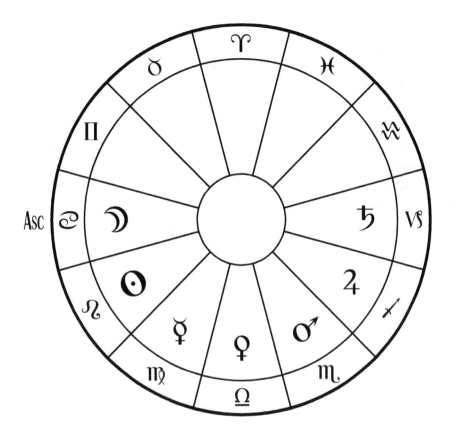

Figure 8.1 - Thema Mundi

In the Thema Mundi, each of the seven traditional planets is located in what became known as one of its "domiciles" or signs that it "rules," and this seems to have been part of the original conceptual basis for the traditional rulership scheme. It begins by assigning the Moon to Cancer and the Sun to Leo, and then the rest of the planets are assigned to the other signs in zodiacal order, based on their relative speed and distance from the Sun. Mercury, which never gets more than one sign away from the Sun before turning retrograde, is assigned to the sign immediately after the Sun, which is Virgo. Venus, which never gets more than two signs away from the Sun, is assigned to the sign two signs from the Sun in zodiacal order, which is Libra. The next furthest visible planet is Mars,

---

making this emendation and putting the Sun in Leo, although it is not clear then why most of the manuscripts put the Sun in its exaltation degree. In discussing this discrepancy, Rafaelli (*L'oroscopo del mundo*, p. 145–6) suggests that the entire chapter in Paulus may have been tampered with by scribes in the Medieval period, influenced by the alternative Persian version of the Thema Mundi that emphasizes the exaltations. It is only really the position of the Sun in Paulus that seems suspect, however.

which is assigned to Scorpio. Jupiter is the furthest planet after Mars, and is assigned to Sagittarius. Finally, Saturn—the furthest, slowest, and dimmest visible planet—is allotted to the sign opposite to the Moon, which is Capricorn.

One of the questions that naturally arises about the Thema Mundi is why Cancer should be the rising sign; what sort of significance did this have for ancient astrologers? Unfortunately, there is little discussion on this point in the surviving texts, but there are two pieces of astrological lore that may be relevant in attempting to explain it.

The first is the belief amongst some late Mesopotamian or early Hellenistic astrologers that the conjunction of all of the planets in the signs of Cancer and Capricorn indicated the periodic creation and destruction of the world. This doctrine was specifically ascribed to Berossus, who evidently said that when all of the planets are aligned in Cancer that the world would be destroyed in a fire, whereas when all of the planets are aligned in Capricorn the world would be destroyed by a flood.[46] This is probably because Cancer coincides with the hottest part of the year in the northern hemisphere, and thus they associated it with fire, whereas Capricorn coincides with the winter, and thus the coldness of water. This may also explain why the two lights or luminaries were assigned to Cancer and Leo as the starting point of the sequence of planets, since these two signs fall just after the summer solstice, during the hottest and brightest part of the year. The distinction between masculine and feminine signs may have already been in place by this point, since the Moon is assigned to the first sign after the solstice, Cancer, which is feminine, while the Sun is assigned to the masculine sign Leo.

Another possible motivation for Cancer rising in the Thema Mundi is that in Egypt, the heliacal rising of the fixed star Sirius in the summertime would indicate the annual flooding of the Nile River, which marked the beginning of the Egyptian calendar.[47] Sirius is the brightest fixed star in the night sky, and in the Hellenistic period its heliacal rising would occur in July just before sunrise when the Sun was in Leo. Thus Sirius would first make an appearance from under the Sun's beams during the summer when Cancer was rising over the eastern horizon in the morning just before the Sun rose in Leo. Thus Cancer becomes the starting point for the Egyptian year, and by extension perhaps for the cosmos in general.

---

[46] Seneca, *Natural Questions*, 3, 29: 1. See the discussion in Van der Sluijs, "A Possible Babylonian Precursor to the Theory of ecpyrōsis."

[47] Bouché-Leclercq first noted this (*L'Astrologie grecque*, pp. 185–6), saying that it betrayed the Egyptian origin of the Thema Mundi. On the Egyptian calendar and the heliacal rising of Sirius see Bomhard, *The Egyptian Calendar*.

The Nativity of God?

Most of the astrologers who mention the Thema Mundi consistently refer to it as the nativity of the cosmos; however, Antiochus apparently referred to it as the "nativity of god" (*theou geneseōs*).[48] This may provide some clues to the philosophical mindset of some of the early Hellenistic astrologers, as there were a few specific philosophical schools that considered the cosmos to be a divine being. In the *Timaeus*, Plato describes the creation of the cosmos and says that it is a living creature with a soul and intelligence.[49] The Stoics adopted this doctrine and took it further, developing a pantheistic philosophy in which the entire cosmos is a sentient, divine being, so that the sensible world is the body of the cosmos, and is infused with the invisible soul of the cosmos that holds everything together:

> They [the Stoics] say that god is mixed with matter, pervading all of it and so shaping it, structuring it, and making it into the world.[50]

Even the term "cosmos," which was often used to refer to the Thema Mundi, was sometimes used by the Stoics to refer to god. According to Diogenes Laertius:

> They [the Stoics] use "world" [*kosmos*] in three ways: of god himself, the peculiarly qualified individual consisting of all substance, who is indestructible and ingenerable, since he is the manufacturer of the world-order, at set periods of time consuming all substance into himself and reproducing it again from himself; they also describe the world-order as "world"; and thirdly, what is composed out of both [i.e. god and world-order].[51]

The notion of the cosmos itself as god is a theme that also comes up in the *Corpus Hermeticum*:

> This entire cosmos, this great god, which is an image of the greater, with whom it is united, preserves the order and will of the Father and is the abundance of life. In this cosmos, throughout the eternal cycle of ages, which issues from the Father, there is nothing, neither of the whole nor of

---

[48] Antiochus, *Summary*, book 2 (CCAG 8, 3, p. 118: 25).

[49] Plato, *Timaeus*, 29e–37a.

[50] Alexander of Aphrodisias, *On Mixture*, 225: 1–2 (SVF 2.310, part), trans. Long and Sedley, *The Hellenistic Philosophers*, vol. 1, 45H, p. 273.

[51] Diogenes Laertius, *Lives*, 7: 137 (SVF 2.525, part), trans. Long and Sedley, *The Hellenistic Philosophers*, vol. 1, 44F, p. 270.

any part, that does not live. In the cosmos not one dead thing has come to be, is, or will be. For the Father willed that as long as it exists it should be a living being. Therefore the cosmos must needs be a god also.[52]

This may imply that for some of the early Hellenistic astrologers the Thema Mundi had some deeper philosophical or religious significance, because in examining the hypothetical birth chart of the cosmos it provided insight not only into the inner workings and development of the universe through the astrological construct, but indeed, it may have given them some sense of insight into the divine itself.

Domicile Rulership

In the astrological texts, the signs of the zodiac were commonly said to be the "houses," "domiciles," or "dwelling places" of the planets, from the Greek word *oikos*. According to this doctrine, each luminary is assigned one sign of the zodiac, and then each of the remaining planets is allocated two signs of the zodiac, one sign being masculine and the other feminine. The domicile of the Sun is the masculine sign Leo, while the domicile of the Moon is the feminine sign of Cancer. Mercury is allotted Gemini and Virgo as its domiciles, Venus is assigned to Taurus and Libra, Mars to Aries and Scorpio, Jupiter to Pisces and Sagittarius, and Saturn to Aquarius and Capricorn.

The domicile assignments set up one of the most important planetary rulership schemes in the Hellenistic tradition, which every major Hellenistic astrologer used.[53] Each planet is said to be the "domicile master" (*oikodespotēs*), "lord" (*kurios*), or "ruler" (*despotēs*) of the sign that it calls home. This is one of the earliest rulership schemes introduced towards the beginning of the Hellenistic tradition, and is one of the most defining features that sets Greco-Roman astrology apart from the earlier Mesopotamian tradition.

What modern astrologers refer to as the twelve "houses" were called "places" or "regions" (*topoi*) in Hellenistic astrology, which we will discuss in more detail in the chapter dedicated to that topic. In order to avoid confusion between these two techniques, I will use the word *domicile* to refer to the Hellenistic concept of planets calling certain signs their "home." While it still essentially means the same thing as "house," by using a different word in English, it should help us to

---

[52] *Corpus Hermeticum*, 12: 15, trans. Salaman et al, *The Way of Hermes*, p. 62.

[53] The concept is explicitly defined in Dorotheus, *Carmen*, 1, 1: 8; *Michigan Papyrus*, col. xvi: 4–20; Ptolemy, *Tetrabiblos*, 1, 18; Porphyry, *Introduction*, 5; Firmicus, *Mathesis*, 1, 2. Others refer to it when discussing the properties of the signs, such as Valens, *Anthology*, 1, 2; Paulus, *Introduction*, 2. The rest take it for granted and use it implicitly as a basic technical concept.

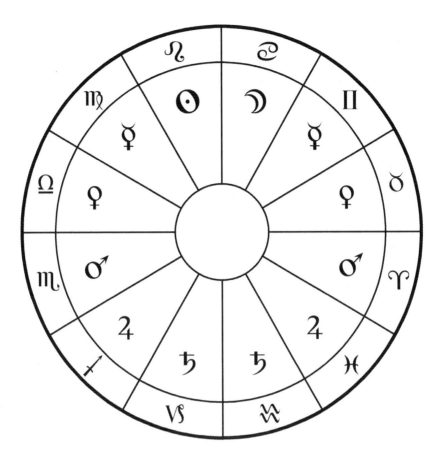

Figure 8.2 - Domiciles of the Planets

maintain some level of clarity when we are discussing the different concepts.

The domicile assignments seem to be derived from the Thema Mundi by creating a mirror image of it with the same planetary sequence projected out—in reverse zodiacal order—from the Moon in Cancer. This results in a symmetrical scheme in which the two luminaries are allocated to the two signs during the warmest and brightest part of the year in the northern hemisphere, and then the rest of the planets are alloted to the signs flanking the luminaries based on their relative speed and distance. Thus, the Moon and Sun are assigned to Cancer and Leo, respectively, as per the Thema Mundi. Then Mercury, which never gets more than one sign away from the Sun, is assigned to the signs immediately adjacent to the two luminaries, which are Gemini and Virgo. Venus, which never gets more than two signs away from the Sun, is assigned to Taurus and Libra, which are both two signs apart from Cancer and Leo. Mars is the next furthest planet out, and is assigned to Aries and Scorpio. Jupiter, the next furthest planet, is assigned to Pisces and Sagittarius. Finally, Saturn is the most distant and slowest visible planet, and is assigned to the two signs that are furthest from the two luminaries, Capricorn and Aquarius.

Ptolemy points out that the luminaries are assigned to the two most northern signs that coincide with the hottest and brightest part of the year, when the days are longest in the northern hemisphere (where Hellenistic astrology was developed).[54] Conversely, he says that Saturn is the furthest visible planet, so it is assigned to the two signs furthest from the luminaries, which coincides with the signs that align with the coldest part of the year just after the winter solstice.[55] While it is true that Ptolemy tends to favor naturalistic rationales that emphasize themes related to heat, light, and moisture, we should be cautious about assuming that these were the only factors that the originator of this scheme took into account when developing it. Nevertheless, these still seem to be some compelling points that create a sort of symbolic affinity between planets and signs.[56]

The seasonal factors described by Ptolemy appear to form a large part of the basis for the traditional rulership scheme; if true, this would mean that seasonal or tropical considerations were taken into account in the early Hellenistic tradition during the composition of the Thema Mundi and domicile rulership scheme. This must be one of the factors that made Ptolemy think that some of the early astrological writers had the tropical zodiac in mind when developing Hellenistic astrology. In point of fact, Firmicus explicitly says that the Thema Mundi was outlined by Nechepso and Petosiris, and that they received the doctrine from Asclepius and Hermes Trismegistus.[57] If this is true, then the Thema Mundi and the domicile assignments become the first instance of a conceptual construct underlying the practice of Hellenistic astrology, which may be traced back to an early set of *de facto* foundational texts.

Alternative Persian Rationale for Assignments

There is an interesting alternative rationale for the domicile assignments that seems to come from the Sassanian Persian tradition, which is preserved in a later

---

[54] Ptolemy, *Tetrabiblos*, 1, 18: 2–3.

[55] Ptolemy, *Tetrabiblos*, 1, 18: 4.

[56] Porphyry has a similar but slightly different rationale in *On the Cave of the Nymphs*, 21, trans. Lamberton, p. 71, where he says: "The summer tropic is in Cancer, the winter one in Capricorn. Since Cancer is very close to us, this constellation is appropriately associated with the Moon, which is the closest of the heavenly bodies to the earth. Since the South Pole remains invisible, Capricorn is associated with the farthest and highest of these bodies, i.e. Saturn."

[57] Firmicus, *Mathesis*, 3, proem: 4; 3, 1: 1–2.

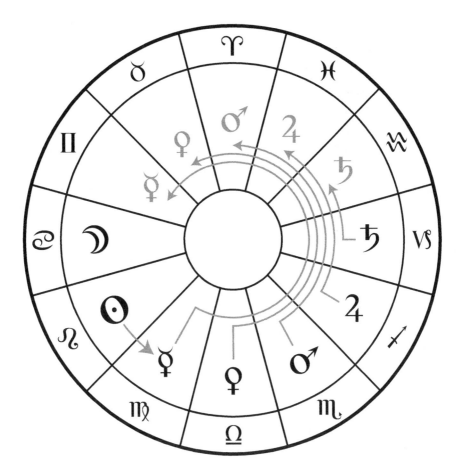

Figure 8.3 - Persian Rulership Rationale

Byzantine Greek translation.[58] The story has an almost mythological quality; it starts with the planets in the positions they held at the birth of the world in the Thema Mundi.[59] Then the Sun is said to have begun moving through the signs in zodiacal order. First it moved from Leo into Virgo, where Mercury, unable to deal with the intensity of the Sun's fiery rays, escaped by moving over into the

[58] From *Vaticanus graecus* 191, ff. 229–231v., edited in CCAG, 5, 2, pp. 130–37, esp. p. 132: 17–30, trans. George, *The Foundation of the Astrological Art*, pp. 1–2. The provenance is discussed briefly in Pingree, *From Astral Omens*, p. 67, and then more extensively with a translation and commentary in Rafaelli, *L'oroscopo del mundo*, pp. 154–160. Rafaelli says that some of the Zoroastrian elements imply that it is probably ultimately derived from Sassanian Persian sources, although the text itself is a Greek translation of an Arabic text.

[59] The mythological character of this account is somewhat reminiscent of the cosmogony outlined in *Corpus Hermeticum* 1, the *Poimandres*, and it leads me to suspect that the original account of the Thema Mundi may have been outlined in a Hermetic text that adopted a similar literary style. This would explain why Firmicus invokes the Hermes, Asclepius, and Nechepso-Petosiris lineage to explain where he obtained the doctrine of the Thema Mundi.

furthest unoccupied sign in zodiacal order, which is Gemini, next to the Moon in Cancer. Next, the Sun began moving from Virgo into Libra, and Venus saw him coming and packed up her bags and moved into the next furthest unoccupied sign, which was Taurus. As the Sun progressed, Mars in Scorpio moved over into Aries, and Jupiter in Sagittarius moved into Pisces. Finally, Saturn in Capricorn, the last planet left, could only move one sign over into Aquarius; when the Sun caught up to him he fell under the beams, which burnt him up, dried him out, and turned him black, whence his dark color.

It is unclear if this story ultimately goes back to Hellenistic sources and played some additional or secondary role as an explanatory rationale for the domicile assignments, or if it was simply an explanation that was developed later in the Sassanian Persian tradition to justify the domicile assignment scheme after the fact. Either way, it provides an interesting additional perspective on the symmetries involved.

Domicile Rulership and the Guest-Host Metaphor

The Hellenistic astrologers appear to have conceptualized planets in their own domiciles with the metaphor of being "at home." When a person is at home they have access to their own resources, they are in their own element, and thus they are able to act more effectively and in a way that is more in accord with their basic nature. However, when a planet is in the domicile of another planet, it has to rely on its host for support, which can be either positive or negative, depending on who the host is and what relationship they have with their guest. Sometimes the host planet will support the guest, while other times a host planet may act as a hindrance or even become hostile towards the guest. This entire metaphor is explained by Firmicus:

> Note also what planet is located in the house or the terms of which particular planet and, if your planet is located in the house of another, look at the ruler of that house to see which houses of the chart it is in. [...] For if the ruler of the sign is well located, that planet about which we are inquiring also shares in a part of the good fortune of the host's joy. But if the ruler of the sign is dejected in any way, that planet about which we are inquiring, even though placed in a fortunate house, will be hindered by the dejection of that other planet which is the ruler of the sign. This also you can easily observe from human behavior. If you enter anyone's home by invitation and the master of the house has just been blessed with an increase in good fortune, you too become a participant in his good fortune,

for you share in the happiness of the good fortune of your host. But if the host is suffering from miserable poverty and is embroiled in the wretched accidents of misfortune, you make yourself also a partner in his grief and trouble, and the adversity in which you share overwhelms you too. This is also true of the planets who are rulers of the signs.[60]

This guest-host metaphor then leads to the concrete interpretive principle that a planet in its own domicile is seen as more positive in a chart than a planet that is not in its own sign. According to Manetho:

All of the stars in their own domiciles at the time of birth are very good; when benefic, they are better, and they give more good things; and when malefic, they give fewer bad things. Accordingly, it is particularly important to consider how many (planets) are seen to be in their own domiciles or bounds. If they are more, they are by far better. But if they are fewer, they grant a lesser glory and profession to one's livelihood.[61]

The underlying premise here seems to be that planets in their own domiciles are viewed as more positive or fortunate because those planets do not have to rely on any other planets for support. This is why Dorotheus describes planets in their own domiciles as being "self-ruled" (*autodespota*) and "having one's own power" (*autexousia*).[62] Similarly, the anonymous author of the *Michigan Papyrus* says "in these signs the stars have their own powers and are vigorous."[63]

Similar sentiments are expressed by other astrologers in terms of planets in their own domiciles being viewed as positive. For example, Antiochus, Thrasyllus, and Firmicus all recommend comparing the birth charts of individuals to the Thema Mundi or to the mirror image of the Thema Mundi, effectively to ascertain how many planets are in their own domiciles in a person's chart.[64] Thrasyllus says that the Thema Mundi is a sort of "standard" or ideal "model" (*kanōn*) that other charts should be compared to or measured against. Antiochus speaks of the Thema Mundi as if it is the nativity of god, and he says that the more planets in their own domiciles that an individual nativity has, the more brilliant or magnificent (*lampros*) the life is, since it approaches or approximates the divine, while those which have none of the same placements

---

[60] Firmicus, *Mathesis*, 2, 20: 9–10, trans. Bram, p. 52.

[61] Manetho, *Apotelesmatika*, 2: 141–147, trans. Lopilato, p. 207, modified.

[62] Dorotheus, *Excerpts*, 8: 1, trans. Gramaglia.

[63] *Michigan Papyrus*, col. xvi: 22–23, trans. Robbins, p. 116.

[64] For Antiochus see CCAG, 8, 3, p. 118: 29–p. 119: 12. For Thrasyllus see CCAG 8, 3, p. 100: 27–30. Firmicus, *Mathesis*, 3, 1.

experience misfortune (*dustuchia*). Firmicus must have drawn on a similar doctrine in his chapter on the quality of nativities:

> This too we should know, that an average chart is that which has a single planet in its own sign, located in an important house of the chart. The man who has a chart with two planets, each in its own sign, is blessed with moderately good fortune. Fortunate and powerful beyond the usual is the one who has three; and he could be near to the gods in happiness who has four planets, each located in its own sign. More than this number the character of the human race does not allow; while on the other hand, he who has no planet in its own sign will forever be unknown, of low-born family, and doomed to a miserable life.[65]

Later, in his discussion of the Thema Mundi, Firmicus says that the early Hellenistic astrologers "wished to prove that the fates of men are arranged in accordance with this birth chart."[66] Elsewhere he says that it "has been handed down to us as an example to follow in the charts of men," and that "man was created in the image of the world."[67]

From a practical standpoint, it seems that a planet's domicile is a place that the planet enjoys being in because it is most well-suited to its own natural expression. In other words, when a planet is at home it can do what it wants, and what it wants to do is signify the things that come naturally to it. A byproduct of this is that when the planet is able to signify the things that come naturally to it, the area of life under the control of that planet will tend to be more fortunate, which results in that area being experienced as more positive by the native. This point will become more clear later when we start looking at some example charts.

Basic Natures of the Planets via the Domicile Assignments

In the Hellenistic tradition we can see some attempts by different authors to describe the core meanings of the planets by establishing certain keywords from which other significations can be derived. None of these attempts to narrow down the diverse significations of the planets into single principles seem to have been completely successful, perhaps due to the impossibility of articulating something as broad or all-encompassing as an archetype, although the different attempts are useful because they help to provide an access point for understanding the rationale underlying some of the individual significations.

---

[65] Firmicus, *Mathesis*, 2, 21, trans. Bram, p. 53.
[66] Firmicus, *Mathesis*, 3, 1: 2, trans. Bram, p. 72.
[67] Firmicus, *Mathesis*, 3, 1: 15, trans. Bram, p. 74.

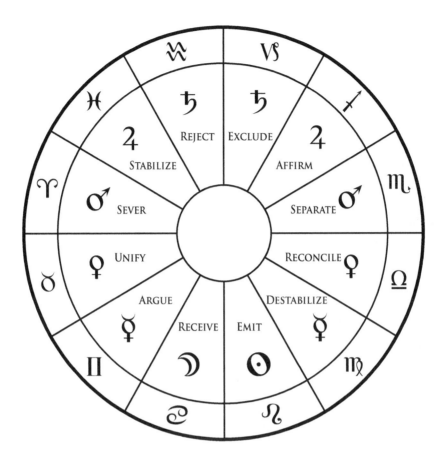

Figure 8.4 - Basic Natures of the Planets

Rhetorius uses the domicile assignments of the planets to the signs of the zodiac as a means of establishing a basic set of core significations for the planets, by contrasting the significations of each planet with those of the planet that rules the opposing zodiacal sign.[68]

In Rhetorius' model the Sun and Moon, from their domiciles of Cancer and Leo, signify light, and this is contrasted with Saturn in its opposing domiciles of Capricorn and Aquarius, which he says signifies darkness. Venus as ruler of Libra and Taurus is said to signify pleasure and desire, and he contrasts this with Mars as ruler of the opposite signs Aries and Scorpio as signifying fear and wrath. Finally, he contrasts Jupiter ruling Sagittarius and Pisces as signifying possessions and abundance with Mercury as the ruler of the opposite signs, Gemini and Virgo, as signifying the intellect and reason. The point here is that some of the significations or meanings of the planets were not developed or

---

[68] Rhetorius, *Compendium*, 8.

conceptualized in isolation, but instead were developed together in pairs by contrasting opposing principles through the domicile assignments.

A similar principle may be at work in Proclus' commentary on Plato's *Timaeus*, when he says that "Venus possess the power of binding things together and harmonizing what has been separated,"[69] presumably contrasting the principles of Venus and Mars, as we have seen Rhetorius do earlier through their domicile assignments. This goes beyond just a mechanical listing of a myriad of different manifestations, such as the one we encountered from Valens earlier; instead it seems to represent an attempt to find an underlying principle that can bind together many different significations. For example, the overarching ideas of "binding together" and "harmonizing" mentioned by Proclus could be applied to some of the following individual significations that Valens gives for Venus: love, friendship, companionship, marriage, reconciliation, making music, pleasant sounds, painting and art in general, decorating, cleaning, order, and so on.

Following this logic, Schmidt took the domicile assignment model of Rhetorius and modified it in order to try to establish a set of overarching significations that could encompass those given in Valens' lists.[70] In his model, the Sun's primary principle is to "select," and it is opposite to Saturn's principle which is to "reject." The Moon's principle is to "gather and include," while Saturn's opposing principle is to "reject." Venus "unifies and reconciles," while Mars "severs and separates." Finally, Mercury "destabilizes and contests" while Jupiter "confirms and stabilizes."

While Schmidt's model does not encompass all of the significations of the planets, it is a useful starting point that covers many of the most fundamental meanings that the Hellenistic astrologers often give. I use a slightly modified version of Schmidt's model, taking a cue from a statement that Olympiodorus makes that the basic nature of the Sun is that it "gives" (*didōsi*) light while the Moon "receives" (*dechetai*) light.[71] Elsewhere, instead of "contest" for Mercury I would say "argue," opposing it to the principle of Jupiter to "affirm," although it should be pointed out that Mercury is the most multifaceted of the planets, and there are a number of other core concepts underlying its significations that could be used as alternative principles. Again, while this model does not cover every possible signification for each of the traditional planets, it is a useful way to see how some of the meanings were arranged in connection with other concepts such as the zodiacal domiciles.

---

[69] Proclus, *Commentary on Plato's Timaeus*, IV, 66: 7–8, trans. Baltzly, vol. 5, p. 133.

[70] Schmidt, *Kepler College Sourcebook*, figure 4.

[71] Olympiodorus, *Commentary on Plato's Gorgias*, 47.4, trans. Jackson et al, p. 299. Greek text edited in Olympiodorus, *Olympiodori in Platonis Gorgiam commentaria*, ed. Westerink.

Ptolemy's Basic Natures of the Planets

It should be noted at this point that Ptolemy also attempted to introduce a model to explain the basic natures of the planets, and while it was not connected to the domicile assignments, it should probably be presented at this point in the discussion. Ptolemy adapted the Aristotelian qualities of hot, cold, wet, and dry and applied them to the planets in order to explain their basic natures.[72] The "powers" (*dunameis*) or qualities he ascribed to the planets are as follows:

SATURN:	cooling and slightly drying
JUPITER:	heating and slightly moistening
MARS:	drying and burning
SUN:	heating and slightly drying
VENUS:	moistening and slightly heating
MERCURY:	alternating between moistening and drying
MOON:	moistening and slightly heating

The fourth century CE philosopher Iamblichus draws on a similar model in the process of explaining how the natural qualities of Mars and Saturn might be experienced as problematic or "malefic" in the lives of individuals, even if the planets themselves are not inherently evil:

> the emanation deriving from Saturn tends to pull things together, while that deriving from Mars tends to provoke motion in them; however, at the level of material things, the passive generative receptacle receives the one as rigidity and coldness, and the other as a degree of inflammation exceeding moderation.[73]

This explanation is derived from the causal astrological model of Ptolemy, where by way of example he explains all of Mars' significations as ultimately deriving from the planet's tendency to dry and burn things:

> The star of Ares has a nature chiefly to dry and to burn, appropriately both for the fiery nature of its color and for its proximity to the Sun, since the solar sphere lies underneath it.[74]

Ptolemy's model was adopted by a number of later astrologers, and became

---

[72] Ptolemy, *Tetrabiblos*, 1, 4.
[73] Iamblichus, *On the Mysteries*, 1, 18, trans. Clarke et al, p. 69.
[74] Ptolemy, *Tetrabiblos*, 1, 4: 4, trans. Schmidt, pp. 14–15.

very influential in the medieval tradition, although it is not clear to what extent he was drawing on an earlier tradition versus creating a new conceptual model within the context of his broader cosmological program.

Exaltations and Depressions

There are certain signs in which each of the planets was said to have their "exaltation," from the Greek *hupsōma*, which refers to something that is raised up, elevated, or at its height. The Sun is said to have its exaltation in Aries, the Moon in Taurus, Saturn in Libra, Jupiter in Cancer, Mars in Capricorn, Venus in Pisces, and Mercury in Virgo.

The sign opposite to a planet's exaltation is the sign of its "depression," from the Greek word *tapeinōma*, which means to lower, depress, or deject something. In late traditional astrology, this position is more commonly referred to as the sign of a planet's "fall," although I follow Schmidt in rendering it as "depression" here, as this seems both more evocative and in line with the underlying concept.[75] The Sun is said to have its depression in Libra, the Moon in Scorpio, Saturn in Aries, Jupiter in Capricorn, Mars in Cancer, Venus in Virgo, and Mercury in Pisces.

There are also a set of specific degrees that are sometimes mentioned in connection with the exaltations. There is some ambiguity due to slight variations in the numbers given in the textual tradition.[76] Nonetheless, the standard set of exaltation degrees is as follows, according to Valens, *Anthology*, 3, 4:

MOON:	3° Taurus
SUN:	19° Aries
MERCURY:	15° Virgo
VENUS:	27° Pisces
MARS:	28° Capricorn
JUPITER:	15° Cancer
SATURN:	21° Libra

It is not clear what the rationale is for the exaltation degrees.[77] Most of the time

---

[75] Schmidt, *Definitions and Foundations*, p. 110.

[76] Pingree gives a list of different variants for the exaltation degrees in *Yavanajātaka*, vol. 2, pp. 220–21. The main discrepancy is whether Saturn should be exalted at 21° or 20° Libra, although it seems like the majority of Hellenistic sources favor 21°. Another variant is that Porphyry, *Introduction*, 6, says that Venus should be exalted at 26° Pisces rather than 27°, although it is the only source for that variant, so this may just be a textual error.

[77] The mid-twentieth century astrologer Cyril Fagan attempted to argue that the exaltation degrees were based on a set of actual planetary alignments that occurred on different dates

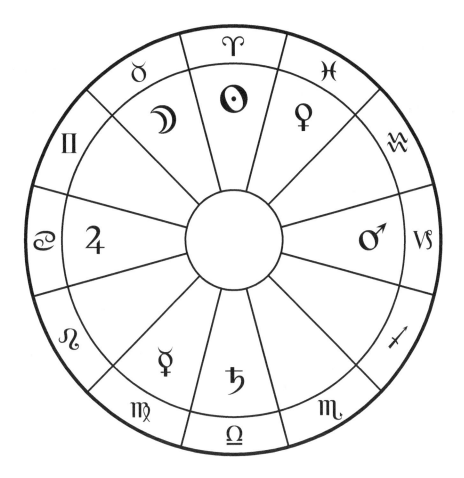

Figure 8.5 - Exaltations

the Hellenistic astrologers seem to focus on the entire sign of exaltation rather than concentrating on the specific degree, with the exception of a few techniques that are specifically designed to take the exaltation degrees into account.[78] It is also notable that most of the rationales given for the exaltations in the textual tradition seem to focus on the entire signs rather than the specific degrees,

---

around 786 BCE, although most of the positions he found are only roughly correct, and it is not clear why these placements would be seen as having a lasting impact from that point forward. He speculates that it was due to the building of a temple to Nabu that year, which was the god associated with Mercury. The argument was originally outlined in Fagan, *Zodiacs Old and New*, which was summarized and defended more recently in Bowser, *An Introduction to Western Sidereal Astrology*, pp. 193–201.

[78] One instance is the "steps" and "winds" technique outlined by Valens in *Anthology*, 3, 4, although he notes that some other astrologers think that this technique is useless. Another instance occurs within the context of a timing technique briefly outlined by Balbillus in CCAG 8, 4, p. 237: 16–22 (trans. Schmidt, *Sages*, p. 70).

which creates some ambiguity surrounding how the concept was developed and whether the exaltation signs or degrees came first.

The concept of exaltations was apparently inherited from the Mesopotamian tradition, although it is integrated into other Hellenistic concepts in surprising and rather striking ways. This raises some questions about the order of the development of some of the doctrines, which we will discuss more later.

Interpretation of the Exaltations

The astrologers sometimes tend to speak of the planets as having more power when they are exalted, and having their power diminished when they are depressed. For example, Firmicus says that exalted planets are "elevated by a certain natural sublimity of magnitude," while planets in their depression are "weakened by the diminished power of their authority."[79] It is not necessarily the case here that the "power" described by Firmicus derives from some sort of energy or force emitted by the planets, as is sometimes assumed; instead, this statement seems to be his attempt to explain an earlier metaphor that associated the exaltations with positions of authority, which by extension were connected with the ability to exercise power. In one of the excerpts from Dorotheus it says that when a planet is in its exaltation it can signify that the native will be "illustrious and remarkable," because

> the star attaining exaltation is a kingly and authoritative figure: whence, if the stars giving the activity are in their own exaltations too, they are entrusted with kingly works, dwell with them, and enjoy the profit therefrom.[80]

There is a similar and somewhat more explicit statement in the *Michigan Papyrus*, where the author refers to the exaltations as "thrones" (*thronous*) and the depressions as "prisons" (*phulakas*):

> And nature assigned them thrones and prisons; their thrones the signs upon which they are exalted and have royal power and prisons wherein they are depressed and oppose their own powers.[81]

Elsewhere Dorotheus treats the exaltations and depressions as if they are conceptually similar to the doctrine of planets being in culminating or declining

---

[79] Firmicus, *Mathesis*, 2, 3: 1, trans. Holden, p. 46.
[80] Dorotheus, *Excerpts*, 8: 2–3, trans. Gramaglia.
[81] *Michigan Papyrus*, col. xvi: 23–27, trans. Robbins, p. 116.

places. Through this he associates the exaltations with things that are raised up to a high point, and thus of a high quality, ennobled, and esteemed, versus the depressions, which indicate things that are brought down low or are falling downward, which are thus of lower quality, cheapened, or made shabby:

> The stars being in their own exaltations, or culminating, indicate that the matters or people are more honorable and of higher repute, especially Jupiter and Venus; Saturn would show them to be honorable, but also sordid or old. In the depressions or declines, they disparage (*eutelizō*) the affairs.[82]

Rationale for the Exaltations

Later in the tradition, Rhetorius emphasizes the conflicting nature of the planets that have their exaltations in diametrically opposing signs, and he presents this as part of the explanatory rationale for why the planets are said to be exalted in certain signs.[83] This dynamic, he then notes, creates three polarities: Sun in Aries opposes Saturn in Libra; Mercury in Virgo opposes Venus in Pisces; Jupiter in Cancer opposes Mars in Capricorn. According to Rhetorius, each planet displays opposing or contrary qualities within the context of this scheme, in much the same way as the domicile lords display contrary natures to their opposing domicile lords. The Sun's qualities of fire, light, and heat are opposed to Saturn's qualities of darkness and cold, with the Sun being exalted in Aries and Saturn being exalted in Libra, and each having their depressions in the sign opposite. Here there is some overlap with Ptolemy, who attempts to provide a similar justification for how the exaltations are tied into the seasons.[84] He says that the Sun is exalted in Aries because this is the sign just after the spring equinox, when the length of the days begins to increase, and thus the heating power of the Sun begins to increase as well. This is opposite to Libra, which comes just after the fall equinox, when the days begin to become shorter and the power of the Sun starts to diminish. Thus, there are symbolic themes of rising up or falling down.

Rhetorius extends a similar rationale to Jupiter and Mars, which are exalted in Cancer and Capricorn, respectively. There he associates Jupiter with the "life-breath" or "vital-breath" (*zōtikou pneumatos*) and abundance, and he contrasts this with Mars as signifying death. After that he contrasts Venus as signifying desire and pleasure with Mercury as signifying the intellectual, saying that

---

[82] Dorotheus, *Excerpts*, 64: 1–2, trans. Gramaglia. In the notes to this translation Dykes pointed out that the word *eutelizō* derives from notions of cheapening or making shabby.

[83] Rhetorius, *Compendium*, 7.

[84] Ptolemy, *Tetrabiblos*, 1, 20.

when the intellectual is raised up it means that the impetus for desire and pleasure is diminished, whereas when desire and pleasure are exalted the intellect is depressed.

The Moon is the only planet in this scheme that has no opposite, since no planet has its exaltation in Scorpio, and Rhetorius says that this is because the Moon is the "fortune of all" (*tuchē esti tou pantos*), and whatever fortune exalts nothing can depress, and whatever fortune depresses nothing can exalt. Here he seems to be emphasizing the overriding nature of the concept of fortune or *tuchē*.

In terms of other possible explanatory rationales, Porphyry points out that in the exaltation scheme, each of the diurnal planets is configured to one of their domiciles by trine when they are in their sign of exaltation, whereas conversely each of the nocturnal planets are configured to one of their domiciles by sextile.[85] For example, the Sun in its exaltation in Aries is configured to its domicile Leo by trine; Jupiter in Cancer is configured to Pisces by trine; and Saturn in Libra is configured to Aquarius by trine. With respect to the nocturnal planets, the Moon in its exaltation of Taurus is configured to its domicile Cancer by sextile; Venus in Pisces is configured to Taurus by sextile; and Mars in Capricorn is configured to Scorpio by sextile. This striking arrangement is suggestive of a deeper underlying attempt to create a logical system of interrelated concepts and techniques, which in this instance integrates the planets, domiciles, and sect with the doctrine of configurations or aspects.

Another interesting discovery about the possible rationale for the exaltations was made by Schmidt, who points out that when you superimpose the exaltations on the Thema Mundi,

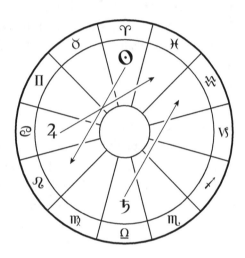

Figure 8.6 - Diurnal Exaltation Trines

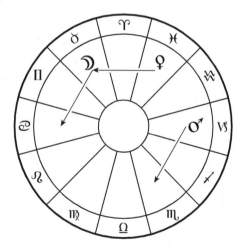

Figure 8.7 - Nocturnal Exaltation Sextiles

---

[85] Porphyry, *Introduction*, 6.

each of the signs of exaltation is configured to the rising sign by one of the five recognized configurations.[86] For example, in the Thema Mundi, the Moon's sign of exaltation, Taurus, is configured to the rising sign, Cancer, by sextile. The Sun in Aries is configured to Cancer by square; Venus in Pisces is configured by trine; Mars in Capricorn by opposition; Saturn in Libra by square; and Mercury in Virgo by sextile. The last remaining planet, Jupiter, has its exaltation in Cancer, which is the rising sign itself. Schmidt suggests that since most of the planetary domiciles in the Thema Mundi are determined based on their phase relationship with the Sun, perhaps the Moon plays a similar role in the exaltations scheme, with its domicile becoming the focal point that all planets are configured to.[87]

Origins of the Exaltations
These symmetries and the way that they seem to incorporate several other concepts into the underlying rationale for the exaltations is perplexing, since the exaltations are one of the few specific technical concepts that are usually thought to have been inherited from the earlier Mesopotamian tradition.[88] Firmicus explicitly says at one point that "the Babylonians called the signs in which the planets are exalted their 'domiciles' (*domicilia*)," and since the early twentieth century, modern scholars have thought the exaltations were associated with what is called in cuneiform texts the *bit nisirti* or *asar nisirti*, which means "secret houses" or "secret places."[89] The extent to which other concepts that are thought to be unique to the Hellenistic tradition—such as domiciles, sect, and aspects, which are integrated into the rationale outlined by Porphyry—raises some serious questions about the order of the development of these doctrines. At least three potential scenarios might be implied:

1. The exaltations were inherited on their own from the Mesopotamian tradition, and then the concepts of domiciles, sect, and aspects were developed around them in the early Hellenistic tradition. At least as

---

[86] Schmidt, *Definitions and Foundations*, p. 110. This point is also made in the same text that contains the Persian story about domicile assignments, so that at one point the planets in their exaltations are superimposed on a chart with Cancer rising. See CCAG 5, 2, p. 133: 18–36.

[87] Schmidt, *Definitions and Foundations*, p. 112.

[88] As discussed in Hunger and Pingree, *Astral Sciences in Mesopotamia*, pp. 28–29; Rochberg-Halton, "Elements of the Babylonian Contribution to Hellenistic Astrology," pp. 53–57; Rochberg, *Babylonian Horoscopes*, pp. 46–50.

[89] Firmicus, *Mathesis*, 2, 3: 4, trans. Bram, p. 34, modified. Rochberg notes that the connection between the Hellenistic exaltations and the Mesopotamian secret places was first established by Ernst Weidner in two papers published in 1913 and 1919. See Rochberg-Halton, "Elements of the Babylonian," p. 53, fn. 13.

far as what we currently have evidence for in terms of which techniques were being employed in the Mesopotamian tradition, this is a somewhat natural conclusion to make, although conceptually it seems somewhat implausible given how well the internal logic underlying the concepts of domiciles, sect, and aspects stands on its own.

2. The exaltation scheme was not inherited from the earlier Mesopotamian tradition, but instead was created in the early Hellenistic tradition alongside the other concepts such as domiciles, sect, and aspects. This would explain why all four concepts seem to be so well integrated, but it would mean that the current scholarly consensus that connects the Hellenistic exaltations with the Mesopotamian secret places would be mistaken. Rochberg does note that most of the evidence used to connect the exaltations with the secret places dates to the Seleucid period, which might imply that the concept could have actually first been developed in the Hellenistic astrological tradition along with the other concepts, after which it was transmitted back into cuneiform sources.[90] However, the apparent existence of earlier, albeit scanty, references to the secret places prior to the Hellenistic/Seleucid period may contradict this hypothesis.[91]

3. The exaltations were developed alongside the domiciles, sect, and the aspect doctrine sometime in the earlier Mesopotamian tradition, and we simply don't have evidence for the use of domiciles, sect, or aspects in the earlier Mesopotamian tradition yet due to the loss of texts.[92]

---

[90] Rochberg, *Babylonian Horoscopes*, p. 48.

[91] For the pre-Hellenistic references see Hunger and Pingree, *Astral Sciences*, p. 28. The late cuneiform references to Aries as a ram or sheep instead of the older name of the "Hired Man" is usually thought to be an indication of influence going from the Hellenistic/Greek tradition into the late Mesopotamian tradition, although this point as well as some other potential instances of reverse transmission were recently summarized and challenged in Steele, "Greek influence on Babylonian astronomy?"

[92] Rochberg said in an early paper that there is evidence that the "trine aspect" was used in Mesopotamia, although the doctrine she cited instead seems to be a forerunner of the Hellenistic concept of grouping the signs into four sets of three now known as "triplicities." Rochberg-Halton, "Elements of the Babylonian," pp. 60–62. The confusion arises from the fact that the Greek astrologers used the same word to refer to both the concept of the "trine aspect" and "triplicities," which was *trigōnon* ("triangle"), even though the two techniques are conceptually distinct. In the same paper Rochberg herself notes (p. 60) that "the Babylonian grouping of three signs seems to be the result simply of the schematic arrangement of twelve elements (here zodiacal signs) into four groups of three elements each, rather than the result of some geometrical or spatial relation." To the extent that this is not viewed as a geometrical or spatial relation between planets, it probably should not be viewed as the existence of the doctrine of "aspects" in the earlier Mesopotamian tradition.

Unfortunately it is unclear what the correct answer is here, but the arrangement underlying the exaltations seems suggestive enough to warrant further research into the origins of the concept.

Adversities

One of the glaring omissions in many texts from the early Hellenistic tradition compared with the later Medieval and Renaissance traditions is the question of how to treat planets that are in signs opposite to their own domiciles. In the later traditions this became known as the concept of a planet's "detriment," and it was generally treated as a problematic or debilitating factor for a planet, similar to the sign of a planet's depression or fall. In most of the introductory Hellenistic texts, while they clearly define the concepts of domicile, exaltation, and depression, there is no corresponding definition of "detriment," which raises some questions about how the position was viewed, and whether it was conceptualized as a debilitating factor or not.[93] This is compounded by the fact that detriment isn't usually viewed as a negative or debilitating factor in most standard traditions of Indian astrology even today, likely as a result of the fact that the position is rarely defined or mentioned in many of the early Hellenistic texts.

Only by the end of the Hellenistic tradition do we see the concept starting to be clearly defined and referred to as a negative factor when determining a planet's condition, primarily in the text of Rhetorius. In Rhetorius he refers to a planet being placed in a sign opposite to one of its own domiciles as *enantiōma*, which according to the LSJ lexicon means "anything opposite or opposed, obstacle, hindrance," or "opposition, incompatibility, conflicting, differences," or "discrepancies."[94] This term has a different range of meaning than the later term "detriment"; it primarily focuses on things that are contrary or opposed. This seems to arise from the rationale that Rhetorius uses for determining the basic meanings of the planets, which emphasizes how the natures of the planets that rule opposing domiciles are often conflicting or contradictory. This appears to be the primary reason why this placement came to be viewed as problematic, because when a planet is placed in the sign opposite to its own domicile, it is ruled by a planet that has contrary significations.

---

[93] Dykes notes that there continued to be some ambiguity surrounding the concept even in the early Medieval tradition, in *Works of Sahl and Māshā'allāh*, pp. xxix–xxxiv.

[94] Rhetorius, *Compendium*, 8. The term is also used consistently in the material on qualities of the signs of the zodiac from Teucer of Babylon that is preserved by Rhetorius, although it seems as if the references to a planet opposite its domicile being problematic may have been inserted by Rhetorius himself. See CCAG, 7, pp. 214–224. Translated in Rhetorius, *Compendium*, trans. Holden, pp. 167–189.

Unfortunately we encounter a bit of a problem in figuring out what to call this condition, because the most literal translation of Rhetorius' term *enantiōma* is "opposition." While this is the most direct translation, it is already a common term used to describe the 180° aspect in modern astrology (which in Greek was typically called the "diameter" rather than "opposition," as we say today). I think that it would cause too much confusion to attempt to call a planet opposite its own domicile the "sign of its opposition," and so this requires us to find an alternative keyword to use in order to refer to this concept. Based on how the placement is often interpreted by the few Hellenistic authors who mention it, there are a few possible words that could be used to refer to the placement: "adversity," "debility," and "exile." In order to explain why these terms might be appropriate, let's take a look at some of the few instances where the concept is referred to in the earlier Hellenistic authors prior to Rhetorius.

While for some reason it is never defined alongside domicile, exaltation, and detriment, there are a few scattered references to planets being placed in the sign opposite to their own domicile in the earlier texts, and it is generally interpreted as a negative or problematic placement. A brief statement about it appears in Hephaestio when he is summarizing or paraphrasing Dorotheus' approach to annual profections: "when the stars are in opposition to their own domiciles, they are corrupted (*kakunontai*)."[95] Schmidt notes in his translation of this passage of Hephaestio that the word he translated as corrupted here "can either mean 'damaged' or 'weakened' in the physical sense; it can also mean 'made evil' in the moral sense."[96] The word "debility" seems as if it would capture the sense of something being physically damaged or weakened quite well, although this term is usually used in a more general sense by later astrologers, especially in the Renaissance tradition. A decade later Schmidt translated the same passage slightly differently: "the stars turn bad (*kakunontai*) when opposed (*enantioumenoi*) to their own domiciles."[97] The *Liber Hermetis* also has a very similar stray sentence in Latin in which it says that planets that are opposite their own domiciles indicate *adversitas*, which means "opposition," "contrariety,"

---

[95] Hephaestio, *Apotelesmatika*, 2, 27: 4, trans. Schmidt, p. 81. The exact same line appears in a Byzantine summary of Serapio's works, but it is probably just derived from this statement in Hephaestio, as Pingree warns that this summary is actually a compilation from several sources (*Yavanajātaka*, vol. 2, p. 441).

[96] Hephaestio, *Apotelesmatika*, 2, trans. Schmidt, p. 81, fn. 208.

[97] CCAG, 8, 4: p. 231: 1, trans. Schmidt, *Definitions and Foundations*, p. 225. This passage is from the *Definitions* of Serapio, although ultimately it seems to derive from Hephaestio, since the wording of the Greek sentence is exactly the same. See the footnote on the previous passage from Hephaestio.

"hostility," "antipathy," "misfortune," or "suffering."[98] Zoller translates it as "adversities," which nicely summarizes some of the general meanings.[99]

Elsewhere, Valens seems to say that when the ruler of the Lot of Spirit is opposite to its own place that the native will come to live in a foreign country and will experience *tarachais*, which means "disturbances," "upheavals," "confusion," "tumults," or "troubles."[100] Valens goes on to say that instead of the native's inheritance staying in their family it ends up going to strangers. Here the words "adversity" or "debility" seem to be rather appropriate for one part of the delineation, although there is also another interpretive element involved with the statement about the native coming to live in a foreign country and their inheritance going to strangers. I believe that these other aspects of the delineation are being derived from the notion of contrasting the concept of "home" or "domicile" with whatever the opposite of that would be, which in this instance means living away from one's homeland or having one's family inheritance given away to others rather than staying in the family or "at home," as it were.

Another passage in Rhetorius seems to support this interpretation, when he says that the Moon being opposed by its domicile lord in a native's chart indicated "flights," "banishment," or "exile" (*fugas*).[101] He then quotes a delineation in verse from an unknown author, perhaps Dorotheus, who says

> Behold the Moon is in the domicile of some star, and if you find that one lurking in opposition, he will also indeed be a fugitive (*fugas*), obscure and a wanderer.[102]

While the Moon's general signification of the native's home and living situation is part of why this particular delineation is tied in with the native being exiled or banished from their home when its ruler is in opposition, there still seems to be an underlying interpretive theme here that has to do with banishment, exile, and being away from home in general with these placements. This is probably because the place opposite to a planet's domicile is the furthest away a planet can get in the zodiac from its home, and therefore it was interpreted symbolically as invoking the exact opposite of the comfort represented by being in one's abode.

On this basis, I would like to suggest the use of the word "exile" as an additional convention that could be used for referring to this placement, both

---

[98] *Liber Hermetis*, 3: 21.

[99] *Liber Hermetis, Part I*, trans. Zoller, p. 19.

[100] Valens, *Anthology*, 2, 20: 7.

[101] CCAG, 8, 4, p. 222: 8–10.

[102] Rhetorius, *Compendium*, 113, trans. Holden, p. 161 (CCAG, 8, 4, p. 222: 12–14).

based on the interpretive precedent in Valens and Rhetorius above, but also because conceptually this provides a nice contrast with the idea of a planet being in its "domicile." Some later Medieval and Renaissance astrologers seem to have picked up on this underlying idea in the earlier tradition and refer to this concept as exile instead of (or in addition to) detriment. This usage then survived into modern times in some Spanish, Portuguese, and French astrological traditions, although for some reason it did not make it into English.

To summarize, I would suggest using the convention of referring to the placement of a planet in the sign opposite to its own domicile as the sign of the planet's "adversity," "debility," or "exile." While the term adversity is probably the least dire-sounding, and also less prone to conflict with terminology already used in later astrological traditions, the other two terms tie in well to the rest of the system conceptually, and should probably be retained and used interchangeably where appropriate.

If this doctrine is accepted, then the signs of adversity are as follows: the Sun has its adversity in Aquarius, the Moon in Capricorn, Mercury in Sagittarius and Pisces, Venus in Scorpio and Aries, Mars in Libra and Taurus, Jupiter in Gemini and Virgo, Saturn in Cancer and Leo. As for why these placements are not typically defined alongside domicile, exaltation, and depression in the early Hellenistic instructional texts, it is not really clear. It is possible that it is something that was seen as self-evident based on the arrangement of the planetary domiciles, and the way that each of the planets naturally rules a sign opposite to another planet with contrary qualities. There seem to be enough references to the concept to conclude that it was generally seen as problematic in one way or another, although as with many areas of Hellenistic astrology, we are often forced to draw inferences about the practice based on a few scattered references that have survived here and there.

Quadruplicities

One of the intrinsic properties of the zodiacal signs that all authors agree upon is their grouping into three sets of four, which I will refer to here as *quadruplicities*, although they are known more commonly in modern times as the *modalities*.[103] The Hellenistic astrologers do not seem to have had a specific term that was used to refer to this concept in general, although Paulus does refer to it as the

---

[103] The concept is defined explicitly in Ptolemy, *Tetrabiblos*, 1, 12; Rhetorius, *Compendium*, preface (trans. Holden, pp. 1–2). It is enumerated as one of several different properties assigned to specific signs in Valens, *Anthology*, 1, 2; Firmicus, *Mathesis*, 2, 10; Paulus, *Introduction*, 2; Hephaestio, *Apotelesmatika*, 1, 1. Other authors mention the concept and take it for granted as a basic principle in delineations.

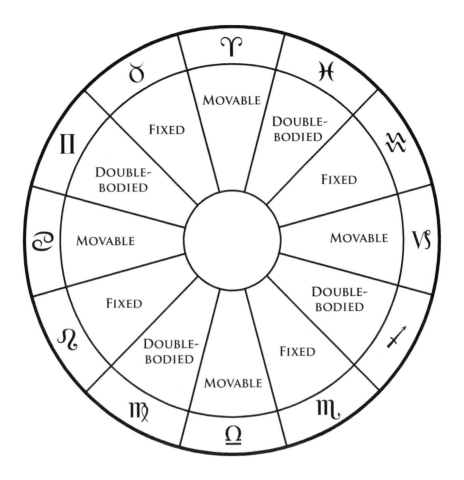

Figure 8.8 - Quadruplicities

grouping of the signs that "stand apart by fours," and so the adoption of the later term quadruplicity seems fitting.[104]

In modern times the three quadruplicities are known as cardinal, fixed, and mutable; however, the Greek terms for the quadruplicities are usually translated as "tropical" (*tropika*), "solid" (*sterea*) and "double-bodied" (*disōma*), respectively. For the purposes of this book I will be referring to them as the "movable," "fixed," and "double-bodied" signs, for reasons that I will explain below. Using this terminology, the standard arrangement of the quadruplicities is as follows:

MOVABLE:	Aries, Cancer, Libra, Capricorn
FIXED:	Taurus, Leo, Scorpio, Aquarius
DOUBLE-BODIED:	Gemini, Virgo, Sagittarius, Pisces

---

[104] Paulus, *Introduction*, 2, ed. Boer, p. 8: 17–p. 9: 1–2.

Although the Greek term *tropikos* is usually translated as "tropical," because the word was originally used to refer to the "tropics" or "solstices" which occur in Cancer and Capricorn, it literally means "pertaining to turning" or "pertaining to change." It is derived from the word *tropē*, which means "turn," "change," or "transformation." Sometimes this quadruplicity is divided into two subsets, with only Cancer and Capricorn being referred to as the "tropical" or "solstitial" signs, since they coincide with the summer and winter solstices, while Aries and Libra are referred to as the "equipartite" or "equinoctial" signs, since they coincide with the spring and fall equinoxes.[105] However, most authors seem to use the term *tropika* as a general term to refer to the entire quadruplicity of all four signs. For that reason, it seems inappropriate for us to continue to refer to them as the "tropical" signs, since technically only two of them contain the tropics, but it seems that the term *tropika* was used to refer to all four signs because the word conveyed some sense of motion or change, which became the primary interpretive keywords for this quadruplicity. In the Indian and Medieval traditions this quadruplicity came to be referred to as the "movable" signs, which seems like a good attempt to convey both the meaning of the Greek term as well as the astrological interpretation, and I will adopt it here for the purpose of referring to this concept.[106]

The Greek term for the "fixed" signs is *stereos*, which means "solid" or "firm," although it can also be used metaphorically to refer to things that are "stiff" or "stubborn." The traditional translation of this term as "fixed" seems close enough in meaning to the original Greek that I don't see the need to attempt to change the contemporary usage here, although I would like to note that in the Indian tradition these are referred to as the "immovable" signs, which provides some important insight into the contrast that was probably originally intended with the "movable" signs.[107]

The Greek term for the "mutable" signs is *disōmos*, which means "double-bodied" or "having two bodies." In some later traditions the word "bicorporeal" is used, which means the same thing. This is partially derived from the fact that some of the constellations that these signs were named after originally had images with two figures that coincided with these signs, such as Gemini and the twins, or Pisces and the two fish. There was also a later rationale that was connected with the seasons, which we will discuss shortly. The Indian

---

[105] Ptolemy, *Tetrabiblos*, 1, 12.
[106] Pingree, *Yavanajātaka*, vol. 2, p. 216. Dykes, *Introductions*, p. 62.
[107] Pingree, *Yavanajātaka*, vol. 2, p. 216.

astrologers refer to this quadruplicity as the "two-natured" signs, which again provides some conceptual insight.[108]

In terms of interpretations, Hephaestio makes a concise statement about the nature of the quadruplicities at one point within the context of inceptional astrology:

> The movable signs foster changes easily (for better or for worse), the fixed ones make the matter that is sought unalterable, the double-bodied ones make the result of the matter sought bipartite.[109]

This seems to be tied in with a broader seasonal metaphor that is outlined more explicitly in Ptolemy and Rhetorius, which is connected to the tropical zodiac.[110] There they say that the movable signs are connected to change because when the Sun moves into those signs it marks the beginning of a new season: Aries being associated with the start of spring in the northern hemisphere, Cancer with summer, Libra with fall, and Capricorn with winter. Each season brings with it a change in the temperature and the length of the days. Then when the Sun moves into the fixed signs these coincide with the middle of the seasons and the weather becomes more steady and unchangeable, and thus fixed or solid. Taurus coincides with the middle of spring, Leo with the middle of summer, Scorpio with the middle of fall, and Aquarius with the middle of winter. Finally, when the Sun moves into the mutable signs, Rhetorius says that the weather becomes more "ambiguous" (*epamphoteros*), as things start to transition from one season into another. For Ptolemy these signs represent a sort of transitional or in-between state, since they are "sharing the specific natural characteristics of the two states of weather at their ends and at their beginnings," and this is why they can be described as double-bodied.[111]

This conceptualization of the division of the signs into quadruplicities in connection with the beginning, middle, and end of the seasons seems to have been the basis for a number of interpretive statements in other authors. In inceptional astrology the movable signs are sometimes interpreted as easily initiating new actions, but having trouble bringing what is initiated to completion, and needing to try again.[112] They are generally interpreted as being

---

[108] Pingree, *Yavanajātaka*, vol. 2, p. 216.
[109] Hephaestio, *Apotelesmatika*, 3, 4: 9, trans. Gramaglia, p. 40, modified.
[110] Ptolemy, *Tetrabiblos*, 1, 12. Rhetorius, *Compendium*, preface (trans. Holden, pp. 1–2).
[111] Ptolemy, *Tetrabiblos*, 1, 12: 5, trans. Schmidt, p. 28.
[112] Dorotheus, *Carmen*, 5, 3.

quick and changeable. The fixed signs are said to be prominent in charts where the matter at hand is stable, unalterable, or permanent.[113] They are generally interpreted as pertaining to matters that are slow or difficult to change, or in some instances not changeable at all. In the Arabic version of Dorotheus it says that the mutable signs indicate digressions in their manner of bringing about events, with two actions taken, so that the second action finishes before the first can be completed.[114] They are generally interpreted as ambiguous, going from stable to changing.

The double-bodied signs are also commonly interpreted as providing two of whatever it is they signify in a particular chart, and at one point this is stated as a rule in the Arabic version of Dorotheus: "Whatever planet you find in a sign having two bodies, double it."[115] This is the principle underlying Ptolemy's statement that having a preponderance of relevant significators in double-bodied signs will lead to the birth of twins.[116] This idea of the quadruplicities indicating numbers or frequency in a chart is sometimes used as a concrete interpretive principle in other areas as well. For example, when Valens addresses the topic of marriage, he says that having Venus in a movable or double-bodied sign can indicate that the native will have multiple marriages or be promiscuous, if compounded by other factors.[117] Dorotheus similarly says that Venus in a double-bodied sign indicates that the native will have more than one marriage.[118] In this way the quadruplicities can modify the expression of the planets by altering the frequency or number of whatever is signified.

Triplicities

In addition to quadruplicities, the signs were also grouped into four sets of three, which were known as "trigons" or "triangles" (*trigōnon*). I will use the later Medieval convention of referring to these groups as "triplicities," which simply means "a group of three things." The four triplicity groups are as follows:

TRIPLICITY 1:	Aries, Leo, Sagittarius
TRIPLICITY 2:	Taurus, Virgo, Capricorn
TRIPLICITY 3:	Gemini, Libra, Aquarius
TRIPLICITY 4:	Cancer, Scorpio, Pisces

---

[113] Hephaestio, *Apotelesmatika*, 3, 4: 9.
[114] Dorotheus, *Carmen*, 5, 4: 1.
[115] Dorotheus, *Carmen*, 1, 11: 5, trans. Pingree, p. 170.
[116] Ptolemy, *Tetrabiblos*, 3, 8.
[117] Valens, *Anthology*, 2, 38: 4.
[118] Dorotheus, *Carmen*, 2, 3: 13.

The Greek terminology here has caused some confusion in the academic scholarship because the word that the astrologers used to refer to the grouping of the signs into four sets of three was *trigōnon*, which means "triangle." The same term was also used to refer to the "trine" aspect, even though the idea of aspects is conceptually distinct from the division of the signs into four sets of three. This is why I have adopted the convention of referring to the groupings of the signs into four sets of three as "triplicities," while referring to the aspect as a "trine."

Astrologers had started to group the signs into four sets of three already in the late Mesopotamian tradition, and even to assign planets to these triplicities.[119] In the Hellenistic tradition the triplicities came to be associated with the four cardinal directions or "winds."[120] Some astrologers also assigned the four classical elements of fire, earth, air, and water to each of the triplicities. There was also a unique system of planetary rulers associated with the triplicities, which is analogous to the domicile rulership scheme, although these assignments were different than the earlier Mesopotamian precursors. The Hellenistic system of triplicity rulers will be discussed in more detail later in this book. For now I will focus on the elemental associations.

Background on the Four Elements and Qualities

Around the sixth century BCE some of the early pre-Socratic Greek philosophers proposed that all things in the universe could be reduced to a single underlying principle.[121] The philosopher Thales argued that this principle was water, while Anaximenes said that is was air, and Heraclitus posited that it was fire. By the fifth century BCE, the philosopher Empedocles outlined a doctrine in which there were four of these principles or, as he called them, "roots" (*rhizōmata*): earth, air, fire and water. These four "roots" were later adopted by the philosopher Plato in the fourth century BCE, who was the first to refer to them as "elements" (*stoicheia*) in his account of the creation of the cosmos, the *Timaeus*.[122] The Greek term for the "elements" was originally used to refer to the "letters" of the alphabet, insomuch as individual letters are the smallest possible components which make up a complete sentence. Elements, similarly, were

---

[119] Hunger and Pingree, *Astral Sciences*, p. 17; Rochberg-Halton, "TCL 6 13;" Rochberg-Halton, "Elements of the Babylonian," pp. 60–61.

[120] I will not be dealing with the directions associated with the signs in this work, but there is a good summary of some of the different schemes in the Hellenistic tradition in Pingree, *Yavanajātaka*, vol. 2, pp. 225–226.

[121] For much of this and what follows see Warren, *Presocratics*, and Barnes, *Early Greek Philosophy*.

[122] Plato, *Timaeus*, 48c.

conceptualized as the smallest components which make up perceptible bodies.[123]

Aristotle, a student of Plato, also adopted the four-element theory, although he expanded it by incorporating the concept that the elements are able to turn into one another rather than being immutable, as Empedocles apparently believed.[124] In order to explain how each of the elements could transform into another, he introduced the idea that there are specific contrasting qualities associated with each of the elements, for without a contrariety of opposing qualities, he argues, there can be no change. Since the elements are the building blocks of perceptible bodies, Aristotle reasoned that the qualities underlying the elements would have to relate to the sense of perception that is the most closely connected to what is tangible, and he concludes that the most obvious candidate for this is the sense of touch. This then results in the premise that physical bodies are differentiated through the contrariety of tangible qualities.

Following this line of thought, Aristotle chose two sets of qualities which possessed reciprocal active and passive components, which led to the establishment of the four primary qualities: hot and cold, dry and wet. These were then associated with each of the four elements in a way that gave them two non-contrary qualities each:

FIRE is hot and dry
AIR is hot and wet
WATER is cold and wet
EARTH is cold and dry

Despite the dual qualities associated with each element, Aristotle said that there was one quality that was most closely associated with each of the four:

FIRE is primarily hot
AIR is primarily moist
WATER is primarily cold
EARTH is primarily dry

---

[123] Plato goes on to describe the elements as geometrical structures which are made up of triangles (*Timaeus*, 53c–57d), which is interesting given the connection between the elements and triplicities/triangles in Hellenistic astrology.

[124] For what follows see Aristotle, *On Generation and Corruption*, 2, 1–4. Aristotle discusses Empedocles' position and contrasts it with his own view that the elements do transform into one another in chapter 6.

Aristotle subsequently posited that while each element is capable of transforming into another, this transformation happens much faster for those elements that share a quality in common. Fire, for example, is hot and dry, and air is hot and wet; fire is thus able to change into air simply by the conversion of a single quality—dry into wet—because it already shares one quality in common with air (i.e. heat). Alternatively, fire, which is hot and dry, would have to change both of its qualities in order to become water, which is cold and wet.

This is, essentially, Aristotle's approach to the theory of the four elements, at least as outlined in his most influential work on the subject, *On Generation and Corruption*. However, despite the weight of his authority, his immediate successors did not necessarily accept the premise of his argument entirely. Theophrastus, the first student to succeed Aristotle as the head of the Lyceum, his school in Athens, rejected his teacher's association between air and heat, opting instead to make air primarily cold and water primarily wet. This brought the four-element theory in line with some contemporary medical doctrines advocated by the physician Philistion of Locri, and it also corrected a basic discrepancy that existed between Aristotle's physical writings and his biological writings, since in the latter he would often treat air as if it was primarily cold or functioned as a refrigerant or cooling agent.[125] This, in turn, likely influenced the later Stoic conceptualization of the four-element theory, since the founder of that school, Zeno of Citium, studied in Athens and eventually set up his own school there not long after Aristotle's death, in close enough proximity to be exposed to some of the changes that Aristotle's successors made to one of his core doctrines.[126]

Beginning with Zeno sometime around the year 300 BCE, the Stoics embraced the four-element theory as a fundamental component of their cosmology. For the Stoics there are two "principles" (*archai*): the active and the passive.[127] The passive principle is the unqualified substance of matter, while the active principle is God, which shapes and qualifies matter with its reason (*logos*). From the union of these two principles arise the four elements of fire, water,

---

[125] For an extensive treatment of this issue see Longrigg, "Elementary Physics in the Lyceum and Stoa," pp. 211–229. A similar account is given in Hahm, *The Origins of Stoic Cosmology*, pp. 91–103. Both point out that already in the fourth century, the Sicilian physician Philistion of Locri had associated fire with hot, air with cold, water with moist, and earth with dry. Both authors also document Aristotle's tendency to associate air with the property of cooling in his biological works, particularly in his theory of respiration, in which air only becomes hot once it enters the body and meets with the internal heat which resides there. See Aristotle, *On Youth and Old Age, On Life and Death, On Breathing*, 480a28–480b6.

[126] This is the basic premise of both Longrigg and Hahm's arguments, cited above.

[127] Diogenes Laertius, *Lives of Eminent Philosophers*, 7: 134–137.

air, and earth. Fire and air were conceptualized as being "active" and capable
of sustaining things, while earth and water were conceptualized as "passive"
and needed to be sustained.[128] They associated each of the elements with one
quality, following the model advocated by Philistion and Theophrastus:

> FIRE is hot
> AIR is cold
> WATER is wet
> EARTH is dry

While following Aristotle in associating each of the four elements with opposing
qualities, they differed from him by setting up air (cold) as the antithesis of fire
(hot), and water (wet) as the antithesis of earth (dry).

This arrangement is important because it seems to have been the Stoic
conceptualization of the elements that prevailed in the Hellenistic astrological
tradition rather than the Aristotelian one. It was not until the Medieval tradition
that Aristotle's conceptualization reemerged and began to displace the Stoic
approach.

Assignment of the Elements to the Triplicities

Several of the Hellenistic astrologers assign each of four classical elements of fire,
earth, air, and water to the signs of the zodiac in accordance with the triplicities.
Despite the prevalence of this doctrine in the later Medieval, Renaissance, and
modern astrological traditions, the assignment of the elements to the triplicities
was not universal amongst the Hellenistic astrologers. In fact, the majority of
the surviving sources are conspicuously silent when it comes to this scheme,
potentially due to philosophical or conceptual disagreements over the rationale
for which signs the elements were assigned to. The rationale for the assignments
seems to be derived from the planetary joys scheme, which will be discussed
later, and if this is true then it does appear to date back to very early in the
Hellenistic tradition, although the origins are still somewhat obscure.

While there does appear to have been a widespread system of grouping the
signs into four sets of three amongst the Hellenistic astrologers (referred to as
"triplicities"), and while these correspond to the same groups of signs that would
later be associated with the elements, several authors seem to be unaware of any
associations between those signs and the four elements. Instead they associated

---

[128] Long and Sedley, *The Hellenistic Philosophers*, vol. 1, 47D, E, F and G, citing respectively
Nemesius, *On the Nature of Man*, 164:15–18, Galen, *On Natural Faculties*, 106: 13–17, Galen,
On Bodily Mass, 7.525:9–14, and Plutarch, *On Common Conceptions*, 1085C–D.

the triplicities with certain cardinal directions, and sometimes assigned certain planets as rulers of the groups. Dorotheus of Sidon in the late first century CE is the most prominent example of this, as he employs the triplicity rulers of the signs frequently in delineations, but he does not seem to mention the elements in connection with the triplicities.

Other authors who discuss the qualities associated with the signs or group them into triplicities but do *not* associate them with elements include Manilius, Thrasyllus, Antiochus, Dorotheus, Manetho, Ptolemy, Porphyry, Paulus, Anonymous of 379, and Olympiodorus.[129] The authors who do assign the four elements to the signs of the zodiac in the standard grouping include Valens, Firmicus, Hephaestio, Julian of Laodicea, and Rhetorius.[130]

Our earliest source for the association of each of the signs of the zodiac with the four elements is in the writings of Vettius Valens in the mid-second century CE.[131] Valens is also our single most extensive Hellenistic source for both the conceptualization of this doctrine and its application in an astrological context. He first introduces the elemental associations in book 1, chapter 2 of the *Anthology*, where he lists the qualities associated with each of the signs. During the course of his descriptions he refers to Aries as "fiery" (*pyrōdēs*), Taurus as "earthy" (*geōdēs*), Gemini as "airy" (*aerōdēs*), Cancer as "watery" (*hudatōdēs*), and so on through the signs. The end result is four groups of three signs which are each associated with one of the four classical elements:

FIERY:	Aries, Leo, Sagittarius
EARTHY:	Taurus, Virgo, Capricorn
AIRY:	Gemini, Libra, Aquarius
WATERY:	Cancer, Scorpio, Pisces

These basic associations have persisted in the western astrological tradition up through the present day.

---

[129] In some of these authors there is an occasional reference to certain signs being watery or other such qualities, although these seem to be derived from the irregular distribution of secondary qualities that are associated with the images of the zodiacal constellations, and not necessarily from the approach to assigning all four elements to the triplicities that became standard later in the tradition. In this way there were two approaches to assigning elemental qualities, although in this approach it is only applied to a few of the signs rather than to all of them.

[130] Valens, *Anthology*, 1, 2; Firmicus, *Mathesis*, 2, 10; Hephaestio, *Apotelesmatika*, 3, 7: 7; Julian in CCAG 4, p. 152: 21–23; Rhetorius, *Compendium*, 3.

[131] This was first pointed out by Robert Hand in Valens, *The Anthology, Book I*, trans. Schmidt, ed. Hand, p. ii.

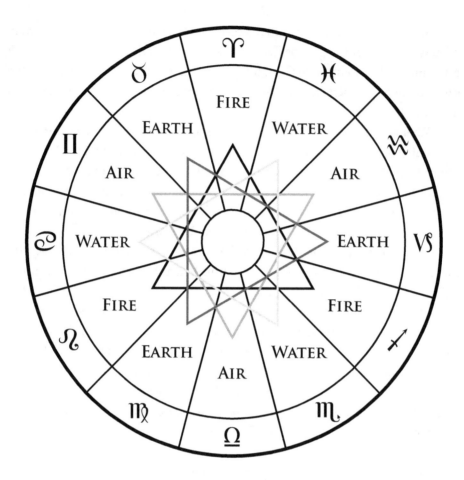

Figure 8.9 - Elements and Triplicities

Interpretation of the Elements

References to how the elements were used in delineations are scarce, although they generally seem to be employed like the gender assignments, in which there is both a very literal way they could be used in interpretations, as well as a broader, symbolic way.

In terms of literal interpretations, Valens invokes the elements a few times in a chapter on indications in a natal chart for violent death. In one chart he uses an example of someone who had the relevant significator in Cancer; he says that the native died from drowning while taking a bath, since Cancer is a water sign.[132] Later he gives the chart of someone who died in a fire, and he points out that one of the main significators in the person's chart was Mars in Leo, which is a fiery sign.[133] In another example he talks about someone who had the relevant

---

[132] Valens, *Anthology*, 2, 41: 49. Cf. Valens, *Anthology*, 2, 41: 63.

[133] Valens, *Anthology*, 2, 41: 66. Possibly exacerbated because Mars is a fiery planet.

significator afflicted in the water sign Pisces, and he evidently met his end in the cargo hold of a ship, presumably by drowning as it sank.[134]

There is a similar set of literal interpretations in book 3 of Hephaestio of Thebes, when he briefly talks about inception charts for the founding of a city, and derives different delineations for the help or harm that will come to a city if there is an eclipse in certain triplicities:

> For it comes to pass that, according to such an inception, there is utter destruction by earthquakes, and very unremitting damage to the cities thus born: in the triplicity of Aries, as it is fiery, [the destruction will come] from fire; in <that of> Taurus, being earth-like, one must suppose harm or aid from earth and agriculture [...] in the triplicity of Gemini, as it is airy by nature, [one must expect] aid or harm from the air; in the [triplicity] of Cancer, as it is watery, aid or harm from waters.[135]

As with the gender assignments, the elements are primarily invoked in literal interpretations when relevant to the delineation. While in many instances they may not be applicable, they can be used in specific circumstances that require a very precise statement about the material fortunes of the native or the inceptional chart under examination.

Elemental Qualities and Temperament Interpretations

In addition to being one of the few Hellenistic sources that mentions the elements in connection with the triplicities, Valens is also one of the only authors who mentions the qualities that he associates with the elements, and here he follows the Stoic conceptualization which makes fire hot, air cold, water wet, and earth dry. This ends up having important implications for the way that the elements are assigned to the signs of the zodiac, because the common scheme amongst astrologers who mention them puts the fire signs opposite to the air signs, and the water signs opposite to the earth signs. Thus the author of this scheme provided a concrete depiction of the Stoic conceptualization of the elemental oppositions, which places fire/hot opposite to air/cold, and water/ wet opposite to earth/dry. For example, in the zodiacal wheel Aries is a hot fire sign, and it is opposite to Libra which is a cold air sign. Next, Taurus is a dry earth sign, and it is opposite to Scorpio which is a wet water sign; and so on.

Valens' primary discussion about the qualities of the elements occurs in book 4 of the *Anthology* within the context of a discussion about a specific facet

---

[134] Valens, *Anthology*, 2, 41: 73–76.
[135] Hephaestio, *Apotelesmatika*, 3, 7: 7, trans. Gramaglia, p. 65.

of the time-lord technique called zodiacal releasing.[136] The part of the technique that Valens is trying to explain is the "loosing of the bond," in which there is a break in the sequence of signs so that the timing period jumps to the opposite sign of the zodiac from where it started. Valens tries to defend this facet of the technique by explaining how the interaction between the opposing signs in the zodiac serves an important, mutually beneficial function, with each opposing element enlivening and helping the other to grow. It is here that Valens discusses the qualities that he associates with each of the signs.

He says that fire and air intermingle with each other since they rise upwards, and in the process of doing so, fire, which is hot, is supported by the more mild temperature of the air, which is cold, while at the same time air is warmed up by the heat of fire so that it does not become overly cold or frigid.[137] Similarly, Valens says that earth, which is dry, is nourished by the moisture of water, which allows the earth to make things grow, while water itself is born from and contained by the earth.[138] Essentially, the moisture of water allows the earth to be fertile, while earth contains and gives form to water. Later, in book 9 of the *Anthology*, Valens returns to this topic, discussing the way in which the elements change into and counterbalance each other:

> In such a way each of the elements changes one to the other according to natural law, transforming itself and taking on its own beauty and its own value to make manifest the universal structure. An element that stays in its own form to encroach on the other elements is nothing but useless and harmful. But when blended with another, it creates a temperate state, and when permeating everything, it is not destroyed by anything.[139]

These interpretations of the qualities associated with the elements seem to provide an access point for understanding their broader interpretive value within the context of Hellenistic astrology, because this is where they integrate into traditional doctrines surrounding the temperaments, which in turn are connected to ancient views surrounding character analysis and the nature of

---

[136] Valens, *Anthology*, 4, 4: 20–31.

[137] Valens, *Anthology*, 4, 4: 24. At first the text inexplicably refers to fire as being "dry," which Schmidt and Hand point out is probably an error in the manuscripts (*Anthology, Book IV*, trans. Schmidt, p. 7, n. 7), and indeed this is confirmed later in the same sentence when Valens contrasts the heating properties of fire with the cooling tendencies of air. I assume that this was the contrast that Valens was originally trying to make throughout this sentence.

[138] Valens, *Anthology*, 4, 4: 25.

[139] Valens, *Anthology*, 9, 8: 40, trans. Riley, p. 158.

the psyche. The first century philosopher, Seneca, gives a useful overview of the Stoic temperament theory:

> There are four elements—fire, water, air, and earth—with matching properties—hot, cold, dry, and moist. Accordingly, the blending of the elements produces variations in places and creatures and bodies and customs; creatures' innate characters incline more in a given direction in direct proportion to the greater force that the preponderance of a given element supplies. Hence we call some areas "moist" and "dry" and "hot" and "frigid." The same distinctions are valid for animals and humans: it makes a difference how much moisture and heat each individual has within him; the element that predominates in him will determine his characteristic behaviors.[140]

Very little survives of Stoic temperament theory, although Seneca gives us some insights into its interpretation. He goes on to say that fire is active and stubborn or intransigent, so that fiery people can be passionate and prone to anger or wrathfulness, whereas people who have a cold temperament are prone to be timid or cowardly, because cold as a quality is sluggish and prone to shrinking.[141] Later he says that while fiery people can be prone to anger, those with wet, dry, or cold temperaments can be panicky, contrarian, feel hopeless, or suspicious.[142] Elsewhere he alludes to water and earth as passive elements, resulting in people who can be listless and sleepy.[143] There are similar statements in some of the Hermetic philosophical material, where it says that if there is an excess of heat the person becomes light and ardent, while an excess of cold will make them heavy and slow.[144]

There are some hints of Valens applying similar principles to the elements when he is discussing a certain timing technique and what happens to the native when it activates signs that are associated with the different elements:

> If the star controlling such a time-lord period is found in a fiery sign with malefics in conjunction or in aspect, he will suffer a great nervous breakdown, and will act against his own will, being mentally unstable. If the star is in an

---

[140] Seneca, *On Anger*, 19: 1–2 (in Seneca, *Anger, Mercy, Revenge*, trans. Kaster and Nussbaum, pp. 46–7).

[141] Seneca, *On Anger*, 19: 2.

[142] Seneca, *On Anger*, 19: 4.

[143] Seneca, *On Providence*, 5: 9 (in Seneca, *Dialogues and Essays*, trans. Davie).

[144] *Corpus Hermeticum*, vol. 3, fragment 20: 5, ed. Nock and Festugière, p. 87.

airy sign or if the sign or its ruler are afflicted, the native will be distracted and troubled, and will suppose that he is accomplishing something other than what he really is. If the star is in an earthy sign, he will bear the blows of fortune nobly, and will survive most things philosophically because of his endurance. If the star is in a watery sign, the native will have a mind which can be easily reassured, will come into vicissitudes in many affairs, but will manage to succeed and be successful in his dealings.[145]

This points to a broader set of interpretive principles underlying the elements that can be used to describe actions and analyze character, in addition to the nature of concrete external events, with the access point being the qualities that are associated with the elements.

Triplicity Rulers

The triplicities were also associated with an alternative form of zodiacal sign rulership in the Hellenistic tradition. These planetary assignments to the triplicities were known as "triplicity lords" (*trigōnokratōr*).[146] In some early texts such as Dorotheus, these almost seem to be used as an alternative form of sign rulership, serving many of the same functions as the domicile rulers. In other authors such as Valens they are used more restrictively for specific purposes or techniques. In the Medieval tradition they eventually became one of the five "essential dignities," ranking just below domicile and exaltation in the order of importance.[147]

Assignment of the Triplicity Rulers

The primary system of assigning the triplicity rulers is the one used by

---

[145] Valens, *Anthology*, 4, 7: 8, trans. Riley, p. 74, modified.

[146] Hephaestio uses the term *trigōnokratōr* a few times (e.g. *Apotelesmatika*, 2, 4: 20; 2, 14: 2), especially when citing Dorotheus, which probably implies that this was the original term that Dorotheus used. Valens tends to use the term *oikodespotēs* (e.g. *Anthology*, 2, 1–2), which in this context just means "master" or "ruler" of a triplicity, although it can be a bit confusing since this is the same term used to refer to the "domcile lord" of a sign. Usually one just has to infer by the context if he is referring to the ruler of the triplicity or the domicile, although typically he will make it easier by adding the word triplicity when he is specifically referring to a triplicity lord.

[147] It should be noted that the essential dignity system that uses a weighted point scheme, which became standard in later Renaissance works, didn't really come into use until the Medieval period. The closest precedent in the Hellenistic tradition are some of the predomination arguments used by Ptolemy in *Tetrabiblos*, 3, 3–5, although he only assigns one point for each "dignity." There is a comprehensive exploration of this topic in the preface and appendices of Hermann of Carinthia, *The Search of the Heart*, trans. Dykes.

Day Rulers						Night Rulers		
1	**2**	**3**				**1**	**2**	**3**
☉	♃	♄	♈	♌	♐	♃	☉	♄
♀	☽	♂	♉	♍	♑	☽	♀	♂
♄	☿	♃	♊	♎	♒	☿	♄	♃
♀	♂	☽	♋	♏	♓	♂	♀	☽

Table 8.1 - Standard Triplicity Rulership Scheme

Dorotheus and Valens, our two main sources for the technique.[148] It is sometimes referred to as the Dorothean triplicity rulership scheme, although Dorotheus was probably not the originator of the technique, as it seems to be relatively standard throughout the Hellenistic tradition. There was an alternative triplicity rulership scheme that was devised by Ptolemy, known as the Ptolemaic triplicity rulers, although this system does not appear to have been very widely adopted in the Hellenistic tradition, as it merely represents a modification of the Dorothean system. Here I will primarily deal with the Dorothean system, and outline Ptolemy's approach separately later.

Each triplicity is assigned three planetary rulers: a day ruler, a night ruler, and a cooperating ruler. This is also sometimes stated as a first ruler, second ruler, and third ruler. The planets that are primary and secondary change places depending on whether it is a day or night chart, while the cooperating ruler always stays the same. The triplicity rulers of the signs are as follows:

1. In the zodiacal signs associated with the fire triplicity (i.e. Aries, Leo, Sagittarius), the primary ruler by day is the Sun, the secondary ruler is Jupiter, and the cooperating ruler is Saturn. In a night chart the primary ruler is Jupiter, the secondary ruler is the Sun, and the cooperating ruler is Saturn.
2. In the earth triplicity (i.e. Taurus, Virgo, Capricorn) the primary ruler by day is Venus, the secondary ruler is the Moon, and the cooperating

---

[148] Dorotheus, *Carmen*, 1, 1: 2–4. Valens, *Anthology*, 2, 1. Cf. Hephaestio, *Apotelesmatika*, 1, 6, who quotes Dorotheus directly from the original verse text, and Rhetorius, *Compendium*, 9.

ruler is Mars. In a night chart the primary ruler is the Moon, the secondary ruler is Venus, and the cooperating ruler is Mars.

3. In the air triplicity the primary ruler by day is Saturn, the secondary ruler is Mercury, and the cooperating ruler is Jupiter. By night the primary ruler is Mercury, the secondary ruler is Saturn, and the cooperating ruler is Jupiter.

4. In the water triplicity the primary ruler by day is Venus, the secondary ruler is Mars, and the cooperating ruler is the Moon. By night the primary ruler is Mars, the secondary ruler is Venus, and the cooperating ruler is the Moon.

Dorotheus says that Mercury may have some role in the earth triplicity as well, although in practice this never seems to be brought into use in any tangible way.[149] Valens does not mention Mercury in connection with the earth triplicity, although he does say that since Mercury is "common" (*koinos*), it works with and assists all of the triplicity rulers.[150]

Rationale for the Triplicity Ruler Scheme

The origins of the triplicity ruler scheme are a little murky from a historical perspective, but it may have originally arisen in connection with another early concept called "joint domicile masters" (*sunoikodespotēs*). This concept seems to have emerged out of an early debate in Hellenistic astrology over whether the domicile lords are the only rulers of the signs, or if there are other ways in which planets can become affiliated with certain signs.[151]

There seem to be two rationales at play in the assignment of the planets to the triplicities, as well as the order of their assignments. The first rationale is discussed by Ptolemy and partially by Valens, and it is predicated on (1) sect, and (2) the number of rulerships each planet has in a triplicity by domicile and exaltation. The second rationale was discovered more recently, and it is

---

[149] In the Arabic translation it seems to imply that Mercury's association with the earth triplicity specifically applies to or is restricted to Virgo. Dorotheus, *Carmen*, 1, 1: 3. However, when Hephaestio quotes the original Greek passage of Dorotheus it seems to say that Mercury has a more general role as an additional ruler of the earth triplicity as a whole. Virgo is probably mentioned in the Arabic because that is the only earth sign in which Mercury has any rulership relation, and thus it is probably part of the reason why Mercury is mentioned at all here. This will be discussed more later in the section on the dignity rationale for the triplicity lords.

[150] Valens, *Anthology*, 2, 1: 10.

[151] See the discussion about different opinions on the concept of joint domicile masters in Antiochus, *Summary*, 5, and Porphyry, *Introduction*, 7. Also see the translation and discussion of these two passages in Schmidt, *Definitions and Foundations*, pp. 119–126.

connected with the joys of the planets. Here we will focus on the dignity rationale, and then return to this topic later after we have introduced the planetary joys in a subsequent chapter.

The dignity rationale for the triplicity rulership scheme is primarily discussed by Ptolemy.[152] The premise of this rationale has four main points:

1. Only diurnal planets can be assigned to the masculine signs which compose the fire and air triplicities, using the scheme in which masculine signs are diurnal and feminine nocturnal, while only nocturnal planets are assigned to the feminine signs which compose the earth and water triplicities. By extension, if a planet is contrary to the sect of the signs associated with that triplicity then it must be excluded from consideration, and cannot be a ruler of that triplicity.

2. If a planet has its domicile or exaltation in a particular triplicity then it is eligible to become a triplicity ruler of those three signs.

3. If the planet has both its domicile and its exaltation in that triplicity then it gets more weight in the final tabulation.

This model, at least as explained by Ptolemy, doesn't really account for the cooperating lords very well, and isn't entirely theoretically consistent. Based on this, I suspect that either it wasn't the original rationale, or at least wasn't the *primary* rationale, when the standard triplicity lords scheme was first devised. However, it still does a reasonably good job of explaining most of the assignments, and the rationale works out as follows.

Fire Triplicity Rationale

The fire triplicity is entirely composed of masculine signs, so only diurnal planets can be taken into consideration as possible rulers. The Sun, Jupiter, and Mars have their domiciles in signs associated with this triplicity (i.e. Leo, Sagittarius, and Aries). Mars must be excluded because it is a nocturnal planet. The Sun is considered to be more diurnal, or more representative of the diurnal sect, and it also has its exaltation in Aries, so it becomes the primary day ruler of the fire triplicity. Jupiter then becomes the secondary or night ruler. Saturn has no dignities by domicile or exaltation in the fire triplicity, but it is the last remaining diurnal planet, so it becomes the cooperating ruler. Thus, in a day chart the order of the fire triplicity lords is: Sun, Jupiter, Saturn.

---

[152] Ptolemy, *Tetrabiblos*, 1, 19.

Earth Triplicity Rationale

The earth triplicity is composed of feminine signs, so the nocturnal planets must be the rulers. The only inherently nocturnal planet which owns a domicile in that triplicity is Venus, which rules Taurus, so it becomes the primary ruler by day. Saturn and Mercury rule the other two domiciles, Capricorn and Virgo, but they are excluded from rulership since they are not nocturnal planets. The Moon is exalted in Taurus and Mars in Capricorn, but since the Moon is considered to be more nocturnal it gets the nocturnal or secondary rulership of the earth triplicity, and Mars becomes the cooperating ruler. Thus, in a day chart the order of the earth triplicity lords is: Venus, Moon, Mars.

Air Triplicity Rationale

The air triplicity is composed of masculine signs, so it should be ruled by diurnal planets. Venus is excluded for being inherently nocturnal. Mercury has its domicile in Gemini, and it is kept in the running despite the fact that it is neutral when it comes to sect. Saturn is the only diurnal planet, and it has both a domicile and an exaltation in this triplicity, so it becomes the primary ruler of the triplicity by day. Mercury becomes the secondary or nocturnal ruler. The Sun and Jupiter are the only two remaining diurnal planets. Jupiter becomes the cooperating lord instead of the Sun for unknown reasons. Thus, in a day chart the order of the air triplicity rulers is: Saturn, Mercury, Jupiter.

Water Triplicity Rationale

The water triplicity is composed of feminine signs, so only nocturnal planets can be taken into consideration. Jupiter is therefore excluded since it is diurnal. Both Mars and the Moon have their domiciles in this triplicity, while Venus has its exaltation. Venus becomes the primary ruler of the water triplicity by day, Mars is made the secondary or nocturnal ruler by night even though the Moon is elsewhere considered to be more nocturnal. The Moon becomes the cooperating ruler. The order of the water triplicity lords in a day chart is: Venus, Mars, Moon.

Conclusions About the Dignity Rationale

The dignity rationale is a little bit too clean to be an accident, but at the same time it is not entirely consistent. If this was the only set of criteria and was followed consistently then the Moon should be the secondary ruler of the water triplicity by day and the primary ruler by night, since she is more nocturnal than Mars. Additionally, Mercury is made a ruler of the air triplicity even though his sect is neutral, presumably because he has a domicile there; but he is rejected

Day	Night			
♈ ♌ ♐	☉	♃
♉ ♍ ♑	♀	☽
♊ ♎ ♒	♄	☿
♋ ♏ ♓	♂ (♀)	♂ (☽)

Table 8.2 - Ptolemy's Triplicity Rulership Scheme

as a primary ruler of earth even though he has both domicile and exaltation in that triplicity. Additionally, it is not clear why Jupiter is made cooperating ruler of air instead of the Sun, since the Sun is more diurnal. Thus, the dignity rationale does not fully explain why certain planets were assigned as rulers of each triplicity, although it goes a long way in doing so. The other missing factor that seems to explain a number of these inconsistencies is the planetary joys scheme, which will be discussed later.

Ptolemy's Alternative Triplicity Ruler Scheme

Ptolemy had an alternative triplicity rulers scheme which was a modified version of the more mainstream one in Dorotheus and Valens.[153] In this approach, Ptolemy only takes the dignity rationale into account, evidently rejecting or unaware of the joys as a secondary explanatory factor, which forces him to change some things in the scheme for conceptual reasons in order to be consistent. For example, he gets rid of the cooperating ruler because the cooperating ruler seldom has domicile or exaltation in the triplicity that it gets assigned to in the other scheme, so he only has two rulers per triplicity.

Mars is the last remaining planet in Ptolemy's scheme once he gets to the triplicity that consists of Cancer, Scorpio, and Pisces, so he makes it the primary ruler both by day and night, and makes some passing remark about Venus becoming a co-ruler by day and the Moon a co-ruler by night. Part of

---

[153] Outlined in Ptolemy, *Tetrabiblos*, 1, 19.

the purpose here seems to be that each planet is only used once in his overall triplicity ruler scheme.

Ptolemy's scheme was never widely adopted in the Hellenistic or Medieval traditions, but instead the standard system outlined by Dorotheus and Valens seems to have been used most of the time. William Lilly is one of the most notable later authors who adopted Ptolemy's scheme, and he cites Ptolemy for it.[154] In a later chapter we will discuss the use of the triplicity rulers within the context of the triplicity rulers of the sect light technique.

Irregular Distribution of Secondary Qualities

Aside from the primary qualities related to gender, domicile, exaltation, triplicity, and quadruplicity, there were also some other secondary qualities attributed to the signs. These qualities usually do not seem to have been assigned using the same logical or geometrical rationales that the primary qualities were based on, but instead they appear to have been assigned in a more irregular fashion based on other considerations. The rationale for these assignments sometimes appears to be derived from the images originally associated with the zodiacal constellations, where different facets of the image are interpreted as having broader symbolic significance for certain things, while other qualities may represent individual characteristics that came to be associated with certain signs based on other considerations. In some instances, the qualities seem to be designed to be used within the context of specific techniques, for example the distinction between barren and fertile signs, which are said to be indicative of the ease with which one can produce children. These specialized characteristics were not fully standardized amongst the Hellenistic astrologers, and different astrologers will sometimes report the qualities slightly differently. Due to this variability and the fact that we will not be using these qualities much in this book I will not give a full account of all of the assignments and the differences between the various authors here. It will suffice to provide an overview of a few of the qualities that are mentioned in connection with the signs.[155]

Four-Footed / Quadrupedal (*tetrapous*): Aries, Taurus, Leo, Sagittarius.

Human in Form / Anthropomorphic (*anthrōpoeidēs*): Gemini, Virgo, Libra, Sagittarius, Aquarius.

---

[154] Lilly, *Christian Astrology*, 1, 18, pp. 103–105.
[155] There is a later summary of many of the qualities in Ludwich, *Maximi et Ammonis*, pp. 105–112.

Prolific (*polugonos*): Cancer, Scorpio, Pisces. This means prolific in the sense of producing many offspring.

Barren (*steirōdēs*): Gemini, Virgo, Sagittarius, Capricorn. In the sense of being sterile or unable to bear children.

Incomplete (*atelēs*): Taurus, Virgo, Sagittarius, Capricorn.

Enigmatical (*ainigmatōdēs*): Sagittarius, Capricorn.

Royal / kingly (*basilikos*): Aries, Leo, Sagittarius.

Other miscellaneous qualities sometimes applied to the signs are: vocal, mute, licentious, outrageous, and others. Many of these qualities clearly seem to be derived from the images of the figures associated with the constellations, although some may be based on other rationales.

Valens uses some of the qualities at one point in a delineation for when a certain configuration of planets in a person's chart indicates a violent death, in order to modify the delineation in a way that specifies how it will come about:

If the stars are in four-footed signs, men will be taken by beasts; if in anthropomorphic signs, by bandits; if in fixed signs, men will die by falls from heights; if in fiery signs, from fires; if in wet signs, by shipwreck; if in movable signs, in the arena.[156]

This example is fairly typical in demonstrating the way in which the primary and secondary zodiacal qualities were sometimes employed in order to describe the manner in which the significations indicated by the planets will come about.

Zodiacal Melothesia

The practice of assigning parts of the body to planets, signs of the zodiac, decans, or other astrological factors is referred to in Greek as *melothesia*, which literally means something like "body part assignment" or "body part arrangement." The zodiacal melothesia is a system of assigning different parts of the body to each of the twelve signs of the zodiac, under the premise that there is a system of sympathetic correspondences between the microcosm of

---

[156] Valens, *Anthology*, 2, 17: 59, trans. Riley, p. 33, modified.

the human body reflecting the macrocosm of the arrangement of the cosmos at the moment of birth.

All systems of zodiacal melothesia begin by starting at the top of the body and assigning Aries to the head, under the premise that Aries is the first sign of the zodiac, and then work their way down the body, assigning signs to other parts of the body in order, eventually ending with the feet, which are assigned to the last sign of the zodiac, Pisces. In the Medieval and Renaissance traditions, illustrations of the signs of the zodiac and their correspondences with different body parts became so common that the concept came to be known as the Zodiac Man or Man of Signs (*Homo signorum*).[157] In the Hellenistic tradition the assignments were relatively standardized, although there were some slight variations between different authors, especially in some of the parts associated with the torso.[158] A standard list of the assignments is as follows:

ARIES:	head
TAURUS:	neck
GEMINI:	shoulders, arms, hands
CANCER:	chest
LEO:	ribs or sides, heart
VIRGO:	belly or abdomen
LIBRA:	hips and buttocks
SCORPIO:	genitalia
SAGITTARIUS:	thighs
CAPRICORN:	knees
AQUARIUS:	lower legs
PISCES:	feet

The zodiacal melothesia were typically used in order to identify parts of the body that might be subject to injury or disease.[159] Dorotheus uses a mathematical point derived from Mars and Saturn known as the Lot of Injury, and says that whatever sign of the zodiac it falls in within a natal chart, the native will experience an injury or chronic illness in the corresponding part of their body at some point in their life.[160] The melothesia were also used in astrological medicine, which

---

[157] Wee, "Discovery of the Zodiac Man," p. 217.

[158] There is very useful set of tables that compares the zodiacal melothesia given by all of the major Hellenistic astrologers in Wee, "Discovery of the Zodiac Man," pp. 220–222. For a survey of Hellenistic texts that deal with the melothesia see Pingree, *Yavanajātaka*, vol. 2, pp. 199–201.

[159] Valens, *Anthology*, 2, 37.

[160] Dorotheus, *Carmen*, 4, 1: 75–76.

was called *iatromathēmatika*, not just in order to identify potential illnesses or injuries, but also sometimes in order to determine how to treat them.[161]

The zodiacal melothesia are usually thought to have been one of the unique developments that occurred in the Hellenistic astrological tradition, although the recent discovery of a cuneiform tablet that preserves the doctrine has raised the possibility that the concept dates back earlier to the late Mesopotamian tradition.[162] Unfortunately this cuneiform tablet cannot be dated beyond a general period relatively late in the Mesopotamian tradition, and so it is not clear if it represents another instance of a doctrine being developed in the earlier traditions and then passed on to the Hellenistic astrologers, or if it is instead a doctrine that was developed by the Hellenistic astrologers and then transmitted back into cuneiform sources.[163]

Subdivisions of the Zodiac

The signs of the zodiac were commonly subdivided into smaller portions, in order to identify smaller ranges of degrees that were associated with different qualities within the same sign. There were several different methods of subdividing the signs in the Hellenistic tradition, with some of these methods playing a greater or lesser role in different parts of the system. The most popular were the divisions of the signs into thirds called "decans," the division into twelfths called "twelfth-parts," and an unequal division usually into five parts called "bounds," "terms," or "confines." In some authors there were also systems for assigning planets to each individual degree of the zodiac, called *monomoiria*, but we will pass over these since they do not appear to have been used as widely.[164]

Bounds

The most important and widely used of the zodiacal subdivisions were known as the "bounds," from the Greek *horia*. The bounds are unequal subdivisions of each of the signs of the zodiac which allot certain spans of influence to each of the planets. For example, in the sign Aries, the first six degrees of the sign are usually said to be ruled by Jupiter, the next six degrees are ruled by Venus, the following eight are ruled by Mercury, the next five by Mars, and the last five by Saturn. There may have been as many as nine different systems of bounds that existed in the Hellenistic tradition, although by far the most widespread and popular set

---

[161] Discussed in Wilson and George, "Anonymi, de Decubitu: Contexts of Rationality."
[162] Wee, "Discovery of the Zodiac Man."
[163] Wee, "Discovery of the Zodiac Man," pp. 232–233.
[164] For *monomoiria* see Paulus, *Introduction*, 32.

among the Greco-Roman astrologers were known as the "Egyptian bounds."[165]

The attribution of this set of bounds to the "Egyptians" is usually thought to imply that it was popularized in the texts attributed to Nechepso and Petosiris.[166] More recently it has been shown that this set of bounds may have had its origins in the earlier Mesopotamian tradition.[167] The Hellenistic authors who used the Egyptian bounds include Dorotheus, Valens, Firmicus, Paulus, and others. Additionally, nearly all of the surviving horoscopes employ the Egyptian bounds.[168] This set of bounds was subsequently transmitted to the Medieval astrologers, where it became the primary approach used in that tradition as well.

The Greek word for this subdivision, *horia*, connotes limitation or restriction, as well as spatial or territorial boundaries. In the Renaissance tradition, this division of the signs became known as the "terms," following the Latin word *termini*, although this doesn't quite convey the restrictive connotations of the Greek term as much as it should, thus the use of the term "bounds" here. Schmidt originally preferred and popularized the convention of referring to the concept as "bounds," but later decided to adopt the word "confines" instead.[169]

The primary technique that the bounds were incorporated into was the length of life technique. It is possible that this is why they were called "bounds" in the first place, because they were supposed to be used to show how long a person would live, with the planets demarcating the bounds or limits of a person's lifetime.[170] Whatever the case, they came to be used more generally as a zodiacal subdivision as the tradition progressed, so that each set of bounds carried certain unique qualities associated with its ruling planet, and planets were thought to be more auspicious when located in their own bounds in a

---

[165] There is a good survey of five of the systems in Pingree, *Yavanajātaka*, vol. 2, pp. 211–215. A more recent survey lists nine separate sets, which includes the version in the *Yavanajātaka*, as well as a set that Apollinarius is cited for which otherwise no longer survives, in Jones and Steele, "A New Discovery of a Component of Greek Astrology in Babylonian Tablets: The 'Terms.'"

[166] Pingree, *Yavanajātaka*, vol. 2, p. 214; Heilen, "Ptolemy's Doctrine of the Terms," p. 46.

[167] Jones and Steele, "A New Discovery." Cf. Steele, "A Late Babylonian Compendium."

[168] Alexander Jones points out that the Egyptian set of bounds is the only one employed in his collection of papyri from Oxyrhynchus. Jones, *Astronomical Papyri from Oxyrhynchus*, vol. 1, p. 11. Neugebauer and Van Hoesen report the same in their collection, with only one exception, from a literary source. Neugebauer and Van Hoesen, *Greek Horoscopes*, p. 12.

[169] Schmidt, *Definitions and Foundations*, p. 113.

[170] Paulus explicitly says in *Introduction*, 3 when he first introduces the bounds that the Egyptian sages (Nechepso and Petosiris?) used the bounds in order to determine the Master of the Nativity, and then from this to determine the length of life. He then goes on to list how many years of life each planet gives when it becomes the operative planet in the length of life technique.

Aries ♈

Degrees	1–6	7–12	13–20	21–25	26–30
Ruler	♃	♀	☿	♂	♄

Taurus ♉

Degrees	1–8	9–14	15–22	23–27	28–30
Ruler	♀	☿	♃	♄	♂

Gemini ♊

Degrees	1–6	7–12	13–17	18–24	25–30
Ruler	☿	♃	♀	♂	♄

Cancer ♋

Degrees	1–7	8–13	14–19	20–26	27–30
Ruler	♂	♀	☿	♃	♄

Leo ♌

Degrees	1–6	7–11	12–18	19–24	25–30
Ruler	♃	♀	♄	☿	♂

Virgo ♍

Degrees	1–7	8–17	18–21	22–28	29–30
Ruler	☿	♀	♃	♂	♄

Libra ♎

Degrees	1–6	7–14	15–21	22–28	29–30
Ruler	♄	☿	♃	♀	♂

Scorpio ♏

Degrees	1–7	8–11	12–19	20–24	25–30
Ruler	♂	♀	☿	♃	♄

Sagittarius ♐

Degrees	1–12	13–17	18–21	22–26	27–30
Ruler	♃	♀	☿	♄	♂

Capricorn ♑

Degrees	1–7	8–14	15–22	23–26	27–30
Ruler	☿	♃	♀	♄	♂

Aquarius ♒

Degrees	1–7	8–13	14–20	21–25	26–30
Ruler	☿	♀	♃	♂	♄

Pisces ♓

Degrees	1–12	13–16	17–19	20–28	29–30
Ruler	♀	♃	☿	♂	♄

Table 8.3 - The Egyptian Bounds
From the original verse text of Dorotheus, via Hephaestio, Apotelesmatika, 1, 1.

given sign.[171] If the entire sign of the zodiac is like the domicile of a planet, then the bounds might be likened to individual rooms within that domicile that are under the control of different planets. Naturally it was seen as more positive for a planet to be under the control of benefics, and less auspicious to be under the rule of malefics.

Despite how widely used they were, there is no clear systematic rationale underlying the distribution of the Egyptian bounds, and so the logic for their allotment remains a mystery. There are a few tantalizing patterns, however. In the Egyptian set only the five planets are given bounds; the Sun and Moon are excluded from having rulership. Paulus notes that the total number of degrees allotted to each of the planets in all twelve signs adds up so that it is equal to the so-called "greater" or "complete" years of the planets: Saturn: 57, Jupiter: 79, Mars: 66, Venus: 82, Mercury: 76.[172] This results in the benefics having a greater number of degrees allotted to them than the malefics. There is also a distinct pattern in which one of the malefics is always assigned to the end of each of the signs. In terms of the ordering and the number of degrees assigned to each of the planets, there is a tendency to assign the planets first based on which one has some form of rulership according to domicile, exaltation, or triplicity. For example, in Taurus, Gemini, Virgo, Scorpio, and Sagittarius the domicile lord of the sign is given the first set of bounds, while in Libra and Pisces the exaltation lord is given priority. Ptolemy notes this loose pattern, but then criticizes it for not being consistent.[173]

After criticizing the Egyptian bounds and then one other set that he attributes to the "Chaldeans," Ptolemy goes on to introduce a third set that he claims to have found in an old damaged manuscript.[174] Ptolemy is usually thought to be inventing his own set of bounds here, probably in order to have a clearer and more consistent rationale for them, which he felt was lacking in the Egyptian and Chaldean sets that he outlines first.[175] As with his triplicity

---

[171] Valens gives delineations for each of the bounds in *Anthology*, 1, 3. That planets are more auspicious when in their own bounds is stated in Paulus, *Introduction*, 3. It is also implied by the inclusion of this placement along with domicile and exaltation for a planet to be considered in its "chariot" in Antiochus, *Summary*, 14; Porphyry, *Introduction*, 25; Rhetorius, *Compendium*, 43.

[172] Paulus, *Introduction*, 3. Cf. Rhetorius, *Compendium*, 49.

[173] Ptolemy, *Tetrabiblos*, 1, 21: 2–4.

[174] Ptolemy, *Tetrabiblos*, 1, 21: 20–30.

[175] For an excellent overview of Ptolemy's set of bounds and some of the issues associated with them see Heilen, "Ptolemy's Doctrine of the Terms and Its Reception." Heilen discusses the question of the authenticity of the manuscript that Ptolemy claims to have found, and concludes the discussion by saying (p. 52): "a definitive answer is impossible, but there is a considerable probability that Ptolemy himself invented the third system of Terms." Cf.

rulership scheme, Ptolemy's bounds found few followers until the Renaissance period, when Lilly and some of his contemporaries adopted and popularized them.[176]

Decans or Faces

Another subdivision that is occasionally employed by the Hellenistic astrologers is the division of each sign into three ten-degree segments called "decans" or "faces." The decans were inherited from the earlier Egyptian astrological tradition, and originally each of the thirty-six decans was associated with specific fixed stars or asterisms, but in the Hellenistic period they became ten-degree subdivisions of the zodiacal signs. The decans then appear sporadically throughout the subsequent Hellenistic astrological tradition, although they seem to have played a much more reduced or subordinate role to the signs of the zodiac in the approaches outlined by most of the later Hellenistic astrologers.

The rising decan that contains the Ascendant in a person's birth chart was sometimes used in order to make general predictions about the native's life. For example, Hephaestio's delineation for the first decan of Virgo states:

> He who is brought forth upon the first decan, then, will be good, fond of laughter, dear to many; he will go through his life in luxury, wifeless because of not remaining with one woman, and his personal daimon and luck will be his protector, and though he will be unhealthy, he will also find medical relief; and after his youth he will be well-favored by women and he will meet with a fine end.[177]

The decans also seem to be used in order to describe the actual appearance of a native, as well as marks on specific parts of their body. Quoting again from the same passage in Hephaestio's delineation of the first decan of Virgo:

> The signs of this decan: His height will be lofty, his soul courageous, the face well-formed, the eyes lovely, the nose snub and a little thick. He will have a mark on his bosom.[178]

Houlding, "The Transmission of Ptolemy's Terms."

[176] The only major exception in the Hellenistic tradition is Hephaestio, who lists Ptolemy's bounds after those of Dorotheus in *Apotelesmatika*, 1, 1. The transmission and reception of Ptolemy's bounds among later astrologers is traced in detail in Heilen, "Ptolemy's Doctrine of the Terms," pp. 67–77.

[177] Hephaestio, *Apotelesmatika*, 1, 1: 109–111, trans. Schmidt, p. 13.

[178] Hephaestio, *Apotelesmatika*, 1, 1: 110, trans. Schmidt, p. 13.

In some of the ancient manuscripts the decans were accompanied by elaborate illustrations or descriptions of figures with striking features, which presumably invoked symbolic associations.[179] This is perhaps why the decans are also sometimes referred to as "faces," from the Greek *prosōpon*, which can also mean "mask," "visage," or "countenance." The *Liber Hermetis* preserves some descriptions from one of these texts, although some are more detailed than others.[180] For example, here is the description of the first decan of Aries:

> It is an armed sign, upright, walking, having the likeness of a man, standing on feet like claws, holding above his head a double sided battle axe with both hands.[181]

There were a few different systems for assigning meanings to the decans in the Hellenistic tradition. Some of the decan systems appear to be attempts to continue some aspects of the older Egyptian associations with the decans, such as Hephaestio's attribution of specific Egyptian names to each of the decans. For example, he says that the first decan of Cancer is named *Sōthis*, the second is *Sit*, and the third is *Chnoumis*.[182] These names are in accord with a list of names that were recorded for the decans in some ancient Egyptian temples, although Neugebauer and Parker note that Hephaestio seems to have conflated two different ancient naming schemes in his list.[183] To the extent that the decans simply became ten-degree subdivisions of the zodiacal signs in the Hellenistic tradition rather than markers that were based on specific fixed stars or asterisms, they largely ceased to be connected with the earlier Egyptian tradition, and it is not clear whether the continued use of some of these names represents anything more than a vestigial carryover from the earlier tradition.

There also seems to have been another system that broke with the previous tradition by attempting to create a schematic arrangement of planetary rulers associated with each of the decans. This system appears around the first century CE with Teucer of Babylon. According to this approach, the first decan of Aries is given the same planetary ruler as the domicile of Aries as a whole, which is Mars. Then the rest of the planets are assigned to subsequent decans in what is usually referred to by later astrologers as descending Chaldean order, which

---

[179] For a discussion of the sources and some of the different images see Pingree, "The Indian Iconography of the Decans and Horâs."

[180] *Liber Hermetis*, chapter 1.

[181] *Liber Hermetis*, 1: 4, trans. Zoller, Part I, p. 2.

[182] Hephaestio, *Apotelesmatika*, 1, 1: 69.

[183] Neugebauer and Parker, *Egyptian Astronomical Texts*, vol. 3, pp. 168–171. Cf. Neugebauer and Van Hoesen, *Greek Horoscopes*, pp. 5–6.

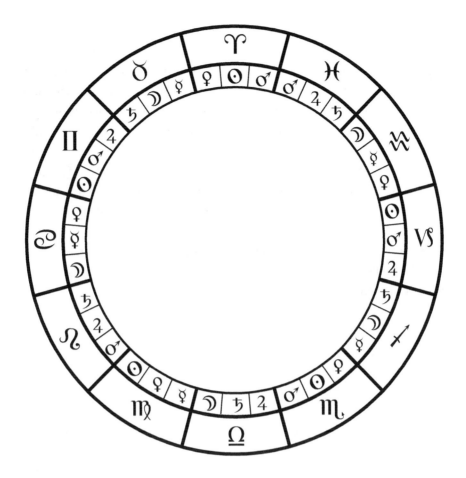

Figure 8.10 - Chaldean Order Decan Scheme

starts with Saturn, then goes to Jupiter, then Mars, then Sun, Venus, Mercury, Moon, before starting over again with Saturn.[184] Thus, since the first decan of Aries is Mars, the second decan is assigned to the Sun, which is the next planet in descending Chaldean order. Then after that the third decan is assigned to Venus. Next, the first decan of Taurus is assigned to Mercury, the next to the Moon, and then the following one to Saturn; and so on. Porphyry gives an example of how this system of decans was used in interpretations, perhaps drawing on Teucer's lost text:

---

[184] This approach is outlined in Paulus, *Introduction*, 4. Instead of referring to the planetary sequence as Chaldean order, he calls it the "seven zone system." This order of planets is also sometimes called "Ptolemaic order" in some contemporary discussions. In the fifth century CE Macrobius refers to it as "the Chaldean system." Macrobius, *Commentary on the Dream of Scipio*, 1, 19: 2. For a more detailed discussion about different planetary order schemes and their sources see Neugebauer, *A History of Ancient Mathematical Astronomy*, pp. 690–693.

For example, suppose the Sun to be in 10 degrees of Aries, in the first decan, the face of Mars; then, since we have said that the Sun signifies the spirit, you will find the spirit of that [person] to be manly, irascible, fond of fighting, fond of weapons, and such like. Again, supposed the Sun to be in the 20th degree of Aries, in the second decan, the face of the Sun; it signifies that [person] to be bright-spirited and ambitious and proud and not at all fond of fighting. Again, suppose the Sun to be in the 30th degree of Aries, in the third decan, the face of Venus; it signifies that [person] to be womanly-spirited, feminine in appearance, shameful, lustful, and such like. See how in a single sign they indicated three differences of spirit.[185]

It is not clear how widespread this system of assigning meanings to the decans was in the Hellenistic tradition, and in some ways it appears to have been in competition with the other approaches. Eventually by the Medieval tradition it seems to have won out, and decan or face became one of the five essential dignities.

Some of the surviving sources mention a further subdivision of the decans into thirds called *leitourgoi*, which means something like "servitors" or "ministers."[186] In some of the Hermetic philosophical material, the *leitourgoi* are characterized as the servants and soldiers of the decans.[187] Unfortunately, the astrological usage and interpretation of these subdivisions is left ambiguous since no interpretive texts for them survive. The decans as a whole are somewhat mysterious in general in terms of their interpretive value in the Hellenistic tradition, although Austin Coppock recently published an excellent book in which he attempted to explore and synthesize some of the different meanings of the decans, as inspired by a number of traditional sources. [188]

While the decans are sometimes referred to as "faces" (*prosōpa*), this should not be confused with a separate doctrine called "proper face" (*idioprosōpia*). A planet is said to be in its proper face when it has the same phase relationship with the Sun or Moon that it holds in the domicile assignments.[189] For example, in the domicile assignments the Sun is in Leo and it is configured to Venus in Libra through a superior sextile, with Venus being later in zodiacal order. If the Sun was in Scorpio and Venus was two signs later in Capricorn, then Venus would be in its "proper face" because it has the same phase relationship to the

---

[185] Porphyry, *Introduction*, 47, trans. Holden, pp. 40–41.

[186] Firmicus, *Mathesis*, 2, 4: 4–5; Anubio, *Carmen*, F1: 10–14.

[187] *Corpus Hermeticum*, vol. 3, fragment 6: 12, ed. Nock and Festugière, p. 36.

[188] See Coppock, *36 Faces: The History, Astrology, and Magic of the Decans*.

[189] Ptolemy, *Tetrabiblos*, 1, 23: 1; Rhetorius, *Compendium*, 54.

Sun by sign as it did in the domicile assignments. Unfortunately the existence of this doctrine sometimes creates some confusion when reading the texts, as it is not always clear when the author is referring to a planet being in its "proper face" versus when they are referring to it being in its own decan according to the Chaldean order assignments.[190] Ptolemy outlines proper face as a favorable condition for a planet to be in and otherwise never mentions the decans, which Schmidt rightly speculates may have been due to his use of the tropical zodiac, which would not be compatible with the older Egyptian associations between the decans and specific fixed stars or asterisms.[191]

Twelfth-Parts

The third major subdivision used in the Hellenistic tradition was known as "twelfth-parts," from the Greek *dōdekatēmorion* (pl. *dōdekatēmoria*). These are subdivisions of each of the signs into twelve smaller increments, usually of two and a half degrees each. This creates a sort of "micro-zodiac" of twelve small signs within each of the twelve larger signs of the zodiac, resulting in a total number of 144 subdivisions. Within a given sign, the first two and a half degrees are ruled by that same sign, while the next two and a half degrees are ruled by the next sign, and so on, following zodiacal order.[192] For example, the first twelfth-part of Aries is Aries-Aries, the second twelfth-part is Aries-Taurus, the third part is Aries-Gemini, and so on. In the sign Taurus the first twelfth-part begins with Taurus-Taurus, the next is Taurus-Gemini, then Taurus-Cancer, and so on.

The twelfth-parts are one of the specific techniques that can be traced back to the Mesopotamian tradition, as references to them survive in some late cuneiform sources.[193] In the Hellenistic tradition, these subdivisions primarily

---

[190] For example, see Valens, *Anthology*, 2, 5: 1, and compare with 2, 6: 1. Schmidt and Hand note the uncertainty in Valens, *The Anthology, Book II, Part 1*, p. 10, fn. 3.

[191] Ptolemy, *Tetrabiblos, Book I*, trans. Schmidt, p. 46, fn. 2.

[192] There is an alternative approach outlined in Paulus (*Introduction*, 22) which involves a thirteenth harmonic calculation, in which you multiply the degree of the placement by thirteen instead of twelve. The difference between the calculations is discussed by Rhetorius (*Compendium*, 18), who mentions Paulus' calculation, but then contrasts it with the approach of Dorotheus and Ptolemy, who multiply by twelve instead of thirteen. For Dorotheus see *Carmen*, 1, 8: 7. For Ptolemy see *Tetrabiblos*, 1, 22: 1. Hephaestio uses the same approach at one point within the context of inceptional astrology (*Apotelesmatika*, 3, 4: 19–34), perhaps following Dorotheus. Olympiodorus discusses the calculation issue a bit in chapter 19 of his Commentary on Paulus. Hand has a good discussion of the twelfth versus thirteenth harmonic issue in the introduction to Valens, *The Anthology, Book I*, trans. Schmidt, pp. vii–xiv.

[193] Rochberg-Halton, "Elements of the Babylonian Contribution," pp. 57–60. Cf. Koch-Westenholz, *Mesopotamian Astrology*, pp. 168–169, Monroe, "The Micro-Zodiac in Babylon and Uruk," and Wee, "Virtual Moons over Babylonia."

appear to have been used in order to determine minute modifications to the status of certain planets and points in a chart, with the nature of the planet or point that falls in a certain twelfth-part being altered by the nature of the ruling planet or the quality of the zodiacal sign associated with that twelfth-part, for better or worse. Firmicus tells us that some astrologers thought quite highly of these subdivisions, from which they could yield hidden information about certain placements:

> Some people think that from these the whole essence of the chart can be found and they claim that whatever is hidden in the chart can be revealed by the *dōdekatēmoria*.[194]

Firmicus goes on to briefly describe certain planets falling in a twelfth-part ruled by benefics or malefics as being more or less favorable for the functioning of that planet in a chart. He points out that even Jupiter's more favorable significations can be hindered by falling in an unfavorable twelfth-part, while Saturn's more problematic significations in a chart can become more acute if it is negatively impacted by its position in an unfavorable twelfth-part, with all other factors also being taken into account.[195] When studying the twelfth-parts in a chart from this perspective, the primary importance would seem to be viewing them within the context of their domicile lord, and the way that the significations of that planet may alter the functioning of a planet in the chart for better or worse.

Elsewhere, Hephaestio preserves a long set of interpretations for all 144 twelfth-parts at one point within the context of inceptional astrology, and specifically knowing what a client will inquire about based on which twelfth-part the Ascendant is located in at the inception of an astrological consultation.[196] Here is his delineation of the twelfth-parts of Leo:

> The first twelfth-part of Leo would give hints on reputation, the desire of things belonging to another, and greediness; the second [Leo-Virgo], on a great matter, and punishment, and injury; the third [Leo-Libra], on battle and greediness and being attacked on both sides; the fourth [Leo-Scorpio], on the completion of a great work; the fifth [Leo-Sagittarius], on matters not small but [rather] kingly, or on founding [something]; the sixth [Leo-Capricorn], on some labor or foreign trade or public revenue; the seventh [Leo-Aquarius], on enemies and the like; the eighth, on a

---

[194] Firmicus, *Mathesis*, 2, 13: 1, trans. Bram, p. 43, modified.
[195] Firmicus, *Mathesis*, 2, 13: 4–5.
[196] Hephaestio, *Apotelesmatika*, 3, 4: 19–34.

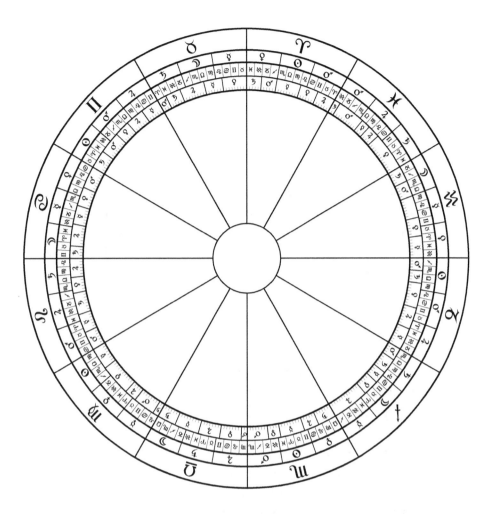

Figure 8.11 - Zodiacal Subdivisions: Decans, Twelfth-Parts, and Bounds

matter belonging to another, or care for another [Leo-Pisces]; the ninth, on fear and uncertainty [Leo-Aries]; the tenth, on a lounging place or country house or living abroad; the eleventh [Leo-Taurus], on battle and things unexpected [Leo-Gemini]; the last one [Leo-Cancer], <on> sacred matters or things of such kind.[197]

Here we can start to get a sense of some of the minute distinctions that the twelfth-parts allowed for in delineations, which become especially important in instances in which births or inceptions happen in close succession, so that there are only small differences in the chart placements.[198] This may have been

---

[197] Hephaestio, *Apotelesmatika*, 3, 4: 27, trans. Gramaglia, p. 45.

[198] Valens talks about this explicitly at one point when discussing the birth of twins

part of the underlying argument that was made by a Roman intellectual and astrologer named Nigidius Figulus in the first century BCE, in response to a skeptical question about natal astrology and the issue of twins who are born close together. Saint Augustine relates the story as follows:

> He revolved a potter's wheel with all the vigour he could command, and while it was spinning he made two very rapid strokes on the wheel with ink, apparently on the same spot. When the wheel stopped those marks were found to be a considerable distance apart on the edge of it. 'In the same way,' said Nigidius, 'the sky whirls round so swiftly that although twins may be born in as quick succession as my two strikes on the wheel, that corresponds to a very large tract of the sky. This would account for all the great divergences alleged in the character of twins and in the events of their lives.'[199]

As an astrologer, Nigidius probably would have been aware of some of the smaller subdivisions of the zodiacal signs, and how the Ascendant and other swift-moving points in the chart can change from minute to minute, which sometimes can make a noteworthy difference in terms of how one placement would be interpreted compared to another.

Interpreting Planets in Signs

Several implicit formulas seem to have been used for interpreting the meaning of planets when they are placed in certain zodiacal signs. Oftentimes these delineations seem to refer back to the domicile lord of the sign in particular. For example, when Mercury is in Sagittarius, this is sometimes interpreted as Mercury doing something related to Jupiter, which is the domicile lord of that sign. This is part of the reason why a planet in its own sign is interpreted as auspicious, since it does not have to rely on another planet to provide significations, but instead it can provide its own significations.

Two of the implicit formulas that were used in delineations can be stated as: "x of y," and "x with y," where x is drawn from the significations of the planet in the sign, and y is drawn from the significations of the domicile lord of the sign. For example, Mercury in a domicile of Jupiter (i.e. Sagittarius or Pisces) is interpreted by Manetho as "messengers of kings."[200] The signification

---

(*Anthology*, 3, 7: 15), and the fact that sometimes a change of one or two degrees can make a big difference with techniques such as the length of life treatment.

[199] Augustine, *City of God*, 5, 3, trans. Bettenson, p. 182.

[200] Manetho, *Apotelesmatika*, 2: 253–265, trans. Lopilato, p. 211.

of "messengers" comes from Mercury, the planet located in the sign, while the signification of "kings" comes from Jupiter, the domicile lord of the sign. Another example from Manetho is Saturn in a domicile of Mercury (i.e. Gemini or Virgo) indicating impediments with speech. This delineation is worth quoting directly from the verse text of Manetho in order to see the type of imagery he draws from Saturn: "Saturn in the signs of gold-shining Mercury dulls the keen ears of men and deprives them of fair speech or fetters their tongue."[201] From Saturn he is drawing keywords like dulling or blunting, depriving, and fetters or restraints, whereas from Mercury he gets the keywords of hearing and speech. When combined, it essentially produces a delineation of "difficulties with hearing" or "impediments with speech."

As we saw earlier, these formulas are also applied to other zodiacal qualities such as quadruplicity, although in these instances the properties derived from the signs usually become modifying factors that dictate the manner in which the planet's significations are expressed. For example, in his chapter on marriage Valens talks about the way in which Venus signifies marriage being modified depending on the quadruplicity of the sign it is in, among other factors: "If Venus is operative in a movable or a double-bodied sign, especially for night births, it makes men oft-married and promiscuous, particularly if Mercury is in conjunction."[202] Since the movable signs are associated with beginning or initiating things, and the double-bodied signs are associated with transitions and the presence of two things at the same time, Valens interprets this as modifying Venus' signification of marriage so that it results in multiple marriages or having multiple partners. The implicit contrast, then, is with Venus in fixed signs, which might be interpreted as more stable and likely to only have one marriage partner or only one love interest at a time. However, these delineations are always modified by the presence of other planets and factors which can either exacerbate or counteract the indication, as we see with his statement about Mercury, which is due to its changeable nature.

---

[201] Manetho, *Apotelesmatika*, 2: 191–193, trans. Lopilato, p. 209.
[202] Valens, *Anthology*, 2, 38: 4, trans. Riley, p. 50, modified.

CHAPTER 9
CONFIGURATIONS

Nor is it enough to know the special shapes of the signs and the individual ordinances which the stars impose on men at their birth; they also affect our destinies through their agreements with each other, for they rejoice in alliances and cooperate with one another according to their natures and locations.[1]

– Manilius

The third area of chart interpretation is known as the doctrine of configurations, which is more commonly referred to in modern astrology as the concept of "aspects." The primary purpose of configurations is that they allow the planets to form relationships and to interact with each other in different ways in the chart.

Reconstructing the Aspect Doctrine

While a number of astrological manuals survive from the Hellenistic tradition, they often take for granted that the reader is already familiar with a number of basic technical concepts, and they seldom define their terminology. This becomes the most problematic when dealing with the Hellenistic aspect doctrine, because many of the terms used for different types of configurations, as well as some of the underlying concepts, can be quite complex.

Sometime in the early Hellenistic tradition, an astrologer named Antiochus wrote a book in which he systematically defined most of the basic technical concepts. For this reason, Antiochus is a key source for reconstructing the Hellenistic doctrine of configurations, and his work appears to have influenced

---

[1] Manilius, *Astronomica*, 2: 270–2, trans. Goold, p. 105.

a number of later authors, including Porphyry, Firmicus, Hephaestio, and Rhetorius. Despite his influence on later authors, Antiochus' original book of definitions did not survive into the present day. Instead, we have three different versions of some of Antiochus' definitions that were either paraphrased, quoted, or adapted to later works. The three surviving works are as follows:

1. THE SUMMARY is a Byzantine synopsis of Antiochus' definitions.[2] The grammar is sometimes uneven, and there are signs that one scribe may have read the text aloud while another wrote the text down and summarized it, resulting in mistakes. The text breaks off prematurely in book two, but otherwise most of the material on the aspect doctrine survives.

2. PORPHYRY'S INTRODUCTION. An introduction to Ptolemy's *Tetrabiblos* is attributed to the third century Neoplatonic philosopher Porphyry of Tyre.[3] It largely consists of definitions that appear to have been taken verbatim from Antiochus. The text has some interpolated definitions from a later Medieval source, Sahl ibn Bishr, and it also seems to end prematurely. Otherwise, it preserves the clearest versions of many of Antiochus' definitions. Hephaestio of Thebes seems to have taken a few of the definitions that appear in the first book of his *Apotelesmatika* from Porphyry's version.

3. RHETORIUS' COMPENDIUM. In the late Hellenistic tradition, perhaps around the early sixth or seventh century, Rhetorius of Egypt incorporated a number of definitions from Antiochus at the beginning of a large compendium of astrological lore that he wrote.[4] He seems to have rewritten many of the definitions, either in order to clarify them, or in order to bring them in line with contemporary practice, as some technical and conceptual changes had occurred by the late Hellenistic tradition. As a result of these rewrites, Rhetorius' definitions are

---

[2] Edited in CCAG 8, 3, pp. 111–119. For a translation see Schmidt, *Definitions and Foundations*, pp. 43–56.

[3] Edited in CCAG 5, 4, pp. 187–228. Most of the aspect definitions are translated in Schmidt, *Definitions and Foundations*. For an alternative translation see Porphyry, *Introduction*, trans. Holden.

[4] The Antiochus definitions from Rhetorius are edited primarily in CCAG 1, pp. 140–164. This segment of Rhetorius was recently re-edited with the addition of a new manuscript tradition in Caballero Sánchez and Bautista Ruiz, "Una paráfrasis inédita de los Tesoros de Antíoco de Atenas: el epítome IIa. Edición crítica, traducción y notas." Most of the aspect definitions are translated in Schmidt, *Definitions and Foundations*. For a full translation see Rhetorius, *Compendium*, trans. Holden.

sometimes at variance with the *Summary* and Porphyry, although in some instances this may help to clarify the intent of the original text.

By comparing these three later versions of Antiochus' definitions, one may be able to reconstruct what the original definitions were. As early as 1985, in a privately circulated translation of Rhetorius, Holden suggested comparing these texts as a method for determining what Antiochus wrote; Schmidt completed the first full attempt at a reconstruction in 2009.[5] Unfortunately, because the three different versions of Antiochus' definitions often disagree with each other, it can lead to radically different reconstructions of the original doctrines. In 2010, I collaborated with Demetra George and Benjamin Dykes on an alternative attempt to reconstruct the aspect definitions of Antiochus in order to see if we could validate Schmidt's reconstruction; we came to a number of different conclusions about the original aspect doctrine. This led us to produce an alternative reconstruction of the original aspect doctrine, and the presentation of this reconstruction will form a large part of the structure of this chapter.

Definition of Witnessing or Testimony

In the Antiochus *Summary* and Porphyry, the series of definitions that deal with planetary configurations starts with the definition of what is called "witnessing" or "testimony" (*epimarturia*).[6] The full definition from Porphyry describes the configurations that connect planets together; their intervals; the nature of the relationship for each particular configuration; the necessity to see if the configurations are "complete," "finished," or "perfect" (*teleia*) by degree and not just by sign; that each configuration has specific degree intervals; and that planets are frequently configured by sign, but "no longer" (*ouketi*) by degree. Here is a translation of this passage by Demetra George:

> They call the configurations of the stars towards each other bearing witness. There are the following figures: the trigon is through five [intervals], whenever there are three zodiacal signs between the two; the tetragon is through four [intervals] whenever there are two zodiacal signs between them, the diameter is through seven [intervals] whenever there are five in the middle, and the hexagon is through three [intervals], whenever

[5] Rhetorius, *Compendium*, trans. Holden, p. xi. Schmidt outlines his methodology for comparing the texts and reconstructing the original definitions in *Definitions and Foundations*, pp. 22–32. Both were partially following the general outline that had first been established by Pingree in 1977 for determining the relationship between the three texts in his article "Antiochus and Rhetorius."

[6] Antiochus, *Summary*, 6; Porphyry, *Introduction*, 8.

there is one between them. And the trigon is sympathetic and helpful, and even if a destructive star is there, it is less damaging. The tetragon is harsh and unsympathetic and capable of causing pain if a destructive star is present. The diameter is adversarial, but worse if a malefic star is present. The hexagon is less efficacious. It is necessary to consider if the figures are perfect by degree and not only by zodiacal sign. The triangular figure is at an interval of 120 degrees, the square at an interval of 90 degrees, the hexagon at an interval of 60 degrees, the diameter at an interval of 180 degrees. For often [stars] are configured according to zodiacal sign, but no longer according to degree.[7]

This definition presents the broadest statement about configurations possible, and subsequent definitions in the Antiochus *Summary* and Porphyry add further nuances and qualifications to the basic concept. Before moving on, it is therefore important to first break down this definition in order to examine the different components at the core of the aspect doctrine.

Aspects as Vision

The first point that is notable about the definition of aspects presented in the Antiochus *Summary* and Porphyry is the use of the term *epimarturia* to refer to the concept, which means "to bear witness" to something. The related term *martureō* is used frequently in the New Testament where it means "to be a witness," "to bear witness," "give evidence," or "bear testimony." The Thayer New Testament lexicon defines it as follows: "to be a witness, to bear witness, i.e. to affirm that one has seen or heard or experienced something, or that he knows it because taught by divine revelation or inspiration."[8] In legal terminology, someone who is giving "witness testimony" has personally witnessed an event and is able to provide information about it. In an astrological context, the use of this term seems to imply that the planets have observed something, either in the chart with respect to other planets, or perhaps about the native's life or fate, and as a result of that they can provide testimony about what they have seen.

Most of the terminology that is used for aspects in the Hellenistic tradition has visual connotations, and serves to denote the ability or inability of the planets to see each other. Thus, in the texts, aspects are frequently referred to with terms like "witnessing," "observing," and "scrutinizing." When the Greek texts are translated literally, it results in sentences like "Zeus witnessing Hermes is favorable for speech and oratory," or "Mars scrutinizing Helios harms the

---

[7] Porphyry, *Introduction*, 8, trans. George, unpublished, modified.
[8] Thayer, *Thayer's Greek-English Lexicon of the New Testament*, p. 390

father." This is because in the Hellenistic tradition, aspects were conceptualized as the means by which the planets could *see* or *not see* each other. The aspect doctrine then is partially based on ancient Greek optical theories that have to do with rays emanating from the eyes, as well as the need for an affinity between the observer and the observed in order for vision to take place.

Although modern astrology has lost these visual connotations associated with aspects, the English word "aspect" itself comes from the Latin term *aspectus*, which means "a seeing, looking at, a look, sight."[9] Thus the visual connotations of the aspect doctrine are still embedded in the modern terminology, despite the fact that this conceptualization is no longer understood in modern astrology today.

Greek Optical Theories

The doctrine of configurations is rooted in developments that took place in the Hellenistic period in the related fields of optics and geometry. Greek optical theories often posited that there was a physical connection between the eye of the observer and that which was seen through vision. This principle is summarized succinctly by the second century physician Galen:

> A body that is seen does one of two things: either it sends something from itself to us and thereby gives an indication of its particular character, or if it does not itself send something, it waits for some sensory power to come to it from us.[10]

While many different theories about vision existed in the Greco-Roman period, historian Mark Smith has identified three broad categories that most fall into.[11] The three categories are as follows:

1. EXTRAMISSION: something is emitted from the eye towards the object being observed.
2. INTROMISSION: the object emits something towards the eye of the observer.
3. INTERMEDIATE THEORIES: both of the above are operative in some way, or sometimes neither, instead incorporating other factors such as notions of affinity or sympathy.

---

[9] Lewis and Short, *A Latin Dictionary*, p. 173.

[10] Galen, *On the Doctrines of Hippocrates and Plato*, 7.5, trans. deLacy, quoted in *Greek Science of the Hellenistic Era*, ed. Irby-Massie and Keyser, p. 202.

[11] Smith, "Ptolemy and the Foundations of Ancient Mathematical Optics," p. 23ff.

In the extramissionist theory, a geometrical ray is emitted from the eye. The objects which the rays fall on are seen, while the objects that the rays are unable to fall on are not seen. This was used to explain why we can't see around corners, because the rays that extend from the eye are straight lines. This approach is outlined concisely by the Greek mathematician Euclid, who in addition to writing a famous work on geometry, also wrote a work on optics:

1. Let it be assumed that lines extended directly from the eye pass through a space of great extent;
2. and that the figure included within our vision-rays is a cone, with its apex in the eye and its base at the limits of our vision;
3. and that those things upon which the vision-rays fall are seen, and that those things upon which the vision-rays do not fall are not seen.[12]

It is not entirely clear which optical theories the Hellenistic astrologers followed, although they seem to posit some sort of extramissionist theory in which rays are emitted from the "eyes" of the planets, and this is part of what allows them to see each other. Porphyry specifically says in chapter nine of his *Introduction* that every planet emits seven rays, and this seems to be part of the rationale for degree-based aspects.

Additionally, the astrologers seem to have incorporated some Platonic and Stoic optical theories, which held that there needed to be some affinity or sympathy between the observer and the observed in order for vision to take place, and this seems to be the theoretical rationale underlying sign-based aspects, as we will see later.

The ability of the planets to see each other comes about as a result of specific geometrical alignments that they make with one another as they move into different signs of the zodiac. The technical term that is used to refer to these geometrical relationships between planets is *schematismos*, which means "configuration," "figure," or "formation." Thus, the aspect terminogy sometimes implies visual connotations, and other times geometrical connotations, since both were linked through the close relationship between geometry and optics in the Hellenistic period.

The Five Configurations

There are five recognized aspects in Hellenistic astrology. From a practical standpoint, the Hellenistic astrologers used both sign-based and degree-based

---

[12] Euclid, *Optics*, definitions 1–3, translated in Irby-Massie and Keyser, *Greek Science of the Hellenistic Era*, p. 181.

aspects, and for that reason configurations are defined both in terms of intervals between signs as well as intervals between degrees.

The first and perhaps original aspect is known as "copresence" (*sumparousia*) or "conjunction," which occurs either when two planets are in the same sign (copresence) or when two planets occupy or are close to occupying the same degree of the zodiac, or in other words have zero degrees of longitudinal separation between them (conjunction). Originally the conjunction was not technically categorized as an "aspect" or "configuration," and the early Hellenistic astrologers seem to have defined it separately from the four proper configurations. This seems to have been because a conjunction is simply the presence of two planets in the same sign, or in the same degree, and they were not necessarily conceptualized as "witnessing" or looking at each other, but rather were simply present together. However, by the later part of the Hellenistic tradition, authors such as Rhetorius began grouping the conjunction together with the other configurations. For the sake of simplicity, I will largely treat the conjunction as a proper aspect here, although the distinction should be kept in mind since it comes up frequently in early authors such as Antiochus.

The other four original configurations are as follows:

1. Hexagon or sextile, which is when planets are either three signs apart or are separated by 60°.
2. Tetragon or square, which is when the planets are four signs apart or separated by 90°.
3. Triangle or trine, which is when the planets are five signs apart or separated by 120°.
4. Diameter or opposition, which is when the planets are seven signs apart or separated by 180°.

From a geometrical standpoint, the hexagon, tetragon, and triangle configurations are one side of a regular polygon that has been inscribed on the zodiacal circle. That is to say, they represent one side of a complete geometrical figure: 60° is one side of a six-sided hexagon; 90° is one side of a four-sided square; and 120° is one side of a three-sided triangle. This is why in Greek the terms used to refer to these aspects literally mean "hexagon," "square," and "triangle." However, for the purpose of this book I will adopt the modern convention of referring to these aspects as the sextile, square, and trine.

The configurations are sometimes simply referred to as "figures" (*schēma*), which primarily refers to the shape of the polygon that each is associated with, although Schmidt points out that this Greek term can also be used to refer to the

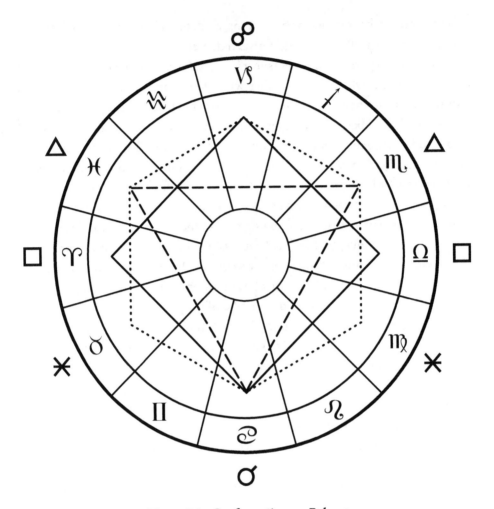

Figure 9.1 - Configurations as Polygons

attitude or bearing that someone adopts towards another person.[13] This implies that the nature of the aspect between planets is partially meant to characterize the attitude that they adopt relative to one another when they are configured. Thus, the configurations may be conceptualized as defining specific types of stances that the planets adopt relative to each other, and some of these stances are more friendly, while others can be more hostile.

Sign-Based Configurations

Porphyry and the *Summary* define the configurations first by sign and then by degree, and the other Hellenistic astrologers generally appear to have used both sign-based and degree-based aspects in practice. Sign-based aspects occur when

---

[13] Schmidt, *Definitions and Foundations*, p. 134.

planets are located in signs that are configured according to one of the recognized configurations. Planets configured by sign share a connection due to an affinity between the qualities associated with the signs they are located in.[14] That is to say, part of the rationale underlying sign-based configurations seems to be that they connect together signs that share the same gender, quadruplicity, or triplicity. Without this affinity they cannot see each other, and thus they cannot relate. This is then connected with some ancient optical theories that were adopted by the Platonists and the Stoics that posited sympathy or affinity as a requirement for vision. For example, the Greek philosopher Theophrastus explains:

> The various opinions concerning sense perception, when regarded broadly, fall into two groups. By some investigators it is ascribed to similarity, while by others it is ascribed to contrast: Parmenides, Empedokles, and Plato attribute it to similarity; Anaxagoras and Herakleitos attribute it to contrast. The one party is persuaded by the thought that other things are, for the most part, best interpreted by similarity; that it is innate to all creatures to know their kin; and furthermore, that sense perception takes place by means of an effluence, and like is born toward like.[15]

The notion that visual perception is due to likeness or affinity first appears in the work of pre-Socratic philosopher Empedocles, who is quoted by Aristotle as saying: "By earth in us we perceive earth; by water in us water; by air in us, the gods' air; and consuming fire by fire in us."[16] This concept later played a central role in the philosopher Plotinus' theory of vision in the third century CE as well, which means that it was a common notion during both the period in which Hellenistic astrology was developed as well as for several centuries while it was being practiced.[17]

The planets are connected with each other through the affinity of sign-based aspects in the following ways. Sextile signs share the same gender, masculine or feminine. For example, a planet in Cancer and a planet in Virgo are configured by a sign-based sextile, because the signs they are in share an affinity by both being feminine. A planet in Sagittarius and a planet in Aquarius would share a

---

[14] This seems to be part of the implicit premise underlying Ptolemy's explanation of configurations and aversions in *Tetrabiblos*, 1, 14 & 17. Manilius makes a similar statement about gender connecting signs through affinity in *Astronomica*, 2, 379–384.

[15] Theophrastus, *On the Senses*, 1, translation from Irby-Massie and Keyser, *Greek Science of the Hellenistic Era*, p. 335.

[16] Quoted in Aristotle, *On the Soul*, 404b8–15, although here I am using the translation of this line in Darrigol, *A History of Optics*, p. 3.

[17] Plotinus' views are discussed in Emilsson, *Plotinus on Sense-Perception*, pp. 36–61.

sign-based sextile because both are in masculine signs. Square signs share the same quadruplicity (movable, fixed, double-bodied), although their genders are different, which causes some contrast. A planet in Taurus is in a sign-based square configuration with a planet in Leo because both are fixed signs, for example. Trine signs share the same gender and elemental triplicity (fire, earth, air, water). For example, a planet in Cancer is in a sign-based trine aspect with a planet in Scorpio because both are feminine water signs. Opposing signs share the same quadruplicity and gender, although from a seasonal standpoint they represent opposite ends of the spectrum (spring opposite fall, and summer opposite winter).

This point about the affinity between zodiacal signs is important because it provides the conceptual justification for sign-based aspects, and explains why the Hellenistic astrologers would still conceptualize two planets as potentially being configured by sign even if they are not closely configured by degree.

Aversion

Planets that are not configured to each other by sign are said to be in "aversion" (*apostrophē*), and "turned away" from or "unconnected" (*asundetos*) to each other, since they share none of these affinities by sign. Ptolemy calls them "estranged" or "alienated" (*apēllotriōmenos*).[18] This is part of the reason why the concepts of the semi-sextile and quincunx aspects of modern astrology were never developed in the Hellenistic tradition, because these intervals were characterized by their lack of affinity, and thus the absence of configuration or aspect.

Sometimes aversion can be negative, but other times it can be positive depending on the circumstances. For example, when you are looking at a specific planet as signifying a topic, it is generally better for the benefics to be configured to that planet, since they can provide help and support. When the benefics are in aversion to a planet they are unable to see it, and therefore unable to lend their aid. Conversely, with the malefic planets it is often better if they are in aversion to a significator, for that way they are unable to obstruct or negate the significations of that planet. It thus depends on context; the key point is that aversion denotes a lack of configuration or relationship between two planets.

One of the interesting rules to keep in mind as a result of this doctrine is that each planet is configured to seven other signs at any given time when it is located in a specific sign of the zodiac, and is simultaneously in aversion to four other signs. For example, if Mercury is located in the sign Cancer, then it has a sign-based sextile with Taurus and Virgo, a sign-based square with Aries and Libra, a trine with Pisces and Scorpio, and an opposition with Capricorn.

---

[18] Ptolemy, *Tetrabiblos*, 1, 17: 1.

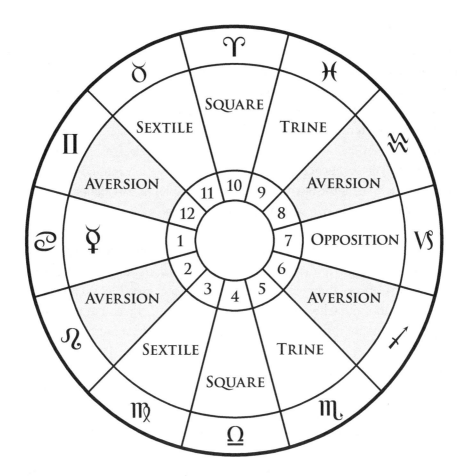

Figure 9.2 - Sign-Based Configurations and Aversions

It would be in aversion to Leo, Sagittarius, Aquarius, and Gemini. If Mercury were to move into Leo then the signs that it is configured to or in aversion with would similarly change as soon as the sign ingress took place, due to different affinities involved in terms of the relationship that Leo shares with other signs.

Copresence

Planets that are in the same sign are said to be copresent with each other, and their significations are blended together in that sign, regardless of the distance between them. For example, if Mercury is located in the sign Cancer along with the planet Saturn, then the two would be considered to be copresent with each other, even if Mercury is at the very beginning of the sign, at 1° Cancer, and Saturn is at the very end of the sign, at 29° Cancer. Copresence is essentially a sign-based conjunction.

The analogy is that when two planets are in the same sign it is like they are living in the same house together. When you are living under the same roof as someone it is difficult to not have an awareness of them and for each to have some influence over the other, even if they are living on different sides of the house. Obviously the relationship would be more intense if the two were living right next to each other in the same room, but from a Hellenistic perspective, even presence in the same sign is enough to create a relationship between the two planets. When this occurs the planets are usually interpreted as mixing or blending their significations together. For example, Valens delineates Jupiter copresent in the same sign with Mercury as follows:

> Jupiter and Mercury are good, in harmony, and supervisory. They make men who are managers, overseers of affairs, in posts of trust and administration. They make men who are successful as secretaries and accountants and who are respected in education. These are approachable people with many friends, judged worthy of pay and stipends.[19]

Elsewhere, Firmicus mentions that his delineation of the conjunction of Venus and Jupiter is applicable whether they are in the same sign or the same degree:

> If Jupiter and Venus are positioned together in the same degree or in the same sign, they denote the insignia of honor with the greatest grace of charm; they also always associate with good and great men in faithful friendships.[20]

Although there is an interpretive distinction between aspects by sign versus those by degree, it is important to understand that the basis of the classical aspect doctrine rests on the notion that it is the signs of the zodiac that provide the basic framework for configurations.

Degree-Based Configurations

Porphyry and the Antiochus *Summary* define configurations first by sign and then by degree. Antiochus seems to have made a specific point at the end of the original definition about this distinction; he says that planets are "often" (*pollakis*) configured by zodiacal sign, but "no longer" (*ouketi*) by degree. I take this simply to refer to the obvious point that sign-based aspects will occur more frequently from a statistical standpoint since the ranges involved in sign-based

---

[19] Valens, *Anthology*, 1, 19: 14.
[20] Firmicus, *Mathesis*, 6, 23: 4, trans. Holden, p. 346.

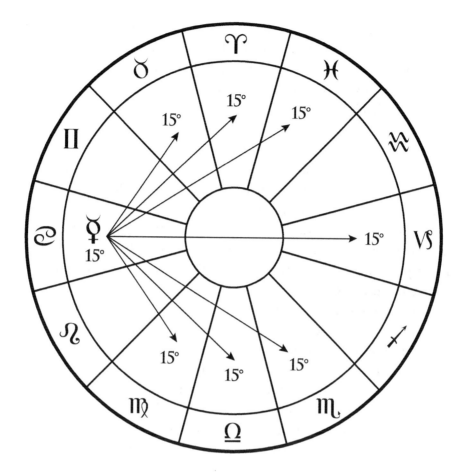

Figure 9.3 - Every Planet Emits Seven Partile Rays

aspects are much broader than those covered by degree-based aspects.[21]

At the heart of the degree-based aspect doctrine is a concept that Porphyry states in definition nine of his *Introduction*, that each planet emits seven rays of vision, from the degree that the planet is located in to the same degree in seven other signs: two sextile rays, two square rays, two trine rays, and one opposition ray. Each planet constantly emits these seven "partile" or degree-based rays. So, for example, Mercury at 10° Cancer casts two sextile rays to 10° Taurus and 10° Virgo, two square rays to 10° Aries and 10° Libra, two trine rays to 10° Pisces and 10° Scorpio, and one opposition ray to 10° Capricorn.

Configurations are said to be "complete" or "perfect" (*teleia*) when the two planets reach the exact degree interval associated with the configuration (e.g. 90°

---

[21] For an alternative interpretation see Schmidt, *Definitions and Foundations*, pp. 130–131. For a critical analysis of Schmidt's argument see Dykes' discussion of the term "testimony" in Hephaestio, *Apotelesmatika*, 3, trans. Gramaglia, pp. 25–6.

for square, 60° for a sextile, etc.). This is when the visual ray of the planet crosses over the body of another planet, and the two planets have the clearest vision of each other. This is defined in chapter ten of Porphyry as "passing by" (*parallagē*): "They call it a 'passing by' whenever stars pass beyond a configuration by degree of an equal-sided figure."[22]

From a practical standpoint, this means that planets establish a relationship as soon as they move into signs that are configured, but these relationships become stronger or more intense when they are also closely configured by degree. In some later Hellenistic astrologers such as Valens, they will often use the more general language of "witnessing" when referring to sign-based configurations, or configurations in general, but will switch to different terms which convey more intense visual connotations when they are specifically referring to degree-based aspects. The most common term that the astrologers will switch to when a degree-based configuration is intended is *katopteuō*, which according to the LSJ lexicon means to "observe closely," "spy out," or "reconnoiter." Schmidt translates *katopteuō* as "scrutinize," which I follow.[23] Underlying this distinction seems to be the notion that the visual ray is most acute right at the very center of where it falls, as this represents the central point of visual focus where things are the clearest, within the broader context of the planet's overall field of vision. When all of this is taken together it seems to imply that the primary distinction between sign- and degree-based aspects is one of visual clarity, and having a close degree-based configuration can intensify the strength of the relationship, for better or worse.

Applying versus Separating

When the two planets are still moving towards an exact degree-based configuration or a conjunction they are said to be "applying" (*sunaphē*), while when they are moving away from an exact configuration or conjunction they are said to be "separating" or "flowing away" (*aporroia*).[24] This is the general usage of the term *sunaphē*, in the sense of applying configurations, as contrasted with separating configurations. However, *sunaphē* is also used to refer to a more specific type of application.

Planets applying to an exact degree-based configuration within three degrees were thought to be in the most intense range of the configuration. According to the *Summary* and Porphyry, when planets are applying within three degrees through a sextile, square, trine, or opposition, it was referred to

---

[22] Porphyry, *Introduction*, 10, trans. Demetra George, unpublished.

[23] Schmidt and Hand, *Project Hindsight Companion to the Greek Track*, p. 46.

[24] Discussed in Porphyry, *Introduction*, 11–13.

as an "engagement" or "joining" (*sunaphē*), whereas when two planets were applying within three degrees to an exact conjunction it was referred to as an "adherence" (*kollēsis*).[25] The use of two separate terms here to refer to the general idea of an applying aspect within three degrees is due to the distinction between the conjunction and the other proper aspects in the early Hellenistic tradition. Porphyry says that the Moon is unique in that its range for an engagement or adherence is thirteen degrees rather than three, which is the average distance it will travel in a twenty-four-hour period. We will return to the concepts of engagement and adherence and talk about their practical applications later in the chapter on bonification and maltreatment, where they become special considerations within the context of that doctrine.

For planets besides the Moon, an additional range was sometimes mentioned for the conjunction, which was more than three degrees but less than fifteen degrees. This range is referred to in the Antiochus *Summary* as an "assembly" (*sunodos*).[26] These ranges, especially the three-degree range for engagement, are the closest that the Hellenistic astrologers seem to have come to developing something like the modern concept of "orbs" of influence for the planets. It appears that something approaching the modern idea of orbs didn't fully develop until the Medieval period.

From an interpretive standpoint, applying configurations were thought to be more powerful than separating configurations, for better or worse. We will see this especially in the context of the bonification and maltreatment conditions. Within the context of inceptional astrology, applying configurations were thought to indicate events and circumstances that will develop in the future, while separating configurations indicate things that have already occurred in the past.[27] Rhetorius summarizes this principle by saying:

> For the separations give judgment on the things that have preceded and have been preserved; and the applications give judgment on the things that are going to be and those that are hoped for.[28]

This is because applying aspects are planetary configurations that are still forming or moving towards being exact by degree, while separating aspects represent configurations that have already completed and are now moving away

---

[25] Antiochus, *Summary*, 8–9; Porphyry, *Introduction*, 11.

[26] Antiochus, *Summary*, 9.

[27] Dorotheus, *Carmen*, 5, 28: 4. Julian of Laodicea cites Petosiris for the same doctrine in CCAG, 1, p. 138: 18–19.

[28] Rhetorius, *Compendium*, 112, trans. Holden, p. 159.

from the exact, degree-based alignment. This leads to the concrete interpretative principle that the outcome of any inception that is initiated when important planets like the Moon are applying to benefic planets will be positive, whereas if the Moon is applying to malefics the outcome will be negative.[29]

From the perspective of a contemporary practitioner of astrology, the main thing to understand about the Hellenistic aspect doctrine which sets it apart from the modern approach is that planets begin "aspecting" each other as soon as they move into signs that are configured. The closer that the planets get to an exact, degree-based aspect, the more intense or acute their relationship becomes. This also applies to transits, as a transit begins as soon as the planets become configured by sign, but grows more intense the closer the transiting aspect gets to completion. Applying within three degrees is the most important or intense range for degree-based aspects between planets, except for the Moon, which is thirteen degrees. We will see some specific instances of this later in chart examples once all of the basic principles have been outlined.

Running in the Void

A condition that is related to the concept of application appears in the Antiochus *Summary* and Porphyry under the definition "running in the void" (*kenodromia*):

> It is called running in the void whenever the Moon is joined to nothing, neither zodiacally nor by degree, not according to figure nor according to bodily adherence nor is it about to make an engagement or assembly within the nearest thirty degrees. These such nativities are undistinguished and make no progress.[30]

This is the origin of the modern concept known as "void of course Moon." The Greek term here is *kenodromia*, which is a compound word formed from *kenos*, which means "empty," "fruitless," or "void," and *dromos*, which means "a course," "running," or a "race." Together it means something like "running in the void" or "running in the emptiness," although the modern phrase "void of course" is accurate as well.

The Antiochus *Summary* and Porphyry both say that running in the void is a condition in which the Moon does not apply to an exact degree-based aspect, either through bodily conjunction or by any other aspect, within the next thirty

---

[29] Julian of Laodicea summarizing Petosiris in CCAG, 1, p. 138: 15–18.

[30] Porphyry, *Introduction*, 23, trans. Demetra George, unpublished, modified. Cf. Antiochus, *Summary*, 11.

degrees.[31] This is quite different from the modern definitions of void of course, where the range involved is usually narrower, and there is sometimes an added stipulation involving the aspect completing before the Moon moves into the next sign. The Hellenistic definition given by Antiochus and Porphyry does not mention anything about a sign boundary, but just that the Moon completes no exact aspect within the next thirty degrees. Such a condition is somewhat rare, although it does happen from time to time. Benjamin Dykes points out that this essentially sets up something like a set of equal houses from the degree of the Moon, and all of the planets would have to be in aversion to the first "house" in this chart in order for this condition to be in effect.[32]

It is not clear why the definition of void of course changed in the later Medieval tradition.[33] It may have had something to do with the expanded development of the practice of interrogational astrology, in which the idea of planets completing their aspects before changing signs started to become more important, as a manner of determining whether the answer to a question was affirmative or negative. Along those lines, it is important to note that running in the void is only defined in terms of the Moon here, and the concept generally does not seem to have been applied to other planets in the Hellenistic tradition.[34]

From an interpretive standpoint, running in the void was usually viewed as an extremely unfavorable indication in a chart in the Hellenistic tradition.[35] It is primarily mentioned as a condition in natal astrology that portends difficulty in making progress in the native's future, presumably because the Moon's inability to complete future aspects was symbolically thought of as a negative omen for the native's own potential in making accomplishments in their life. This idea of being unable to accomplish things may be the reason why Porphyry says that natives with this placement are undistinguished and make no progress.

Qualities of the Configurations

The statements that Porphyry makes about the qualities of the different configurations in the definition of witnessing are generally consistent with

---

[31] Rhetorius initially defines void of course in chapter 39 of his *Compendium*, but there he does not specify the degree range involved. Later in chapter 112 he defines it again, and this time he does specify the 30-degree range.

[32] Dykes, *Introductions to Traditional Astrology*, p. 144.

[33] For a comparison with some later medieval authors see Dykes, *Introductions to Traditional Astrology*, pp. 142–143.

[34] The only exception to this is a brief statement that Rhetorius makes in *Compendium* 112 in which he says something about planets having certain configurations with the Sun also sometimes being said to be void of course, although I'm not entirely clear about what is being referred to here.

[35] There are some delineations of running in the void in Firmicus, *Mathesis*, 4, 8.

how other astrologers describe those aspects. Generally speaking, the trine and sextile were thought to be easy or positive configurations, while the opposition and square were thought to be challenging or negative.

The trine is usually considered to be the most positive configuration, and Porphyry calls it "sympathetic" (*sumpathēs*) and "helpful" or "beneficial" (*ōphelimos*). The hexagon or sextile is usually thought to be similar to the trine in being positive, but it is seen as weaker or less efficacious. For example, after giving delineations for Venus trine Saturn, Valens goes on to say "if these stars are sextile with each other, their effects are the same as those attributed to the trine configuration, but dim and weak."[36] Other authors make similar statements for other planets when configured by sextile.[37] Both the trine and the sextile configurations were thought to be very positive when the planets involved are benefics, whereas malefics were said to be incapable of doing harm when configured by trine or sextile.[38]

Porphyry and the *Summary* refer to the diameter or opposition as "adversarial" (*antizēlos*), using a word that can also mean "rivaling" or "controversial." Malefics are thought to be particularly difficult or damaging when configured to other planets by opposition, while benefics are typically seen as less positive when configured in this way.[39] Within the context of a discussion about synastry, Dorotheus interprets the opposition as indicating estrangement, discord, and hostility.[40]

The square or tetragon is referred to as "hard" or "harsh" (*sklēros*) and "inharmonious" (*asumphōnos*) by Porphyry. Malefics are thought to be particularly difficult when configured by square, while benefics are interpreted as being either somewhat problematic or potentially beneficial under certain circumstances when configured by square. The ambiguity about how to treat benefics that are configured by square arises from the fact that this configuration was also viewed as being very powerful despite being challenging, and if the benefic has the upper hand in the square then it is able to use that

---

[36] Valens, *Anthology*, 2, 17: 67, trans. Riley, p. 33.

[37] Dorotheus, *Carmen*, 2, 17: 1; Manilius, *Astronomica*, 2: 358.

[38] Porphyry and the Summary both seem to say that the malefics are "less" harmful when configured by trine, although elsewhere the astrologers seem consistent in treating the malefics as not causing harm to planets they are configured with in this way. For example, the *Michigan Papyrus* says that the malefics are "harmless" (*ablabēs*) when configured by trine. See *Michigan Papyrus*, col. xviii: 17–19.

[39] The *Michigan Papyrus* says that malefics are capable of injuring other planets through the opposition, whereas benefics are more "slack" (*atonōteroi*), which Robbins interprets as meaning "less effective." See *Michigan Papyrus*, col. xviii: 17–21.

[40] Dorotheus, *Carmen*, 5, 16: 38–39.

power for good. This point is made quite explicitly in a Greek fragment that is somewhat doubtfully attributed to Petosiris:

> Everyone supposes that the triangular sides are harmonious throughout our [lives] and the cause of good things, but they are in error. For, the squares have the strongest activity whether they should be indicative of good things or base. And the triangle often makes neither a good [figure] that is well-fitted, nor a bad one. Again, of the squares the ones on the right are more active than those on the left. And in the diameters malefics are difficult, but diametrical benefics are never bad, neither with each other nor with the lights. And Kronos and Ares are exceedingly malefic in this figure if they are able to act while stationing.[41]

While the attribution of this passage to Petosiris is usually doubted, the sentiments expressed are largely consistent with the approaches that many of the Hellenistic astrologers seemed to take, so it may represent a view that was generally accepted, regardless of who actually wrote it.[42] Indeed, Hephaestio makes a similar statement at one point when he says:

> the diametrical figures have rivalry and opposition, the triangular figures are harmonious and sympathetic, though not as strong as the square figures. The hexagons are much weaker, and more vaguely help or hinder.[43]

Similarly, Valens says at one point that squares and oppositions are the most "powerful" or "potent" (*dunastikos*) types of configurations.[44] We will see specifically how the distinction between squares on the right or left works shortly, when discussing the concept of overcoming.

Finally, the conjunction or copresence is usually treated as neutral, and can be positive when it involves good planets, or negative when it involves bad ones.[45] Thus, a conjunction with Venus or Jupiter would generally be interpreted

---

[41] CCAG, 6, p. 62: 9–17, trans. Schmidt, *The Astrological Record*, p. 18.

[42] Pingree ("Petosiris," p. 549, n. 33) says that he doubts the attribution of the passage.

[43] Hephaestio, *Apotelesmatika*, 3, 41: 5, trans. Gramaglia, p. 119.

[44] Valens, *Anthology*, 4, 16: 23.

[45] One exception to this is Paulus, *Introduction*, 10, who says that the conjunction is harmonious and effective, likening it to the trine in terms of its power, evidently because he is contrasting the conjunction with the opposition. While this seems true when it comes to positive conjunctions or copresences, it seems like when it involves malefics this placement is generally interpreted as being a bit more difficult, so it is not clear that Paulus' view is fully representative of the tradition in this instance.

as positive, while a conjunction with Mars or Saturn would generally be seen as negative, other factors aside. Much of the interpretation of the conjunction seems to depend on the planets involved, since there are some conjunctions that are interpreted in a very positive way, while there are others that are interpreted in a very negative way. Sometimes this has to do with underlying theories about the temperamental qualities associated with certain planets, and the potential for each to balance or neutralize the other, which in some instances leads to interpretations of certain combinations like Mars and Saturn that are surprisingly positive.[46] This was not true of all authors, though; Valens interprets the conjunction of Mars and Saturn as essentially negative, unless mitigated by other factors.[47] In this way the neutral nature of the conjunction seems to have encouraged variant interpretations among the astrologers due to different philosophical and conceptual perspectives.

Domicile Assignment Configuration Rationale

Ptolemy relates the natures of the configurations to the domicile assignments. He demonstrates that if you place all of the planets in their respective domiciles, the nature of the planet is largely in accord with the quality of the configuration relative to each of the luminaries.[48] The scheme is as follows: first, each of the planets are assigned to their respective domiciles, and then the zodiac is divided into two halves along the axis between Cancer and Leo. This results in a solar half of the zodiac running from Leo to Capricorn, and a lunar half of the zodiac running from Cancer to Aquarius. If you draw aspect lines from each of the luminaries to each of the planets in their respective hemispheres, you connect each of the aspects to one of the benefics or malefics. The resulting breakdown is as follows:

> Venus is associated with the sextile
> Mars with the square
> Jupiter with the trine
> Saturn with the opposition

Because the sextile and trine connect to the two benefics, Venus and Jupiter, these configurations were thought to be positive; the square and opposition, in contrast, connect to the two malefics, Mars and Saturn, and these configurations

---

[46] For example, in Dorotheus, *Carmen*, ed. Pingree, pp. 368: 25–30–p. 369: 1–3, quoted earlier, in the philosophy chapter.

[47] Valens, *Anthology*, 1, 19: 3.

[48] Ptolemy, *Tetrabiblos*, 1, 18.

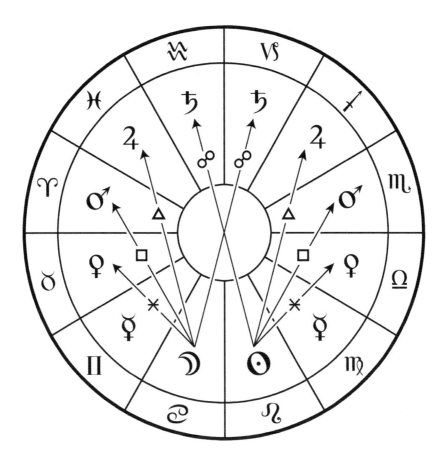

Figure 9.4 - Quality of the Configurations via Domiciles

were generally thought to be negative or challenging. This seems to imply that the basic natures of the configurations are partially derived from the relationships between the planets and the luminaries in the domicile assignment scheme, which in turn is derived from the Thema Mundi. Firmicus Maternus talks about this schematization briefly during his treatment of the Thema Mundi, which may imply that these concepts were all tied together originally via the mythical birth chart of the cosmos.[49]

Right versus Left

In chapter nine of his *Introduction*, Porphyry introduces an important distinction between configurations on the right side of a planet versus configurations on the left side of a planet:

---

[49] Firmicus, *Mathesis*, 3, 1: 2–7.

> They say that the trine, square, and sextile from which a star has come are on the right, but those towards which the star is going are on the left. [...] For each of the stars sends forth seven rays, three upwards and three downwards, and one towards the diameter, of which the upward ones are on the right side, but the downward ones are on the left side.[50]

This is connected with the doctrine that each planet casts seven partile rays, with three of those rays being sent to signs that are earlier in zodiacal order, and another three rays being sent to signs that are later in zodiacal order. Zodiacal order goes in a counter-clockwise direction, which is the direction that the planets move through the signs most of the time, when they are direct in motion.

According to the distinction outlined here, the three rays that a planet casts to signs that are earlier in zodiacal order relative to the planet's location are said to be on the right side. So, for example, if Mercury is in Cancer then it casts a sextile to its right side to the sign of Taurus, a square to Aries, and a trine to Pisces. These aspects are all sent to signs that are earlier in zodiacal order relative to Mercury, and therefore are conceptualized as being right-sided aspects. Conversely, the three rays that a planet casts to signs that are later in zodiacal order relative to the planet are said to be on the left side. For example, if Mercury is in Cancer then it casts a sextile ray to its left side to Virgo, a square to Libra, and a trine to Scorpio. These aspects are all sent to signs that are later in zodiacal order relative to Mercury, and therefore are conceptualized as being on the left side of Mercury.

An easier way to see this distinction in individual nativities is to imagine yourself standing in the middle of a round chart wheel, with the zodiac all around you. When you turn toward and look at a specific planet while standing in the center of the wheel, any planets to your right will be on the right side of the planet, and any planets on your left will be on the left side of the planet. Thus right and left is partially conceptualized as an observational consideration that is measured relative to the perspective of the observer looking up at the planets in the zodiac, rather than from the perspective of the planet looking down at the earth.

The distinction between right and left only applies to the sextile, square, and trine configurations. The opposition and the conjunction are neither right nor left, since they fall right on the dividing line between the two hemispheres.

In Greek the authors typically use the euphemism "the well-named side" (*euōnumos*) to refer to the "left," since from very early times the Greeks held the right side to be auspicious and the left to be inauspicious.[51] This will become

---

[50] Porphyry, *Introduction*, 9, trans. Demetra George, unpublished, modified.

[51] For a concise discussion of some early Greek views see Hall, *The Sinister Side*, pp. 14–21.

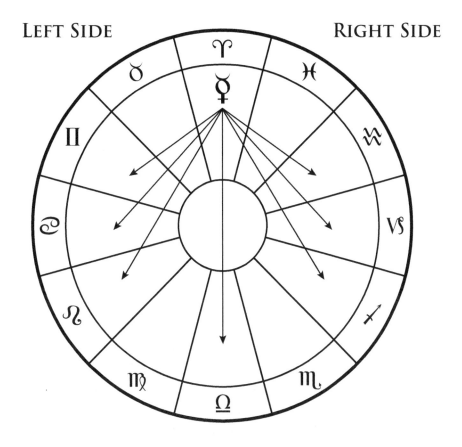

Figure 9.5 - Right versus Left-Sided Configurations

relevant later as an interpretive principle once we introduce the concept of overcoming. The distinction between aspects on the right or left side survived into the Renaissance tradition, where they used the Latin terms *dexter* and *sinister*, which simply mean "right" and "left."

Overcoming

In definition ten of the Antiochus *Summary* and chapter twenty-one of Porphyry they introduce the extremely important concept known as "overcoming" (*kathuperterēsis*). According to this distinction, when two planets are configured according to a trine, square, or sextile, the one that is on the "right" side exerts a more dominant influence over the planet that is on the "left" side. Here is Porphyry's definition of overcoming:

> Every star, the one which is lying on the right trine or square or sextile overcomes the one on the left, for it is going towards it. Thus, some star

which is in Capricorn overcomes one in Taurus by trine figure and one in Aries by square figure and one in Pisces by sextile figure; it itself is overcome by a star in Libra and by one in Virgo and by one in Scorpio. They say that overcomings are more powerful when [the stars] are either configured by trine or square. For in this way the star that is overcoming is stronger, whether it should be a benefic or malefic, or angular. For a benefic shows the nativity to be eminent, but a destroyer shows the nativity to be undistinguished. And in general every star on the right overcomes one on the left, toward which it travels.[52]

The term for overcoming, *kathuperterēsis*, is derived from a word that is sometimes used metaphorically in non-astrological texts to refer to someone "having the upper hand" or being in the "upper" or "superior position." It thus has connotations of being on top of or above something, and the LSJ lexicon uses an example of "a wrestler who falls atop of his opponent."

In Porphyry this definition builds on the earlier distinction between right and left sided configurations by introducing the notion that the planet on the right is stronger than the planet on the left. The planet on the right is characterized as being in the superior position, and therefore it overcomes the planet that is in the inferior position.

The only point that is problematic in this definition is Porphyry's statement that the planet on the right is stronger because it "goes towards" the planet on the left. This statement could be interpreted in a number of different ways, but I take it to mean that he is referring to the typical movement of the planets in zodiacal order, and the fact that in a general sense they all eventually move towards the place that is on their left side relative to their present location.[53]

From a practical standpoint, in the Hellenistic texts a planet that is overcoming another planet is always given more weight as having the greater impact in the interpretation of the configuration between two planets.[54] The overcoming planet dominates the relationship between the two planets, for better or worse. If a benefic has the upper hand, then it promotes a positive outcome to the configuration, while if a malefic has the upper hand it typically promotes a more negative or difficult outcome. For example, if Jupiter is in Taurus and Mars is in Leo, then Jupiter overcomes Mars, and thus Jupiter has the upper hand and is able to force Mars to behave in a more positive manner

---

[52] Porphyry, *Introduction*, 21, trans. Demetra George, unpublished, modified.

[53] For an alternative interpretation see Schmidt, *Definitions and Foundations*, p. 184ff.

[54] For examples see the delineations in Firmicus, *Mathesis*, 6, 3–14. Cf. Anubio, *Carmen*, ed. Obbink, T8: 1–207.

than it would otherwise. Conversely, if Mars is in Taurus and Jupiter is in Leo, then Mars overcomes Jupiter, and thus Mars has the upper hand and is able to force Jupiter to act in a way that is worse than it would be otherwise.

In the surviving delineation material, the astrologers would often give different interpretations for the same configuration between planets depending on which one is overcoming the other. For example, Firmicus' delineation of Mars square Jupiter:

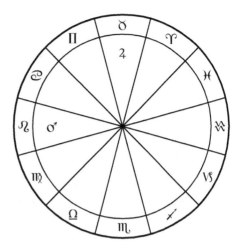

Figure 9.6 - Jupiter Overcomes Mars

> Jupiter and Mars in square aspect with Jupiter in the superior position indicate great fame, good reputation, and high position. Some will be involved in military activities; others assigned to royal households with high government position. From these duties they will gain important promotions. But they are never able to preserve their paternal inheritance; they will

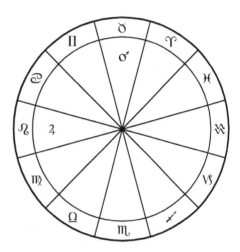

Figure 9.7 - Mars Overcomes Jupiter

have children late and suffer constant grief from accidents to children. If Mars is in the superior place, this causes extreme mental anxiety. The natives will be involved in various kinds of errors and difficulties. They will suffer from royal or government actions and will be attacked by hostile accusations of dangerous enemies.[55]

Note how the interpretation of Mars square Jupiter is mostly positive as long as Jupiter is in the superior position, overcoming Mars, but the delineation becomes entirely negative when the situation is reversed, when Mars is overcoming Jupiter. There is a similar reversal in the interpretations even

---

[55] Firmicus, *Mathesis*, 6, 10: 1–2, trans. Bram, p. 189, modified.

when more neutral planets are involved. For example, Firmicus' delineation of Moon square Mercury:

> The Moon and Mercury in square aspect with Mercury superior, indicate wisdom, learning, fluent speech, and facility in oratory. But trouble often comes from popular uprisings. [...] But if the Moon is in the superior position, the natives will be unstable in mind; their plans are inconsistent and their minds are not able to carry on a reasonable train of thought.[56]

Here, Mercury overcoming the Moon is delineated relatively positively, but the Moon overcoming Mercury is interpreted more negatively. A similar principle is applied to all other interpretations of aspects between planets that are configured by sextile, square, or trine.

Upon the Tenth or Domination

As Porphyry said, overcoming was thought to be the most powerful when it occurs through a trine or a square. In fact, overcoming through the superior square was thought to be so powerful that it was sometimes given a separate designation of its own, called "upon the tenth" (*epidekateia*).[57] This condition occurs when one planet is in the tenth sign relative to another planet, which is the same as being in a sign-based square. The planet that is upon the tenth is overcoming the other planet through a superior sign-based square, which makes this a specific version of overcoming or being in a superior position. Being upon the tenth occurs by sign, regardless of what degrees the planets are in. It is a purely sign-based type of configuration.

The term *epidekateia* is complicated because it appears to carry double meanings.[58] On the one hand, it primarily means being "upon the tenth," referring to the fact that the planet in this position is literally in the tenth sign relative to another planet. There may also be a secondary meaning of "tithing," or the action of taking a tenth of something from another planet. Unfortunately, it is hard to find an English word that conveys both of these meanings. Schmidt refers to this condition as "decimation," which strictly speaking means to remove or kill a tenth of something, from a practice employed in the Roman army for punishing soldiers.[59] The problem I have with this translation is that in modern times, the term "decimate" has come to more broadly mean to kill, destroy, or remove a

---

[56] Firmicus, *Mathesis*, 6, 14: 1–3, trans. Bram, p. 192, modified.
[57] Porphyry, *Introduction*, 20. Cf. Antiochus, *Summary*, 10.
[58] Discussed in Schmidt, *Definitions and Foundations*, pp. 181–183.
[59] Schmidt, *Definitions and Foundations*, p. 182.

large percentage or part of something. This is problematic because while it is true that the malefics were usually interpreted as being particularly harmful when in this position in a chart, the benefic planets can also take up the position of being "upon the tenth," and the interpretations are usually quite positive in those instances.[60] Therefore, it doesn't seem appropriate to say that when the benefics are doing something favorable to other planets that they are "decimating" them. As a result of this I prefer to refer to this condition as "domination," which I think presents a more neutral meaning that still conveys a position of power and authority, which can then be used for good or ill. Holden used a similar term, referring to this condition as "dominance" in his translation of Rhetorius.[61]

Thus, domination occurs when one planet is in the tenth sign relative to another planet, which is the superior square. If the planet that is upon the tenth is a benefic then this is quite a positive configuration for the planet in the inferior position, especially if the planet in the superior position is the benefic that is of the sect. For example, if Jupiter was in Scorpio in a day chart while Mercury was in Aquarius, then Jupiter would be upon the tenth relative to Mercury, and thus in a position to dominate him. However, if the planet that is upon the tenth is a malefic, then this is a particularly negative configuration for the inferior planet, especially if the malefic in the superior position is contrary to the sect: for example, if Saturn was in Taurus in a night chart while the Moon was in Leo. We will return to this concept later and see how it works in some example charts after introducing the conditions of bonification and maltreatment.

Mitigations and Alternative Aspect Doctrines

The conceptual premise underlying sign-based aspects—that there needs to be an affinity or similarity between two signs in order for them to share a relationship—seems to have been the basis for some other alternative schemes for determining connections between signs.

Sometimes these schemes were used as exceptions to the concept of aversion, in order to show how certain signs could still share a relationship even though they don't have any affinities based on gender, quadruplicity, or triplicity. One such exception is in the concept of "like-engirding" (*homozōnia*), which are signs that share the same domicile lord.[62] According to this doctrine, signs that have the same domicile lord are not completely in aversion even if they

---

[60] An instance of upon the tenth being used in a positive sense when it involves a benefic occurs in Valens, *Anthology*, 2, 32: 3, in some material that Valens seems to have excerpted from an older author named Timaeus.

[61] Rhetorius, *Compendium*, trans. Holden, p. 21.

[62] Paulus, *Introduction*, 12.

otherwise would be, based on the standard configurations. This applies to the following zodiacal pairs: Aries and Scorpio, Taurus and Libra, and Capricorn and Aquarius. In some sense these signs have a sort of mitigated aversion. A similar concept concerns those signs which have the same ascensional times, which are known as equally ascending signs.[63] The equally-ascending signs are:

Aries–Pisces
Taurus–Aquarius
Gemini–Capricorn
Cancer–Sagittarius
Leo–Scorpio
Virgo–Libra

A related concept is the doctrine of "antiscia," which are signs or degrees that are equidistant from the solstices. These signs will experience roughly the same length of daylight when the Sun transits through them, thus they share some affinity or similarity. The term antiscia is essentially just a transliteration of the Greek word *antiskion*, which is a compound word formed from the Greek terms for "shadow" (*skia*) and "opposite" or "counter" (*anti*), thus meaning something like "counter-shadow." Lacking a better translation for this, and given the longstanding convention of referring to this doctrine as antiscia, I will retain that convention here for the purpose of this discussion. The signs that straddle the solstices are as follows, starting from the summer solstice, which is at the beginning of Cancer in the tropical zodiac:

Cancer–Gemini
Leo–Taurus
Virgo–Aries
Libra–Pisces
Scorpio–Aquarius
Sagittarius–Capricorn

In some authors like Firmicus the antiscia become almost like an alternative aspect doctrine, in which planets are said to be capable of sending their influence from the degree they are in to the corresponding degree in the antiscia sign.[64] The idea that the relationship is almost like an alternative to the standard aspect doctrine seems to be reinforced by Ptolemy, who says that the antiscia signs

[63] Paulus, *Introduction*, 12. Sometimes called "contra-antiscia" in later authors.
[64] Firmicus, *Mathesis*, 2, 29.

are able to "see" (*blepein*) each other.[65] One wonders then whether this and similar doctrines just represent logical extensions of the premise underlying the standard aspect doctrine that were developed at the same time, or whether they represent an alternative or even competing doctrine in the early tradition that lost out to or was somehow displaced by what became the standard method of determining interactions between planets based on geometrical relations. Many of the later Hellenistic astrologers seem to want to reconcile the different doctrines, although in doing so it seems as if they often ended up relegating the antiscia and related concepts to a secondary status as mitigating factors, rather than as primary conditions that were typically used on their own.

---

[65] Ptolemy, *Tetrabiblos*, 1, 16: 1.

CHAPTER 10
THE TWELVE PLACES

———— ✸ ————

The twelve "places" are sectors or regions in a chart, which are primarily used to designate different areas of a person's life. They are connected with the diurnal rotation of the planets, which can be visualized most clearly through the daily movement of the Sun, which rises over the eastern horizon each morning at sunrise, culminates overhead towards the middle of the sky around noon, and finally sets over the western horizon in the evening at sunset. After the Sun sets it goes under the earth from our perspective and then reaches anti-culmination around midnight, before eventually reemerging the next morning by rising over the horizon and starting the cycle over again. This daily cycle is not unique to the Sun; the Moon and the other planets follow the diurnal rotation in rising, culminating, setting, and anti-culminating each day as well.

In the Hellenistic tradition, diurnal rotation became a secondary reference system in addition to the zodiac. Like the zodiac, it was divided up into twelve segments or sectors, which became known as "places" or "regions" (*topoi*). In a birth chart, the places primarily indicate areas or topics in the native's life, although they can also indicate other things such as how active or "busy" a planet is in producing its significations, as well as timing information about when a planet's significations will manifest.

In the later traditions, the terminology between the twelve "places" and the signs of the zodiac became conflated, which eventually resulted in the places coming to be referred to as "houses" in modern astrology, even though originally it was the signs of the zodiac that were called the "houses" or "domiciles" (*oikoi*) of the planets. As we get further into this chapter I will largely maintain the Hellenistic convention of referring to these twelve sectors as "places" in order to preserve the conceptual distinction with the concept of the domiciles, although I will make some concessions to contemporary terminology when discussing the issue of what modern astrologers refer to as "house division."

The Whole Sign House System

One of the more notable findings that has resulted from the recovery of Hellenistic astrology in the astrological community over the past three decades is the rediscovery of the form of house division called the whole sign house system. In 1982, James Holden published a paper in the American Federation of Astrologers *Journal of Research* pointing out that the original form of house division in the Hellenistic tradition was whole sign houses.[1] The existence and popularity of the whole sign house system in the Hellenistic tradition was later confirmed by Schmidt and Hand in the mid-1990s during the process of translating texts under the auspices of Project Hindsight.[2] Through Schmidt and especially Hand, whole sign houses started to become popularized again in the astrological community in the late 1990s and 2000s.

Prior to this research, western astrologers were not aware that the whole sign house system was the original system of house division used in the western tradition, nor was it even recognized as a form of house division at all, as the concept had been lost in the west at some point during the Medieval and Renaissance periods.[3] While whole sign houses did continue to be used as the

---

[1] Holden, "Ancient House Division." Holden called it the "Sign-House system." On p. 22 he says "this was the first system of house division." Later, in his book *A History of Horoscopic Astrology*, Holden referred to it as "the original system of houses" (p. 94).

[2] Hand already noted the use of whole sign houses as a distinctive feature of Hellenistic astrology in the introduction to the very first Greek astrological translation published by Project Hindsight in 1993. See Paulus, *Introductory Matters*, trans. Schmidt, pp. iii–iv. Schmidt later did a survey of different approaches to house division in the Hellenistic tradition in the introduction to Ptolemy, *Tetrabiblos, Book III*, trans. Schmidt, pp. viii–xvi. Hand later published a monograph in 2000 titled *Whole Sign Houses, The Oldest House System*, followed by a more academic treatment in his 2007 paper "Signs as Houses (Places) in Ancient Astrology."

[3] For example, in his 1986 academic work on the history of different forms of house division in traditional astrology titled *Horoscopes and History*, J. D. North does not mention and did not seem to be aware of whole sign houses as a concept, despite surveying more than a dozen different forms of house division from the first through the seventeenth century. In fact, he concludes from the absence of calculated midheavens or intermediate house cusps in the vast majority of the surviving Greek horoscopes, which are not necessary in whole sign houses, that the Hellenistic astrologers "did not attach such importance to the houses as later Islamic and Christian astrologers were to do" (p. 7), which is patently false. Other books on house division from the 1970s astrological community such as Dona Marie Lorenz's *Tools of Astrology: Houses* or Ralph Holden's *The Elements of House Division* similarly do not mention whole sign houses, since it was not known as a concept in western astrology at that point in time. Technically a form of the whole sign system was used by some writers of Sun-sign

primary form of house division in the Indian astrological tradition ever since the transmission of the *Yavanajātaka* around the second century CE, it was not until more recently that it has started to become popularized again in the west, largely due to the revival of Hellenistic astrology in the past two decades. It is perhaps one of the most significant rediscoveries of a basic technique or concept that has been made in recent times as a result of the study of the early tradition.

Calculating Whole Sign Houses

In order to calculate whole sign houses in a chart, the first step is to determine what sign of the zodiac the Ascendant is located in. The Ascendant is the degree of the ecliptic which intersects the eastern horizon at any given moment in time, or roughly the region of the sky where the Sun rises over the horizon in the morning each day. Whatever sign of the zodiac the Ascendant is located in becomes marked or designated as the first "house" or "place," from zero to thirty degrees of that sign, regardless of how early or late the Ascendant is in the sign. The entire rising sign itself then becomes the first house or place. Then the next sign in zodiacal order (counterclockwise) becomes the second house or place, from zero to thirty degrees of that sign. After that, the following sign becomes the third house, and so on. Eventually you end up with twelve signs, and twelve houses/places, with each house consisting of thirty degrees.

By way of example, let us take a chart in which the Ascendant falls somewhere in the zodiacal sign of Cancer. With whole sign houses, Cancer would become the first house in this chart, from zero to thirty degrees, because the Ascendant is located in that sign. Leo would become the second house, Virgo the third house, Libra the fourth, Scorpio the fifth, Sagittarius the sixth, Capricorn the seventh, Aquarius the eighth, Pisces the ninth, Aries the tenth, Taurus the eleventh, and finally Gemini the twelfth. There are twelve houses/places, and each coincides perfectly with one of the twelve signs. Indeed, this is probably the reason why there are twelve houses in western astrology to begin with, rather than some other number such as eight or thirty-six, because the houses were originally meant to coincide with the signs. In this way the signs of the zodiac continue to provide the backbone or structure for the entire system, as we saw that they did with the aspect doctrine.

The Hellenistic astrologers usually refer to the Ascendant as the "Hour-Marker" (*hōroskopos*) in Greek. The implication seems to be that the Ascendant

---

horoscope columns since the mid-twentieth century, although this involves using derived houses from the Sun as a matter of necessity or convenience, whereas using whole sign houses from the Ascendant was not otherwise usually known as a standard approach to house division in the west prior to the revival of whole sign houses in the late twentieth century.

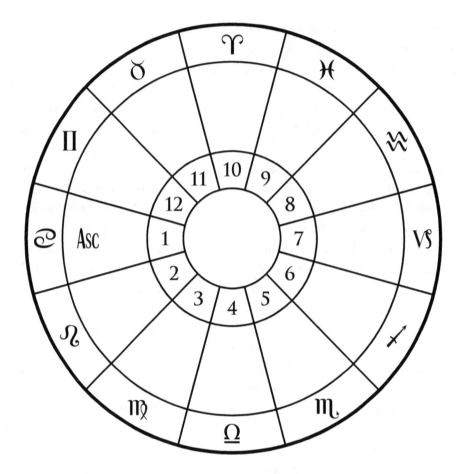

Figure 1.6 - Whole Sign Houses

or Hour-Marker "marks" or designates the sign that becomes the first "place" or "house," and as a consequence, the subsequent signs in zodiacal order become the other eleven houses.[4] In this way the Hour-Marker always acts as the starting point in establishing the sequence of the houses, and this is why Paulus calls it the "beginning and foundation of the twelve places."[5] There is also a Greek term

---

[4] Schmidt originally argued that this was the correct interpretation of the term *hōroskopos* in his translation of Paulus, *Introduction*, pp. xiii-xiv. The Greek term may derive from the earlier Egyptian use of the decans in order to mark different hours of the night, as argued by Greenbaum and Ross, "The Role of Egypt," p. 160ff. It is also perhaps worth noting that in the second century, Clement of Alexandria referred to a specific type of Egyptian priest as the "hour-marker" (*hōroskopos*), which is connected with an older Egyptian tradition of hour-priests whose role was to keep track of time in order to know when to perform temple rituals, as discussed in Dieleman, "Stars and the Egyptian Priesthood in the Greco-Roman Period," pp. 138–140.

[5] Paulus, *Introduction*, 24 (ed. Boer, p. 53: 23–25), trans. Greenbaum, p. 44.

that was sometimes used which can be translated as "Ascendant" (*anatellon*), meaning "rising up" or "ascending," although it is much more common to see the word Hour-Marker used in most Greco-Roman texts.[6] This close association between the Hour-Marker and the first place sometimes leads the astrologers to use the term interchangeably to refer to the entire first whole sign house, and not just the degree of the Ascendant. Thus, when the astrologers say that a planet is "in the Hour-Marker" or "marks the hour" (*hōroskopeō*), this usually means anywhere in the rising sign.[7] When the astrologers are referring to the exact degree of the Ascendant they will usually qualify the statement, as Valens does at one point in a chart example where he says that Venus was "marking the hour by degree" (*moirikōs hōroskopousa*).[8]

Names of the Places

Each of the places was numbered from one to twelve, in zodiacal or counterclockwise order, beginning with the rising sign. Sometimes they were simply referred to according to the number associated with each, such as the "eleventh place" or the "seventh place" relative to the rising sign. However, the places also had specific names, and the Hellenistic astrologers would frequently refer to the places by their given names rather than their numbers.

FIRST PLACE	Hour-Marker, Helm (*oiax*), the Hour (*hōra*), Ascension (*anaphora*), Ascendant (*anatellon*), Rising (Gk. *anatolē*, Lat. *ortus*),[9] Hour-Divider or Hour-Regulator (*hōronomos*).[10]
SECOND PLACE	Gate of Hades (*Haidou pulē*)
THIRD PLACE	Goddess (*Thea*)
FOURTH PLACE	Subterraneous (*hupogeion*)
FIFTH PLACE	Good Fortune (*agathē tuchē*)
SIXTH PLACE	Bad Fortune (*kakē tuchē*)
SEVENTH PLACE	Setting (*dusis*)

---

[6] For the use of *anatellon* see Thrasyllus in CCAG 8, 3, p. 100: 31.

[7] E.g. Valens, *Anthology*, 2, 4: 1–6; Paulus, *Introduction*, 24, first paragraph, ed. Boer, p. 54: 1–14.

[8] Valens, *Anthology*, 2, 32: 36–37, trans. Schmidt, p. 40.

[9] For *anaphora* and *anatellon* see Thrasyllus in CCAG 8, 3, p. 100: 31, trans. Schmidt, *Definitions and Foundations*, p. 343. For *ortus* see Firmicus, *Mathesis*, 2, 15: 1.

[10] Hephaestio, *Apotelesmatika*, 2, 2: 11, quoting Anubio, *Carmen*, F2, ed. Obbink. Also Hephaestio, *Apotelesmatika*, 3, 26: 1 and 3, 30: 1, quoting Dorotheus.

EIGHTH PLACE	Idle (*argos*)
NINTH PLACE	God (*Theos*)
TENTH PLACE	Midheaven (*mesouranēma*)
ELEVENTH PLACE	Good Spirit (*agathos daimōn*)
TWELFTH PLACE	Bad Spirit (*kakos daimōn*)

Importantly, the names for most of the angular places, such as the tenth, seventh, and fourth, are purely descriptive in terms of the astronomical properties associated with each of those three regions: the Midheaven occupies the middle of the sky or heavens; the seventh place is connected with the western horizon where planets set and sink out of sight under the horizon; the subterraneous place is the region that is at the lowest point below the earth from the observer's perspective.

Conversely, the names for many of the remaining places are not derived from astronomical considerations. Instead they appear to be derived from the planetary joys, which is a scheme for assigning the planets to specific places that will be discussed later.

Conceptual Models Underlying the Places

From a conceptual standpoint, the meanings or significations of the places are primarily derived from three factors: (1) the concept of angularity and the angular triads; (2) configuration to the rising sign; and (3) association with the planetary joys.

The modern astrological convention which treats the meanings of the planets, signs, and houses as interchangeable doesn't seem to have existed in the Hellenistic tradition. For example, modern astrologers associate the first sign of the zodiac, Aries, with the first house, as well as with the ruler of Aries, which is Mars. The significations of all three are then seen to be similar and essentially interchangeable, so that the resulting formula becomes Aries = Mars = first house, or Taurus = Venus = second house, and so on. Modern astrologers will often then resort to borrowing significations from Aries and Mars and applying them to the first house in order to develop an understanding of what the first house means.

It is important to understand from the outset that this approach does not appear to have existed in the Hellenistic tradition; they did not equate the planets, signs, and houses. Instead, there was a specific set of conceptual and symbolic considerations that were used in order to develop the meanings of the houses or places. As a result of this, some of the Hellenistic significations of the houses are quite different when compared with the later traditions. For example, the eighth house is not associated with sex in the Hellenistic tradition, since they did not associate the eighth house with Scorpio. Many other such differences could be pointed out, although for our purposes the important point here is simply to clear away any preconceived notions about what the houses mean, and to see how the significations may have developed originally based on specific astronomical and symbolic considerations.

The Angles or Pivots

The four angles or pivots (*kentra*) are the first, fourth, seventh, and tenth places, otherwise known as the Hour-Marker, the subterraneous place, the setting place, and the Midheaven. In whole sign houses, this is the rising sign, the fourth sign in zodiacal order relative to the rising sign, the seventh sign, and the tenth sign. These are undoubtedly the four most important places or regions, and they represent the foundation of each individual chart or nativity.

The primary term used to refer to these four places was *kentron*, which has three separate but related meanings in Greek.[11] The first and primary meaning of *kentron* is a "sharp point," especially one that acts as a "goad," which prods or excites something into action, like a cattle prod. The second meaning of *kentron* is geometrical, standing for the "center" of something, such as the center of a circle. Finally, the third meaning is a "pivot," or the place around which something turns, such as the fixed leg of a compass. Unfortunately, there is no English word that fully encompasses all three of these different meanings. Schmidt has advocated the translation convention of "pivot" for *kentron*, which is a good word that covers the second and third meanings of the Greek term quite well, although it does not convey the idea of being a sharp point or goad.[12] This meaning is clearly what Firmicus or his Latin sources chose to emphasize by referring to these places as *cardines* in Latin, which means "pivot" or "hinge."[13] At one point, Ptolemy uses the Greek term *gōnia*, which means "corner" or "angle," as a synonym for *kentron*; this partly explains the origin of the modern convention of referring to these regions as the four "angles" or "angular houses."[14] I think that this arises partially from the fact that the four angular whole sign houses form a complete geometrical square in the chart, and each of the individual angles was conceptualized as a

---

[11] Discussed in Schmidt, *Definitions and Foundations*, pp. 281–283.

[12] Schmidt, *Definitions and Foundations*, p. 281, citing his adoption of "pivot" as a convention for *kentron* in 1993, where it appears in his translation of Paulus, *Introductory Matters*, trans. Schmidt, p. 85. Bouché-Leclercq also used the term pivot as a translation for *kentron* at one point in *L'Astrologie grecque*, p. 258.

[13] Firmicus, *Mathesis*, 2, 15.

[14] Ptolemy, *Tetrabiblos*, 1, 11: 1.

peak or high point where the planets are more prominent, while the two adjacent places were thought of as building up to or sloping away from the peak, as we will see later. The notion of the four pivots as angles is also helpful in terms of conceptualizing them as sharp points that can goad the planets into action. In the Indian tradition, the author of the *Yavanajātaka* translated *kentron* into Sanskrit as "spike" (*kantaka*) at one point, evidently choosing to emphasize the goading connotations, while the medieval astrologers similarly translated it into Arabic as "stake" (*watad*).[15] In what follows I will alternate between "angle" and "pivot" when referring to this concept, in order to better convey all of the meanings involved, although with a preference for the term angle, given that it is the standard modern convention.

The four angles are the only places that have symbolic connotations that are independent of other schematic factors, and as a result of this they act as the foundation for the meanings of the other places. This is because each of the four angles has some unique astronomical property that makes it stand out, and this becomes very important when interpreting the astronomical phenomena from a symbolic perspective. For example, the Hour-Marker is unique because that is the part of the sky where the Sun and other planets rise over the horizon each day. The Midheaven is the sign of the zodiac that contains the highest point of the ecliptic, where planets reach the middle of the sky and are at their most visible. The setting place is where the planets and stars set each day and sink out of sight. Finally, the subterraneous place is the area opposite the Midheaven, where the planets are at their most hidden. These four positions and their symbolic meanings become the foundation of many of the basic interpretations of the places, with the significations of the other places largely being derived from their relationship with the angles.

From a historical perspective, the concept of the four angles was probably developed first, and may have had some history behind it before the concept and significations of the rest of the places were developed. On a fundamental level, this can be confirmed by the focus that the ancient Egyptians placed on the rising and culminating decan in order to time religious rituals; by the time of the *Salmeschiniaka* in the Ptolemaic period, the rising, culminating, setting, and anti-culminating decans were all being singled out and given specific interpretive values within the context of astrology.[16] The rising decan was said to signify birth, the culminating decan was said to signify life or livelihood (*bios*), the setting decan injury, and the subterraneous decan death. This intermediate

---

[15] *Yavanajātaka*, 1: 61, with a brief comment by Pingree on p. 221 of vol. 2. For a discussion about *watad*, see Dykes, *Works of Sahl and Māshā'allāh*, pp. xxxviii–lix.

[16] Based on the summary in Hephaestio, *Apotelesmatika*, 2, 18: 75–6, quoted earlier.

stage in the development of the places, in which only the four angles were used, can probably be confirmed by the electional rules preserved by Dorotheus and Hephaestio, which almost exclusively focus upon the four angular places in order to produce interpretations about the outcome of most topics, largely ignoring the other places.[17]

One of the interpretive techniques that was probably developed independently at this stage, when the four angles were used exclusively, is a timing technique that is connected with the diurnal rotation. There were some variations of this technique in the Hellenistic tradition, but the general idea is that the life of the native is divided into four stages, with each stage being represented by one of the angles.[18] Since the planets and stars first become visible when they rise over the horizon, the Ascendant and first place became associated with the first stage of life, which is youth. After rising over the horizon the planets will move towards the Midheaven and tenth place, eventually culminating there, and so this angle is associated with the second part of life, which is middle age. After that, the stars and planets will sink underneath the horizon at the setting place, and so this angle becomes associated with the third stage of life, which is old age. Finally, the cycle is completed when planets reach the subterraneous place, which represents the fourth and final stage of life, which is death. This sequence seems to be implicit already in the meanings associated with the four angular decans in the *Salmeschiniaka*, which assigns them in the following order: birth, life, injury, death.

Another related principle that is employed by some astrologers is the idea that planets located in the first and tenth places will manifest their significations earlier in the native's life, while planets located in the seventh and fourth places will manifest their significations later in the native's life.[19] This is again tied in with the concept of different stages in the diurnal rotation demarcating different stages in the native's life, although it represents a simpler version of the technique.

Aside from their value in timing, the angular places were conceptualized as having two primary roles: (1) the power to goad the planets into action, and (2) the function of acting as a center or pivot around which the planets revolved in a sequence of three places, which we turn to next.

---

[17] See Dorotheus, *Carmen*, 5, and Hephaestio, *Apotelesmatika*, 3.

[18] Different versions are discussed by Pingree in *Yavanajātaka*, vol. 2, pp. 219–220. The most common approach is the one outlined in Porphyry, *Introduction*, 52, where the Ascendant signifies the first age of life, the Midheaven middle age, the Descendant old age, and the subterraneous place death and things that follow after death. Cf. Paulus, *Introduction*, 24; Serapio, *Definitions*, p. 231: 24–33.

[19] This principle comes up frequently in Rhetorius, *Compendium*, 57.

Angular Triads

The four angular places acted as the center or pivot in a sequence of three places, which we will refer to here collectively as an "angular triad," following Schmidt.[20] The angles form a cross of four places, and each of these places is flanked by one place that rises before the angle, and one place that rises after the angle, thus creating a sequence of three places centered on each angle.

In the diurnal rotation, where the signs rotate in a clockwise direction each day, each of the four angles is preceded by what is known as a "decline" (*apoklima*) or declining place. This is the equivalent of what modern astrologers call a "cadent" house. The term "cadent" is derived from the Latin word *cadō*, which means "to fall down" or "to decline," which is quite an accurate rendering of the original Greek concept. The four declining places are the third, sixth, ninth, and twelfth. Planets that are in the declines are falling or declining away from the angles, because the diurnal rotation carries the planets away from them. This can be visualized the most clearly in the ninth place, since planets in that place are declining or falling away from the Midheaven at the top of the chart.

Each angle is then followed by a "post-ascension" (*epanaphora*), which is the equivalent of what is called a "succedent" house in modern astrology. The term succedent means "to follow after," which is a good rendering of the idea underlying the original Greek concept, so I will retain it here. The post-ascensions or succedent places are the second, fifth, eighth, and eleventh places. Planets in the succedent places are conceptualized as rising up towards or following after the angles or pivots.

To summarize, the breakdown of the places is as follows:

DECLINES:	third, sixth, ninth, twelfth
ANGLES:	first, fourth, seventh, tenth
SUCCEDENTS:	second, fifth, eighth, eleventh

When you combine all three of these types of places together into a sequence, the result is what we call an angular triad. An angular triad consists of a decline, an angle, and a succedent place. There are four angular triads in every chart, and each is centered around a pivot or angle. There is one angular triad that is centered around the Ascendant or rising sign, and it consists of the twelfth (decline), first (angle), and second place (succedent). The next angular triad is centered around the Midheaven, and it consists of the ninth, tenth, and eleventh

---

[20] I believe that the terminology of referring to these groupings as "angular triads" was first introduced by Schmidt and Black in "Peak Times and Patterns in the Life of Dane Rudhyar," p. 40.

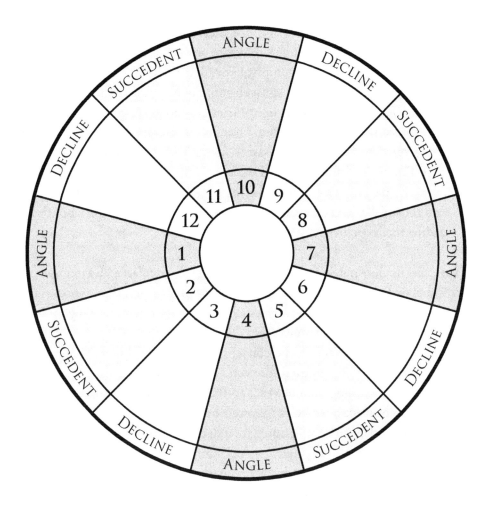

Figure 10.2 - Angular, Succedent, and Declining Places

places. After that comes the angular triad centered around the Descendant or setting place, which consists of the sixth, seventh, and eighth places. Finally, the last angular triad is centered around the subterranean place, and it consists of the third, fourth, and fifth places.[21]

Olympiodorus provides a useful demonstration of this concept by using the Thema Mundi:

it is necessary to seek also the post-ascensions and the declines, and whether the stars are post-ascending or declining... The post-ascensions

---

[21] The ordering of the angular triads is clearly the motivation for the sequence in which the places are named in Sextus Empiricus, *Against the Professors*, 5, 15–20. It is also evident in the sequence of life applied to the twelve places attributed to Serapio in CCAG, 8, 4, p. 231: 24–33, and in the way the places are outlined in *Liber Hermetis*, 14.

are taken from the pivots. For since there are four pivots — the Hour-Marker, Midheaven, Setting, Subterraneous — one must know that the leading zodiacal sign for each pivot is called a decline. The one which is following the pivot [is] a post-ascension. Such as: for the nativity of the Cosmos, let Cancer mark the hour, Aries culminate, Capricorn set and let the Subterraneous Pivot be Libra. Pisces is the decline of Aries, Taurus the post-ascension; Leo is the post-ascension of Cancer, Gemini the decline, since Cancer is following. And Scorpio is the post-ascension of Libra, Virgo the decline. One must take [it] in the same way for each nativity. And those following from the pivots are called post-ascensions, but those leading them declines.[22]

What this demonstrates is that the concept of angularity was originally predicated on the angular triad scheme, and was used within the context of the whole sign house system to identify which zodiacal signs were moving towards or away from the four angular places.

The angular triads seem to be conceptualized in two different ways, with different terminology being used for each. The first conceptualization follows a clockwise order through the places, and starts with the ascent of the planets at the succedent places, which is followed by a summit at the angular place, and is finally brought to completion with a decline at the cadent place. So this order is: (1) succedent, (2) angle, (3) decline. The second conceptualization follows the counterclockwise zodiacal order, starting with the decline or cadent place, which is sometimes also called "pre-ascension" (*proanaphora*), followed by the angular place, which is sometimes called "ascension" (*anaphora*), and is finally brought to completion in the succedent place, which is called the "post-ascension" (*epanaphora*). Thus, this second sequence is: (1) decline, (2) angle, (3) succedent. Both sequences have independent symbolic value because one describes the order in which the planets move through the diurnal rotation each day when they rise, culminate, set, and anti-culminate, while the other describes the order with which the planets move through the signs, which is in zodiacal order or counterclockwise. As we will see later, the astrologers took both sequences into account when developing the meanings of the places.

From an interpretive standpoint, within the context of the angular triads, the four angular places primarily seem to be associated with the notion of permanence or that which is in the present moment in time. The succedent places tend to be associated with gain and building things up, especially the eleventh

---

[22] Olympiodorus, *Commentary*, 7, trans. Greenbaum, p. 84, modified.

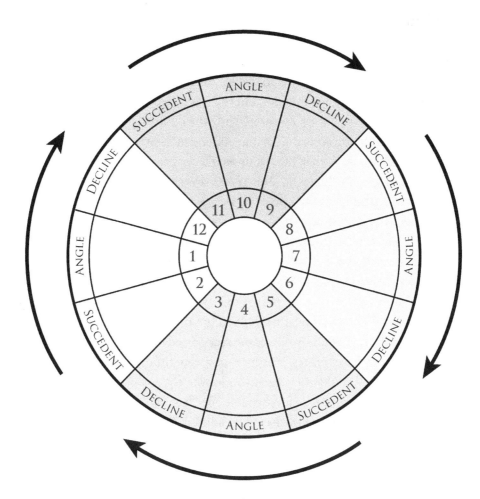

Figure 10.3 - Angular Triads

and fifth places, while the declines tend to indicate loss and dissipation, especially the twelfth and sixth places. This is tied in with a temporal conceptualization of the angular triads, which results in the declines being associated with the past, the angles being associated with the present, and the succedent places being associated with the future.[23] In some authors such as Serapio, this becomes an elaborate timing technique, while in others it is simply one of the subtle underlying properties of the places which are used to generate meanings.[24]

---

[23] Hephaestio applies this temporal scheme to the angular triads explicitly at one point in a limited sense by saying that the ninth place in an inceptional chart signifies the past, the tenth the present, and the eleventh the future (*Apotelesmatika*, 3, 4: 2–3). However, Julian of Laodicea states this as a more general principle that applies to all of the angular triads (CCAG, 4, p. 104–p. 105: 1). Discussed briefly in Greenbaum, *The Daimon*, pp. 66–67.

[24] For Serapio see *Definitions*, p. 231: 24–33.

Good and Bad Places

The first place is the region of the chart that is most closely associated with the native, and their health and physical vitality. This is because it is the sign that is rising at birth, and is thus symbolically connected to the native's emergence from the mother's womb at the moment of birth. According to Porphyry, some astrologers believed that the soul entered into the body through a cosmic stream or portal that was connected with the Ascendant at the moment of birth.[25] Indeed, Antiochus says that the Hour-Marker represents "the entrance into physical life" (*tēs zōēs eisodos*).[26] This is perhaps symbolically fitting since the degree of the Ascendant is the point in a chart where the sky meets the earth, and thus by extension where the soul enters the material world. Whatever the motivations, in natal astrology the first place came to have uniquely personal associations with the native who was born at that moment in time, whereas the other places came to be associated with other people or areas in the native's life.

In addition to the angular triads, the meanings of the places were also determined based on their relationships to the rising sign. Any places that are configured to the first place by one of the recognized configurations were called the "favorable" or "good places," because they were thought to be supportive of the life and physical vitality of the native. Conversely, any places not configured to the rising sign were called "unfavorable" or "bad places," because they were thought to be unsupportive of the native's life.[27] This results in the following scheme:

GOOD PLACES:
    third, fourth, fifth, seventh, ninth, tenth, and eleventh
BAD PLACES:
    second, sixth, eighth, and twelfth

The result of this scheme is that the good places are generally associated with positive significations or topics in the native's life (e.g. siblings, parents, children, partners, travel, career, friends), while the bad places tend to be associated with negative significations (e.g. illness, death, loss).

---

[25] Porphyry, *To Gaurus On How Embryos are Ensouled*, 16: 5.

[26] Antiochus, *Summary*, 24 (CCAG, 8, 3, p. 117: 1–2), trans. Schmidt, *Definitions and Foundations*, p. 305.

[27] Discussed in Firmicus, *Mathesis*, 2, 16–19. Firmicus refers to the power of these places as being "favorable" versus "feeble and debilitated." The implicit contrast is favorable versus unfavorable, or good versus bad, as demonstrated by the standard names of the fifth, sixth, eleventh, and twelfth places.

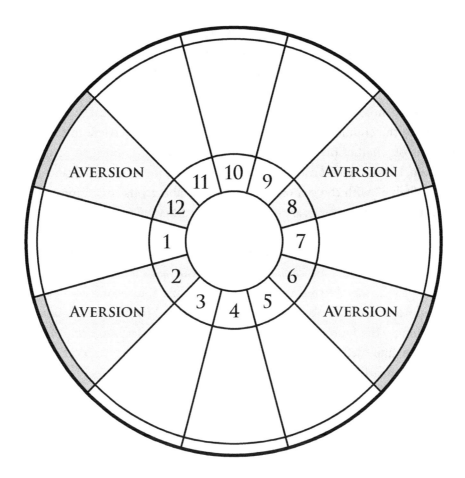

Figure 10.4 - Good and Bad Places

Busy or Advantageous Places

Another important classification of the places are those that are called *chrēmatistikos* and *achrēmatistikos*. The Greek term *chrēmatistikos* is frequently used in the Hellenistic astrological texts to designate a specific set of places that were either considered to be more advantageous for the native, or were considered to make the planets more active, busy, or energized in producing their significations. These two different interpretations seem to have arisen from conflicting uses of the same term in two early foundational texts, as well as some ambiguity in the meaning of the original Greek term itself.

The word *chrēmatistikos* primarily has mercantile connotations having to do with money-making, and one of the primary meanings in the LSJ lexical entry refers to something that is "belonging to or fitted for the dispatch of public business," which Schmidt abbreviates as "conducive to business."[28] When this

---

[28] Schmidt, *Definitions and Foundations*, p. 279ff.

word is used in the astrological texts to describe the activity of the planets, it seems to describe them as being "active," "busy," "energetic," "effective," or "operative." The reverse of this is when the planets are *achrēmatistikos*, which in this context would mean "inactive," "lazy," "unenergetic," "ineffective," or "inoperative."

The secondary meaning of *chrēmatistikos* in the astrological texts seems to pertain to the condition of the planets insomuch as they relate to the native, in terms of whether or not they are in a position that is positive or negative for them. In this context *chrēmatistikos* takes on the meaning of "advantageous" or "profitable," with the opposite being "disadvantageous" or "unprofitable."[29] These two sets of meanings are both relevant in different contexts depending on how the term is being used in the texts.

In the early Hellenistic tradition, there were two different approaches to defining which places are *chrēmatistikos* or *achrēmatistikos*, broadly speaking. One approach was derived from Nechepso, while the second was evidently derived from a text ascribed to Hermes, as reported by Timaeus.[30] According to Nechepso, the four angles and the four succedent places are *chrēmatistikos*, while the four declining places are *achrēmatistikos*. This conceptualization seems to primarily relate to the notion of the *chrēmatistikos* places being "busy," "active," or "energetic," as a result of the goading nature of the angles, which are able to spur or incite the planets into action, thus making them "operative." The declines, then, are conceptualized as "inactive," "idle," and "unenergetic," thus making planets in them "inoperative." Thus the Nechepso version seems to focus on the meaning of *chrēmatistikos* that has to do with the planets being "energetic" or "unenergetic," and that will be our primary set of keywords for referring to this meaning of the term *chrēmatistikos*.

According to Hermes and Timaeus, the *chrēmatistikos* places are the four angles, the two places configured by trine to the Hour-Marker (the fifth and ninth places), and the succedent place from the Midheaven (the eleventh). The rest of the places are *achrēmatistikos* (second, third, sixth, eighth, twelfth). This approach seems to be a blend of both the notion that the angular places are more energetic because they act as goads, as well as the notion that the places configured to the rising sign are positive or supportive of the native. This shift in focus towards the ascending sign or first place in this conceptualization means

---

[29] Benjamin Dykes prefers to use the term "unadvantageous" rather than "disadvantageous" for *achrēmatistikos*. Dykes, *Introductions*, p. 118.

[30] According to the Antiochus *Summary*, the author Timaeus attributed this doctrine to Hermes, while Antiochus himself attributed the second approach to Nechepso. See CCAG 8, 3, p. 116: 3–12. For a translation and discussion of this passage see Schmidt, *Definitions and Foundations*, pp. 279–289, and Dykes, *Introductions*, pp. 118–213.

that in this approach, the places are primarily defined in terms of whether they are "advantageous" or "disadvantageous" from the perspective of the native.

Both of these conceptualizations need to be kept in mind in the future when discussing the *chrēmatistikos* places, using the two primary keywords "energetic" and "advantageous."

Ranking of the Places

Some astrologers rank the places from best to worst. These rankings are usually closely connected with the doctrine of the *chrēmatistikos* places, especially the Hermes variant, with some other undertones being factored in from the joys of the planets as well, which we will discuss next. According to Hephaestio, the ranking of the places from best to worst is as follows:

First, tenth, eleventh, fifth, seventh, fourth, ninth, second, third, eighth, sixth, twelfth.[31]

There is some ambiguity with the third place, where it sometimes switches with the second in the lists. Some authors say that the third is the least bad of the bad places, while others says that it is the least good of the good places.[32] This is because the third is a decline that is only weakly configured to the rising sign through an inferior sextile. However, most interpretations of the third place are typically positive, often moreso than the second, so I would be inclined to revise Hephaestio's numbering as follows:

First, tenth, eleventh, fifth, seventh, fourth, ninth, third, second, eighth, sixth, twelfth.

The rankings become useful in certain contexts when it is important to be able to distinguish between one placement being more advantageous than another, such as for example in inceptional astrology when one is trying to select an auspicious chart, or in natal astrology when trying to calculate the overall ruler of the chart, called the Master of the Nativity.

---

[31] Hephaestio, *Apotelesmatika*, 1, 12.

[32] Serapio says that the "benefic" places are first, tenth, eleventh, fifth, ninth, and third, while the "malefic" places are the second, fourth, sixth, seventh, <eighth>, and twelfth. Serapio, *Definitions*, p. 226: 20–23. Valens gives a similar ranking as Hephaestio for the first few places at one point, except he says that the third, ninth, seventh, and fourth places are all "middling" (*Anthology*, 4, 11: 49). Dorotheus on the other hand twice groups the third together with the bad places, in *Carmen*, 1, 10: 28 and 1, 13: 4.

Joys of the Planets

Each of the planets has a specific place which is called the place of its "joy."[33] The joys of the planets are as follows:

> The Sun has its joy in the ninth
> The Moon has its joy in the third
> Jupiter has its joy in the eleventh
> Venus has its joy in the fifth
> Mars has its joy in the sixth
> Saturn has its joy in the twelfth
> Mercury has its joy in the first

From an interpretive standpoint, there seems to be a general notion, especially in Valens, that the benefics become more benefic in the places of Good Spirit and Good Fortune, while the malefics become less malefic.[34] Conversely, the malefics become more malefic in the places of Bad Spirit and Bad Fortune, while the benefics become less benefic.[35] In later authors such as Paulus, planets are interpreted as being well-situated when they are located in the specific place associated with their joy, but only if they are also otherwise well-situated according to zodiacal sign and sect as well.[36]

---

[33] The joys are outlined the most clearly in Paulus, *Introduction*, 24; Olympiodorus, *Commentary*, 23; Firmicus, *Mathesis*, 2, 15–19; Rhetorius, *Compendium*, 54. Manilius is the only ancient author who describes an alternative scheme for the joys, where Venus rejoices in the tenth rather than the fifth place, and Saturn in the fourth rather than the twelfth (*Astronomica*, 2: 918–938). The rest of the joys he lists are the same as in other authors. Unfortunately, since Manilius' text is the only one which contains this alternative scheme, it is unclear whether his arrangement represents a genuine variant tradition, an error in the textual transmission, or an idiosyncratic modification of the standard system that he made on his own. Houlding attempted to defend Manilius' variant as genuine, largely based on his antiquity as a source (*The Houses*, p. 35ff). On the other hand, Schmidt dismissed Manilius' treatment of the houses as "sketchy" and "aberrant" within the context of the rest of the Hellenistic tradition, and challenged Houlding's argument by citing Thrasyllus as being a more reliable early source for the doctrine of the places and joys (*Facets of Fate*, p. 126, fn. 11). More recently, see the discussion in Greenbaum, *The Daimon*, pp. 57–58. There she discusses a possible Egyptian precedent for associating Venus with the tenth place, based on a Demotic text that calls the tenth the "house/place of the goddess," although Greenbaum notes that it is not clear whether this refers to Venus or the Moon. Due to the ambiguity, this connection should probably be treated with caution. For the text see Neugebauer, "Demotic Horoscopes," p. 117, which is also discussed in Ross, "A Survey of Demotic Astrological Texts," p. 24.

[34] Valens, *Anthology*, 2, chapters 6 and 12.

[35] Valens, *Anthology*, 2, chapters 5 and 11.

[36] Paulus, *Introduction*, 24.

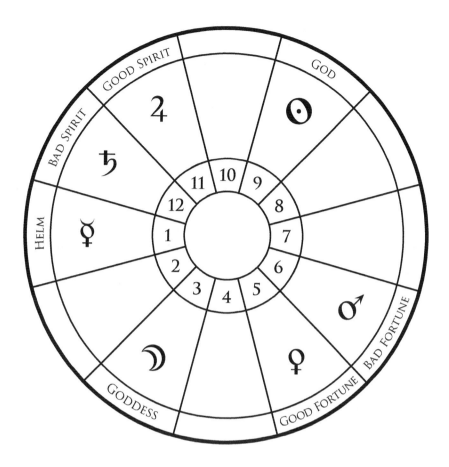

Figure 10.5 - Joys of the Planets

Joys as a Conceptual Construct

The joys appear to have acted as a conceptual construct from which a number of other important basic concepts were derived, similar to the Thema Mundi.[37] Some aspects of the schematic nature of the joys can be seen easily at first glance; for example, the diurnal planets all have their joys in places above the horizon, while the nocturnal planets have their joys below the horizon. Mercury, which is neutral with respect to sect, has its joy in the first place, which in the whole sign system can be either above or below the horizon. Other traces of the schematic nature of the joys are more subtle; the luminaries, for example, are both configured to the two malefics by difficult aspects, a square, while they are configured to both of the benefics by easy aspects, the trine and sextile.

---

[37] Much of this argument was first presented in Brennan, "The Planetary Joys and the Origins of the Significations of the Houses and Triplicities." It was based on a series of discoveries that I made with Benjamin Dykes in April of 2012, much of which is presented in what follows.

Schmidt noted that the joys are actually the triplicity rulers grouped around each of the four angular triads.[38] At the top of the chart are the Sun and Jupiter, the two principal rulers of the fire triplicity, located in the angular triad that surrounds the Midheaven. Towards the bottom are the Moon and Venus, the two primary rulers of the earth triplicity, which are grouped around the angular triad that is centered on the subterraneous pivot. On the left are Saturn and Mercury, which are the two rulers of the air triplicity, grouped around the angular triad that is centered on the rising sign. Finally, we find the last planet, Mars, one of the primary rulers of the water triplicity, over on the right side of the chart in the angular triad associated with the setting place.

What is interesting about the association of the triplicity rulers with each of these four angular triads in the joys is that it may have provided the original rationale for the assignment of the four classical elements to the signs of the zodiac, as it seems to be arranged in a way that imitates Aristotle's doctrine of "natural place." According to Aristotle, each element has a natural tendency to move either upwards or downwards, either towards the center of the cosmos or away from the center of the cosmos, with the Earth being at the center.[39] Fire rises up to the highest region, while earth moves down to the lowest region. Air rises upwards and settles in a position just below fire, while water settles down and rests on top of earth. The hierarchy of elemental layers according to Aristotle's doctrine of natural place is therefore:

1. FIRE
2. AIR
3. WATER
4. EARTH

This ordering of the elements in terms of the positions they were thought to hold in the cosmos was later adopted by the Stoic and Hermetic philosophical schools, and so it would have been very widespread and familiar during the Hellenistic period.[40]

When viewed in this context, the arrangement of the joys represents a depiction of the doctrine of natural place with the planets themselves

---

[38] Private communication, January 2008.

[39] Aristotle, *On Generation and Corruption*, 1: 2–3.

[40] For the Stoic adoption of this elemental hierarchy, see the report by Diogenes Laertius, *Lives of Eminent Philosophers*, 7: 137. For the Hermetic tradition, see the cosmogony in *Corpus Hermeticum*, 1: 4, where fire and air are said to move upwards and water and earth downwards. Copenhaver (*Hermetica*, p. 98) interprets the language in this passage as having been influenced by the Stoic treatment of the elements.

representing each of the four elements in their proper place in the cosmos. The two planets associated with fire are at the very top of the cosmos, clustered around the place that is called "Midheaven" (*mesouranēma*). The two planets associated with earth are at the very bottom of the cosmos, clustered around the place that is called "subterraneous" (*hupogeion*). The two planets associated with air are located near the first house, because planets rise over the horizon at the Ascendant and then move upwards towards the Midheaven. The placement of the air planets here cleverly creates a situation where air is symbolically pushed upwards, towards the element of fire. Conversely, Mars, the planet associated with water, is located near the seventh house, called the "setting" place (*dusis*), because planets in this sector of the chart set and sink downwards towards the subterraneous place. The placement of the element of water here pushes water downwards towards the element of earth.

The end result is that fire and earth form the upper and lower extremes, while air and water have middling positions, but the diurnal rotation pushes air upwards towards fire and water downwards towards earth. Thus it perfectly recreates the doctrine of natural place, with fire, air, water, and earth all in their respective positions in the cosmos. This then provides a rationale for assigning each of the four groups of planets to each of the four classical elements, and I would argue that these associations were then probably imported from the joys into the zodiacal signs, so that the elements that the triplicity rulers were associated with in the joys scheme came to be associated with those signs of the zodiac and the triplicities as well.

The idea that the joys played a foundational role in informing different aspects of the early Hellenistic astrological system is probably further affirmed by the fact that the names of several of the places appear to be derived from the joys. For example, the ninth is called the place of God, and this is the place where the Sun has his joy. Opposite the ninth is the third place, which is called Goddess, and this is the place where the Moon has her joy. The two benefic planets, Venus and Jupiter, are associated with the two good places, which are the place of Good Fortune and the place of Good Spirit, respectively. Conversely, the two malefic planets, Mars and Saturn, are associated with the two bad places, which are the places of Bad Fortune and Bad Spirit, respectively. This connection between the names and the joys is confirmed by Firmicus, who says that the fifth place "is called Good Fortune, *because* it is the place of Venus."[41] Similarly, he says the sixth place is called Bad Fortune "because it is the place of Mars."[42] Paulus similarly calls the third the "place of the Moon," the fifth "the place of Venus,"

---

[41] Firmicus, *Mathesis*, 2, 21: 6, trans. Holden, modified, emphasis added.
[42] Firmicus, *Mathesis*, 2, 21: 7, trans. Holden, modified.

the sixth the "place of Mars," and so on.[43] This close association between the planets and certain places seems to have resulted in the significations of some of the places being derived directly from the planetary joys.

One final point of interest about the joys relates to the position that Mercury occupies in the scheme relative to the two luminaries. To begin with, it is interesting in and of itself that the joys may be traced back to a text in the first century BCE (or slightly earlier) attributed to Hermes Trismegistus, for in the joys scheme we find Mercury or Hermes prominently located in the first place, acting as an intermediary between the upper and lower hemispheres of the chart, a bridge between the celestial and terrestrial realms which are united at the degree of the Ascendant. We have already seen that in the joys, the luminaries are both configured by favorable aspects to the benefics and difficult aspects to the malefics, but what about Mercury? If aspect lines are drawn from the two luminaries in their joys to Mercury in the first place, one finds that Mercury is configured to the Sun by a trine, while he is configured to the Moon by sextile. We have notably seen this before in the exaltation scheme, in which Porphyry mentions that all of the diurnal planets are exalted in signs that are configured by trine to one of their domiciles, while all of the nocturnal planets are exalted in signs that are configured by sextile to one of their domiciles. Could this be a coincidence? Or is it evidence of something more deliberate on the part of an early group of founders of Hellenistic astrology? It seems too clean to be an accident. But if it was intentional, it raises serious questions about how many major components of the Hellenistic system were created at the same time as part of a deliberate and elaborate technical construct sometime around the first century BCE.

Significations of the Places

The earliest and perhaps original attempt to ascribe significations to all twelve of the places appeared in a text attributed to Hermes Trismegistus.[44] This system was known to later authors either as the *dōdekatropos*, which means "twelve-turning," or possibly as the *dōdekatopos*, which means "twelve-place" or "twelve-topic" system. The manuscripts are ambiguous about which is the correct title, and either would make sense.[45] The publication of this text was followed by another book ascribed to Asclepius that outlined an additional or revised set

---

[43] Paulus, *Introduction*, 24. Rhetorius makes similar statements in *Compendium*, 57.

[44] As cited by Thrasyllus in the early first century CE in CCAG, 8, 3, p. 101: 16–30.

[45] It is called the *dōdekatropos* in Valens, *Anthology*, 4, 12: 3 and 9, 3: 4. However, it is called *dōdekatopos* at one point in the second epitome of Hephaestio, *Apotelesmatika*, ed. Pingree, vol. 2, p. 79: 25, as well as in CCAG, 8, 1, p. 246: 21–22. In one of the fragments that Valens quotes from Nechepso (*Anthology*, 7, 6: 212) where the places are being discussed he seems to refer to it as the "turning" (*tropos*), which probably confirms that *dōdekatropos* is the correct name.

of significations for just the first eight places in zodiacal order starting from the rising sign, which was known either as the *oktatropos* ("eight-turning") or *oktatopos* ("eight-place" system).[46] Schmidt has pointed out that many of the later treatments of the places by astrologers such as Valens appear to represent a synthesis of these two earlier systems.[47] I will outline both of the early systems separately below, followed by a synthesized version from Valens.

Significations of the Dōdekatropos According to Hermes

A summary of the significations of the *dōdekatropos* of Hermes is preserved in a summary of Thrasyllus' *Tablet*.[48] According to that summary, the significations of the twelve places are as follows:

FIRST:	Helm, fortune, soul, way of life,[49] siblings.
SECOND:	hopes/expectations (*elpidōn*).
THIRD:	action (*praxis*), siblings.
FOURTH:	Foundation of happiness, paternal possessions, slaves.
FIFTH:	Good Fortune.
SIXTH:	Daimonic [Fortune],[50] punishment (*poinēs*), injury.
SEVENTH:	death, wife.
EIGHTH:	life (*zōē*), livelihood (*bios*).
NINTH:	travel, living abroad.
TENTH:	fortune, livelihood (*bios*), life (*zōē*), children, procreation (*sporan*),[51] action/occupation (*praxis*), esteem, authority (*archas*), ruling (*hegemonias*).
ELEVENTH:	Good Spirit.
TWELFTH:	Bad Spirit, pre-ascension, livelihood (*bios*), submission of slaves.

---

[46] It is called the *oktatopos* in the Antiochus *Summary*, 1, 25 (CCAG, 8, 3, p. 117: 21), although it is referred to as the *oktatropos* in Valens, *Anthology*, 9, 3: 5.

[47] Schmidt, *Kepler College Sourcebook*, p. 77.

[48] CCAG, 8, 3, p. 101: 16–30. For a translation see Schmidt, *Definitions and Foundations*, pp. 344–345. My translation of the keywords below has been influenced by Schmidt's translation.

[49] *tropou zōēs*. Or possibly "manner," "direction," or "course of life."

[50] *daimonian*. Following Greenbaum (*The Daimon*, pp. 140–141), who cites Hübner and Housman in emending *daiman* to *daimonian*, and then viewing this word "as a feminine adjective modifying an implied *tuchēn*," due to a parallel construction with the fifth place of "Good Fortune." Alternatively, Schmidt thinks that the original word in the text was *daimoniē*, based on a comparison with the *Michigan Papyrus*, which he interprets to mean "demonic possession." Schmidt, *Definitions and Foundations*, p. 345, fn. 125.

[51] Alternatively, "sowing" or "conception" of children.

One of the things that becomes clear about the Hermes significations is that most of the names that later became associated with the places are already present, since he calls the first place the Helm, the fifth place Good Fortune, the sixth possibly something similar to Bad Fortune, the eleventh Good Spirit, and the twelfth Bad Spirit. If it is true that the names of the places really are derived from the planetary joys, which they seem to be, then this implies that the joys scheme was already in place by the time this text attributed to Hermes was written. This not only makes it the earliest text to implicitly refer to the joys, but it is potentially the original text that introduced the scheme to begin with. Since Thrasyllus wrote in the early first century CE, this means that the Hermes text that he cited for this original set of significations must have been written sometime in the first century BCE or earlier.

I believe that this theory about the Hermes text as the source of the planetary joys scheme can be confirmed by the fact that the topic of siblings was evidently ascribed to the first place in this text. Later astrologers tended to instead focus on the third place as signifying siblings most of the time.[52] However, it makes sense that the Hermes text would propose siblings for the first place if the joys scheme existed and significations were being derived from it, because Mercury has its joy in the first place, and one of Mercury's general significations is brothers.[53] I believe this demonstrates that the joys scheme had already been introduced by the time of, or perhaps within, the Hermes text itself, and that it was being used as a conceptual construct for determining some of the significations of the places.

Significations of the Oktatropos According to Asclepius

Sometime around or not long after the Hermes text was written, another influential and early text on the significations of the places was written and attributed to Asclepius. This text only gave a list of significations for the first eight places, arranged in zodiacal order starting with the rising sign, which became known as the *oktatropos*.[54]

---

[52] E.g. Valens, *Anthology*, 2, 40: 4; Paulus, *Introduction*, 24, ed. Boer, p. 55: 6.

[53] Valens, *Anthology*, 1, 1: 38; Dorotheus, *Carmen*, 1, 18: 2.

[54] In some academic and astrological literature in the twentieth century, the *oktatropos* was sometimes mistakenly said to have been a division of the entire chart into eight houses or sectors rather than twelve (e.g. Bouché-Leclercq, *L'Astrologie grecque*, p. 276ff; Fagan, *Astrological Origins*, pp. 161–170; (Ralph) Holden, *The Elements of House Division*, p. 49; Tester, *A History*, p. 26). Already in 1927 A. E. Housman, one of the editors of Manilius, pointed out to Frank Egleston Robbins in a letter that the *oktatropos* was not an eight-fold division of the entire diurnal rotation, but simply an alternative system for assigning significations to the first eight places: "The *octatropos*, wherever it occurs, is simply an incomplete *dodecatropos*: it never divides the circle into eight equal parts." From *The Letters of A. E. Housman*, ed. Burnett, vol. 2, p. 154. Housman's assessment has been echoed more recently by Goold (Manilius,

According to the Thrasyllus summary, the *oktatropos* is as follows:[55]

FIRST: life (*zōē*)
SECOND: livelihood (*bios*)
THIRD: siblings
FOURTH: parents
FIFTH: children
SIXTH: injury
SEVENTH: wife
EIGHTH: fortune, death

Schmidt pointed out that one of the unique features of the *oktatropos* is that it contains a full set of significations for all of the different members of one's family: siblings, parents, children, and wife.[56] This seems to be one of the main features that makes the *oktatropos* unique, and perhaps provides a motivation for why its author felt the need to compose an addendum to the *dōdekatropos* of Hermes. However, it is not clear if these additional family members are completely absent from the *dōdekatropos*, or if they were just assigned to different places according to an alternative rationale that the author of the Asclepius text disagreed with. There is a passage in Valens where family members are attributed to each of the places based on the joys scheme:

> [The place of] God gives signs for the father; Goddess for the mother; Good Spirit for children; Good Fortune for marriage; Bad Spirit for suffering; Bad Fortune for injuries; Lot of Fortune and *Hōroskopos* for life and living; [the Lot of] Spirit for mind; Midheaven for action; [the Lot of] Eros for desire; [the Lot of] Necessity for enemies.[57]

It is not clear if this alternative scheme for assigning family members to the places represents a later attempt to derive them based on the joys, or if it is something that was in the original Hermes text and just not fully represented in Thrasyllus. Thrasyllus' summary only preserves a very brief list of significations from the Hermes text, so it is possible that some are missing.[58] Regardless, the

---

Astronomica, pp. lxi–lxii) and Schmidt (*Definitions and Foundations*, p. 308f).

[55] CCAG, 8, 3, p. 101: 3–9. Cf. Firmicus, *Mathesis*, 2, 14.

[56] Schmidt, *Definitions and Foundations*, p. 309.

[57] Valens, *Anthology*, 2, 16: 1, trans. Schmidt, p. 18, modified.

[58] Antiochus, *Summary*, 24, seems to have a more well-fleshed out yet still early set of significations for the *dōdekatropos*, in CCAG, 8, 3, p. 116: 32–p. 117: 1–20. I focused on the version from Thrasyllus here, though, because it can be dated more reliably.

purpose of the Asclepius text appears to have been to introduce an alternative set of significations that is based on a completely different symbolic rationale.

One of the more notable and consequential differences in the Asclepius text is that it places the topic of death in the eighth place. In the Hermes text, death was assigned to the seventh place, but Asclepius moves it forward one sign. Interestingly, this is another instance where later authors tended to follow the Asclepius text more, so that the eighth came to be the primary place that was often associated with death, and Hermes' association of the seventh with death was gradually forgotten as the tradition progressed.

Significations According to Valens

Valens discusses the significations of the places several different times in the *Anthology*, but at one point during his treatment of annual profections he gives a concise list of the basic significations that seems representative of the later synthesis of the Hermes and Asclepius systems.[59] The entire passage is worth quoting in full:

> Let the beginning be from the HOUR-MARKER, which is life, helm, body, spirit.[60] SECOND: livelihood, Gate of Hades,[61] shaded,[62] giving,[63] receiving, sharing.[64] THIRD: siblings,[65] living abroad, queen, authority, friends, relatives, revenue,[66] slaves. FOURTH: reputation, father, children, one's own

---

[59] Valens, *Anthology*, 4, 12: 1–2. Compare alternative translations in Valens, *The Anthology, Book IV*, trans. Schmidt, pp. 32–33; Valens, *Anthology*, trans. Riley, p. 80; Holden, *A History*, pp. 55–56. Annual profections is a timing technique that will be explored in detail in a later chapter.

[60] Literally "breath" or "life-breath" (*pneuma*).

[61] Or "Gate of the Underworld."

[62] *Kataskion.* Or "shadowy."

[63] In the sense of a gift or a payment.

[64] *Koinōnia.* The term means "contributory help," "participation," "sharing in (something)," "communion," "fellowship." In *Corpus Hermeticum*, 13: 9, this term is used in contrast with pleonexia, which means "greed." The contrast there seems to be between "generosity" and "greed." "Generosity" or "charity" may be a correct alternative meaning here as well.

[65] *Adelphoi.* Technically it means "brothers," although the masculine plural form is sometimes used in Greek to refer to both brothers and sisters. In Christian texts the word sometimes means "fellow-believers," "brethren," those belonging to the same people, countrymen, etc.

[66] Following Holden's suggestion of reading *epikarpia* instead of the otherwise undocumented *epikardia* (*A History*, p. 55, fn. 137). I think that this makes more sense in terms of some of the financial connotations associated with the third place in authors such as Rhetorius, as we will see later. However, if the term *epikardia* really was the correct word in the manuscript, it literally means something like "upon-the-heart." Holden interprets the *epi-* prefix as an intensifier, and *kardia* metaphorically to refer to feelings, so he translates it as "strong feelings." Or perhaps "loved-ones."

woman, and elder persons,[67] action (*praxis*), one's city, home, property, dwellings,[68] the results of actions,[69] changes of place, dangers, death, confinement, secret matters.[70] FIFTH: the place of children, friendship, generosity,[71] the freeing of emancipated slaves, any act of good or beneficence.[72] SIXTH: of slaves, injuries, enmities, sufferings,[73] sickness.[74] SEVENTH: marriage, success, union with a woman,[75] friendship,[76] living abroad. EIGHTH: death, benefits from death, Idle place,[77] punishment,[78]

---

[67] With an implied sense of dignity and wisdom.

[68] *Monai*. Or perhaps "lodgings" (Riley).

[69] *Metatropai*. This word has a few different meanings, and it is not clear which one is correct. The LSJ lexicon cites this passage and says the word means "changes," which makes sense for *tropos*, but doesn't take into account the meta- prefix, which has a wide range of meanings, including "that which follows" or "comes after" something. If that was the correct interpretation then it could mean something like "the results of changes" or more broadly "the results of actions," which leads to other meanings in the lexical entries such as "retribution" or "punishment." I went with "the results of actions" here based on how frequently the fourth place is associated with the end result of matters in inceptional astrology in book 3 of Hephaestio. On the other hand, if the primary meaning of *metatropai* really is just something like "changes," then other entries in the Brill lexicon may be more apt, such as: "vicissitudes," "alterations," or "changes of fortune." See Montanari, *The Brill Dictionary of Ancient Greek*.

[70] *Mustika pragmata*. Or "matters pertaining to the mysteries." The word *mustikos* is often used to refer to the mystery religions, insomuch as their teachings were secret. *Mustikos* more directly refers to matters that are private or secret.

[71] *Koinōnias*. This is the same word as the last signification Valens gives for the second place. According to the BDAG lexicon, the primary meaning is a "close association involving mutual interests and sharing," but a secondary meaning is an "attitude of good will that manifests an interest in a close relationship," which can include making a sign of fellowship with a gift or contribution.

[72] Or perhaps "act of kindness."

[73] *Pathous*. This term usually refers either to something that befalls a person, such as a calamity or mishap, or it can refer to something that afflicts the mind or soul. Hellenistic philosophers tended to characterize *pathos* as a disease of the soul. Since it is the sixth place, there are probably undertones of physical suffering. Schmidt thinks it means "ailments," Holden opts for "sickness," and Riley, "disease."

[74] *Astheneias*. The term also means "weakness" or "feebleness," although the primary meaning is "illness," "sickness," "disease."

[75] *Gunaikos epiplokēs*. Or "intercourse with a woman." Literally "interweaving with a woman." If this is definitely a euphemism, then evidently he is associating sex with the seventh place.

[76] *Philias*. Or perhaps "affection."

[77] *Argos topos*. Or "inactive place."

[78] *Dikēs*. Alternately "justice" or "penalty."

weaknesses.[79] NINTH: friendship, travel,[80] benefits from foreign things,[81] (the place) of God, king, sovereign, astrology,[82] oracular decrees, the appearance of gods,[83] divination,[84] mystical or occult matters,[85] fellowship.[86] TENTH: (the place) of what one does,[87] reputation, advancement, children, spouse,[88] change, innovative activities.[89] ELEVENTH: friends, hopes,[90] gifts, children, emancipation of slaves. TWELFTH: (place of) foreign lands,[91] enmities, slaves, injuries, dangers, judgments,[92] suffering, death, sickness.[93] Therefore each place signifies its own particular outcomes, but the nature of the opposite place works together with it.

His concluding remark about each place working together or cooperating with the significations of the opposing place is interesting, since there are a number of instances in which the places share the same or similar significations with the opposite place.

---

[79] *Astheneias.* This word is also used as the last signification of the sixth place, which I translated as "sickness" earlier.

[80] *Apodēmias.* The word means "being away from home." In the astrological texts, it usually has an underlying sense of traveling to or being in a foreign land. For example, Ptolemy, *Tetrabiblos*, 4, 8: 2.

[81] This may simply mean "benefits from foreigners," but it could also mean things which are foreign in a broader sense, including foreign places.

[82] *Astronomias.* Which includes astronomy.

[83] As in the sudden appearance or manifestation of deities to a worshipper.

[84] *Manteias.* Or "prophecy."

[85] *Mustikōn ē apokruphōn pragmatōn.* Alternatively, "secret or occult matters." The first signification is the same one that came up in the fourth place, which is that which pertains to the mysteries. The second signification means "hidden," "concealed," "secret" or "obscure" matters.

[86] *Koinōnias.* This same signification came up in the second and fifth places as well, although I translate it here using one of the other meanings of the term.

[87] Following Schmidt's rendering of praxis. Alternatively, one's "occupation," "business," or "action."

[88] *Gunaikos.* Literally, "woman" or "wife."

[89] *Kainismou pragmatōn.* This phrase is kind of difficult, and it isn't entirely clear what it means. The first word seems to mean that which is "new," or an "innovation," or perhaps a "renewal." The second word is just a general term for one's circumstances, affairs, or business. The phrase seems to relate to the initiation of new affairs, businesses, or circumstances.

[90] *Elpidōn.* Or "expectations."

[91] *Xenēs.* This is a bit of an odd declension with the feminine form of xenos. Holden translated it as "a foreign woman," although I don't think that this really makes sense. Later in the same chapter Valens says all four of the declining places are associated with foreign lands/foreign countries (*Anthology*, 4, 12:13).

[92] *Kritērion.* As in court judgments, referring to legal courts and the results of trials.

[93] *Astheneias.* Or "weakness."

Figure 10.6 - Significations of the Places According to Valens

Derived Place Meanings

One additional conceptual model underlying some of the significations of the places that should be mentioned is a doctrine that modern astrologers refer to as "derived," "derivative," or "turned" houses. This concept appears to date back very early in the Hellenistic tradition, although our sources do not have a specific name for it, so I will refer to it here as the doctrine of derived places.

In the Hellenistic tradition this concept was primarily used in natal astrology in order to (1) look at the chart from the perspective of different people in the native's life, or (2) to generate additional significations for the places based on the positions they occupy relative to each other in the chart. This involves figuratively "turning the chart" in order to imagine that the Ascendant is in one of the other places besides the first, and then reading the chart from the perspective of the person associated with that place, deriving a secondary set of places relative to the new starting point.

For example, if I am looking at a person's birth chart and they have Taurus rising, then in the whole sign system Taurus would be the first place, Gemini the second place, Cancer the third place, Leo the fourth, and so on. If I wanted to study the topic of siblings in this person's chart using the doctrine of derived places then I could "turn" the chart and look at it from the perspective of Cancer, which is the third place in this instance. Using derived places, Cancer would become the first place from the perspective of the native's sibling, Leo would become the second place, Virgo would become the third place, Libra the fourth place, and so on. This is then used to generate additional significations for certain places relative to the person you are looking at. For example, the seventh place relative to the third place of siblings would signify the marriage partner of the native's sibling, while the tenth place relative to the third would signify the occupation of the sibling, and so on. It essentially creates a secondary set of significations for the places that are derived by treating other places as starting points rather than the Ascendant.

This doctrine is not invoked as frequently in the Hellenistic tradition as it is in the later Medieval and Renaissance traditions, although it may be the source of some stray significations for the places in different authors. For example, Paulus says that the topic of children is associated with the fourth, fifth, tenth, and eleventh places.[94] The fifth place is commonly given as the primary place that signifies children, I suspect because it is the post-ascension or succedent place that follows after the fourth place in terms of the angular triads, and thus represents the continuation of the lineage of one's parents. The tenth place may have relevance for the matter of children because it is the place of *praxis*, which means "action," "occupation," or "what one does." To the extent that producing children or raising one's children might be viewed as connected with or a part of one's overall vocation in life, the attribution of this signification to the tenth might make some sense. The attribution of children to the eleventh and fourth places, however, may result from derived meanings, since these would be the fifth and tenth places relative to the seventh place, which is associated with one's marriage partner. However, sometimes it is difficult to say for sure whether certain significations are the result of derived places being employed, or if there are other symbolic considerations at play that could explain the attributions

---

[94] Paulus, *Introduction*, 25, first paragraph, possibly drawing on Ptolemy, *Tetrabiblos*, 4, 6: 1, who mentions the same four places in connection with children. Hephaestio says that Ptolemy drew on Petosiris for his treatment of the topic of children, so it may represent a more general approach (*Apotelesmatika*, 2, 22: 8).

instead. For example, the eleventh place could instead be associated with children because Jupiter has its joy there, and one of the very first significations that Valens gives for Jupiter is "the begetting of children."

Valens preserves a long treatment of derived places at one point in book 9 of the *Anthology*.[95] He begins this section by mentioning Asclepius, and saying that this author wrote the most about the topic of the *dōdekatropos*, and that he was subsequently followed by many Egyptians and Chaldeans.[96] Then there is a brief statement at the end of this sentence which says "similarly for the *oktatropos*," and then the text launches into giving an extended set of significations for each of the twelve places along with their derived meanings. Here is the entire passage from Valens:

> The places starting from the Hour-Marker are as follows:
>
> THE FIRST: life, the foundation of time, the spiritual breath (that is to say, the Hour-Marker itself). Relative to the place of siblings this is the Good Spirit and the place of friends.[97] Relative to the place of parents it is the place of occupation. Relative to the place of the spouse it is the marriage-bringer.[98] Relative to the place of children it is the ninth.
>
> THE SECOND: livelihood, income from property. Relative to the place of siblings it is the Bad Spirit and the place of slaves and enemies and the cause of afflictions. Relative to the place of parents it is the Good Spirit and the place of friends. Relative to the place of children it concerns occupation and reputation. Relative to the place of the spouse it is the place of death. [...]
>
> THE THIRD: concerning the life of brothers. Relative to the place of parents, it concerns enemies and slaves. Relative to the place of the spouse it is the ninth place. It is also the place of the Goddess and of the Queen.
>
> THE FOURTH: the place concerning the life of parents, mystical or secret matters, foundations, property, and discoveries.[99] Relative to the place of siblings it concerns livelihood. Relative to the place of the spouse it concerns reputation and occupation.

---

[95] Valens, *Anthology*, 9, 3: 6–18.

[96] Valens, *Anthology*, 9, 3: 5.

[97] It is the eleventh place from the third place, so it indicates the friends of the native's siblings.

[98] Or "marriage-maker."

[99] *Heurēmatōn*. Riley translates this as "treasure-troves." It can also mean "invention" or "unexpected discovery," usually with other underlying connotations of there being good luck or a windfall involved. Presumably the fundamental symbolic meaning is just uncovering something that was buried or hidden.

THE FIFTH: the place concerning the life of children, and the place of Good Fortune. Relative to the place of siblings it is the place of bastard- and half-siblings.[100] Relative to the place of the spouse it is the Good Spirit.

THE SIXTH: concerning injuries, illness, and afflicting causes. Relative to the place of parents it concerns siblings. Relative to the place of siblings it concerns step-parents and guardians.[101] Relative to the place of the spouse it concerns enemies and slaves.

THE SEVENTH: the marriage-bringer of the nativity; concerning the life of the spouse.[102] Relative to the place of siblings it concerns children and is the place of Good Fortune. Relative to the place of parents it concerns parents, foundations, property, discoveries, and mystical matters.

THE EIGHTH: similarly, for the native this place concerns death. Relative to the place of siblings it concerns injuries and sickness. Relative to the place of parents it concerns bastard children. Relative to the place of the spouse it concerns livelihood.

THE NINTH: concerning travel, God, king, divination, and oracular dealings.[103] Relative to the place of siblings it is the marriage-bringer. Relative to the place of parents it concerns injuries, sickness, and afflicting causes. Relative to the place of the spouse it concerns siblings. Relative to the place of livelihood it concerns death.

THE TENTH: concerning occupation and reputation. Relative to the place of the spouse it concerns foundations, property, mystical undertakings, and the place of parents.

THE ELEVENTH: the place of Good Spirit, friends, desires, and acquisition. Relative to the place of siblings it concerns God, king, divination, and oracular dealings. Relative to the place of parents it concerns death. Relative to the place of children it is the marriage-bringer. Relative to the place of the spouse it concerns step-children.

---

[100] Riley says "step-siblings."

[101] *Epiplastōn*. Riley says "supposititious parents." The LSJ says that the word is a metaphor that means "feigned" or "false."

[102] I have consistently translated *gunaikos* as "spouse" here, although it more commonly means "wife" or "woman."

[103] *Chrēmatistikēs*. This is the same word as the astrological concept discussed earlier, *chrēmatistikos*. It primarily has mercantile connotations and means "conducive to business," or, as Riley translates it, pertaining to "money matters." However, one of the submeanings is "oracular" or "prophetic," and when discussing the significations of the Sun earlier in *Anthology*, 1, 1: 1, Valens uses the same word to say "dealings with the gods" (*theōn chrēmatismon*). That together with the proximity of this signification to the previous one which means "divination" leads me to interpret this as meaning having dealings with an oracle. Naturally there is some uncertainty, though.

THE TWELFTH: concerning enemies, slaves, and afflicting causes. Relative to the place of siblings it concerns occupation and reputation. Relative to the place of parents it concerns travel, God, king. Relative to the place of children it concerns death. Relative to the place of the spouse it concerns injuries and sickness.

There is good reason to believe that this set of delineations of the places and some of the section that follows may either be an excerpt or a paraphrase that Valens made from the earlier text on the places attributed to Asclepius. The reference to Asclepius and the *oktatropos* when he first introduces it is already suggestive, but more compelling is the fact that in the interpretations they only generate derived meanings from the first eight places.

For example, in the section on the meanings of the first place, the text says that the first is the eleventh place relative to the third place, the tenth relative to the fourth place, the seventh relative to the seventh place, the ninth relative to the fifth place. Thus the text only ended up looking at derived place meanings relative to the third, fourth, seventh, and fifth places, not going beyond the eighth. A similar pattern holds for the delineations of the next place, where the text says that the second place is the twelfth relative to the third place, the eleventh relative to the fourth place, the tenth relative to the fifth place, and the eighth relative to the seventh place, and then again, it stops counting, not going past the eighth. It is the same with the interpretations for the rest of the twelve places; the text never gives the derived place significations for what any place means beyond the eighth place. It seems then that the concept of the *oktatropos* or eight-turning system, which is associated with Asclepius, is intimately tied in with the delineations given in this chapter, and the excerpt represents a merging of that system with the *dōdekatropos*.

This is further confirmed by the fact that all of the derived significations given are consistent with those associated with the *oktatropos* in other authors. For example, Firmicus says that the significations of the *oktatropos* are life, money/hope, siblings, parents, children, illness, spouse, death.[104] These are essentially the only significations used in the different derived place meanings in the delineations from Valens above. Thus, what we seem to have here in Valens is something closely connected to the original Asclepius text, and it may provide more insight into why the *oktatropos* was constructed so as to only include significations for the first eight places, as it may have been tied in to the process of turning the chart in order to generate derived place meanings.

Valens then goes on to briefly discuss some other points related to the

---

[104] Firmicus, *Mathesis*, 2, 14.

places and their interpretation after the excerpt quoted above, and some of this material is similar to Firmicus' treatment of the places in book two of the *Mathesis*, which again seems to emphasize the idea that what we have here are later authors drawing on or summarizing an early source text attributed to Asclepius on the places.[105]

Survey of Each of the Twelve Places

While the passages cited from Valens above are a good source for the significations of the twelve places, it is also important to review the significations provided by a variety of Hellenistic astrologers, including later ones such as Rhetorius. Doing this should help us to develop a more well-rounded understanding of the meanings of the places across the entire Hellenistic astrological tradition.

At the same time, I would like to use this as an opportunity to talk about the conceptual motivation underlying certain significations, and to explore what the symbolic rationale may have been for assigning specific meanings to certain regions of the chart. This is an important process for contemporary practitioners of astrology, because it seems clear that once the underlying concepts are understood, it is easier to understand how this material can be applied in a modern context.

This process can also be useful in terms of understanding how additional significations were developed and added to the places in the later Medieval and Renaissance traditions. In some instances, these additions were based on logical extensions of earlier Hellenistic rationales, while in other instances they were based on conceptual motivations that did not exist yet in the Hellenistic tradition.[106]

In terms of sources, in this section I will be primarily synthesizing different comments about the places that are made in longer chapters that provide interpretations for each of the places in authors such as Dorotheus, Valens, Firmicus, Paulus, and Rhetorius.[107] I will also incorporate some other stray comments about the nature of the places from other authors. This will not be a completely comprehensive or methodical survey, although it should be sufficient for our purposes.[108]

---

[105] Firmicus, *Mathesis*, book 2, especially chapter 20, although much of the preceding material from chapters 14–19 may come from the same source, as he begins his entire treatment of the places here by starting with the oktatropos. We will return to this topic again later in the chapter on house division.

[106] Some of the medieval innovations are discussed in Schmidt, "The Facets of Fate."

[107] Especially Dorotheus, *Carmen*, 2, 20–27; Valens, *Anthology*, 2, 4–16; Firmicus, *Mathesis*, 3, 2–13; Paulus, *Introduction*, 24; Rhetorius, *Compendium*, 57.

[108] For another useful survey see Schmidt, "The Facets of Fate."

The First Place

The first place is usually called "the Hour-Marker" and the "Helm." The Helm is the part of a ship from which it was steered, and forms part of a nautical metaphor that will be discussed in more detail later. It was also called the rising and Ascendant, because it coincides with the region of the sky where the Sun, planets, and stars rise over the horizon and emerge into view each day. As a result of this it came to be associated with anything that emerges, begins, or is born at a specific moment in time.

In natal charts the first place becomes the place most closely associated with the native, whereas the other places represent different areas or people in the native's life. In some sense, the first is the place of self, while the rest of the places represent others. Similarly, in inceptional astrology the first place is the one most closely associated with whatever was born or initiated at that moment in time, as well as the one who initiated it, while other places like the seventh represent the person who is on the receiving end of the action.[109]

The first is the place where Mercury has its joy, because it is the place where the sky and earth unite, and thus Mercury brings together what are seen as contrasting or opposing realms. The upper hemisphere of the chart that contains the sky seems to have been generally associated with the realm of spirit, while the lower hemisphere of the chart seems to have been associated with matter and the physical realm. I believe that this is why the eleventh and twelfth places are given the names Good Spirit and Bad Spirit, while the fifth and sixth places are called Good Fortune and Bad Fortune. Elsewhere Valens associates the Lot of Spirit with the Sun, the mind, and the spirit, while he associates the Lot of Fortune with the Moon and things that pertain to the body.[110] The first place is unique from this perspective because when using the whole sign house system, part of it will be above the horizon in the realm of the spirit, and part of it will be below the horizon in the realm of matter. As a result of this, the first place takes on significations related to both the spirit and body of the native.

The first is sometimes called the place of life (*zōē*), which refers to physical or biological life. As mentioned earlier, according to Porphyry, some astrologers believed that the soul entered the body at the moment of birth through the Hour-Marker; this is probably why Antiochus called the first place the entrance point into physical life. The first place is often said to signify the native's body and things related to their health and physical constitution, sometimes including physical appearance.

The first place is also associated with the spirit (*pneuma*) or soul (*psuchē*)

---

[109] For examples see Hephaestio, *Apotelesmatika*, book 3, chapters 6, 7, 9, 26, and 37.

[110] Valens, *Anthology*, 4, 4: 1–2.

of the native. In the *oktatropos* Asclepius seems to have associated it with the "spiritual breath" (*psuchikon pneuma*), based on a citation Valens gives at one point in the section on derived places.[111] At one point Valens himself relates the Hour-Marker and its domicile lord to the "actualizations of the soul" (*psuchēs energēmata*).[112] By extension, it also becomes associated with character traits and behavior.

In terms of timing, in Rhetorius the first place is frequently interpreted as signifying circumstances surrounding the first part of the native's life, as opposed to the seventh place which indicates things that come about later on. Since the Hour-Marker and first place always dictate the start of the sequence of the rest of the places, it is referred to as the beginning (*archē*) and foundation (*basis*) of the places.[113]

The Second Place

The second is called the place of *bios*, which in this context means "livelihood," "means of living," or "manner of living." In other words, it has to do with the resources needed to maintain life, or one's means of subsistence. Since the second place succeeds or follows after the first place in terms of the order of the angular triads, it broadly signifies that which follows the birth of the native or is attendant upon physical life. Essentially, it is what happens after you are born and your soul enters or descends fully into the material world.

This notion of descending into the material world is probably the primary conceptual motivation underlying the primary significations that the second place is associated with, which are material possessions, money, and property. Paulus provides an additional rationale, saying that the second is one of the places that is connected to the native's "occupation" or "what one does" (*praxis*) as a result of the fact that it is configured by trine to the Midheaven.[114] Valens adds that the second also has to do with giving and receiving, or perhaps spending money and making money, as well as a third word that means either "sharing," "generosity," or "charity" (*koinōnia*).[115]

Since the second is a succedent place or post-ascension that follows after the first in terms of the angular triads, it represents that which develops as time goes on, and is sometimes said to signify hopes or expectations for the future, similar to the eleventh place.

---

[111] Valens, *Anthology*, 9, 3: 7.
[112] Valens, *Anthology*, 7, 2: 6.
[113] Paulus, *Introduction*, 24 (ed. Boer, p. 53: 23–25).
[114] Paulus, *Introduction*, 24 (ed. Boer, p. 54: 16–28).
[115] Valens, *Anthology*, 4, 12: 1.

The second place is commonly called the Gate of Hades or the Gate of the Underworld. This is probably because the second place is the last region that the planets have to travel through in the diurnal rotation before they rise over the eastern horizon at the degree of the Ascendant and thus emerge from under the earth each day. Valens also calls it "shadowy" or "shaded." Perhaps in connection with these names, the second is sometimes attributed negative significations by some authors, where it is said to indicate things such as idleness, sluggishness, prisons, bonds, cemeteries, and death. This is likely due to the fact that it is in aversion to the rising sign, and lies opposite to the eighth place of death, and thus participates in some of its significations. The association with Hades or the underworld may also provide a secondary motivation for some of the associations with financial matters, since in Greek mythology Hades was also referred to as Pluto (*Ploutōn*), and was associated with riches and wealth.

The Third Place

The third is called the place of "Goddess," and the Moon has her joy here. Rhetorius calls it a "good decline," since it is configured to the rising sign by a sextile, and declines away from the subterraneous angle. The third place is generally said to signify siblings, friends, and relatives.

As a declining place it is also associated with travel, foreign places, and living abroad. In the Hellenistic tradition all four of the declines were associated with travel, because planets in these places are symbolically moving away from the stability represented by the angles. In the Medieval tradition, astrologers began distinguishing between short distance travel (applied to the third place) and long distance travel (applied to the ninth). This is probably partially because the Moon has her joy in the third place, and she moves much more quickly than the Sun. While there are no surviving textual references from the Hellenistic tradition that indicate that they recognized this distinction, it would have been easy to make, and we will see in the chart examples later that issues having to do with short distance travel and mobility often come up prominently when planets are placed in the third.

Another major theme associated with the third place is religious observance, worship, sacred places, and temples, as well as priests and priestesses. When malefics afflict the third place, one of the delineations is sometimes blasphemy, or speaking against the gods. Along similar lines, the third place is also associated with divination and dreams.

The third place can also signify authority over cities or other positions of power as held by administrators, governors, royalty, the queen, and as a consequence, having followers. This is different from the later tradition which tended to place more emphasis on the tenth place for matters of authority, and it probably derives from the fact that the two luminaries have their joys in the third and ninth, which was then given much more emphasis in terms of conferring authority and related concepts.

This connection with temples and authorities is probably part of what led the third to also sometimes have other associations with banking, wealth, riches, or treasuries. Some of this is tied in with Greco-Roman culture, since in the Hellenistic period proper, kings and queens promoted ruler cults and were seen as divine, especially in Egypt where this was used to legitimize the rule of the Ptolemaic dynasty.[116] These ruler cults were modeled after how gods were worshiped in Greek culture, and there were both large scale, state supported expressions of the cult, as well as smaller scale, local versions promoted by individual cities. Sacrifices were offered annually on the ruler's birthday, as well as monthly on the same day. These celebrations included a procession, in which religious songs would be sung and everyone in the city would watch or participate. This helped the cities to build a relationship with the monarch, and express gratitude and recognition for past and future benefactions. Some of these practices were later continued in the Roman Empire. It is tempting to think that some of the Hellenistic astrologers would have associated the third place with local versions of the ruler cult, and the ninth with the larger national version, and from this other symbolic associations may have also been made. Thus, the cultural context of the society during this time period becomes very important for understanding what in some instances may seem like obscure significations for certain places, especially from the perspective of the later tradition, during which some of these significations were moved around to other places due to shifting cultural trends.

The Fourth Place

The fourth is called the subterraneous or underground place, or sometimes the anti-midheaven or bottom of the heavens. Since it occupies the very bottom of the chart under the earth, it appears to have become symbolically associated with the native's roots or foundations, and in the astrological texts, the fourth is commonly said to signify the native's parents, inheritance, and patrimony.

As the most hidden or private part of the chart, which is opposite to the most visible or public part of the chart associated with the Midheaven, the fourth also becomes associated with one's home, dwellings, household goods, and the house in which one is born. This is then extended to include things like one's city, property, lands, estates, fatherland, and nobility of birth. Finally, the

---

[116] For this discussion see Chaniotis, "The Divinity of Hellenistic Rulers."

notion that the fourth indicates one's foundations is also sometimes extended to include broader ideas of stability or permanence.

The notion of the fourth place being under the earth and opposite to the most public part of the chart often results in symbolic associations with things that are hidden or matters that are secret, as well as religious or mystical matters, treasures, or sometimes confinement. Essentially, if the tenth is where things are the most public, then the fourth is where things are the most secret, private, or hidden.

The fourth is commonly associated with old age, the end of life, death, funerals, and things after death. In my personal research I was surprised by how often the fourth place was activated in years in which the native either died or had to deal with issues related to mortality, as we will see later in the chapter on annual profections.

Valens and Ptolemy say that the fourth is one of the places that signify children, perhaps because it is the tenth place relative to the seventh, and thus according to the technique of derived places it signifies that which the marriage partner does or produces (*praxis*).

The Fifth Place

The fifth is called the place of Good Fortune, and it is the joy of Venus. The primary signification associated with the fifth place is children, evidently introduced in the Asclepius text. While other places are also sometimes said to signify children, the fifth became the primary place associated with that topic by most authors.

The fifth is the post-ascension of the fourth place according to the sequence of angular triads, as it follows after that angle, and planets placed there are moving towards the subterranean pivot. In the delineation material the fifth is generally associated with an increase of things pertaining to livelihood, especially in terms of the native's material fortunes and personal wealth. The nature of the planets associated with the fifth signify the means of the native's advancement or success. Negative placements connected with the fifth are associated with a loss of personal assets through misfortune.

Delineations connected with the fifth often have to do with themes of good fortune, eminence, honor, and power. Benefics are usually interpreted as being more benefic, while the malefics are viewed as being less malefic. Valens generally associates the fifth with "any act of good or beneficence," including things like the freeing of slaves, generosity, or friendship.

The Sixth Place

The sixth is called the place of Bad Fortune, and it is the joy of Mars. Later authors refer to the sixth as a bad decline, because it is declining away from the setting angle while also being in aversion to the rising sign.

The sixth place is primarily associated with injury, sickness, suffering, and troubles, and this may be partially because it precedes the seventh and eighth places in the order of the angular triads, and thus it indicates that which comes before death. In the Antiochus *Summary*, it specifies "injuries to the body," and there may be more of an emphasis on physical rather than mental afflictions associated with this place since it is below the horizon, in the hemisphere associated with fortune and the body.[117]

The sixth is also commonly associated with slaves, and later authors also associate it with quadrupeds, or four-footed animals. I suspect that this may be because the sixth place declines from the seventh place. If the first place represents the native or the self, and the seventh represents the other or the partner, then the sixth place may have been conceptualized as the "other" that is in a subservient role or relationship relative to the native, since this place declines away from the seventh. Thus it might have been conceptualized as signifying "others" who are in a lower social position, although this is somewhat speculative. The sixth place is also generally associated with enemies, plots, and insurrections.

Travel is sometimes mentioned as an association with the sixth, as it is with all of the declining places, although in the sixth the quality of the travel is usually given negative connotations. In some instances this is expanded to include things like banishment.

Paulus says that the sixth is connected to one's occupation because it is configured to the Midheaven through a superior trine.[118] Valens makes a similar statement at one point when he says that the place of Bad Fortune is better than the place of Bad Spirit because it is configured to the Midheaven by trine.[119] The implication seems to be that while neither place is very helpful for bodily matters since they are both in aversion to the first place, the sixth is more useful for other matters pertaining to one's occupation due to the favorable configuration to the tenth place.

Other keywords and themes in the Hellenistic delineations of the sixth place include oppression, subordination, wasting, dissipation, being unlucky, low-born, and crippled.

---

[117] CCAG 8, 3, p. 117: 26.

[118] Paulus, *Introduction*, 24, ed. Boer, p. 58: 5–9. Rhetorius makes a similar statement in the first paragraph of his entry for the sixth place in *Compendium*, 57.

[119] Valens, *Anthology*, 4, 11: 50.

The Seventh Place

The seventh is called the "setting" place, because it coincides with the region of the sky where the planets and stars sink under the horizon around the degree of the Descendant. Because it is opposite the first place, which represents the "self," the seventh generally signifies the "other," and as a result it primarily becomes known as the place that signifies marriage, the marriage partner, and sexual union.

In terms of the different stages of life, it is usually said to indicate old age, or events and circumstances that take place later in life in general. Some authors following Hermes associate the seventh with death, and the quality of death, probably since this is where the Sun and other planets disappear from view each day, symbolically dying before being reborn again when they reemerge from beneath the earth at the Ascendant.

Valens says that the seventh signifies living abroad, and others mention it in connection with long periods abroad as well.

It is sometimes mentioned in connection with hidden parts of the body, probably because the setting of the Sun and other planets here is symbolically conceptualized as going into concealment or things that are concealed or hidden. In this way it is almost treated as loosely analogous to the concept of being under the beams, which is also sometimes referred to as "setting" as well.

In Rhetorius there are some statements about malefics being placed here indicating injury, dangers, or violent death, probably because they would then oppose the first place, which can be a very damaging configuration when involving malefics. Conversely, when benefics are placed here it is sometimes associated with inheritance, acquiring the property of others, and benefits from death. Some of these significations show up more prominently in the eighth place, and some of the crossover between the two may have to do with debates between the Hermes and Asclepius traditions over whether to assign death to the seventh or eighth place.

The Eighth Place

The eighth is called the Idle place, which conveys a sense of not being in motion or doing anything, perhaps because this is the last phase of the angular triad associated with the Descendant where planets set each day. The eighth is the post-ascension of the setting angle, so some of its significations are derived from following after the seventh.

Following the Asclepius text, in the later tradition the eighth place primarily came to be associated with the topic of death, and then secondarily things that are connected with or derived from death, such as benefits from death, or inheritance. In the derived place scheme mentioned by Valens, which probably comes from Asclepius, the eighth is said to signify the livelihood of the marriage partner, since it is the second place relative to the seventh, and thus it may have some financial connotations.

Notions of idleness, laziness, weakness, dullness, inactivity, and squandering what is gained are commonly mentioned in delineations of planets in the eighth place. Valens also mentions punishment or justice (*dikē*).

The Ninth Place

The ninth is called the place of God, and it is the place where the Sun has its joy. Some also call it "good decline," since it is a declining place that is falling away from the Midheaven, but is configured to the rising sign by a superior trine.

The ninth is associated with many topics, although it becomes one of the primary places that signifies travel, journeys, being away from home, foreign lands, and foreigners. Since it is a good place, these topics are usually delineated as being positive or productive, although negative placements in the ninth can indicate difficulties with these same topics.

The ninth place is also commonly associated with religion, religious observance, piousness, righteousness, philosophers, and priests. When malefics are placed here it is commonly delineated in the Hellenistic texts that the natives become despoilers of temples, impious, or blasphemers. Some of these religious associations lead to other significations such as divination, mystical or occult matters, oracular decrees, astrology/astronomy, and prophets.

Like the third place, the ninth takes on some significations having to do with authorities, including kings and sovereigns. This represents a bit of a tension in the conceptual structure of some of the significations associated with the places, because while the tenth place was seen as commanding and having some connection with ideas of authority or leading, the joys scheme that placed the luminaries in the ninth and third dictated that authority should reside in those places. This was also complicated by the tendency for religion and politics to be intertwined during the Hellenistic period, with ruler cults that served both religious and administrative functions.

The Tenth Place

The tenth place is called the Midheaven, or sometimes the "place at the peak," from the Greek word *koruphē*, which means "head," "top," "peak," or "summit."[120] Within this context it is sometimes said to represent the peak or summit of one's life and livelihood. It is primarily said to signify *praxis*, which means action, but more broadly, astrologers often seem to have taken this to mean "what one

---

[120] For an example see Ptolemy, *Tetrabiblos*, 4, 6: 1.

does," or in other words one's occupation. Antiochus specifically relates it to one's skill or trade (*technē*).[121]

The tenth place is usually conceptualized as the highest or most visible place in the chart, and as a result it comes to be associated with significations related to the native's reputation and rank, as well as advancement, change, and innovation in general. In the Hermes text this was evidently extended to broader notions of honor, ruling, and leading.[122] Generally, the tenth and its ruler are also associated with how effective or successful the native is.[123]

The tenth is sometimes listed as one of the places associated with children, probably tied in with the idea that children can be one of the things that a native does or produces as a result of their actions or as a sort of occupation.

The Eleventh Place

The eleventh is called the place of Good Spirit, and it is the joy of Jupiter. It is the post-ascension or succedent place that follows after the Midheaven, and a number of the significations derive from the idea of rising up towards or aspiring to reach the highest position in the chart, or alternatively that which helps or supports the actions that the native takes in the tenth place.

The eleventh place becomes the primary one associated with the topic of friendship, and this is often extended to other related notions such as alliances, patronage, and becoming friends with powerful people.

As a post-ascension that is rising up to or carrying planets towards the Midheaven, the eleventh is commonly associated with hopes, desires, and expectations. It is essentially that which the native aspires towards. Antiochus says that it signifies "the increase of things in the future."[124] In the delineation material it is commonly invoked as a place related to acquisition, gifts, honors, dignity, and wealth.

The eleventh is one of the places associated with children by some authors, presumably partially because it is the fifth from the seventh, although perhaps for other reasons as well. The statement quoted earlier from Valens about each place drawing some of its significations from the place opposite to it may provide an alternative or additional rationale.

The Twelfth Place

The twelfth is called the place of Bad Spirit, and it is the joy of Saturn. The

---

[121] Antiochus, *Summary*, 24 (CCAG, 8, 3, p. 117: 15).
[122] As cited by Thrasyllus in CCAG, 8, 3, p. 101: 28.
[123] Valens, *Anthology*, 2, 7: 3.
[124] Antiochus, *Summary*, 24, trans. Schmidt, *Definitions and Foundations*, p. 306.

twelfth is also called the pre-ascension of the Hour-Marker, since it is the sign that rises just prior to the native's birth. Rhetorius calls it the place "between worlds" (*metakosmios*), and says that it signifies "everything that happens before the moment of the native's birth, both for the mother and the child, since this sign rises prior to the separation of the two."[125]

In the texts of the Hellenistic astrologers the twelfth becomes the primary place associated with enemies. More broadly, it is associated with loss and misfortune, and in the delineation material it is commonly associated with suffering, ailments, injuries, dangers, weakness, death, and troubles. Much of this derives from the fact that it is a declining place that is in aversion to the rising sign, as well as the fact that in declining from the rising it may have been thought to signify that which detracts from the life and/or spirit of the native.

Antiochus says that one of the significations of the twelfth is necessity, which is sometimes given as a signification of Saturn, and generally some of the delineations deriving from this seem to fall under the general rubric of that which comes about by force or restraint. In some authors this is extended to things like trials or judgments.

The twelfth is also associated with slaves or servants, as well as quadrupeds or four-footed creatures. As one of the declining places it is also associated with travel, although because it is a bad place it is usually given negative connotations of travel that does not go well, or is difficult for some reason, such as being banished from one's country.

Interpreting Planets in Places

The logic underlying the interpretation of planets when they fall in certain places is similar to the logic underlying planet-sign combinations. The first part of the delineation typically involves one of the significations associated with the planet, while the second part denotes the significations associated with the place, although sometimes this order is reversed. For example, one of the delineations that Rhetorius gives for the Sun in the sixth place is that the father of the native (Sun) is a slave (sixth place).[126] Elsewhere he says that the Moon in the ninth place might indicate that the native's mother (Moon) is a foreigner (ninth place).[127] Planets may also signify actions instead of people. For example, Rhetorius delineates Venus in the sixth place as the native having relationships with subordinates, or relationships with those who are physically disabled.[128]

---

[125] Rhetorius, *Compendium*, 57 (CCAG 8, 4, p. 216: 18–p. 127: 1–2).
[126] Rhetorius, *Compendium*, 57 (CCAG, 8, 4, p. 155: 3–5).
[127] Rhetorius, *Compendium*, 57 (CCAG, 8, 4, p. 164: 3–4).
[128] Rhetorius, *Compendium*, 57 (CCAG, 8, 4, p. 155: 14–16).

This is because the sixth place signifies both subordinates or slaves as well as injuries.

The multiple meanings associated with each of the places sometimes creates some ambiguity over the specific way that certain placements will manifest, because there are often numerous scenarios associated with the same placement, as demonstrated above by the passage from Rhetorius where he gives two delineations for Venus in the sixth place. In some instances, the specific manifestation can be narrowed down by taking into account other factors or variables which can affirm that the focus of the placement is on one particular outcome rather than another. In other instances, the native may have several experiences at different points in their life that conform to the different possible outcomes associated with the placement. In the scenarios mentioned by Rhetorius, for example, at one point in the native's life they might have a relationship with someone who is physically disabled, but at another time they might have a relationship with someone who is a subordinate. In some instances, multiple meanings can be combined in the same outcome: for example, the native might have a relationship with a subordinate who is also physically disabled. Thus, while the symbolism can often be constrained or narrowed down to some extent, there is still a certain level of uncertainty about the specific manifestation or outcome of each placement.

Location of the Most Positive and Negative Planet by Place

One of the simplest starting points for chart interpretation is looking at which of the twelve places the benefic and malefic planets are located in a given chart. These placements are frequently interpreted in the delineation texts as indicating positive or negative circumstances surrounding the area of life or the people associated with that particular place in the chart. This approach can be sharpened by determining which of the benefics and malefics are of the sect or contrary to the sect of the chart.

Generally speaking, the place that the benefic of the sect is located in within a chart will tend to be an area of good fortune and ease in the life of the native. This would be the place that contains Jupiter in a day chart or Venus in a night chart, which will tend to express their most positive significations. For example, if Jupiter is located in the seventh place in a day chart, we would expect the topic of marriage to go well for the native, indicating that they will in fact get married at some point in their life, or that they will have a successful marriage. If Venus is located in the eleventh place in a night chart, this would indicate that the topic of friendship would go well for the native, or that the native's friends would play a positive role in their life, or they might experience good fortune as a result of their friends.

Conversely, the place that contains the malefic that is contrary to the sect will tend to be an area of difficulty, hardship, and sometimes misfortune in the native's life. This would be the position of Saturn in night charts, or Mars in day charts. Saturn in the seventh place in a night chart, for example, might indicate difficulties with respect to the topic of marriage; the native might never get married, or may experience hardship or loss with respect to the marriage partner. Alternatively, if Mars is in the eleventh place in a day chart, it might indicate that the topic of friendship does not go smoothly, that the native's friends play a negative role in the native's life, or that they experience misfortune as a result of their friends.

All of these placements can be mitigated for better or worse based on other conditions, but generally speaking the rule holds true that the location of the benefics and malefics in the places indicates topics or areas of life that are experienced as more subjectively positive or difficult in the native's life, and this is especially true for the most positive and negative planets in the chart as determined by sect. The benefics and malefics that are more neutral in a given chart due to sect will also have a tendency to manifest positive or negative significations in the sphere of life associated with the place they are located in, but these significations will be much more moderate or restrained. With the benefics this would be Jupiter in a night chart and Venus in a day chart, while with the malefics this would be Saturn in a day chart and Mars in a night chart. A benefic contrary to the sect of the chart and located in the seventh place might indicate positive things with respect to the topic of marriage, but it will not be as positive as the benefic of the sect in favor; as a consequence, this will not typically be the most positive area of the native's life. Similarly, when one of the malefics is of the sect in favor and located in the seventh place, it will typically indicate some difficulties in the area of marriage or relationships, but these will tend to be surmountable difficulties that the native is able to overcome, and it will not usually turn out to be the most difficult area of the native's life. In this way we can start to see how some of the different components of the chart begin to work together in order to produce specific interpretations.

CHAPTER 11
THE ISSUE OF HOUSE DIVISION

While the whole sign system appears to have been the primary form of house division in the Hellenistic tradition, it was not the only form, and other methods of dividing the diurnal rotation into different sectors were developed and employed for different purposes. Many of the modern debates about house division have their origins in the ambiguous way in which different house systems were used by the Greco-Roman astrologers, and even the precise role of the different forms of house division is still a matter of ongoing debate amongst those who research Hellenistic astrology today. Here I will attempt to provide an overview of some of the main points related to the house division issue and suggest some tentative conclusions, although I consider this to be an area of ongoing research and debate.

I want to first begin this section by citing a couple of later Medieval sources for their characterization of the earlier Hellenistic tradition as they were looking back on it a few centuries later. In the critical edition of the commentary on Paulus by the sixth-century astrologer Olympiodorus, there is a short chapter in Greek that explains how to calculate quadrant houses.[1] The editor, Emilie Boer, set this chapter in a smaller typeface in the critical edition, essentially bracketing it as possibly not belonging to the original text at all, and instead potentially being a later Medieval insertion.[2] While this excerpt probably comes from a later

---

[1] Olympiodorus, *Commentary*, 23, ed. Boer, pp. 75–78; trans. Greenbaum, pp. 118–120.

[2] That this passage was probably a later Medieval interpolation was recently pointed out by Schmidt, *The So-Called Problem of House Division*, pp. 56–58. This was necessary because it had recently generated some discussion as possible evidence for quadrant houses in the late Hellenistic tradition since it appears in Olympiodorus (e.g. Hand, *Whole Sign Houses*, pp. 16–

Medieval source, perhaps as late as the fourteenth century, the opening remarks that the author makes are illuminating, because they explicitly acknowledge that the earlier astrologers used the whole sign house system:

> There has come to be a certain amount of difference and ambiguity for the astrologers concerning the division and separation of such twelve places. For they define the whole place as the zodiacal sign (*zōidion*) itself, whose degree is found marking the hour or culminating.[3]

There is a similar statement in a Medieval text called the *Book of Aristotle*, which its editors attributed to the late eighth century astrologer Māshā'allāh.[4] In this passage the author says that there has been disagreement amongst the astrologers about the concept of the Ascendant, and that some say that the first house begins around the actual degree of the Ascendant, while others say that the entire sign that contains the Ascendant is the first house, even if the Ascendant is located in the very last degree of the rising sign.[5] This seems to establish that, at least by the Medieval tradition, astrologers were wrestling with a dual inheritance: a tradition in which sometimes houses began with the rising sign, and other times with the rising degree. How did this confusion come about?

The Midheaven and the Three Forms of House Division

Broadly speaking, there were three different approaches to house division in the Hellenistic tradition: (1) whole sign houses, (2) equal houses, and (3) quadrant houses. All three appear to have originated very early in the Hellenistic tradition, although they are not all mentioned with the same frequency in the surviving texts. Additionally, sometimes one approach or the other is mentioned more

---

17), and because the bracketing convention in the critical edition that flagged it as a possible interpolation was not properly conveyed in the Greenbaum translation of the chapter. In the critical apparatus for this passage Boer says that this chapter only exists in the β manuscript tradition, which was evidently produced in the fourteenth century in the school of John Abramius (as noted in Pingree, *Yavanajātaka*, vol. 2, p. 428). Pingree had warned elsewhere that in copying other texts such as Hephaestio, "Abramius has felt free to make extensive changes, omitting long passages, adding many others, and altering both the expression and sometimes the contents of a large number of passages." Pingree, "The Astrological School of John Abramius," p. 202. Thus, this chapter cannot be taken for granted as being by Olympiodorus, but instead may derive from a later Byzantine source. I am indebted to Levente László for clarifying some of the manuscript details for me.

[3] Olympiodorus, *Commentary*, 23, ed. Boer, p. 75: 24–27, trans. Greenbaum, p. 118, slightly modified.

[4] *The Liber Aristotilis of Hugo of Santalla*, 1, 4, ed. Burnett and Pingree.

[5] For a translation see Dykes, *Persian Nativities*, vol. 1, p. 15.

frequently within the context of certain techniques or measurements, which may imply that some house systems were originally developed for the purpose of specific techniques, and may not have been used at all times for more general purposes.

The existence of three different approaches to house division seems to partially have its origins in the fact that there are three different ways of defining the concept of the "Midheaven." Many of the early Hellenistic astrologers tend to focus on the tenth sign relative to the rising sign, and typically when the Midheaven is mentioned without qualification this seems to be what they are referring to: the tenth whole sign house. The second point that can be referred to as the "Midheaven" is the degree that is at the top of the chart, exactly 90° from the degree of the Ascendant, which is sometimes known in modern times as the nonagesimal, from the Latin word for ninetieth. In the equal house system the nonagesimal becomes the cusp or starting point of the tenth house. Finally, the third point that is called the "Midheaven" is the degree of the meridian, which is the point where the north-south axis or *meridian* intersects the ecliptic. The Ascendant and Descendant are not always exactly due east or due west, but instead will shift slightly over the course of a day. The meridian or north-south axis, however, does not shift and is always exactly due north-south. Therefore, the relationship of the meridian and the point opposite to it (the IC) shifts with respect to the Ascendant-Descendant axis, and quadrants of varying size created by these two axes are the result. Since the Ascendant and horizon become a fixed reference point, when viewed on a two-dimensional diagram, the intersection of the meridian and the ecliptic becomes a specific degree of the zodiac that moves around the top half of the chart relative to the Ascendant-Descendant axis, and does not necessarily always fall in the tenth sign relative to the rising sign. In quadrant house systems the degree of the meridian becomes the starting point of the tenth house. For the sake of clarity, in what follows I will refer to this point as the "meridian," "meridian-Midheaven," or "quadrant Midheaven."

These three different approaches to defining what the Midheaven is leads to three different ways of calculating the houses. The first approach to house division is whole sign houses, where, as outlined above, once the rising sign is identified, each of the twelve houses are measured out relative to it by assigning one house to each sign of the zodiac, so that each house starts and ends with the beginning and end of the signs. In other words, what modern astrologers refer to as the "cusp," which is the beginning of each house, becomes the dividing line between the signs in this approach. Each house consists of exactly thirty degrees, since that is the length of each of the signs of the zodiac. Additionally, there are exactly twelve houses because there are twelve signs, and this is probably the

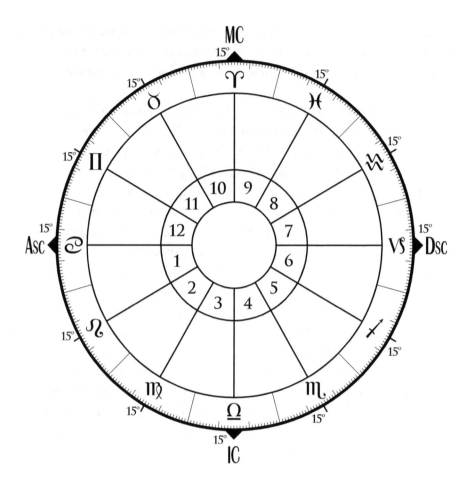

Figure 11.1 - Equal House System

reason why there are twelve houses in western astrology to begin with, rather than some other number such as eight or thirty-six.

The second approach to house division is known today as the equal house system. In order to calculate equal houses in a chart, you start with the degree of the Ascendant and then measure forward 30° in zodiacal order (counterclockwise). That entire span of degrees, from the degree of the Ascendant to the same degree in the next sign becomes the first "house" or sector. Then you measure out each of the subsequent houses in thirty-degree increments from that degree. For example, if the Ascendant is located at 15° of Cancer in a chart, then in equal houses the first house will extend from 15° Cancer to 15° Leo, the second house will extend from 15° Leo to 15° Virgo, the third house from 15° Virgo to 15° Libra, and so on.

The third approach I will refer to as quadrant house systems. In quadrant houses you first determine the exact degree of the Ascendant, the meridian,

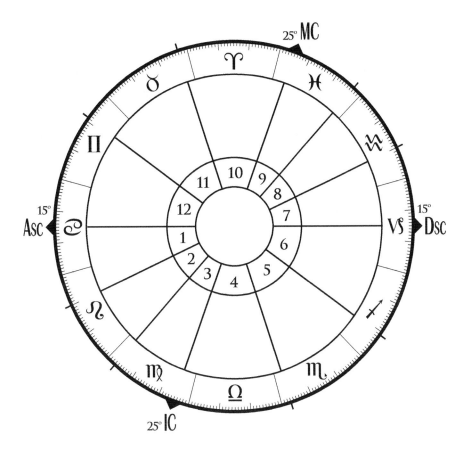

Figure 11.2 - Quadrant House System

the Descendant, and the point opposite the meridian, which we will call the *Imum Coeli* or IC, following the modern convention. You then trisect the arc between these four pairs of degrees, in each of the four quadrants that they establish in the chart. In the most common method in the Hellenistic tradition, which is known today as Porphyry houses, each quadrant is divided evenly into thirds by degrees on the ecliptic. So, for example, you would take the degree of the Ascendant and the degree of the meridian, and then divide the space between them into three parts evenly, depending on how many degrees lie between them in a given chart. You then repeat the same process for the other three quadrants, with the degrees between the meridian and Descendant, the degrees between the Descendant and IC, and then finally the degrees between the IC and Ascendant. The result is that each quadrant is broken up into thirds, and each of those thirds becomes one of the twelve houses. Unlike whole sign houses and equal houses, in this approach the houses will not usually consist of exactly thirty degrees each, but will tend to vary in size.

Broadly speaking, these are the three different approaches to house division that were used by the Hellenistic astrologers. In what follows I will make the argument that all three approaches were introduced very early on in some of the foundational texts of the Hellenistic astrological tradition: whole sign houses in the Hermes text, equal houses in the Asclepius text, and quadrant houses in the Nechepso-Petosiris text(s). The whole sign house system became the primary form of house division, while the quadrant and equal house systems were typically used as a secondary overlay, oftentimes only within the context of specific techniques, such as the method for determining the length of life. Eventually this usage was expanded so that they came to be used for more general purposes alongside whole sign houses in the late Hellenistic tradition, although still evidently as secondary overlays. The Medieval astrologers initially continued this tradition of using both whole sign and quadrant houses together, but eventually quadrant houses completely eclipsed the whole sign approach in the later Medieval and Renaissance traditions for reasons that are unclear.[6] After the ninth century, knowledge of the whole sign house system as a concept was slowly forgotten.

General Survey of Surviving Horoscopes

I want to begin by first providing a general survey of the use of each of the three approaches to house division, based on the evidence that survives in horoscopes from the first century BCE through the sixth century CE. What we will find is that the whole sign house system is the only approach that could have been used in the vast majority of the surviving horoscopes.

One of the most compelling pieces of evidence about the pervasiveness of whole sign houses in the Hellenistic tradition is the fact that while hundreds of horoscopes survive, the vast majority of them only list the sign that the Ascendant was located in at the time of the native's birth, and they usually do not mention the exact degree of the Ascendant, nor do they record the degree of the meridian-Midheaven.[7] This point is important because the whole sign system is the only approach where you only need to know the rising sign in order to calculate the twelve houses. The exact degree of the Ascendant is required in order to calculate equal houses, while both the exact degree of the Ascendant and meridian-Midheaven are needed in order to calculate quadrant houses. Let's take a look at some specific numbers in the surviving horoscopes in order

---

[6] For an analysis of the use of whole sign houses and quadrant houses together in the early Medieval tradition see Dykes, *Works of Sahl and Māshā'allāh*, pp. xxxviii–lix.

[7] This point was originally made in Hand, "Signs as Houses," pp. 135–143.

to get a sense of how many charts are involved when I say that the majority only list the rising sign.[8]

A number of standalone charts or horoscopes survive from the Hellenistic tradition and have been published in different collections. These "horoscopes" are usually just small pieces of papyrus that only record the positions of the planets in a person's birth chart. During an astrological consultation, the recorded positions from the papyrus would be recreated on a horoscope board by the astrologer in order to present the delineation.[9] Thus the surviving individual horoscopes that we have are the raw data needed in order to interpret a chart, and they are essentially the ancient equivalent of a modern printed astrological chart that a client might take to different astrologers in order to have them interpret it. In Neugebauer and Van Hoesen's collection, *Greek Horoscopes*, there are approximately thirty-eight standalone charts that only record the sign of the Ascendant, and thus could only be used to calculate whole sign houses.[10] Most of the planetary positions in these charts are only given by sign. For example, here is a chart written on a piece of papyrus that has been dated to March 11 or 12, 150 CE:

> Nativity of Philoe. Year 13 of Antonius.
> Caesar the Lord. Phamenoth 15
> to 16. 4th hour of the night, Sun in
> Pisces, Jupiter and Mercury in Aries,
> Saturn in Cancer, Mars in Leo,
> Venus (and) Moon in Aquarius.
> Scorpio is the Hour-Marker.[11]

Most of the other standalone charts look very similar to this one. This particular chart is interesting because it actually says that the sign Scorpio is itself the Hour-Marker or first place, thus acknowledging the power of the Ascendant to mark or designate the first sign in the sequence of whole sign houses. In contrast

---

[8] Robert Hand originally proposed a similar approach and tallied up the number of charts that contained references to the Ascendant or Midheaven in "Signs as Houses," pp. 138–142. One of the points that he noted is that while most Greek horoscopes contain the Ascendant, few of them explicitly record the position of the Midheaven. I decided to recount all of the horoscopes in some of the major collections myself in order to be clear about when specific degrees are mentioned versus just signs, and the numbers that follow are based on that research.

[9] As pointed out in Evans, "The Astrologer's Apparatus," pp. 3–4.

[10] These are called "original documents" in Neugebauer and Van Hoesen, *Greek Horoscopes*, pp. 14–75. The dates range from the late first century BCE to the late fifth century CE.

[11] Neugebauer and Van Hoesen, *Greek Horoscopes*, No. 150, pp. 47–48, translation slightly modified to say "Hour-Marker" instead of the printed "Horoscopos."

with the thirty-eight standalone charts in *Greek Horoscopes* that simply record the Ascendant by sign, there are only seven standalone charts that give the actual degree of the Ascendant. These charts could have been used to calculate either whole sign or equal houses, in theory, although in practice most of these likely would have employed whole sign houses as well. Finally, there are only three standalone charts in *Greek Horoscopes* that included both the degree of the Ascendant and the degree of the meridian-Midheaven, and thus could have been used to calculate quadrant houses. Even here there is some ambiguity, since sometimes, even when an author calculated the degree of the Ascendant and meridian, they would still use whole sign houses, as we will see later in Valens. Nonetheless, it is only in these three charts that quadrant houses could have been calculated at all, whereas there are seven charts that could have been used to calculate equal houses or whole sign houses, and thirty-eight charts where only the whole sign house system could have been used.

We find similar numbers in another collection of standalone charts by Alexander Jones titled *Astronomical Papyri from Oxyrhynchus*. These charts all come from the same Greco-Roman city in Egypt, with dates ranging from the first through the fourth century CE, thus right in the heart of the Hellenistic astrological tradition.[12] By my calculation, there are thirty-four charts in this compilation that only record what sign the Ascendant is located in, and thus only could have been used to calculate whole sign houses. As with the charts in *Greek Horoscopes*, most of the planetary positions are also only given by sign. There were only three charts that gave the degree of the Ascendant, and thus could have been used for equal or whole sign houses. Finally, there was only one chart in this collection that gave both the degree of the Ascendant and degree of the meridian-Midheaven.

There are also a number of smaller collections of standalone horoscopes, and the results here are similar. Neugebauer and van Hoesen published a supplement to *Greek Horoscopes* in 1964 in which they added three additional standalone charts or "original documents" that only list the Ascendant by sign, and one additional chart that provides the degree of the Ascendant but no meridian-Midheaven.[13] Later, a scholar named Donata Baccani published another supplement to *Greek Horoscopes*, and this work contains sixteen additional charts that only recorded the Ascendant by sign, and one chart that gives the actual degree of the Ascendant, but no meridian.[14]

Elsewhere, Neugebauer published six standalone horoscopes written in

---

[12] Jones, *Astronomical Papyri from Oxyrhynchus*, vol. 2, pp. 371–447.
[13] Neugebauer and Van Hoesen, "Astrological Papyri and Ostraca," pp. 67–70.
[14] See Baccani, *Oroscopi greci*.

Demotic Egyptian in 1943, and all of them only recorded the sign that the Ascendant was located in, with five of them also listing the signs of the other three angles, all of which are consistent with whole sign house placements (i.e. the signs square or opposite to the rising sign).[15] Neugebauer and Parker published two more Demotic horoscopes in 1968, one of which only lists the Ascendant and other planets by sign, and the other which lists the actual degrees of the planets, as well as the degrees of the Ascendant and meridian-Midheaven.[16] Later, Micah Ross published a collection of Demotic horoscopes written on ostraca or potsherds from the Greco-Roman city of Medînet Mâdi in Egypt, which contained at least fourteen horoscopes that explicitly record the position of the Ascendant by sign, and one chart that provides the degree of the Ascendant but no meridian-Midheaven.[17] This compilation contains an additional fifteen separate horoscopes that use a more economical style of writing, where only the positions of eight zodiacal signs are listed in a row, which then implicitly refers to the placements of the seven traditional planets plus the sign of the Ascendant.[18] All of these charts date to a period around the second century CE.[19] Ross concludes elsewhere that the Demotic charts that are known about at the present time generally conform to whole sign house placements.[20]

As stated earlier, these standalone charts had been calculated for individual clients, and they would have been the raw data used in a consultation to set up the chart on a horoscope board. The fact that only the sign of the Ascendant is recorded in the vast majority of the surviving charts implies that the majority of astrologers felt that the whole sign house system was sufficient for the purpose of delineating a chart most of the time, in terms of the typical practice of Hellenistic astrology. The fact that neither the degree of the Ascendant nor the degree of the meridian were recorded in the vast majority of surviving horoscopes means that neither equal houses nor quadrant houses could have possibly been calculated in these charts, since those degrees are required prerequisites in those systems of house division. Therefore, only whole sign houses could have been used in the vast majority of standalone horoscopes. Since the dating of these standalone charts range from the first century BCE through the fifth century CE, this implies the whole sign house system was the primary or predominant form of

---

[15] Neugebauer, "Demotic Horoscopes," pp. 115–121. He notes on p. 120 that most of these charts date to the first half of the first century CE.

[16] Neugebauer and Parker, "Two Demotic Horoscopes."

[17] Ross, *Horoscopic Ostraca from Medînet Mâdi*, pp. 47–143.

[18] Ross, *Horoscopic Ostraca from Medînet Mâdi*, pp. 145–266.

[19] Ross, *Horoscopic Ostraca from Medînet Mâdi*, pp. 268–9.

[20] Ross, "A Survey of Demotic Astrological Texts," p. 25.

house division during the majority of the Hellenistic astrological tradition.[21]

Aside from the standalone charts that survive on pieces of papyrus or ostraca, there are also a number of "literary horoscopes" that are preserved in astrological manuals and other books from the Hellenistic tradition. The literary charts should be treated separately from the standalone charts, since oftentimes large groups of them will come from the same author. The vast majority of these charts come from Vettius Valens in the second century, since he used over a hundred example charts in order to demonstrate different concepts and techniques in the *Anthology*, sometimes using the same chart multiple times. In the literary charts collected in Neugebauer and Van Hoesen's *Greek Horoscopes*, there are approximately eighty-eight charts that only record the sign that the Ascendant is located in, six charts that list the degree of the Ascendant but no meridian, and approximately twenty-four charts that list both the degree of the Ascendant and the degree of the meridian-Midheaven.[22] Of the twenty-four charts that list the Ascendant and meridian-Midheaven, four of the charts also explicitly calculate intermediate house cusps, thus clearly employing quadrant houses. It should be noted that the majority of these twenty-four charts that list both the Ascendant and meridian-Midheaven in this collection date to the later part of the Hellenistic tradition, and originate from two sources in particular, Rhetorius and another source known as "Palchus."[23] If one excludes charts that date to the fifth century CE or later from this tabulation, then that leaves only six literary charts in *Greek Horoscopes* that include both the degree of the Ascendant and the meridian-Midheaven. This is worth noting, since as we will see later, quadrant houses and equal houses may have become more prominent later in the Hellenistic tradition than they were during the earlier centuries.

Additionally, some of these numbers with respect to the literary charts would be altered by including astrological manuals that contain charts that were discovered after *Greek Horoscopes* was published by Neugebauer and Van Hoesen in 1959. For example, Pingree published a critical edition of the

---

[21] This conclusion agrees with Holden's assessment that the whole sign house system "was used by the majority of classical astrologers for half a millennium." Holden, "The Sign-House System of House Division," pp. 3–4. Greenbaum similarly says that the whole sign system was "by far the most prevalent among Hellenistic astrologers." Greenbaum, *The Daimon*, p. 400, fn. 6.

[22] The "literary" horoscopes are presented in Neugebauer and Van Hoesen, *Greek Horoscopes*, pp. 76–160.

[23] For an important discussion about the identity of Palchus see Pingree, "The Astrological School of John Abramius," who argues that "Palchus" is a pseudonym used by a fourteenth century Byzantine astrologer/scribe named Eleutherius Zebelenus of Elis. Pingree says that Eleutherius preserved much material from earlier Greek sources, although he would sometimes make changes to the texts he copied.

Arabic version of the lost text of Dorotheus in 1976, and this text contains nine additional literary horoscopes from the first century CE. There are eight charts in this text that only record the Ascendant by sign, and one chart that mentions the actual degree of the Ascendant but still uses whole sign houses.[24] A number of other stray charts could be added, but the results would remain largely the same, and I think that the general point about the prevalence of the whole sign house system in the surviving horoscopes has been sufficiently demonstrated in this broad survey.[25] We will now turn to an analysis of the surviving astrological manuals in order to get a sense of the context in which the different forms of house division were used.

References to Whole Sign Houses in the Manuals

The primary factor that makes whole sign houses unique compared with other forms of house division is that in this system, the signs of the zodiac become the houses. Therefore, one of the ways that you can tell when one of the Hellenistic astrologers is using whole sign houses is that they will refer to the "houses" or "places" as if they are zodiacal signs, treating the two concepts as interchangeable. This is clearly not done when an author is using another form of house division such as quadrant or equal houses, as the Hellenistic astrologers will generally go out of their way to be clear when they are using a different form of house division, and they will stop referring to the places as signs.[26] This point is also important because when the astrologers qualify their statements about other forms of house division, it implicitly acknowledges that whole sign houses was the standard or primary system. Especially in the early Hellenistic astrologers, we find frequent instances of the use of whole sign houses through the references to the houses as zodiacal signs (plural: *zōidia*, singular: *zōidion*). Let's take a look at some examples.

---

[24] The one chart that mentions the degree of the Ascendant is the example used in Dorotheus, *Carmen*, 3, 2. This is the chart that Pingree originally dated to 281 and assumed was an interpolation, but Holden later re-dated to October 2, 44 CE (Holden, *A History*, p. 35). In the diagram the Ascendant is said to be around 6° Scorpio, and the Midheaven is not given. The Sun and Moon are said to be cadent in the delineation, which is true by sign, with the Sun in Libra and Moon in Cancer. Mars is said to be in the place of Good Fortune, by which is meant the eleventh place, which is again true by sign. This example is interesting, then, because even though he is using degrees here because he is demonstrating the length of life technique, he is still evidently measuring the angularity of the planets by sign. Holden notes Dorotheus' use of whole sign houses even in instances where he discusses the Midheaven on p. 34 of *A History*.

[25] Those who wish to conduct a more comprehensive survey should make use of the catalogue of all known ancient horoscopes that was recently published in Heilen, *Hadriani Genitura*, vol. 1, pp. 204–333.

[26] E.g. Valens, *Anthology*, 3, 2.

Our first piece of testimony is from the second-century CE skeptic named Sextus Empiricus, who wrote a long attack on astrology in which he outlined several of the core technical doctrines of the subject before critiquing it. His statements about the places are worth quoting at length here because he tries to be very deliberate about articulating how the places are determined, and in the process he clearly defines them in terms of whole sign houses:

> However, of all these zodiacal signs (zōidia) those which are dominant at each nativity for the production of outcomes (apotelesmatōn) and from which they principally frame their prognostications are, they say, four in number; and to these they give the general name of "angles" (kentra), and more specifically they call them "Hour-Marker," "Midheaven," "Setting," "Subterranean" or "Anti-Midheaven," this last being also in the middle of the heavens. Now, the "Hour-Marker" is [the sign][27] which happens to rise up at the time when the birth is completed; the "Midheaven" is the fourth zodiacal sign (zōidion) therefrom, it being included; the "Setting" is that opposite to the "Hour-Marker"; and the "Subterranean" or "Anti-Midheaven" is that opposite to the "Midheaven": thus (for an example will make it clear), when Cancer is the "Hour-Marker" Aries is the "Midheaven," and Capricorn is the "Setting," and Libra is the "Subterranean."[28]

---

[27] The word "sign" is implied here grammatically through a men/de construction that connects the beginning of the sentence with the use of the term "sign" (zōidion) later in the same sentence when Sextus talks about the Midheaven. R. G. Bury, the translator of the Loeb edition of Sextus, recognized this and translates the beginning of this passage as "Now the 'horoscope' is the sign which happens to arise at the time when the birth is completed..." Nonetheless, since the word sign technically isn't printed in the Greek text until later in the sentence, I have put it in brackets here. If you omit it then the sentence reads awkwardly: "Now, the 'Hour-Marker' is [blank] which happens to arise..." It becomes even clearer that he is talking about a sign being the subject of the sentence later in the paragraph when he gives the example where Cancer is the Hour-Marker, or again later when he refers to "the sign of the Hour-Marker" towards the end of the passage. Spinelli similarly adds in the word "sign" in brackets in the Italian translation due to the grammar: "Oroscopo è (il segno) che si trova a sorgere al tempo in cui viene portata a compimento la nascita..." Sextus Empiricus, Contro Gli Astrologi, trans. Spinelli, p. 59.

[28] The translation of this passage here and in what follows is a modified version of the translation in Sextus Empiricus, Against the Professors, 5: 12–19, trans. Bury, pp. 327–331, with some help from the edition and Italian translation of the passage in Sextus Empiricus, Contro Gli Astrologi, trans. Spinelli, pp. 59–61. For the most part my translation follows Bury's very closely, although I use my own terminology for the names of the places, and he is generally more liberal about inferring when the signs are being referred to, due to the way the grammar is constructed in this passage. I have taken a slightly more conservative approach here due to the context in which I am using the passage, although I think his translation is correct, and I would recommend comparing it with what I have here.

This passage is important because it shows that all four of the angles were being defined in terms of signs relative to the rising sign, including the Midheaven, and it shows that even an educated external observer of the astrological tradition understood this to be the case in the second century. As the passage continues, Sextus outlines the doctrine of angular triads in terms of which signs of the zodiac are either moving away from (declining) or following after (succedent) the angular signs, just as we saw Olympiodorus doing in the last chapter:

> Moreover, in the case of each of these "angles" (*kentra*) they call the preceding zodiacal sign "decline" (*apoklima*) and the following one "succedent" (*epanaphora*). Also they say that which ascends before the sign (*zōidion*) of the Hour-Marker, and is in view, is that of "Evil Spirit," and that after it, which follows the "Midheaven," is that of "Good Spirit," and that which precedes the "Midheaven" is "downwards region" (*katō merida*) and "single-degree" (*monomorion*) and "God," and that which comes to the "Setting" is the "Idle" zodiacal sign (*zōidion*) and "dominion of death," and that which comes after the "Setting," which is out of view and it is opposite to the "Evil Spirit," is "punishment" and "Bad Fortune," and that which comes to the "Subterranean" is "Good Fortune," being opposite to the "Good Spirit," and that which comes next after the "Anti-Midheaven," towards the east, is "Goddess," being opposite to the "God," and that which comes next to the "Hour-Marker" is "ineffective" (*argon*), and it again is opposite to the "Idle."

Finally, he summarizes the entire arrangement one more time even more explicitly in terms of the angular triads:

> Or, to speak more concisely, the "decline" of the zodiacal sign (*zōidion*) of the "Hour-Marker" is called the "Evil Spirit," and its "succedent" [is called] "ineffective"; similarly, the decline of the "Midheaven" is "God," and its succedent "Good Spirit"; and in the same way the decline of the "Anti-Midheaven" is "Goddess," and its succedent "Good Fortune"; likewise, the decline of the "Setting" is "Bad Fortune," and its succedent "Idle."

Sextus' clear enumeration of the places as signs here is an important piece of evidence because he is clearly articulating something that is otherwise often taken for granted by the astrologers themselves, because it was such a basic or obvious astrological doctrine at that point in time. Once this is understood, many of the statements that the astrologers themselves make about the places become clear, and the fact that they are often taking whole sign houses for granted is evident.[29]

In terms of the astrologers themselves, one of our earliest sources for the doctrine of the twelve places is Thrasyllus, and in the summary of his work that survives, when he talks about the places he clearly treats them as signs, for example saying that the Hour-Marker is an "advantageous zodiacal sign" (*chrēmatizon zōidion*), and then enumerating the other angles in terms of their configuration to the rising sign by whole sign aspect:

> the one diametrical to it is said to be the Setting; and the one pre-ascending the Hour-Marker in a square figure on the right the Midheaven; and the remaining pivot the Anti-Midheaven, which is also called the subterraneous pivot and one that is square to the Hour-Marker on the left.[30]

It must have been astrologers like Thrasyllus and his predecessors that the first-century BCE astronomer, Geminus, had in mind when he criticized certain unnamed people who always treat the sign of the zodiac that is square to the rising and setting signs as if it is the Midheaven:

> The squares, too, are used, as has been said, for sympathies in the nativities. Moreover, the arrangement of the squares is used by some for another purpose. For they supposed that, when one of the signs of the selfsame square is setting, the next sign culminates <in> the hemisphere above the Earth, <the next rises, and the last culminates in the hemisphere beneath the Earth,> as when Capricorn is setting, Aries culminates, Cancer rises, and Libra culminates beneath the Earth. The same logic applies to the remaining squares.[31]

Later, towards the end of the *Summary*, Thrasyllus begins recounting the significations of the *dōdekatropos*, which he mentions as being derived from

---

[29] Compare this passage in Sextus Empiricus with Olympiodorus, *Commentary*, 7, where the angular triads are also explicitly defined in terms of zodiacal signs that precede or follow after the four angular signs.

[30] CCAG, 8, 3, p. 100: 30–34, trans. Schmidt, *Definitions and Foundations*, pp. 343–4. I have modified Schmidt's translation slightly by having it say "square" instead of "tetragonal" for the sake of clarity, although it means the same thing.

[31] Geminos, *Introduction*, 2: 18–19, trans. Evans and Berggren, p. 129. The bracketed words are in the translation, and were added by the editor of the text. For the rest of Geminus' argument read through the entirety of 2: 18–26. On dating Geminus to the first century BCE, see Geminos, *Introduction*, trans. Evans and Berggren, pp. 15–22.

Hermes Trismegistus, and there he specifically refers to each of the places as being a "twelfth-part" (*dōdekatēmorion*) in the chart, using the synonym for zodiacal sign that we have seen Ptolemy and others using earlier.[32] He goes on to enumerate the houses starting with the first place, and later confirms the equivalency between zodiacal sign and place when the summary says "the eleventh zodiacal sign (*zōidion*) in the chart he calls Good Spirit."[33] This is important because it is the earliest testimony we have to the text on the twelve places that was attributed to Hermes Trismegistus, which may have introduced the earliest set of meanings for each of the twelve houses, as well as the names of the places and the planetary joys scheme. If Thrasyllus is saying that Hermes treated each of the twelve places as zodiacal signs, then it implies that the earliest and perhaps original text on the twelve places used the whole sign house system. This would then partially explain why whole sign houses subsequently became the predominant system of house division in the Hellenistic tradition.

This theory seems to be confirmed in the treatment of the places in other early authors such as Antiochus. At one point in the *Summary* of Antiochus' text he discusses the concept of advantageous (*chrēmatistikos*) and disadvantageous places, and he first gives the opinion of Hermes Trismegistus, as reported by Timaeus. What is interesting here is that he defines the places in terms of the zodiacal signs they occupy relative to the rising sign:

> Following Timaeus, they say that seven zodiacal signs (*zōidia*) lend themselves to conduct of advantageous business – I mean the four pivots (*kentra*): the Hour-Marker and Midheaven and Descendant and Anti-Midheaven; the two trigonal figures to the Hour-Marker, and the post-ascension of the Midheaven. The remaining are without ability to bring advantage.[34]

If Antiochus and Timaeus were drawing on the same text on the places attributed to Hermes Trismegistus that Thrasyllus was drawing on, then this seems to further confirm that the conceptual premise of that treatise was primarily predicated on viewing the twelve places as zodiacal signs.[35] Serapio makes a similar statement when he ranks the twelve places from best to worst,

---

[32] CCAG, 8, 3, p. 101: 16–18. For this usage of "twelfth-part" see Ptolemy, *Tetrabiblos*, 1, 14: 1.

[33] CCAG, 8, 3, p. 101: 28–29: "To de ia' en tōi diathemati zōidion agathon ekalei daimona…"

[34] Antiochus, *Summary*, 19, trans. Schmidt, *Definitions and Foundations*, p. 279, modified slightly to say "zodiacal signs" instead of Schmidt's preferred translation of *zōidia* as "images."

[35] This passage goes on to make a statement about the ability of the succedent place from the rising sign to be jointly advantageous that we will come back to later.

saying that the "benefic signs" (*agathopoia zōidia*) are "the Hour-Marker, the Midheaven, eleventh, fifth, God, Goddess," while the "malefic" ones are the "second, fourth, sixth, seventh, <eighth>, and twelfth."[36] Later in the Antiochus *Summary*, he recounts the names and significations of the *dōdekatropos*, likely derived from the same Hermes text that Thrasyllus cited, and there he clearly refers to the places as signs. For example, Antiochus says that "the eighth is called After-Setting and Idle zodiacal sign (*zōidion*)."[37] In other authors such as Valens, the eighth is called the "Idle place" (*argos topos*) as a specific name or designation, whereas here it is the "Idle sign" (*argon zōidion*), again showing the equivalency of the two.[38]

In terms of other early first-century CE authors, Manilius is sometimes assumed to have used some form of quadrant house division.[39] Admittedly, there is some ambiguity in the text that arises from the fact that Manilius wrote it in the form of a poem, and thus he uses a number of poetical allusions and idealized metaphors when he describes the twelve places, rather than just outlining them in a more straightforward manner.[40] Some of this is compounded by Goold's somewhat loose translation of the text, where for example Manilius will use the word *locus* which means "place," and Goold will sometimes instead translate this as "temple" or occasionally as "point."[41] However, when one reads the actual Latin verses of Manilius carefully, the language that he uses to describe the places is consistent with the other Hellenistic astrologers, and he never outlines any specific method for trisecting the quadrants. As a result of this, it seems likely that he followed the same approach as the other early astrologers of his era

---

[36] CCAG 8, 4, p. 226: 20–23.

[37] Antiochus, *Summary*, 24, CCAG, 8, 3, p. 117: 11–12.

[38] For an example of the eighth as the "Idle place," see Valens, *Anthology*, 4, 12: 1.

[39] Houlding, *The Houses*, pp. 95 & 100, who cites Jones, "Celestial and Terrestrial Orientation: The Origins of House Division in Ancient Cosmology." Jones' paper was published in 1989, which was prior to the widespread rediscovery of whole sign houses as a concept. Many of the arguments she makes about Manilius using the Campanus house system are equally applicable to the whole sign house system, and one wonders if the same argument would still be made today given the advancements in our understanding of the Hellenistic tradition that have occurred since that time.

[40] For his main treatment of the places see Manilius, *Astronomica*, 2: 788–970.

[41] Throughout Manilius, *Astronomica*, 2: 788–970, trans. Goold, pp. 145–159. Pingree also called attention to Goold's misuse of the term "zenith" in his review of this translation, which has important implications for understanding how Manilius describes the houses, saying that in Manilius the term zenith "refers to the point on that sphere directly above the observer." See Pingree, "Review of Manilius, Astronomica," p. 265. Along the same lines, Greenbaum points out that in the main passage where Manilius outlines the houses, that "one would think, reading Goold's translation of this section, that Manilius uses 'templum' in every other sentence. This is not the case. It only appears twice..." Greenbaum, *The Daimon*, p. 57, fn. 50.

in using the whole sign house system.

In later authors of the first and second centuries CE, the trend of equating the places and signs that we saw earlier continues. As stated previously, in the late first century Dorotheus only uses whole sign houses in his example charts, and the instructions that he gives in the different procedural chapters of his work also commonly equate the signs and places. For example, Hephaestio paraphrases Dorotheus' treatment of the topic of injury by saying:

> The [treatments] of Dorotheus are likewise in accord with these. One must examine these [figures], he says: If the sixth zodiacal sign (zōidion) is bestial or moist, or the lord of this domicile is itself in such a place, it causes injury.[42]

There are similar statements throughout Dorotheus' text for other topics. For the topic of marriage, Hephaestio paraphrases Dorotheus by saying that you look at "the seventh zodiacal sign (zōidion) from the Hour-Marker."[43] The Arabic translation of the same passage of Dorotheus is even more explicit:

> If you find the malefics aspecting the sign of wedding, which is the seventh from the Ascendant, and you find the lord of this place cadent or corrupted by the aspect of the malefics or by a bad position, then it indicates what I will tell you.[44]

Elsewhere, in his treatment of the topic of siblings in the Arabic version of Dorotheus, he instructs the reader to "look from the third sign from the Ascendant about the matter of brothers."[45] In describing financial matters, he says "I instruct you to look at the sign which is the second place from the Ascendant. If you find a malefic in it or in opposition or quartile to it, then judge a decline in property and livelihood."[46] On the topic of children, he says:

> Look from the fifth, from the sign which is the sign of children, and its lord – in what place it is, whether it is a benefic or a malefic [...] If a

---

[42] Hephaestio, *Apotelesmatika*, 2, 13: 24–25, trans. Schmidt, pp. 50–51, slightly modified. This corresponds with Dorotheus, *Carmen*, 4, 1: 65–66, which says virtually the same thing. I quote from Hephaestio here because it is sometimes closer to the original Greek version than the Arabic translation is.

[43] Hephaestio, *Apotelesmatika*, 2, 21: 33.

[44] Dorotheus, *Carmen*, 2, 1, 16, trans. Pingree, p. 198.

[45] Dorotheus, *Carmen*, 1, 21: 8, trans. Pingree, p. 180.

[46] Dorotheus, *Carmen*, 1, 27: 4–5, trans. Pingree, p. 193.

benefic aspects the fifth place and its lord is in a good place aspecting the Midheaven, then this is an indication of the abundance of [his] children and their goodness.[47]

A similar pattern of equating signs and places is followed by Dorotheus in the treatment of the rest of the standard topics that correlate with each of the twelve places. Interestingly, Hephaestio says at one point that Dorotheus drew on the work of Nechepso when treating certain topics such as marriage, and if this is true then it implies that the early foundational text attributed to Nechepso and Petosiris may have also employed whole sign houses for studying specific topics.[48]

The situation is similar in the work of Vettius Valens in the second century. When he talks about the places he frequently alternates between calling them places (*topoi*) and signs (*zōidia*). For example, when he first introduces the twelfth place, at one point he says "benefics found in this place (*topos*) will not bestow their benefits," but then in the very next sentence he switches to calling it a sign: "Whenever these three stars fall in this zodiacal sign (*zōidion*)..."[49] With the eleventh place, he says "if the benefics are in the sign (*zōidion*) of the Good Spirit, appropriately situated (*epitopōs keimenoi*) and in their proper faces, they make men illustrious and rich from youth..."[50] Elsewhere, he begins the

---

[47] Dorotheus, *Carmen*, 1, 12: 17–19, trans. Pingree, p. 211.

[48] Hephaestio, *Apotelesmatika*, 2, 21: 26.

[49] Valens, *Anthology*, 2, 5: 2–3, trans. Riley, p. 28.

[50] Valens, *Anthology*, 2, 6: 1, trans. Riley, p. 28, modified. The word *epitopōs* clearly means "appropriately" or "upon its place" in Valens, which primarily means being in a zodiacal sign that it has some rulership over or familiarity with, such as its domicile, *contra* Schmidt, *The So-Called Problem of House Division*, pp. 14–18; p. 33. The opposite is *atopōs*, which means "inappropriately" or "not upon its place." The meaning is similar to a statement in Hephaestio (*Apotelesmatika*, 2, 18: 12) when he is paraphrasing Dorotheus (*Carmen*, 1, 25: 6) and mentions planets being in their "proper place" or "familiar place" (*oikeiois topois*). Valens uses a similar term several times later when he refers to planets being in their "proper place" (*idiotopeō*), which demonstrates that sometimes topos can mean "zodiacal sign" (e.g. *Anthology*, 2, 17: 23; 2, 20: 5, etc.), and I see no reason to treat *epitopos* as much more than a synonym. For example, at one point in an example chart that Valens gives where Jupiter is in Pisces (*Anthology*, 2, 22: 37), he refers to Jupiter being in its "proper place" (*idiotopeō*). Similarly, in the very first example chart that Valens gives in the same chapter (*Anthology*, 2, 22: 1–9), he explains how the three main planets he is examining in the chart are all in their own domiciles (*idiōi oikōi*) and not in declining places, and he concludes by saying that it is obvious that the native will be eminent, because all three of the rulers are configured "appropriately" or "upon their places" (*epitopōs*). In this example the planets are also well-situated by whole sign house, so the term may have a more general meaning of being well-situated by sign and place, but this still does not support Schmidt's interpretation that this keyword is used to invoke a secondary overlay using the equal house system. Furthermore,

section on the eighth by referring to it as a place, saying "benefics appearing in this place (*topos*) are ineffectual and weak," but then switches to referring to it as a sign: "if Mercury alone is in this zodiacal sign (*zōidion*)..."[51] In a later chapter on the topic of marriage he says "the place (*topos*) of marriage is naturally considered to be the seventh zodiacal sign (*zōidion*) from the Hour-Marker."[52] He continuously alternates between saying sign and place as he goes through the rest of the places. Eventually he introduces dozens of example charts later in book 2 of the *Anthology*, and in all of them he consistently demonstrates the use of the whole sign house system.

The other major astrologer who lived in the second century is Claudius Ptolemy. One of the things that makes Ptolemy's work unique is that he has a distinct tendency to focus primarily on the planets as significators for certain topics such as parents, marriage, character, etc., while at the same time he has a tendency to not use the places or lots for topical purposes, which is what his contemporaries like Dorotheus and Valens did.[53] This tendency to emphasize the planets and deemphasize the use of the places for topical purposes is so marked that at one point one of his translators notes that "Ptolemy says little about the 'places' (less correctly 'houses') of a geniture."[54] Now, this is true to a certain extent, but only for topical purposes. For example, Ptolemy never mentions the seventh place in association with the topic of marriage, while both Dorotheus and Valens do, as we have seen. However, Ptolemy does refer to the places quite frequently when it comes to the concept of the angular triads. Angularity (whether a planet is angular, succedent, or declining) was partially conceptualized as providing information about how active and prominent a planet is in a chart, and Ptolemy says at one point that angular and succedent planets are effective, while planets that are in declines are weak.[55] There is almost not a single chapter in books 3 and 4 of the *Tetrabiblos* in which Ptolemy does not refer to this concept of angularity. To the extent that this is related

---

my understanding of *epitopos* as a general term that means well-situated by sign and place seems to be supported by a gloss in one of the appendices of Valens (*Anthology*, Appendix, 11: 35), where the text uses the word *epitopos* and then makes the parenthetical remark: "that is to say, not declining (*apoklinōn*) and not situated without dignity (*adoxōs*)." This is likely a Medieval gloss, but that does not mean that it is without merit, and discussion of this gloss as well as many other instances where Valens himself uses the term *epitopos* are conspicuously absent in Schmidt's argument about the "original" or "intended" meaning of the term.

[51] Valens, *Anthology*, 2, 9: 1 and 5, trans. Riley, p. 28.

[52] Valens, *Anthology*, 2, 38: 2.

[53] Ptolemy makes a dismissive remark about the use of lots by other astrologers in *Tetrabiblos*, 3, 4: 4.

[54] Ptolemy, *Tetrabiblos*, trans. Robbins, p. 267, fn. 3.

[55] Ptolemy, *Tetrabiblos*, 3, 4: 7.

to the concept of the places, which it is closely, Ptolemy actually is using the places quite frequently, just not for topical purposes, but rather primarily for determining how "busy," "energetic," or "operative" the planets are.

That being said, it is not the case that Ptolemy does not use the places for topical purposes at all. In fact, there are several places where he explicitly uses them for topical purposes, and his usage is largely in line with the significations that other Hellenistic astrologers ascribe to those same places. For example, at certain points in books 3 and 4 he makes the following associations:

HOUR-MARKER with the appearance of the native.[56]
SIXTH PLACE with injuries.[57]
MIDHEAVEN with occupation.[58]
TWELFTH PLACE with slaves.[59]
TENTH, ELEVENTH, FOURTH, AND FIFTH PLACES with children.[60]

These are the only instances that I've found in which he associates specific topics with the places, and the rest of the places are not mentioned within the context of their topical significations. To some extent this seems to result from Ptolemy's tendency to act as a reformer of the tradition, and thus it is possible that his silence on the significations of some of the places represents a rejection of the traditional associations that many of his contemporaries took for granted. For example, why doesn't he mention the third place in his chapter on siblings, or the seventh place in his chapter on relationships? On the other hand, his treatments of many of these topics are exceedingly brief, and perhaps it is the case that he would have used more of the traditional topics associated with the places if he had chosen to write a larger, more detailed exposition of each topic. Unfortunately, we cannot say for sure.

All of that being said, while Ptolemy's tendency to focus on the planets and downplay the use of the places for topical purposes means that there are not many instances in the *Tetrabiblos* that we can study in order to infer what type of house division he used, the instances where he does discuss the places often seem to indicate that he was using the whole sign house system as his primary approach. Let's take a look at a few specific instances.

In chapter 4 of book 3 of the *Tetrabiblos*, Ptolemy provides a broad overview

---

[56] Ptolemy, *Tetrabiblos*, 3, 12: 2ff.
[57] Ptolemy, *Tetrabiblos*, 3, 13: 1ff.
[58] Ptolemy, *Tetrabiblos*, 4, 4: 1ff.
[59] Ptolemy, *Tetrabiblos*, 4, 7: 10.
[60] Ptolemy, *Tetrabiblos*, 4, 6: 1.

of his general approach to natal astrology, which he then attempts to employ systematically in subsequent chapters. In the second to last paragraph he says that planets are most effective in a nativity when they are angular or succedent. It is here that we find his first reference to what appears to be whole sign houses:

> And they are most effective with respect to the nativity whenever they should be passing through the pivots and the post-ascensional twelfth-parts (*dōdekatēmorion*), and especially the primary pivots (I mean those ascending and culminating).[61]

Ptolemy should say "places" here if he was using some other approach to house division besides whole sign houses. In that case the sentence would say something like "whenever they should be passing through the angles and the succedent places." Instead he refers to the succedent places as "twelfth-parts" or "signs." This doesn't make a lot of sense from the perspective of quadrant or equal houses, but it seems quite natural if we understand his approach within the context of the whole sign house system. Elsewhere, Ptolemy says that the topic of slaves is studied by looking at:

> the zodiacal sign (*zōidion*) occupying the Evil Spirit, and from the natural fitness of the stars regarding this place (*topos*) in the nativity itself and by ingress or diametrical opposition, and especially whenever the stars having lordship over this twelfth-part (*dōdekatēmorion*) should be either harmonious with the authoritative places of the nativity or should make configurations which are opposite.[62]

This is an unequivocal reference to whole sign houses, because he says the "sign" occupying the Evil Spirit, and then later refers to it as both a "place" and a "twelfth-part."

In the following chapter on the topic of travel, Ptolemy begins by saying that the primary criteria for travel is the relationship between the two luminaries and the angles. What he ends up establishing is that all of the "declining" places are associated with travel, as is the seventh place. Ptolemy then begins giving some specific examples or placements which indicate travel. First he says that when

---

[61] Ptolemy, *Tetrabiblos*, 3, 4: 7, trans. Schmidt, p. 12. The Robbins translation says "whenever they are passing through the angles or signs that rise after them, and especially the principal of these, by which I mean the signs ascendant and culminating." Ptolemy, *Tetrabiblos*, trans. Robbins, p. 239.

[62] Ptolemy, *Tetrabiblos*, 4, 7: 10, trans. Schmidt, p. 33, slightly modified.

the Moon is declining or setting that it causes travel. Then he says that when Mars is setting or declining from the Midheaven, which means being in the ninth place, that it also causes travel. Finally, at the end of this paragraph he says:

> And if the Lot of Fortune also should fall out in the zodiacal signs (*zōidia*) that cause being away from home, [the natives] will continue to have their whole lives and their dwelling and their activities in a foreign land.[63]

This is another explicit reference to whole sign houses, because no specific zodiacal signs were mentioned at this point in the chapter. The only areas associated with travel that were mentioned so far were the places—specifically the four declines and the seventh place. Ptolemy explicitly refers to these "places" as "signs" here, thus there is good reason to think that he was like his contemporaries in that he used the whole sign house system much of the time for the purpose of studying certain topics.

While there are many other instances of whole sign house usage that we could look at in these and other authors, for our purposes I think that this survey is sufficient to establish that the use of the whole sign system was prevalent not only in the surviving horoscopes, but also in the technical manuals of the astrologers themselves. Furthermore, we can see now that the overwhelming use of whole sign houses in the horoscopes was not merely the result of technical restrictions, such as issues related to the accuracy of recorded birth times, or the astronomical precision with which one could calculate the degree of the Ascendant in ancient times. Instead, what we can see here is that there was something fundamental about the way that the places were conceptualized from very early on in the tradition that made it so that they were closely connected to the signs of the zodiac. The question then is, if that is the case, where did the other forms of house division come from, and how were they used?

Quadrant Houses and Dynamic Strength

As we have seen, the Hellenistic astrologers generally tend to treat the zodiacal signs as places, especially when discussing specific topics or areas of life associated with them. However, sometimes when the places are used within the context of determining how "busy" or "energetic" (*chrēmatistikos*) the planets are, this is when other forms of house division were sometimes employed. Schmidt first noted this tendency among the Hellenistic astrologers in the preface to his translation of book 3 of Ptolemy, and introduced the convention of referring to the use of houses in order to determine topics or areas of life as a "topical"

---

[63] Ptolemy, *Tetrabiblos*, 4, 8: 2, trans. Schmidt, p. 33, slightly modified.

application of the concept, while the use of the houses to determine planetary strength or activity was referred to as a "dynamic" application.[64] While this is not a perfect distinction, since sometimes there can be overlap between the two categories, for the most part it is a useful and necessary one to keep in mind in order to understand how and why some of the different forms of house division were first introduced and used in the Hellenistic tradition.

This distinction initially appears to have developed out of a notion that we find in some early texts where the power of the degree of the Hour-Marker to "energize" the planets was thought to extend or radiate downward for several degrees in zodiacal order, even if this involved crossing a sign boundary. For example, in the Arabic version of Dorotheus, in a discussion about identifying planets that are *chrēmatistikos*, it says:

> If you find a planet [such that there are] fifteen degrees between it and the Ascendant, then, even if it is in the second sign from the Ascendant, reckon its power as if it were in the Ascendant. But if it goes beyond this, it has no strength in the Ascendant.[65]

The conceptual impetus underlying this seems to be the fact that the degrees that follow immediately after the exact degree of the Ascendant are the ones that will rise in the near future, so that even if a planet is not exactly on the degree of the Ascendant at the moment of birth, if it is only a short interval below the Ascendant it will rise not long after. There is a similar statement in the summary of Antiochus, later in the same passage where the *chrēmatistikos* places were outlined earlier, as derived from Hermes via Timaeus:

> But often, should the majority of the degrees of the Hour-Marker pre-ascend while the last degrees mark the hour, then the post-ascensional zodiacal sign (*zōidion*) will lend itself jointly to the conduct of advantageous business with the Hour-Marker.[66]

This passage is similar to the statement in Dorotheus in that it is saying that the power of the degree of the Ascendant can extend beyond the rising sign, but it is unique in that it says that in those instances both the rising sign and the second sign in zodiacal order become marked as "busy" or *chrēmatistikos*, referring to

---

[64] Ptolemy, *Tetrabiblos, Book III*, trans. Schmidt, p. viii. Cf. Schmidt, "The Facets of Fate," pp. 84–85, and p. 106, fn. 3.

[65] Dorotheus, *Carmen*, 1, 7: 7–8, trans. Pingree, p. 165. Cf. *Carmen*, 1, 26: 1–9.

[66] Antiochus, *Summary*, 19, trans. Schmidt, *Definitions and Foundations*, p. 50.

them as "jointly-busy" or "co-active" (*sunchrēmatizon*).

This conceptualization of the degree of the Ascendant extending its power downward in zodiacal order seems to have provided part of the motivation for the development of the other forms of house division, and it is notable that other forms of division besides the whole sign system are often only introduced by earlier authors during discussions that involve determining whether a planet is *chrēmatistikos* or not. In particular, discussions about other forms of house division usually first come up when discussing the specific technique that was used in order to determine the length of a native's life. For example, Valens uses dozens of example charts in book 2 of the *Anthology* that all use whole sign houses, but then when he gets to the length of life technique in book 3, he suddenly introduces a form of quadrant house division for the first time (the so-called Porphyry house system), and explains how to use it to determine which planets are "busy" (*chrēmatistikos*) and which are not, within the context of this specific technique.[67] This use of quadrant houses for dynamic purposes occurs when finding the "predominator" (*epikratētōr*), which is the planet that is strong enough to represent the native's vitality in the length of life technique, although it is also sometimes used in other techniques such as finding the Master of the Nativity as well. Once Valens completes the discussion of the length of life technique in book 3, he reverts back to using whole sign houses in his example charts for the rest of the *Anthology*.

Interestingly, when Valens first introduces the use of quadrant houses for dynamic purposes, it is not necessarily even a full set of quadrant houses in the conventional sense; at first he says that when you trisect the arc between the degrees of the angles in all four of the quadrants, then the first third following after the angles will be "busy" (*chrēmatistikos*), while the remaining two thirds in each quadrant will not be busy.[68] This results in what is essentially a division of the quadrant houses into eight functional sectors: the four areas immediately after the angles which are busy, and then the four areas that follow which are not busy. However, he then introduces what may be his own modification of this approach, and says that it seems better to him to treat the first third of the quadrant after the degrees of the angles to be the most "busy," and then the second third to be moderate or middling, and then the last third to be unenergetic.[69] Essentially this is the extension of the concept of angular, succedent, and declining places from the whole sign house framework into the quadrant framework, although it is striking that in Valens' time in the second century such an extension was

---

[67] Valens, *Anthology*, 3, 2.

[68] Valens, *Anthology*, 3, 2: 1–14.

[69] Valens, *Anthology*, 3, 2: 15–19.

evidently an innovation. At the end of this discussion there is a statement that an author named Orion "expounded all this in his book," which indicates that Valens was drawing on an earlier source for some of this material on quadrant houses, although presumably this does not include the modification that Valens seems to have introduced himself.[70]

This can be compared with another passage in Dorotheus where he says that the power of the degrees of the angles radiates outward in zodiacal order in fifteen-degree increments, apparently in degrees of ascension.[71] This is presented within the context of the triplicity rulers of the sect light technique, and he says that the first fifteen degrees after the angles are powerful, the second fifteen degrees are similarly powerful, the third fifteen-degree segment is middling, and then any placements beyond that range all the way up until the degree of the next angle will have no power. It is unclear if he is talking about the degrees of the equal house angles here or quadrant angles. In either case, though, this again reiterates that the three standard gradations of angular, succedent, and cadent were not always directly applied to the quadrant or equal house overlays in the early tradition. Instead that classification appears to have originally been used within the context of the whole sign house system, and then later astrologers eventually began applying it to the secondary divisions.

This chapter from Valens, taken together with the passage in Dorotheus, seems to indicate that the degrees of the quadrant angles may have originally been conceptualized as extending their power over a certain range following the angles, but this did not necessarily always translate into a full division of the quadrants into twelve sectors that included three gradations of maximum, moderate, and weak power (i.e. strictly following the angular, succedent, and declining distinction). Instead there was just a general notion that the regions following the exact degrees of the angles had the power to energize the planets and make them "busy," but there were different methods for establishing what these ranges were. It seems as if much of this may go back to different interpretations of some of the early source texts that the later authors were drawing on, such as the Nechepso text, which, according to Antiochus, said that the four angles and the four succedent places are *chrēmatistikos*, while the four declining places are not.[72]

Like Valens, Ptolemy waits until he deals with the length of life technique in book 3, chapter 11 of the *Tetrabiblos* to first introduce his alternative form of house division. Which specific form of house division Ptolemy describes in

---

[70] Valens, *Anthology*, 3, 2: 20, trans. Riley, p. 59.
[71] Dorotheus, *Carmen*, 1, 26: 1–9.
[72] Antiochus, *Summary*, 19.

this chapter has historically been the subject of controversy, although in recent times both Schmidt and Holden have interpreted this passage as outlining a form of equal houses that begins five degrees above the degree of the Ascendant.[73] This appears to be how Hephaestio initially interprets this passage in Ptolemy two centuries later, and he seems to say that others follow a similar approach for the purpose of this particular technique.[74] However, he then goes on to cite an early commentator on Ptolemy named Pancharius who evidently interpreted the passage differently, as outlining a form of quadrant house division.[75] Here Pancharius outlines what is either a modified form of the Porphyry house system, or possibly a version of what later became known as the Alcabitius house system.[76] In his *Introduction* to the *Tetrabiblos*, Porphyry similarly interpreted this passage of Ptolemy as referring to quadrant houses for the purpose of the length of life technique.[77] In this chapter, Porphyry recommends trisecting the four quadrants proportionally into thirds, resulting in the approach that is known today as the Porphyry house system, although the same approach was already described by Valens in the second century, as we saw earlier. Thus, we can see that this passage in Ptolemy was used as the justification for the promotion of quadrant house systems by at least two different authors within a few centuries after his death, based on different interpretations of what Ptolemy himself meant to say, but also likely with the awareness that other early astrologers such as Valens were already using quadrant house systems rather than equal houses for the purpose of the length of life technique.

The question then naturally arises: why are the Hellenistic astrologers such as Valens and Ptolemy only first introducing these alternative forms of house division within the context of this particular technique for determining the length of life? The answer to this seems to be that the standard length of life technique that was used in the Hellenistic tradition, which involves finding a predominator and then moving it forward in the chart using primary directions, can be traced back to the Nechepso and Petosiris texts. In the late first century, Pliny reports that a technique for determining the length of a person's life

---

[73] Ptolemy, *Tetrabiblos, Book III*, trans. Schmidt, pp. xii–xiv. Holden, "Ancient House Division," pp. 22–24. Elsewhere Holden remarks that this chapter of Ptolemy "has occasioned more astrological controversy than any other ever written" (*A History*, p. 49).

[74] Hephaestio, *Apotelesmatika*, 2, 11: 6–7.

[75] Hephaestio, *Apotelesmatika*, 2, 11: 8ff.

[76] Schmidt identifies the system that Pancharius uses as a modified form of Alcabitius in Hephaestio, *Apotelesmatika*, 2, trans. Schmidt, p. v. However, Holden describes Pancharius' system as a modified form of the Porphyry house system, in "House Division II," p. 33, instead saying that Rhetorius was the first to mention Alcabitius houses a few centuries later.

[77] Porphyry, *Introduction*, 43.

was handed down by Nechepso and Petosiris, and that it is called the theory of "quarters," because it holds that no person can live longer than the time it takes for the predominating planet to move ninety degrees forward in primary directions from its position in the natal chart.[78] This doctrine was widely reported by later authors, such as Manetho, who summarizes it by saying "a quartile side bounds every prorogation. For this is pleasing to the Fates as the longest end of mortals."[79] Valens cites this same doctrine and criticizes it early in his treatment of the length of life technique, saying that he has seen nativities that lived longer than the side of a square, even though "the old one" (*palaios*) specifically said that this was not possible.[80] Ptolemy must have drawn on the same text, as he opens his chapter on the length of life by saying that this technique should be applied before all others because, according to "the ancient one" (*archaion*), it is ridiculous to make predictions about events in the future for a person who will not live long enough to see them.[81] While Pliny attributes the technique to both Nechepso and Petosiris, I suspect that Petosiris was the one more closely associated with it, since already by the first century CE he was satirized in an epigram by the poet Lucillius:

> Aulus the astrologer, after making out his own nativity, said that the fatal hour had come and that he had still four hours to live. When it reached the fifth hour and he had to go on living convicted of ignorance, he grew ashamed of Petosiris and hanged himself, and there up in the air he is dying, but he is dying ignorant.[82]

The implication of this piece of satire is that the astrologer was so embarrassed that Petosiris' length of life technique didn't work that he decided to kill himself. This may be why Valens and Ptolemy both refer to this mysterious ancient author in the singular as "the old one" or "the ancient one," because the specific technique that became popular among later astrologers for determining the length of life was originally published in a text attributed to Petosiris. This would explain, then, why both Ptolemy and Valens introduce alternative forms of house division when they start talking about this specific technique, since that must have been what the Petosiris text did as well. By extension then, this

---

[78] Pliny, *Natural History*, 7, 49: 160.

[79] Manetho, *Apotelesmatika*, 3: 427–8, trans. Lopilato, p. 237.

[80] Valens, *Anthology*, 3, 3: 2.

[81] Ptolemy, *Tetrabiblos*, 3, 11: 1.

[82] This is epigram number 164 in vol. 11 of the *Palatine Anthology*, which is T3 in Riess, *Nechepsonis et Petosiridis*, p. 330. The translation is from *The Greek Anthology*, trans. Paton, vol. 4, p. 151.

may be another instance of a technique that was written about in an ambiguous manner, which left room for different authors to come to different interpretations about what form of house division was intended for this particular technique, similar to some of the issues that arose from differing interpretations of Nechepso's statements about how to calculate the Lot of Fortune.[83] For Ptolemy, he may have interpreted it as outlining equal houses, whereas for Valens and others it may have been interpreted as referring to quadrant houses. The general point of agreement, though, was that the source text seemed to imply that for the purpose of this specific technique, the houses needed to be calculated by degree rather than just by sign. We may be able to get some sense of the sort of language that was used in the original source text from the Antiochus *Summary*, which preserves a short passage for determining the predominator (*epikratētōr*), which was a precursor for calculating the length of life in later authors:

> But more precisely, in the case of a diurnal nativity, when the Sun chances to be in the east, it also has the predomination itself because it rules over the day; but when it is declining westward by day, if the Moon is in the east, the Moon itself will predominate. Similarly, even if the Moon itself chances to be in the post-ascension of the Hour-Marker while the Sun is declining from the east, the Moon itself will have predomination. But with both of them declining westward, the Hour-Marker will assume the predomination.[84]

This sort of vague directional language is somewhat unique here, and when Valens lists a very similar set of rules in his chapter on finding the predominator, presumably drawing on a common source (Petosiris?), he translates the directional terminology into more specific placements within the twelve houses.[85] It is possible then that it was the vagueness of some of this language that gave rise to different systems for dividing up the houses within the context of this specific technique. In particular, one wonders if the way that the Midheaven was described was ambiguous enough to leave room for different interpretations. Whatever the case, all of this taken together effectively means that some of the alternative forms of house division, quadrant house systems in particular, may have developed out of comments made by Petosiris within the context of the length of life technique very early in the Hellenistic tradition. Moreover, there seems to have been a tendency to use these systems as a secondary overlay for

---

[83] As discussed in the beginning of Valens, *Anthology*, 3, 11.

[84] Antiochus, *Summary*, 1, 29, trans. Schmidt, *Definitions and Foundations*, p. 54.

[85] Valens, *Anthology*, 3, 1.

dynamic rather than topical purposes, although there were some exceptions to this, which we will look at next.

Topical Significance of the Degree of the Midheaven

While Valens seems to restrict the use of quadrant house systems to the length of life technique, and otherwise employs whole sign houses in his example charts, at one point in book 5 of the *Anthology* he does have a brief digression about the topical significance of the meridian-Midheaven and the point opposite to it (the degree of the IC).[86] He says that those degrees carry significations related to the tenth and fourth places, and they import those significations into whatever whole sign house they fall in, so that it doubles up the topics associated with those signs. This is similar to the way the lots are used, as we will see later, where the degree of a sensitive point falling in a specific zodiacal sign will mark the entirety of that sign with its significations, rather than just a restricted range of degrees that follow after the placement. Valens gives an example at one point in order to explain what he means:

> As with the Hour-Marker in Gemini, the Midheaven in Aquarius by degree. This place, then, possesses the relation concerning activity and reputation and children, and also that concerning a foreign land and god since zodiacally it is found in the 9th from the Hour-Marker [...] Similarly also, the diameter of Aquarius (that is, Leo), which is the subterranean pivot, possesses the relation concerning foundations, buildings, and parents, as well as that concerning god and siblings and a foreign land.[87]

He goes on to say that the same is true in other placements of the meridian-Midheaven, such as when it falls in the eleventh whole sign house. This becomes an important principle when working with the whole sign house system in practice, because it means that the degree of the meridian-Midheaven and IC are still taken into account, but their positions are interpreted as importing significations into whatever whole sign house they fall in. In this way it seems to represent an early attempt to reconcile the whole sign and quadrant house systems, although it is worth noting that Valens only applies this to the degree of the meridian-Midheaven and IC, and he does not seem to say anything about calculating intermediate house cusps within the context of quadrant houses in this chapter, instead evidently just focusing on the degree of the meridian and the point opposite to it.

---

[86] Valens, *Anthology*, 5, 6: 65–69.
[87] Valens, *Anthology*, 5, 6: 66–67, trans. Schmidt, p. 30.

We see Valens apply this concept in one example chart later in book 7 of the *Anthology,* where he interprets the activation of Saturn in the ninth whole sign house but copresent with the meridian-Midheaven as indicative of a period of troubles in the native's life, although he also takes into account that Mars was also being activated in another way in the tenth whole sign house as being a similar contributing factor as well.[88] In this way we can see that even in some of the surviving horoscopes where the degree of the Ascendant and the degree of the meridian-Midheaven are calculated, it cannot be taken for granted that they would have used some form of quadrant house division, because sometimes the astrologers were incorporating these degrees as sensitive points into what was still fundamentally a whole sign house framework.

Dynamic Power of the Degrees of the Angles

Another important way in which there was some overlap between the whole sign and quadrant house systems towards the middle of the Hellenistic tradition is mentioned by Paulus of Alexandria in the fourth century, when he introduces the idea that the degrees of the Ascendant and meridian-Midheaven have the power to goad other planets into action and render them *chrēmatistikos* or "busy" by being closely configured to them.[89] Paulus mentions this as a mitigating condition for planets that fall in one of the declining or cadent whole sign houses, as a way for the planet to be made "busy" despite falling in a place that is otherwise partially characterized by the fact that it renders planets unenergetic. He says that in order for this mitigating factor to be in effect, the planet in a declining or cadent place has to aspect the exact degree of an angle by a trine within three degrees. He then gives an example where the Ascendant is at 14 degrees of Leo and Jupiter is at 15 degrees of Aries. He says that Jupiter in this example is in a decline since it is in the ninth place relative to the rising sign; however, Jupiter's condition in this instance is made more "busy" or energetic as a result of the fact that it is configured to the degree of the Ascendant by a trine within three degrees.[90]

Paulus then goes on to give another example in order to show how this

---

[88] Valens, *Anthology,* 7, 6: 111–116. Chart no. L 111, IX in Neugebauer and Van Hoesen, *Greek Horoscopes.*

[89] Paulus, *Introduction,* 27.

[90] Levente László has pointed out to me privately that these examples in Paulus are missing from the primary manuscripts, as well as from the excerpt made by Rhetorius, and so it is possible that they comprise a later interpolation. He points out that the example used in the Olympiodorus commentary is more reliable from a philological standpoint, which has the Hour-Marker at 15° Scorpio and the Sun at 15° Cancer in the ninth place. I've retained the Paulus example here for the sake of demonstration, since it is consistent with the principle outlined by both Paulus and Olympiodorus, although compare this with Olympiodorus, *Commentary,* 26.

works with the degree of the Midheaven. He says to imagine that the Midheaven is at 14 degrees of Taurus and Venus is at 15 degrees of Capricorn. Venus would be in the sixth whole sign place, and thus in a decline, but since it is configured to the degree of the Midheaven by trine within three degrees, Venus becomes "advantageous" and "busy." Presumably here Paulus is referring to the degree of the meridian-Midheaven, since he later gives instructions on how to calculate it in chapter 30 of the *Introduction*, although technically in this example the Midheaven would be exactly 90 degrees from the Ascendant, and thus the same as the cusp of the equal house Midheaven, if the previous example with the Ascendant at 14 degrees of Leo is meant to be the same chart. Like Valens, Paulus notes in the later chapter that the degree of the meridian-Midheaven does not always fall in the tenth sign from the Hour-Marker, but sometimes it falls in the ninth or the eleventh.

That Paulus was integrating the degrees of the Ascendant and meridian-Midheaven into what was otherwise a whole sign house approach can be seen from the way that he repeatedly describes the places as zodiacal signs in chapter 24 of his *Introduction*. For example, he calls the second place the "succedent of the Hour-Marker," and then in the next sentence when he gives the delineations of planets in this place, he begins by saying "In this zodiacal sign (*zōidion*), when the benefic planets are present there…"[91] In the next paragraph when he talks about the third place, he refers to it being opposite to "the zodiacal sign (*zōidion*) that concerns gods," by which he means the ninth place. He resumes talking about the third, and says that "in this sign the Moon rejoices."[92] A similar pattern where he alternates between referring to the houses as places and signs continues for the rest of the chapter.

In this way we see another instance in which there was some overlap between the whole sign and quadrant house systems towards the middle of the Hellenistic tradition, or at least where even when working within the framework of whole sign houses, the actual degrees of the Ascendant and meridian would still be incorporated into the interpretation of the chart, in this instance for dynamic purposes. As we will see later when we start looking at chart examples, this is actually a very useful and important mitigating factor to take into account when interpreting planets that are in difficult places in a chart.

Equal Houses and the Asclepius Text

While Ptolemy may have used equal houses for dynamic purposes where others used quadrant houses within the context of the length of life technique, he was

---

[91] Paulus, *Introduction*, 24, ed. Boer, p. 54: 16–19.
[92] Paulus, *Introduction*, 24, ed. Boer, p. 55: 9–12.

not the only Hellenistic astrologer who mentioned the equal house system. Outside of Ptolemy, equal houses also show up in two other major sources from the Hellenistic tradition, Valens and Firmicus. In Valens, the concept is only referenced briefly once in book 9 of the *Anthology*, immediately after Valens first introduces the delineations for derived house meanings, which I presented earlier.[93] As I argued previously, much of this short chapter in Valens (which starts with the derived house meanings) appears to be a summary or a paraphrase of material from the early text attributed to Asclepius which dealt with the *oktatropos*, and there are some parallels in the early chapters of Firmicus' *Mathesis* where he introduces the places by starting with the *oktatropos*.[94] The fact that Valens actually mentions Asclepius at the beginning of this section as someone who wrote much on both the *dōdekatropos* and *oktatropos* before giving the derived place meanings was probably meant to signal that he was summarizing material from elsewhere, in the same way that a chapter or so of material on the topic of parents appears to be summarized earlier in the *Anthology* after the heading "on parents, from Timaeus" appears.[95] Or again elsewhere, when Valens cites Abraham for the topic of travel and then gives some specific delineations for placements that indicate it.[96] After introducing the derived place meanings in this same chapter of book 9 of the *Anthology*, the text makes some brief statements about the interpretation of the places and their rulers, and then discusses their use within the context of an unspecified time-lord technique (which sounds like annual profections).[97] This is followed by a sudden digression wherein the equal house system is introduced:

> First of all, it is necessary to calculate the positions of the places in degrees: count from whatever point has been determined to be the Ascendant until you have completed the 30° of the first place; this will be the Place of Life. Then proceed until you have completed another 30°, the Place of Livelihood. Continue in the order of signs. Often two places will fall in one sign and will indicate both qualities according to the number of degrees each one occupies. Likewise examine in which sign the ruler of the sign is and which place it controls (according to its degree-position in the horoscope). With these procedures, the turn (*tropos*) can readily be

---

[93] Valens, *Anthology*, 9, 3.

[94] Firmicus, *Mathesis*, 2, 14–20.

[95] Valens, *Anthology*, 2, 32.

[96] Valens, *Anthology*, 2, 29–30. Riley notes that Abraham's terminology is slightly different than that of Valens, and suggests that most of chapter 30 is a summary (*A Survey of Vettius Valens*, p. 8).

[97] Valens, *Anthology*, 9, 3: 19–20.

interpreted. If it is calculated that each place exactly corresponds to each sign in the chart as a whole (a circumstance which is rare), then the native will be involved in confinement, violence, and entangling affairs.[98]

This appears to be a clear explanation of the equal house system, as well as an admission that sometimes a planet can fall in one place according to the whole sign house system and another according to equal houses, and that the qualities of both will become relevant somehow in the delineation. The text then starts to say something about what happens when the places are exactly aligned with the zodiacal signs, but then unfortunately the text becomes garbled and some sort of natal delineation is given, followed by an abrupt transition to a new timing procedure in the very next sentence:

> If the star of Mercury is associated with these chronocrators (i.e. with the sign of the sun or with the signs belonging to the star of Mars), then this circumstance indicates that the attack or the confinement occurs because of documents. And so on. Be aware of the transits of the stars and their changes of sign at the various chronocratorships, as I have described. It is necessary to calculate as follows: add a number of days to the birth date equivalent to the age (in years) of the native. Then, having first determined the date, whether in the following month or in the birth month itself, cast a horoscope for that day.[99]

Schmidt has recently interpreted the statement at the end of the previous passage as an admonition against only using whole sign houses, although since the text becomes garbled and transitions into specific natal placements and timing techniques right at this point, it is not clear if that is necessarily what was intended here, nor is it clear whether the statement was originally made

---

[98] Valens, *Anthology*, 9, 3: 21–25, trans. Riley, p. 154, modified. Riley translates the term tropos towards the end of the sentence as "place," probably since the places were referred to as the "twelve-turning" (*dōdekatropos*) earlier, although elsewhere Valens uses this term to mean "change." It literally means "turn." Valens once quotes Nechepso for using the term tropos in a way that seems to mean "place" (*Anthology*, 7, 6: 212), so it very well may simply be a synonym for *topos* here, but we should be careful since if it instead means "change" then the sentence might carry a different interpretation.

[99] Valens, *Anthology*, 9, 3: 26–28, trans. Riley, p. 154. The timing procedure outlined here appears to be the first and only reference to secondary progressions that I am aware of in the Hellenistic tradition. This is notable since Holden says that the earliest author he is aware of who mentions secondary progressions is Johannes Kepler in the seventeenth century. Holden, *A History*, p. 173.

by Valens or Asclepius.[100] The only points that are clear about the passage are that it occurs immediately after the first and only extended treatment of derived places in the *Anthology*; it is sandwiched in between two fragmentary discussions of separate timing techniques (which appear to be profections and secondary progressions), and it makes a statement that two places can coincide with the same sign. What is not made clear in this brief paragraph is whether the doubling up of two places on one sign is envisioned in terms of topics, such as when Valens mentions in book 5 that the degree of the meridian can import additional topics into whatever whole sign house it falls in, or whether instead it is being used purely for dynamic purposes, such as the way that Valens uses quadrant houses as a secondary overlay in book 3 of the *Anthology*, or how Ptolemy uses equal houses for dynamic purposes in book 3 of the *Tetrabiblos*.

Unfortunately, Valens never seems to use the equal house system in any of the 100+ chart examples that he gives in the *Anthology*, and so we are left somewhat in the dark about whether this was actually a technique that he regularly employed in practice, as a secondary overlay on top of what appears to be his primary system, whole sign houses. If most of this chapter is in fact a paraphrase of some part of the lost text of Asclepius, then one explanation for the absence of equal houses elsewhere in the *Anthology* may be that this represents a piece of lore that Valens found in an earlier text, but otherwise did not use himself in practice. One possible explanation for this is that the equal house system may have been the original secondary overlay that was meant to be used for dynamic purposes in order to render the planets *chrēmatistikos*, as this is clearly how Ptolemy uses it, but then the Petosiris text later introduced some form of quadrant houses for determining which planets are *chrēmatistikos*, and that became a competing system that subsequently turned out to be the more popular one to use as a secondary overlay for dynamic purposes. This would partially explain why later commentators like Pancharius and Porphyry kept reinterpreting Ptolemy's equal house system as a quadrant system for dynamic purposes. The fact that Valens introduces a quadrant house system for determining which planets are *chrēmatistikos* within the context of the length of life technique, whereas Ptolemy used equal houses for the same treatment, implies that by the second century, the two systems had become different approaches for accomplishing the same thing. If that was the case, then Valens doesn't use equal houses elsewhere in the *Anthology* probably because he preferred to use quadrant houses for that specific purpose instead, although when summarizing some material from the Asclepius text in book 9 he still dutifully recorded the paragraph in which equal

---

[100] For Schmidt's recent discussion of this passage see *The So-Called Problem of House Division*, pp. 27–32; 59–61.

houses were outlined as a concept.

Even if Valens himself did not use the equal house system in practice, that does not detract from the fact that the presence of this statement in the Asclepius text would imply that equal houses were introduced very early in the tradition. In point of fact, Hephaestio's description of the Egyptian decan text called the *Salmeschiniaka* implies that it probably would have used a quasi-equal house system, but only for the four angles in order to identify the rising, culminating, setting, and anti-culminating decans.[101] This would result in a whole-decan house system, where the "angles" would be ten-degree segments that coincide with those four "angular" decans. In Hephaestio's short synopsis of the *Salmeschiniaka*, the culminating decan that deals with "livelihood" is said to be the twenty-eighth decan relative to the Hour-Marker, and this decan would contain the nonagesimal degree. This would not be a division of the diurnal rotation into twelve segments; only the four angular degrees would have been used to establish the four pivotal decans. It seems as if the full division of the chart into twelve segments with the equal house angles as the starting point was the unique innovation that the Asclepius text introduced later, as a spinoff of the twelvefold division of the houses that was based on the signs, as introduced by Hermes. The decans do not really provide a good motivation for dividing the diurnal rotation into twelve sectors, but the twelve-fold division of the zodiac does, and that provides an additional reason from a logical standpoint for why the equal house division would necessarily have developed after the introduction of the whole sign house system as a concept. Specifically how equal houses were meant to be employed as a secondary overlay may have been a matter of debate, though, as we see Ptolemy using it in the length of life technique for dynamic purposes, whereas Firmicus may have used it for topical purposes, as we will see next.

Firmicus, Rhetorius, and the Two Delineation Texts

Firmicus appears to have drawn on the Asclepius text as his primary source for material on the places, and as a result he appears to have emphasized the approach outlined in that text more than some of the other Hellenistic

---

[101] As described in Hephaestio, *Apotelesmatika*, 2, 18: 75–6, quoted earlier. The dating of this text is uncertain, although it is usually assumed to have preceded Nechepso and Petosiris. However, this is partially based on the mistaken notion that Nechepso cited the *Salmeschiniaka* at some point, which itself seems to be based on a misreading of the Hephaestio passage above. Heilen clarifies this point in his treatment of the *Salmeschiniaka* in *Hadriani Genitura*, p. 1333ff. Heilen notes that Porphyry and Iamblichus mention it in connection with the Egyptian priest Chaeremon, who lived in the first century CE, so the best we can say is that the *Salmeschiniaka* was probably written around or somewhere before that time, probably in the Ptolemaic period.

astrologers did. One of the pieces of evidence for this is the fact that when Firmicus first introduces the concept of the twelve places and their meanings in book 2 of the *Mathesis*, he begins with a brief chapter outlining the significations of the *oktatropos*.[102] Interestingly, Firmicus initially outlines the significations of the *oktatropos* in terms of whole sign houses:

> Generally, the Place of Life is in that sign (*signum*) where the Hour-Marker is located, the Place of Hope or Money in the second sign (*signum*) from the Hour-Marker, that of Brothers in the third, that of Parents in the fourth, that of Children in the fifth, that of Illness in the sixth, that of the Spouse in the seventh, [and] that of Death in the eighth.[103]

He goes on to say that this is how the concept of places is defined generally (*platicus*), but he also explains how it is defined according to degrees as well.[104] These later seem to become Firmicus' keywords for talking about whole sign houses versus equal houses, as argued by Schmidt.[105] Rhetorius uses similar language a few centuries later when he alternates between using whole sign houses and quadrant houses in one of his example charts, and so this may represent a more general trend in terms of how some of the later Hellenistic astrologers would invoke additional forms of house division by referring to the places "by sign" versus the places "by degree."[106] In the following chapter Firmicus defines the four angular places both in terms of signs and in terms of degrees:

> But so that you may more readily understand, measure from the degree of the Hour-Marker through the other signs 180 degrees, and in whatever sign the 181st degree is found, in that very sign, <namely the seventh, it is found by degree. Which, so that you may understand it more clearly, in that very sign> or degree of the nativity the Setting is located. The Midheaven is in fact the tenth sign from the Hour-Marker, but now and then the Midheaven is also found by degree in the eleventh sign from the Hour-Marker. But so that you may more readily understand, measure 270

---

[102] Firmicus, *Mathesis*, 2, 14.

[103] Firmicus, *Mathesis*, 2, 14: 3, trans. Holden, p. 61, modified. I have changed Holden's translation of locus as "house" to "place," and also rendered Firmicus' use of the Latin word horoscopus as "Hour-Marker" instead of Holden's "ASC." I will continue modifying these words in the other passages that follow from Firmicus in order to keep them in line with the conventions I have adopted in this book.

[104] Firmicus, *Mathesis*, 2, 14: 4.

[105] Schmidt, *The So-Called Problem of House Division*, pp. 33–35.

[106] Rhetorius, *Compendium*, 113.

degrees from the degree of the Hour-Marker through the other signs that follow, and in whatever sign the 271st degree is found, that is allotted the Midheaven...[107]

This passage is interesting because Firmicus appears to be emphasizing that the Midheaven is the tenth sign relative to the rising sign, although, like Paulus, he notes that the degree of the meridian-Midheaven does not always fall in the tenth sign from the rising sign. He continues referring to the places as signs in the next chapter when he gives the traditional names for the places, as perhaps first introduced in the Hermes text:

Goddess is the third place, i.e. the third sign from the Hour-Marker; that place is called *Thea* by the Greeks as we just mentioned. But the sign is called God that is located in opposition across from that [previous] sign— that is to say the ninth sign from the Hour-Marker. That place is called *Theos* by the Greeks.[108]

Again, in the following chapter in which he defines the good and bad places, he seems to do so in terms of the signs they occupy relative to the rising sign:

Moreover, the first of these four remaining places is that which is located in the second sign from the Hour-Marker, which place is called the Gates of Hades or *anaphora*. The place that is in opposition to this sign, i.e. in the eighth sign from the Hour-Marker, is called *epikataphora*. But the last <places> are those of Bad Fortune and the Bad Spirit. And the Bad Fortune is located in the sixth <sign> from the Hour-Marker, but the Bad Spirit is placed in the twelfth sign from the Hour-Marker. But the Greeks call the Bad Fortune *Kake Tuche*. The Bad Spirit, which is the twelfth sign from the Hour-Marker, the Greeks call *Kakos Daimon*.[109]

Finally, in chapter 19, Firmicus explicitly defines each of the places in terms of the equal house system, beginning by saying that he is now going to explain the "particular" (*specialiter*) significations of the twelve places in this chapter, which seems to harken back to the way that he outlined the places by sign earlier

---

[107] Firmicus, *Mathesis*, 2, 15: 3–4, trans. Holden, pp. 62–63, modified. The section in brackets is in Holden's translation, which he added from manuscript N.

[108] Firmicus, *Mathesis*, 2, 16: 2, trans. Holden, p. 63, modified.

[109] Firmicus, *Mathesis*, 2, 17: 1, trans. Holden, p. 64, modified. All text in brackets is included in Holden's translation. He says that manuscript A adds "sign," while manuscript N adds "place."

as "general" (*platicus*). As in book 9 of Valens, Firmicus defines each equal house as beginning at the degree of the Hour-Marker, and then he says that it extends its "power" (*vires*) through the remaining 30 degrees, until eventually the second equal house begins at the same degree in the following sign. In the chapter that follows, Firmicus gives instructions for interpreting the places and their rulers, and much of the material here sounds like an expanded version of the short synopsis that Valens summarizes in book 9 of the *Anthology*, just after explaining how to calculate equal houses.[110] I suspect what we are seeing here is Firmicus paraphrasing the same source as Valens, which is the lost text of Asclepius, and this would explain why Firmicus is unique among the Hellenistic astrologers in introducing equal houses very early on in his work, whereas for Valens this material is only summarized briefly in a chapter later on in the *Anthology*. Firmicus seems to have prioritized this material from Asclepius more than Valens did for some reason.

In book 3 of the *Mathesis*, Firmicus provides an extended set of interpretations for what the planets mean when they are located in each of the twelve places. This material should be useful for getting a clearer understanding of how Firmicus used the places, although it is complicated because he evidently translated many of the interpretations in this book into Latin from an unknown Greek source text. Unfortunately, it is not always clear which parts represent the original source text versus which comments are additions by Firmicus. Parallels between Firmicus' delineations and some fragments that have survived from the work of Anubio were originally interpreted as meaning that Firmicus translated the delineations from Anubio directly.[111] However, Heilen has recently argued that instead, Anubio and Firmicus independently drew on a separate source text for these delineations.[112] Generally, the delineations in Firmicus are wordier than those that survive from Anubio, and sometimes there are different interpretations for the same placement.[113]

More importantly, Holden notes that there are many close parallels between the delineations of planets in the places in this book of Firmicus and a chapter that deals with the same topic in Rhetorius, which led him to conclude that "plainly, both Firmicus and Rhetorius derived these statements from the same source."[114] This becomes important because then the delineations in Firmicus must be read together with the parallel delineations in Rhetorius in order to

---

[110] Compare especially Firmicus, *Mathesis*, 2, 20: 3–7 with Valens, *Anthology*, 9, 3: 20.

[111] Parallel delineations are noted in Anubio, *Carmen*, ed. Obbink.

[112] Heilen, "Anubio Reconsidered," p. 131ff.

[113] As discussed by Heilen, "Anubio Reconsidered," p. 131–133.

[114] Firmicus, *Mathesis*, trans. Holden, p. 95, fn. 2. Holden notes a number of additional parallel passages in the footnotes of Rhetorius, *Compendium*, 57, trans. Holden.

understand what the original source text said, as well as to clarify how it was being interpreted by later authors, including Firmicus.

Rhetorius' primary treatment of the meanings of the twelve places occurs in chapter 57 of his *Compendium*. This is an extremely long chapter, where Rhetorius starts with the twelfth place and then works his way through the rest of the places in zodiacal order. He introduces a new place each time by listing the different names associated with it, as well as some of its general significations. Then he goes through each of the planets and gives a set of interpretations for what they mean when they are located in that particular place in a natal chart. Rhetorius then does something unique: after finishing the first set of interpretations, he then starts the process over again and gives a second set of delineations for each of the planets in the same place. This second set of interpretations is significantly different than the first set. He goes through this same process for all twelve places, where he presents two different sets of delineations for each of the planets. What is even more interesting about this is that the first set of delineations that Rhetorius gives has some close parallels with the chapters on the same topic in Dorotheus, Valens, and Paulus, while the second set of delineations that Rhetorius gives often closely matches the corresponding passages in book 3 of Firmicus.[115] With the second set of delineations, it seems clear that Rhetorius and Firmicus were drawing on the same underlying source text, whereas with the first set of delineations it is not clear if Rhetorius had access to the original source text underlying them or if he is just compiling the delineations directly from Dorotheus, Valens, and Paulus, since we know that he had access to all three of their texts.[116] I would argue that the fact that there are similarities between the delineations in Valens and Paulus (and to a lesser extent Dorotheus) to begin with, as well as the fact that Rhetorius treats them as a distinct tradition of its own, implies that there probably was some sort of specific underlying delineation text that originally motivated the interpretations that they provide. What this results in, then, is effectively two major variant traditions among the Hellenistic astrologers for how to interpret the planets in the twelve places.

---

[115] For the first set of delineations in Rhetorius, *Compendium*, 57, compare Dorotheus, *Carmen*, 2, 20–27; Valens, *Anthology*, 2, 4–15; Paulus, *Introduction*, 24. For the second set of delineations in Rhetorius compare Firmicus, *Mathesis*, 3, 2–13.

[116] Pingree described this chapter of Rhetorius as "a late conflation of material from Valens, Firmicus (or his source), Paulus, and others. Uses Dorotheus and Critodemus." Pingree, "Antiochus and Rhetorius," p. 211. Elsewhere Pingree says that Rhetorius may have drawn on the same source text as Valens for this material, rather than from Valens directly (Pingree, *Yavanajātaka*, vol. 2, p. 431). Rhetorius mentions Dorotheus, Valens, and Paulus by name at different points elsewhere in his *Compendium*.

The identification of these two variant traditions for delineating planets in places is important within the context of the discussion about house division, because in variant one (represented by Dorotheus, Valens, Paulus, and Rhetorius), the places are always discussed in terms of signs—i.e. whole sign houses—whereas in variant two (Firmicus and Rhetorius), the places are sometimes discussed in terms of signs and sometimes in terms of degrees. I suspect that the difference between these two traditions has something to do with the variance between the text attributed to Hermes Trismegistus that introduced the *dōdekatropos* and the text attributed to Asclepius that introduced the *oktatropos*. It is hard to be certain, however, since later authors tended to conflate the two systems, whereas earlier authors such as Thrasyllus and Antiochus tended to present them separately. The fact that the Asclepius text seems to have introduced the concept of equal houses, as we have seen in Valens and Firmicus, might explain why there seems to be some additional focus on the places both in terms of signs and in terms of degrees in the delineations in variant two of Firmicus and Rhetorius. Some of the specific details surrounding the use of the places in terms of degrees in the source text of Firmicus and Rhetorius are a bit murky, though. Let's take a look at how both authors treat this issue.

Firmicus opens book 3 of the *Mathesis* with a treatment of the Thema Mundi. Just before he gives some extended interpretations of it, he cites the title of a specific book by Asclepius that he says dealt with the topic, called *Infinite Nativities (Myriogenesis)*.[117] Elsewhere, Firmicus says that this same book gave delineations for the Ascendant at each degree and minute of the zodiac.[118] If this is true, then it may partially explain the greater preoccupation with the exact degrees of the angles in the Asclepius tradition. At the end of this chapter, Firmicus completes the discussion of the Thema Mundi, and then prepares to transition into giving delineations for the planets in the twelve places for the rest of book 3 of the *Mathesis*, but first he makes an important prefatory statement:

> Now, because these things have been stated and demonstrated, it ought to be defined what the individual stars denote in the individual places of the nativity. [...] But even though these things are thought by some to be defined only generally (*platicus*), many things should also be stated by degrees (*partiliter*) in this book. For the stars will then have their own efficacy, if they are also located precisely in their own individual places.[119]

---

[117] Firmicus, *Mathesis*, 3, 1: 2.
[118] Firmicus, *Mathesis*, 5, 1: 36–38.
[119] Firmicus, *Mathesis*, 3, 1: 19, trans. Holden, p. 94, modified.

In other words, Firmicus acknowledges here that some astrologers only define the places by sign (i.e. whole sign houses); however, he says that he thinks they should also be defined by degree, because the planets are more "efficacious" or "powerful" (*efficacia*) when they are located precisely in the degrees of certain places. The language he uses here sounds reminiscent of the way that some of the other Hellenistic astrologers would use the Greek word *chrēmatistikos* to describe how the planets become more "busy" or "energetic" the closer they get to the exact degrees of the angles, as we have seen earlier.

In the following chapter, Firmicus begins giving the delineations for the planets located in each of the places, starting with Saturn. What is interesting and unique about these delineations is that in all four of the angular places Firmicus always starts the delineation by using some specific wording that seems to refer to the degree of the angle. For example, for Saturn he begins by saying:

> Saturn partilely (*partiliter*) posited in the Hour-Marker by day, i.e. if he is in that very degree in which the Hour-Marker is, will make the birth to occur with a very loud outcry.[120]

The Latin word that Firmicus uses here, *partiliter*, is distinctive and important, although there is some ambiguity about what it means. It is derived from the Latin word *pars*, which means "portion," which in this context is probably equivalent to the Greek term *moira*, which also means "portion," although in an astrological context it usually means "degree." *Partiliter* is an adverb, so it means something like "to-the-degree." Holden interprets this as meaning that the placement is on the very degree of the angle, while Schmidt has recently argued that this wording is used by Firmicus to refer to his use of equal houses as a secondary overlay.[121] Firmicus uses the same language with the other three angles as well, for example saying "Saturn being established to-the-degree (*partiliter*) in the fourth place from the Hour-Marker, that is, in the IC," or "Saturn being established in the seventh place from the Hour-Marker, that is in the setting, to-the-degree," or "Saturn being established in the tenth place from the Hour-Marker, to-the-degree in the MC."[122] However, for some reason Firmicus never uses this language when discussing the intermediate houses in book 3 of the *Mathesis*; instead he just refers to those places according to their number relative to the rising sign, or occasionally even refers to the intermediate places

---

[120] Firmicus, *Mathesis*, 3, 2: 1, trans. Holden, p. 95, modified.

[121] Holden talks about the meaning of partiliter briefly in Firmicus, *Mathesis*, trans. Holden, p. xxviii. Schmidt, *The So-Called Problem of House Division*, p. 33ff.

[122] Firmicus, *Mathesis*, 3, 2: 8; 3, 2: 14; 3, 2: 20.

as signs (*signum*).[123] For example, when Firmicus starts talking about Saturn in the second place he says "when Saturn occupies the second place (*locus*) from the Hour-Marker," but then when he moves on to the third place he says "Saturn established in the third sign (*signum*) from the Hour-Marker."[124] This creates an odd situation in which Firmicus is somehow emphasizing the exact degrees when he talks about the four places associated with the angles, but he does not emphasize the degrees associated with the other eight places. This then leaves us with some uncertainty about whether Firmicus' delineations of the four angles "to-the-degree" (*partiliter*) are meant to be interpreted as only referring to the exact degree occupied by the angles, or if they are meant to refer to the entire thirty-degree range that follows the exact degree of the angles, which would be the range associated with the four angular places using the equal house system that Firmicus outlined earlier in book 2.

In the parallel delineations in Rhetorius that match the ones in Firmicus, he tends to refer to the places in terms of their number rather than referring to them explicitly as signs. This may be notable since Rhetorius talks about the places as if they are signs much more frequently in the first set of delineations that match Dorotheus, Valens, and Paulus, as well as in his introductory remarks about each of the places. The only exceptions to this in the second set of delineations that he shares with Firmicus are when Rhetorius talks about the first and tenth places, which he does tend to refer to as signs. For example, compare Firmicus' statement about Saturn in the Hour-Marker "to-the-degree" quoted above with this parallel passage in Rhetorius:

> When the [star] of Saturn chances to be in the Hour-Marking sign (*hōroskopountos zōidiou*), it will produce a loud outcry...[125]

In Firmicus, this placement is given as relating to the degree or possibly degrees associated with the Hour-Marker, whereas in Rhetorius the delineation is situated within the context of the rising sign. Similarly, compare Firmicus' delineation of Jupiter in the tenth place:

> Jupiter posited in the tenth place, i.e. the MC partilely (*partiliter*) by day, will make principal managers of public affairs. And it will make one of the First Ten of the greatest nations, and those on whom the greatest honors

---

[123] Thanks to Benjamin Dykes for noting this point about the intermediate places.

[124] Firmicus, *Mathesis*, 3, 2: 4 & 7. For other examples see Firmicus, *Mathesis*, 3, 2: 8; 3, 3: 12; 3, 4: 24.

[125] Rhetorius, *Compendium*, 57 (CCAG, 8, 4, p. 135: 10), trans. Holden, p. 51, modified.

are conferred by the people, distinguished persons and those who would always like to avail themselves of the grace of ostentation...[126]

In Rhetorius the parallel delineation for Jupiter in the tenth reads:

Jupiter chancing to be in the sign (*zōidion*) of the Midheaven by day denotes athletic contestants, directors of public affairs, those esteemed by the people, famous, well-known, or those who are entrusted by kings and magnates with [the management of] their affairs, [or] those who wear crowns throughout their whole lives.[127]

The delineations are both clearly drawing on some similar underlying source text, but for some reason Rhetorius seems to be emphasizing the culminating sign, whereas Firmicus has some language about a specific degree or degrees being involved. Is the difference then that Rhetorius was using whole sign houses, while Firmicus was using equal houses? If that is the case, then what did the underlying source text originally say? The fact that there are some delineations of specific placements given in Firmicus that would only be possible in whole sign houses implies that the original source text did take whole sign placements into account to some extent.[128] For example, at one point Firmicus gives a delineation for the Sun in the first place in a day chart, although this would only be possible using the whole sign house system, since in the equal and quadrant house systems the first place lies entirely underneath the horizon.[129]

While this seems to establish that the whole sign house system was used in the original source text to some extent, that does not necessarily mean that this was the only system that was used. There are a few isolated instances elsewhere in the same chapter of Rhetorius where he also uses language that might imply that specific degrees are involved with the angles, using the uncommon Greek word *homokentros*. Rhetorius only uses this word a few times in his entire treatment of the places in this chapter, but there are two points that are clear: (1) the term only appears in the second set of delineations that are from the same source as Firmicus, and (2) the term only appears when Rhetorius is

---

[126] Firmicus, *Mathesis*, 3, 3: 18, trans. Holden, p. 107, modified.

[127] Rhetorius, *Compendium*, 57 (CCAG, 8, 4, p. 168: 6–9), trans. Holden, p. 93, modified.

[128] As noted in Holden, *A History*, p. 74, fn. 170.

[129] Firmicus, *Mathesis*, 3, 5: 3. The parallel passage in Rhetorius starts by talking about the Sun in the rising sign in what is implicitly a day chart, and then halfway through it explicitly switches to talking about it in a night chart. Rhetorius, *Compendium*, 57 (CCAG, 8, 4: p. 136: 9–20).

talking about the first and tenth places. The word *homokentros* seems to correspond to Firmicus' use of the word *partiliter* when talking about the four angular places. Surveying other authors that use the same term, Valens uses *homokentros* twice in the *Anthology*, and both times it seems to refer to when two planets are "located at the same angular place."[130] It is also used twice in Hephaestio/Antigonus, in the example chart of Hadrian, where it is used to refer to the placement of the Moon and Jupiter in the chart, which are both conjunct the Ascendant, and thus "located at the same angular place."[131] It is perhaps worth noting that in this example, the Moon and Jupiter are both conjunct the exact degree of the Ascendant in the first degree of Aquarius, and this may help us to understand Firmicus' usage of this concept. There may have been a general sense of the term *homokentros* which simply involved two planets being in the same angular whole sign house, and then there may have been a more idealized version of the placement in which the two planets were exactly conjoining each other to the degree while also being exactly on the degree of the angle. If that is the case, then Firmicus may have been emphasizing the degree placement each time in his delineations because that was the most idealized form of the specific placement, when it was angular both by sign and by degree.

Rhetorius only uses the term *homokentros* when talking about the first and tenth places. As stated earlier, these are also the only places in the second set of delineations that he shares with Firmicus where the places are explicitly described as signs, although Rhetorius seems to use the word *homokentros* as his keyword occasionally to modify the delineation by referring to the specific degrees associated with those angles. The end result is that Rhetorius presents two delineations for the same placement: one in which the planet is in the angular place just by sign, and another when it is in the angular place to the exact degree. The distinction seems to be one of intensity, since the placements by degree generally seem to be interpreted as more extreme or idealized, whereas the placements by sign are toned down a bit. An example of this is when Rhetorius gives two delineations back-to-back for the Moon in the tenth place, with the first referring to the idealized placement of the Moon on the Midheaven degree, and the other just in the Midheaven sign:

> The Moon chancing to be of the sect, in the Midheaven sign (*zōidion*), on the same spot as the angle (*homokentros*), will produce great rulers, kings, rulers of life and death. Chancing to be in the Midheaven place [only]

---

[130] Valens, *Anthology*, 2, 4: 1; 2, 38: 16.
[131] Hephaestio, *Apotelesmatika*, 2, 18: 33; 48.

according to sign (*zōidiakōs*): those who are great in their actions and in those efforts with which they are entrusted or which they do for their own benefit, those who receive money.[132]

Firmicus has a very similar although somewhat expanded delineation in the parallel passage for the same placement:

> The Moon posited in the tenth place from the Hour-Marker, i.e. the MC, if it was found partially in this place in a nocturnal nativity in those signs in which it is exalted or in which it rejoices—namely, increasing in light, and with Jupiter protecting it with fortunate aspects—it will make the greatest Emperors or powerful administrators, to whom the power of life and death is entrusted in ready fashion. When posited thus, it also gives ordinary consulates. But if it either precedes or follows the MC degree in the next place (*locus*) and is located in nearby degrees, it will produce generals, tribunes, and administrators; but if it is plactically posited in the same sign (*signum*), it yields those who are great in all their actions and adorned with various kinds of good fortune.[133]

What is interesting here is that both authors are emphasizing the exact degree of the Midheaven as indicating the most ideal and powerful placement, while indicating gradations for anything outside of that. Both agree that one of those gradations is just being in the sign associated with the Midheaven; Firmicus adds an additional one of being in the vicinity of the degree of the Midheaven but in a different place. If the Midheaven degree that Firmicus is using here is the equal house Midheaven that he outlined in book 2, then this implies that he is using whole sign houses and equal houses together in this chapter. It is interesting that Rhetorius does not mention this additional gradation, leaving it unclear whether it was in the original text or whether this was added in by Firmicus himself due to his personal emphasis on using equal houses as a secondary overlay.

The other instances of the use of the word *homokentros* in Rhetorius occur when he is talking about the first place. Most of the delineations of planets in the first place in this chapter are given by Rhetorius in terms of the entire rising sign, but when he talks about the Sun and Moon he gives different gradations again based on the proximity to the exact degree of the Ascendant:

---

[132] Rhetorius, *Compendium*, 57 (CCAG, 8, 4: p. 170: 5–9), trans. Holden, p. 95, modified.
[133] Firmicus, *Mathesis*, 3, 13: 9, trans. Holden, p. 169, modified.

The Moon being of the sect in the sign of the Hour-Marker, making application to none [of the planets], will be judged to be not good. But chancing to be on the same angle (*homokentros*) of the Hour-Marker, she will produce those in command, rulers, magnates, kings [...] But chancing to be of the sect in the Hour-Marking sign (*zōidion*), she will produce priests who handle temple funds or high priests or those who preside over the sacred games or who have actions and benefits in sacred things [...] And in general, when the Moon is void of course in the important places (*topoi*) of the nativity, no good will be produced. You are helped to decide [by noting] in which place (*topos*) of the nativity she is [and] what phase she was allotted; for, if she chances to be in the sign of the Hour-Marker by day, on the same spot as the angle (*homokentros*), she will produce ship-masters or pirates or those in charge of places that are difficult to traverse.[134]

Again, Rhetorius is alternating between interpreting the placement just by sign versus when it is exactly on the angle by degree, and the interpretation when the placement is exact by degree often involves themes of greater eminence or power. The parallel delineation in Firmicus is shorter and seems to focus more on the placements being exact to the degree:

The Moon partilely (*partiliter*) posited in the Hour-Marker in a nocturnal nativity, if it was full and found in those signs in which it rejoices, denotes great increases of good fortune. It makes the native to be put first among his brothers, both by age always and by merit. But if it was found partilely in this place by day, it will make pilots of major ships.[135]

What we seem to be seeing here is a tension in the later Hellenistic tradition, where Rhetorius is describing the places largely as signs and then occasionally in terms of specific degrees, whereas Firmicus has a distinct tendency to emphasize the degrees associated with the angular places, and then only occasionally mentions them in terms of signs. Clearly the underlying source text that both Rhetorius and Firmicus were drawing on said something in the original delineations about planets in the four angular places being the most powerful when they are located at the exact degrees associated with the angles, but it seems as if Firmicus may have extended this so that the power of the equal houses as a secondary overlay was conceptualized as spreading beyond the sign boundary in some instances,

---

[134] Rhetorius, *Compendium*, 57 (CCAG, 8, 4: p. 138: 3–22), trans. Holden, pp. 54–5, modified.

[135] Firmicus, *Mathesis*, 3, 13: 1, trans. Holden, p. 166, modified.

certainly for dynamic purposes, and perhaps even for topical purposes. Rhetorius seems less clear on this point, as he almost seems to want to restrict his use of the secondary overlay as being for dynamic purposes, since the discussion of the degree of the angle is typically limited to the specific sign that is involved in, as a range of degrees within that sign that confer additional power and intensity to the delineation. At one point when he gives the delineation for the Sun in the first place, he situates it within the context of the entire rising sign, but he does distinguish between the "angular" part of the sign and what is presumably the non-angular part of the sign:

> The Sun being upon the sign (*zōidion*) of the Hour-Marker, on the same spot as the angle (*homokentros*), will produce kings or commanders [...] But by night this god being upon the sign (*zōidion*) of the Hour-Marker indicates that the parents will be lower class. [...] But always the Sun, when he is present in the angular (*epikentros*) portions of the signs will become the destroyer of the elder brothers, but it also indicates that some [of the natives] are first born or first nourished.[136]

There is also some uncertainty surrounding which house system Rhetorius would have used in these delineations when it comes to determining what the range is after the degrees of the angles that would be considered more active, although we do know from elsewhere in his *Compendium* that he used quadrant houses as his secondary overlay for dynamic purposes. For example, later in the *Compendium* Rhetorius delineates an example chart of a native who was a scholar that suffered a downfall after taking part in a revolt.[137] Rhetorius outlines all of the placements in the chart, and then when he proceeds with the delineation he jumps back and forth between analyzing the placement of the planets by whole sign house, which he calls "by sign," and then by quadrant house, which he calls "by degree." Here is the first part of the delineation:

> Investigating the foregoing nativity, I found the Moon and Saturn and Venus and Mars by degree to have been declining, but by sign the Moon

---

[136] Rhetorius, *Compendium*, 57 (CCAG, 8, 4: p. 136: 9–20), trans. Holden, pp. 52–3, modified. The editors of the CCAG emended the text and added Saturn as being *homokentros* with the Sun on the degree of Ascendant based on a comparison with the parallel passage in Firmicus. I am not clear if this was an appropriate insertion to make, as Rhetorius could have just been talking about the Sun being on the degree of the angle, as he did with the Moon. On the other hand, the delineation here is a bit more negative than one might expect, so perhaps Saturn was originally supposed to be mentioned in the text.

[137] Rhetorius, *Compendium*, 113.

and Saturn and Venus angular, and the Sun and Mercury and Jupiter by sign to have been declining, but by degree the Sun chanced to be in the succedent of the Setting [place]. I see then Saturn being ruler of the Hour-Marker and first ruler of the triplicity of the Hour-Marker and of the [sect] light, signifying the first age, in the decline of the Subterraneous angle and retrograde and aspected by Mars with an equal-sided trine, but also Venus, ruler of it and of the Moon posited in opposition to her. How could he have not had a troublesome first age...[138]

The important point here is that Rhetorius was using quadrant houses as his secondary overlay for dynamic purposes, whereas Firmicus seems to have been using equal houses. This is similar then to the parallel we find with Valens and Ptolemy, where the former used quadrant houses and the latter used equal houses for dynamic purposes. It is left ambiguous what the original source text that Firmicus and Rhetorius shared in common would have used, since it only seems to have emphasized the degrees of the four angles, and used them to determine which planets were the most "busy" or powerful within the broader context of whatever whole sign house they were placed in. The point that is clear, however, is that by the time of Firmicus and Rhetorius in the later Hellenistic tradition these secondary overlays were being used for more general purposes in order to interpret the basic placement of planets in the birth chart, and they were no longer restricted to only being used within the context of certain techniques. While there was still a tendency to use the secondary overlays more for dynamic purposes rather than for topical purposes, by the later part of the Hellenistic tradition, the other forms of house division had become integrated into the system to such an extent that they were always used alongside whole sign houses.

Concluding Remarks

At this point I think we can understand some of the statements by the later Medieval astrologers that I opened this discussion with, about how there seemed to be some confusion in the inherited tradition regarding whether the first house began with the rising sign or the rising degree. This issue had its origins in the earliest strata of the Hellenistic tradition, where we find the whole sign house system being introduced in the text attributed to Hermes

---

[138] Rhetorius, *Compendium*, 113, trans. Holden, p. 160–161, modified. Holden says that Rhetorius uses the so-called Alcabitius house system here (p. 160, fn. 5). Levente László points out privately that while Alcabitius may be used in one other nativity in Rhetorius' *Compendium*, it is not clear if this example uses the Alcabitius or Porphyry house system.

Trismegistus, the equal house system being introduced in the text of Asclepius, and some form of quadrant houses likely being described in the compilation of Nechepso-Petosiris. While I believe that it is still safe to say that the whole sign house system was the original and the primary form of house division in the Hellenistic tradition, it is clear that from a very early stage, other foundational authors thought it was necessary to introduce other forms of house division to use alongside whole sign houses as a secondary overlay. It does appear that most of the time these secondary overlays were used for dynamic purposes, in order to gauge angularity and planetary strength, whereas whole sign houses tended to be used more for determining topics or areas of life. I would suggest that this has to do with the fact that many of the significations associated with the places are closely tied in with the sign-based aspect that each of the whole sign places have with the rising sign as well as to each other. To the extent that the aspect doctrine was originally intertwined with the signs of the zodiac in the Hellenistic tradition, many of the basic meanings that were first developed for the twelve houses in the Hellenistic tradition are conceptually predicated on the framework of whole sign houses.

That being said, it is also clear that from a very early period in the Hellenistic tradition, there was an attempt to integrate and reconcile the different frames of reference that equal houses and quadrant houses represent. The reason for this is that each of these frames of reference has some independent symbolic value, and this provided the early astrologers with an impetus to integrate them in some way. Moreover, even if there was a tendency to use equal houses and quadrant houses mainly for dynamic purposes in the Hellenistic tradition, we can also clearly see that steps were being made towards using them for topical purposes, such as Valens' use of the meridian to import tenth house topics into other whole sign houses, or Firmicus' apparent desire to treat equal houses as a secondary overlay for topical purposes, perhaps motivated by statements going back to the Asclepius text. In this way the eventual transition towards using quadrant or equal houses for topical purposes in the later Medieval tradition seems to represent the next step in a process that was already occurring in the Hellenistic tradition. An unfortunate side effect of this process was that the discussion eventually shifted entirely towards determining which form of quadrant house division was the most accurate, and in the process the concept of whole sign houses as a system was completely forgotten as the tradition progressed. This was an unfortunate loss because of the important conceptual and practical role that the whole sign house system plays in the overall system, as well as the fact that it was always meant to be used together with the other systems of house division.

In what follows I will continue to use whole sign houses as my primary approach to house division in this work, since many of the techniques of Hellenistic astrology were originally developed and practiced within the context of that approach, and I consider it to be the most representative of the Hellenistic tradition in general, for reasons that should be clear at this point. Part of the purpose of this book, then, is to demonstrate the efficacy of the whole sign house system, and to teach the reader how to use that approach in practice. However, I will occasionally incorporate Valens' topical use of the degrees of the meridian-Midheaven and IC, as well as Paulus' use of close configurations to the degrees of the Ascendant and meridian-Midheaven as mitigating factors, as I have found both of these considerations to be very useful in practice. I encourage the reader to explore the house division issue more deeply, since ultimately a hybrid approach that incorporates some elements of the whole sign and other house systems is desirable in terms of the contemporary practice of astrology, and we can see that this was the direction that the tradition was headed by the time of Rhetorius. It is not clear whether this synthesis is something that was fully accomplished during the Hellenistic tradition, though, so it is not my place to present such an innovation here.

Chapter 12
The Domicile Lord
of the Hour-Marker

———— ❊ ————

In Hellenistic astrology there were several methods for identifying different planetary rulers in a chart that play an important role in shaping the quality and direction of a native's life. One of the most important chart rulers is the domicile lord of the Hour-Marker: the planet that rules the rising sign. Valens singles out the domicile lord of the Hour-Marker as one of the first things that should be considered when examining a birth chart:

> For every nativity, after the stars have been accurately charted, it will be necessary to examine how the domicile lord is configured, which stars it has witnessing it, whether it is rising or setting [under the beams], and whether it has a familiar or foreign relation to the sect.[1]

Because the first place is the part of the chart that is most closely associated with the native, the domicile lord of the Hour-Marker becomes one of the most important planets in the chart for describing the focus, topics, and dominant themes of the native's life. Valens refers to this at one point as relating to the "actualizations of the soul" (*psuchēs energēmata*):

> To begin with, one must survey the hour-marking pivot, and how the master of this was figured. For if it chances to be present in the Hour-Marker or present familiarly in another, it is good for the vital times and for the actualizations of the soul. But if it chances to be setting or is figured

---

[1] Valens, *Anthology*, 7, 2: 2, trans. Riley, p. 24, significantly modified.

oppositely or unfamiliarly, it is difficult; for having completed either the ascensional time of the hour-marking zodiacal sign, or the ascensional time of the zodiacal sign upon which it is present, or the period of that star whose zodiacal sign it is, it abandons the times [of life]. And if it chances to be so, it makes those who are short-lived.[2]

Here we can see that Valens is associating the first place both with the spirit as well as the body or physical vitality of the native. This association between the ruler of the Ascendant and the native's health and longevity comes up in other places in the *Anthology* as well. For example, at one point in the second book Valens says:

In general, malefics which behold the luminaries and the Hour-Marker with no benefics configured make men short-lived. If the ruler of the Hour-Marker lies in its proper place or in its own sect, it becomes the bestower of long lifespans. If it is configured with the lord of the Lot of Fortune, the native becomes full of years and fortunate. If the ruler happens to be setting, the native becomes short-lived.[3]

The domicile lord of the Hour-Marker also has some role to play in informing character traits on the part of the native. In his discussion of the qualities associated with the signs of the zodiac, Valens lists a number of traits for "those born in" or "born under" each sign, which seems to mean that the native is born with the Hour-Marker in that particular sign.[4] For example, for Taurus he says:

Men born under this sign are noble, energetic, toilsome, good at keeping things, pleasure-loving, music-loving, generous. Some are laborers, propagators, planters.[5]

However, Valens says that these interpretations can be modified for better or worse based on the condition of the domicile lord of the sign:

If benefics incline toward this place or if the domicile lord is favorably situated, men become priests and school superintendents, as well as those

---

[2] Valens, *Anthology*, 7, 2: 5–7, trans. Schmidt, modified.

[3] Valens, *Anthology*, 2, 4: 13–14, trans. Riley, p. 27, modified.

[4] The parallel delineations from Teucer/Rhetorius explicitly say that they are for those who were born with the Ascendant or Moon in that sign of the zodiac (CCAG 7, p. 196: 4).

[5] Valens, *Anthology*, 1, 2: 16, trans. Riley, p. 3, modified.

judged worthy of crowns and of the purple, of monuments and statues; also supervisors of temples and distinguished and brilliant individuals.[6]

Here the delineation is improved, and many of the most positive facets of Taurus and Venus are brought to the forefront in the native's life when benefics are configured to the first place, or when the domicile lord of the Hour-Marker is well-situated in the chart. Valens makes some similar statements when talking about Aries:

> Depending on its relationship with the domicile lord, men born under this sign will be brilliant, distinguished, authoritarian, just, hard on offenders, free, governing, bold in thought, boastful, great-hearted, restless, unstable, haughty, inflated, intimidating, quickly changing, wealthy. When the domicile lords are favorably situated and have benefics witnessing, kings and powerful men are born, those having the say over life and death.[7]

Here the characteristics of Aries and its domicile lord, Mars, become personal character traits of the native because they are related to the first place: the place of self. However, some of the most positive interpretations are only made when the domicile lord of the Ascendant is well-situated and configured to benefic planets. Valens later summarizes this principle by saying that the significations of the domicile lord will tend to manifest in the respective signs that the planet rules, but that these significations can be altered for better or worse depending on the condition of the planet:

> In general, whatever the domicile ruler usually produces according to its own nature, whether good or bad, greater or lesser, this it produces in each of the signs according to the advantageous or disadvantageous figure-description of the domicile lord.[8]

This principle goes back to the conceptual notion of the planets treating the signs of the zodiac as their homes or domiciles, but here we have an additional modification of this doctrine that states that the quality of the significations that are expressed through the zodiacal signs can be modified depending on the condition of the ruler of the sign. This is important because it implies that while each of the signs have certain core properties, the way that those qualities

---

[6] Valens, *Anthology*, 1, 2: 16, trans. Riley, p. 3, modified.

[7] Valens, *Anthology*, 1, 2: 1–2, trans. Riley, p. 2, modified.

[8] Valens, *Anthology*, 1, 2: 20, trans. Riley, p. 3, modified.

manifest will always vary from chart to chart depending on the placement of the ruling planet. Nowhere is this more pronounced or more important than when it comes to the analysis of the domicile lord of the Hour-Marker.

The Nautical Metaphor

The first place is commonly referred to in ancient astrological texts as the "Helm" (*oiax*), which is a designation that evidently goes back to the original Hermes text on the *dōdekatropos*, as cited by Thrasyllus.[9] Originally the Greek term referred to the handle of the rudder or tiller on a ship, although it came to mean more broadly the "helm" or the position on a ship from which it is steered. In an astrological context, the question arises: if there is a helm in a natal chart, then what is the ship, and who exactly is steering it?

Schmidt took this reference to the first place as the Helm and another reference to nautical themes at one point in Porphyry's *Introduction* as evidence of an elaborate interpretive metaphor that may have been used by ancient astrologers in order to understand the function of different components of the chart.[10] Some of the references to nautical themes in the surviving texts certainly seem suggestive, although it is not entirely clear how far the Hellenistic astrologers took them.

One piece of evidence that seems to support the existence of an extended nautical metaphor in chart interpretations occurs in one of the surviving papyrus horoscopes from Oxyrhynchus.[11] This horoscope is fragmentary, but it refers to the Hour-Marker as the Helm, and in the next line there is a broken reference to a "steersman," "pilot," or "captain" (*kubernētēs*). This seems to imply that the planet in charge of the Helm would be considered the steersman of the ship. The natural candidate for this is the domicile lord of the Hour-Marker, since that is the primary planet that is in charge of the rising sign at the moment of birth. The role of the domicile lord of the Hour-Marker, then, is that it is in control of the Helm, and its purpose is to steer the native's life towards a specific place or destination. Thus, the steersman acts as a sort of navigator or guide.

The Steersman of the Ship

In his text on embryology, Porphyry argues that the soul enters the body at the moment of birth, and in support of this argument he says that this was also the view of the astrologers in his time.[12] He makes the analogy that the gestation

---

[9] CCAG, 8, 3, p. 101: 16–18.

[10] Schmidt, *Definitions and Foundations*, p. 325. Cf. Porphyry, *Introduction*, 30.

[11] Jones, *Astronomical Papyri from Oxyrhynchus*, horoscope 4277 (vol. 2, p. 421).

[12] Porphyry, *To Gaurus on How Embryos are Ensouled*, 16: 5–6.

of the physical body is like a ship being built, and that birth is like the launch of the ship; it is here that the captain or steersman (*kubernētēs*) gets on board to navigate.[13]

This analogy is complicated somewhat by the existence of other rulers of the chart. In his *Introduction* to Ptolemy's *Tetrabiblos*, Porphyry distinguishes between the "Master" (*oikodespotēs*) and the "Lord" (*kurios*) of the nativity, which were thought to be two separate rulers that had dominion over the entire chart (and thus the life of the native).[14] Porphyry emphasizes that the Master and Lord of the nativity are distinct rulers that have separate roles, and then he compares them to the different jobs of a captain (*kubernētēs*) and shipowner (*nauklēros*). Schmidt takes this passage as further evidence of the use of a complex nautical metaphor as an underlying interpretive principle in Hellenistic astrology.[15] Nautical analogies were not uncommon in Greek literature, especially amongst the Platonists, but Porphyry may simply have been making a general analogy here rather than outlining a specific interpretive principle in astrology in this chapter. Unfortunately it is not clear. Thus, the only firm textual support we have for the nautical metaphor seems to be the association of the domicile lord of the Hour-Marker with the steersman of the ship.

The Domicile Lord in the Twelve Places

One of the most important interpretive principles when examining the domicile lord of the Hour-Marker is to ascertain which of the twelve places it is located in. Oftentimes the native's life will somehow be focused on or directed towards the topics associated with that particular place, often in a way that stands out as being more important or more distinct than other areas of the native's life. When Valens first introduces the twelve places in book two of the *Anthology*, the interpretations he gives for each place are partially predicated on having the domicile lord of the Hour-Marker located there, since when that happens those topics were understood as becoming more notable in the overall direction of the native's life.[16]

For example, individuals that have the domicile lord of the Hour-Marker in the tenth place will sometimes be led towards focusing on their occupation and reputation, which are significations of the tenth place. A modern example of someone with this placement is J. Paul Getty, who was the founder and owner of a major oil company in the mid-twentieth century. He was born with Capricorn

---

[13] Porphyry, *To Gaurus*, 10: 4.
[14] Porphyry, *Introduction*, 30.
[15] Schmidt, *Definitions and Foundations*, p. 325.
[16] Valens, *Anthology*, 2, 4–15.

rising, and Saturn exalted in Libra in the tenth place in a day chart. He was the richest person in America in the 1950s, and then in the entire world by the 1960s. His obituary in the *New York Times* described his focus on his career and reputation:

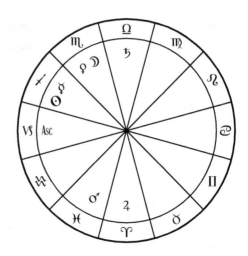

Chart 1 - J. Paul Getty

'I don't think there is any story in being known as a moneybags,' he asserted in his Oklahoma drawl. 'I'd rather be considered a businessman.' Indeed, business was Mr. Getty's life. One of his former wives once remarked, perhaps astringently, that business was his 'first love' and that wealth was merely a byproduct. Describing how he often worked 16 and 18 hours a day to handle the complex transactions of his multifarious business dealings, Mr. Getty seemed to agree. 'I can't remember a single day of vacation in the last 45 years that was not somehow interrupted by a cable, telegram or telephone call that made me tend to business for at least a few hours,' he wrote in 1965. 'Such work schedules and the need for devoting the majority of my time to business have taken a heavy toll on my personal life.' [...] He thought of himself as a man who yearned for privacy. Yet certainly after Fortune emblazoned his wealth, he courted publicity.[17]

Individuals with the domicile lord of the Hour-Marker in different places find their focus directed towards other topics or areas of their life. For example, someone with the domicile lord in the fourth place might find issues surrounding their home or parents to be more prominent in guiding or dictating the course of their life compared to other people. An example of this is Prince Charles, who was born with Leo rising, and the Sun in Scorpio in the fourth whole sign place. He is the eldest child of Queen Elizabeth II, and heir apparent to the British throne. There has been a lingering question for much of his life about when or if he will inherit the throne from his mother and become king. His mother became Queen when he was three years old, more than sixty years ago; not only is he the longest-serving heir apparent in British history, the Queen herself has recently

---

[17] Alden Whitman, "J. Paul Getty Dead at 83; Amassed Billions From Oil," *New York Times*, June 6, 1976.

become the longest-reigning British monarch in history. This has led to some frustration on his part that his reign has not yet begun. Although the Queen is the Head of State, Charles will often travel for other official business on behalf of his mother, or on behalf of the United Kingdom.

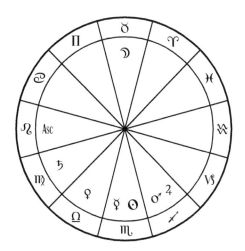

Chart 2 - Prince Charles

Sometimes when the ruler of the Ascendant is located in one of the more difficult places, the topics that the native's life is directed towards can be more challenging or problematic. For example, Che Guevara was born with Aries rising, and Mars in Pisces in the twelfth place. When he was in college he took two long journeys across South America that had a major impact on his life direction. After witnessing widespread poverty, illness, exploitation, and disenfranchisement throughout Latin America, he decided that the only solution was armed revolution. He subsequently became a major figure in the Cuban Revolution, and later traveled the world attempting to foment revolutions in other countries,

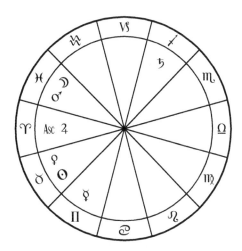

Chart 3 - Che Guevara

but was eventually captured and executed by foreign enemies while fighting in Bolivia. Here we see some of the major themes of the twelfth place becoming prominent in his life, such as suffering, enemies, and travel. In different ways each of these became important factors in shaping his life direction in a very unique way.

Another example of difficulties manifesting in connection with the placement of the ruler of the rising sign is Franklin D. Roosevelt, who was the thirty-second President of the United States, from 1933 to 1945. He was born with Virgo rising, and Mercury in Aquarius in the sixth place. He contracted polio in his late thirties, which resulted in permanent paralysis from the waist down. He returned to politics after recovering, eventually becoming President, but since people with disabilities were looked down upon at that time in history, he kept his condition a secret. He was the first President of the United States with a significant physical disability. For the rest of his life he was committed to finding a way to rehabilitate himself as well as others afflicted with polio. The foundation that he established eventually went on to fund the development of the polio vaccine, which led to the near eradication of polio as a disease only a few decades

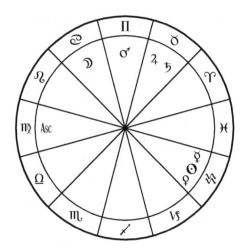

Chart 4 - Franklin D. Roosevelt

later. In this way the domicile lord of the Hour-Marker can show themes and struggles that are prominent in the native's personal life, but sometimes it can also indicate areas where the native's life has a broader or more lasting impact on the world around them.

Sometimes the positive or negative themes that a native encounters within the context of the place arise from the presence of benefics or malefics in that place, copresent with the domicile lord of the Hour-Marker. For example, Christopher Reeve, a famous actor best known for having played Superman in movies in the 1970s and 80s, was born with Leo rising and the Sun in the third place (Libra). He had a night chart, and his Sun was copresent with both Venus (benefic of the sect) and Saturn (malefic contrary to the sect). With the domicile lord of the Hour-Marker in the third, themes involving travel seem to have been prominent throughout his life; he was fond of flying planes and sailing in his spare time. With the malefic contrary to the sect in this place we would also expect it to coincide with some of his greatest difficulties. In 1995 he was

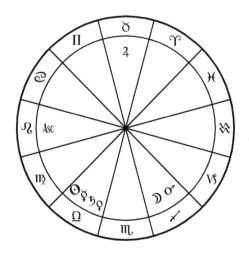

Chart 5 - Christopher Reeve

injured in a horse riding accident that left him quadriplegic. He subsequently used his fame to draw attention to people with spinal injuries and disabilities, and he founded the Christopher and Dana Reeve Foundation, which is dedicated to curing spinal cord injuries by funding research, as well as improving the quality of life for people living with paralysis. In the years following his injury, Reeve did much to promote research on spinal cord injury, as well as other neurological disorders. Here the symbolic theme of travel associated with the third place seems to have been extended to broader themes of mobility in general, as well as his physical health in connection with the ruler of the Ascendant.

The ability of the placements to have very literal personal meanings to the native as well as broader symbolic meanings pertaining to the world at large comes up in just about every place. For example, oftentimes placements in the fifth can indicate circumstances surrounding the native's own children or the subject of childbirth, but sometimes these placements can relate more broadly to themes surrounding the topic of children in general in the native's life. A good example of this is Judy Blume, who is a famous author who writes books for children and teenagers. She was born with Libra rising, and Venus in Aquarius in the fifth place in a night chart. In 1996 she won the prestigious Margaret A. Edwards Award from the American Library Association, and her books have sold over eighty million copies and have been translated into more than thirty languages. She began writing children's books while her own children were in preschool, and at the present time she has written over two dozen books.

The placement of the domicile lord of the Hour-Marker seems to show an area of the person's life that they sometimes gravitate towards or become fascinated with, even if it is an area that others might consider

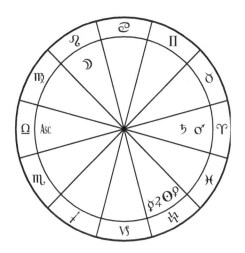

Chart 6 - Judy Blume

to be odd or unappealing. Sometimes having the domicile lord of the Hour-Marker in an inauspicious place, such as the eighth, can mean that the topics of that place, such as death, have a broader, more abstract role in the person's life. The late astrologer Richard Houck was born with Capricorn rising and Saturn in Leo in the eighth place in a night chart. Today he is perhaps most well known for a book he published in 1994 entitled *The Astrology of Death*. In the book he blended modern western and Indian astrology, and said that it was the first book ever written in the history of astrology solely on the topic of death. As a result of his own premature death at the age of 53, his book *The Astrology of Death* ended up representing a large part of his legacy in the astrological community.

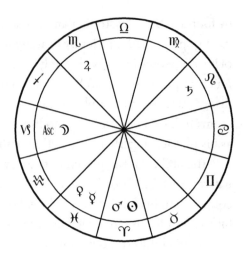

The ruler of the Ascendant can also reveal areas or people in the native's life that are somehow necessary to work with in order to arrive at their intended destination in life, or that can help the native accomplish whatever their life's focus is. For example, scientist Carl Sagan was born with Taurus rising and

Chart 7 - Richard Houck

Venus in Scorpio in the seventh place. He was married three times, first to Lynn Margulis from 1957–1963, then to Linda Salzman from 1968–1981, and finally to Ann Druyan from 1981–1996. His focus on his career was a contributing

factor to the breakup of his first two marriages, with Saturn in Aquarius in the tenth place squaring the Scorpio stellium in the seventh. His second two marriages became more tied in with his career and overall life direction. He collaborated with Margulis on the design of the plaques on the Pioneer 10 and 11 space probes (she did the artwork). He was able to find a way to compromise by the time of his third marriage by working together with his wife on professional projects. They co-wrote a few books together, and also

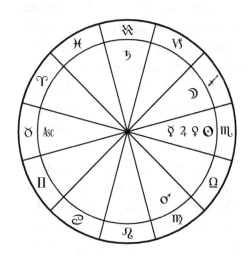

Chart 8 - Carl Sagan

worked together on the *Cosmos* television series, which he hosted and became well known for around the world. She carried on some of his work after he died in 1996, becoming a producer on the movie *Contact*, based on the book they co-wrote; she was later credited as a creator, producer, and writer of the follow-up series in 2014, *Cosmos: A Spacetime Odyssey*. Relationships and marriage thus became notably linked up to Sagan's overall life direction in a unique way.

Mitigation of Difficult Placements

The difficult nature of the bad places can make the placement of the domicile lord of the Hour-Marker in these sectors coincide with challenging experiences for natives, although a spectrum of positive or constructive manifestations can still play out, especially when mitigating factors are present. For example, issues surrounding health and illness seem to come up prominently with planets in the sixth place. Sometimes this can be positive when the placement is mitigated, but if unmitigated, then illness and injury can become dominant themes. One of the things that makes the sixth place problematic is the fact that it is a decline, and as a result, planets are not *chrēmatistikos* or "busy," which weakens the planets so that they cannot manifest significations that are advantageous to the native. However, this situation can be altered under certain circumstances. As discussed earlier, in his treatment of the sixth place Paulus says that planets there can be rendered "busy" (*chrēmatistikos*) if they are configured to the meridian-Midheaven within three degrees, or even to a planet that is in an angular place such as the tenth. Paulus explains this as a general principle that applies to all of the declining places:

> One must know that there are four pivots, four post-ascensions, and four declines, and that sometimes the declines are operational (*chrematizō*) and make activity which is not random in regard to the reckoning concerning outcomes. This is whenever any of the stars which happen to be present on one of the declines should bring rays within three degrees to a figure actually being harmonious to it by triangle, either with a pivot or a star.[18]

Paulus goes on to use an example showing how this can be applied to planets in the ninth or sixth place. I've found that it seems to be helpful as a general mitigating factor for other placements as well, including the twelfth and second places. The sixth place in particular seems to manifest its significations in starkly different ways depending on whether this mitigation is present.

For example, a native who was born with Pisces rising and Jupiter in Leo has Jupiter declining in the sixth place; this is mitigated, however, because it is configured to the degree of the meridian-Midheaven within three degrees by trine, and is also being overcome by Venus in a night chart, with no difficult aspects from malefics. Thus, the ruler of the Ascendant is in the sixth, but it is mitigated and relatively well-situated. The native is a medical doctor with an interest in enhancing patient care, gravitating towards physician leadership

---

[18] Paulus, *Introduction*, 27, ed. Boer, p. 76: 13–19, trans. Greenbaum, pp. 58–9.

roles. At one point in her career she became the head of a hospital. The native's life is clearly focused on the sixth place topic of illness, but not in a way where she herself has become afflicted; instead, she spends her time helping others who are ill.

Mitigating factors are thus important to pay attention to, as they seem to help planets that are in bad places, or further improve the condition of planets that are in good places. This is especially the case when they are made busy through their configuration to the degrees of the angles.

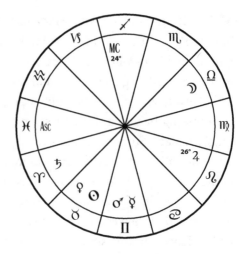

Chart 9 - Doctor

Ruler of the Hour-Marker in the First Place

When the domicile lord of the Hour-Marker is itself located in the first place it takes control of the Helm directly. What this means in practical terms is that the natural significations of the planet that is the domicile lord come to the forefront in characterizing the native's life direction and focus. For example, in his delineations of different planets ruling the Hour-Marker, Valens says:

> If Saturn is allotted the Hour or the Lot <of Fortune> and is in the Hour-Marker, with Mars not in opposition, the native will be fortunate in activities controlled by Saturn.[19]

That is to say, the native will excel or be fortunate in the activities that are proper to Saturn, since Saturn here would be in its own domicile and in the first place while ruling the Hour-Marker. A planet enjoys being in its own domicile because of the affinity that it shares with that sign, and thus it is a place that is most well-suited to its natural expression. When that planet is also the ruler of the Ascendant, it means that the native will tend to gravitate towards and excel at the things associated with that planet in terms of the overall course of their life.

An example of this is Pope Benedict XVI, Joseph Ratzinger, who has Pisces rising, with the domicile lord of the Hour-Marker also in Pisces, in the first place. When he was inaugurated as Pope, Ratzinger became the head of the Catholic

---

[19] Valens, *Anthology*, 2, 4: 1, trans. Riley, p. 27, modified.

Church. This clearly matches one of the significations that Valens gives for Jupiter, which signifies "heads of holy places."[20]

Another example is William Rehnquist, who had Sagittarius rising, with Jupiter in Sagittarius in the first place in a day chart. He was an American lawyer, jurist, and political figure who served as an Associate Justice of the Supreme Court of the United States, and later became the sixteenth Chief Justice. He was the head of the Supreme Court for about nineteen years, which is the highest court in the United States. According to Valens, Jupiter also signifies "justice, authorities, governments, honors [...] and the arbitration of trials."[21]

Moving on to other planets, the American poet T. S. Eliot was born with Libra rising and Venus ruling the Hour-Marker, copresent with Mercury in the first place. In this instance, the combination of Venus and Mercury results in poetry, or aesthetically pleasing speech. The favorable placement of Venus in its own domicile indicated that he would excel in the arts; he won the Nobel Prize for Literature in 1948 for his pioneering contributions to contemporary poetry.

Filmmaker George Lucas was born with Taurus rising and Venus ruling the Hour-Marker in the first

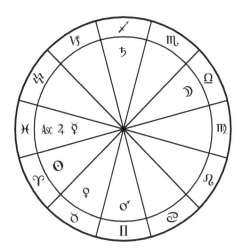

Chart 10 - Pope Benedict XVI

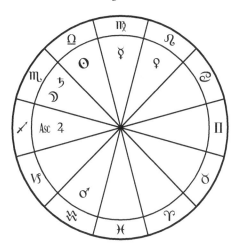

Chart 11 - William Rehnquist

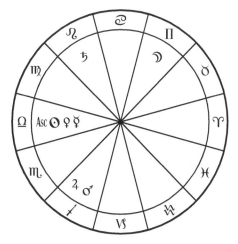

Chart 12 - T. S. Eliot

[20] Valens, *Anthology*, 1, 1: 17.
[21] Valens, *Anthology*, 1, 1: 17.

place. He became interested in making movies while in college, and received a Bachelor of Fine Arts in film. He went on to become a director, being most well known for his role in creating the Star Wars and Indiana Jones films. An interesting additional Venusian theme with Lucas is that his movies incorporated many themes, ideas, and aesthetics from other earlier films and shows, perhaps due to the unifying principle of Venus.

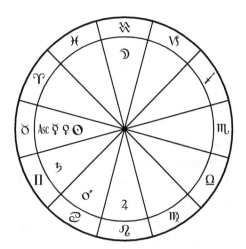

Chart 13 - George Lucas

Steve Wozniak provides a good example of Mercury rising while in its domicile and thus ruling the Hour-Marker (Mercury in Virgo in the first place). Wozniak is a computer programmer who co-founded Apple Computer, Inc. with Steve Jobs. He was the programmer and technical genius, while Jobs was the visionary and marketing guru. According to Rhetorius, "Mercury in the Hour-Marker makes the natives intelligent, prudent, [and] ingenious."[22] Mercury in Virgo especially tends to excel at technical activities, which in a modern context can include things such as programming and computers.

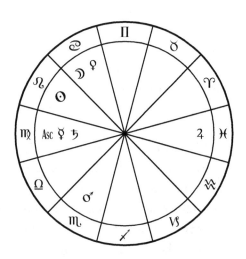

Chart 14 - Steve Wozniak

One of the general points here is that there are a range of different ways in which the archetype of a planet can manifest as a specific career or focus in life, although in each instance the life focus does end up being directed towards something that is under the general dominion of that specific planet.

Planets in the First and Physical Appearance or Character

Planets in the first can sometimes describe or typify the native's physical appearance, including distinguishing features about the native's physicality.[23]

---

[22] Rhetorius, *Compendium*, 57, trans. Holden, p. 48, modified.

[23] This is something that Ptolemy talks about especially in *Tetrabiblos*, 3, 12. Cf. Hephaestio,

For example, Venus in the first is sometimes associated with people who are particularly physically attractive, since the first place represents the body and physical appearance, while Venus represents beauty and things that are aesthetically appealing. Angelina Jolie, for example, was born with 28° Cancer rising, with Venus conjunct the degree of the Hour-Marker, also at 28° Cancer. In 2006 she was listed as the most beautiful person in the world in *People* magazine's "100 Most Beautiful People" issue.

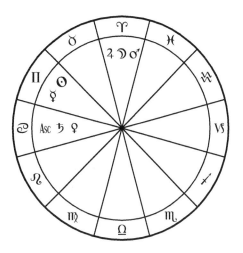

Chart 15 - Angelina Jolie

Another example is Paul Newman, who was born with 13° Capricorn rising, with Venus at 14° Capricorn in a night chart. In his obituary, the *New York Times* described him as "a strikingly handsome figure of animal high spirits and blue-eyed candor whose magnetism was almost impossible to resist."[24]

Conversely, malefics in the first place can sometimes indicate ailments or injuries to the body.[25] For example, Mars can indicate cuts or scars, while Saturn can indicate chronic illness. Planets in the first place can also indicate or modify the native's character or behavior. Since these planets are in the Helm, they can sometimes take a more significant contributing role in helping to direct the native's life, for better or worse.

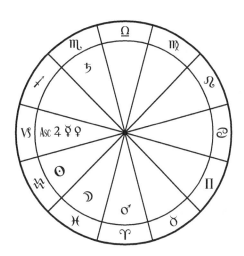

Chart 16 - Paul Newman

Apotelesmatika, 2, 12: 1.

[24] Aljean Harmetz, "Paul Newman, a Magnetic Titan of Hollywood, Is Dead at 83," *New York Times*, September 28, 2008.

[25] Ptolemy mentions the Ascendant as one of the places to examine for injury in *Tetrabiblos*, 3, 13: 1. He goes on to talk about malefics being present in this and other related places as indicating injuries or ailments. Cf. Hephaestio, *Apotelesmatika*, 2, 13: 3.

The Sect of the Ruler

The malefic that is contrary to the sect is usually the most difficult planet in the chart, and it tends to work against the interests of the native. When this planet is also the domicile lord of the Hour-Marker, sometimes the native takes on the role or agency of the malefic, since the first place is the part of the chart that represents the self. I have observed that people who have the malefic that is contrary to the sect as the ruler of the Hour-Marker sometimes tend to undermine themselves or work against their own best interests. In other words, instead of difficulties coming from other people or situations in the native's life, sometimes the difficulties come from within.

An example of this is Ted Kennedy, who was born with Capricorn rising, and Saturn in late Capricorn in the first place in a night chart. He was the younger brother of U.S. President John F. Kennedy and Robert F. Kennedy, and he was expected to succeed his brothers in becoming President of the United States after they were both assassinated in the 1960s. However, his opportunity to become President was ruined due to his involvement in a car accident, possibly while intoxicated, which resulted in the death of a woman who was with him at the time. He still went on to have a long and successful career in the United States Senate, but he never became President, largely due to this specific incident and the mistake that he made.

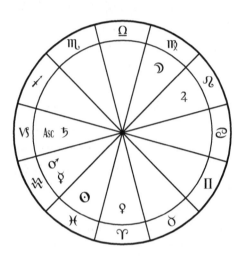

Chart 17 - Ted Kennedy

A native with Capricorn rising and Saturn in the second place (Aquarius) in a night chart was born in America during the Great Depression. The native and his family had a hard time financially when he was growing up, and he was raised very frugally. A common family

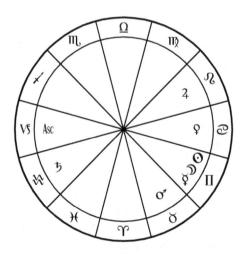

Chart 18 - Financial Anxieties

phrase around his house was "that's all we have." As a result of this, as he grew up he was always very aware of every penny he had, to the point of being somewhat obsessive. As he got older he continued to be very cautious about spending, sometimes in a way that became problematic or difficult to deal with for his family. He was eventually able to have a long and successful business career as an adult, and he was able to create a comfortable life for his family financially, although he still sometimes had concerns or anxieties surrounding money. This placement had relevance both for the native's objective external circumstances with respect to his experience of financial matters early in his life, but also his attitude or certain character traits that he developed with respect to money as a result of these experiences. The fact that Saturn was in one of its own signs helped to mitigate the negative effect that this placement might otherwise have on his finances though, so it is not the most extreme example.

The Degree of the Midheaven in Other Places

As stated previously, the degrees of the quadrant Midheaven and IC import tenth and fourth place significations into the whole sign place that they fall in. They also render the planets that they are present with both more advantageous, as well as "busy" or "energetic" (*chrēmatistikos*). In some instances, being conjunct the exact degree of the quadrant Midheaven also seems to be an eminence indicator, similar to having it in the tenth whole sign place, even if it is not in the tenth sign.

An example of this is the current Emperor of Japan. Emperor Akihito was born with Sagittarius rising, and Jupiter at 20° Libra in the eleventh sign, but conjunct the degree of the quadrant Midheaven at 16° Libra. He became Emperor in 1989 after his father Hirohito died, and while the power of the Emperor in Japan was reduced after World War II to the role of a figurehead, it is interesting to see the placement in a modern-day royal nativity.

Elizabeth II, the current Queen of the United Kingdom and other Commonwealth realms, was born with Capricorn rising and Saturn at 24° Scorpio in the eleventh whole sign place, conjunct the degree of

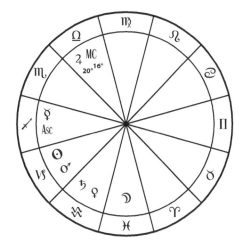

Chart 19 - Emperor Akihito

the quadrant MC at 25° Scorpio. She ascended the throne upon the death of her father in 1952, and recently became the longest-reigning British monarch in history.

Her oldest grandson, Prince William, Duke of Cambridge, has a similar placement, with Sagittarius rising and Jupiter located at 0° Scorpio in the twelfth sign, but conjunct the degree of the quadrant Midheaven at 2° Scorpio. He is second in line to succeed his grandmother, Elizabeth II, after his father Charles.

Prince William's younger brother, Prince Henry of Wales, also has a similar placement. He was born with Capricorn rising, and Saturn at 12° Scorpio in the eleventh place, conjunct the degree of the MC at 17° Scorpio.

Prince Henry was born on September 15, 1984; strangely, another prince was born just a few months earlier with similar placements. Prince Andrea Casiraghi, of the royal family of Monaco, was born June 8, 1984, with Capricorn rising, and Saturn at 10° Scorpio in the eleventh place, conjunct the degree of the MC at 9° Scorpio. As of 2016 he is currently the fourth in the line of succession in his family. Interestingly, although born just a few months prior to Harry, they have approximately the same rising degrees, and the same domicile lord of the Hour-Marker again conjunct degree of the quadrant Midheaven.

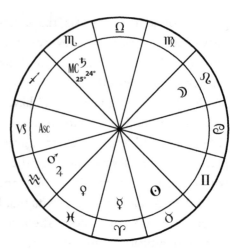

Chart 20 - Queen Elizabeth II

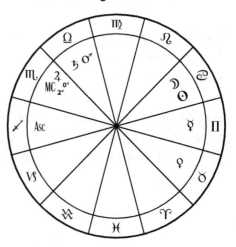

Chart 21 - Prince William

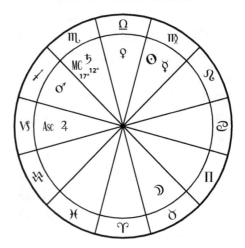

Chart 22 - Prince Henry

These examples underscore the importance of paying attention to the degree of the quadrant Midheaven, and both the topical and dynamic qualities that it can import into whatever sign in which it falls. This concept also extends to the degree of the quadrant IC, both in terms of the topical and dynamic qualities that it can import into the sign in which it falls. In this way we can start to see how the quadrant and whole sign house systems can be integrated or reconciled in some way, as well as why it is important to do so.

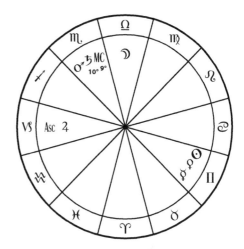

Chart 23 - Prince Andrea Casiraghi

CHAPTER 13
RULERS OF THE PLACES

———————— ✸ ————————

In book two of the *Anthology*, Valens outlines an important interpretive principle in connection with the rulers of the twelve places:

> If anyone researches thoroughly the places and the rulers, he will determine quite easily the area in which the nativity is fortunate and the area in which it is unfortunate. Whenever any star that has a relationship with the nativity (i.e. one that controls livelihood, life, injury, disease, occupation, or any of the other areas of concern) is afflicted in one respect, in that respect it will harm the nativity.[1]

Each of the planets becomes the "ruler" or "lord" of the place that coincides with the sign of the zodiac that it rules as domicile lord. For example, if Gemini coincides with the fifth place in a chart, then Mercury becomes the ruler of the fifth place. Already we have seen how this works with the domicile lord of the Hour-Marker, which is the first place, but in this chapter we will focus on how the concept of rulership can be extended to the rest of the twelve places as well. Through this, we will start to see how different parts of the chart work together.

The planet that rules a place becomes the primary representative in the chart for the significations associated with that place, even if the significations associated with that place are not ones naturally associated with that particular planet. For example, if Aquarius coincides with the seventh place, which is the

---

[1] Valens, *Anthology*, 2, 41: 13–14, trans. Riley, p. 55, modified.

place of marriage, then Saturn will come to signify the topic of marriage in that particular chart, even though marriage is not otherwise a signification that would naturally be associated with Saturn.

While planets that are actually located in places often signify things about that topic more immediately, the ruler of the place is often treated as if it is ultimately more important for the outcome of any situations associated with the place. For example, in delineating the ruler of the ninth place, Rhetorius says:

> The good [stars] being in this place make good fortune in foreign places and pious persons and righteous in religious observance, especially if the ruler of the place is also well situated and in its own domicile or exaltation and not contemplated by the malefics.[2]

Similarly, when discussing the tenth place, Valens singles out the ruler of the place as the primary determining factor for how successful or unsuccessful the native is in their work and actions: "When the ruler of this place is well situated, it makes those who are effective; but when it is poorly situated, those who are unsuccessful."[3]

The rulers of the places often seem to have been emphasized as being more important for specific topics than the general planetary significator of the same topic. So the ruler of the seventh, for example, is sometimes given more emphasis for the topic of marriage than the planet Venus. This is likely because the ruler is more individually relevant to the native, since it derives from the location of the Ascendant at the moment of birth, whereas the general planetary significator is the same for everyone who was born on the same day.

Interpretive Principles for Studying the Rulers

There are three main interpretive principles that are used when examining the rulers of the places in a chart:

1. The first principle concerns the symbolic meaning involved when the ruler of one place is located in another place, and how the significations of each place are combined. For example, if the ruler of the fifth place is in the eighth, then that evokes a specific range of interpretations. For example, Rhetorius says that the ruler of the fifth place of children in the eighth place of death can signify the death of children.[4] Elsewhere,

---

[2] Rhetorius, *Compendium*, 57, trans. Holden, p. 87, modified.
[3] Valens, *Anthology*, 2, 7: 3, trans. Schmidt, p. 11.
[4] Rhetorius, *Compendium*, 57 (CCAG, 8, 4, p. 152: 25–27).

the ruler of the seventh place of marriage in the ninth place of foreign travel is said to indicate that the native may get married to a person from a foreign country.[5]

2. The second consideration is whether the topics associated with the ruler of the place will have fortunate or unfortunate circumstances surrounding them, based purely on whether the ruler is located in a good or bad place. If the ruler is located in a good place, then the outcome will tend to be positive; if the ruler is located in a bad place, the outcome will tend to be negative. For example, if the ruler of the seventh is in the eleventh place, then that would usually be interpreted positively, since the eleventh is a good place. Conversely, if the ruler of the seventh is in the twelfth place then that would generally be interpreted negatively, since the twelfth is a bad place.

3. The third consideration is to take into account the overall condition of the ruler, such as for example whether it is in its own domicile or exaltation, if it is being bonified or maltreated, and thus whether the topics it wants to signify are being affirmed or denied, supported or corrupted, etc.

The conditions of bonification and maltreatment will be discussed in the next chapter. Here we will primarily focus on the first two considerations.

Preliminary Remarks

Before we get into the delineations of the planets in the places from Rhetorius and start looking at example charts, I want to make a few preliminary remarks about some conceptual and philosophical issues that are relevant to this topic. Many of the following points came up while I was researching this topic and working with different case studies over the past several years, and I feel that some of them need to be spelled out clearly in order to understand what we are looking at when trying to use this technique or research this specific area of astrology.

Placements as Archetypal Scenarios

One of the things that we will be focusing on here is how placements indicate possible scenarios that may play out in a person's life. By "scenario" I mean a postulated development or sequence of events. Sometimes these are one-off scenarios, while other times they recur repeatedly throughout a person's life. I have provisionally designated these as "symbolic scenarios" or "archetypal scenarios," for lack of a better term. These scenarios often indicate something

---

[5] Rhetorius, *Compendium*, 57 (CCAG, 8, 4, p. 159: 8).

that is dynamic, like a process or a sequence of events, but that play out on a symbolic level that can manifest itself in different ways.

One of the most important points about interpreting charts from a Hellenistic perspective in general, and with respect to the rulers of the places in particular, is that you must learn how to understand and interpret symbolism. Symbolism is multivalent, and can be interpreted in a number of different ways within the overall context of what is being symbolized. The symbolism can often be narrowed down or constrained by taking additional variables into consideration, since each additional variable limits the range in which the symbolism is able to manifest. But generally speaking, it is important to understand that there are a range of possible ways that a single placement can manifest itself. As we will see when we turn to the delineations in Rhetorius, we are usually presented with a few possible outcomes for any given placement or combination of placements.

The present chapter will focus primarily on what the place itself symbolizes, and how it can be symbolically combined with the meaning of another place. In the next chapter, we will spend more time demonstrating how to constrain the symbolism and squeeze out more specific interpretations by taking into account additional variables that relate to a planet's condition in the chart.

Personal versus Universal Meaning

In some instances, placements will describe the native's subjective experience of certain events in their life, while in other instances they describe things that the native's life becomes known for or contributes to the world in general. A distinction can therefore be made between (1) what the placements indicate about the person's life from a personal or subjective standpoint, versus (2) what the placements signify about the broader meaning or impact of the person's life on the world at large, i.e. in a universal or objective sense. We have seen some examples of this already through the domicile lord of the Hour-Marker, and this will continue to be a recurring theme in the rulers of the places. In some instances we will see both subjective and objective meanings occur, and while it may be possible to distinguish between the two, determining how to do so will not be our focus in this chapter.

The Self versus Others in the Chart

Modern psychological astrology tends to treat every part of the chart as an extension of the native's psyche. From a Hellenistic standpoint, however, certain parts of the chart represent the native, while other parts represent other people in the native's life in a more concrete sense. For example, the ruler of the Ascendant or Hour-Marker specifically pertains to the native, while the rulers of the other places often indicate other people, things, or situations in the native's life.

In some instances we can determine information about how those people will interact with the native, or what types of roles they will play in the native's life. This is an important distinction, because while sometimes these placements can describe how the native feels about the roles that other people play in their life, more often than not, what it describes are objective circumstances and events that take place involving other people around the native. Thus, in order to maintain clear interpretations, it is important to distinguish between that which pertains to the native in the chart, versus that which pertains to people around the native. It is also important to distinguish between the subjective experience of the native versus the objective reality of their life, as these two things are not always one and the same.

Isolated versus Persistent Themes

The placements in a person's chart indicate potential outcomes or scenarios in the person's life. Not all of these will manifest continuously throughout the course of the life. Some placements represent isolated events or situations that will only occur once, while others will manifest in different forms a few times, and still others will become persistent or recurring themes throughout life.

It is sometimes difficult to predict whether the events or themes signified by a placement will represent isolated or persistent themes. However, there may be a way to deal with this to a certain extent from a technical standpoint, since some considerations in the astrological texts supposedly indicate the persistence of a theme or lack thereof. For example, the quadruplicities are commonly mentioned in connection with the frequency with which certain placements will manifest in the life of the native. At one point Rhetorius interprets the ruler of the seventh place connected with the ruler of the eighth as indicating that the native will be widowed or divorced, and he says that this will only happen once if the configuration takes place in fixed zodiacal signs, twice if in double-bodied signs, and many times if in movable signs.[6] Additionally, in some instances, placements that indicate scenarios that will occur only once or a few times will manifest when the placements are activated as time-lords or by certain types of transits, as we will discuss later.

However, the general point here is that we need to avoid viewing everything as if it must be relevant for the entire duration of the native's life, rather than just being an important event that takes place once. The birth chart gives a set of omens that indicate what will become distinguishing characteristics about

---

[6] Rhetorius, *Compendium*, 57 (CCAG, 8, 4, p. 159: 4–6).

the native's life. Sometimes some of the most notable things that will occur in a person's life are one-time events.

Sources for the Delineations

Delineations of planets ruling places occur sporadically throughout the astrological literature in the Hellenistic tradition. For example, Valens gives some short delineations for the ruler of the Hour-Marker in each of the places (*Anthology*, 2, 4–15), but he only gives interpretations for the other rulers occasionally in this section. For some unknown reason, Rhetorius is the only source who preserves a full chapter that contains delineations for most of the rulers of the places when they are located in different places (*Compendium*, 57). It is not entirely clear where he compiled the delineations from, although they tend to fall towards the end of the first variant derived from Dorotheus, Valens, and Paulus, so he may have collected them either from some scattered references in those authors, or from a common source. Despite how late Rhetorius is, it is likely that in this instance he is preserving genuine material from earlier in the tradition that represents a common Hellenistic approach to chart delineation.

The Ruler of the Second Place

In the previous chapter we already discussed how to delineate the ruler of the first place, the domicile lord of the Hour-Marker, so here we will move straight to the second place. Although there are no delineations of the ruler of the second place in Rhetorius, in his section on the second place he does outline a general interpretive principle for how to use the ruler of a place in order to understand what will happen when it is afflicted by a malefic:

> And it seems to me that in each domicile and place that is damaged by a malefic that the loss is shown forth by the nature of the ruler of the sign, if it is a malefic, and the significations by the place.[7]

Rhetorius derives this general principle from a statement made by Dorotheus about how a loss of livelihood can come about in a native's life if malefics are configured to the second place through a sign-based aspect.[8] Rhetorius summarizes this principle from Dorotheus in the preceding paragraph: "If a malefic beholds the second place by square or opposition or conjunction, it signifies the loss of livelihood for the native."[9] He then gives some interpretations

---

[7] Rhetorius, *Compendium*, 57 (CCAG, 8, 4, p. 141: 13–16), trans. Holden, p.58.

[8] Dorotheus, *Carmen*, 1, 27: 4–12.

[9] Rhetorius, *Compendium*, 57 (CCAG, 8, 4, p. 140: 23–24), trans. Holden, p.57.

of what each planet would signify as the source of the loss of livelihood depending on the ruler of the second place:

> VENUS: losses for the sake of women or through the agency of women.
> MERCURY: for the sake of learning or calculations or inheritances or separations.
> JUPITER: he will have his loss from magnates or public affairs.
> MARS: from military affairs or suchlike persons, or from war, or burning, or a fight or from robbery or from highway robbers.
> SATURN: say that the loss is from old people or slaves or freedmen, for the sake of land or inheritance, or from tombs or the affairs of the dead, or from worthless persons.
> SUN: it will make the loss to be from the father, or from paternal relatives or elders, or on account of loans, or some monies, or business affairs.
> MOON: on account of the mother, or the maternal kindred, or the step-mother, or suchlike persons.[10]

The general interpretive principle here is that when a malefic is located in the second place, or configured to the second by square or opposition, that it will indicate problems with respect to the native's finances and livelihood. The source of the loss of livelihood will thus be signified by the planet that rules the second place.

Examples of the Ruler of the Second

While the delineations that Rhetorius gives for the rulers of the places are not fully comprehensive, they do clearly demonstrate how to approach the subject in general. I would like to use some modern example charts in order to show how the rulers of the places can be employed to identify distinct characteristics in the lives of contemporary individuals. As we will see, the ruler of the second place is particularly useful for studying matters pertaining the native's livelihood and finances.

MAURIZIO GUCCI

A native who was born with a night chart, and Cancer rising, with Leo on the second whole sign place. The Sun is ruling the second place, located in Libra in the fourth place, exchanging signs with Venus. Maurizio Gucci had the ruler of

---

[10] Rhetorius, *Compendium*, 57 (CCAG, 8, 4, p. 141: 1–12), trans. Holden, pp.57–8. These and the other delineations that follow are adapted from Holden's translation of Rhetorius, *Compendium*, 57, modified after comparing the Greek text.

the second place of livelihood in the fourth place of parents and family. The native's grandfather was Guccio Gucci, the founder of the Gucci fashion empire. The native inherited a fifty percent stake in the family business when his father died of cancer on May 16, 1983. During the 1980s, he engaged in a hostile takeover of the business, eventually ousting his uncle and three cousins from the board. He was notorious for his lavish spending, and in 1993 he sold his stock in the company for $170 million. Here the

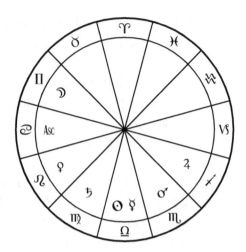

Chart 24 - Maurizio Gucci

delineation of the ruler of the second place in the fourth might be: "the native makes their money through their family" or "inherits money from their family." His personal finances and livelihood became wrapped up in the family business, and the paternal inheritance, which is signified by the fourth place.

STEVE WOZNIAK

Another example. A day chart with Virgo rising, and Libra on the second place. Venus is the lady of the second place, located in Cancer (eleventh place), copresent with the Moon and overcome by a superior trine from Jupiter. The chart belongs to Apple Computer co-founder, Steve Wozniak, who is an excellent example of someone born with the ruler of the second place in the eleventh place. Wozniak started out as friends with Steve Jobs around the time they

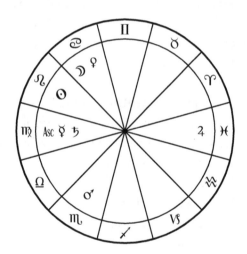

Chart 25 - Steve Wozniak

finished high school, and eventually he became rich as a result of this friendship. The essential delineation of the ruler of the second in the eleventh is: the native becomes wealthy as a result of friends; or more broadly: his livelihood is tied in with his friendships. However, it should be noted that the ruler is relatively well-situated in this case, especially in terms of its configuration with Jupiter, and thus the outcome is more positive. Conversely, if the ruler of the second was in the eleventh but not in good condition, then the delineation might be: the native loses money or has problems with their livelihood as a result of their friends.

The Ruler of the Third Place

In Rhetorius the ruler of the third is generally associated with friends, travel, foreign places, and siblings. Here are some of the delineations that Rhetorius gives for the ruler of the third place and related placements:

> *Ruler of the sixth or twelfth place in the third place:*
>> Hypocrisies and betrayals by friends and damages by enemies. Or injury and sickness while traveling in a foreign country.
>
> *Ruler of the third in the second or sixth place:*
>> Assaults by bandits on the road.
>
> *Ruler of the fifth or eleventh in the third place:*
>> Good and profitable sojourns abroad and friendships.
>
> *Ruler of the seventh in third place:*
>> Foreign marriages.
>
> *Ruler of third in a fertile zodiacal sign and configured to a benefic:*
>> Many siblings.
>
> *Ruler of the third in the second or eleventh or ninth or tenth place:*
>> Younger and elder brothers.
>
> *Ruler of the third in the first:*
>> The native is first-born or an only child.
>
> *Ruler of the third in the twelfth:*
>> The brothers and friends of the native become enemies.
>
> *Ruler of the third in the sixth place:*
>> The native is mistreated by his friends or brothers, or the brothers are injured.[11]

In terms of modern examples, the third place is very useful for studying the topic of siblings. The charts of Ted Kennedy and Vincent van Gogh demonstrate how the ruler of the third can operate when it falls in a bad place versus a good place (the eighth versus the tenth, respectively).

TED KENNEDY

Ted Kennedy was born at night with Capricorn rising, Pisces on the third place, and Jupiter (ruler of the third) in Leo (eighth place), retrograde, contrary to

---

[11] These and the other delineations that follow are adapted from Holden's translation of Rhetorius, *Compendium*, 57, done in comparison with the Greek text.

the sect, and opposed by Mars. Not only did he have the ruler of the third place in the eighth, but also the ruler of the eighth place in the third. He was the brother of U.S. President John F. Kennedy. With the ruler of the third in the eighth, he experienced the death of his siblings, and these events became some of the most notable turning points in his life. When he was younger, his oldest brother, Joseph P. Kennedy Jr., died fighting in World War II. A few years later his sister Kathleen died in

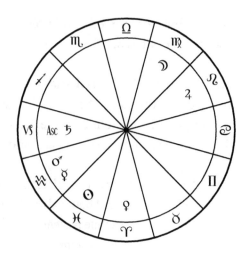

Chart 26 - Ted Kennedy

an airplane crash. Later, in 1963, his brother, President John F. Kennedy, was assassinated. In 1968, his brother Robert F. Kennedy was also assassinated shortly after entering the presidential race that year. Thus, the ruler of the third place of siblings in the eighth place of death indicated some major and recurring themes in Ted Kennedy's life.

VINCENT VAN GOGH

A diurnal chart with Cancer rising, Virgo on the third place, and Mercury (ruler of the third) in Aries (tenth place). Vincent van Gogh was a famous Dutch painter. Although he was not very successful during his lifetime, his younger brother, Theo van Gogh, supported Vincent's work and made it possible, both financially and emotionally. With the ruler of the third place of siblings in the tenth place of career, the

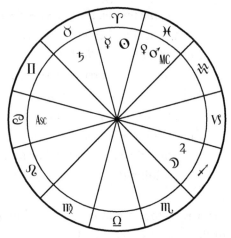

Chart 27 - Vincent van Gogh

most general statement we could make is that the siblings will be involved in the native's occupation or career, which in this case is true in a very vivid and literal way. Interestingly, Vincent also had the ruler of the tenth whole sign place in the ninth, conjunct the degree of the meridian-Midheaven. Recall that in his section on derived places, Valens says that "relative to the [third place] of siblings it [the ninth place] is the marriage-bringer."[12] That is to say, since the ninth place is the seventh from the third, it relates to the marriage partner of the sibling. Vincent's brother Theo died only months after Vincent did, and it was Theo's wife, Johanna van Gogh-Bonger, who promoted Vincent's work after his death and was eventually successful in making him as widely recognized for his artwork as he is today. Without her, it is not clear whether Vincent's work would have achieved the level of recognition that it eventually did.

Thus, one of the points that we have to be aware of is that sometimes there can be overlapping levels of meaning that relate to the placement of different rulers in the chart, and sometimes some levels of meaning can only be fully accessed by looking at the placements in terms of derived places. While in most cases it is impractical or even impossible to take into account all of the possible derived place meanings for different placements, it is still an important additional level of symbolism to be aware of.

The Ruler of the Fourth Place

Rhetorius only has one delineation for the ruler of the fourth place, and it deals with matters surrounding the native's death:

> If the domicile lord [of the fourth] is opposing this place, or is in the sixth, eighth or the twelfth: [the native] will die abroad.[13]

He adds a similar additional delineation under the section on the twelfth place: "And if the ruler of the subterraneous angle is found there [in the twelfth], predict his end abroad."[14] The text literally says that native's "end" will occur abroad, evidently focusing on the fourth place associations with death and the end or conclusion of matters. As we have seen elsewhere, the fourth place can also be useful for studying matters pertaining to the native's parents and home or living situation, and the next two chart examples show how these themes can manifest in very vivid ways in the native's life.

REINHOLD EBERTIN

The famous astrologer Reinhold Ebertin was born with a nocturnal chart that had Capricorn rising, Aries on the fourth place, and Mars, ruler of the fourth, in Virgo in the ninth place. Mars belongs to the sect of the chart, and is configured by a close degree-based trine to Jupiter at 5° Capricorn from its position at 5° of Virgo.

---

12 Valens, *Anthology*, 9, 3: 15.
13 Rhetorius, *Compendium*, 57 (CCAG, 8, 4, p. 150: 7–8).
14 Rhetorius, *Compendium*, 57 (CCAG, 8, 4, p.128: 5–7), trans. Holden, p. 44.

His mother was Elsbeth Ebertin, a famous astrologer in Germany, who made a noted prediction about the rise of Hitler in the early 1920s based on his birth chart. Reinhold did not grow up with an interest in astrology, but Elsbeth taught it to him after he took an interest in it in his early 20s. Eventually he would go on to found an influential approach to astrology known as Cosmobiology. With the ruler of the fourth place of parents in the ninth place of astrology and divination, it is thus noteworthy that

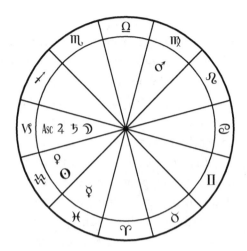

Chart 28 - Reinhold Ebertin

his mother was an astrologer, and that he learned the subject from her.

RULER OF FOURTH IN NINTH

The ruler of the fourth can also typify the home and living situation. For example, a native who was born with a night chart, Virgo rising, and Sagittarius on the fourth place. Jupiter is the ruler of the fourth, and it is located in Taurus, which is the ninth place. With the ruler of the fourth in the ninth, the native grew up with a strong desire to live in a foreign country. When this placement became activated after the native became an adult, they permanently moved to a foreign country. This particular placement was also emphasized by the ruler of the ninth being in the fourth. That is, the rulers of the ninth and fourth were exchanging signs, an arrangement that accentuates the connection between the two places, as we saw already in the chart of Ted Kennedy.

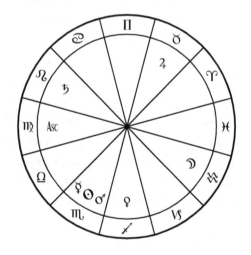

Chart 29 - Ruler of Fourth in Ninth

The Ruler of the Fifth Place

The ruler of the fifth is often described as being associated with the circumstances surrounding the native's children, or the topic of children in general. Rhetorius has the following delineations for the ruler of the fifth place:

> *Ruler of the twelfth in the fifth place, or ruler of fifth in twelfth:*
>   The native will be a step-father or foster-father of the children of others.[15]
> *Ruler of the fifth or ruler of the Lot of Children in the eighth:*
>   Childless persons or the death of children.
> *Ruler of the place of marriage or Lot of Marriage in fifth:*
>   It makes happily married men, and one who takes a widow having a son.

In terms of modern chart examples, the ruler of the fifth is often useful for describing things that happen in the native's life with respect to the topic of children, or sometimes in the lives of the native's children in general.

RULER OF FIFTH IN NINTH

Here is an example of a native who was born with a diurnal chart, Leo rising, Sagittarius coinciding with the fifth place, and Jupiter in Aries. With the ruler of the fifth in the ninth, one of the native's children became very religious as an adult, and subsequently patterned her life around her religion, moving away from home to follow her pastor and open a new church in a different part of the country. The native's other child grew up in the United States, but had a fascination with Asian culture

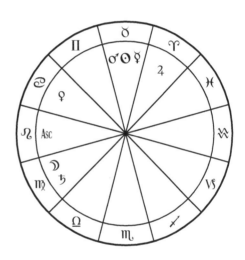

Chart 30 - Ruler of Fifth in Ninth

from a very early age and studied Japanese in school. As soon as he became an adult he moved to Asia, and has lived in different Asian countries for the entirety of his adult life. Eventually he renounced his United States citizenship, and became a citizen of a foreign country. This example is interesting because it illustrates two different facets of the ninth place significations manifesting in the lives of each of the native's children.

---

[15] This is also a signification of Saturn according to Valens, which may be relevant here since the twelfth is where Saturn has its joy.

RULER OF FIFTH IN EIGHTH

A native who was born with Taurus rising, and Virgo on the fifth place. Venus (ruler of the Ascendant) is in Virgo, and Mercury (ruler of the fifth) is in Sagittarius (eighth place). With the ruler of the fifth in the eighth, the native had three children; two died prematurely, one in infancy, and the other at the age of twenty. The native's husband was born with Cancer rising, and Scorpio on the fifth place. The ruler of the fifth was Mars, located in Aquarius in the eighth place. Thus, there were indications in both parents' charts for the death of children.

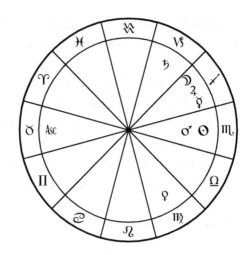

Chart 31 - Ruler of Fifth in Eighth

The Ruler of the Sixth Place

Rhetorius gives a few different delineations for poorly placed planets ruling the sixth place, resulting in different types of illnesses or injuries:

> *Jupiter ruling the sixth place, maltreated and badly placed in sixth or twelfth:*
>   Liver complaints, impairments from wine.
> *Venus ruling the sixth place:*
>   Those who are mad for women, and suffer bad things as a result of it.
> *Mercury ruling the sixth place:*
>   Injuries to the hearing, speech, or throat.

He also gives a few general delineations of the ruler of the sixth place:

> *Ruler of the fourth in the sixth, or the ruler of eighth or ninth in sixth:*
>   It makes wanderers and those who die abroad.
> *Ruler of the seventh in the sixth:*
>   The native has intercourse with slave-girls, cripples, or wretched women.
> *Ruler of the third in the sixth:*
>   The native is mistreated by his friends or brothers, or the brothers are injured.

In contemporary charts the sixth place and its ruler are often useful for studying matters pertaining to physical injury and illness.

ERNEST HEMINGWAY

The famous American writer Ernest Hemingway was born with a day chart, Virgo rising, Aquarius as the sixth place, and Saturn in Sagittarius. With the ruler of the sixth place in the fourth place, he inherited a genetic disorder from his father that later contributed to his suicide. His father may have had the same disease (hemochromatosis), and he also committed suicide. Hemochromatosis stops the body from metabolizing iron, which results

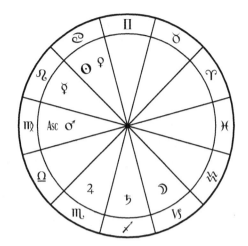

Chart 32 - Ernest Hemingway

in mental and physical deterioration, and Hemingway's behavior before he died was evidently similar to his father's. In this instance the delineation of the ruler of the sixth in the fourth is: inheriting an illness or disease from the father. The association of the fourth with the end of life and death is also relevant, as this illness contributed to his eventual demise.

MICHEL FOUCAULT

The prominent French philosopher, Michel Foucault, was born with a day chart, Scorpio rising, Aries on the sixth place, and Mars in Taurus in the seventh. He died in 1984 due to complications related to HIV/AIDS, which he contracted sexually while he was a visiting professor in California in the early 1980s. His longtime partner Daniel Defert founded the first national HIV/AIDS organization in France shortly after Foucault's death, and subsequently became a well-known

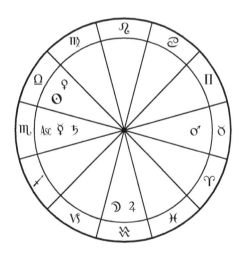

Chart 33 - Michel Foucault

AIDS activist. On the one hand the ruler of the sixth in the seventh seems to indicate contracting an illness from a sexual partner. On the other hand, the placement also reflects the influence that Foucault's tragic illness had on his partner after his death.

The Ruler of the Seventh Place

Rhetorius gives the following delineations for the ruler of the seventh place, which often involve marriage, the spouse, or sexual intercourse:

> *Ruler of the seventh in the twelfth, or ruler of twelfth in seventh:*
> Bad fortune with marriage, or marriage to a slave.
> *Ruler of the seventh configured to the ruler of eighth:*
> Widowers or divorced persons, once if in a solid sign, twice in a
> bicorporeal sign, but many times in a tropical sign.
> *Ruler of the seventh in the tenth and ruler of twelfth in fourth:*
> Those who marry slaves or those who purchase their own wives.[16]
> *Ruler of the seventh in the ninth:*
> A foreign or religious wife.
> *Ruler of the seventh under the beams or in the fourth or afflicted by malefics:*
> Intercourse with prostitutes or slave-girls.

In modern nativities the ruler of the seventh is useful for studying matters pertaining to relationships and marriage in general, and sometimes the placement of the ruler can come to define important events that will take place at some point within the context of the native's love life. I want to use the first two examples here as an opportunity to look at how the same placement manifested in similar ways in the lives of two different individuals.

JOHNNY CARSON

The talk show host Johnny Carson was born with a day chart, Scorpio rising, Taurus coinciding with the setting place, and Venus in Sagittarius. Thus, he had the ruler of the seventh in the second place. He was the host of The Tonight Show for thirty years, from 1962 until 1992. Towards the end of his career his annual salary was $25 million per year, and he was worth around $300 million by the time he died. He was married four times. His second

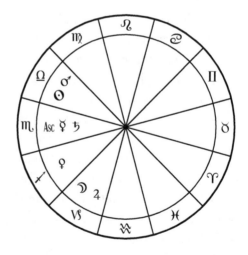

Chart 34 - Johnny Carson

---

[16] There might be some corruption here because the interpretation of the ruler of the seventh in tenth is more positive later on in Rhetorius' text.

wife received $500,000 in cash and art when they were divorced, and lifetime alimony payments of $100,000 a year. His third wife filed for divorce in 1983, and since they were married in California she was entitled to fifty percent of all the assets accumulated during their marriage. She ended up receiving $20 million in cash and property after the settlement. Before marrying his fourth wife, he is reported to have said "Look, I'm not going through this bullshit again. If I ever get married again, put a .38 to my head, and if we don't have a prenup, pull the damn trigger."[17] Thus the ruler of the seventh in the second clearly shows a recurring theme surrounding marriage and personal finances in Carson's life.

STEVEN SPIELBERG

The director Steven Spielberg was born with a nocturnal chart, Cancer rising, Capricorn on the seventh place, and Saturn in Leo. Thus, he had a similar placement as Carson, with the ruler of the seventh in the second, although the difference is that in this case the ruler is Saturn in a night chart and in a fixed sign. When he was in the process of getting a divorce from his first wife, the judge voided their prenuptial agreement because it was written on a napkin. As a result,

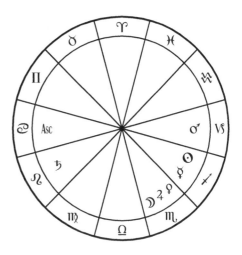

Chart 35 - Steven Spielberg

she received around $100 million dollars in the settlement, which was half of his fortune. At the time, this was reported as one of the most costly celebrity divorces in history.

ADOLF HITLER

Adolf Hitler was born with a day chart, Libra rising, Aries coinciding with the seventh, and Mars in Taurus. With the ruler of the seventh in the eighth, he committed suicide with his wife Eva Braun shortly after getting married. His honeymoon consisted of watching his wife commit suicide, shooting himself in the head, then

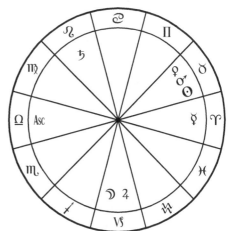

Chart 36 - Adolf Hitler

---

[17] Bushkin, *Johnny Carson*, p. 229.

having their bodies burned and dumped in a ditch. One of his presumed earlier lovers, his niece Geli Raubal, committed suicide with his gun in his apartment while he was away on a trip. Thus in Hitler's chart, the ruler of the seventh in the eighth closely ties the topic of death to the topic of relationships.

RULER OF SEVENTH IN ELEVENTH

A more positive example. A native who was born with a day chart, Scorpio rising, and Taurus on the seventh place. Venus, the ruler of the seventh, is in Virgo, the eleventh place. With the ruler of the seventh in the eleventh, the native first encountered her future marriage partner through an online social network, and then they were introduced later in person through a mutual friend. At first they were just friends, and later got into a long-term romantic relationship, and then eventually were married.

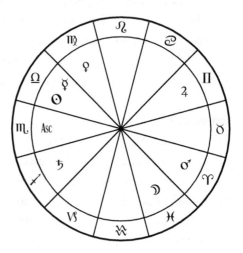

Chart 37 - Ruler of Seventh in Eleventh

The Ruler of the Eighth Place

Rhetorius' delineations of the eighth place are usually focused on issues surrounding death and inheritance:

> *Ruler of the eighth place in a decline:*
> The native dies abroad.
> *Ruler of the fourth place in the eighth place:*
> Also native dies abroad.[18]
> *Ruler of the eighth place in the tenth, eleventh, or fifth place:*
> Native grows rich from matters having to do with the dead, especially when in its own domicile or exaltation, not under the beams, and moving swiftly. But if it is under the beams, it makes an inheritance, but the native immediately squanders it.
> *Ruler of the third place in eighth place:*
> Siblings die before the native.
> *Ruler of the fifth place in the eighth place:*
> Childlessness.

---

[18] This seems a bit odd, and seems like it should instead be "death at home."

Ruler of the twelfth or sixth place in eighth place:
    The deaths of enemies and slaves.

Rhetorius has an entire section here where he deals with the eighth place in determining the quality of the native's death, evidently derived from Critodemus:

> Saturn as ruler of the eighth, beholding it, destroys by water, and abroad, mainly when in a watery sign, or maltreated in another sign. If Saturn is in a dry sign, he destroys on a mountain. Simply examine the ruler of each sign of the eighth, in which sign it is, for of such quality the death will be. The Sun as ruler of the eighth, maltreated in the sign of another, if the eighth place itself were corrupted, it destroys [by a fall] from a height, according to the nature of the sign. Mars as ruler of the eighth, while the place is corrupted, produces a violent death; some other times, also hound-leaders. Venus corrupted as ruler of the eighth, this place itself being corrupted, makes a violent death from [drinking] much wine, or from poisoning by women. Mercury as ruler of the eighth, this place being corrupted, produces death by slaves or by writing. Jupiter ruler of the eighth, being this place itself corrupted, makes death from kings and great men; and if they were found <in> their own domicile, triplicity or exaltation, in one's own country; but if in other signs, abroad.[19]

Let's look at two contemporary example charts to see how the ruler of the eighth place described the circumstances surrounding the native's death.

ERNEST HEMINGWAY

Returning to the example of Ernest Hemingway, we have seen that he experienced mental and physical deterioration towards the end of his life due to an illness he inherited from his father. In his chart these issues were complicated by the fact that he had Aries coinciding with the eighth place, and Mars in Virgo in the first, in a day chart. Connections between

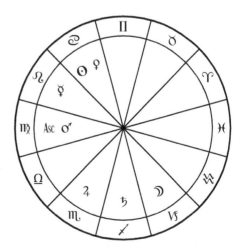

Chart 38 - Ernest Hemingway

---

[19] Rhetorius, *Compendium*, 57 (CCAG, 8, 4, p. 162: 1–15), trans. Eduardo Gramaglia, unpublished.

the eighth place and the first place were commonly associated with suicide in the Hellenistic tradition, since the first place is the place of self, and so having the ruler of the eighth there is sometimes interpreted to mean that the native's death is somehow partially the result of their own actions. Hemingway did in fact commit suicide by shooting himself in the head with a shotgun. In this case the placement of the ruler of the eighth in the first is made more problematic by the fact that it is the malefic that is contrary to the sect, and thus the most difficult planet in the chart.

PRINCESS DIANA

Another example of the ruler of the eighth indicating the quality of death occurs in the chart of Princess Diana. She was born with a day chart, Sagittarius rising, and Cancer on the eighth place. The ruler of the eighth is the Moon, which is located in the third place, applying to an out of sign opposition with Mars in a day chart within thirteen degrees. This is a condition of maltreatment, which we will discuss in the next chapter. She also has the ruler of the ninth place of

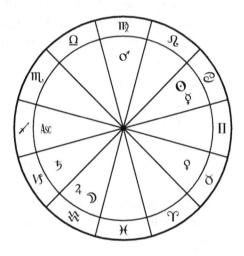

Chart 39 - Princess Diana

travel in the eighth place. She died in a widely publicized car accident while in a foreign country.

The Ruler of the Ninth Place

Rhetorius's delineations of the ninth place generally involve foreign travel, foreigners, and religious matters:

> *Ruler of the eighth place in the ninth place:*
> Death abroad.
> *Ruler of ninth well-situated and not under the beams, in its own sign or exaltation:*
> Good fortune abroad.
> *Ruler of the ninth in the sixth or second or third or twelfth or eighth:*
> Those who wander about abroad.
> *Ruler of the seventh place in the ninth place:*
> A foreign or pious spouse.

I will limit myself to one example here, in order to demonstrate the way in which notions of "that which is foreign" can be imported into different places by the ruler of the ninth.

RULER OF NINTH IN FOURTH

A native who was born at night with Scorpio rising, Cancer in the ninth place, and the Moon in Aquarius in the fourth. With the ruler of the ninth in the fourth, the native was born in the United States, but his mother and her family are from the Philippines. Because his family came from a different culture than the one grew up in, he developed a general interest in other cultures. His mother's family is located in different parts of the world, and he visits them

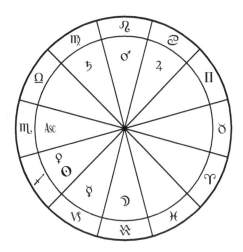

Chart 40 - Ruler of Ninth in Fourth

periodically. With the Moon ruling the ninth and placed in the fourth, the delineation might be stated: the native's mother is a foreigner, or the mother's side of the family lives abroad.

The Ruler of the Tenth Place

Rhetorius does not have many delineations of the ruler of the tenth in that specific section, although we do find the following in chapter 57 in general:

> *Ruler of the seventh place in the tenth place:*
> Good marriages.
> *Ruler of the eighth place in the tenth place:*
> Increases through inheritances.
> *Ruler of the ninth place in the tenth place:*
> Good fortune abroad.

Elsewhere, Valens has the following delineation of the ruler of the tenth place: "When the ruler of this place is well situated, it makes those who are effective; but when it is poorly situated, those who are unsuccessful."[20] In contemporary charts the ruler of the tenth can sometimes be useful in describing the nature of the native's career or occupation.

---

[20] Valens, *Anthology*, 2, 7: 3, trans. Schmidt.

ANONYMOUS (DOCTOR)

A native who was born at night with Pisces rising, Sagittarius coinciding with the tenth place, and Jupiter in Leo in the sixth. Jupiter is configured to the degree of the quadrant Midheaven within three degrees, and is overcome by Venus (benefic of the sect), which is a condition of bonification, which will be discussed in the next chapter. With the ruler of the tenth place well-situated in the sixth place, the native is a doctor, and later became the head of a hospital.

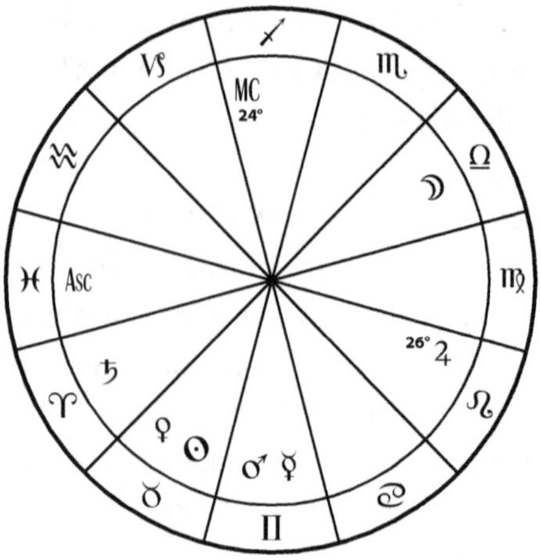

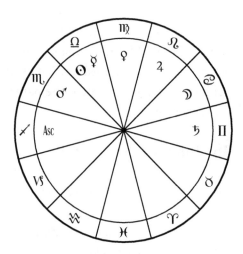

Chart 41 - Doctor

ELEANOR ROOSEVELT

Eleanor Roosevelt, the wife of U.S. President Franklin D. Roosevelt and First Lady of the United States, was born during the day with Sagittarius rising, Virgo occupying the tenth place, and Mercury in Libra. Having the ruler of the tenth in the eleventh place seems to have emphasized themes related to friends and alliances within the context of her career. Both before and after Roosevelt's death she was deeply involved in politics, with a strong focus on social issues (which might be broadly connected

Chart 42 - Eleanor Roosevelt

to the eleventh house as the place of friends and alliances). She was a key figure in several of the most important social reform movements of the twentieth century in the U.S., including the Progressive Movement, the New Deal, the Women's Movement, the Civil Rights Movement, and the United Nations. She was appointed as a delegate to the United Nations General Assembly shortly after the creation of the U.N., and she became the first chairperson of the United Nations Commission on Human Rights. Her focus on this area is emphasized by the fact that Mercury at 2° Libra is conjunct the degree of the meridian-Midheaven at 7° Libra, and it also exchanges signs with Venus in Virgo.

The Ruler of the Eleventh Place

Rhetorius has the following delineations for the ruler of the eleventh place:

> *Every ruler in the eleventh signifies good things;*
>> Unless it is afflicted or poorly-situated in some way, in which case the positive indications are weakened.
>
> *Ruler of the eleventh in the first and ruler of twelfth in the seventh:*
>> It makes the native's life easy or smooth in his youth, but then more moderate circumstances in old age.
>
> *Ruler of eleventh in seventh and ruler of twelfth in first:*
>> Moderate circumstances in youth, and then smoother ones in old age.

The topic of friends is often very closely associated with the ruler of the eleventh in contemporary charts, and sometimes this can describe the unique role that friendship plays in different parts of the native's life.

TIGER WOODS

The eminent golfer, Tiger Woods, has the ruler of the eleventh in the fourth. His father played a very influential and supportive role in shaping his life and career, and Tiger considered him to be his best friend. When his father died in 2006, Tiger wrote: "My dad was my best friend and greatest role model, and I will miss him deeply [...] I'm overwhelmed when I think of all of the great things he accomplished in his life. He was an amazing dad, coach, mentor, soldier, husband and friend. I wouldn't

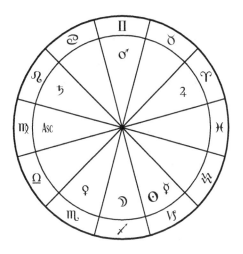

Chart 43 - Tiger Woods

be where I am today without him, and I'm honored to continue his legacy of sharing and caring."[21] Tiger's birth name is actually Eldrick Tont Woods, but he was nicknamed "Tiger" in honor of his father's friend, Col. Vuong Dang Phong, who was known as Tiger Phong. In this way there are sometimes multiple overlapping outcomes that can result from the same placement, with each manifesting the same underlying symbolism in a unique way.

---

[21] Londino, *Tiger Woods: A Biography*, p. 28.

Ruler of Eleventh in Eighth

A native who was born during the day with Sagittarius rising, Libra occupying the eleventh place, and Venus in Cancer with Mars. Thus, the ruler of the eleventh is in the eighth, and it is rendered more problematic by the fact that it is copresent with the malefic that is contrary to the sect. For most of her life, she had only one close friend, a girl she grew up with. The friend tragically died of cancer when the native was in her thirties. The death of her friend was particularly traumatic for the native, as she doesn't have any other friends, nor is she interested in developing other friendships.

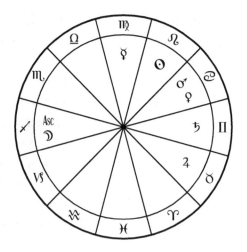

Chart 44 - Ruler of Eleventh in Eighth

The Ruler of the Twelfth Place

One of the ideas that some of the delineations of the ruler of the twelfth seem to share in common is the idea of importing misfortune or loss into the place that the ruler is located in. Rhetorius has a number of delineations for the twelfth:

> *Ruler of the third place in the twelfth place:*
>   Brothers and friends of the native become enemies.
> *Ruler of the fourth place in the twelfth place:*
>   Death abroad.
> *Rulers of the twelfth place and the fifth exchange signs:*
>   The native becomes the father of the children of others.
> *Ruler of the seventh in the twelfth place:*
>   Bad marriages, marriages with slaves, loss (*zemias*) or damage (*blabas*) as a result of marriage.
> *Ruler of the eighth in the twelfth place:*
>   Damage from matters related to death (inheritances, legacies), or death in a foreign land.
> *Ruler of ninth in twelfth:*
>   Wandering in a foreign land. Probably in a negative sense. Maybe "wandering aimlessly" or "being led astray."
> *Ruler of the ninth in the twelfth, with Saturn present in the twelfth:*
>   Shipwrecks or dangers in the sea, unless mitigated by benefics.

Ruler of the ninth in the twelfth, with Mars present in twelfth:
>The native is attacked by soldiers or robbers (alternatively: pirates, thieves) while abroad or traveling.

Ruler of the twelfth place in the first place:
>The native will have a wearisome or toilsome youth.

Ruler of the twelfth in the seventh place:
>The native will suffer hardships in old age.

Saturn or Mars as the ruler of the twelfth while located in the first place:
>The native is eaten by dogs or wild beasts, or is fond of hunting.

Ruler of the twelfth place with the Sun:
>The father is worthless, or the inheritance from the father is destroyed.

Ruler of the twelfth place with the Moon:
>Same as for the Sun, except applied to the mother.

This general idea of the ruler of the twelfth importing themes having to do with loss or misfortune in general into the place that it falls sometimes works out in strange and interesting ways in contemporary charts.

JOHN F. KENNEDY JR.

The native was the son of U.S. President John F. Kennedy, and he was born seventeen days after his father was elected President in November 1960. He had a night chart with Virgo rising, Leo occupying the twelfth place, and the Sun in Sagittarius in the fourth. President Kennedy was assassinated on November 22, 1963, and his state funeral was held three days later, on November 25, which happened to be his son's third birthday. In this instance, the ruler of twelfth in the fourth indicated loss or misfortune surrounding the parents, and since the Sun was the ruling planet, it evidently signified the father in particular.

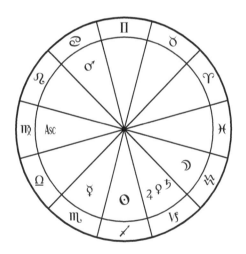

Chart 45 - John F. Kennedy Jr.

GEORGE LUCAS

The film director George Lucas was born shortly before sunrise, with Taurus rising, Aries occupying the twelfth place, and Mars in Cancer in the third place.

He was born close enough to sunrise that his chart seems to behave as a day chart, which would make Mars the malefic that is contrary to the sect of the chart. Lucas grew up having a fascination with cars, and wanted to become a professional race car driver. However, just after he turned eighteen years old, he was involved in a terrible car accident and was almost killed three days before graduating from high school. He was thrown from the car, which saved his life, because the car was crushed against

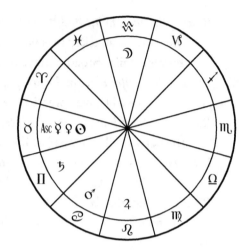

Chart 46 - George Lucas

a tree. He was badly injured though, and his friends thought that he was dead when he was first found. He spent forty-eight hours in a coma, followed by two weeks in intensive care. For those first three days he hung between life and death. Lucas later said "You can't have that kind of experience and not feel that there must be a reason why you're here. I realized I should be spending my time trying to figure out what that reason is and trying to fulfill it."[22] Thus, with the ruler of the twelfth in the third, Lucas was severely injured and came close to death while traveling. As a result of this experience he decided to stop racing and go to college, where he developed the interest in filmmaking that would later come to define his career.

---

[22] Pollock, *Skywalking*, p. xvi.

CHAPTER 14
CONDITIONS OF
BONIFICATION AND MALTREATMENT

Already we have seen several different ways that the conditions of the planets in a chart can be determined, based on their position by sign, place, and configuration with other planets. In the Hellenistic tradition there were also a special set of considerations that were used to identify planetary condition which gave the benefics and malefics special roles in the birth chart, and these were known as the conditions of bonification and maltreatment.

References to the concepts of bonification and maltreatment are scattered throughout the surviving corpus of ancient astrological literature, although as with many other techniques, it is only in the book of definitions by Antiochus and its derivatives that the concepts are actually defined. Unfortunately, the three surviving versions of the Antiochus definitions are all slightly different, and as a result of this the actual technical concepts must be reconstructed by piecing together different definitions from the lost work of Antiochus. The purpose of this chapter is to present the reconstruction of the conditions of bonification and maltreatment that I completed with Demetra George and Benjamin Dykes in 2010, as well as to demonstrate how the conditions can be used in practice.[1]

---

[1] Our reconstruction of the conditions resulted from an attempt to check and verify the reconstruction presented by Schmidt in *Definitions and Foundations*, p. 266ff. We ended up coming to different conclusions about how the bonification and maltreatment conditions were probably originally defined in Antiochus though. Nonetheless, our reconstruction was partially predicated on the work that Schmidt did, and the reader should compare our reconstruction with his and then draw their own conclusions.

The Purpose of the Conditions

The conditions of bonification and maltreatment are predicated on the notion that the benefics and malefics have special roles that they play in a chart. The primary purpose of the conditions is that they establish the means by which the benefics and malefics can affirm or deny what other planets want to signify in the chart. As discussed previously, one of the primary roles of the benefics is to affirm or say "yes" to what other planets want to signify in a chart, whereas conversely, the primary role of the malefics is to negate or say "no" to what other planets want to signify. The conditions of bonification and maltreatment become the primary means through which the benefics and malefics are able to perform this special role, because they provide a specific set of conditions that must be present in order for them to be able to fully exercise their power. This becomes extremely useful for the topical analysis of different parts of the chart in order to see if certain events will come about in the native's life, such as whether they will have children, whether they will be married, whether they will have friends, and so on.

Additionally, the conditions of bonification and maltreatment can also alter the quality of how a topic is expressed in a native's life. Bonification affirms, stabilizes, or improves the condition of other planets, while maltreatment negates, destabilizes, or corrupts. This is particularly useful when looking at the rulers of the places, as it can provide additional information about how certain topics or areas of life will play out during the course of the life of the native.

Because bonification and maltreatment represent a very specific set of conditions, when they are present in a chart they tend to indicate extreme scenarios of positive or negative manifestations of whatever planet is the focal point. Sometimes this results in what are essentially best-case or worst-case scenarios with respect to the placement of a planet. However, sometimes the conditions can also play a mitigating role, either improving the condition of planets that are already poorly-situated, or conversely, worsening the condition of planets that are otherwise well-situated. This is especially evident when a planet is being both bonified and maltreated at the same time.

Finally, it is important to note that the conditions affect both the general significations of a planet as well as the place(s) it rules in a chart. For example, if Venus is being maltreated then this may negate Venus' general signification of marriage in that particular chart. If Venus is also the ruler of the fifth place, then it may also negate the topic of children in the chart as well. While in this chapter we will tend to focus on the rulers of the places, it is important to keep in mind that the conditions can also affect the way in which a planet manifests its natural or general significations as well.

The Inequities of Fortune

All charts are not created equal. Just as everyone's life is not equal in terms of the quality of the events that they experience in their lives, so too is it true that some people are more fortunate than others. Indeed, some people have lives than can be characterized as *particularly* fortunate or unfortunate. Moreover, some people may be particularly fortunate in one area of their life, but markedly unfortunate in another area. These are important points to realize from the outset in order to understand what we are seeing when we begin analyzing the conditions of bonification and maltreatment in a birth chart.

In some charts the benefics have the upper hand, while in other charts the malefics do. Part of the purpose of the conditions is to determine which planets have the upper hand in a chart, and which parts of the life this applies to. In some instances, it will be restricted to a specific area of life, while in other instances the benefics or the malefics can dominate the entire chart, thus characterizing the quality of life as a whole (e.g. one can have a "hard life" or a "good life").

Definition of Maltreatment

Maltreatment is defined in three places: definition 17 of the Antiochus *Summary*; chapter 28 of Porphyry's *Introduction*; and chapter 27 of Rhetorius' *Compendium*. The technical term used for this concept is *kakōsis*, which according to the LSJ lexicon means: ill-treatment, oppression, suffering, distress, or the effects of disease, damage, misfortune. It is derived from the verb *kakoō*, which the LSJ defines as: to treat ill, maltreat, afflict, distress; to suffer ill, be in ill plight, be distressed; to spoil, ruin.

Schmidt translates the term as "maltreatment," which I have adopted as well.[2] An alternative term that could be used is "affliction," since this is the origin of the use of the word affliction as a technical term in the later astrological tradition. However, because the term affliction has taken on such a general meaning in modern astrology, referring to anything that is poorly-situated, it is necessary to use a more specialized term here in order to designate a specific type of affliction that stands out as particularly unique or extreme. We will use the term maltreatment to refer to this concept.

In the Antiochus *Summary*, Porphyry, and Rhetorius, no corresponding set of positive conditions are ever systematically defined to accompany the negative set of conditions for maltreatment. However, when many of the concepts related to maltreatment are defined earlier in these texts, there are clear allusions to a corresponding set of positive conditions, which often involve substituting the

---

[2] Schmidt, *Definitions and Foundations*, p. 266ff.

benefic planets in the place of the malefics in the conditions of maltreatment. The Greek term *agathunō*, which means "to make good," is used occasionally by astrologers such as Dorotheus to refer to the positive influence of the benefics over other planets, and Schmidt has used this as the starting point to propose the use of the term "bonification" to refer to the corresponding set of positive conditions that complement the term "maltreatment."[3] I will adopt that convention here as well.

Out of the three surviving discussions, Porphyry gives the clearest definition of maltreatment, which is as follows:

> It is called 'maltreatment' whenever some [star] is struck with a ray by destroyers or enclosed or is in an engagement or adherence with a destructive star or opposed or overcome or is ruled by a badly-situated destroyer, it itself declining in disadvantageous places.[4]

In the original Antiochus text, this definition of maltreatment evidently came at the end of a series of definitions of several other concepts, and so in order to understand each individual condition, all of the other definitions prior to this one must also be understood. In this way, the definition of maltreatment can also be used as a sort of benchmark in order to check the reconstruction of many of the other definitions in Antiochus, especially the ones related to the doctrine of configurations.[5] We have already encountered several of the concepts mentioned in this definition before, such as adherence and overcoming, while others have not been introduced yet, such as striking with a ray and enclosure. In this chapter we will go through each individual condition and see what each looks like when it is used as a condition of maltreatment.

Six clearly distinguishable conditions are mentioned in the first part of the definition in Porphyry. However, there is some ambiguity over whether the last part of the definition is describing a single additional condition, or whether it is outlining two separate conditions. The grammar is ambiguous and could be interpreted in one of two ways, and unfortunately the Antiochus *Summary* is of little help for comparisons due to even more problematic grammatical issues. In the first interpretation, it could simply be describing a single condition, which is essentially same as the definition of "counteraction" (*antanalusis*, which is when a planet is ruled by a poorly-situated planet, in this case a malefic); it then

---

[3] Schmidt, *Definitions and Foundations*, p. 272. Cf. Dorotheus, *Carmen*, ed. Pingree, p. 380: 11.
[4] Porphyry, *Introduction*, 28, trans. Demetra George, unpublished, modified.
[5] As suggested by Schmidt, *Definitions and Foundations*, p. 267.

specifies that the malefic must be (1) in a decline and (2) in a disadvantageous place, which would narrow it down to just the sixth and twelfth places. In the second interpretation, these may be two separate clauses: one defining counteraction as a condition of maltreatment; the other defining a planet in the sixth or twelfth place as a condition of maltreatment on its own.[6] I believe that the first interpretation, in which both statements form part of the same condition, is correct, and that this can be demonstrated by the way that Rhetorius rewrote the last part of the definition in order to attempt to clarify this point. Here is Rhetorius' version of the definition of maltreatment:

> It is called maltreatment whenever some star is struck with a ray or looked upon (*epitheoreō*)[7] or enclosed by malefics, or is joined to a destructive star or in an adherence with it, or opposed, or ruled by some star badly disposed in the disadvantageous places, the second from the Hour-Marker, the sixth, the eighth, and the twelfth. These are the idle and disadvantageous places.[8]

Rhetorius' rewriting of the last part of the definition appears to be an attempt to clarify what was an ambiguous point in the original definition from Antiochus, and while he expands the disadvantageous places specified to include the second and eighth, it is clear that the intent is to clarify how the last part of the definition represents a single condition. If this interpretation is correct, then there were seven conditions of maltreatment in the original definition by Antiochus:

1. Being "struck with a ray" (*aktinobolia*) by a malefic.
2. Being "enclosed" (*emperischesis*) by malefics.
3. Being in an "engagement" (*sunaphē*) with a malefic.
4. Being in an "adherence" (*kollēsis*) with a malefic.
5. Being opposed by a malefic.
6. Being overcome by a malefic.
7. Being ruled by a poorly-situated malefic.

By inference and by comparison with other definitions such as overcoming and enclosure, where corresponding positive conditions are mentioned together with the negative ones, the conditions of bonification can be established as follows:

---

[6] This is Schmidt's preferred interpretation in *Definitions and Foundations*, p. 272.

[7] In Rhetorius *epitheoreō* is the functional equivalent of overcoming.

[8] Rhetorius, *Compendium*, 27 (following the edition that incorporates epitome IIa, ed. Caballero Sánchez and Bautista Ruiz, "Una paráfrasis," p. 225), trans. Demetra George, unpublished, modified.

1. Being "struck with a ray" by a benefic.
2. Being "enclosed" by benefics.
3. Being in an "engagement" (*sunaphē*) with a benefic.
4. Being in an "adherence" (*kollēsis*) with a benefic.
5. Being trined by a benefic.
6. Being overcome by a benefic.
7. Being ruled by a well-situated benefic.

We will cover each of these conditions individually in this chapter, beginning with those that focus on sign-based configurations between planets, and then moving on to the more complicated, degree-based considerations.

Overcoming

Overcoming has already been treated earlier in the chapter on configurations, where it was established that planets that are earlier in the order of signs are in a superior position and "overcome" other planets that they are configured to that are later in zodiacal order. All that we need to address here are the specific circumstances under which overcoming becomes a condition of bonification or maltreatment, and what it looks like in practice.

In his definition of overcoming, Porphyry says that all planets on the right side overcome planets that they are configured to on the left side; however, he also says that overcoming through a square or trine is regarded as particularly powerful:

> They say that overcomings are more powerful when [the stars] are either trine or square. For in this way the star that is overcoming is stronger, whether it should be a benefic or malefic, or angular. For a benefic shows the nativity to be eminent, but a destroyer shows the nativity to be undistinguished.[9]

Taken together with the separate rule that the malefics are not harmful when configured by trine or sextile, which is alluded to in the definition of witnessing (Porphyry, *Introduction*, 8), this condition seems to stipulate that benefics are able to bonify other planets when they are overcoming them through a superior sign-based trine or square, while malefics are only able to maltreat other planets when they are overcoming them through a superior sign-based square. Both the superior trine and square qualify as overcoming, while the square itself is so powerful that it is given a special name: being "upon-the-tenth," or "domination."

---

[9] Porphyry, *Introduction*, 21, trans. Demetra George, unpublished, modified.

It is important to note that overcoming and domination were viewed as such powerful positions for planets to be in that they only have to be configured to other planets by sign when in these positions, and not by degree. While it is also positive when a benefic overcomes another planet through a superior sextile, the sextile is usually characterized as weaker than the trine; it is thus uncertain whether this would be powerful enough to count as a full-fledged condition of bonification.

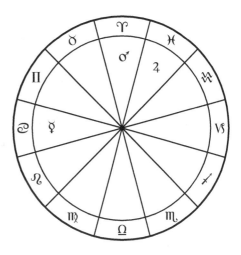

Figure 14.1 - Mars Maltreats and Jupiter Bonifies Mercury via Overcoming

To give an example, if Mercury was located in Cancer, and Jupiter was in Pisces or Aries, then Jupiter would be in a position to overcome Mercury through a superior trine or square, respectively; as a result, Jupiter would be in a position to bonify Mercury. Conversely, if Mercury was in Cancer, while Mars or Saturn were placed in Aries, they would be in a position to overcome Mercury through a superior square, thus maltreating Mercury.

Sect as a Mitigating Factor

Another important factor that must be kept in mind here is the role of sect, because it can either intensify or mitigate the power of the benefics and malefics to bonify or maltreat other planets. Sect plays this role in all of the bonification and maltreatment conditions, because it is the consideration that identifies whether the benefics and malefics are acting to the fullest extreme in their natural inclinations as benefics or malefics, or conversely whether they are acting in a more restrained way, and thus less beneficially or less maleficently than they otherwise could be.

From a practical standpoint, one of the main things that we can gain from sect is the ability to identify the planet that has the most potential for harming or maltreating other planets in the chart, as well as the planet that has the most potential for helping or bonifying other planets. Other factors aside, the planet that has the most potential to harm other planets through maltreatment is the malefic that is contrary to the sect, which would be Mars in a day chart or Saturn in a night chart. Conversely, the planet that has the most potential to help other planets through bonification is the benefic that is of the sect, which is Jupiter in a day chart or Venus in a night chart. The malefic that is of the sect is generally not as damaging when maltreating other planets. Similarly, the benefic that is contrary to the sect is generally not as helpful when bonifying other planets in a chart. This sets up a spectrum or gradation when determining which planets are being bonified or maltreated in a given chart, and whether it is the most extreme scenario or somewhere in between.

Examples of Bonification and Maltreatment via Overcoming

Valens uses the concept of overcoming numerous times in example charts at different points in the *Anthology*, although these examples are often tied in with demonstrating other techniques that have not been introduced yet in this book, such as the triplicity rulers of the sect light or the Lot of Fortune.[10] As a result of that, here we will focus on contemporary examples of bonification and maltreatment through overcoming.

RULER OF THIRD MALTREATED

A native who was born with a diurnal chart, and Cancer rising. Virgo occupies the third place, and the ruler, Mercury, is in Gemini in the twelfth. Mars is in Pisces, overcoming and dominating Mercury through a superior, sign-based square. Here the diurnal sect of the chart accentuates the malefic nature of Mars. The native's older sister had a very good life, and was very successful, which is represented by Mercury being well-situated in its own domicile. She was

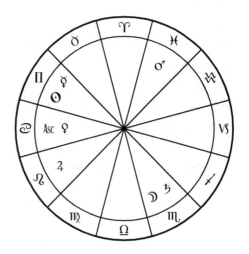

Chart 47 - Ruler of Third Maltreated

described as "a classic overachiever," was president of her class in high school, and president of the student union in college. The native described her sister as pretty and popular, the superstar who their mom lived through vicariously. But the native's sister was diagnosed with cancer at the age of thirty-three, and died at the age of thirty-five. In this instance, the ruler of the third place of siblings in its own zodiacal sign indicated the positive qualities and potential that the sibling had in her life, but the placement in the twelfth and the maltreatment by Mars indicated loss and being cut down while in her prime.

---

[10] E.g. Valens, *Anthology*, 2, 27: 8–12 (Neugebauer, *Greek Horoscopes*, No. L 101, III); *Anthology*, 2, 37: 48–51 (No. L 85, XI); *Anthology*, 2, 37: 60–62 (No. L 92, XI).

STEVE WOZNIAK

We have seen previously that Steve Wozniak's second-place ruler, Venus, located in the eleventh seemed to explain how he became very wealthy as a result of his friendship with Steve Jobs when they founded Apple Computer. We can add an additional level of information by noting that Venus is also being overcome by Jupiter in Pisces through a superior trine in a day chart. Thus, Jupiter is fully benefic, and he is overcoming Venus through the most positive

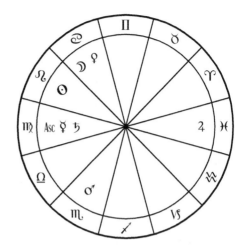

Chart 48 - Steve Wozniak

configuration possible, the trine. Thus, not only is there a connection between the native's finances and his friends with the ruler of the second in the eleventh, but the outcome is also positive because the ruler is being bonified.

CHE GUEVARA

Previously used as an example of someone with the ruler of the Hour-Marker in the twelfth place, Che Guevara also has the rulers of the eighth and fourth in the twelfth. He died in a foreign country after being captured and executed by his enemies. Here we can add an additional detail by noting that he has a night chart with Saturn in Sagittarius in the ninth place, overcoming and dominating Mars and the Moon in Pisces in the twelfth, which are the rulers of the

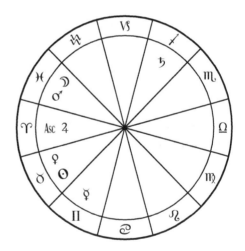

Chart 49 - Che Guevara

first, eighth, and fourth places, respectively. Thus, the outcome is negative or difficult in terms of his personal experience, since the rulers are maltreated.

ANONYMOUS (DOCTOR)

Returning to the chart of a doctor who became the head of a hospital, it was previously noted that the ruler of the first and tenth places was Jupiter, which was located in Leo in the sixth place, and configured to the degree of the quadrant

Midheaven within three degrees. We can now see an additional reason why this position worked out positively: Jupiter is also being overcome or dominated by Venus in Taurus in a night chart through a superior sign-based square. In this way there can sometimes be multiple mitigating conditions which can enable placements that would otherwise be difficult to manifest in a constructive and beneficial manner.

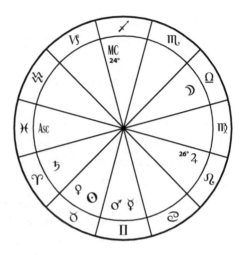

Chart 50 - Doctor

PHILIPPE POZZO DI BORGO

Philippe Pozzo di Borgo provides a mixed case of bonification and maltreatment with respect to the same significator. He was born with a day chart, Cancer rising, and the Moon in Gemini in the twelfth place. The Moon is overcome by Mars in Pisces in the ninth, as well as by Jupiter and Venus in the same sign, through a superior sign-based square. Di Borgo was a wealthy French businessman who was involved in a paragliding accident that left him paralyzed. Around the same time, his wife was diagnosed with cancer and died while he was still in recovery. He fell into a deep depression, and attempted suicide, but failed. He was saved by a foreign caretaker from Algeria who was initially hired to help him with basic tasks, but subsequently helped to

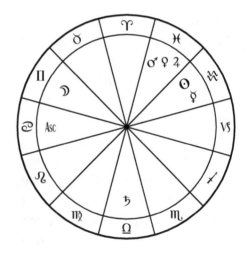

Chart 51 - Philippe Pozzo di Borgo

reinvigorate his life with meaning and purpose. Di Borgo wrote a book about this experience in 2001 called *A Second Wind* (*Le Second Souffle*), which was subsequently turned into a successful film in 2011. The point of this example is that sometimes, when a significator is being both bonified and maltreated, it can result in both extremely positive and negative events with respect to that part of life. Alternatively, in other instances this can have a mitigating effect which lessens the severity of a bonified or maltreated planet.

Opposition and Trine

Porphyry specifies being opposed by a malefic as one of the conditions of maltreatment. This seems to refer to a sign-based opposition with a malefic, rather than requiring a degree-based opposition. The opposition seems to generally be regarded as the most difficult configuration in the literature, and in some ways it becomes the special aspect of the malefics by which they are capable of doing the most harm. In the Thema Mundi, the opposition is specifically associated with Saturn.

In terms of inferring what the corresponding condition of bonification is here if the malefics are able to maltreat through a simple sign-based opposition, I would suggest that the answer is the trine. In the previous condition of overcoming, it was notable that while the malefics could only maltreat by overcoming through a superior sign-based square, the benefics could bonify by overcoming through a superior square or trine. Thus in the previous condition, the benefics had two configurations, while the malefics only had one. The addition of the opposition in this condition balances things out, as it gives the malefics two sign-based configurations by which they can maltreat other planets. By extension, the special aspect of the benefics is the trine, which is generally regarded in the texts as the more powerful and more beneficent of the two positive aspects, and it is implied here that the trine is the special configuration by which the benefics can bonify other planets. In the Thema Mundi, the trine is associated with Jupiter. For the purpose of bonification this this probably only requires a sign-based superior trine, rather than needing to be a close, degree-based trine.

Example of Maltreatment through Sign-Based Opposition

The power of the superior trine to bonify has already been demonstrated in the previous section, so here we will focus on an example of maltreatment through a sign-based opposition.

MICHAEL PATRICK MACDONALD

Michael Patrick MacDonald is an American writer who was born with a diurnal chart and Taurus rising. His Libra Moon in the sixth place rules the third place of siblings, and it is opposed by Mars in Aries. This wide, sign-based opposition from Mars in Aries in the twelfth place is made more difficult because Mars is contrary to the sect. The placement is slightly offset by being overcome by Jupiter in Gemini, resulting in the native having many siblings, but unfortunately many of them had tragic ends. One sibling died as an infant. Another of his brothers committed suicide by slitting his wrists and jumping off a building. A sister was pushed off a building due to a dispute over drugs; although she survived the fall, she suffered brain damage and paralysis. Another brother was shot during a bank robbery, and then subsequently strangled to death by his partners in crime in order to protect their identities. Another brother was hung in jail, which may have been a murder or a suicide. Finally, another younger brother was implicated in the murder of a friend at the age of thirteen. Thus, with the ruler of the third in the sixth,

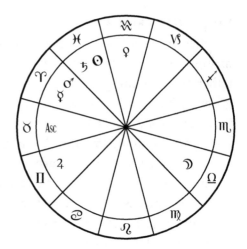

Chart 52 - Michael Patrick MacDonald

maltreated by an opposition from Mars in a day chart, the native's siblings were involved in injuries, accidents, and general misfortunes.

Counteraction

The last condition mentioned in the definition of maltreatment is a planet being ruled by a poorly-situated malefic. This is defined earlier in the Antiochus *Summary* and in Porphyry as "counteraction" (*antanalusis*).[11] Counteraction is defined in the following way by Porphyry:

> It is called counteraction whenever the diurnal stars occupy the domiciles or exaltations of the nocturnal stars or the nocturnal stars occupy the domiciles or exaltations of the diurnal stars, or whenever stars that lie upon zodiacal signs operate advantageously, but the rulers of those signs are in a state of maltreatment, being disadvantageous (*achrēmatistoi*).[12]

The second part of this explanation, which focuses on the domicile lord of the sign being located in a disadvantageous place, is used in the definition of maltreatment. This concept seems to have had wide currency in the Hellenistic tradition, and is also mentioned by Valens and Firmicus.[13] The general underlying premise is that when a planet is not in its own zodiacal sign, it has to rely on the host of that sign for support. "Counteraction" occurs when the domicile lord of a planet is in a condition in the chart that is contrary to the initial planet's

---

[11] Antiochus, *Summary*, 16. Porphyry, *Introduction*, 27.
[12] Porphyry, *Introduction*, 27, trans. Demetra George, unpublished.
[13] Valens, *Anthology*, 2, 2: 26–28. Firmicus, *Mathesis*, 2, 20: 7–9.

condition. In the case of maltreatment, counteraction occurs when a planet is ruled by a poorly-situated malefic that is in one of the bad places, especially the sixth or twelfth, which are the two worst places. Rhetorius applies the concept of counteraction to all of the bad places, which may have some merit, although the worst-case scenario will probably only occur when the ruler is situated in what are generally agreed to be the worst places.

By inference, the inverse scenario for this condition that would constitute a positive case of bonification through counteraction would be when a poorly-situated planet is ruled by a benefic that is in one of the good places, especially the first, tenth, eleventh, or fifth. Thus, bonification via counteraction essentially occurs when a planet is ruled by a favorably placed benefic planet that is in one of the good or advantageous places.

Since the bonification and maltreatment conditions tend to represent extremes, different combinations can be helpful or harmful. The important thing to keep in mind is that a planet depends on its domicile lord for support, based on the guest-host metaphor discussed earlier.

Tiger Woods

A contemporary example of maltreatment through counteraction occurs in the chart of the eminent golfer, Tiger Woods, who was born with a nocturnal chart, Virgo rising, and Mercury in Capricorn in the fifth place. Mercury is relatively well-situated: Venus overcomes it through a close, superior, degree-based sextile from Scorpio. Mercury is also configured by a square to Jupiter, and is in aversion to both malefics.

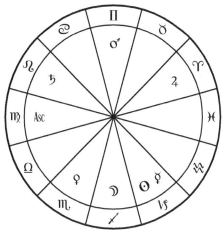

Chart 53 - Tiger Woods

However, while Mercury is relatively well-situated, it is not in its own sign, but instead it is in the domicile of Saturn; it must thus depend on Saturn for support. Unfortunately, Saturn is not well-situated in this chart: it is a malefic planet located in the twelfth place, retrograde, contrary to the sect, and in the sign of its adversity. Thus Mercury—the domicile lord of the Hour-Marker—is being maltreated through the counteraction of its domicile lord. Woods was a child prodigy who was introduced to the sport of golf at a very early age, and eventually became one of the most successful and highest-paid athletes in the world. However, when his many extramarital affairs were revealed in late 2009, it created major turmoil in his life. This resulted in the loss of his marriage, the loss of sponsorships, and ultimately impacted his ability to play golf successfully. While he attempted to make a comeback, the necessity of back surgery left him struggling to regain his former success. By 2016 he had dropped out of the top 500 ranked golfers in the world for the first time in his career.

This example demonstrates two important characteristics of counteraction. The first is that they tend to be characterized by reversals, especially when one planet is extremely well-situated and the ruler is extremely-poorly placed, or vice versa; the second is that the placement of the first planet usually describes the initial set of circumstances or how things proceed in the beginning, while the condition of the ruler describes how things develop later on. As an interpretive principle, this is most pronounced in extreme cases of counteraction. It also comes up in electional texts, such as a statement attributed to Petosiris in which the condition of the Moon in an electional chart indicates the first part of the matter, while the condition of the Moon's ruler indicates the outcome.[14]

Enclosure

"Enclosure" (*emperischesis*) is the Hellenistic equivalent of the Medieval concept of "besiegement," which is when a planet is surrounded either bodily or by ray by both malefics, or both benefics. This concept is defined in the Antiochus *Summary*, in Porphyry, and in Rhetorius.[15] There is both a sign-based version of the concept as well as a degree-based version, as well as a third circumstance that can set up the conditions to nullify both. We will examine all three here.

The sign-based version of this concept is known as *perischesis*, which according to the LSJ lexicon means "surrounding," "taking in flank," or "blockade." I will follow Schmidt's convention in translating the term as "containment."[16] The concept is only defined in Porphyry and Hephaestio (who is probably following Porphyry).[17] According to these authors, containment occurs when a planet is in a sign that is surrounded by the sign-based aspects of another planet, with no other planet sending in an interposing sign-based aspect to the contained planet. As an example, Porphyry uses the Moon in Virgo and Mars in Aries. The Moon is said to be "contained" by the rays of Mars, who sends a sign-based trine ray to Leo, and a sign-based opposition ray to Libra. Since Leo and Libra are the two signs on either side of Virgo, the Moon is said to be contained by Mars's rays, and this is considered to be destructive. Porphyry adds that if a benefic

---

[14] Julian of Laodicea summarizing Petosiris in CCAG, 1, p. 138: 2–15.

[15] Antiochus, *Summary*, 12; Porphyry, *Introduction*, 15, Rhetorius, *Compendium*, 41.

[16] Schmidt, *Definitions and Foundations*, pp. 195–196.

[17] Porphyry, *Introduction*, 14; Hephaestio, *Apotelesmatika*, 1, 15: 1–2.

is configured to the planet that is contained, then it can offset the destructive nature of the containment from a malefic. While Porphyry only uses a negative example, adding that a benefic could break the containment, presumably the reverse scenario—a benefic containment—could also be true.

There is also a degree-based version of this condition that is mentioned more frequently in the surviving literature, called *emperischesis*. The LSJ lexicon refers to this as "hemming in," although I will follow Schmidt's convention in calling it "enclosure."[18] It is defined by Porphyry as follows:

> It is called 'enclosure' whenever two stars enclose one between them when no other star casts a ray in the intervening space, and further when even other [stars] cast rays according to figure either onto the seven degrees which the star has passed or onto the seven degrees toward which it is proceeding, or when even the same and one star casts its rays from different figures, as was mentioned previously. And this such containment when occurring under the agency of destructive stars is harsh, but when by benefic stars is beneficent.[19]

Two forms of enclosure are defined here. The first is when either two benefics or two malefics are on either side of a planet by bodily conjunction. The second is when either two benefics or two malefics surround a third planet with their degree-based rays, within seven degrees on each side. Both types of enclosure can be nullified by the presence of a third condition known as "intervention" (*mesembolēsis*). Intervention occurs when a planet intervenes in an enclosure, either bodily (by getting in between a planet that is attempting to enclose another planet), or by casting its rays in the intervening degrees between the encloser and the enclosed planet.[20] What this means is that in both instances of enclosure, the two benefics or two malefics must be the only planets on either side of the planet that is being enclosed; otherwise the enclosure will be broken up and it will not count as a case of bonification or maltreatment. Intervention seems to be defined broadly enough that it is applicable any time a planet gets in the way of some sort of degree-based aspect between planets, thus it may also be applicable to other conditions that we will discuss later, such as "adherence."

While a degree range is mentioned for enclosure by ray, it is not specified for bodily enclosure by conjunction. This makes it uncertain whether there can be an extremely large range (as long as no other planet sends an intervening

---

[18] Schmidt, *Definitions and Foundations*, p. 197.

[19] Porphyry, *Introduction*, 15, trans. Demetra George, unpublished.

[20] As defined in Porphyry, *Introduction*, 16, and to a lesser extent Rhetorius, *Compendium*, 36.

ray), or if it should be restricted to seven degrees on either side. It is also unclear if sign boundaries are a factor that should be taken into account here, although it seems likely that they would have been, and that most of these configurations were assumed to be taking place in the same sign.

CHRIS FARLEY

There is an example of enclosure in the birth chart of Chris Farley, who was a comedian and actor popular in the early 1990s. He was born with a day chart, the Ascendant at 5° Leo, and the Sun at 26°14' Aquarius. The Sun is enclosed bodily between Saturn at 25° Aquarius and Mars at 26°30' Aquarius. The malefic enclosure in his chart is exacerbated because it is a day chart, and the Sun—the domicile lord of the Hour-

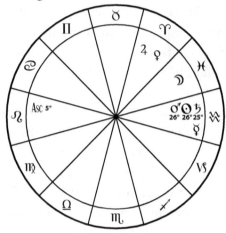

Chart 54 - Chris Farley

Marker—is applying to Mars, which means that the Sun is also in an adherence with the malefic contrary to sect, with no interventions present. Farley was a regular on the weekly television comedy show *Saturday Night Live*, and played the lead role in comedies that grew in popularity by the mid-1990s. However, he struggled with drug and alcohol abuse, and died on December 18, 1997 at the age of thirty-three due to a cocaine and morphine overdose.

ROBIN WILLIAMS

Another example of enclosure occurs in the birth chart of Robin Williams, who was a famous actor and comedian. His chart provides an interesting case because there is a benefic enclosure that mitigates and improves the condition of the most difficult planet in the chart. He was born with a day chart, Scorpio rising, and Mars in Cancer in the ninth place. Mars is contrary to the sect, and in the sign of its depression. Since it is the ruler of the Ascendant, we would expect him to take on or embody the agency of the malefic in some way, or have it manifest partially within the context of the significations associated with the first place. While in his public life, Williams was a comedian and entertainer, privately he suffered from depression and struggled with drug and alcohol addiction, which is relevant in terms of Mars also ruling the sixth place of illness. He lived a relatively long and successful life, though, due to the fact that Mars' condition is mitigated as a result of being enclosed by the rays of the benefics.

Mars is at 11° Cancer, while Venus is at 10° Virgo and Jupiter is at 13° Aries. Venus sends a sextile ray to 10° Cancer, which lands just before Mars, while Jupiter sends a square ray to 13° Cancer, which falls just after Mars. Thus, Mars is enclosed by the rays of both benefics, within seven degrees on each side, and as a result Mars is bonified. This mitigation seems to have allowed him to manage and overcome many of the issues that he struggled with for years. However, in his final years he

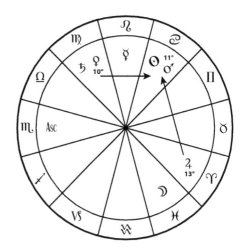

Chart 55 - Robin Williams

began experiencing the effects of Lewy body dementia and Parkinson's disease. In the end he committed suicide by hanging at the age of sixty-three. Despite his personal struggles, he is generally regarded as having had a positive influence on many people. While in some sense it is true that the malefic qualities of Mars expressed themselves through his internal struggles and illnesses, the point of this example is that the enclosure from the benefics seems to have moderated the severity of some of these issues, and given him the help and support necessary to lead a largely successful and happy life.

Adherence

Adherence (*kollēsis*) is defined in the Antiochus *Summary* and Rhetorius as an applying bodily conjunction that is within three degrees of being exact.[21] Porphyry adds that for the Moon, the range is thirteen degrees, which is the average distance it will travel in a twenty-four-hour period.[22] The definition of maltreatment says that a planet is maltreated when it is in an adherence with a malefic.

While the general sense of this condition of maltreatment is clear, there are some ambiguities surrounding the specifics. If an adherence is an applying conjunction within three degrees, does that mean that another planet has to apply to the malefic in order to be maltreated, or does the malefic have to apply to the planet in order to maltreat it? In other words, which planet has to move towards the other according to this condition? Or is the condition still in effect either way, regardless of which planet applies to the other? The grammar in the

---

[21] Antiochus, *Summary*, 9; Rhetorius, *Compendium*, 34.

[22] Porphyry, *Introduction*, 11. Cf. Rhetorius, *Compendium*, 35.

Antiochus *Summary* seems to imply that it is the other planet that must apply to the malefic. However, Rhetorius appears to say that it is the malefic that must apply to the planet. Finally, Porphyry is more ambiguous, and could be interpreted either way.

Contemporary solutions to this problem have gone in different directions. Schmidt prefers the interpretation in which the malefic must apply to another planet in order to maltreat it.[23] My objection to this interpretation is that this would mean that Saturn would never be able to maltreat other planets by adherence, and Mars would only be able to maltreat Jupiter and Saturn. In order for a planet to apply or move towards an exact conjunction with another planet, it has to be able to move faster than it. Thus, if the malefics had to apply to other planets in order to maltreat them, it would largely make this condition of maltreatment functionally useless.[24] I therefore prefer the interpretation in which a planet can be maltreated when it applies *to* a conjunction with a malefic. In this scenario, all of the planets are capable of being maltreated by Saturn via adherence, because Saturn is the slowest moving visible planet, and thus any of the other planets can apply to a conjunction with him within three degrees. While this interpretation does make it so that Jupiter and Saturn cannot normally be maltreated by Mars through adherence, since they cannot move fast enough to apply *to* Mars, all of the other planets—Venus, Mercury, Sun, Moon—can be maltreated by Mars by applying to a conjunction with him.

This interpretation is also appealing conceptually because it coheres with the general concept of application and separation, which was introduced earlier in the Antiochus text prior to the definition of maltreatment.[25] As discussed earlier, in texts on inceptional astrology, applying configurations are usually interpreted as signifying events and circumstances that will take place in the future, while separating configurations are interpreted as describing conditions that have taken place in the past. This is why applying aspects are sometimes

---

[23] Schmidt, *Definitions and Foundations*, pp. 269–270.

[24] There is, however, one possible piece of textual support for this interpretation in Valens, *Anthology*, 2, 31: 20, where he seems to make a statement in a parenthetical remark that "overcoming" can occur when planets are in the same sign or opposed, and that the planet that approaches overcomes the one that is later. It is not clear if this was standard doctrine or if it was Valens' own opinion though. Overcoming is typically only applied to the square, trine, and sextile, and that seems to be why Valens makes this remark in the first place, since it is a non-standard view. There is also still a conceptual issue because outer planets like Saturn would not move towards or apply to the later planet, because Saturn moves slower than the other planets. Thus, whether this is sufficient justification to interpret Antiochus' condition of maltreatment through adherence as occurring when a malefic applies to another planet is unclear.

[25] See especially Porphyry, *Introduction*, 12.

given more weight in texts on electional astrology, since they indicate the future of whatever is being initiated at that moment in time. With regard to the doctrine of adherence, any planets moving towards an exact conjunction with a malefic would presage difficult circumstances in the future.

If this interpretation is correct, maltreatment by adherence takes place when a planet applies to a bodily conjunction with a malefic within three degrees. For example, if Mercury was at 18° Cancer and Saturn was at 20° Cancer, then Mercury would be maltreated by Saturn, because it is applying to a conjunction within three degrees. Conversely, by inference, bonification through adherence occurs when a planet applies to a bodily conjunction with a benefic within three degrees. For example, if Mercury was at 18° Cancer and Jupiter was at 20° Cancer, then Mercury would be bonified by Jupiter, because it is applying to a conjunction with him within three degrees. All of the planets except for Saturn would be able to be bonified by Jupiter in this way, and Venus would usually be able to bonify the Sun, Moon, and Mercury. Retrograde periods create a special set of conditions in which planets that might not otherwise be able to apply to other planets through an adherence may be able to do so.

RULER OF ELEVENTH MALTREATED

Let's return to an example from the previous chapter, a native who had the ruler of the eleventh place of friends in the eighth place of death, and lost her only friend prematurely due to cancer. The ruler of the eleventh is Venus, which is at 9° Cancer, and it is applying to a conjunction with Mars at 12° Cancer, within three degrees. Mars is also the malefic that is contrary to the sect, since this is a day chart. Thus, the ruler of the eleventh is not just located in a bad place, but

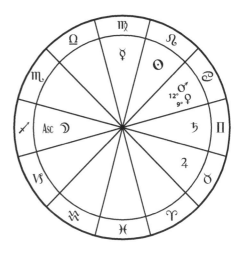

Chart 56 - Ruler of Eleventh Maltreated

it is also being maltreated by the most difficult malefic in the chart through adherence. This is a useful example because it demonstrates how sometimes the worst-case scenarios only come about as a result of a combination of multiple factors. Even here there was some mitigation due to superior sign-based sextile from Jupiter in Taurus, and while this was not enough to completely cancel out the adherence, it was enough to ensure that the native's early life was not completely devoid of friendship.

MAYA ANGELOU

Eminent American writer and poet Maya Angelou had two instances of bonification via adherence in her chart. She was born with a day chart, Leo rising, and the Sun at 14° Aries in the ninth place in an adherence with Jupiter at 16° Aries. In addition to the Sun and Jupiter, she also had Mercury at 20° Pisces in an adherence with Venus at 21° Pisces. Thus both the domicile lord of the Hour-Marker and Mercury were bonified. As with the earlier example

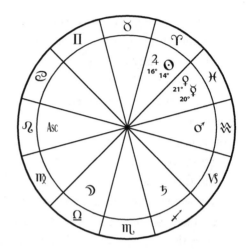

Chart 57 - Maya Angelou

of T. S. Eliot, whose success in the field of poetry was indicated by his Mercury-Venus conjunction in Libra on the degree of the Ascendant, Maya Angelou provides a parallel example of another successful poet with that combination prominent in her chart. In her case Venus is the ruler of the tenth place of career and reputation, and it is exalted in Pisces, with Mercury in an adherence with it. During the course of her life she received many awards and honors for her writings, including the Presidential Medal of Freedom from President Obama in 2011, which is the highest award that a civilian can receive in the United States.

JAMES EAGAN HOLMES

James Eagan Holmes was a mass murderer who killed twelve people and injured seventy others in a gun massacre at a theater in Aurora, Colorado, on July 20, 2012. At the trial he pled not guilty by reason of insanity, although the shooting had been meticulously planned out, and he was eventually convicted and sentenced to life in prison without the possibility of parole. He was born with Leo rising and the Sun at 21° Sagittarius in an adherence with

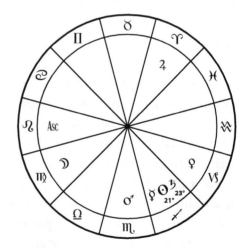

Chart 58 - James Eagan Holmes

Saturn at 23° Sagittarius. Thus, the domicile lord of the Hour-Marker is being maltreated by Saturn, and it is made worse by the fact that it is a night chart.

This case is interesting because it raises some questions about what we are seeing here. Did the maltreatment of the ruler of the Hour-Marker indicate the corruption of the native in this instance? Did the native essentially become or take on the agency of the malefic as a result of the adherence with Saturn? Or did the maltreatment of the ruler of the Ascendant just foreshadow his being sentenced to life in prison at the age of 27 years old, shortly before his first Saturn return would begin?

LIFE INSURANCE FROM FATHER

One last example of adherence, a native who was born during the day with Leo rising and the Sun at 22° Pisces in the eighth place, in an adherence with Jupiter at 24° Pisces. The native's father died suddenly and unexpectedly of a heart attack when she was twenty-six years old. The father had a sizable life insurance policy which the native received, since she was an only child and her father and mother had divorced years earlier. The native invested some of the money in a mutual fund that did

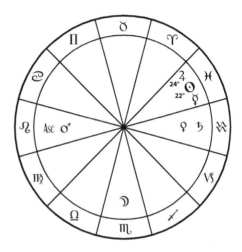

Chart 59 - Life Insurance from Father

well for a time, and this allowed her to spend more than a decade finding her life direction. This example shows how some of the standard themes associated with the eighth place regarding death and inheritance can manifest in a very literal way. It is also important because it demonstrates some of the specific circumstances under which difficult events can sometimes have positive outcomes, which can ultimately help to shape the course of the native's life in a constructive fashion.

Striking With A Ray

"Striking with a ray" (*aktinobolia*) is one of the most difficult yet important concepts to reconstruct and understand in the series of definitions of different configurations from the lost work of Antiochus. The reconstruction of what this concept means is complicated by that fact that different astrologers seem to define or use the term in different ways throughout the Hellenistic tradition. It is defined in the Antiochus *Summary*, Porphyry, and Rhetorius.[26] Part of our

---

[26] Antiochus, *Summary*, 13; Porphyry, *Introduction*, 24, Rhetorius, *Compendium*, 20–22.

challenge here will be understanding the general usage of the term, as well as the specific way that it was used in the original Antiochus text as a condition of maltreatment. Here is the core of the definition, according to Porphyry:

> A leading star 'hurls a ray' at a following star according to an aspect (*schēma*). For example, the star in Aries hurls a ray at a star in Capricorn according to the square, and at a star in Sagittarius according to the trine; the star following looks upon (*ephoraō*) the star leading and even overcomes it, being carried towards it, as has been previously mentioned, but it does not hurl a ray. For every beam (*augēs*), the sight (*opsis*) is carried towards the star ahead, but the ray (*aktis*) to the star behind. And then it is necessary to observe whether it hurls a ray only zodiacally or if it is also joining (*sunaptei*) by degree.[27]

The Greek term for this concept is *aktinobolia,* which is a compound word formed from *aktina,* "ray" or "beam," and *ballō,* "throw," "cast," "hurl," or "strike." As a specific technical term *aktinobolia* seems to mean either "hurling a ray," when the process itself is the focus, or alternatively "striking with a ray," as Schmidt puts it, when the end result of the process is the focus.[28] Oftentimes authors will use *aktina* and *ballō* separately to refer to the general notion of "casting a ray," such as when Porphyry says that each planet emits seven partile rays; but when the two words are put together to create a compound word it seems to refer to a specific technical concept, which is "striking with a ray" or "hurling a ray."

Earlier in the series of definitions in Antiochus and Porphyry, the configurations or aspect rays that are directed forwards in the order of signs were defined as "overcoming." That is to say, planets that are earlier in zodiacal order were said to overcome planets that are later in zodiacal order when they are configured. The definition of *aktinobolia* seems to suggest that configurations or rays that are sent backwards in zodiacal order are called "hurling rays" or "striking with a ray." It thus distinguishes between planets that send "aspects" forward in zodiacal order, which are able to "look upon" (*ephoraō*) other planets, versus planets that send aspects backwards in zodiacal order, which "hurl a ray." The *Summary* and Rhetorius use an example with a planet in Aries hurling a ray backwards in zodiacal order to a planet in Capricorn. Porphyry uses the same example, but then adds that a planet in Aries would also hurl a ray at a planet in Sagittarius. Thus, at the most fundamental level "hurling a ray" or "striking with a ray" was originally defined as an aspect that is cast backwards in the order of

---

[27] Porphyry, *Introduction*, 24, first half, trans. Demetra George, unpublished, modified.

[28] Schmidt, *Definitions and Foundations*, pp. 207–208.

signs; it is thus bound to similar distinctions such as right versus left, as well as overcoming and domination.

Matters become more complicated when we look at this definition in the context of the conditions of maltreatment, because there, overcoming and striking with a ray are both said to be conditions of maltreatment. As we have seen previously, maltreatment by overcoming can only occur through the superior sign-based square, since the trine and sextile are generally seen as incapable of doing harm. The same restriction applies when we look at striking with a ray as an aspect cast backwards in the order of signs; as a condition of maltreatment it could only refer to an inferior square cast backwards in the order of signs.

At this point we run into a contradiction: the definition of overcoming says that the planet that is earlier in the order of signs is always in the superior position, thus its ability to maltreat the planet on the inferior end of the square. If we were to take the definition of maltreatment at face value, it would mean that malefics are capable of maltreating by square whether they are in a superior or inferior position; in other words, whether they are earlier or later in the order of signs. This is problematic conceptually because it seems to negate the earlier distinction between superior and inferior aspects.

The solution to this issue seems to lie in an additional statement that Porphyry makes towards the end of the definition, where he says "it is necessary to observe whether it hurls a ray only zodiacally or if it is also joining (*sunaptei*) by degree." This harkens back to the statement in the definition of testimony where it is said that witnessing can occur both by sign and by degree. This seems to imply that we may be talking about degree-based aspects here rather than just sign-based ones, and in fact in later authors this concept is often mentioned within the context of primary directions, where specific degree ranges are necessary.[29] Even the term "striking with a ray" or "hurling a ray" evokes the concept mentioned earlier by Porphyry that every planet emits seven degree-based rays, from the degree that it is in, to the same degree in seven other signs.

Thus I would suggest that the solution to the seeming contradiction in the definition of maltreatment is that malefics that are earlier in zodiacal order and thus in the superior position are capable of maltreating other planets through a simple sign-based square, whereas a malefic that is later in zodiacal order and thus in the inferior position must send a close degree-based aspect backwards in the order of signs through a square in order to be in a position to maltreat another planet. This allows us to retain the distinction introduced earlier that planets that are earlier in zodiacal order play a dominant role in the aspect relationship between two planets, while at the same time adding an exception to

---

[29] E.g. Valens, *Anthology*, 3, 1: 2ff.

this rule that only happens infrequently, by allowing a certain set of conditions whereby an inferior planet can become capable of fighting back or turning the tables despite its inferior position.

Looking at the concept of *aktinobolia* from this perspective, I would suggest that when the term is used without reference to an object, it simply means "to send an aspect backwards in the order of signs," but when a specific planet is specified it means "to cast a ray backwards in the order of signs to strike another planet." Thus, even though the same term is used in both instances, the way *aktinobolia* should be read in the texts is context specific. Sometimes the phrase "hurling a ray" is the most appropriate way to render it, when the author is referring to a sign-based aspect cast backwards in the order of signs, but other times the phrase "striking with a ray" is more appropriate when the author is referring to a degree-based aspect that hits another planet.

This seems to explain some ambiguities in the second part of Porphyry's definition of striking with a ray, where he talks about there being two different schools of thought on the definition of striking with a ray:

> There are two schools of thought concerning this matter. For some state that the star hurls a ray in accordance with a square from the leading sign at the star which is departing from the following sign. For example, a star in Cancer hurls a ray at a star in Aries, but a star in Aries looks upon a star in Cancer, which they go so far as to say that it destroys if it should be a malefic. For, the star that hurls a ray destroys, not the star that looks upon. The star configured by opposition both hurls a ray and looks upon, however the star configured according to the trine never hurls a ray. For the star fixes its ray upon the square which is nearer than the trine, so that the affinity of the star is more beneficent upon the trine. And that is how it is in these matters.
>
> However, Thrasyllus says that the hurling of rays is destruction, and those [planets] destroy which are configured to one another according to the square or the opposition figures in the interval of the Hour-Marking degree, provided that the testimony of the trine configuration is not taken as destructive. He says it does not make a difference whether the ray is carried forth from the right or the left side into the succedent place of the Hour-Marker or whether the ray is borne forth from the star having the rulership of the Moon. He says that even if the Moon happens to have the domicile master [conjoined] with her or opposed to her that the releasing will be made from the domicile master. For example, if the Moon should

be in Sagittarius with Jupiter, or if Jupiter is in Gemini with the Moon herself being in Sagittarius, we will release (*aphēsis*) from Jupiter.[30]

This commentary is evidently by Porphyry, as there is no parallel in the Antiochus *Summary*. The main thing that I take from it is that one school primarily views striking with a ray as a square ray that is cast backwards in the order of signs, while the other school (deriving from Thrasyllus) believes striking with a ray can occur on the right or the left side of the planet. This seems to be because originally striking with a ray was defined in terms of an aspect cast backwards in the order of signs, especially as a degree-based aspect; but that as the tradition went on the integration of the concept of striking with a ray into primary directions made the directionality of the aspect less important, since it became a general term used to describe any type of degree-based aspect. That is to say, the notion that each planet emits seven degree-based rays became conflated with the concept of striking with a ray. This seems to have created some confusion in the subsequent tradition, which is still evident when reading many of the texts.

The next question that arises is whether there are any ranges involved for a planet to be considered "struck" by the ray of another planet. Unfortunately, Antiochus, Porphyry, and Rhetorius leave this point ambiguous. However, in the *Anthology* Valens discusses *aktinobolia* at one point within the context of the length of life technique, and there he specifies a three-degree range on either side of a planet that is susceptible to "striking with a ray."[31] This is interesting because three degrees is also the range for adherence (*kollēsis*) and engagement (*sunaphē*), and I strongly suspect that this is the implied range for striking with a ray as well, although this is never made explicit in the different versions of the Antiochus definitions themselves. Nonetheless, if Valens' range is at all representative of what other astrologers were using, then within the context of the definition of maltreatment, striking with a ray would be defined as a degree-based aspect that is cast by a malefic backwards in the order of signs, which strikes another planet within three degrees on either side of an exact aspect.

The final distinction here is whether the aspect needs to be applying or separating. It is worth noting again Porphyry's statement towards the end of his definition of striking with a ray, where he says that it is important to see if the planet is only hurling a ray by sign or if it is actually "joining (*sunaptō*) by degree." The word *sunaptō* is usually used in other definitions derived from Antiochus in order to describe the process in which planets in degree-based configurations

---

[30] Porphyry, *Introduction*, 24, second half, trans. Demetra George, unpublished, heavily modified.

[31] Valens, *Anthology*, 3, 3: 42–43.

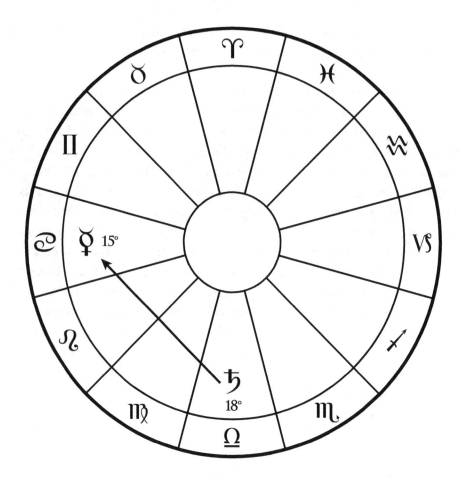

Figure 14.2 - Saturn Strikes Mercury with a Ray

"join" together while they are in the process of forming an exact aspect. It is used especially in the definition of *sunaphē* and *kollēsis*, which both involve applying aspects that are within three degrees. The use of the term "joins" here seems to imply that it was somehow important to determine if the ray is actually in the process of joining to or "perfecting" the configuration with the planet that is being struck with the ray. This seems to imply that either (1) striking with a ray requires an applying configuration within three degrees that will "perfect," or (2) striking with a ray requires an applying configuration that will perfect *at some point* in the future, although there is no restriction on how wide it can be.

I believe this suggests that the idealized form of striking with a ray is an applying configuration within three degrees that is cast backwards in the order of signs, eventually connecting with the planet in the superior position, and thus striking it with the ray of the inferior planet. This was seen as particularly dangerous when the malefic is hurling the ray because then the faster planet is moving towards the slower planet when it runs into its ray.

This ties together multiple concepts, such as hurling rays as an aspect cast backwards in the order of signs; application as being more powerful for the future compared to separation; and "engagement" (*sunaphē*), which involves applying within three degrees to an exact joining, as a particularly important range. While striking with a ray might still be in effect within three degrees on either side of an exact configuration, as per Valens, the most idealized or powerful version of the condition is when it is still applying to an exact aspect within three degrees.

Maltreatment and Bonification via Striking with a Ray

If the foregoing reconstruction is correct, then maltreatment via striking with a ray occurs when a malefic casts an exact degree-based square aspect backwards in the order of signs, and the ray "strikes" another planet, especially through an applying aspect within three degrees. Conversely, bonification through striking with a ray occurs when a benefic casts a trine, square, or possibly sextile ray backwards in the order of signs and strikes another planet, especially if it is an applying aspect within three degrees.

MARTIN LUTHER KING JR.

An example of maltreatment via striking with a ray occurs in the chart of the American civil rights activist, Martin Luther King Jr. He was born with a day chart and the Moon at 19° Pisces, applying to an exact degree-based square with Mars at 21° Gemini. Even though the Moon is earlier in zodiacal order and thus in the superior position, it is moving towards an exact square with Mars, and thus Mars is striking the Moon with its ray, maltreating it. Because it is a day chart, Mars is also the

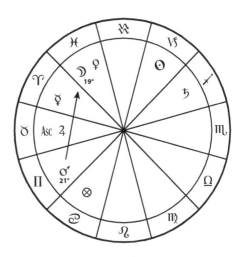

Chart 60 - Martin Luther King Jr.

malefic that is contrary to the sect. This creates a problematic indicator in terms of vitality because the Moon is a general significator of the body, and in this particular chart it also happens to rule the Lot of Fortune in Cancer (which will be discussed later). It is thus one of the major factors in his chart that appears to foreshadow his assassination at the age of thirty-nine.

Albert Einstein

An example of bonification occurs in the chart of the scientist Albert Einstein. He was born with a day chart, Cancer rising, and the Moon at 14° Sagittarius in the sixth place, applying to a trine with Venus at 16° Aries in the tenth place. His Moon is thus being bonified by Venus through striking with a ray. This bonification, combined with the configuration of the Moon to the degree of the quadrant Midheaven at 12° Pisces, heavily mitigated the otherwise

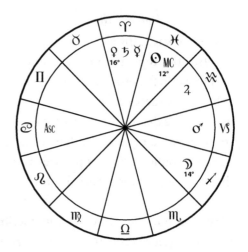

Chart 61 - Albert Einstein

potentially challenging placement of having the domicile lord of the Hour-Marker in the sixth place. This resulted in a lifetime devoted to his successful work in the field of scientific research.

Engagement

The final condition of maltreatment to address is called "joining together," "union," or "engagement" (*sunaphē*). According to the Antiochus *Summary*:

> Engagement (*sunaphē*) is whenever the stars join together (*sunaptō*) by degree or are about to join within three degrees. The engagement of the Moon is said to be whenever it is about to join within thirteen degrees.[32]

Engagement is thus an applying degree-based aspect that is within three degrees of being exact. In my reconstruction, I have made this the final condition, because it is simply a more intense version of some of the other sign-based conditions of maltreatment. From this perspective, maltreatment through engagement occurs when a planet applies to a malefic within three degrees, either by square or opposition, since those are the two aspects by which the malefics do harm.

The three conditions in which there is an overlap with engagement (i.e. overcoming, opposing, and striking with a ray) each have a general range in which the placement is effective, but what this condition stipulates is that they are the *most* effective when they are also in an engagement (i.e. applying to an exact aspect within three degrees). Thus the sign-based opposition that was mentioned as a condition of maltreatment earlier becomes even more damaging

---

[32] Antiochus, *Summary*, 8, trans. Demetra George, unpublished, modified.

when it is a tighter, degree-based opposition through engagement. Similarly, a malefic that is overcoming through a superior sign-based square becomes even more harmful when it is also in an engagement. Finally, the condition of striking with a ray, which seemed to allow for a three-degree range on either side of the planet, becomes more intense when the two planets are also involved in an engagement, so that the planet applies within three degrees to an exact square with a malefic that is in the inferior position.

Bonification via engagement would occur when a planet applies to an exact aspect with a benefic within three degrees by trine, square, or possibly sextile. It is unclear if the opposition would allow for bonification in the most positive sense due to the difficult nature of this configuration, although applying aspects to benefics seem generally to be viewed as positive, so it very well might.

ROBERT F. KENNEDY

An example of maltreatment by engagement occurs in the chart of Robert F. Kennedy. He was born with Taurus rising and the Moon at 28° Capricorn, applying to an out-of-sign degree-based square with Mars at 4° Scorpio in a day chart. Recall Antiochus' statement that the range of engagement for the Moon is thirteen degrees, but three for the rest of the planets. Thus in this instance, the Moon is being maltreated via engagement with Mars, the malefic contrary to the sect. With the ruler of the third maltreated in this way, it shows misfortune in the area of siblings: the native's oldest brother was killed in WWII, his sister died in a plane accident, and his next-oldest brother, President John F. Kennedy, was assassinated while in office. The Moon is also ruling the Lot of Fortune in Cancer in his chart, as it was in the chart of Martin Luther King Jr., and the native would later be assassinated himself while running for President.

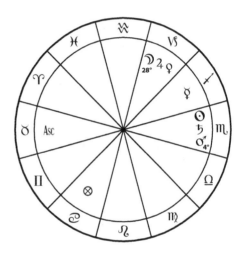

Chart 62 - Robert F. Kennedy

ANDRE ROMELLE YOUNG (DR. DRE)

An example of bonification via engagement occurs in the chart of the rapper and music producer Dr. Dre. He was born with Gemini rising, the Moon at 7° Libra, and Venus at 16° Aquarius. In his chart the Moon rules the second place of financial matters, and it is located in the fifth place of Good Fortune, while applying to a trine with Venus within thirteen degrees (while being received in the domicile of Venus, which will be discussed below). The ruler of the second is thus being bonified by Venus via striking with a ray. Interestingly, Venus herself applies to a square with Jupiter at 18° Taurus within three degrees, also with reception, and thus Venus is

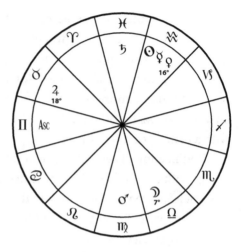

Chart 63 - Dr. Dre

also being bonified via striking with a ray. In 2014, the sale of a company he co-founded, Beats Electronics, made him one of the richest rappers in the world.

JACQUELINE KENNEDY ONASSIS

An example of maltreatment through engagement in an opposition occurs in the chart of Jacqueline Kennedy Onassis. She was born with a day chart, Scorpio rising, and Taurus occupying the seventh place of marriage. The ruler of the seventh is Venus, which is located at 21° Gemini, in the eighth place of death. Venus is applying to an opposition with Saturn at 24° Sagittarius, and thus the ruler of the seventh is being maltreated via engagement with a malefic. Her husband, U.S. President John F. Kennedy, was assassinated while they were riding

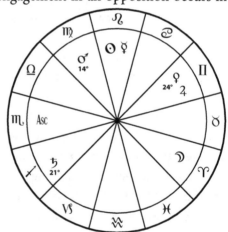

Chart 64 - Jacqueline Kennedy Onassis

in the same car together, and she held him as he died. This instance is worsened by the fact that Mars is located at 14° Virgo, so that Venus is also enclosed by the rays of both malefics. This underscores the point that oftentimes there can be multiple overlapping conditions of bonification or maltreatment in the same chart, which can intensify the quality of the outcome, for better or worse.

Mitigating Conditions: Reception

I would like to close this chapter by mentioning a couple of additional mitigating conditions that are important to take into account when applying some of these techniques in practice: reception, and exchanging domiciles or mutual reception. While these concepts were apparently only explicitly defined starting in the early Medieval tradition in authors such as Māshā'allāh and Sahl ibn Bishr, conceptually they have their roots in the earlier Hellenistic tradition. Moreover, both concepts are so well-defined already by the time that they appear in these two early Medieval authors that I suspect they were drawing on a practice that already existed in the late Hellenistic tradition, which we simply don't have much documentation of. From a practical standpoint I have found them to be very important factors to take into account in my personal practice. For those reasons I feel comfortable discussing the concepts here, with those caveats about their origins being borne in mind.

Implicit in the concept of the signs as domiciles is the idea that the ruler of a sign acts as a host who welcomes any planets that are placed in its sign as guests in its home. An extension of this concept seems to be that it is better when the ruler of a sign is also configured to any guest planets staying in its home; this helps to engender a more favorable or supportive relationship between the domicile lord and planets placed in its sign. Valens for example says at one point in book seven of the *Anthology*:

> One star in another's zodiacal sign and having some relationship with it is productive and beneficial during the applicable timelordship.[33]

This concept was later formalized in the early Medieval tradition as the technical doctrine known as "reception."[34] While the term reception wasn't used or explicitly defined until Medieval times, I will use it here since the concept clearly has a Hellenistic precedent. In a Medieval context, reception is usually defined as an applying aspect that will perfect or become exact between two planets, in which one of the planets has some form of zodiacal rulership over the other.[35] While this concept is not as explicitly defined in the Hellenistic tradition, it clearly has its roots in the guest-host relationship model, and the notion that it is more positive for a planet to be configured to its domicile lord, while being more problematic for a planet to be unconfigured or in aversion to its

---

[33] Valens, *Anthology*, 7, 2: 34, trans. Riley, p. 125, modified.

[34] For the early Medieval definition of the term see Sahl, *Introduction*, 5.8, or Māshā'allāh, *On Reception*, in: Dykes, *Works of Sahl and Māshā'allāh*.

[35] Sahl, *Introduction*, 5.8.

domicile lord. In the Hellenistic tradition, reception was probably originally conceptualized as simply occurring between a planet and its domicile lord; the two only needed to be configured by sign, and not necessarily applying by a degree-based aspect, as demonstrated by the quote from Valens above. Thus, the definition of reception that we will be using here is a bit looser than the Medieval definition.

Valens says that when reception occurs, it is productive and beneficial during the times in a person's life when those planets are activated as time-lords, and this seems consistent with the general Medieval notion that reception helps to build a stronger and more favorable relationship between two planets, since then they share more in common. A general rule in the Hellenistic tradition seems to be that the more two planets share in common, the more favorably they will act towards each other, because it makes the planets behave as if they are family members, and people are less inclined to harm members of their own family. This seems to be part of the rationale underlying the concept known as "neighboring" (*homorēsis*), which is defined in Porphyry as follows:

> It is called 'neighboring' whenever stars are in the same bounds, either according to an adherence (*kollēsis*) which has come about, or according to any figure whatsoever they look upon each other while in the bounds of the same star.[36]

This definition essentially says that when two planets are aspecting each other while being in the bounds of the same planet, then it is like they become neighbors with each other, with positive or friendly undertones. Definitions like this seem to act as a sort of precursor to the way that reception was defined in the Medieval tradition, since it shows that planets were conceptualized as being more friendly with each other when they both aspected each other while sharing something in common in terms of the zodiacal signs they are in.

In practice, one of the major functional roles of reception is that it can help alleviate the negative effects of a difficult configuration between two planets, or alternatively to strengthen the positive effects of a favorable configuration. More specifically, I've found that when a planet is being maltreated by another planet, if one of the planets is in the domicile of the other so that there is reception, the maltreatment will be less severe and often more manageable than it would be otherwise. Similarly, when one planet is bonifying another planet, if one of the planets is in the domicile of the other so that there is reception,

---

[36] Porphyry, *Introduction*, 22, trans. Demetra George, unpublished, modified. Cf. Antiochus, *Summary*, 11; Rhetorius, *Compendium*, 40. Cf. Schmidt, *Definitions and Foundations*, p. 187ff.

the positive effects of the bonification will be enhanced beyond what would otherwise normally occur. Of course, this only becomes relevant in the specific forms of bonification and maltreatment that involve the planets being in configuration with each other, whereas it is not as relevant in other forms.

Exchanging Signs (Mutual Reception)

In the Medieval tradition a "mutual reception" was more strictly defined as occurring when two planets are in each other's domiciles (or other dignities) and are configured, especially through an applying degree-based aspect. In the earlier Hellenistic tradition this concept appears to have existed in some form as well, although it was simplified: they noted only the simple exchange of zodiacal signs between two planets that are in each other's domiciles. The technical term used to refer to this in Greek was *enallassō*, which simply means "exchange." Planets are said to "exchange" domiciles or sometimes bounds when they are each in signs ruled by the other.[37]

There is some ambiguity about how the exchange of domiciles was interpreted, although generally it seems to have been viewed as mutually beneficial for the two planets involved, because they are both seen as supporting each other. Here is an example where Valens mentions two planets exchanging signs within the context of a delineation for Jupiter trine Mars:

> Jupiter trine with Mars, if one is the Master of the Nativity and the other is the Lord (*despozontos*), indicates great men, leaders and dictators, especially when these stars are in their own signs, triplicities, or degrees, in advantageous signs, or when they have exchanged domiciles or bounds, especially if they rule the Lot of Fortune or its domicile lord.[38]

Here Valens clearly mentions the exchange of domiciles as a lesser sort of positive zodiacal placement, comparable to planets being in their own signs, albeit probably slightly less auspicious.[39]

---

[37] No explicit definition of the concept survives from the Hellenistic tradition, although it is mentioned sporadically by Valens within the context of the delineation of different placements and configurations. See *Anthology*, 2, 17: 46; 2, 17: 84; 2, 23: 8. It is also mentioned by Firmicus in *Mathesis*, 2, 29: 18–19.

[38] Valens, *Anthology*, 2, 17: 84, trans. Riley, p. 34, modified.

[39] It is perhaps worth noting that there is also one instance at the end of Valens' delineation of Mercury square Mars where he seems to say that the exchange of signs between these two planets could produce a more negative delineation. Valens, *Anthology*, 2, 17: 59. This may imply that in some instances whether the exchange was viewed as positive or not partially depends on which planets are involved, although I'm not entirely certain whether this is the correct interpretation of this passage.

The exchange of signs is of course better when the two planets are configured to each other, because then there is also the presence of reception, and the two planets receive each other into their domiciles. For example, in a chart with the Sun at 20° Aries and Mars at 22° Leo, the Sun and Mars would be exchanging signs, since they are in each other's domiciles, but they would also have reception, since they are also configured. Alternatively, in a chart with Mercury in Taurus and Venus in Gemini, the two planets are exchanging domiciles, and thus there is some mutual support, although it is not quite as good as it could be since they are not configured, and thus there is no reception. That this could still be seen as beneficial even without a configuration seems to be demonstrated by Firmicus when he gives an example of an exchange between Saturn in Virgo and Mercury in Aquarius.[40]

From a functional perspective, reception and the exchange of domiciles are important factors to take into account, because they can improve the relationship between two planets that are configured, and they can also provide an additional level of support or familiarity that is akin to what later astrologers refer to as "dignity," even when the planets are in zodiacal signs that are otherwise not their homes.

---

[40] Firmicus, *Mathesis*, 2, 29: 18–19.

CHAPTER 15
TRIPLICITY RULERS OF THE SECT LIGHT

Previously we have seen how the placement and condition of the domicile lord of the Hour-Marker can be used in order to make some statements that are generally applicable to the native's life as a whole. This chapter will focus on an additional technique that is also used to make broad statements about the native's life, and to determine the level of stability and prosperity the native will enjoy at different times, through the analysis of the triplicity lords of the sect light. As we have seen earlier, the triplicity rulers are an alternative form of sign rulership, similar to the domicile rulers, but assigned according to a different rationale.

Sources for the Technique

Our two primary sources for the triplicity rulers of the sect light technique are Valens and Dorotheus.[1] Valens gives the more extensive treatment, and it is the very first technique that he introduces in book two of the *Anthology*, after introducing material on basic concepts like the nature of the planets and signs in book one.

Dorotheus' approach to this technique is very similar to Valens', although Valens only looks at the triplicity rulers of the sect light, whereas Dorotheus looks at triplicity lords for other planets and places as well. Dorotheus' view of

---

[1] First introduced in Valens, *Anthology*, 2, 1–2, and then used off and on throughout the rest of book 2. First introduced in Dorotheus, *Carmen*, 1, 1, and then used off and on throughout the rest of book 1. Rhetorius briefly mentions the technique as well, and uses it in a chart example in *Compendium*, 113.

the importance of the triplicity rulers is stated quite emphatically in the opening of his work:

> I tell you that everything which is decided or indicated is from the lords of the triplicities, and as for everything of afflictions and distress which reaches the people of the world and the totality of men, the lords of the triplicities decide it.[2]

Valens seems to restrict the use of the triplicity rulers to the sect light technique, although he attributes quite a bit of importance to this particular analysis, and he frequently refers back to it in different parts of the *Anthology* as the method for determining what he calls the "general support" (*katholikos hupostasis*) or "foundation" (*katabolē*) of the nativity.[3] Both authors relate the technique to the stability, support, and fortune of the native, sometimes also connecting it with the eminence (*doxa*) or brightness (*lampros*) of the nativity as well.[4] Valens addresses it under the general topic of "happiness" (*eudaimōnia*), although within this context he seems to mean something more like "prosperity," as determined by the level of material support and stability that the native enjoys in different parts of their life.[5] Thus, for Valens, at least in this part of the *Anthology*, the concept of happiness appears to be partially predicated on conventional goods such as health, wealth, and stability.

Identifying the Triplicity Rulers of the Sect Light

The first step in the technique is to identify the sect light, which is the Sun by day or the Moon by night, and what zodiacal sign it is located in. The three triplicity rulers of that sign are then identified. According to Valens, these three planets will provide the "general support" or "foundation" of the nativity. If they are well-situated in the chart, then the native's life will be stable, fortunate, and potentially eminent. If they are in more neutral positions, then the conditions of the life will be more moderate or middling. Finally, if the triplicity rulers are poorly-situated, then the native's life will be unstable, unfortunate, and undistinguished.

The triplicity lords of the sect light are also said to divide the life into different parts, with the quality of each part being determined by the condition

---

[2] Dorotheus, *Carmen*, 1, 1: 4, trans. Pingree, p. 162.

[3] For *hupostasis* see Valens, *Anthology*, 2, proem: 2ff. For the use of *katabolē* as a synonym, see Valens, *Anthology*, 6, 2: 29.

[4] Valens, *Anthology*, 2, 2: 1–12.

[5] Valens, *Anthology*, 2, 2: 1.

of the triplicity lord that controls it. According to Dorotheus and Valens, the primary triplicity lord rules the first part of the life, the second lord rules the second part of the life, and the third lord cooperates during both parts of the life.[6] This is an important point because this is one of the significant areas in which the Hellenistic and Medieval traditions diverged from a technical standpoint, since in the Medieval authors the triplicity lords are taken as dividing the life up into three parts rather than two, with the first third ruled by the first triplicity lord, the second third by the second lord, and the final third by the cooperating lord.[7] This appears to have been a departure from the Hellenistic practice of dividing the life into two parts, and may have occurred due to textual issues with the Persian-Arabic translation of Dorotheus. Let's take a look at how this may have come about, because it provides a useful example of some of the issues we have to be aware of when using different versions of these texts.

Throughout his work Dorotheus seems to follow the standard Hellenistic approach of using the triplicity lords to divide the life into two parts. However, at one point in the discussion of the topic of marriage, when Dorotheus instructs the reader to look at the triplicity rulers of Venus, the Persian-Arabic translation of the text seems to indicate that the technique is dividing the life into thirds:

> If the first of the lords of Venus's triplicity is in a good place and the second in a bad place, then this condition in the matter of women is good in the beginning of his age, and in the last it is bad, because the first of the lords of Venus's triplicity indicates the first years, the second indicates the middle years and the third indicates the end of life.[8]

However, Hephaestio of Thebes happens to preserve Dorotheus' treatment of the same topic in Greek, and when this is compared to the Arabic version, it

---

[6] Valens, *Anthology*, 2, 2; Dorotheus, *Carmen*, 1, 22. Compare with the chart examples given by both authors in later chapters.

[7] The only possible exception that I am aware of in the Hellenistic tradition is in one example chart in Valens, *Anthology*, 2, 22: 24–25 (no. L 72 in Neugebauer and Van Hoesen, *Greek Horoscopes*), where Valens seems to mention the cooperating lord in connection with the later part of the native's life. However, this example is complicated because he also mentions the ruler of Lot of Fortune and Exaltation as being relevant at the same time. Since the lot itself was often interpreted as pertaining to the first part of the life while the ruler of the lot was interpreted as pertaining to the second part of the life, it may be that it is the lords of the lots that are the primary factor here in describing the later part of the native's life. As a result of this, we should probably be careful about using this example as justification for the later medieval approach.

[8] Dorotheus, *Carmen*, 2, 3: 21, trans. Pingree, p. 200.

becomes clear that in the original text Dorotheus was in fact only dividing the life into two parts rather than three:

> Again, we make a synopsis, by putting together the discussions of Nechepso and others in the verses of Dorotheus [...] And whenever the first trigon-lord is well situated, but the second ill, it signifies the that first years of wedlock are good, but the last poor; and it signifies the opposite when things hold in the opposite way.[9]

It thus appears that this delineation was changed subtly in the Persian-Arabic translation of Dorotheus, perhaps due to a misunderstanding or translation error, and this went on to change the way that the doctrine was practiced in the later Medieval tradition in a very significant way.

The Importance of Angularity

One thing that Valens and Dorotheus seem to agree on is that angularity is key when analyzing the condition of the triplicity lords of the sect light. Both emphasize the concept of angularity as the primary condition to look at when judging the triplicity rulers, even to the point of disregarding what would in other contexts be a challenging placement, such as being in the eighth place, in favor of emphasizing the angular and succedent places as universally more favorable than the declines.[10]

According to this approach, when one of the triplicity rulers is located in one of the angular or pivotal places (first, fourth, seventh, tenth), it is interpreted as good. When one of the rulers is located in a succedent place (second, fifth, eighth, eleventh), it is interpreted as moderate or middling. Finally, when a triplicity ruler is located in a declining place (third, sixth, ninth, twelfth), it is interpreted as being negative or bad. The motivation for this emphasis on angularity within the context of this technique seems to be that the triplicity lords were conceptualized as being related to the native's fortune and prosperity, and being angular symbolically represents the height of fortune, succedent placements signify increasing fortune that is building up or growing, while declines signify a decreasing or diminishing fortune.

Dorotheus and Valens both use whole sign houses in their example charts when demonstrating the technique, emphasizing the importance of having more angular placements. Dorotheus does talk about looking at how close

---

[9] Hephaestio, *Apotelesmatika*, 2, 21: 26; 29, trans. Schmidt, p. 69.

[10] This comes up the most prominently in the example charts given in Dorotheus, *Carmen*, 1, 24, and Valens, *Anthology*, 2, 22.

the triplicity rulers are to the degrees of the angles at one point in order to determine the magnitude of the native's fortune, and establishes a series of gradations measured out in fifteen-degree increments after the degrees of the angles, although this appears to be according to ascensional times rather than strict degrees of longitude.[11] As a result of this it is not entirely clear if the secondary overlay he is describing here is the equal house system or if he is talking about the quadrant angles. When Rhetorius applies the triplicity rulers of the sect light technique in one of his chart examples, he seems to mention the angularity of the rulers both in terms of their whole sign placement and quadrant placement, and ultimately one of the conclusions that he draws about the condition of one triplicity lord seems to place more emphasis on the fact that the planet is declining according to the quadrant placement.[12] As usual with Rhetorius, it is not clear if this is an instance in which he is doing things differently due to changes towards the end of the Hellenistic tradition, or if he is simply being more explicit about something that was already implicitly being used early on. This seems to be an area where it would be good to research both the whole sign and the quadrant placements, especially due to the heavy emphasis on the concept of angularity, in order to clarify which works better in practice.

The Sequence of the Native's Life

There are several different scenarios about how the sequence of the native's life will unfold once it has been divided into two parts based on the triplicity rulers and their conditions. If the first triplicity ruler of the sect light is well-placed, for example, but the second triplicity lord is poorly-placed, then it was thought to indicate that things will go well in the first part of the native's life but poorly later on. Conversely, if the first triplicity ruler is poorly-placed but the second triplicity ruler is well-placed, then the first part of the native's life will be difficult but the second part will go smoothly. If both triplicity rulers are well-placed, then the native will be fortunate from the beginning to the end of their life, whereas if both rulers are poorly-placed, the native would be unfortunate throughout their life. Finally, there are corresponding variations when any of the above placements are switched with succedent placements, which indicate more moderate circumstances, and there are also variations based on the condition of the cooperating lord, and whether it is improving the condition of the two primary lords, or dragging them down through counteraction.

Valens points out that you have to pay attention to the domicile lord of the

---

[11] Dorotheus, *Carmen*, 1, 26: 1–9.
[12] Rhetorius, *Compendium*, 113.

		Day	Night	Cooperating
♈ ♌ ♐		☉	♃	♄
♉ ♍ ♑		♀	☽	♂
♊ ♎ ♒		♄	☿	♃
♋ ♏ ♓		♀	♂	☽

Table 15.1 - Triplicity Rulers

triplicity lord, and whether it is well-situated.[13] He says that a good placement can be undone by a poorly-situated domicile lord, and vice versa. This is essentially the concept of "counteraction," as applied to studying the condition of the triplicity rulers of the sect light, and it becomes very useful here in terms of reversing the condition of triplicity lords that are otherwise situated well or poorly.

Examples from Valens and Dorotheus

Let us look at some examples from Valens and Dorotheus in order to better understand how they applied the technique in practice. Valens gives an example

of an anonymous chart that he says has the Hour-Marker and Venus in Libra, the Sun, Mercury, and Mars in Scorpio, Jupiter in Sagittarius, and the Moon in Cancer.[14] According to Valens, this is a nocturnal chart, so the Moon is the sect light. The Moon is located in the zodiacal sign of Cancer, so we look to the rulers of the water triplicity. Mars is the primary ruler of the water triplicity by night, Venus is the secondary ruler, and the Moon is the cooperating ruler. Mars is in a succedent place, in his own domicile,

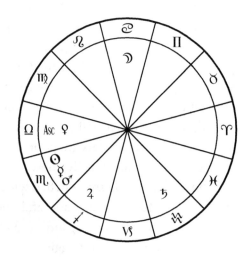

Chart 65 - Valens Triplicity Example 1

---

[13] Valens, *Anthology*, 2, 2: 26–28.

[14] Valens, *Anthology*, 2, 22: 1–9. No. L 50 in Neugebauer, *Greek Horoscopes*.

triplicity, and of the sect. It is thus interpreted as a middling to good placement. Venus is the secondary triplicity ruler, she is located in an angular place, and in her own domicile. This is interpreted as a very good placement. Finally, the Moon as the cooperating triplicity lord is also in an angular place, and in her own domicile, which is interpreted as very auspicious. Valens says that the native was "distinguished" or "estimable" as a result of the placement of their triplicity rulers.

Valens gives another example with Leo rising, the Moon and Jupiter in Scorpio, the Sun, Mars, Venus, and Mercury in Aquarius, and Saturn in Aries.[15] Walking us through the example, Valens explains that because it is a day chart, the Sun is the sect light; the Sun is in Aquarius, so we look to the rulers of the air triplicity, which in a day chart makes Saturn the primary ruler, Mercury secondary, and Jupiter the cooperating ruler. Saturn is in a decline, which is interpreted as a bad placement. Mercury is in an angular

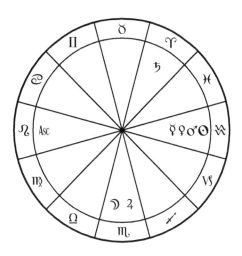

Chart 66 - Valens Triplicity Example 2

place, which is interpreted as a very good placement. Finally, Jupiter is also in an angle, which is taken to be an excellent placement. Thus, according to Valens, the native went from a depressed or mediocre fortune to a more positive one, since the lord of the first part of life was poorly-placed and the lord of the second part was well-placed.

In another example, Valens gives a chart of a native who has the Ascendant and Venus in Cancer, Jupiter in Scorpio, the Moon in Capricorn, Mars and Saturn in Aquarius, and the Sun and Mercury in Gemini.[16] This is a day chart, so the Sun is the sect light; the Sun is in Gemini, so we look to the rulers

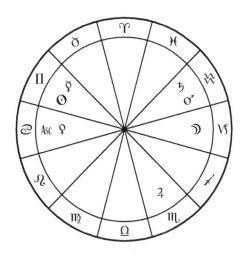

Chart 67 - Valens Triplicity Example 3

---

[15] Valens, *Anthology*, 2, 22: 13–16. Neugebauer, *Greek Horoscopes*, L 85 II.

[16] Valens, *Anthology*, 2, 22: 43–44. Neugebauer, *Greek Horoscopes*, L 109.

of the air triplicity. Saturn is primary, Mercury secondary, and Jupiter is the cooperating ruler. Saturn is in a succedent place, which is a middling placement. Mercury is in a decline, which is a very poor placement. Jupiter is in a succedent place, which is middling. Valens says that the native was born a slave, but he was able to obtain a political office through his family connections. But later his livelihood suffered and he fell into debt. The example illustrates that the native wasn't born into great circumstances to begin with, but he was still able to make some advancement in the first part of his life, but later on ran into trouble due to the poor condition of the secondary triplicity ruler.

Dorotheus gives an example with Gemini rising, the Sun and Venus in Leo, Mercury in Virgo, the Moon and Saturn in Scorpio, Mars in Aquarius, and Jupiter in Taurus.[17] He says that this is a night chart, so the Moon is the sect light. The Moon is in Scorpio, so we look to the rulers of the water triplicity. Mars is primary, Venus secondary, and the Moon is the cooperating ruler. Mars is in the ninth, a declining place, which is interpreted as a bad placement. Venus is also in a declining place, the third, which is also interpreted negatively. Lastly, the Moon is also in a declining place, the sixth, giving three negative placements. Dorotheus says that the native was "needy, poor, not finding his daily bread, miserable."[18]

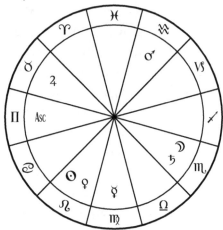

Chart 68 - Dorotheus Example 1

Another example from Dorotheus has the Ascendant and Moon in Scorpio, Mars in Aquarius, Mercury in Pisces, Sun in Aries, Venus in Taurus, and Jupiter and Saturn in Virgo.[19] It is a night chart, so the Moon is the sect light. The Moon

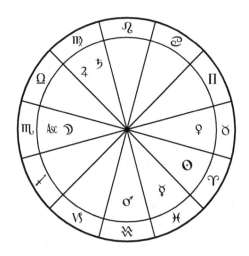

Chart 69 - Dorotheus Example 2

---

[17] Dorotheus, *Carmen*, 1, 24: 1–4. Chart "octava" in Pingree.
[18] Dorotheus, *Carmen*, 1, 24: 3, trans. Pingree, p. 185.
[19] Dorotheus, *Carmen*, 1, 24: 9–11. "Septima" in Pingree.

is located in Scorpio, so we look to the rulers of the water triplicity, which makes Mars the primary triplicity lord, Venus secondary, and the Moon the cooperating ruler. Mars is in an angular place, the fourth, which is a very good placement. Venus is also in an angular place, the seventh, which is likewise interpreted as a very auspicious placement. Finally, the Moon is also in an angular place, the first, which is interpreted as positive. Dorotheus says that since all three rulers are angular, this man was "mighty in eminence, powerful in leadership so that crowns of gold and silver are placed on him and he is praised."[20]

Integration with Other Techniques

Valens used the triplicity lords of the sect light together with other techniques, such as the domicile lord of the Hour-Marker, and the Lots of Fortune, Exaltation, and Foundation. Valens and Dorotheus both seem to agree that when the triplicity lords are poorly-situated one must default to the Lot of Fortune and its lord, and if this is well-situated, the native may still be able to get by as a result of luck.[21] The Lots of Exaltation and Foundation and their lords were also used by Valens as additional factors in order to determine whether the native would be eminent. It is important to note that Valens did not introduce any example charts until he had outlined all of these techniques. He also takes the other techniques into account in every chart in which he demonstrates the use of the triplicity lords, since the lots were sometimes viewed as mitigating factors. We will deal with the lots in the next chapter, but for now it is necessary to point out that while the triplicity lords of the sect light technique is presented on its own here for the sake of instruction, it is not necessarily something that should be used in isolation from other techniques and considerations.

Modern Examples

Let's take a look at how the triplicity rulers of the sect light technique works within the context of a few modern nativities. The foregoing description provides us with a number of things to take into account when analyzing the triplicity rulers:

1. Is the triplicity ruler in an angular, succedent, or declining place?
2. Is it in its own domicile, exaltation, or triplicity?
3. Is it of the sect in favor or contrary to the sect?
4. Is it favorably configured to the benefic of the sect?

---

[20] Dorotheus, *Carmen*, 1, 24: 11, trans. Pingree, p. 187.
[21] Dorotheus, *Carmen*, 1, 26: 10; Valens, *Anthology*, 2, 2: 18.

5. Is it unfavorably configured to the malefic contrary to the sect?
6. Is the triplicity ruler visible, or is it under the beams?
7. What is the condition of the domicile lord of the triplicity ruler?
8. Is it otherwise bonified or maltreated?

NAPOLEON BONAPARTE

Napoleon was born with a day chart, Scorpio rising, and the Sun in Leo. The primary triplicity lord is the Sun itself, which is angular in the tenth place, in its own domicile and triplicity, and of the sect in favor. The secondary triplicity lord is Jupiter, which is also angular, although it has no rulership in Scorpio. Jupiter is also ruled by Mars, which is less well-situated, in a succedent place in the eleventh, and contrary to the sect. The cooperating lord is Saturn, which

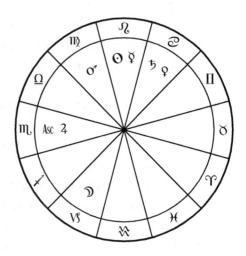

Chart 70 - Napoleon Bonaparte

is declining in Cancer in the ninth place. Napoleon is an interesting example in terms of the potential for the technique to indicate eminence; he famously became the Emperor of France and attempted to conquer large parts of Europe in the early nineteenth century. Ultimately, the second triplicity lord seems to have brought him down, since, despite its moderate angularity, it is ruled by the malefic that is contrary to the sect, and ultimately he lost power and died in exile.

DIED IN INFANCY

This was a native who was born with a day chart, Cancer rising, and the Sun in Aquarius. The primary triplicity ruler is Saturn, which is declining in the third place. The secondary triplicity ruler is Mercury, which is succedent in the eighth. The cooperating triplicity lord is Jupiter, which is angular because it is in the seventh place. The child never made it past the first triplicity rulership,

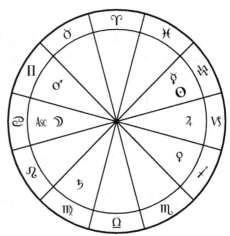

Chart 71 - Died in Infancy

and died in infancy. Saturn, the primary lord, is declining, retrograde, has Mars overcoming it through a superior sign-based square in a day chart, and is thus maltreated. The inferior trine from Jupiter in Capricorn to Saturn offers some mitigation, but evidently not enough. The native died by choking on a piece of food shortly before his second birthday.

ROBERT DOWNEY JR.

The actor Robert Downey Jr. was born with a day chart, Leo rising, and the Sun in Aries. The Sun is the primary triplicity ruler and is exalted, in its own triplicity, and in an adherence with a benefic, but declining. Jupiter is the secondary triplicity ruler, angular, and the benefic of the sect. The cooperating lord is Saturn, which is succedent. His early life and career was filled with many ups and downs, largely

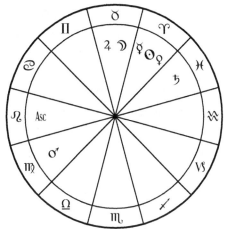

Chart 72 - Robert Downey Jr.

due to issues with drug abuse, which resulted in much instability. Later in life, he was able to get his addiction issues under control, and he became more stable and eminent, eventually becoming one of the highest-paid actors in Hollywood.

KURT COBAIN

The musician and songwriter Kurt Cobain was born with a night chart, Virgo rising, and the Moon in Cancer. The primary triplicity lord is Mars, which is declining in Scorpio, in its own domicile and triplicity. The secondary triplicity lord is Venus, which is angular and exalted in Pisces. The cooperating lord is the Moon in Cancer in the eleventh. All three triplicity rulers are well-situated by sign, although Venus is being maltreated by Saturn

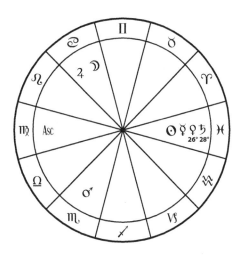

Chart 73 - Kurt Cobain

via adherence. Cobain had a troubled and somewhat unstable youth. He later achieved success and eminence as a musician in his twenties, but committed suicide due to depression and substance abuse issues at the age of twenty-seven.

BILL CLINTON

U.S. President Bill Clinton was born with a day chart, Libra rising, and the Sun in Leo. The Sun is the primary triplicity lord, is in a succedent place, in its own domicile, triplicity, and of the sect in favor. The secondary triplicity lord is Jupiter, which is angular, and copresent with Venus and Mars. The cooperating triplicity lord is Saturn, which is succedent. His primary lord is middling in terms of angularity, but otherwise well-situated by sign. The second lord

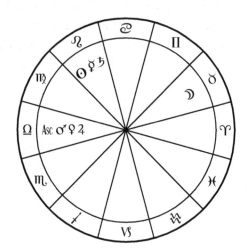

Chart 74 - Bill Clinton

is very well-placed in terms of angularity, but there is some discord due to its copresence with Mars. Note however that Mars isn't capable of fully maltreating Jupiter, since there is no adherence, which implies that it is not the worst-case scenario. He became the forty-second President of the United States at the age of forty-six years old, and while scandals nearly brought him down, he ultimately served two complete four-year terms in office.

WHITNEY HOUSTON

The singer Whitney Houston was born at night, with Pisces rising and the Moon in Aries. Jupiter is the primary triplicity lord, in a succedent place, and in its own triplicity. The Sun is the secondary triplicity lord, in its own domicile, but in a decline, and applying to an exact opposition with Saturn in about three degrees. Saturn is the cooperating lord, and it is in its own domicile and triplicity, but also in a decline. While she was a very successful singer and musician from

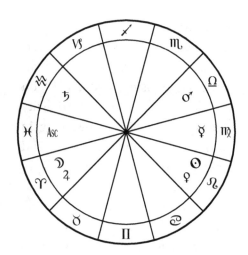

Chart 75 - Whitney Houston

around the age of twenty, her life became increasingly unstable after developing a drug habit. She drowned in a hotel bathtub at the age of forty-eight.

HANS CHRISTIAN ANDERSEN

The Danish author Hans Christian Andersen was born with a nocturnal chart, Sagittarius rising, and the Moon in Taurus. The Moon is the primary triplicity ruler, exalted, but declining in the sixth place by whole sign. Venus is the secondary triplicity ruler, angular in the fourth place, and exalted. The cooperating triplicity lord is Mars, declining in Leo in the ninth. He was born into poverty, but later in life he became one of the most celebrated writers in Europe.

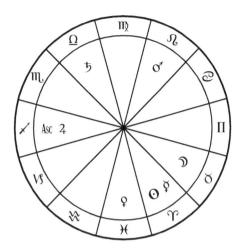

Chart 76 - Hans Christian Andersen

Timing the Changeover Between Triplicity Lords

Valens says that you can time the changeover between the primary and secondary triplicity ruler by using what is known as planetary periods and ascensional times of the zodiacal signs:

> For nativities which are badly situated (whether day or night births), if the predominant triplicity ruler is unfavorably located, but its successor is at an angle or otherwise configured well, the native will experience ups and downs during his early years until the ascensional time of the sign or until the cyclical return of the chronocrator, but will afterwards be vigorous and effective—except for being unsteady and anxious. If the preceding triplicity ruler is favorably situated and the succeeding one unfavorably, the native will fulfill his promise well at first, but afterwards will be brought low, starting at the time of the ascension of the sign in which the succeeding triplicity ruler is unfavorably situated.[22]

The "cyclical return of the chronocrator" or "circular period" of the planet that Valens refers to above is probably what is known elsewhere as the "minor," "lesser," or "least years" of the planets. These associate a specific number of years with each of the planets.[23] The periods are mostly derived from synodic or

---

[22] Valens, *Anthology*, 2, 2: 6–8, trans. Riley, p. 25, modified.

[23] The lesser years of the planets are outlined in Valens, *Anthology*, 3, 11: 6, Rhetorius, *Compendium*, 49, and Balbillus (CCAG 8, 4, p. 237: 16–22). They are used either explicitly or implicitly by many other authors, and they are integrated into several time-lord techniques.

recurrence cycles with the Sun, which is when a planet and the Sun will return to the same area of the zodiac at roughly the same time. According to most Hellenistic sources, the planetary periods are as follows:

SUN:	19
MOON:	25
MERCURY:	20
VENUS:	8
MARS:	15
JUPITER:	12
SATURN:	30

Rationales for these periods have been explored by Hand and others.[24] The nineteen-year period of the Sun is connected to the metonic cycle, in which every nineteen years an eclipse will take place around the same part of the zodiac. The period of the Moon is based on a combination of the Egyptian calendar, which had exactly 365 days, and the lunation cycle, where every twenty-five Egyptian years the Moon will have the exact same phase relationship with the Sun on the same days of the year. Hand notes that the Sun and Moon derive their cycles from each other. The twenty-year period of Mercury is derived from its recurrence cycle, in which roughly every twenty Egyptian years the Sun and Mercury will form a conjunction on the same date roughly to the degree. Venus' period is connected to its synodic cycle, where roughly every eight years it will conjoin the Sun around the same date. The rest are also recurrence cycles: Mars conjoins the Sun roughly around the same date every fifteen years, Jupiter takes twelve years, and Saturn takes thirty. Hand notes that the conjunctions of Mars, Jupiter, and Saturn with the Sun are by sign rather than by degree.[25]

The ascensional times of the signs are based on the fact that each of the signs of the zodiac takes a different amount of time to rise over the horizon depending on where you are on Earth. Some signs rise very quickly, while others rise very slowly, and this is the basis of the doctrine of the signs of long or short ascension. The amount of time that it takes for each of the signs to rise in different northern or southern latitudes is listed in the table of ascensional times that I have attached to this chapter. The values are given as a number of degrees in right ascension, and the number of degrees can be converted directly to a number

---

[24] For this and most of the explanations that follow, see Hand's preface to Valens, *The Anthology, Book II, Part 1*, trans. Schmidt, pp. v–vii. Cf. Neugebauer and Van Hoesen, *Greek Horoscopes*, pp. 10–11; Pingree, *Yavanajātaka*, vol. 2, pp. 334–335.

[25] Ibid., p. vii.

| North | ♈ - ♓ | ♉ - ♒ | ♊ - ♑ | ♋ - ♐ | ♌ - ♏ | ♍ - ♎ |
South	♍ - ♎	♌ - ♏	♋ - ♐	♊ - ♑	♉ - ♒	♈ - ♓
0°	27.91	29.90	32.18	32.18	29.90	27.91
5°	26.89	29.08	31.84	32.51	30.73	28.92
10°	25.86	28.24	31.50	32.85	31.56	29.96
15°	24.79	27.38	31.15	33.20	32.43	31.02
20°	23.67	26.47	30.77	33.58	33.34	32.14
21°	23.44	26.27	30.69	33.66	33.53	32.37
22°	23.20	26.08	30.61	33.74	33.72	32.61
23°	22.97	25.89	30.53	33.82	33.92	32.85
24°	22.72	25.69	30.45	33.90	34.12	33.09
25°	22.48	25.48	30.36	33.99	34.32	33.34
26°	22.23	25.28	30.28	34.07	34.53	33.59
27°	21.97	25.06	30.19	34.16	34.74	33.84
28°	21.71	24.85	30.10	34.25	34.96	34.10
29°	21.45	24.63	30.01	34.34	35.18	34.36
30°	21.18	24.40	29.91	34.44	35.40	34.63
31°	20.90	24.17	29.81	34.54	35.63	34.91
32°	20.62	23.94	29.71	34.64	35.87	35.19
33°	20.34	23.69	29.61	34.74	36.11	35.48
34°	20.04	23.44	29.50	34.85	36.36	35.77
35°	19.74	23.19	29.39	34.96	36.62	36.07
36°	19.43	22.92	29.28	35.07	36.88	36.38
37°	19.11	22.65	29.16	35.19	37.16	36.70
38°	18.79	22.37	29.04	35.31	37.44	37.03
39°	18.45	22.08	28.91	35.44	37.73	37.36
40°	18.10	21.78	28.78	35.57	38.03	37.71
41°	17.75	21.47	28.64	35.71	38.34	38.07
42°	17.38	21.14	28.49	35.86	38.66	38.43
43°	17.00	20.81	28.34	36.01	39.00	38.81
44°	16.61	20.45	28.18	36.17	39.35	39.21
45°	16.20	20.09	28.01	36.34	39.72	39.61
46°	15.78	19.71	27.83	36.52	40.10	40.03
47°	15.34	19.30	27.64	36.71	40.50	40.47
48°	14.88	18.88	27.44	36.91	40.92	40.93
49°	14.41	18.44	27.23	37.12	41.37	41.40
50°	13.91	17.97	27.00	37.35	41.84	41.90
51°	13.40	17.48	26.75	37.60	42.33	42.42
52°	12.85	16.95	26.49	37.87	42.86	42.96
53°	12.29	16.39	26.19	38.16	43.42	43.53
54°	11.69	15.79	25.88	38.47	44.01	44.12
55°	11.06	15.15	25.53	38.82	44.65	44.75
56°	10.40	14.46	25.14	39.21	45.35	45.41
57°	9.70	13.71	24.70	39.65	46.09	46.11
58°	8.96	12.90	24.21	40.14	46.91	46.85
59°	8.17	12.01	23.64	40.71	47.80	47.64
60°	7.33	11.03	22.97	41.38	48.78	48.48
61°	6.44	9.94	22.18	42.17	49.87	49.38
62°	5.47	8.71	21.20	43.15	51.10	50.34
63°	4.44	7.32	19.94	44.41	52.49	51.37
64°	3.32	5.71	18.25	46.10	54.10	52.49
65°	2.11	3.82	15.70	48.65	55.99	53.70
66°	0.80	1.53	10.88	53.47	58.28	55.02

Table 15.2 - Ascensional Times of the Zodiacal Signs
Compiled by Benjamin Dykes, based on Duffett-Smith, Practical Astronomy

of years, with one degree equaling one year of life. For example, if a sign of the zodiac lists an ascensional time of twenty-one degrees, then this can be converted directly into twenty-one years of life. Each of the values changes depending on the latitude of the native.

Valens says that the triplicity rulers become activated at the completion of the period of the planet, or at the completion of the ascensional time of the zodiacal sign that the triplicity lord is in.[26] This occurs in the year leading up to the birthday associated with that year in the native's life, using ordinal numbers. For example, the planetary period of Mars is fifteen years, which means that Mars becomes activated in the native's fifteenth year, which occurs from the age of fourteen to fifteen years old.

Although Valens is our main source for material on timing through ascensional times and planetary periods, he seems to have drawn on Nechepso and Petosiris for some of the details; there are also references to the technique in Dorotheus and Rhetorius.[27] Valens initially treats the subject in *Anthology* 2, 28, but then in book seven he returns to the subject and gives it a much more elaborate treatment, with many citations from Nechepso. There he demonstrates how different combinations of planetary periods and ascensional times can be added together to provide specific years in which different placements can be activated, showing how planetary periods and ascensional times can be used to time the activation of other planets besides the triplicity rulers of the sect light.[28] He also shows how to divide the resulting years by a third, a half, and two-thirds to find other times in a person's life of lesser importance.[29]

A full treatment of the use of planetary periods and ascensional times is beyond the scope of this book.[30] There are other timing techniques that I have found to be more effective, and these will be explored in later chapters.

As we have seen, the triplicity rulers of the sect light are useful for getting a broad sense of the native's life and identifying important planets in the birth chart. Although I've demonstrated the use of the technique on its own for purposes of clarity, it is important to reiterate that it was never meant to be used in isolation. Rather, it is to be used in conjunction with other techniques, such as the lots, to which we now turn.

---

[26] This is demonstrated by Valens throughout the example charts in book seven, although at one point in *Anthology*, 7, 6: 193–194, he seems to say that the outcome occurs after the ascensional times and planetary periods are completed.

[27] Dorotheus, *Carmen*, 1, 23. Rhetorius briefly mentions using ascensional times and planetary periods in accordance with the Egyptians in *Compendium*, 54, trans. Holden, p. 37.

[28] Valens, *Anthology*, 7, 1–5.

[29] Valens, *Anthology*, 7, 6.

[30] See book seven of Valens' *Anthology* for more information about this approach.

CHAPTER 16
LOTS

One of the more important yet mysterious concepts in the Hellenistic tradition are the mathematical points sometimes used in chart interpretations known as "lots" (*klēroi*). The lots are mathematically derived from the positions of other placements, and their purpose is to mark the signs of the zodiac with additional topics or significations in a way that is analogous to the twelve places. The lots appear to date back to the earliest strata of the Hellenistic tradition, and they act as one of the major cornerstones of chart delineation and prediction.

The lots are the Hellenistic equivalent of what are known in modern astrology as the so-called "Arabic parts," with the most famous one being the Part of Fortune. The term "Arabic part" is a misnomer, however, as the Medieval Arabic tradition of astrology only began around 775 CE, while this technique had already been in use in the Greco-Roman astrological tradition since at least the first century BCE. The fact that the Arabic astrological authors expanded the number of lots beyond what they inherited from the Hellenistic tradition seems to have contributed to the later misconception that the Arabic authors had invented the concept. The twelfth-century author al-Bīrūnī dryly remarked that the number of lots that were being invented for different purposes increased daily.[1]

In the Hellenistic tradition, these mathematical points were originally referred to as "lots," from the Greek word *klēros*. This was connected to the ancient practice of casting or drawing lots, which is somewhat similar to the modern practice of entering into a "lottery." The casting of lots was done in order to decide matters by leaving the outcome up to chance or fortune (*tuchē*).

---

[1] al-Bīrūnī, *The Book of Instruction*, 476, trans. Wright, p. 66.

"Kleromancy," or lot-divination, was used as a method of ascertaining the will of the divine through the casting of lots. Part of the rationale for this type of divination was the notion that there is some sort of divine agency at work in the seemingly random acts of chance or fortune.[2] There is a prominent instance of this belief in the New Testament when the apostles have to replace Judas after his betrayal of Jesus.[3] There were two contenders for the position: Joseph and Matthias. The eleven apostles prayed to god for guidance, and then they cast lots. The lot fell to Matthias, so he was chosen. Thus, kleromancy was similar to other forms of divination in using a system in which both (1) the result is completely outside of the control of questioner, and (2) appears completely random, but assumes the appropriate answer will be provided through divine agency.

The astrological concept of lots plays a similar role in charts, in that they are used as a sort of wild card or unpredictable factor that can assign topics and outcomes in a more random fashion than the twelve places do, although even here the apparently random acts of fortune are still evidently seen as being guided by the providential hand of fate.

Calculation and Conceptualization

Lots are usually calculated by measuring the distance between two planets, and then measuring the same distance from the degree of the Ascendant. In modern times, lots are usually presented as abstract algebraic formulas, such as the following calculation for the Lot of Fortune:

DAY: Fortune = Ascendant + Moon - Sun
NIGHT: Fortune = Ascendant + Sun - Moon

However, in the Hellenistic astrological texts, lot calculations are usually described in a way that could be characterized as more geometrical in nature; one measures the distance from point A to point B, and then measures the same distance from the Ascendant. Here is Paulus' description of how to calculate the Lot of Fortune:

> First is the Lot of Fortune which, for those born by day, it will be necessary to count from the solar degree to the lunar degree, and one must cast out the collected number from the degree-number of the Hour-Marker, giving 30 degrees to each sign. And where the collected number leaves off, say

---

[2] Cicero says "under divine influence it may happen that they can be drawn so as to fall appropriately." Cicero, *On Divination*, 1: 34, trans. Wardle, p. 57.

[3] *Acts*, 1: 24–26.

that at that place is the Lot of Fortune. For those at night, the reverse, that is from the lunar degree to the solar. And likewise one must cast out the remainder from the degree of the Hour-Marker.[4]

In other words, in order to calculate the Lot of Fortune in a day chart, you measure the distance from the Sun to the Moon, and then measure the same distance from the Ascendant. In a night chart you reverse the order of the first two points, and instead measure the distance from the Moon to the Sun, and then again measure the same distance from the Ascendant. The degree that you come to in the last part of the measurement will be the location of the Lot of Fortune in the chart. The inversion of the calculation according to sect is true for many of the early lot formulas. Viewing the lot calculations as geometrical measurements rather than abstract algebraic equations is important, because it provides an access point for understanding the rationale for their formulas, as we will see later.

The default method of calculation that is usually presented in the texts is always counted in zodiacal order, which is counter-clockwise, starting with the distance from point A to point B, and then again when measuring the same distance from the degree of the Ascendant (also in zodiacal order).[5] An alternative method that makes it easier to calculate the lots at a glance is to measure the *shortest* distance from point A to point B, whatever direction that is in the chart, and then measure the same distance from the degree of the Ascendant, going in the same direction as the direction you needed to go in order to calculate the shortest distance between the two starting points. This method is easier to do visually, and it results in the same placements from a mathematical standpoint, although it does not necessarily fully match the way that Paulus and others appear to have calculated lots most of the time.

---

[4] Paulus, *Introduction*, 23, ed. Boer, p. 47: 15–18, p. 48: 1–5; trans. Greenbaum, p. 41, modified.

[5] This is clearly the case in Paulus (*Introduction*, 23), and seems to be in most other authors as well, although there is a brief discussion in Hephaestio (*Apotelesmatika*, 2, 11: 23–25) that seems to imply (if Pingree's textual emendations are correct) that there may have been some ambiguity surrounding whether Nechepso and Petosiris projected the distance backwards from the Ascendant in some instances. In Pingree's translation of the Arabic version of Dorotheus there seem to be some instances where he reverses the direction that is projected from the Ascendant by day and night rather than the direction between the two planets that compose the lot, although Benjamin Dykes has pointed out to me that the Arabic text itself does not seem to say anything about reversing the direction from the Ascendant, and it is not clear why Pingree framed it this way in his translation. Nonetheless, it is an important issue to be aware of, because even though only reversing the direction from the Ascendant rather than between the two points that compose the lot would result in the same thing mathematically as reversing the two initial points, it could have other important conceptual ramifications if it was in fact being done this way by some early authors.

Part of the rationale underlying the lots, which can be seen from the way they are calculated, is that they take the relationship or distance between the two primary planets involved, and then they personalize that relationship by projecting the same distance from the Ascendant. If the two planets are configured to each other by trine, then the lot will be configured to the Ascendant through a trine. If the two planets are configured by a square, then the lot will be configured to the Ascendant by a square as well. Finally, if the two planets are in aversion to each other, then the lot will be in aversion to the Ascendant as well. Thus, whatever relationship the two planets share with each other will be replicated in the configuration of the lot to the Ascendant.

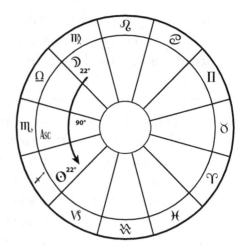

Fig. 16.1 - Nocturnal Fortune Calculation Step 1: Measure from Moon to Sun

Projecting the distance between the two planets from the Ascendant personalizes it for the native by tying it to the most personal point in the chart. While two people born in the world on the same day will have the planets in their charts in roughly the same configurations to each other,

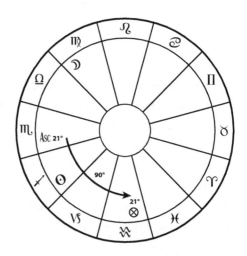

Fig. 16.2 - Nocturnal Fortune Calculation Step 2: Project distance from Ascendant

their lot placements will be different because the degree of the Ascendant is going to be different in separate locations. The Ascendant also moves very rapidly from moment to moment compared to the planets, and as a result of this the positions of the lots change relatively frequently as well. Thus, part of the conceptual motivation for the lots appears to have been an attempt to personalize the relationships between the planets in the native's chart.[6]

---

[6] This idea of the Lot of Fortune being more personal to the native even than the Ascendant seems to be implied in a comment that Valens makes at one point when he refers to the angles from the Ascendant as "universal" (*kosmikos*) and the angles from the Lot of Fortune

The Use of Lots in Natal Astrology

Lots were primarily used in the Hellenistic tradition in order to assign additional topics to the signs of the zodiac and the places. Wherever a lot falls in a chart, it marks that sign with the specific topics associated with that lot. For example, if the Lot of Marriage falls in Scorpio in the second place in a chart, then that sign and its ruler will have some bearing on the topic of marriage in that particular chart, even though neither the second place nor Scorpio normally have any natural association with that topic. In this way, the lots become a secondary system for assigning topics to the places in a chart, based on a different and somewhat random or chance-like rationale rather than the typical one that always assigns certain topics to certain places or regions in the chart. In fact, when discussing lots, the Hellenistic astrologers will sometimes alternate between referring to them as "lots" versus referring to them as "places" (*topoi*). For example, Valens gives the calculation for a lot composed of Mars and Saturn, and refers to the sign it falls in as the "Place of Accusation."[7] Elsewhere, Firmicus consistently refers to the lots as "places" (*loci*) in Latin, for example referring to the "Place of the Father" (*loco patris*), Place of the Mother (*loco matris*), Place of Brothers (*loco fratrum*), and so on.[8] This raises some interesting historical questions about whether the lot doctrine represented a rival method of assigning topics to places in the early Hellenistic tradition, although the fact that the Antiochus *Summary* attributes a discussion about the lots to Hermes Trismegistus already by the first century CE implies that the concept could have been introduced around the same time as the *dōdekatropos*, or perhaps even in the same text.[9]

Part of the purpose of the lots also seems to have been to create a point that emphasizes or isolates a specific signification associated with one of the planets involved in the calculation. For example, one of the many significations that Valens gives for the Moon is the body, and this becomes one of the primary significations associated with the Lot of Fortune.[10] One of the significations that he gives for the Sun is intelligence (*phronēsis*), and this becomes one of the primary significations given for the Lot of Spirit.[11]

Sometimes the lots were also used in order to particularize people or topics in a way that was more specific than the significations that could be derived

---

as "genethlialogical" or "natal" (*genethlialogikos*). Valens, *Anthology*, 2, 18: 6.

[7] Valens, *Anthology*, 5, 1: 2–5.

[8] Firmicus, *Mathesis*, 6, 32.

[9] Antiochus, *Summary*, 1, 26–27 (CCAG 8, 3, p. 117: 28 – p. 118: 1–2).

[10] Compare Valens, *Anthology*, 1, 1: 4 with 4, 4: 1–3.

[11] Compare Valens, *Anthology*, 1, 1: 1 with 4, 4: 1–4. Paulus specifically uses the term *phronēsis* in *Introduction*, 23.

from the standard twelve places. For example, the fourth place seems to have been taken as referring to both parents in general, but then in order to distinguish between each parent the Lot of the Father or the Lot of the Mother could be used. Dorotheus says that if you want to know which of the native's parents will die first, look at whether the Lot of the Father or the Mother is with the malefics, or whether the malefics are configured to one of those lots by square or opposition.[12]

From a practical standpoint, the use of lots often ends up being the third area that the astrologers would look at within the context of analyzing a specific topic in a native's life, such as the topic of children, marriage, career, etc. The first step would often be the analysis of the planet that matches that topic, such as Venus when studying marriage. The second step would be the analysis of the place that matches that topic, such as the seventh place and its ruler in the case of marriage. Finally, the third step would be the analysis of the lot that corresponds to that topic, such as the Lot of Marriage and its ruler. I believe that this was implicitly part of a "rule of three" for studying topics, which holds that if something is indicated once, then the outcome is possible, if it is indicated twice, the outcome is likely, and if it is indicated three times, then the outcome is certain. This concept is stated already in a section on weather omens at the end of Aratus' *Phaenomena*, which can be dated to the Hellenistic era:

> It is a good idea to observe one sign after another, and if two agree, it is more hopeful, while with a third you can be confident. [...] If you have watched for these signs all together for the year, you will never make an uninformed judgement on the evidence of the sky.[13]

This was also the way that some of the early Medieval astrologers understood the structuring of the approach to dealing with different topics that they inherited from the Hellenistic tradition. For example, in the early ninth century, the astrologer Abū 'Ali al-Khayyāt describes a rule of three towards the end of his book, *On the Judgments of Nativities*:

> In whatever is signified, this must chiefly must be noted: if it has only one testimony, it is routine (*vulgare*); if two, it will be stronger; if three, complete—only if the lords themselves or the significators are strong and not impeded.[14]

---

[12] Dorotheus, *Carmen*, 1, 15:1.
[13] Aratus, *Phaenomena*, 1142–1154, trans. Kidd, p. 157.
[14] Abū 'Ali al-Khayyāt, *On the Judgments of Nativities*, 50, trans. Dykes, *Persian Nativities*,

Lots could also be used for other purposes, such as comparing the charts of two people through synastry, or in specialized timing techniques such as zodiacal releasing, which will be discussed later.

Steps in Analyzing a Lot

From a functional standpoint, the lots are used in a way that is very similar to how the places and their rulers are used, in order to determine the outcome of the topics associated with the place.[15] There are four broad steps when analyzing the placement of a lot and trying to determine what it means for the topics associated with it:

1. Examine the sign the lot falls in. What is the nature of the sign? For example, if the Lot of Children is in a masculine sign, this is often seen as an indication for the birth of male children, while the placement of the lot in a feminine sign is an indication for the birth of females. Other qualities of the signs become relevant depending on the context of the lot being studied.

2. Examine which of the twelve whole sign places the lot falls in. What is the nature of the place? Is it advantageous or disadvantageous? A good place or a bad place? The nature of the place will be taken as an auspicious or inauspicious indication with respect to the topic associated with the lot.

3. Determine which planets are configured to the sign of the lot by a sign-based aspect. Planets that are configured to the lot will contribute something to the quality of the topics associated with the lot, while planets that are in aversion will contribute nothing. Are the planets that are configured benefic or malefic? Is the configuration easy or difficult? Are the planets of the sect or contrary?

4. Examine the condition of the domicile lord of the lot. What is the nature of this planet? Is it well-situated by sign, place, and configuration with other planets? Is it configured to the lot that it rules, or is it in aversion? Is the ruler bonified or maltreated?

The end result is a checklist of sorts that can be used in order to determine whether the placement of a lot is auspicious or inauspicious. Here are some of the relevant considerations:

---

vol. 1, p. 331.

[15] Valens gives a concise set of rules that are supposed to be applicable to interpreting the condition of the lords of places, lots, and triplicity rulers in *Anthology*, 1, 20: 40.

GOOD	BAD
1. Lot in a good place.	1. Lot in a bad place.
2. Benefics copresent with lot.	2. Malefics copresent with lot.
3. Benefics configured to lot.	3. Malefics configured to lot.
4. Malefics in aversion to lot.	4. Benefics in aversion to lot.
5. Lord of the lot a benefic.	5. Lord of the lot a malefic.
6. Lord well-placed by sign.	6. Lord poorly-placed by sign.
7. Lord in a good place.	7. Lord in a bad place.
8. Lord configured to the lot.	8. Lord not configured to lot.
9. Lord configured to benefics.	9. Lord in aversion to benefics.
10. Lord in aversion to malefics.	10. Lord configured to malefics.
11. Lord being bonified.	11. Lord not being bonified.
12. Lord not being maltreated.	12. Lord being maltreated.
13. Lord not under the beams.	13. Lord under the beams.

There are also a few other miscellaneous rules related to lots that can be picked up from different authors. An implicit delineation principle in some texts holds that configurations to the lot indicate the initial state of the matter, but the condition of the lord indicates circumstances later on.[16] This is an extension of the doctrine that is sometimes mentioned within the context of the condition of counteraction, in which the initial state of a placement indicates the initial circumstances surrounding the matter, but the condition of the lord indicates the outcome.

When the lord of a lot falls under the beams, it sometimes means that secrecy will be involved in that topic. For example: the domicile lord of the Lot of Marriage under the beams is delineated by Rhetorius as indicating that the native will be involved in secret marriages.[17] Elsewhere, Hephaestio quotes Dorotheus for the statement that when the lord of a lot is under the beams or even about to go under the beams, whatever is signified by the lot will "dry up," "waste away," or "wither" (*marainetai*).[18]

The Lot of Fortune

The Lot of Fortune (*klēros tuchēs*) is mentioned by just about every major Hellenistic astrologer, and it may have been the first lot that was introduced

---

[16] This may be the implicit principle underlying Dorotheus, *Carmen*, 2, 4: 34–35. This also seems to be implied towards the end of Valens' initial discussion of the Lot of Exaltation in *Anthology*, 2, 19: 5. It is also probably the motivation for the very last statement in Valens, *Anthology*, 2, 27: 12. Eventually the rule is stated explicitly by Rhetorius in *Compendium*, 54 (CCAG 8, 4, p. 122: 19–20).

[17] Rhetorius, *Compendium*, 48.

[18] Hephaestio, *Apotelesmatika*, 2, 18: 18.

when the concept of lots was originally developed. Valens refers to the Lot of Fortune as the "archetypal lot" (*archetupon klēron*), probably acknowledging its status as the original lot, but perhaps also because the concept of chance or fortune was seen as part of the underlying conceptual paradigm for lots in general.[19] Dorotheus and Valens both first mention the Lot of Fortune as the point that is defaulted to if the triplicity lords of the sect light are poorly placed, saying that if the Lot of Fortune and its lord are well-situated, the native may still be able to have some success and happiness in life as a result of luck, despite otherwise having an unstable foundation.[20] In this way, the Lot of Fortune appears to have been integrated into the approaches of some astrologers as a means of determining the role that chance or fortune played in the lives of individuals. Here they may have followed the Stoic belief that chance is simply a cause that is obscure to human reasoning, although through astrology they could attempt to make the underlying causes and outcomes associated with fortune accessible to reason.[21]

Debates Surrounding the Calculation of Fortune

There seem to have been some debates surrounding what the correct calculation was for the Lot of Fortune throughout the Hellenistic tradition, which resulted in some variant calculations.[22] The standard calculation that seems to have been used and advocated by most authors was to measure the distance from the Sun to the Moon by day, but the Moon to the Sun by night, and then measure the same distance from the Ascendant in zodiacal order. This is the calculation that appears to have been preferred by Dorotheus, Valens, Paulus, and others.[23]

Valens has a chapter on the Lot of Fortune that preserves a cryptic passage from Nechepso about how to calculate the lot.[24] Valens says that a

---

[19] Valens, *Anthology*, 2, 13: 1. A similar statement is attributed to Serapio in *Definitions*, p. 227: 17.

[20] Dorotheus, *Carmen*, 1, 26: 10; Valens, *Anthology*, 2, 2: 18.

[21] The Stoic doctrine is described and criticized by Alexander of Aphrodisias in *On Fate*, 8. This view of chance was already described in Aristotle (*Physics*, 2.4 196b5), and the Stoics merged it with other views that incorporated notions of necessity and providence, as discussed in Dudley, *Aristotle's Concept of Chance*, p. 12. There is some brief discussion about the Stoic conceptualization of chance and its relation to divination in *The Cambridge History of Hellenistic Philosophy*, ed. Alegra, pp. 535–4, as well as Bobzien, *Determinism and Freedom in Stoic Philosophy*, pp. 174–5.

[22] For a discussion of this see Greenbaum, "Calculating the Lots of Fortune and Daemon in Hellenistic Astrology," pp. 172–184.

[23] Dorotheus, *Carmen*, 1, 26: 11; for Valens see the chart examples, especially in book 2; for Paulus see the passage quoted already above.

[24] Valens, *Anthology*, 3, 11: 1–5.

number of authors have commented on this passage and come to different conclusions about it. He then gives his own interpretation: in day charts the diurnal calculation for the Lot of Fortune should be used, while in night charts the nocturnal calculation should be used—but only if the Moon is above the horizon (otherwise it defaults to the diurnal formula). Although Valens presents this as his own interpretation of this passage from Nechepso, in later example charts he doesn't seem to use the rule in practice; instead he uses the day or night calculations regardless of what side of the horizon the Moon is on. Valens' personal preferences aside, what this passage seems to demonstrate is that some of the later disagreements about the calculation of the Lot of Fortune may have arisen as a result of different interpretations of early source texts that were written in an obscure way.

Ptolemy is somewhat unique in saying that the calculation for the Lot of Fortune should not be reversed by day and night; instead, the distance from the Sun to the Moon should always be measured and then projected from the Ascendant.[25] This effectively means using what is the diurnal formula for other authors in both day and night charts. Despite Ptolemy's reputation, most later Hellenistic and Medieval astrologers did not follow him; it was only during the Renaissance that this approach became more popular due the perception that Ptolemy represented the older and more authoritative version of the tradition.

There is also a short passage attributed to Serapio that has several different considerations for calculating the Lot of Fortune. While the wording is somewhat difficult to understand in places, it seems to echo the Nechepso passage in that it also treats the calculation of the lot as dependent on certain factors in the chart:

Many times [the Lot of] Fortune becomes [the Lot of] Spirit: such as when the sect light is found in the bounds of [a star] that is contrary to the sect; or, according to the masculine and feminine—that is, when the Sun is in a feminine sign by day, or when the Moon in a masculine sign by night; or when the sect light is not eastern in the hemisphere of the sect. And when both luminaries happen to be in the hemisphere under the earth, and the other stars are found in an unfamiliar condition, then [The Lot of] Fortune is taken from the luminary in a superior position, that is, in the preceding signs, in the direction of the following one.[26]

---

[25] Ptolemy, *Tetrabiblos*, 3, 11: 5.

[26] Serapio, *Definitions*, p. 228: 10–16, trans. Gramaglia, p. 5, modified. Compare with the translations in Greenbaum, "Calculating the Lots of Fortune and Daemon in Hellenistic Astrology," p. 180, and Schmidt, *Definitions and Foundations*, p. 311.

The exact meaning of this passage is uncertain, especially in the final clause, but the general point is that some authors may have taken other factors into account when determining whether to reverse the calculation for the Lot of Fortune. In commenting on this passage, Schmidt wonders whether issues of calculation like this were simplified by later authors, thus leading to the standardization of the formula that seems evident in Dorotheus, Valens, Paulus, and others.[27] This is possible, but then leads us to consider the conceptual motivation underlying the calculation that became prevalent under the later authors: what made it compelling enough to become widely adopted? For this we must turn to the symbolism underlying the calculation itself.

Rationale Underlying Fortune and Spirit Calculations

After the Lot of Fortune, the second most widely used lot in the Hellenistic tradition was known as the Lot of Spirit (*klēros daimonos*).[28] In most Hellenistic authors, the Lot of Fortune is primarily associated with the body, while the Lot of Spirit by contrast is associated with the soul and intellect of the native. Valens, for example, says:

> The Lot of Fortune and of Spirit will have much power over the imposing and turning back of actions. For, the one shows matters concerning the body (*sōma*) and handicrafts, but Spirit and its domicile master matters concerning the soul (*psuchē*) and the intellect (*dianoia*), and actions through discourse and through giving and receiving.[29]

These meanings seem to be tied up with an implicit contrast between the concept of light being associated with the mind and soul, and darkness being associated with the body and physical incarnation. This distinction can be teased out of the calculations of the Lots of Fortune and Spirit by seeing what both calculations have in common in both the day and night formulas, according to the version of the calculation advocated by most authors.

For example, the standard calculation of the Lot of Fortune says that we should measure the distance from the Sun to the Moon in a day chart, or from the Moon to the Sun in a night chart, then measure the same distance from the Ascendant. According to the texts, both of these calculations determine the

---

[27] Schmidt, *Definitions and Foundations*, pp. 311–12

[28] Greenbaum says that out of about 300 surviving charts from the Hellenistic tradition, 91 calculated the Lot of Fortune, while 33 calculated the Lot of Spirit. Greenbaum, "Calculating the Lots of Fortune and Daemon," p. 164.

[29] Valens, *Anthology*, 2, 20: 1, trans. Schmidt, p. 30.

Lot of Fortune. The question then is, what do these two calculations share in common? That is to say, what is still true even though the points being used are inverted depending on the sect of the chart? In both instances, the calculation can be rephrased in the following way: count from the sect light to the luminary that is contrary to the sect, and then project the same distance from the Ascendant. Thus, the commonality between the calculations in both instances is that you are counting from the luminary that is providing light during that part of the day, to the luminary that is in some way darkened or eclipsed during that part of the day. The underlying conceptual premise for the calculation of the Lot of Fortune symbolically proceeds from light to darkness.

Interestingly, the calculation and conceptualization underlying the Lot of Spirit is the reverse. There it is said that we should measure the distance from the Moon to the Sun in a day chart, or from the Sun to the Moon in a night chart, then measure the same distance from the Ascendant. The commonality between these two calculations seems to be that in both instances we are starting with the luminary that is contrary to the sect and then measuring the distance to the luminary that is of the sect. The underlying idea is that we are symbolically proceeding from darkness to light. Thus, the basic contrast between the Lots of Spirit and Fortune is that one is associated with light and the other is associated with darkness; the Lot of Spirit is thus associated with the soul and mind, while the Lot of Fortune is associated with the body.

This provides us with an interesting access point for understanding the motivation underlying the calculations for the lots, and it also shows that there were probably some specific conceptual or philosophical reasons underlying their construction and usage. Schmidt points out that it is doubtful that the lots were developed empirically, because it seems implausible that the original inventors would have noticed that a sensitive point kept coming up in charts and then inferred or reverse engineered the calculations from there.[30] I think that the preceding discussion demonstrates the types of considerations that must have motivated the development of some of the early lots, and it may provide a useful access point for astrologers who are trying to determine which calculation to use today. In what follows I will use the standard calculations for the Lots of Fortune and Spirit that reverse them for day and night charts, as advocated by Dorotheus, Valens, and Paulus.

Easy Fortune Rules to Memorize
Using the standard approach to calculating the Lot of Fortune that reverses the calculation for day and night charts, there are some rules that make it easy to

---

[30] Schmidt, *Kepler College Sourcebook*, p. 10.

calculate its position. As discussed earlier, the Lot of Fortune always has the same configuration to the Ascendant that the luminaries have to each other. In other words, the Ascendant will have the same number of degrees between itself and the Lot of Fortune as the Sun and Moon have relative to each other. This results in the following rules that can be memorized:

1. At a New Moon, which is when the Sun and Moon are conjunct, the Lot of Fortune will always be conjunct the Ascendant.
2. At a Full Moon, when the luminaries are in opposition, Fortune will always be opposite the Ascendant (on the Descendant).
3. At the First or Third Quarter Moon, which is when the luminaries are square each other, Fortune will always be square the Ascendant (around the fourth or tenth whole sign place).

Understanding the relationship between the lunation cycle and the placement of the Lot of Fortune in the chart is both a useful tool for calculation and a helpful additional access point for understanding the purpose and nature of the lot.

Derived Places from the Lot of Fortune

The Lot of Fortune was sometimes used as an alternative Ascendant or Hour-Marker in order to set up a secondary system of derived houses or places. According to this approach, the sign that contains the Lot of Fortune becomes the first place, and then the sign after that in zodiacal order becomes the second place, and so on. In Valens, the places derived from Fortune are given similar significations as the places derived from the Ascendant, although there may be some underlying implications that they have to do with things that befall the native, their circumstances, and their bodily matters.[31] Valens puts particular emphasis on the eighth place from Fortune as indicating the quality of the native's death, and in all of the example charts he uses in order to demonstrate how the natal chart depicts instances of violent deaths, his discussion is largely focused on the eighth place from Fortune.[32] Elsewhere he focuses on the eleventh place from Fortune being what he calls the "Place of Acquisition," which is capable of bestowing property and goods when it is well-situated, by having benefics located in or configured to that sign.[33]

The location of the domicile lord of the Lot of Fortune relative to the twelve places derived from Fortune were thought to indicates major topics that will

---

[31] As first outlined in Valens, *Anthology*, 2, 18.
[32] Valens, *Anthology*, 2, 41.
[33] Valens, *Anthology*, 2, 21.

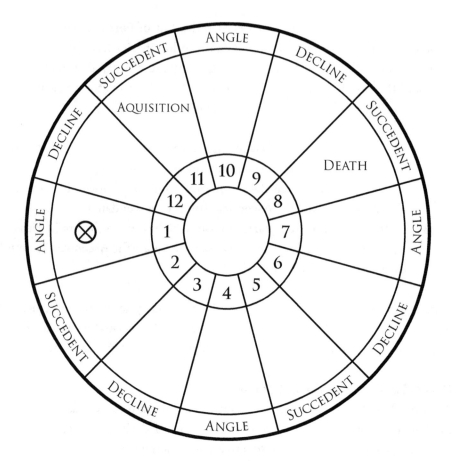

Figure 16.3 - Derived Places from the Lot of Fortune

arise or somehow come to characterize the native's life, similar to the domicile lord of the Hour-Marker. When Valens gives delineations for the domicile lord of the Hour-Marker in the places, he also gives delineations for the ruler of Fortune in the places at the same time.[34]

In some timing techniques, such as zodiacal releasing, derived places from the Lot of Fortune are more important than the places derived from the Ascendant. We will discuss this in more detail in a later chapter.

Survey of Other Lots Used

By far the most widely used lot in the Hellenistic tradition was the Lot of Fortune, followed by the Lot of Spirit. There were also a small handful of other lots for basic topics such as parents, children, marriage, siblings, etc., that seem to have been introduced very early on, probably in one of the foundational texts of the early Hellenistic tradition. Once the concept had been introduced

---

[34] Valens, *Anthology*, 2, 4–15.

it seems like there were multiple early authors that either introduced new lots, or suggested alternative calculation schemes for the same lots. This resulted in multiple variant calculations for some lots, such as the Lot of Marriage.

In the following sections I will give a list of the calculations of some of the more commonly used lots that show up in some of the major authors, including some discussion about variant calculations. This is not meant to be a comprehensive survey, but more of a cursory look at some of the main lots used in the Hellenistic tradition.

The Seven Hermetic Lots

Paulus presents a set of seven lots that are each associated with one of the seven planets, which he says derive from a work known as the *Panaretus*, which means something like "all-virtuous."[35] The scholia on Paulus' text and the commentary by Olympiodorus both say that the *Panaretus* was a work attributed to Hermes Trismegistus.[36] The calculations and descriptions of the Hermetic lots presented below follow Paulus:

LOT OF FORTUNE

Measure from the Sun to the Moon, and then the same distance from the Ascendant by day. By night, from the Moon to the Sun, and then the same distance from the Ascendant. Paulus says that the Moon is the planet associated with the Lot of Fortune, and that the lot itself signifies the body, the things one does for one's livelihood (*tas kata bion praxeis*), possessions, reputation, and privilege.

LOT OF SPIRIT

Measure from the Moon to the Sun by day, but by night from the Sun to the Moon, then the same distance from the Ascendant. Paulus says that the Lot of Spirit is associated with the Sun, and that it signifies the soul, temper, intelligence (*phronēsis*), the exercise of every power (*dunasteia*), and is sometimes relevant in terms of determining what one does in their occupation (*praxis*).

LOT OF EROS

Measure the distance from the Lot of Spirit to Venus by day, but by night from Venus to the Lot of Spirit, then the same from the Ascendant. It is associated with Venus, and it is said to signify appetites (*orexis*), desires (*epithumia*) that

---

[35] Paulus, *Introduction*, 23.

[36] For the scholia, see Paulus, *Introduction*, ed. Boer, p. 118: 24–26 (scholia 48). For the commentary see Olympiodorus, *Commentary*, ed. Boer, p. 51: 13-15.

arise by choice, as well as friendship and favor (*karitos*). The word *eros* means "love" or "desire." Eros was also the name of the Greek god of love, sexual desire, and attraction, and is otherwise known in modern times through his Roman counterpart, Cupid.

Lot of Necessity
Measure from Mercury to the Lot of Fortune by day, but by night from the Lot of Fortune to Mercury, then the same from the Ascendant. He associates the Lot of Necessity (*anankē*) with the planet Mercury, and says that it signifies constraints (*sunochē*), subordinations,[37] battles (*machas*), wars, enmities, hatreds, condemnations, and all other constraining circumstances.

Lot of Courage
From Mars to the Lot of Fortune by day, but by night from the Lot of Fortune to Mars, then the same from the Ascendant. Paulus associates the Lot of Courage (*tolma*) with Mars, and says that it signifies boldness, treachery, strength,[38] and all evildoing (*kakourgias*).

Lot of Victory
From the Lot of Spirit to Jupiter by day, but by night from Jupiter to the Lot of Spirit. He associates the Lot of Victory (*nikē*) with Jupiter, and says that it signifies faith (*pisteōs*), good hope, contests, all kinds of generosity (*koinōnias*), enterprise, and success (*epituchias*).

Lot of Nemesis
From Saturn to the Lot of Fortune by day, but by night from the Lot of Fortune to Saturn. He associates the Lot of Nemesis with Saturn, and says that it signifies spirits of the underworld, things which are concealed (*kekrummenōn*), exposure (*apodeixeos*),[39] weakness, banishment, destruction (*apōleias*),[40] sorrow (*penthos*), and quality of death. Holden refers to it as the Lot of Retribution in his translation of Paulus.

Alternative Eros and Necessity Calculations
It is not clear if the seven "Hermetic" lots in Paulus are from earlier or later in

---

[37] *hupotagē*. Or "subjections."

[38] *ischuos*. Or maybe "brute force."

[39] Greenbaum points out that Olympiodorus has "exposure of hidden things," which helps to clarify the probable meaning (Olympiodorus, *Commentary*, trans. Greenbaum, p. 42, n. 6).

[40] Or "loss."

Diurnal   Nocturnal

Diurnal		Nocturnal
☉ ⟶ ☽	**Fortune**	☽ ⟶ ☉
☽ ⟶ ☉	**Spirit**	☉ ⟶ ☽
Φ ⟶ ♀	**Eros**	♀ ⟶ Φ
Φ ⟶ ♃	**Victory**	♃ ⟶ Φ
☿ ⟶ ⊗	**Necessity**	⊗ ⟶ ☿
♂ ⟶ ⊗	**Courage**	⊗ ⟶ ♂
♄ ⟶ ⊗	**Nemesis**	⊗ ⟶ ♄

Φ = Lot of Spirit   ⊗ = Lot of Fortune

Table 16.1 - Hermetic Lot Calculations from Paulus

the tradition, as the calculations that he gives for the Lots of Eros and Necessity are different than those given by earlier authors such as Dorotheus, Valens, and Firmicus. I suspect that this means that the text on the lots that Paulus drew from was written sometime between the second and fourth centuries CE (i.e. after Valens but before Paulus). According to Valens, the earlier calculations for the Lots of Eros and Necessity are as follows:

LOT OF EROS

By day, measure the distance from the Lot of Fortune to the Lot of Spirit, and then the same distance from the Ascendant. By night, measure from the Lot of Spirit to the Lot of Fortune, and then the same from the Ascendant.[41] Valens says that Eros signifies desire (*epithumia*).[42] Hephaestio says that Dorotheus described the Lot of Eros as being used by some astrologers in order to

---

[41] Valens, *Anthology*, 4, 25: 13. Pingree mistakenly bracketed this sentence as an interpolation in the manuscripts, probably based on the assumption that the Paulus version of the Lot of Eros was the standard calculation. I wish to thank Dorian Greenbaum for pointing this out to me at a conference in 2008.

[42] Valens, *Anthology*, 2, 16: 1.

determine the matter of friendship (*philias*), and Hephaestio includes it in his chapter on friends and enemies.[43]

Lot of Necessity

By day, measure the distance from the Lot of Spirit to the Lot of Fortune, and then measure the same distance from the Ascendant. By night, measure the distance from the Lot of Fortune to the Lot of Spirit, and then the same distance from the Ascendant.[44] Valens says that Necessity signifies enemies (*echthrōn*).[45] One of the fragments of Dorotheus seems to indicate that he used the same calculation for Eros as Valens.[46] Firmicus similarly gives the calculations for Eros and Necessity as only involving the Lot of Spirit and Fortune, although he has the calculations inverted, which is presumably an error.[47] None of the authors prior to Paulus in the fourth century mention the Lots of Courage, Victory, or Nemesis. All of this seems to imply that the original calculations that were used earlier in the Hellenistic tradition were the ones given by Valens and Dorotheus, and then at some point later in the tradition the alternative Eros and Necessity calculations were introduced along with the three other planetary lots, evidently in a text attributed to Hermes Trismegistus, which Paulus used.

When confronted with this discrepancy in the later Medieval tradition, Abū Ma'shar seems to have dealt with it by merging the two traditions, using Valens and Dorotheus' calculations for the Lots of Eros and Necessity, and Paulus' calculations for the Lots of Courage, Victory, and Nemesis.[48] This mixed set of calculations was then passed on to later Medieval astrologers such as Bonatti.[49]

Lots for Family Members

There are several lots for different family members. I will mention only some of the more prominent or common ones here, largely derived from Dorotheus, Valens, Paulus, and Firmicus.

Lot of the Father

According to Dorotheus and Paulus, the Lot of the Father is calculated in a day chart by measuring from the Sun to Saturn, and then the same distance from the Ascendant. By night it is measured from Saturn to the Sun, and then

---

[43] Hephaestio, *Apotelesmatika*, 2, 23: 10–18.

[44] Valens, *Anthology*, 4, 25: 16.

[45] Valens, *Anthology*, 2, 16: 1.

[46] Dorotheus, *Excerpts*, 16: 6.

[47] Firmicus, *Mathesis*, 6, 32: 45–46.

[48] Abū Ma'shar, *The Abbreviation*, 6.

[49] Bonatti, *Book of Astronomy*, tr. 8, pt. 2, ch. 2 (trans. Dykes, vol. 2, pp. 1043–49).

the same distance from the Ascendant. Both Dorotheus and Paulus say that if Saturn is under the beams in the chart, then instead measure the distance from Mars to Jupiter, and then project that from the Ascendant.[50] Paulus says that the measurement from Mars to Jupiter is done the same way both in day and night charts, and evidently Dorotheus agrees.[51] Firmicus has the same calculation, although he doesn't say anything about defaulting to Mars and Jupiter if Saturn is under the beams.[52] Valens also says that the Lot of Father is measured from the Sun to Saturn in an excerpt apparently derived from the astrologer Timaeus, although the text becomes corrupted around the point that he would have discussed the reversal.[53]

LOT OF THE MOTHER

From Venus to the Moon by day, and then the same distance from the Ascendant, but by night from the Moon to Venus.[54] Paulus, Dorotheus, and Firmicus all have the same calculation.[55] Valens also has the same calculation by day, apparently drawing on Timaeus, but the text has become corrupted in a section where it should otherwise mention the nocturnal calculation.[56]

LOT OF SIBLINGS

According to Valens and Firmicus, the Lot of Siblings is calculated by measuring the distance from Saturn to Jupiter by day, and then the same distance from the Ascendant, but by night from Jupiter to Saturn.[57] However, Dorotheus and Paulus say that the calculation should not be reversed for day and night charts, but that you should always measure from Saturn to Jupiter.[58] In instances like this it is unclear if we are dealing with differences of opinion over the calculation motivated by conceptual issues, whether there were textual errors that led to

---

[50] Dorotheus, *Carmen*, 1, 13; Paulus, *Introduction*, 23, ed. Boer, p. 52: 9–17.

[51] Dorotheus, *Carmen*, 1, 13: 1–6. Pingree's English translation of the Arabic version of Dorotheus is apparently untrustworthy here, as Benjamin Dykes has pointed out to me privately that there is nothing about reversing the calculation at night according to the Arabic, despite what the English translation seems to say.

[52] Firmicus, *Mathesis*, 6, 32: 3–20.

[53] Valens, *Anthology*, 2, 32: 10.

[54] Paulus, *Introduction*, 23, ed. Boer, p. 52: 17–19.

[55] Dorotheus, *Carmen*, 1, 14: 1; Firmicus, *Mathesis*, 6, 32: 21.

[56] Valens, *Anthology*, 2, 32: 11.

[57] Valens, *Anthology*, 2, 40: 7; Firmicus, *Mathesis*, 6, 32: 23.

[58] Dorotheus, *Carmen*, 1, 19: 1; Paulus, *Introduction*, 23, ed. Boer, p. 52: 20–22. Again, Pingree's English translation of the Arabic version of Dorotheus is evidently untrustworthy here; Benjamin Dykes points out that there is nothing about reversing the calculation at night according to the Arabic, despite Pingree's translation saying otherwise.

divergences, or whether this represents another instance of variations in the later tradition based on differing interpretations of an enigmatic source text.

This lot is often referred to as the Lot of Brothers in most translations, although it appears to be the lot used for siblings in general. Part of the confusion arises from the fact that the Greek term for brothers can also be used to refer to siblings of either gender.

LOT OF MARRIAGE

There were several different calculations for the Lot of Marriage in the tradition, and we often find multiple calculations in the same author. Dorotheus and Paulus say that for males you should always measure from Saturn to Venus, and then the same distance from the Ascendant, but for females you always measure from Venus to Saturn.[59] This issue with different calculations for different genders leads to a few different specialized calculations in different authors. Firmicus uses a similar but slightly different calculation for the Lot of Marriage, in which he says to measure the distance from Saturn to Venus by day, and then measure the same distance from the Ascendant, but by night from Venus to Saturn.[60] Presumably this is only in the charts of males, because Firmicus has a separate calculation for the Lot of the Husband in the charts of females, where the distance from Mars to Venus is measured by day, then presumably reversed by night, although there is some textual uncertainty with this reversal.[61]

The Arabic version of Dorotheus preserves two other marriage lots. The first he calls the Lot of Pleasure and Wedding, which he says is calculated from Venus to the "degree of the seventh sign," and then the same distance from the Ascendant, evidently both by day and night.[62] In the next chapter it gives another Lot of Wedding, which is measured from the Sun to the Moon; this distance is then projected from the degree of Venus, evidently with no reversal.[63] A few lines later in the text, he seems to imply that this is the calculation for male nativities, but in the charts of women you substitute Mars for Venus, so that you measure

---

[59] Dorotheus, *Carmen*, 2, 2: 1 and 2, 3: 1. Paulus, *Introduction*, 23, ed. Boer, p. 52: 24–p. 53: 1–5. As with the Lot of Siblings, there is an issue with Pingree's English translation of Dorotheus where it seems to indicate a reversal for the Lot of Marriage for males, although in the Arabic text itself this does not seem to be stated.

[60] Dorotheus, *Carmen*, 2, 2: 1–2; Firmicus, *Mathesis*, 6, 32: 27–28.

[61] Firmicus, *Mathesis*, 6, 32: 32.

[62] Dorotheus, *Carmen*, 2, 5: 4, trans. Pingree, p. 204. Pingree's translation is again untrustworthy with respect to the reversal.

[63] Dorotheus, *Carmen*, 2, 6: 1. Similar issues with Pingree's translation as before.

the distance from Mars to the degree of the seventh sign.[64] This is tied in with a long-standing belief, mentioned by Firmicus and others, that in the charts of males Venus signifies the wife, but in the charts of females Mars signifies the husband.[65] This is probably the source of some of the disagreements about how to calculate the Lot of Marriage: whether the lot should be different for men and women, and which planets or significators should be used based on the native's gender.

Valens gives a few different marriage lots. For the first one he says measure the distance from Jupiter to Venus for day charts, and then the same distance from the Ascendant, but for night charts from Venus to Jupiter.[66] Later in the same chapter he gives an alternative calculation that depends on the gender of the chart. He says that for male charts the distance from the Sun to Venus is measured, and then projected from the Ascendant, but in female charts the distance from the Moon to Mars is measured.[67] Evidently there is no reversal based on the sect of the chart.

LOT OF CHILDREN

There were several different calculations for the Lot of Children. In Dorotheus and Paulus the calculation is to measure from Jupiter to Saturn, and then the same distance from the Ascendant, both by day and by night.[68] This is the reverse of their calculation for the Lot of Siblings. Valens gives two different lots for male and female children when discussing the Lot of Children.[69] In order to calculate the lot for male children, which we will call the Lot of Sons, he says measure the distance from Jupiter to Mercury, and then the same distance from the Ascendant. To calculate the lot for female children, which we will call the Lot of Daughters, he says measure the distance from Jupiter to Venus, and then the same from the Ascendant. Evidently there is no reversal in Valens' calculations. Firmicus' Lot of Children also involves Venus and Mercury, although he has a unique calculation which begins with the planet that is earlier in zodiacal order and proceeds to the one that is later; this distance is then projected from the Ascendant.[70]

---

[64] Dorotheus, *Carmen*, 2, 6: 5.

[65] Firmicus, *Mathesis*, 6, 32: 32.

[66] Valens, *Anthology*, 2, 38: 51.

[67] Valens, *Anthology*, 2, 38: 56.

[68] Dorotheus, *Carmen*, 2, 10: 1; Paulus, *Introduction*, 23, ed. Boer, p. 52: 22–24. Pingree's English translation of the Arabic Dorotheus again mistakenly implies that there is a reversal.

[69] Valens, *Anthology*, 2, 39: 2–3.

[70] Firmicus, *Mathesis*, 6, 32: 33–35.

Lots Derived from Places

There are several lots that are partially derived from the places. For example, Dorotheus and Hephaestio mention the Lot of Livelihood, in which the distance from the ruler of the second place to the second place itself is measured, and then added to the Ascendant.[71] Presumably this means from the lord up to the beginning of the sign that coincides with the second whole sign place, which is how Schmidt interpreted it.[72] Evidently there is no reversal based on the sect of the chart.

Another is the Lot of Death. Hephaestio quotes Dorotheus' calculation, which measures from the Moon to the eighth sign relative to the Ascendant (i.e. the eighth whole sign place), and then projects the same distance from Saturn.[73] The examination of this place, its ruler, and the planets configured to this place was supposed to describe the circumstances surrounding the native's death.

The Lot of Illness or Accusation

A particularly difficult lot mentioned by several early authors is composed of the two malefics. It involves measuring the distance from the malefic that is of the sect to the malefic that is contrary to the sect. The calculation is as follows: in a day chart, measure the distance from Saturn to Mars, and then the same distance from the Ascendant. In a night chart measure the distance from Mars to Saturn, and then the same distance from the Ascendant.

There appear to be a few different names for this lot in the tradition. In the Arabic version of Dorotheus it is called the Lot of Chronic Illness, and he says that the sign that it falls in indicates the part of the native's body where they will develop a chronic illness in.[74] For example, if it falls in Aries, the illness will be in the head, if in Taurus, the neck, and so on. Hephaestio has a chapter where he mentions the same lot shortly before citing Dorotheus, and there he calls it the Lot of Illness (*sinos*).[75] The Greek term means "hurt," "harm," "injury," etc. Presumably this is the original Greek name that Dorotheus used for the lot. Firmicus calls it the Place of Bodily Defects and Illness.[76]

Valens also preserves a brief discussion of this lot, although the name that he uses for it is somewhat obscure.[77] He calls it the *aitiatikos* place, which means

---

[71] Dorotheus, *Carmen*, 1, 27: 19; Hephaestio, *Apotelesmatika*, 2, 18: 16–17.

[72] Hephaestio, *Apotelesmatika*, 2, trans. Schmidt, p. 56, fn. 137.

[73] Hephaestio, *Apotelesmatika*, 2, 25: 16.

[74] Dorotheus, *Carmen*, 4, 1: 75–76.

[75] Hephaestio, *Apotelesmatika*, 2, 14.

[76] Firmicus, *Mathesis*, 6, 32: 40.

[77] Valens, *Anthology*, 5, 1: 2–5.

"causal" or "accusative." Riley translates this as the "Crisis-Producing Place," while Schmidt calls it the Lot of Accusation. Schmidt is probably correct, as Firmicus has a variant of the same lot, which he calls the Place of Accusations (*accusationis locum*).[78] Valens says that it signifies fear, danger, and imprisonment. He goes on to say that if malefics are ruling the lot, placed in the same sign, or are otherwise configured to it, that it indicates danger to the native, so that their lives are precarious and easily destroyed. But if benefics are configured to the lot then it will lessen the problems and allow the native to escape from major crises.

Exaltation and Foundation

Valens introduces two important lots that he uses together with the triplicity rulers of the sect light and the Lots of Fortune and Spirit in order to determine the stability and eminence of the native's chart.

LOT OF EXALTATION

The first lot is called the Lot of Exaltation, which is calculated by day from the Sun to Aries, then the same distance from the Ascendant, but by night from the Moon to Taurus, then the same from the Ascendant.[79] In both instances the calculation involves measuring the distance from the sect light to the sign of its exaltation. Valens says to examine the sign the lot falls in, as well as the status of its ruler. If the lord of the lot falls in the first or tenth place, the native may end up being royal or eminent, especially if it falls in a sign that is angular to the Lot (of Fortune, I believe he means), and as long as the foundation of the nativity, as indicated by the triplicity lords of the sect light, agrees.

LOT OF FOUNDATION (LOT OF BASIS)

Later Valens introduces a second lot within the context of a discussion about eminence, which he calls the Lot of Foundation (*basis*). He appears to say that it is calculated by measuring the shortest distance from the Lot of Fortune to the Lot of Spirit by day, and then projecting that from the Ascendant, or from the Lot of Spirit to the Lot of Fortune by night.[80] This is similar to the calculation that Valens gives elsewhere for the Lots of Eros and Necessity, except that by always measuring the shortest distance between Fortune and Spirit this means that the Lot of Foundation will always be either Eros or Necessity, and it will always fall somewhere in the bottom half of the chart. Indeed, this is probably one of the reasons it was named the Lot of Foundation. Since the

---

[78] Firmicus, *Mathesis*, 6, 32: 53.
[79] Valens, *Anthology*, 2, 19: 1.
[80] Valens, *Anthology*, 2, 23: 7.

Lot of Foundation is necessarily also equivalent to Valens' calculations for either the Lot of Eros or the Lot of Necessity, it also implies that Eros or Necessity become foundational principles in the native's life in some broader sense. Valens then goes on to list many different combinations of how the interactions between the Lots of Spirit, Fortune, and Foundation (and their rulers) can indicate different types of eminence in a native's chart. The application of these lots can be understood through a careful study of the example charts used throughout book two of the *Anthology*.

CHAPTER 17
ANNUAL PROFECTIONS

Time-Lord Techniques

A number of different timing techniques were used in the Hellenistic tradition to determine when certain events would occur in the life of an individual. These techniques are sometimes referred to generally as establishing the "divisions of the times," because they are usually designed to divide up the native's life into different chapters and subsections, each possessing different qualities and characteristics. Each of these chapters is ruled by a specific planet in the chart, and these planetary rulers are referred to as "time-lords," from the Greek word *chronokratōr*. In contemporary discussions, these different methods for determining the division of the times have come to be known as time-lord techniques.

The basic premise underlying the time-lord techniques is that not all placements in a person's birth chart are activated at all times. Instead, certain placements lie dormant during the course of a person's life until they become awakened as time-lords. In these periods, the latent natal potential in a placement becomes activated in the native's life, for better or worse.

The time-lord systems are the western equivalent of the *dasha* systems that are still used in Indian astrology to this day. Most of the time-lord systems that were used in the Hellenistic tradition were lost during the course of the transmission of western astrology over the past 2,000 years, and it is only in the past twenty years that western astrologers have started to recover and use them again through translations of ancient texts.

Annual Profections

The most widespread time-lord technique in the Hellenistic tradition is known today as annual profections. Nearly every major astrologer whose work survives from the Hellenistic tradition either demonstrates or at least mentions the technique in passing. The primary sources for treatments of annual profections in the Hellenistic tradition are as follows (arranged chronologically):

> Manilius, *Astronomica*, book 3: 510–525.
> Dorotheus, *Carmen Astrologicum*, book 4.
> Ptolemy, *Tetrabiblos*, book 4, chapter 10.
> Valens, *Anthology*, books 4, 5, and 6.
> Firmicus, *Mathesis*, book 2, chapter 27.
> Paulus, *Introduction*, chapter 31.
> Hephaestio, *Apotelesmatika*, book 2, chapters 27–28.

The most extensive surviving treatment of profections is in the work of Valens. In books 4, 5, and 6 of his *Anthology*, he presents a method of using profections that is more complex than many other authors. Valens seems to have drawn parts of his advanced method of profections from the lost work of Critodemus.[1] He also cites different considerations related to profections from works attributed to Hermes and Nechepso, which seems to indicate that the technique was widely used even among the earliest authors.[2]

The basic method of calculating annual profections is rather simple. Beginning with the rising sign, count one sign per year from that sign in zodiacal order for every year of the native's life. Whatever sign is reached in a given year, the domicile lord of that sign becomes activated as the time-lord for the year.

By way of example, if a person was born with Cancer rising, then Cancer would be activated for the first year of their life. From the moment of birth until their first birthday, the Moon is activated as the time-lord for that year. On the person's first birthday, when they are one year old, the profection would then advance to the next sign in zodiacal order, which would be Leo, thus activating the Sun as the lord of the year. The year after that it would move to Virgo, thus activating Mercury, and so on. Eventually the profection makes its way around the wheel and then returns to the rising sign when the native turns

---

[1] The summary of a work on annual profections attributed to Critodemus in CCAG, 8, 3, p. 102 is very similar to the treatment of annual profections that Valens gives in book 4 of the *Anthology*, especially chapters 17–24 where delineations are given for each of the planets.

[2] For Hermes see Valens, *Anthology*, 4, 27. For Nechepso see Valens, *Anthology*, 5, 4: 1, which deals with monthly profections.

twelve. At that point, Cancer and the Moon would again become activated for a year, as the cycle returns to its beginning point. Thus, every twelve years, the profection returns to the rising sign, which occurs at the ages of twelve, twenty-four, thirty-six, forty-eight, sixty, seventy-two, eighty-four, ninety-six, and so on.

Like most of the time-lord systems, the Hellenistic astrologers didn't seem to have a specific name for this technique, although it was sometimes described as the method for determining the ruler or lord of the year. The term "profection" is derived from the Latin word that was used in the Medieval period to describe this technique, *profectio*, which means "a going away," "setting out," "departure," or "advance." This is because annual profections "depart" from the rising sign in order to "advance" the chart at the rate of one sign per year. Profections can also be advanced on a monthly, daily, or even hourly level, although for the purposes of this chapter we will focus on the yearly approach.

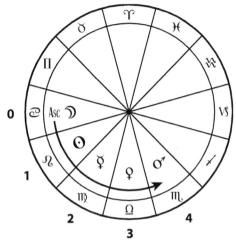

Figure 17.1 - Annual Profections 1
Count one sign per year from rising sign

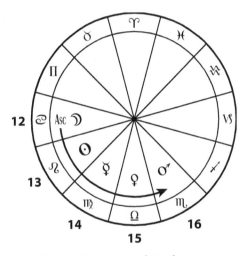

Figure 17.2 - Annual Profections 2
Cycle repeats itself beginning at age 12

Activation of the Places

When the annual profection comes to a specific place in a chart, the topics associated with that place become activated during the course of that year of the native's life. For example, if the profection comes to the sign that coincides with the second place, then topics such as the native's finances and livelihood would become part of the focus of that year. If the profection comes to the seventh place, then relationships would become part of the focus of the year. If it activates the tenth place, career matters would become highlighted, and so on.

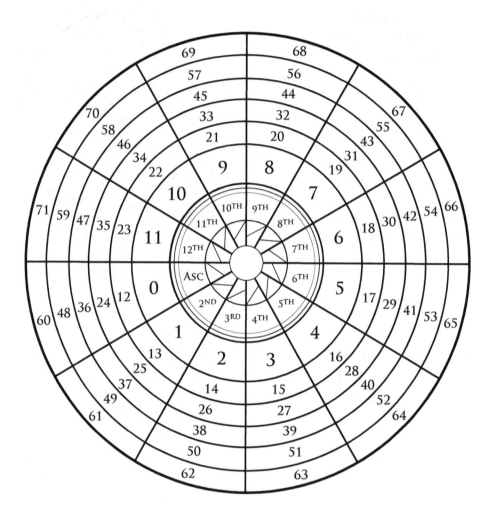

Figure 17.3 - Annual Profections Wheel

An abbreviated way of referring to certain profection years is by referring to them according to the place that is being activated. So, for example, if the tenth place is being activated, then we might call it a "tenth place profection year." If the seventh place is being activated, then it would be a seventh place profection year, and so on. While this terminology is not necessarily used in the Hellenistic texts themselves, it is consistent with the way that they used profections, and it helps to make discussions about the technique easier.

Let's take a look at some examples of how different individuals experienced different profection years, in order to get a sense for how some of the significations associated with the places can become more prominent during certain years.

LISA MARIE PRESLEY

Lisa Marie Presley is a good example of a second place profection year. She is the daughter of the famous singer Elvis Presley, who died when she was nine. Her inheritance was held in a trust until she turned twenty-five. On the day she turned twenty-five she inherited her father's estate, which was estimated to be worth around $100 million. Thus, when she moved into a second place profection year, financial matters became the focus.

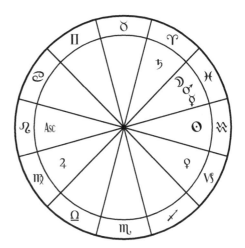

Chart 77 - Lisa Marie Presley

ROBERT F. KENNEDY

Robert F. Kennedy, the brother of U.S. President John F. Kennedy, turned thirty-eight on November 20, 1963, thus moving into a third place profection year. His brother, John, was assassinated two days later on November 22, 1963. Thus, shortly after he moved into a third place profection year, the focus of the year became one of his siblings, and the aftermath of his assassination.

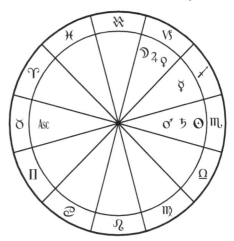

Chart 78 - Robert F. Kennedy

RECONCILIATION WITH MOTHER

A native who turned fifty-one and moved into a fourth place profection year suddenly felt the need to reconcile with her mother, from whom she had been estranged for some time. This estrangement commenced during her previous fourth place profection year twelve years earlier. The native sought outside help from a mediator, and the mother eventually embraced her

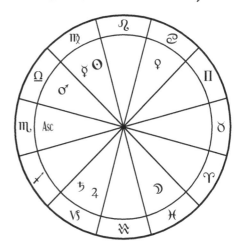

Chart 79 - Reconciliation with Mother

with open arms. She finished the year feeling a greater sense of appreciation for her mother as a person, and had developed an actual relationship with her. However, later in the same profection year, her father died. Thus, in her fourth place profection year, her parents became the focus.

BIRTH OF CHILD

Another native turned twenty-eight years old, and thus moved into a fifth place profection year. He learned that his girlfriend was pregnant around that time, and they had their first and only child five months later.

MICHAEL J. FOX

Actor Michael J. Fox started noticing concerning medical symptoms when he was twenty-nine years old. He was in a sixth place profection year. According to his autobiography, he woke up to his finger twitching uncontrollably on November 13, 1990, and this eventually led him to get his symptoms tested.[3] He was diagnosed with Parkinson's disease.

MET FUTURE HUSBAND

Another native turned eighteen in 1951, moving into a seventh place profection year. She met her future husband and began a relationship with him that year. With the benefic of the sect in the seventh, they have been married for over sixty years.

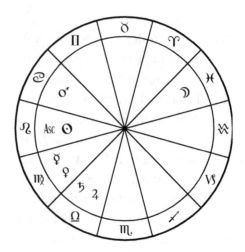

Chart 80 - Birth of Child

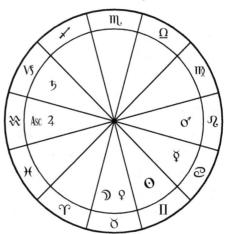

Chart 81 - Michael J. Fox

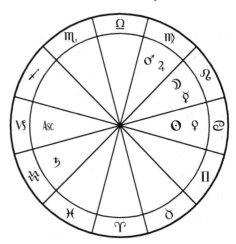

Chart 82 - Met Future Husband

---

[3] Fox, *Lucky Man*, p. 4.

PATRICK SWAYZE

When the actor Patrick Swayze turned fifty-five, he moved into an eighth place profection year, and in that year was diagnosed with stage four pancreatic cancer. He was widely reported to be close to death in the tabloids. He underwent surgery to remove part of his stomach, and had his will rewritten, in addition to transferring his property to his wife. Thus, there was a lot of focus that year on his own mortality, as well as issues surrounding inheritance. Although he recovered from the cancer, he relapsed a year later and died shortly afterward.

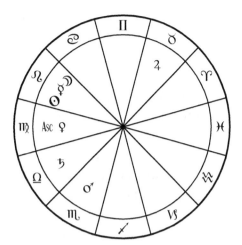

Chart 83 - Patrick Swayze

AMANDA KNOX

Amanda Knox was an American who went to study abroad in Italy for a year shortly after she turned twenty years old, which was a ninth place profection year. A few months into her stay, her roommate was murdered, and Knox and her boyfriend were accused of being involved. Initially they were convicted and sentenced to twenty-six years in prison, although a few years later they were acquitted and exonerated.

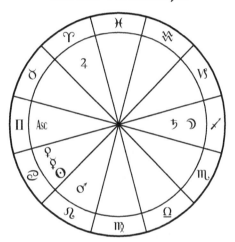

Chart 84 - Amanda Knox

CARL SAGAN

The famous astronomer, cosmologist, and astrophysicist, Carl Sagan, co-wrote and starred in the original *Cosmos* television series, which premiered in the fall of 1980. He was in a tenth place profection year at the time. The series was viewed by more

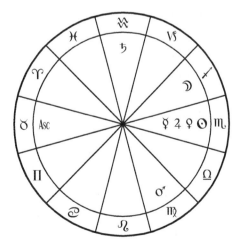

Chart 85 - Carl Sagan

than half a billion people in sixty countries, subsequently making him one of the most famous scientists in the world in the 1980s and early 1990s.

ANTHONY LOUIS

The astrologer Anthony Louis published a book on traditional interrogational astrology in 1991. It was one of the first books to come out of the early revival of traditional astrology that began to take root in the late 1980s and early 1990s. In April of 1992, he unexpectedly received a Regulus Award for the book at the United Astrology Conference in Washington D.C. He was forty-six years old, and thus in an eleventh place profection year. The

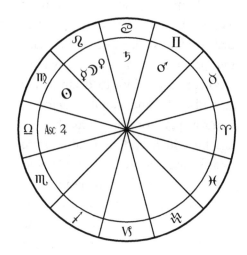

Chart 86 - Anthony Louis

award was sponsored by three major astrological organizations. It was the first time he attended a major national astrological conference, and he said that he met many people at that conference that became lasting friends for decades. It is worth noting that the book was published the previous year, in 1991, during a tenth place profection.

RUDOLF HESS

Rudolf Hess was a high ranking Nazi official before and during World War II. He was essentially Hitler's second in command. On May 10, 1941, he flew a solo mission from Germany to the U.K. to negotiate a peace deal with the British. He was apprehended and imprisoned, and he spent the next forty-six years of his life behind bars; he died on August 17, 1987, apparently by hanging himself. He was born April 26, 1894, and had

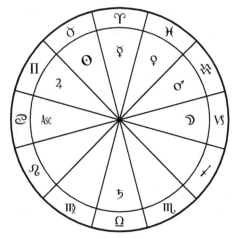

Chart 87 - Rudolf Hess

just turned forty-seven two weeks before his flight to the U.K. The twelfth place profection year that he moved into thus marked what would be the beginning of the rest of his life, imprisoned in a foreign country.

Condition of the Lord of the Year

The condition of the planet that is activated as the lord of the year can dictate the quality of the year, and whether the topics surrounding it will have a positive or negative outcome. While the place activated may provide some information about what topics will become part of the focus of that year, the condition of the ruler answers questions like "how will the year go," or "will the native experience fortunate events or unfortunate events," and so on.

The general principle here is one that is commonly stated in Indian astrology, which is that whatever the planet promises in the natal chart will manifest when it becomes activated as a time-lord. If the planet promises good things because it is well-situated in the chart, then good things will be delivered when it becomes activated, while if negative things are promised because the planet is in poor condition in the chart, then those things will become manifest when that planet is awakened. Thus, it is imperative to understand the condition of the planet, as well as any mitigating factors that may alter its constitution, for better or worse. This becomes particularly notable when planets that are bonified or maltreated become activated according to annual profections. Two examples suffice to demonstrate the concrete effects of the ruler's condition.

ANDRE ROMELLE YOUNG (DR. DRE)
The rapper and music producer Dr. Dre made an estimated $620 million in 2014 due to the sale of the headphones company he co-founded, Beats Electronics, to Apple computers. Apple acquired Beats on August 1, 2014, when the native was forty-nine years old, and thus in a second place profection year. He has the sign Cancer on the second place, thus activating the Moon as the lord of the year. The Moon is natally placed in Libra in the fifth place, and

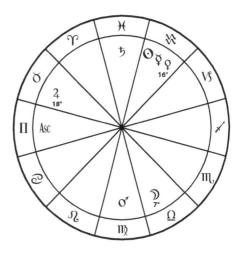

Chart 88 - Dr. Dre

is bonified through an applying trine with Venus within thirteen degrees, which is enhanced due to the presence of reception, since the Moon is in Venus' sign. Thus, the native's second place profection year was clearly directed towards finances; moreover, it went extremely well for him because the lord is well-situated natally. In that year the full natal potential of his well-placed ruler of the second became awakened.

ROBERT F. KENNEDY

Robert F. Kennedy was used as an example earlier, where we saw how his brother was assassinated two days after he moved into a third place profection year. His third whole sign place coincides with Cancer, and the Moon is located in late Capricorn, applying within thirteen degrees to an out-of-sign square with Mars in a day chart. Thus, the Moon is maltreated by the malefic that is contrary to the sect, and in the year in which it became activated he experienced a tragic event in relation to the topic signified by the third place.

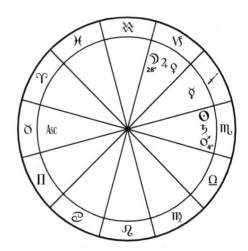

Chart 89 - Robert F. Kennedy

Activation of the Place Containing the Ruler

The significations of the place that the lord of the year is located in also become relevant in describing the topics, themes, and events that will arise during the course of a given year. This technique thus integrates the earlier method of interpreting the rulers of the places. For example, if a person is in a seventh place profection year, and the ruler of seventh is located in the eleventh place, then it may be a year in which relationships or partnerships with friends become part of the focus of the year.

LISA MARIE PRESLEY

Previously I showed how Lisa Marie Presley inherited her father's estate the day she turned twenty-five, thus beginning her second place profection year. Virgo coincides with the second whole sign place, and the ruler, Mercury, is located in Pisces in the eighth, the place of death and inheritance. Thus the position of the ruler helps to clarify where she would receive the financial windfall from in that year, and that it would be from an inheritance.

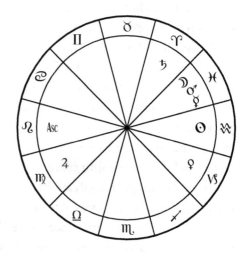

Chart 90 - Lisa Marie Presley

STEVE WOZNIAK

Similarly, Steve Wozniak was also twenty-five when he founded Apple Computer with his friend Steve Jobs on April 1, 1976. He was in a second place profection year, with the ruler of the second, Venus, in the eleventh place of friends, bonified by Jupiter via overcoming. Eventually Wozniak would become rich as a result of this partnership with his friend, which began with the activation of the ruler of the second place that year.

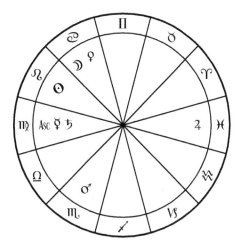

Chart 91 - Steve Wozniak

RELOCATED TO FOREIGN COUNTRY

A native who was born with a night chart, and Virgo rising. Taurus is the ninth place, and the ruler of the ninth, Venus, is in Sagittarius in the fourth place. When she turned thirty-two years old, she moved into a ninth place profection year, thus activating Venus in the fourth. In that year she moved to a foreign country to live permanently. In this way you must always pay attention to both the topics associated with the place that the profection has come to, as well as

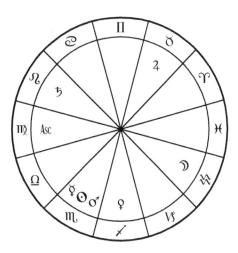

Chart 92 - Relocated to Foreign Country

the topics associated with the place that the lord of the year is located in.

Repetitions and Transits

As we have seen, the profection cycle repeats itself every twelve years, which means that the same places and rulers will be reactivated in twelve year increments. When these repetitions happen, there are often similar themes that come up in the native's life, which arise from the activation of the same place or the ruler of that place. What changes are the transits and the other time-lords that are active in different twelve-year periods. These can intensify or counteract the qualities associated with certain placements, or make them more positive or negative.

Working with transits requires looking at where the planets are or will be in the sky at some point in the future, often relative to where they were originally located in the natal chart. The typical term for a transit in Greek is *epembasis*, which means "to step onto," "to walk upon," "embark" or "transit." In Hellenistic astrology, transits are largely sign-based. They begin as soon as a planet ingresses or moves into a sign that is configured to a natal placement. The effect of the transit intensifies the closer it is to the exact aspect or configuration, in the same way that there is a general distinction between sign-based and degree-based aspects.

In modern astrology, for example, the Saturn return is usually seen to begin when Saturn returns to the exact degree that it was in when a person was born. This first occurs when the native is around the age of twenty-eight. However, in the Hellenistic tradition, this transit would actually begin as soon as Saturn ingressed back into its natal sign, and it would not end until Saturn departs from that sign for the final time in that cycle. To give a specific example, if someone had Saturn at 15° Libra, their Saturn return would begin as soon as Saturn ingresses into 0° Libra, and it would end as soon as it leaves 29° Libra. There may be a particularly important or defining event that occurs when Saturn approaches the exact degree of the return (15° Libra), but the events and circumstances surrounding the transit already begin to develop as soon as it enters the sign, and they are not fully concluded until Saturn leaves the sign. Other transits follow a similar, sign-based approach.

Annual profections work together with transits because the planet that becomes activated as the lord of the year is activated both in its natal position as well as in its transits. This point is explained by Hephaestio, who is probably drawing on Dorotheus when he says:

> Before all, it is necessary to investigate the lord of the year and its mixture and position and phase, and the planets that see it by fixity and by transit, and how it was situated at the nativity, and how it was found at the time of the transit.[4]

This means that all transits involving the planet that is activated as lord of the year will become more important in that year. This includes:

1. Transits *to* the lord of the year in the natal chart
2. Transits *by* the lord of the year to natal planets
3. Transits through the profected sign that year

---

[4] Hephaestio, *Apotelesmatika*, 2, 27: 6, trans. Schmidt, p. 81.

The purpose of using annual profections together with transits is that it helps the astrologer to filter out which transits will coincide with an actual event in a given year, versus transits which will not. A text on transits attributed to Dorotheus, and perhaps partially derived from his work, says explicitly at one point that "one need not examine the ingresses of all of the stars, but rather only those of the time-lords."[5] A text on transits attributed to Anubio similarly states: "for the indications of the effects are steady at the time when the ingressing planets are also the time-lords."[6]

The profections technique restores an important missing piece to astrology. Without profections, we are unable to distinguish in any real way which transits will coincide with something important in the native's life, versus those that will come and go without anything substantial manifesting. Profections thus allow the astrologer to evaluate and rank which transits are more important versus those that will be less important in a given year. Sometimes transits that otherwise wouldn't seem very important or might be fleeting can gain much more weight if the lord of the year is involved.

HOUSE FIRE

A native turned thirty-nine years old in 2014 and thus moved into a fourth place profection year (Capricorn). Later in the year transiting Mars ingressed into Capricorn, the profected sign of the year. A few days later his house caught fire and burned to the ground along with all of his possessions, and he suffered burns on twenty percent of his body. Transiting Mars was at two or three degrees Capricorn at the time, conjunct the degree of the quadrant IC, and square

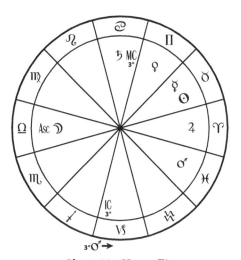

Chart 93 - House Fire

the degree of his Ascendant. Because the profection for the year activated his fourth place, it highlighted the home and living situation; the ingress of Mars into the profected sign for the year by transit brought Mars-related problems with respect to that area. This was worsened due to his day chart, in which Mars is contrary to the sect. The point to take away here is that transits through the profected sign are more important than unactivated transits.

---

[5] CCAG, 2, p. 198: 14–15, trans. Schmidt, *Teachings on Transits*, p. 6.
[6] CCAG, 2, p. 203: 14–15, trans. Schmidt, *Teachings on Transits*, p. 13.

JONATHAN BRANDIS

Jonathan Brandis was an actor who achieved success early in life as a child and teenager, but struggled as his acting career declined during the course of his twenties. He hung himself on November 11, 2003, at the age of twenty-seven. This was a fourth place profection year, activating Aquarius. Saturn was thus activated as lord of the year, which was made more problematic because he was born with a night chart. Transiting Saturn was at 12° Cancer

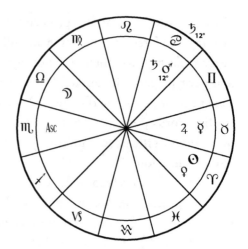

Chart 94 - Jonathan Brandis

when he died, conjunct his natal Mars at 12° Cancer, the ruler of the Ascendant. Thus, the lord of the year came to conjoin the natal ruler of the Ascendant by transit. This demonstrates how transits that the lord of the year makes to other planets in the chart can stand out as more important in a given year.

GEORGE LUCAS

As we have seen earlier, filmmaker George Lucas was involved in a major car accident on June 12, 1962, when he was eighteen years old. This was during a seventh place profection year, activating Scorpio, and thus Mars as the lord of the year. Transiting Mars was at 11° Taurus at the time of the accident, conjunct his natal Venus at 11° Taurus in the first place, which was the ruler of the Hour-Marker. The car accident was very violent, and he almost died, but he was luckily thrown from the

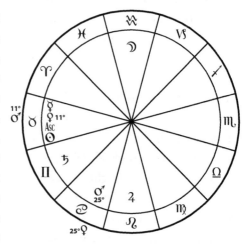

Chart 95 - George Lucas

car before it was crushed against a tree. It is worth noting in this regard that transiting Venus was at 25° Cancer the day of the car accident, conjunct his natal Mars at 25° Cancer, thus acting as a positive or ameliorating transit that offset the transit of Mars to the natal ruler of the Ascendant.

PARTNER'S SUICIDE

A twenty-three year old native's girlfriend committed suicide by shooting herself in the heart while the two were in their apartment together. She died in his arms. The native was in a twelfth place profection year, activating Scorpio, and thus Mars as the lord of the year. Transiting Mars exactly conjoined the native's natal Mercury at 16° Gemini the very night that his girlfriend died, with Mercury being the lord of the seventh place in the natal chart. The Sun had only

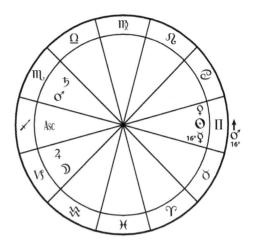

Chart 96 - Partner's Suicide

recently set in this nativity, so it may still be considered a day chart, which would then make Mars the malefic that is contrary to the sect.

Advanced Method of Profections in Valens

In books 4, 5, and 6 of the *Anthology*, Valens introduces a more advanced or complex method of annual profections. He begins with a long personal digression about how he became dissatisfied with some of the other time-lord techniques that he had at his disposal, and he went in search of a better technique for studying smaller increments of time.[7] Eventually, after much struggle, he found a teacher who taught him the technique in Egypt. The technique he found may have been partially derived from the lost work of Critodemus, based on a summary of that work that has survived which seems strikingly similar, and since Valens otherwise mentions him frequently at different points in the *Anthology*.[8]

Activation of Planets in the Profected Sign

One of the things that characterizes Valens' method is his approach to natal planets located in the sign that the profection has come to. For Valens, these planets become activated and are emphasized. This is also true in Dorotheus' approach, although Valens is unique in that he seems to emphasize this point even further.[9] The quality of the planet then characterizes the quality of the outcome for that year. If there are benefics in the sign that the profection

---

[7] Valens, *Anthology*, 4, 11: 1–10.

[8] Critodemus summary edited in CCAG 8, 3, p. 102, trans. Schmidt, *Sages*, p. 49. Compare with Valens, *Anthology*, 4, 11–24.

[9] Dorotheus, *Carmen*, 4, 1: 22–39.

has arrived at, then the outcome will be good or easy. Conversely, if there are malefics, the outcome will be bad or difficult. For example, a tenth place profection year where Saturn is located in the tenth place natally in a night chart would generally be interpreted as a year in which there are difficulties within the context of the native's occupation. If a benefic was there, however, then positive events would occur within the context of the career.

CHARLIE SHEEN

The actor Charlie Sheen turned forty-five in September 2010, thus activating the tenth place (Pisces) until September 2011. He has Saturn in Pisces in a night chart. According to Valens' approach, Saturn would thus become activated and would characterize a large part of the quality of that year. Sheen ended up destroying his own career in early 2011, getting himself fired from a television show that he had starred in for a number of years, and which

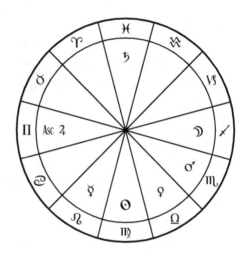

Chart 97 - Charlie Sheen

had made him the highest-paid actor on television. He became self-destructive with drug and alcohol abuse, as well as bizarre public displays and negative media exposure. During this period he was also diagnosed as HIV positive. The important point here is that Saturn in a night chart was activated by being in the sign of the profection, and thus characterized a large part of the year.

LISA MARIE PRESLEY

Returning to the example of Lisa Marie Presley, we have previously seen that she inherited her father's $100 million estate the day she turned twenty-five, which was a second place profection year. She also had her natal Jupiter in the second place in a day chart. Thus, the general delineation for that year is that it would be a good year for financial matters.

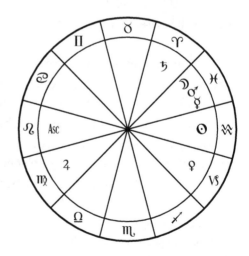

Chart 98 - Lisa Marie Presley

HUSBAND'S DEATH

Another example is a native who was born with Taurus rising, and Mars in Scorpio in the seventh place in a day chart. Her husband died of cancer shortly after the native turned thirty years old. Thirty is a seventh place profection year, thus activating the native's natal Mars in the seventh, and awakening the latent potential of that placement. Contrast this with the following example.

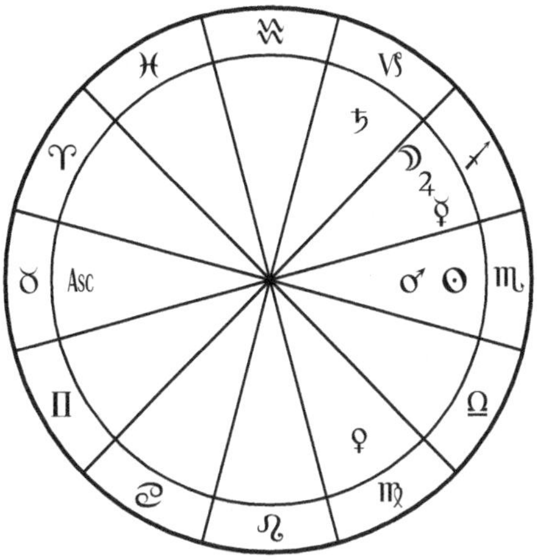

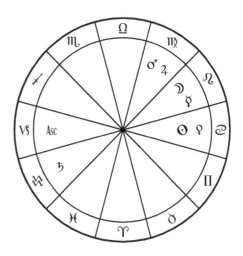

Chart 99 - Husband's Death

BEGAN SUCCESSFUL RELATIONSHIP

A native was born with Capricorn rising and Venus in Cancer in the seventh place in a night chart. When she turned eighteen she moved into a seventh place profection year, thus activating Venus, the benefic of the sect. She met her future husband and began a relationship with him that year, and they were subsequently married for more than sixty years, spending the rest of their lives together.

Chart 100 - Started Relationship

Valens' approach is radically different than the other astrologers because the planet located *in* the sign takes over *instead* of the ruler.[10] Although Dorotheus mentions that planets placed in the sign of profection are activated, he does not seem to suggest that they take over the role of the ruler. This seems to create a tension in the tradition between two different schools or approaches.

From an empirical standpoint, it may be mentioned that over the past ten

---

[10] Valens outlines this approach when he first introduces profections and gives his first chart example demonstrating the technique in *Anthology*, 4, 11: 18–26. A few sentences later he says that if the sign is empty then the ruler takes over (4, 11: 28). Later he says that if a transiting planet is moving through the empty sign then that planet will take over (4, 11: 31).

years I have followed Valens' approach, but eventually came to the conclusion that *both* the planet(s) in the sign *and* the ruler become activated (rather than it being an either/or situation). As with any instance in which the tradition is at variance, it is important for each astrologer not only to be aware of the distinctions and tensions in the tradition, but also to form their own conclusions about them in light of their own practical experience.

Profecting from Other Starting Points

Using Valens' approach, we can profect from any planet, place, or point in the chart, not just the Ascendant.[11] The starting point provides the context, while the end point indicates the outcome. In this approach, when we want to study a specific topic, we begin the profection from the place or planet that matches that topic, rather than from the rising sign. For example, if we want to study marriage, we might profect from the seventh place, and then count one sign per year from that sign until we reach the sign that matches the age of the native. The planet(s) activated in the sign that the profection highlights will tell us how the year will be for the native relative to that topic. Thus, profections provide a topical time-lord system that can be used to determine how specific areas of the native's life will go in a given year.

In this method, the focus is on profecting from all of the places and planets, although according to Valens, the three most important starting points are (1) the sect light, (2) the Hour-Marker, and (3) the luminary that is contrary to the sect.[12] For Valens, these three will set the tone for the entire year. In practice, I often find that when something is not shown in the profections from the Ascendant, it will be clearly indicated in the profections from the sect light.

Valens' advanced method of profections can become incredibly complicated, and I've only given it the barest of treatments here because I think that for the most part, simple profections from the Ascendant can provide more than enough information to give some overall sense of the tone of the year. For those who would like to go deeper into the advanced method, I would recommend exploring books 4, 5, and 6 of Valens' *Anthology*.

---

[11] Valens makes this point repeatedly throughout *Anthology*, 4, 11–12.

[12] Valens, *Anthology*, 5, 7: 1. Cf. *Anthology*, 4, 11: 28; 4, 16: 15.

CHAPTER 18
ZODIACAL RELEASING

One of the most impressive and powerful time-lord techniques that has been recovered from the Hellenistic tradition so far is known today as zodiacal releasing. This technique only survives in the work of Vettius Valens, and when he first introduces it he calls it a "powerful" or "potent" technique. Indeed, it is easily the most remarkable one I've found.

The best analogy for describing the technique is that it divides the native's entire life up into different chapters and paragraphs, as if the life was a book. More specifically, the technique identifies some of the most important chapters in a person's life with respect to different topics, such as career or health, and it can also provide information about the quality of those chapters.

Zodiacal releasing represents an excellent example of one of the more advanced time-lord techniques that were used by the Hellenistic astrologers, not only because it is more complicated than annual profections in the way that it is calculated, but also because it was designed in order to make predictions over longer spans of time in the native's life. Rather than being restricted to specific years, zodiacal releasing periods often span decades.

The level of precision that one can achieve in making predictions with zodiacal releasing can be a bit startling at first, and it raises a number of philosophical and ethical issues, which astrologers will have to wrestle with as they begin to use the technique in contemporary practice.

My goal in this chapter is to provide a broad overview of the technique, and to use some example charts in order to demonstrate how different facets of it work when applied to contemporary nativities.

Source of the Technique

Valens is our only surviving source that outlines zodiacal releasing.[1] His primary treatment of it is in book four of the *Anthology*, although he originally introduces it earlier, in book two, within the context of a discussion about travel.[2] There he cites an earlier text attributed to Abraham for some instructions on how to use the technique to predict when a native will travel. While the technique may have originally been developed in the context of studying travel, in the full treatment of the technique given in book four, Valens demonstrates that it can also be used to study a number of other overarching themes in a person's life.

Zodiacal releasing uses the Lot of Spirit and the Lot of Fortune as starting points in calculating timing periods, and within the context of his discussion about this technique, Valens associates the Sun with the Lot of Spirit and the Moon with the Lot of Fortune.[3] We have a secondary account of the astrological work attributed to Abraham in Firmicus, who also links him to the doctrine of lots. Abraham is listed as one of the later expositors in Firmicus' hierarchy of the founders of Hellenistic astrology, but his name also comes up again in Firmicus' work when he introduces the Lot of Fortune and Spirit. In his discussion of the Lot of Fortune, Firmicus tells us that "Abraham called it the Place of the Moon," and similarly with respect to the Lot of Spirit, Firmicus tells us that "Abraham called it the Place of the Sun."[4] This seems to imply that Valens and Firmicus were drawing on the same source text, a work on the lots attributed to Abraham, although Firmicus doesn't address zodiacal releasing in his surviving work. Nonetheless, from this we can gather that the zodiacal releasing technique was developed at some point prior to Valens' time in the second century, and that it was used by other astrologers besides Valens. Indeed, at one point in his discussion of zodiacal releasing, Valens spends a bit of time refuting one variant approach to the technique that was apparently advocated by some unnamed astrologers that he disagreed with.[5]

Calculating Zodiacal Releasing Periods

Valens opens his treatment of zodiacal releasing by saying that in order to calculate zodiacal releasing periods, you start with the sign that contains the Lot of Spirit or the Lot of Fortune, depending on what you want to study. The lot

---

[1] The only other astrologer who mentions it is Rhetorius, who briefly cites book four of Valens for the technique in *Compendium*, 97, trans. Holden, p. 147.

[2] Valens, *Anthology*, 4, 4–10; Valens, *Anthology*, 2, 30: 5–7.

[3] Valens, *Anthology*, 4, 4: 1–2.

[4] Firmicus, *Mathesis*, 4, 17: 5; 4, 18: 1.

[5] Valens, *Anthology*, 4, 4: 23–31.

that you start with provides the context for the resulting time periods that are produced by the technique. The basic distinction is that you start from the sign that contains the Lot of Spirit in order to study matters that pertain to the mind, while you start from Fortune for matters that pertain to the body:

> When, then, we seek times for bodily matters, such as crises or weaknesses or bloodshed, falls, injuries, sufferings, and whatever appertains to the body, for strength, enjoyment, pleasure, beauty, and loveliness, then it is necessary to project zodiacally from the Lot of Fortune [...] If we are inquiring about action or reputation, then we will make the beginning of the releasing zodiacally from the Lot of Spirit.[6]

In practice, I have found releasing from the Lot of Spirit to be effective for determining periods in a person's life related to career and overall life direction, while releasing from the Lot of Fortune is primarily useful for matters pertaining to the native's health and physical vitality.

Once you have determined which lot you want to start from, each sign of the zodiac is then attributed a certain number of years based on the planetary period of its domicile lord.[7] The periods that are associated with each of the signs within the context of zodiacal releasing are as follows:

CANCER:	25
LEO:	19
GEMINI AND VIRGO:	20
TAURUS AND LIBRA:	8
ARIES AND SCORPIO:	15
PISCES AND SAGITTARIUS:	12
CAPRICORN:	27
AQUARIUS:	30

Note that the periods associated with each of the signs are the normal planetary periods that we are already familiar with, although within the context of this technique, the period associated with Capricorn is 27 years rather than the normal 30 for Saturn.[8]

---

[6] Valens, *Anthology*, 4, 4: 3–4.

[7] Valens, *Anthology*, 2, 30: 5–7.

[8] Valens gives a brief explanation for this that has to do with the "final" or "maximum" years of the planets, which is another system for determining planetary periods, in *Anthology*, 4, 6: 1–4. He says that the final years of the Sun are 120, and half of this equals 60, and that the Sun imparts half of this to the sign opposite to its own domicile, which is 30 years to Aquarius. The

Whatever sign the lot you want to study is located in, the first chapter or period of a person's life lasts for the number of years associated with that sign. For example, if you wanted to study matters related to the native's career and they had the Lot of Spirit in Scorpio, then the first chapter of their life with respect to that topic would last for fifteen years, which is the period of Scorpio/Mars. When the period of that sign is completed, the next sign in zodiacal order and its ruler become activated for the number of years associated with the

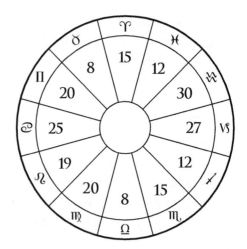

Figure 18.1 - Zodiacal Releasing Periods

number of years associated with that sign. So after Scorpio comes Sagittarius, which would become activated for twelve years. Once the period of that sign is finished, the next sign in zodiacal order becomes activated. The periods keep moving forward at this variable rate for as long as the native is alive.

Like most time-lord systems, Valens didn't have a name for the technique; he refers to it as the method that involves "releasing" from the zodiacal signs of Fortune and Spirit.[9] He uses the technical term *aphesis*, which means "release," "letting go," "dismissal," or "discharge." Schmidt originally argued for "releasing" as the correct rendering of *aphesis* in his translator's preface to book four of Valens.[10] He suggested that the word may have deeper meanings within an astrological context related to being released from a debt. However, it may simply describe the process of "releasing" a significator from its fixed position in the birth chart and allowing it to move around the chart according to a certain rate. Valens' use of the word *apoluō* as a synonym for *aphesis* seems to confirm that "releasing" is the correct way to translate the word, since it means "to loose from," "to set free from," or "to release."[11] The term *aphesis* is also applied to primary directions, usually in the context of the length of life technique, which shows that zodiacal releasing is just one "releasing" technique out of many.[12] Since the rate in this instance is determined by the signs in zodiacal order, we call it zodiacal releasing.

Moon has a 108 final years, half of which is 54, and that it distributes half of these to the sign opposite to its domicile, which results in 27 years to Capricorn.

[9] Valens, *Anthology*, 4, 4: 3–4. Elsewhere he seems to allude to it as one of the methods of dividing the times in accordance with the minor periods of the planets (*Anthology*, 4, 11: 6).

[10] Valens, *Anthology*, 4, trans. Schmidt, pp. xiii–xvi.

[11] Valens, *Anthology*, 4, 8: 3.

[12] Valens, *Anthology*, 3, 3.

For example, let's say that we wanted to study the career periods for a native that was born in 1946. First we would want to identify the sign that contains the Lot of Spirit, which in this case would be Libra. Since the Lot of Spirit is in Libra in this chart, the first general period or chapter of the native's life would last for eight years, which is the period associated with Libra and its ruler, Venus. Once the Venus period is complete (1954) they would move on to the next sign in zodiacal order,

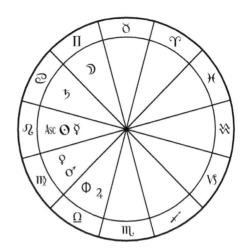

Chart 101 - Spirit in Libra Example

Scorpio, for 15 years (1954 to 1969). Once that 15-year period is finished, the releasing would then move to Sagittarius for 12 years (1969 to 1981). Next would come a 27-year Capricorn period (1981 until 2007) followed by 30 years in Aquarius (2007 until 2037), and so on. All of the periods calculated in order would look something like this:

LIBRA:	1946–1954
SCORPIO:	1954–1969
SAGITTARIUS:	1969–1981
CAPRICORN:	1981–2007
AQUARIUS:	2007–2037

An important note about calculating zodiacal releasing periods is that within the context of this technique, Valens used an idealized year of 360 days, and 30 day months.[13] In this way each month is exactly one twelfth of a year. This causes each zodiacal releasing year to be slightly shorter than a normal calendar year of 365 days, which can sometimes add up over time, although for the purpose of this discussion I will still refer to these as "years" and "months."

Calculating Subperiods

Within each of the general periods that last for one or two or even three decades, there are also subperiods in which additional signs of the zodiac can be activated for a much shorter duration.[14] Zodiacal releasing periods are generally divided

---

[13] Valens, *Anthology*, 4, 9.

[14] The subperiods are outlined the most clearly in Valens, *Anthology*, 4, 10: 1–6.

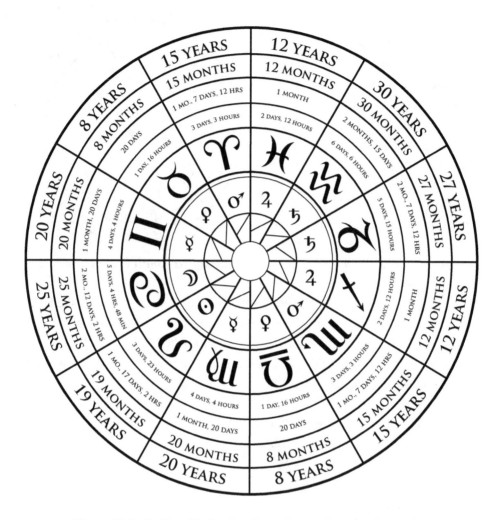

Figure 18.2 - Zodiacal Releasing General Periods and Subperiods

into four levels: "years," "months," "weeks," and "days." The end result is four different levels moving around the zodiac at different speeds, like a clock with four hands. Every sub-level is exactly one twelfth of the duration of the level above. This results in the following breakdown:

Level 1:   360-day "years" (general period).
Level 2:   30-day "months" (first subperiod).
Level 3:   2.5 day "weeks" (second subperiod).
Level 4:   5-hour "days" (third subperiod).

The length of time associated with each sign of the zodiac on all four levels is given in a diagram above. For the purpose of this book, I'm going to focus on the yearly and monthly levels, which are the general period and first subperiod; I will not go into the calculations of the other subperiods. There are a number of different software applications available for calculating zodiacal releasing periods, and I would recommend exploring these in order to gain a better understanding of the breakdown of the different subperiods.

In the last chapter we used annual profections in order to focus on individual years. In this chapter I would like to demonstrate the usefulness of zodiacal releasing in studying entire decades of a person's life.

Interpreting Zodiacal Releasing Periods

Valens gives a few different interpretive principles for looking at zodiacal releasing in his chapters on the subject, but generally speaking there are three main things to focus on in order to determine the quality of a specific period:

1. The nature and position of the sign of the zodiac that has become activated in the chart, including the quality of any natal planets placed in that sign.
2. The nature of any planets that are configured to the zodiacal sign that has become activated.
3. The condition of the ruler of the activated sign.

In his initial introductory remarks about zodiacal releasing, Valens seems to emphasize the ruler of the sign more than the sign itself, but then in the actual chart examples he seems to highlight planets placed in the activated sign or configured to it as being more important in terms of interpreting the quality of the period.[15] In using the technique over the past decade, I have found that planets aspecting the sign that has become activated in the natal chart tend to be much more useful in describing the quality of different periods, and in much of what follows I will tend to emphasize that approach, although the reader should be aware that there are additional nuances and levels of detail that can be accessed through studying the rulers of the activated signs as well.

Peak Periods

One of the interpretive principles that Valens mentions when discussing zodiacal releasing from the Lot of Spirit is the idea that when the signs that are angular from the Lot of Fortune are activated, these will be periods of greater activity and eminence in the native's life:

---

[15] The two chart examples are given in chapters 8 and 10 of book 4 of the *Anthology*.

If, then, the division should come from Spirit to the Midheaven of the Lot of Fortune, or even to the Lot itself ... the native will come into leadership and great reputation, and will be notable and fit for rule and highly visible for those times.[16]

Valens goes on to say that within the context of this technique the places that are angular to the Lot of Fortune are more "energetic" or "efficacious" (*energesteroi*) compared to the natal angles.[17] Thus, the first step when studying the career periods derived from Spirit is to identify the four signs that are angular from the sign that contains the Lot of Fortune. This would be the first, fourth, seventh, and tenth signs relative to Fortune in the natal chart. These are what we will call the Fortune angles, or the places that are angular from the Lot of Fortune.

The approach that Valens outlines here involves starting the timing technique from the sign of the Lot of Spirit, and then counting through the signs until it reaches one of the angles from Fortune. I find that when releasing from Spirit, the activation of the angles from Fortune tend to coincide with periods of heightened importance and activity within the life of the native, especially within the context of the native's career and overall life direction. As a result of this, I refer to periods when the Fortune angles are activated when releasing from Spirit as "peak periods."

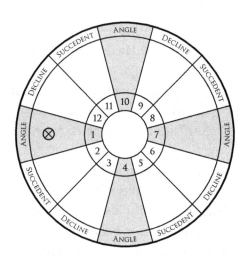

Figure 18.3 - Fortune Angles

When I arrived at Project Hindsight in the summer of 2005 they were just starting to figure out how zodiacal releasing worked and how powerful it was. Two of the chart examples we used in study sessions at that time were of the then-current United States President George W. Bush and former U.S. Vice President Al Gore. These two charts still represent a couple of the most striking examples of how the peak periods work in action.

Let's start with Bush's chart. He has the Lot of Spirit in Taurus, and the Lot

---

[16] Valens, *Anthology*, 4, 7: 14-15, trans. Schmidt.

[17] Valens, *Anthology*, 4, 7: 15. He specifically says that the places "square" to the lot are more energetic, although the contrast with the natal angles makes it clear that he is referring to all four of the Fortune angles.

George W. Bush - Spirit Periods

♉ L1/L2 - 7/6/1946
   Ⅱ L2 - 3/3/1947
   ♋ L2 - 10/23/1948
   ♌ L2 - 11/12/1950
   ♍ L2 - 6/4/1952
   ♎ L2 - 1/25/1954
Ⅱ L1/L2 - 5/25/1954
   ♋ L2 - 1/15/1956
   ♌ L2 - 2/3/1958
   ♍ L2 - 8/27/1959
   ♎ L2 - 4/18/1961
   ♏ L2 - 12/14/1961
   ♐ L2 - 3/9/1963
   ♑ L2 - 3/3/1964
   ♒ L2 - 5/22/1966
   ♓ L2 - 11/7/1968
   ♈ L2 - 11/2/1969
   ♉ L2 - 1/26/1971
   ♐ L2 - 9/23/1971 - LB
   ♑ L2 - 9/17/1972
♋ L1/L2 - 2/9/1974
   ♌ L2 - 2/29/1976
   ♍ L2 - 9/21/1977
   ♎ L2 - 5/14/1979
   ♏ L2 - 1/9/1980
   ♐ L2 - 4/3/1981
   ♑ L2 - 3/29/1982
   ♒ L2 - 6/16/1984
   ♓ L2 - 12/3/1986
   ♈ L2 - 11/28/1987
   ♉ L2 - 2/20/1989
   Ⅱ L2 - 10/18/1989
   ♑ L2 - 6/10/1991 - LB
   ♒ L2 - 8/28/1993
   ♓ L2 - 2/14/1996
   ♈ L2 - 2/8/1997
   ♉ L2 - 5/4/1998
♌ L1/L2 - 10/1/1998
   ♍ L2 - 4/23/2000
   ♎ L2 - 12/14/2001
   ♏ L2 - 8/11/2002
   ♐ L2 - 11/4/2003
   ♑ L2 - 10/29/2004
   ♒ L2 - 1/17/2007
   ♓ L2 - 7/5/2009
   ♈ L2 - 6/30/2010
   ♉ L2 - 9/23/2011
   Ⅱ L2 - 5/20/2012
   ♋ L2 - 1/10/2014
   ♒ L2 - 1/30/2016 - LB
♍ L1/L2 - 6/23/2017

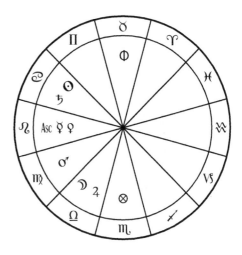

Chart 102 - George W. Bush

of Fortune in Scorpio. Since Fortune is in Scorpio, we know that his peak periods will coincide with the four fixed signs: Scorpio (sign of Fortune), Leo (tenth from Fortune), Taurus (seventh from Fortune), and Aquarius (fourth from Fortune). If we start the releasing from the Lot of Spirit in order to study his career periods, Bush started off in an eight year Taurus period (1946–1954). This is a peak period, since it is angular from Fortune, but he is too young to accomplish anything significant. After that he moves into a twenty-year Gemini period (1954–1974). This period is not angular from Fortune, thus it is not a peak period. Next he moved into a twenty-five year Cancer period (1974–1998). Then in 1998 he started a new nineteen-year Leo period, which is the tenth sign relative to the Lot of Fortune, and thus a peak period. A few months after this period began, he launched his presidential campaign in June of 1999, and was inaugurated as the forty-third President of the United States in January of 2001. He served out two four-year

Al Gore - Spirit Periods

♏ L1/L2 - 3/31/1948
    ♐ L2 - 6/24/1949
    ♑ L2 - 6/19/1950
    ♒ L2 - 9/6/1952
    ♓ L2 - 2/23/1955
    ♈ L2 - 2/18/1956
    ♉ L2 - 5/13/1957
    ♊ L2 - 1/8/1958
    ♋ L2 - 8/31/1959
    ♌ L2 - 9/19/1961
♐ L1/L2 - 1/12/1963
    ♑ L2 - 1/7/1964
    ♒ L2 - 3/27/1966
    ♓ L2 - 9/12/1968
    ♈ L2 - 9/7/1969
    ♉ L2 - 12/1/1970
    ♊ L2 - 7/29/1971
    ♋ L2 - 3/20/1973
♑ L1/L2 - 11/10/1974
    ♒ L2 - 1/28/1977
    ♓ L2 - 7/17/1979
    ♈ L2 - 7/11/1980
    ♉ L2 - 10/4/1981
    ♊ L2 - 6/1/1982
    ♋ L2 - 1/22/1984
    ♌ L2 - 2/10/1986
    ♍ L2 - 9/3/1987
    ♎ L2 - 4/25/1989
    ♏ L2 - 12/21/1989
    ♐ L2 - 3/16/1991
    ♋ L2 - 3/10/1992 - LB
    ♌ L2 - 3/30/1994
    ♍ L2 - 10/21/1995
    ♎ L2 - 6/12/1997
    ♏ L2 - 2/7/1998
    ♐ L2 - 5/3/1999
    ♑ L2 - 4/27/2000
♒ L1/L2 - 6/21/2001
    ♓ L2 - 12/8/2003
    ♈ L2 - 12/2/2004
    ♉ L2 - 2/25/2006
    ♊ L2 - 10/23/2006
    ♋ L2 - 6/14/2008
    ♌ L2 - 7/4/2010
    ♍ L2 - 1/25/2012
    ♎ L2 - 9/16/2013
    ♏ L2 - 5/14/2014
    ♐ L2 - 8/7/2015
    ♑ L2 - 8/1/2016
    ♌ L2 - 10/20/2018 - LB
    ♍ L2 - 5/12/2020
    ♎ L2 - 1/2/2022

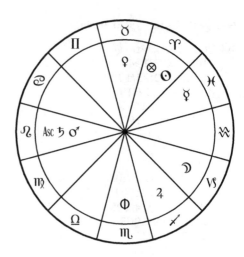

Chart 103 - Al Gore

terms before stepping down in 2009 due to term limits. Thus, Valens' statement about the native coming into power and eminence when the releasing periods from the Lot of Spirit come to the tenth sign relative to the Lot of Fortune would be quite accurate in this instance.

Bush's opponent during the 2000 presidential election in the United States was Al Gore. Gore was born with the Lot of Spirit in Scorpio and the Lot of Fortune in Aries. The Fortune angles in his chart will be the four movable signs: Aries, Capricorn, Libra, and Cancer. The releasing begins from Spirit in Scorpio, starting with a fifteen-year period which lasts from his birth in 1948 until 1963. Once that period was completed, the releasing periods moved to Sagittarius for about twelve years (1963–1974). In 1974 he moved into a twenty-seven-year-long Capricorn period, which is important because it is the tenth sign relative to Fortune, and thus a peak period. Gore began his political career not long after this general period began, when he was elected to the

United States Congress in late 1976. In 1992 Bill Clinton selected him as his running mate during that year's U.S. presidential election, and a few months later he became the Vice President of the United States, which is likely the highest political appointment that he will attain in his lifetime. Gore was still in his twenty-seven-year Capricorn peak period during the presidential race in the year 2000 when he ran against Bush, but the peak period came to an end in June of 2001, which was just a few months after he lost the election and Bush was inaugurated as President.

What is striking about these two examples is that you can see the peak periods of both men coinciding with the times in their lives in which they became eminent as politicians, just as Valens said. It is also remarkable to see one of their peak periods beginning just as his political ambitions were coming to fruition, while the other had his peak period come to an end just as his time of greatest political eminence came to a close.

The implications of what this technique could do were startling to me when I first encountered it in 2005. Over the past ten years I've seen it consistently produce other extraordinary results, and I hope to provide some glimpse of that here, although my treatment must necessarily be somewhat cursory. In what follows I will provide an outline of some of the other main points of the technique, which were developed partially from studying the way in which Valens outlines it in his text, but also partially based on my own experience and observations in working with it over the past decade.

Ranking the Fortune Angles
Just as some angles from the Ascendant were seen as more powerful than others in the Hellenistic tradition, so too are some angles from the Lot of Fortune more powerful than others. The first and tenth signs relative to the Lot of Fortune are the two most powerful or energetic signs, and these are the two that are initially singled out by Valens in his initial statement about the Fortune angles.[18] When these are activated in the subperiods, I usually refer to them as "major peak periods." The next most powerful is the seventh sign from Fortune, which I refer to as a "moderate peak period." The last is the fourth sign from Fortune, which I refer to as a "minor peak period." This follows the usual Hellenistic ranking of the places, which typically has the first and tenth places as the most powerful, followed by the seventh, and then finally the fourth.

The distinction between major, moderate, and minor peak periods mainly becomes relevant when looking at the shorter durations of time in the subperiods. Not every native will reach the tenth sign from Fortune or the

---

[18] Valens, *Anthology*, 4, 7: 14.

sign of Fortune itself on the yearly or general level in the Spirit periods during their lifetime, although that is not necessary in order to have a career peak. Hitting any angle from the Lot of Fortune in the general periods will usually coincide with a period of heightened activity and importance in the native's career and overall life direction, even if it is not the tenth or first. Whatever angle that is, it will tend to be the peak of that part of the person's life, relative to whatever that person's career or life's work is.

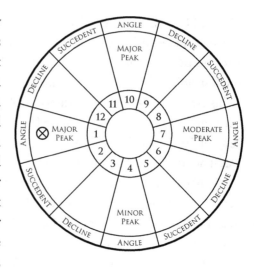

Figure 18.4 - Ranking Fortune Angles

As we will see in the following examples, the technique seems to work across a large range of different career fields. I should also note at this point that there are many other considerations besides Fortune angles that are important interpretive factors that can sometimes become even more crucial than the Fortune angles, as we will discuss later. Before we get to that, however, let's take a look at a few more instances of Fortune angles coinciding with career peaks.

GEORGE LUCAS

George Lucas was born with Spirit in Virgo and Fortune in Aquarius.[19] He started out in a twenty-year Virgo period (1944–1964), followed by a Libra period (1964–1971). In 1971 he entered a fifteen-year Scorpio period, which is the tenth sign from Fortune, and thus his major peak period.

The subperiods of this general peak period began with a fifteen-month Scorpio period (December 1971–March 1973), followed by twelve months in Sagittarius (March 1973–March 1974). This was followed by twenty-seven months in Capricorn (March 1974–May 1976). In May of 1976 he went into a thirty-month Aquarius period, which is the sign of the Lot of Fortune itself. In May 1977 the movie *Star Wars* was released, which developed into a hugely successful film series. At this time, he was in peak periods on both

---

[19] In his chart I am using the diurnal calculations for the lots, since his Sun is only a few degrees below the degree of the Ascendant, and I have found that charts begin to behave like diurnal charts when the Sun is this close to rising in the morning. I've also adjusted his time by moving it forward by a minute and a half to place Spirit in Virgo rather than late Leo, which seems acceptable since the recorded birth time of 5:40 AM may have been slightly rounded.

George Lucas - Spirit Periods

♍ L1/L2 - 5/14/1944
   ♎ L2 - 1/4/1946
   ♏ L2 - 9/1/1946
   ♐ L2 - 11/25/1947
   ♑ L2 - 11/19/1948
   ♒ L2 - 2/7/1951
   ♓ L2 - 7/26/1953
   ♈ L2 - 7/21/1954
   ♉ L2 - 10/14/1955
   ♊ L2 - 6/10/1956
   ♋ L2 - 1/31/1958
   ♌ L2 - 2/20/1960
  ♓ L2 - 9/12/1961 - LB
   ♈ L2 - 9/7/1962
   ♉ L2 - 12/1/1963
♎ L1/L2 - 1/30/1964
   ♏ L2 - 9/26/1964
   ♐ L2 - 12/20/1965
   ♑ L2 - 12/15/1966
   ♒ L2 - 3/4/1969
   ♓ L2 - 8/21/1971
♏ L1/L2 - 12/19/1971
   ♐ L2 - 3/13/1973
   ♑ L2 - 3/8/1974
   ♒ L2 - 5/26/1976
   ♓ L2 - 11/12/1978
   ♈ L2 - 11/7/1979
   ♉ L2 - 1/30/1981
   ♊ L2 - 9/27/1981
   ♋ L2 - 5/20/1983
   ♌ L2 - 6/8/1985
♐ L1/L2 - 10/1/1986
   ♑ L2 - 9/26/1987
   ♒ L2 - 12/14/1989
   ♓ L2 - 6/1/1992
   ♈ L2 - 5/27/1993
   ♉ L2 - 8/20/1994
   ♊ L2 - 4/17/1995
   ♋ L2 - 12/7/1996
♑ L1/L2 - 7/30/1998
   ♒ L2 - 10/17/2000
   ♓ L2 - 4/5/2003
   ♈ L2 - 3/30/2004
   ♉ L2 - 6/23/2005
   ♊ L2 - 2/18/2006
   ♋ L2 - 10/11/2007

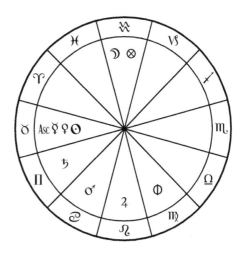

Chart 104 - George Lucas

the general period (level 1) as well as the subperiod (level 2).

The Aquarius subperiod ended in November 1978 and he started a twelve-month Pisces period, followed by a fifteen-month Aries period from November 1979. In January 1981 he entered an eight-month Taurus period, which is the fourth sign from Fortune, and thus another peak period (albeit a less significant one). His movie *Raiders of the Lost Ark* was released in June 1981, and became the second most well-known movie franchise that he was involved in creating. Eventually, in 1986, this fifteen-year peak period (Scorpio) came to an end. What this shows is that two of the biggest highlights of George Lucas' film career occurred precisely when he reached peak periods in zodiacal releasing, both at the general level and in the subperiods.

STEVE WOZNIAK

Wozniak was born with Spirit in Libra and Fortune in Virgo. With Fortune in Virgo, the mutable signs become the peak periods. He started out in an eight-year Libra period (1950–1958), followed by fifteen years in Scorpio (1958–

Steve Wozniak - Spirit Periods

Ω L1/L2 - 8/11/1950
 ♏ L2 - 4/8/1951
 ♐ L2 - 7/1/1952
 ♑ L2 - 6/26/1953
 ♒ L2 - 9/14/1955
 ♓ L2 - 3/2/1958
♏ L1/L2 - 6/30/1958
 ♐ L2 - 9/23/1959
 ♑ L2 - 9/17/1960
 ♒ L2 - 12/6/1962
 ♓ L2 - 5/24/1965
 ♈ L2 - 5/19/1966
 ♉ L2 - 8/12/1967
 ♊ L2 - 4/8/1968
 ♋ L2 - 11/29/1969
 ♌ L2 - 12/19/1971
♐ L1/L2 - 4/12/1973
 ♑ L2 - 4/7/1974
 ♒ L2 - 6/25/1976
 ♓ L2 - 12/12/1978
 ♈ L2 - 12/7/1979
 ♉ L2 - 3/1/1981
 ♊ L2 - 10/27/1981
 ♋ L2 - 6/19/1983
♑ L1/L2 - 2/8/1985
 ♒ L2 - 4/29/1987
 ♓ L2 - 10/15/1989
 ♈ L2 - 10/10/1990
 ♉ L2 - 1/3/1992
 ♊ L2 - 8/30/1992
 ♋ L2 - 4/22/1994
 ♌ L2 - 5/11/1996
 ♍ L2 - 12/2/1997
 Ω L2 - 7/25/1999
 ♏ L2 - 3/21/2000
 ♐ L2 - 6/14/2001
 ♋ L2 - 6/9/2002 - LB
 ♌ L2 - 6/28/2004
 ♍ L2 - 1/19/2006
 Ω L2 - 9/11/2007
 ♏ L2 - 5/8/2008
 ♐ L2 - 8/1/2009
 ♑ L2 - 7/27/2010
♒ L1/L2 - 9/20/2011
 ♓ L2 - 3/8/2014
 ♈ L2 - 3/3/2015

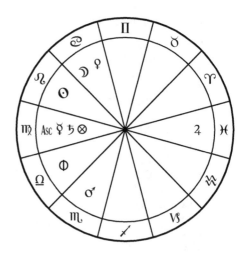

Chart 105 - Steve Wozniak

1973). In 1973 he moved into a twelve-year Sagittarius period, which is the fourth sign from Fortune, and thus a peak period. In the same year his friend Steve Jobs had Wozniak make a circuit board for another company, and this led the two to start collaborating on electronics projects. By 1975, Wozniak had developed the prototype for the first Apple computer, and in 1976, Wozniak and Jobs founded Apple Computer, Inc. Wozniak worked at Apple for about a decade before eventually leaving in early 1985, making his departure official in 1987. His twelve-year Sagittarius peak period that began in 1973 ended in 1985, and thus his peak period clearly coincided with his time at Apple, which became a pioneer in the field of personal computers.

CHRIS BRENNAN

I was born with Fortune in Gemini and Spirit in Scorpio. I started out in a fifteen-year Scorpio period in 1984, and in 1999 I began a twelve-year Sagittarius period, which was a peak period, since Sagittarius is seventh from Fortune. Shortly after that Sagittarius period began, I started studying astrology, which became my main focus in life. In the subperiods of

Chris Brennan - Spirit Periods

♏ L1/L2 - 11/1/1984
    ♐ L2 - 1/25/1986
    ♑ L2 - 1/20/1987
    ♒ L2 - 4/9/1989
    ♓ L2 - 9/26/1991
    ♈ L2 - 9/20/1992
    ♉ L2 - 12/14/1993
    ♊ L2 - 8/11/1994
    ♋ L2 - 4/2/1996
    ♌ L2 - 4/22/1998
♐ L1/L2 - 8/15/1999
    ♑ L2 - 8/9/2000
    ♒ L2 - 10/28/2002
    ♓ L2 - 4/15/2005
    ♈ L2 - 4/10/2006
    ♉ L2 - 7/4/2007
    ♊ L2 - 2/29/2008
    ♋ L2 - 10/21/2009
♑ L1/L2 - 6/13/2011
    ♒ L2 - 8/31/2013
    ♓ L2 - 2/17/2016
    ♈ L2 - 2/11/2017
    ♉ L2 - 5/7/2018
    ♊ L2 - 1/2/2019
    ♋ L2 - 8/24/2020
    ♌ L2 - 9/13/2022
    ♍ L2 - 4/5/2024
    ♎ L2 - 11/26/2025
    ♏ L2 - 7/24/2026
    ♐ L2 - 10/17/2027
  ♋ L2 - 10/11/2028 - LB
    ♌ L2 - 10/31/2030
    ♍ L2 - 5/23/2032
    ♎ L2 - 1/13/2034
    ♏ L2 - 9/10/2034
    ♐ L2 - 12/4/2035
    ♑ L2 - 11/28/2036
♒ L1/L2 - 1/22/2038

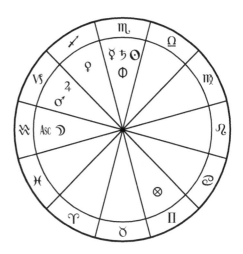

Chart 106 - Chris Brennan

that twelve-year Sagittarius period, I entered a twelve-month Sagittarius period from August 1999 to August 2000, followed by twenty-seven months in Capricorn until October 2002, and thirty months in Aquarius until April 2005. In April 2005 I entered a twelve-month Pisces period, which is the tenth sign from Fortune, and thus a major peak period. In May 2005 I was invited to live at Project Hindsight in order to help with a library they were building. That summer I was able to start reading all of the translations of Hellenistic texts that they had made until that point, and I began studying Valens and zodiacal releasing. Thus, I was in one of my highest peak periods when I discovered this very technique. One could say that an astrologer knows that they have found a powerful technique when the technique itself tells them that they have found it.[20] Interestingly, I am in the same major peak period in Pisces again this year as I finish writing this book.

---

[20] There is a passage in Valens where he tells a story about finding a time-lord technique, and it was originally interpreted by Schmidt to mean that Valens was saying that he could only discover the technique when the technique itself said he would discover it, and that is how he knew that he had found a valid technique. See Valens, *Anthology*, 4, 11: 7–10, trans. Schmidt, p. 23, fn. 6. However, others have interpreted the passage as Valens instead saying that he was led to the technique by providence and his guardian spirit or *daimōn*. See Komorowska, *Vettius Valens of Antioch*, p. 347; Greenbaum, *The Daimon*, p. 36.

Interpreting the Quality of a Period

Peak periods are more active and important, but not necessarily positive or negative. The main considerations which determine what the quality of the period will be like are (1) the nature of any natal planets placed in the sign that has become activated, (2) the nature of any natal planets configured to the sign, especially by square or opposition, and (3) the condition of the ruler of the sign. As stated earlier, we will mainly focus on the first two, as I've found them to be more important, and Valens seems to emphasize them more in his two chart examples.

In his examples, Valens only mentions planets that are configured to the activated sign when they are either located in the sign or are configured to it by a square or opposition. It is not clear if this is deliberate or accidental. It may be connected with a doctrine attributed to Petosiris in which hard aspects such as squares were viewed as more powerful than soft aspects such as trines, either for good or ill (depending on the planets involved).[21] Valens himself mentions that squares and oppositions are more powerful at one point within the context of a discussion about annual profections.[22]

By experience, I've found that the angles from the benefics and malefics tend to be the most useful for determining the periods that will be experienced as the most positive or negative on the part of the native. Here sect is especially useful for determining which signs will be experienced as the most positive or negative, i.e. by identifying the benefic that is of the sect and the malefic that is contrary to the sect. The four signs that are angular relative to the most positive benefic indicate periods that are experienced as positive or easy, and when favorable or preferable events will tend to occur. Conversely, the angles from the most negative malefic in the chart indicate periods that are generally experienced as difficult or challenging, and in these periods unfavorable or unpreferable events will tend to occur. An important point that bears emphasizing here is that planets can aspect empty signs, and when a sign becomes activated, so do any natal configurations that are made to that sign, for better or worse.[23]

---

[21] CCAG, 6, p. 62: 9–17.

[22] Valens, *Anthology*, 4, 16: 23.

[23] That planets can aspect empty signs is demonstrated by Valens in his first zodiacal releasing chart example, where at one point he mentions that Mercury and Mars are witnessing or testifying to Aquarius, which describes the quality of the period (*Anthology*, 4, 8: 18). In the chart, Mercury is in Leo and Mars is in Scorpio, and there are no planets in Aquarius. It may also be worth noting that Mercury is in aversion to its domicile lord in this chart, the Sun, which I believe contradicts Schmidt's conjecture that a planet must also be configured to its domicile lord in order to lend its testimony to an empty sign within the context of zodiacal releasing. Cf. Schmidt, "Two Conjectures about the Hellenistic Concept of Testimony."

Each planet has a stronger or weaker influence over certain signs that it is configured to. Again, mixing experience with standard Hellenistic aspect doctrine, the ranking seems to be as follows: a benefic or malefic will have the greatest power over the sign that it is placed in. After that, the sign that it has the second most powerful influence over is the sign that it overcomes through a superior square. After that, the sign that the planet is opposite to. Finally, a planet has the weakest influence over the sign that it sends an inferior square to. This ranking mainly becomes important in terms of characterizing and differentiating subperiods, or determining which planets have more power over a specific sign when there are multiple planets configured to it, thus determining what the dominant theme will be in a given period.

CHARLIE SHEEN

The actor Charlie Sheen was born with a night chart, Gemini rising, Venus in Libra, Saturn in Pisces, Fortune in Aquarius, and Spirit in Virgo. Releasing from the Lot of Spirit for career, Sheen started out in a twenty-year Virgo period (1965–1985), followed by eight years in Libra (1985–1993). This Libra period was his most subjectively positive one, because it contained the benefic Venus in a night chart. Early in this period he got his first major role in the 1986 film *Platoon*, and by the end started getting cast in other movies.

In 1993 he started a fifteen-year Scorpio peak period, the tenth sign from Fortune. This sign contained Mars, but since it is a night chart, Mars is of the sect in favor, and thus not very difficult. The keyword that I find often comes up when the malefic that is of the sect is activated is "surmountable difficulties." Since this was a fifteen-year peak period, it seems to have coincided with the height of his acting career. He got a star on the Hollywood Walk of Fame in 1994, shortly after the period began, and he took the leading role in several major movies throughout the rest of the 1990s. In the early 2000s, he transitioned into television, starting with the show *Spin City* in 2000, and then the show *Two and a Half Men* in 2003. He received Emmy and Golden Globe award nominations for his role on this show, and eventually became the highest-paid actor on television by the end of the decade.

When the fifteen-year peak period ended in 2008, he began a new twelve-year Sagittarius period. Not only was Sagittarius no longer a peak period, it was square to Saturn in Pisces in a night chart, thus making it one of his most difficult signs. His career and life began to unravel at this point. He was arrested for assaulting his wife in December 2009, attempted rehab in early 2010, was arrested again in October 2010, and then got himself fired from the highly-paid

Charlie Sheen - Spirit Periods

♏ L1/L2 - 9/4/1965
    ♎ L2 - 4/27/1967
    ♏ L2 - 12/23/1967
    ♐ L2 - 3/17/1969
    ♑ L2 - 3/12/1970
    ♒ L2 - 5/30/1972
    ♓ L2 - 11/16/1974
    ♈ L2 - 11/11/1975
    ♉ L2 - 2/3/1977
    ♊ L2 - 10/1/1977
    ♋ L2 - 5/24/1979
    ♌ L2 - 6/12/1981
    ♓ L1/L2 - 1/3/1983 - LB
    ♈ L2 - 12/29/1983
    ♉ L2 - 3/23/1985
♎ L1/L2 - 5/22/1985
    ♏ L2 - 1/17/1986
    ♐ L2 - 4/12/1987
    ♑ L2 - 4/6/1988
    ♒ L2 - 6/25/1990
    ♓ L2 - 12/11/1992
♏ L1/L2 - 4/10/1993
    ♐ L2 - 7/4/1994
    ♑ L2 - 6/29/1995
    ♒ L2 - 9/16/1997
    ♓ L2 - 3/4/2000
    ♈ L2 - 2/27/2001
    ♉ L2 - 5/23/2002
    ♊ L2 - 1/18/2003
    ♋ L2 - 9/9/2004
    ♌ L2 - 9/29/2006
♐ L1/L2 - 1/22/2008
    ♑ L2 - 1/16/2009
    ♒ L2 - 4/6/2011
    ♓ L2 - 9/22/2013
    ♈ L2 - 9/17/2014
    ♉ L2 - 12/11/2015
    ♊ L2 - 8/7/2016
    ♋ L2 - 3/30/2018
♑ L1/L2 - 11/20/2019

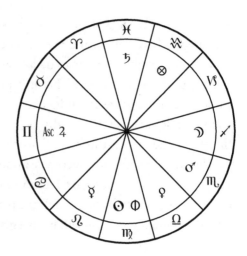

Chart 107 - Charlie Sheen

show that he starred in as a result of bizarre behavior and derogatory remarks about the creator of the series. He then had a much-publicized meltdown over the course of the next year or two. The important point here is that while the peak periods often represent periods of heightened activity and importance in a native's life, it is the angles from the benefics and malefics that indicate periods that are experienced as more subjectively positive or negative. When a person reaches a difficult period within the context of the zodiacal releasing periods from the Lot of Spirit, it can indicate a difficult period in the person's life with respect to their career.

VANESSA WILLIAMS

Another example is the model, singer, and actress Vanessa Williams. She was born with a day chart, Cancer rising, Jupiter in Pisces, Mars in Leo, Spirit in Libra, and Fortune in Aries. Releasing from Spirit for career, she began with an eight-year Libra period (1963–1971), followed by fifteen years in Scorpio (1971–1985). Towards the end of the Scorpio period (September 1983) she was the first African American to win the Miss America beauty pageant. A few

Vanessa Williams - Spirit Periods

♌ L1/L2 - 3/18/1963
    ♏ L2 - 11/13/1963
    ♐ L2 - 2/5/1965
    ♑ L2 - 1/31/1966
    ♒ L2 - 4/20/1968
    ♓ L2 - 10/7/1970
♏ L1/L2 - 2/4/1971
    ♐ L2 - 4/29/1972
    ♑ L2 - 4/24/1973
    ♒ L2 - 7/13/1975
    ♓ L2 - 12/29/1977
    ♈ L2 - 12/24/1978
    ♉ L2 - 3/18/1980
    ♊ L2 - 11/13/1980
    ♋ L2 - 7/6/1982
    ♌ L2 - 7/25/1984
♐ L1/L2 - 11/17/1985
    ♑ L2 - 11/12/1986
    ♒ L2 - 1/30/1989
    ♓ L2 - 7/19/1991
    ♈ L2 - 7/13/1992
    ♉ L2 - 10/6/1993
    ♊ L2 - 6/3/1994
    ♋ L2 - 1/24/1996
♑ L1/L2 - 9/15/1997

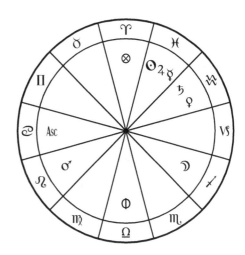

Chart 108 - Vanessa Williams

months later, however, she entered into a nineteen-month Leo subperiod starting in July 1984, activating the sign of the malefic contrary to the sect, and around this time she was forced to resign as Miss America after a magazine published nude photographs of her. A year later, the Leo subperiod and also the entire general period ended, and she moved into a new twelve-year Sagittarius period, which is angular to her natal Jupiter in Pisces. She hired a new manager who helped her reinvent herself, and shortly thereafter became a successful singer, releasing her first album in February 1988 under a twenty-seven-month Capricorn peak period (on level two). A few years later, in August of 1991, she released her second and most successful album during a level two Pisces period, the sign that contains her Jupiter. In this way we can clearly contrast one of the most difficult events that occurred in her career, which happened when the sign containing the malefic contrary to the sect was activated, with one of the most positive times in her career, which occurred when the sign containing the benefic of the sect was activated.[24]

---

[24] This is also a good example of a rule that I have found to be useful in practice, where sometimes the focal point or most important events in a general period will occur when the sign that contains the ruler of the general period is activated on the subperiod level. In this instance the defining event of the fifteen-year Scorpio period occurred when the subperiods came to the sign that contained Mars, and then later her most successful album was released during the twelve-year Sagittarius period when the sign that contained Jupiter was activated on the subperiod level. This is similar to a technique that Robert Zoller shared with me in 2007 within the context of annual profections, which holds that when the monthly profection comes

Up until now we have focused on releasing from the Lot of Spirit in order to show periods that pertain to the native's career. However, Valens also says that you can use zodiacal releasing in order to study periods related to the native's health and body by releasing from the Lot of Fortune. He also demonstrates this in his first example chart when he shows that the releasing from Fortune coming to the sign containing Saturn in a night chart resulted in the native experiencing shipwrecks, illness, and ultimately death.[25] I have also found releasing from Fortune to be useful in connection with studying periods of injury, illness, and sometimes death. I will use two examples:

Nicole Brown Simpson - Fortune Periods

♎ L1/L2 - 5/19/1959
    ♏ L2 - 1/14/1960
    ♐ L2 - 4/8/1961
    ♑ L2 - 4/3/1962
    ♒ L2 - 6/21/1964
    ♓ L2 - 12/8/1966
♏ L1/L2 - 4/7/1967
    ♐ L2 - 6/30/1968
    ♑ L2 - 6/25/1969
    ♒ L2 - 9/13/1971
    ♓ L2 - 3/1/1974
    ♈ L2 - 2/24/1975
    ♉ L2 - 5/19/1976
    ♊ L2 - 1/14/1977
    ♋ L2 - 9/6/1978
    ♌ L2 - 9/25/1980
♐ L1/L2 - 1/18/1982
    ♑ L2 - 1/13/1983
    ♒ L2 - 4/2/1985
    ♓ L2 - 9/19/1987
    ♈ L2 - 9/13/1988
    ♉ L2 - 12/7/1989
    ♊ L2 - 8/4/1990
    ♋ L2 - 3/26/1992
♑ L1/L2 - 11/16/1993
    ♒ L2 - 2/4/1996
    ♓ L2 - 7/23/1998
    ♈ L2 - 7/18/1999
    ♉ L2 - 10/10/2000
    ♊ L2 - 6/7/2001

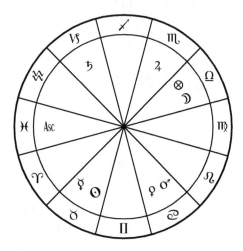

Chart 109 - Nicole Brown Simpson

NICOLE BROWN SIMPSON

This is a night chart, with Saturn in Capricorn, Fortune in Libra. The native began in an eight-year Libra period (1959–1967), followed by Scorpio for fifteen years (1967–1982), and Sagittarius for twelve years (1982–1993). In November of 1993 she began a twenty-seven-year Capricorn period. This is the sign that contains Saturn in a night chart, so we would expect it to be her most difficult. A few months later, in June of 1994, she was murdered.

to the sign that contains the lord of the year, that will indicate the most important month in the native's life in that particular year.

[25] Valens, *Anthology*, 4, 8: 1–13.

Car Accident - Fortune Periods

♏ L1/L2 - 5/6/1987
   ♐ L2 - 7/29/1988
   ♑ L2 - 7/24/1989
   ♒ L2 - 10/12/1991
   ♓ L2 - 3/30/1994
   ♈ L2 - 3/25/1995
   ♉ L2 - 6/17/1996
   ♊ L2 - 2/12/1997
   ♋ L2 - 10/5/1998
   ♌ L2 - 10/24/2000
♐ L1/L2 - 2/16/2002
   ♑ L2 - 2/11/2003
   ♒ L2 - 5/1/2005
   ♓ L2 - 10/18/2007
   ♈ L2 - 10/12/2008
   ♉ L2 - 1/5/2010
   ♊ L2 - 9/2/2010
   ♋ L2 - 4/24/2012
♑ L1/L2 - 12/15/2013

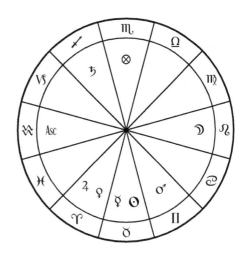

Chart 110 - Car Accident

CAR ACCIDENT

The native had a night chart, with Saturn in Sagittarius, and Fortune in Scorpio. She started with a fifteen-year Scorpio period (1987–2002), followed by a twelve-year Sagittarius period in 2002, which activated the sign containing the malefic that is contrary to the sect, Saturn. On the subperiods level (L2), the new twelve-year Sagittarius period started with a twelve-month Sagittarius subperiod, followed by a twenty-seven-month Capricorn subperiod, and then thirty months in Aquarius. On October 18, 2007, she started a twelve-month Pisces subperiod, which was overcome by Saturn in Sagittarius in the natal chart. Two days after the subperiod began she died in a car accident.

Angular Triads Relative to Fortune

In my experience, the concept of angular triads as applied to the places derived from the Ascendant also seems to be applicable to the places derived from the Lot of Fortune. Indeed, this seems to be implied by Valens to the extent that he constructs derived places from Fortune, and treats the angular signs from Fortune as pivots or *kentra*.[26] According to this scheme, the signs can be broken up into four sets of three, grouped around four angles from Fortune.

Each angular triad represents a sequence that has a beginning, middle, and end. The sign immediately preceding a Fortune angle represents the beginning of the sequence, and I have observed that events that take place under it are often anticipatory or preparatory, acting as precursors for the events that will take place during the following two signs. Next is the Fortune angle itself, which

---

[26] Valens, *Anthology*, 2, 18: 5–7 (*kentra* being the plural of *kentron*).

represents a period of heightened
activity and importance in the
middle of the sequence, when the
events initiated under the previous
sign become fully active. The final
part of the angular triad is the
sign that comes after the Fortune
angle, which represents the end of
the sequence, wherein events and
themes initiated during the previous
two signs are carried forward and
brought to completion. In this way,
each angular triad has a beginning,
a middle, and an end. The sequence
repeats itself at the beginning of the
next angular triad.

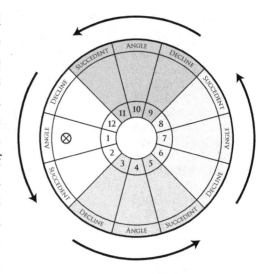

Figure 18.5 - Angular Triads from Fortune

DEMETRA GEORGE

The astrologer Demetra George was born with a day chart, Spirit in Libra,
and Fortune in Cancer. Releasing from Spirit for career, Demetra started in
an eight-year Libra period (1946–1954), followed by fifteen years in Scorpio
(1954–1969), after which she entered a twelve-year Sagittarius period in 1969.
This Sagittarius period represents the start of an angular triad that would last
almost her entire adult life, since it is the sign that comes before and builds up to
Capricorn, the seventh sign from Fortune. At the start of the Sagittarius period,
she was about to graduate from college and become a mathematics teacher, but
in early 1970 she left school and joined a commune; by 1971 she had started
studying astrology through books that were available in the commune library.
Her interest in astrology increased over the next decade, and later in the general
period she attended her first astrological conference where she was given a
copy of a newly published ephemeris for the asteroids. She began to study the
asteroids in charts, and developed interpretations and a system for using them.

In January 1981 she completed the twelve-year Sagittarius period and moved
into a twenty-seven-year Capricorn peak period (angular from Fortune). That
same month she began writing a book on the asteroids, which would eventually
be published in 1986 under the title *Asteroid Goddesses*. The release of this book
helped to launch her career as an astrologer, and cemented her reputation as
one of the more prominent astrologers of the late twentieth and early twenty-
first centuries. During the rest of this period, she published other books, and

Demetra George - Spirit Periods

♎ L1/L2 - 7/25/1946
    ♏ L2 - 3/22/1947
    ♐ L2 - 6/14/1948
    ♑ L2 - 6/9/1949
    ♒ L2 - 8/28/1951
    ♓ L2 - 2/13/1954
♏ L1/L2 - 6/13/1954
    ♐ L2 - 9/6/1955
    ♑ L2 - 8/31/1956
    ♒ L2 - 11/19/1958
    ♓ L2 - 5/7/1961
    ♈ L2 - 5/2/1962
    ♉ L2 - 7/26/1963
    ♊ L2 - 3/22/1964
    ♋ L2 - 11/12/1965
    ♌ L2 - 12/2/1967
♐ L1/L2 - 3/26/1969
    ♑ L2 - 3/21/1970
    ♒ L2 - 6/8/1972
    ♓ L2 - 11/25/1974
    ♈ L2 - 11/20/1975
    ♉ L2 - 2/12/1977
    ♊ L2 - 10/10/1977
    ♋ L2 - 6/2/1979
♑ L1/L2 - 1/22/1981
    ♒ L2 - 4/12/1983
    ♓ L2 - 9/28/1985
    ♈ L2 - 9/23/1986
    ♉ L2 - 12/17/1987
    ♊ L2 - 8/13/1988
    ♋ L2 - 4/5/1990
    ♌ L2 - 4/24/1992
    ♍ L2 - 11/15/1993
    ♎ L2 - 7/8/1995
    ♏ L2 - 3/4/1996
    ♐ L2 - 5/28/1997
    ♋ L2 - 5/23/1998 - LB
    ♌ L2 - 6/11/2000
    ♍ L2 - 1/2/2002
    ♎ L2 - 8/25/2003
    ♏ L2 - 4/21/2004
    ♐ L2 - 7/15/2005
    ♑ L2 - 7/10/2006
♒ L1/L2 - 9/3/2007
    ♓ L2 - 2/19/2010
    ♈ L2 - 2/14/2011
    ♉ L2 - 5/9/2012
    ♊ L2 - 1/4/2013
    ♋ L2 - 8/27/2014
    ♌ L2 - 9/15/2016
    ♍ L2 - 4/8/2018

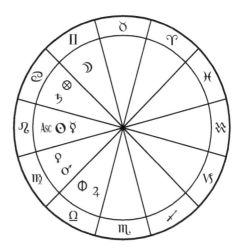

Chart 111 - Demetra George

experienced the most active part of her career in terms of teaching and consulting, as well as recognition that she received for her work. About halfway through the period, she obtained a Masters Degree in Classics and consequently developed an interest in Hellenistic astrology. In the mid-2000s, she began teaching one of the first classes in modern times exclusively focused on Hellenistic astrology.

In 2007, the twenty-seven-year Capricorn period ended, and she moved into a thirty-year Aquarius period. This is the sign after the peak period, in which previous themes are carried forward and brought to completion. A year later, in 2008, she published the book *Astrology and the Authentic Self,* which represented one of the first successful attempts to blend modern and ancient astrology, merging her earlier work on the asteroids and modern psychological astrology with her later work on Hellenistic astrology. Later in this period she plans to publish one of the first major textbooks on Hellenistic astrology.[27] In this way she brought

---

[27] Demetra George, *Ancient Astrology: A Practitioner's Guide* (provisional title), forthcoming.

to completion many of the events and themes that had been initiated under the previous two signs in the angular triad.

Loosing of the Bond

Valens explains at one point that on any subperiod level, if the cycle comes back to the original sign where it started at the beginning of the general period, then instead of starting the cycle over again, the subperiod jumps to the opposite sign from the general period and then begins moving forward again from there.[28] Valens refers to this as the "loosing of the bond" (*sundesmōn luseis*), or the "breaking of the sequence."[29] The loosing of the bond only occurs on the general level in signs longer than 17½ years, since that is approximately how long it takes for all of the level two subperiods to be completed if you add them up.[30] As a result of this, the loosing of the bond only takes place in the signs Gemini, Cancer, Leo, Virgo, Capricorn, and Aquarius. In my research of zodiacal releasing from the Lot of Spirit, I have found that the loosing of the bond usually indicates a major transition in terms of the person's career and life direction. This is one of the stranger facets of the technique, but it also tends to be one of its more notable and reliable aspects as well.

Loosing of the Bond Example

       ♋ L1/L2 - 4/4/1965
         ♌ L2 - 4/24/1967
         ♍ L2 - 11/14/1968
         ♎ L2 - 7/7/1970
         ♏ L2 - 3/4/1971
         ♐ L2 - 5/27/1972
         ♑ L2 - 5/22/1973
         ♒ L2 - 8/10/1975
         ♓ L2 - 1/26/1978
         ♈ L2 - 1/21/1979
         ♉ L2 - 4/15/1980
         ♊ L2 - 12/11/1980
    ♑ L2 - 8/3/1982 - LB
         ♒ L2 - 10/21/1984
         ♓ L2 - 4/9/1987
         ♈ L2 - 4/3/1988
         ♉ L2 - 6/27/1989
   ♌ L1/L2 - 11/24/1989

To give an example, let's imagine a person who is born in 1965 with their Lot of Spirit in Cancer. They begin their life in a twenty-five-year Cancer period. In the subperiods on level two, they begin with a twenty-five-month Cancer period, followed by nineteen months in Leo, twenty months in Virgo, eight months in Libra, fifteen in Scorpio, twelve in Sagittarius, twenty-seven in Capricorn, thirty in Aquarius, twelve in Pisces, fifteen in Aries, eight in Taurus, and twenty in Gemini. At this point, all of the signs of the zodiac have been activated in the subperiods, and the releasing should return to the sign where it started, Cancer, but instead it jumps to the opposing sign, Capricorn. Here it starts the cycle over again at the halfway point: twenty-seven months

---

[28] Valens, *Anthology*, 4, 4: 20–22.

[29] Valens, *Anthology*, 4, 5: 1.

[30] Valens, *Anthology*, 4, 4: 22.

Figure 18.6 - The Loosing of the Bond

in Capricorn, thirty in Aquarius, twelve in Pisces, and so on. Thus, the loosing of the bond is the point at which the subperiods jump to the sign opposite that of the general period, instead of returning to where they started.

This loosing of the bond only occurs on any level one time in a general period, and if the subperiods return to the sign that they started from a second time, then it will activate the original sign once again rather than making a second jump. Only the signs Capricorn and Aquarius are long enough for those signs to be activated again after the loosing of the bond. When this happens, it can actually be quite significant, because the subperiods are returning to the sign that they started at in the beginning of the general period, which was "skipped" at the loosing of the bond. When this occurs in Capricorn and Aquarius, I refer to it as a "completion period," and there is usually some sense of things coming full circle in the native's life at that time.

George Lucas - Spirit Periods

♍ L1/L2 - 5/14/1944
    ♎ L2 - 1/4/1946
    ♏ L2 - 9/1/1946
    ♐ L2 - 11/25/1947
    ♑ L2 - 11/19/1948
    ♒ L2 - 2/7/1951
    ♓ L2 - 7/26/1953
    ♈ L2 - 7/21/1954
    ♉ L2 - 10/14/1955
    ♊ L2 - 6/10/1956
    ♋ L2 - 1/31/1958
    ♌ L2 - 2/20/1960
    ♓ L2 - 9/12/1961 - LB
    ♈ L2 - 9/7/1962
    ♉ L2 - 12/1/1963
♎ L1/L2 - 1/30/1964

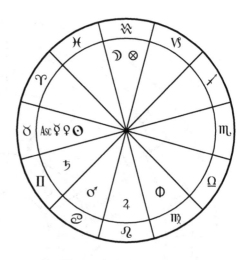

Chart 112 - George Lucas

George Lucas - Fortune Periods

♒ L1/L2 - 5/14/1944
    ♓ L2 - 10/31/1946
    ♈ L2 - 10/26/1947
    ♉ L2 - 1/18/1949
    ♊ L2 - 9/15/1949
    ♋ L2 - 5/8/1951
    ♌ L2 - 5/27/1953
    ♍ L2 - 12/18/1954
    ♎ L2 - 8/9/1956
    ♏ L2 - 4/6/1957
    ♐ L2 - 6/30/1958
    ♑ L2 - 6/25/1959
    ♌ L2 - 9/12/1961 - LB
    ♍ L2 - 4/5/1963
    ♎ L2 - 11/25/1964
    ♏ L2 - 7/23/1965
    ♐ L2 - 10/16/1966
    ♑ L2 - 10/11/1967
    ♒ L2 - 12/29/1969
    ♓ L2 - 6/16/1972
    ♈ L2 - 6/11/1973
♓ L1/L2 - 12/8/1973

GEORGE LUCAS

George Lucas was born with Spirit in Virgo and Fortune in Aquarius, and he experienced a loosing of the bond with both lots when he was eighteen. He grew up wanting to be a race car driver, and spent his teen years preparing for a career in racing after high school. In the Spirit periods he started out in a twenty-year Virgo period. His subperiods began with twenty months in Virgo, and then he went through Libra, Scorpio, Sagittarius, Capricorn, Aquarius, Pisces, Aries, Taurus, Gemini, Cancer, Leo. He then reached a loosing of the bond for twelve months when the periods jumped from Virgo to Pisces, starting in September 1961. A few months later, in June 1962, Lucas was involved in a car accident that almost killed him. He was in the hospital for several weeks. This event signaled a major transition in terms of his career and overall life direction, and afterward he no longer wanted to race. Instead, he decided to go to college, where he developed an interest in filmmaking and ultimately became a famous filmmaker. In this instance, it is notable that Spirit and Fortune are both in signs that are long enough to have a loosing of the bond start simultaneously at about seventeen-and-a-half years in. This loosing was a major transition both in terms of his career and his body or health.

Schwarzenegger - Spirit Periods

⚹ L1/L2 - 7/30/1947
    ♑ L2 - 7/24/1948
    ♒ L2 - 10/12/1950
    ♓ L2 - 3/30/1953
    ♈ L2 - 3/25/1954
    ♉ L2 - 6/18/1955
    ♊ L2 - 2/13/1956
    ♋ L2 - 10/5/1957
♑ L1/L2 - 5/28/1959
    ♒ L2 - 8/15/1961
    ♓ L2 - 2/1/1964
    ♈ L2 - 1/26/1965
    ♉ L2 - 4/21/1966
    ♊ L2 - 12/17/1966
    ♋ L2 - 8/8/1968
    ♌ L2 - 8/28/1970
    ♍ L2 - 3/20/1972
    ♎ L2 - 11/10/1973
    ♏ L2 - 7/8/1974
    ⚹ L2 - 10/1/1975
  ♋ L2 - 9/25/1976 - LB
    ♌ L2 - 10/15/1978
    ♍ L2 - 5/7/1980
    ♎ L2 - 12/28/1981
    ♏ L2 - 8/25/1982
    ⚹ L2 - 11/18/1983
    ♑ L2 - 11/12/1984
♒ L1/L2 - 1/6/1986
    ♓ L2 - 6/24/1988
    ♈ L2 - 6/19/1989
    ♉ L2 - 9/12/1990
    ♊ L2 - 5/10/1991
    ♋ L2 - 12/30/1992
    ♌ L2 - 1/19/1995
    ♍ L2 - 8/11/1996
    ♎ L2 - 4/3/1998
    ♏ L2 - 11/29/1998
    ⚹ L2 - 2/22/2000
    ♑ L2 - 2/16/2001
  ♌ L2 - 5/7/2003 - LB
    ♍ L2 - 11/27/2004
    ♎ L2 - 7/20/2006
    ♏ L2 - 3/17/2007
    ⚹ L2 - 6/9/2008
    ♑ L2 - 6/4/2009
    ♒ L2 - 8/23/2011
    ♓ L2 - 2/8/2014
    ♈ L2 - 2/3/2015
♓ L1/L2 - 8/2/2015
    ♈ L2 - 7/27/2016
    ♉ L2 - 10/20/2017

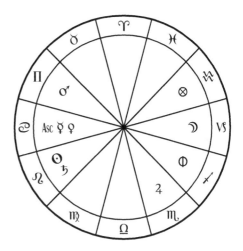

Chart 113 - Arnold Schwarzenegger

ARNOLD SCHWARZENEGGER

The loosing of the bond can often signal a transition from one career field to another. For example, Arnold Schwarzenegger was born with Spirit in Sagittarius and Fortune in Aquarius. He had his first major loosing of the bond from 1976–78, which was around the time that he retired from being a professional bodybuilder and began to make the transition to becoming a professional actor. Years later he had his second loosing of the bond from 2003–2004, when the releasing periods jumped to Leo, which is the seventh sign from Fortune, and thus a peak period. Ever since the mid-1980s, when he started his thirty-year Aquarius peak period, he had built up a career as a world-famous actor. But in May 2003, shortly after he started the loosing of the bond, he suddenly entered the race to become governor of the state of California, which he won. So within a few months, virtually overnight, he went from being an actor to a politician during the loosing of the bond.

Schwarzenegger also has a good example of what I call a "completion" period, because

Linda Goodman - Spirit Periods

♏ L1/L2 - 4/9/1925
    ♐ L2 - 7/3/1926
    ♑ L2 - 6/28/1927
    ♒ L2 - 9/15/1929
    ♓ L2 - 3/3/1932
    ♈ L2 - 2/26/1933
    ♉ L2 - 5/22/1934
    ♊ L2 - 1/17/1935
    ♋ L2 - 9/8/1936
    ♌ L2 - 9/28/1938
♐ L1/L2 - 1/21/1940
    ♑ L2 - 1/15/1941
    ♒ L2 - 4/5/1943
    ♓ L2 - 9/21/1945
    ♈ L2 - 9/16/1946
    ♉ L2 - 12/10/1947
    ♊ L2 - 8/6/1948
    ♋ L2 - 3/29/1950
♑ L1/L2 - 11/19/1951
    ♒ L2 - 2/6/1954
    ♓ L2 - 7/25/1956
    ♈ L2 - 7/20/1957
    ♉ L2 - 10/13/1958
    ♊ L2 - 6/10/1959
    ♋ L2 - 1/30/1961
    ♌ L2 - 2/19/1963
    ♍ L2 - 9/11/1964
    ♎ L2 - 5/4/1966
    ♏ L2 - 12/30/1966
    ♐ L2 - 3/24/1968
♋ L2 - 3/19/1969 - LB
    ♌ L2 - 4/8/1971
    ♍ L2 - 10/29/1972
    ♎ L2 - 6/21/1974
    ♏ L2 - 2/16/1975
    ♐ L2 - 5/11/1976
    ♑ L2 - 5/6/1977
♒ L1/L2 - 6/30/1978
    ♓ L2 - 12/16/1980
    ♈ L2 - 12/11/1981
    ♉ L2 - 3/6/1983
    ♊ L2 - 11/1/1983
    ♋ L2 - 6/23/1985
    ♌ L2 - 7/13/1987
    ♍ L2 - 2/2/1989
    ♎ L2 - 9/25/1990
    ♏ L2 - 5/23/1991
    ♐ L2 - 8/15/1992

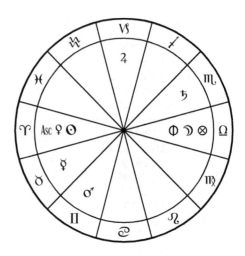

Chart 114 - Linda Goodman

when Aquarius was eventually activated again on level two between 2011 and 2014, his time as governor came to an end, and he made a transition back to acting. Thus, things came full circle in some sense, and he found himself doing what he had been doing at the start of the general period in the mid-1980s, and which he had stopped doing when Aquarius was skipped at the loosing of the bond.

Peak periods like Schwarzenegger's that jump to signs that are angular from the Lot of Fortune also tend to represent the native's hitting a high point in their career field. An example of this is Al Gore, who had been a politician since the mid-1970s when he began his twenty-seven-year Capricorn peak period on level 1 (see the list of periods outlined for him earlier in this chapter). When he reached the loosing of the bond on level 2 in 1992, however, he achieved his highest political appointment, becoming Vice President of the United States.

Similarly, the astrologer Linda Goodman was in a twenty-seven-year Capricorn peak period, which was the fourth sign from Fortune, starting in

Bill Gates - Spirit Periods

VS L1/L2 - 10/29/1955
    ♒ L2 - 1/16/1958
    ♓ L2 - 7/4/1960
    ♈ L2 - 6/29/1961
    ♉ L2 - 9/22/1962
    ♊ L2 - 5/20/1963
    ♋ L2 - 1/9/1965
    ♌ L2 - 1/29/1967
    ♍ L2 - 8/21/1968
    ♎ L2 - 4/13/1970
    ♏ L2 - 12/9/1970
    ♐ L2 - 3/3/1972
    ♋ L2 - 2/26/1973 - LB
    ♌ L2 - 3/18/1975
    ♍ L2 - 10/8/1976
    ♎ L2 - 5/31/1978
    ♏ L2 - 1/26/1979
    ♐ L2 - 4/20/1980
    VS L2 - 4/15/1981
♒ L1/L2 - 6/9/1982
    ♓ L2 - 11/25/1984
    ♈ L2 - 11/20/1985
    ♉ L2 - 2/13/1987
    ♊ L2 - 10/11/1987
    ♋ L2 - 6/2/1989
    ♌ L2 - 6/22/1991
    ♍ L2 - 1/12/1993
    ♎ L2 - 9/4/1994
    ♏ L2 - 5/2/1995
    ♐ L2 - 7/25/1996
    VS L2 - 7/20/1997
    ♌ L2 - 10/8/1999 - LB
    ♍ L2 - 4/30/2001
    ♎ L2 - 12/21/2002
    ♏ L2 - 8/18/2003
    ♐ L2 - 11/10/2004
    VS L2 - 11/5/2005
    ♒ L2 - 1/24/2008
    ♓ L2 - 7/12/2010
    ♈ L2 - 7/7/2011
♓ L1/L2 - 1/3/2012
    ♈ L2 - 12/28/2012
    ♉ L2 - 3/23/2014
    ♊ L2 - 11/18/2014
    ♋ L2 - 7/10/2016
    ♌ L2 - 7/30/2018

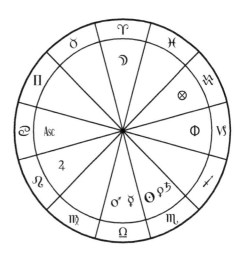

Chart 115 - Bill Gates

1951. In 1969, when she reached the loosing of the bond on the subperiod level, it activated the tenth sign from Fortune in her chart, and suddenly she achieved her greatest level of fame after publishing the book *Sun Signs* at the end of 1968. This became the highest-selling astrology book of all time, and her most well-known and influential work.

Other examples include Bill Gates, who decided to pursue the idea of creating a software company after reading an article in an issue of an electronics magazine in early 1975, during his first loosing of the bond. Not long afterward, he went on to found the company Microsoft, which eventually became the world's largest software maker by the 1980s and 1990s. Years later, Gates had his second loosing of the bond from 1999–2001, and during this time he stepped down as the CEO of Microsoft and founded the Bill and Melinda Gates Foundation, which later became the largest private philanthropic foundation in the world. With the Lot of Fortune in Aquarius, it was the second loosing of the bond (angular from Fortune) that represented the more significant peak of the two.

Elizabeth II - Spirit Periods

ठ L1/L2 - 4/21/1926
   Ⅱ L2 - 12/17/1926
   ♋ L2 - 8/8/1928
   ♌ L2 - 8/28/1930
   ♍ L2 - 3/20/1932
   ♎ L2 - 11/10/1933
Ⅱ L1/L2 - 3/10/1934
   ♋ L2 - 10/31/1935
   ♌ L2 - 11/19/1937
   ♍ L2 - 6/12/1939
   ♎ L2 - 2/1/1941
   ♏ L2 - 9/29/1941
   ♐ L2 - 12/23/1942
   ♑ L2 - 12/18/1943
   ♒ L2 - 3/7/1946
   ♓ L2 - 8/23/1948
   ♈ L2 - 8/18/1949
   ठ L2 - 11/11/1950
   ♐ L2 - 7/9/1951 - LB
   ♑ L2 - 7/3/1952
♋ L1/L2 - 11/25/1953
   ♌ L2 - 12/15/1955
   ♍ L2 - 7/7/1957
   ♎ L2 - 2/27/1959
   ♏ L2 - 10/25/1959
   ♐ L2 - 1/17/1961
   ♑ L2 - 1/12/1962
   ♒ L2 - 4/1/1964
   ♓ L2 - 9/18/1966
   ♈ L2 - 9/13/1967
   ठ L2 - 12/6/1968
   Ⅱ L2 - 8/3/1969
♑ L2 - 3/26/1971 - LB
   ♒ L2 - 6/13/1973
   ♓ L2 - 11/30/1975
   ♈ L2 - 11/24/1976
   ठ L2 - 2/17/1978
♌ L1/L2 - 7/17/1978
   ♍ L2 - 2/7/1980
   ♎ L2 - 9/29/1981
   ♏ L2 - 5/27/1982
   ♐ L2 - 8/20/1983
   ♑ L2 - 8/14/1984
   ♒ L2 - 11/2/1986
   ♓ L2 - 4/20/1989
   ♈ L2 - 4/15/1990
   ठ L2 - 7/9/1991
   Ⅱ L2 - 3/5/1992
   ♋ L2 - 10/26/1993
   ♒ L2 - 11/15/1995 - LB

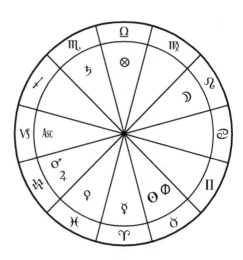

Chart 116 - Queen Elizabeth II

Another example is Queen Elizabeth II, whose father died on February 6, 1952, during her loosing of the bond, thus resulting in her accession to the throne of the United Kingdom.

A similar situation happened with Emperor Hirohito of Japan, whose father died in December of 1926, during Hirohito's loosing of the bond, thus making him Emperor. Twenty years later he experienced another loosing of the bond from 1946–48. This loosing of the bond jumped from Cancer to Capricorn, which contained Saturn in his night chart, and it occurred immediately after the defeat of Japan in World War II. During this time, he was forced to reject the previously accepted divine status of the Emperor, becoming a constitutional monarch instead of imperial sovereign, and thus essentially an influential figurehead in terms of political power. This brings up the point that it is important to see whether benefics or malefics are either located in

Hirohito - Spirit Periods

♉ L1/L2 - 4/29/1901
   ♊ L2 - 12/25/1901
   ♋ L2 - 8/17/1903
   ♌ L2 - 9/5/1905
   ♍ L2 - 3/29/1907
   ♎ L2 - 11/18/1908
♊ L1/L2 - 3/18/1909
   ♋ L2 - 11/8/1910
   ♌ L2 - 11/27/1912
   ♍ L2 - 6/20/1914
   ♎ L2 - 2/10/1916
   ♏ L2 - 10/7/1916
   ♐ L2 - 12/31/1917
   ♑ L2 - 12/26/1918
   ♒ L2 - 3/15/1921
   ♓ L2 - 9/1/1923
   ♈ L2 - 8/26/1924
   ♉ L2 - 11/19/1925
   ♐ L2 - 7/17/1926 - LB
   ♑ L2 - 7/12/1927
♋ L1/L2 - 12/3/1928
   ♌ L2 - 12/23/1930
   ♍ L2 - 7/15/1932
   ♎ L2 - 3/7/1934
   ♏ L2 - 11/2/1934
   ♐ L2 - 1/26/1936
   ♑ L2 - 1/20/1937
   ♒ L2 - 4/10/1939
   ♓ L2 - 9/26/1941
   ♈ L2 - 9/21/1942
   ♉ L2 - 12/15/1943
   ♊ L2 - 8/11/1944
   ♑ L2 - 4/3/1946 - LB
   ♒ L2 - 6/21/1948
   ♓ L2 - 12/8/1950
   ♈ L2 - 12/3/1951
   ♉ L2 - 2/25/1953
♌ L1/L2 - 7/25/1953
   ♍ L2 - 2/15/1955
   ♎ L2 - 10/7/1956
   ♏ L2 - 6/4/1957
   ♐ L2 - 8/28/1958
   ♑ L2 - 8/23/1959
   ♒ L2 - 11/10/1961
   ♓ L2 - 4/28/1964
   ♈ L2 - 4/23/1965

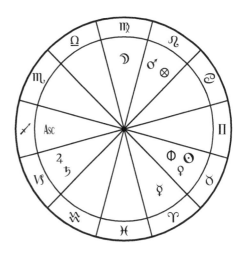

Chart 117 - Emperor Hirohito

or configured to the sign that the loosing of the bond jumps to, since oftentimes this will dictate whether the transition will be experienced as positive or negative.[31]

In this way there are at least three distinct or readily identifiable scenarios that often occur during the loosing of the bond. The first is the person who is established in a specific career field, but then reaches the loosing of the bond and subsequently jumps to another career field entirely, or leaves a career. Examples of this that we have seen include George Lucas and Arnold Schwarzenegger. Another example of this that will occur soon is in the chart of U.S. President Barack Obama, who is due to begin a loosing of the bond in May of 2017, shortly after completing his second and final term of office as President. This was actually part of the basis of a prediction that I made in 2012: that he would be elected to a second

---

[31] Valens makes this point as well, and also says to pay attention to the nature of the ruler of the sign that is becoming activated at the loosing of the bond, as well as its condition in the chart (*Anthology*, 4, 5).

Barack Obama Spirit Periods

♐ L1/L2 - 8/5/1961
   ♑ L2 - 7/31/1962
   ♒ L2 - 10/18/1964
   ♓ L2 - 4/6/1967
   ♈ L2 - 3/31/1968
   ♉ L2 - 6/24/1969
   ♊ L2 - 2/19/1970
   ♋ L2 - 10/12/1971
♑ L1/L2 - 6/3/1973
   ♒ L2 - 8/22/1975
   ♓ L2 - 2/7/1978
   ♈ L2 - 2/2/1979
   ♉ L2 - 4/27/1980
   ♊ L2 - 12/23/1980
   ♋ L2 - 8/15/1982
   ♌ L2 - 9/3/1984
   ♍ L2 - 3/27/1986
   ♎ L2 - 11/17/1987
   ♏ L2 - 7/14/1988
   ♐ L2 - 10/7/1989
♋ L2 - 10/2/1990 - LB
   ♌ L2 - 10/21/1992
   ♍ L2 - 5/14/1994
   ♎ L2 - 1/4/1996
   ♏ L2 - 8/31/1996
   ♐ L2 - 11/24/1997
   ♑ L2 - 11/19/1998
♒ L1/L2 - 1/13/2000
   ♓ L2 - 7/1/2002
   ♈ L2 - 6/26/2003
   ♉ L2 - 9/18/2004
   ♊ L2 - 5/16/2005
   ♋ L2 - 1/6/2007
   ♌ L2 - 1/25/2009
   ♍ L2 - 8/18/2010
   ♎ L2 - 4/9/2012
   ♏ L2 - 12/5/2012
   ♐ L2 - 2/28/2014
   ♑ L2 - 2/23/2015
♌ L2 - 5/13/2017 - LB
   ♍ L2 - 12/4/2018
   ♎ L2 - 7/26/2020
   ♏ L2 - 3/23/2021

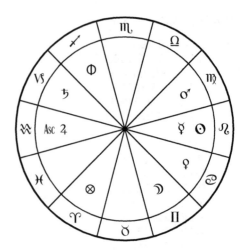

Chart 118 - Barack Obama

term of office later that year, because it was clear that the loosing of the bond indicated a career transition in early 2017, and thus it seemed likely that he would be completing a second term of office at that time.[32]

The second typical scenario for a loosing of the bond is the person who is established in a specific career field early in the general period who hits the high point of their chosen field when they reach the loosing of the bond. Examples of this that we have reviewed so far include Al Gore and Linda Goodman.

Finally, a third scenario that we have not reviewed is one in which the person took one step towards a specific career field earlier in the general period, prior to the loosing of the bond, but then once they reach the loosing of the bond they take the final step and fully dive into the field. Instances of this that I've seen come up a few times in client charts have involved people who receive their master's degree earlier in the general period, and complete their PhD once they reach the loosing of the bond, at which point they transition fully into their career field.

---

[32] Brennan, "An Introduction to Hellenistic Astrology, Part 2," pp. 79–80, which was published by *The Mountain Astrologer* magazine in April of 2012.

One thing that seems to be helpful for determining which scenario will play out in a given instance is to pay attention to the location of the loosing of the bond within the overall context of the angular triads. If the loosing of the bond takes place in the beginning or preparatory sign of the angular triad then it usually indicates a transition that is necessary in order to put the native on the career path that they will then follow after that point for several decades, as in the case of George Lucas. If the loosing of the bond takes place in the middle part of the angular triad during a peak period, then usually this will represent the scenario where the native hits the highest point in their chosen field at this time, as in the case of Al Gore or Linda Goodman. Finally, if the loosing of the bond takes place in the last sign of the angular triad, then it often seems to represent the closing down and bringing to completion of the last phase of a career that the native had been focused on for a few decades up to that point, which will be the case shortly for President Obama.

One observation that I've found particularly useful in terms of determining what the focus of the loosing of the bond will be ahead of time is to identify the sign that will be activated at the loosing of the bond, and then see what was occurring in the native's life and career around the time that the same sign was activated about eight years earlier. I refer to the first activation of this sign prior to the loosing of the bond as the "foreshadowing period." The foreshadowing period occurs when you reach the subperiod that is halfway through the cycle from the general period, or in other words the sign opposite to the general period, prior to the loosing of the bond. The first time this sign is activated there is usually some sort of foreshadowing of events that will later occur at the loosing of the bond. Oftentimes it takes the form of something that almost happens but then doesn't come to fruition. For example, the native thinks about leaving one field and getting into another at the foreshadowing period, and sometimes even starts working towards making the change, but ultimately stops and doesn't fully make the transition at that time. Then, several years later, they reach the loosing of the bond, and the repetition of the same sign brings a return to similar themes and circumstances, but the second time around the person almost always follows through and makes the change, thus leading to a major transition in their career and life direction. Thus, if you are paying careful attention, you can often see what that change will be by investigating what happened during the foreshadowing period.

While we have focused on releasing from the Lot of Spirit here, the loosing of the bond can also indicate a major and sometimes very abrupt transition in terms of the native's health and material circumstances when it takes place in the releasing from the Lot of Fortune. For example, Princess Diana was born with a

Princess Diana - Fortune Periods

♌ L1/L2 - 7/1/1961
   ♍ L2 - 1/22/1963
   ♎ L2 - 9/13/1964
   ♏ L2 - 5/11/1965
   ♐ L2 - 8/4/1966
   ♑ L2 - 7/30/1967
   ♒ L2 - 10/17/1969
   ♓ L2 - 4/4/1972
   ♈ L2 - 3/30/1973
   ♉ L2 - 6/23/1974
   ♊ L2 - 2/18/1975
   ♋ L2 - 10/10/1976
  ♒ L2 - 10/30/1978 - LB
♍ L1/L2 - 3/23/1980
   ♎ L2 - 11/13/1981
   ♏ L2 - 7/11/1982
   ♐ L2 - 10/4/1983
   ♑ L2 - 9/28/1984
   ♒ L2 - 12/17/1986
   ♓ L2 - 6/4/1989
   ♈ L2 - 5/30/1990
   ♉ L2 - 8/23/1991
   ♊ L2 - 4/19/1992
   ♋ L2 - 12/10/1993
   ♌ L2 - 12/30/1995
  ♓ L2 - 7/22/1997 - LB
   ♈ L2 - 7/17/1998
   ♉ L2 - 10/10/1999
♎ L1/L2 - 12/9/1999

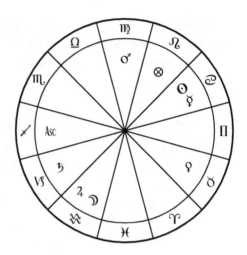

Chart 119 - Princess Diana

day chart with Mars in Virgo, and Fortune in Leo. She started out in a nineteen-year Leo period, from 1961 to 1980. She then moved into a twenty-year Virgo period in 1980. Seventeen and one-half years into this general period, she experienced a loosing of the bond, in which the subperiod jumped from Virgo to Pisces, and thus a twelve-month period beginning in late July 1997. The fact that the loosing of the bond in the Fortune periods was taking place in the sign opposite to Mars in her day chart was problematic for health and bodily matters. Only a month after the loosing of the bond began, she died in a car accident.

Spirit and Fortune in the Same Sign

Another strange yet important rule that Valens mentions within the context of zodiacal releasing pertains to those cases in which the Lot of Fortune and the Lot of Spirit fall together in the same sign in a person's chart. If you want to release from Spirit, you should move the lot forward one sign in zodiacal order and then begin the releasing from there.[33] This will typically occur when the native is born near an exact New Moon or Full Moon, since the lots will be together near the Ascendant or Descendant, respectively. For example, if a

---

[33] Valens, *Anthology*, 4, 4: 7. Valens says that some unnamed astrologers also move Spirit forward one sign when the lots are in opposition to each other, although he says that this doesn't make sense to him (*Anthology*, 4, 4: 9–10).

John Kerry - Spirit Periods

♋ L1/L2 - 12/11/1943
    ♌ L2 - 12/30/1945
    ♍ L2 - 7/23/1947
    ♎ L2 - 3/14/1949
    ♏ L2 - 11/9/1949
    ♐ L2 - 2/2/1951
    ♑ L2 - 1/28/1952
    ♒ L2 - 4/17/1954
    ♓ L2 - 10/3/1956
    ♈ L2 - 9/28/1957
    ♉ L2 - 12/22/1958
    ♊ L2 - 8/19/1959
  ♑ L2 - 4/10/1961 - LB
    ♒ L2 - 6/29/1963
    ♓ L2 - 12/15/1965
    ♈ L2 - 12/10/1966
    ♉ L2 - 3/4/1968
♌ L1/L2 - 8/1/1968
    ♍ L2 - 2/22/1970
    ♎ L2 - 10/15/1971
    ♏ L2 - 6/11/1972
    ♐ L2 - 9/4/1973
    ♑ L2 - 8/30/1974
    ♒ L2 - 11/17/1976
    ♓ L2 - 5/6/1979
    ♈ L2 - 4/30/1980
    ♉ L2 - 7/24/1981
    ♊ L2 - 3/21/1982
    ♋ L2 - 11/11/1983
  ♒ L2 - 11/30/1985 - LB
♍ L1/L2 - 4/24/1987
    ♎ L2 - 12/14/1988
    ♏ L2 - 8/11/1989
    ♐ L2 - 11/4/1990
    ♑ L2 - 10/30/1991
    ♒ L2 - 1/17/1994
    ♓ L2 - 7/5/1996
    ♈ L2 - 6/30/1997
    ♉ L2 - 9/23/1998
    ♊ L2 - 5/21/1999
    ♋ L2 - 1/10/2001
    ♌ L2 - 1/30/2003
  ♓ L2 - 8/22/2004 - LB
    ♈ L2 - 8/17/2005
    ♉ L2 - 11/10/2006
♎ L1/L2 - 1/9/2007
    ♏ L2 - 9/6/2007
    ♐ L2 - 11/29/2008
    ♑ L2 - 11/24/2009
    ♒ L2 - 2/12/2012
    ♓ L2 - 7/31/2014
♏ L1/L2 - 11/28/2014

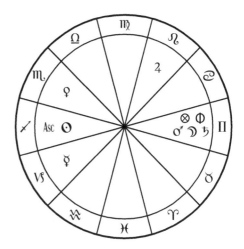

Chart 120 - John Kerry

native was born with both Spirit and Fortune in Scorpio, then you would move Spirit forward one sign, to Sagittarius, for the purpose of releasing from Spirit, while Fortune would stay in Scorpio.

This is admittedly a rather odd and seemingly unintuitive facet of the technique, although I have repeatedly found it to be useful and accurate when working with client charts and researching other nativities. Many of these charts would only make sense when this rule is implemented in their Spirit periods, whereupon they all line up perfectly. Linda Goodman is one example of this, since Spirit and Fortune both fall in Libra in her chart. Thus the periods that I used earlier (in which her loosing of the bond coincided with the release of her most popular book) were based on moving Spirit forward one sign to Scorpio. Former U.S. Secretary of State, John Kerry, is another example, as he has both lots in Gemini, and his Spirit releasing works perfectly if you move it forward one sign, beginning from

Cancer, so that his nearly-successful attempt to become President in 2004 perfectly coincides with a loosing of the bond during a level one Fortune peak period. Another example is the politician Ted Kennedy, who was born with Spirit and Fortune in Cancer. If you move Spirit forward one sign for releasing, then the assassination of his brother Robert in 1968 perfectly coincides with a loosing of the bond.

Many other such examples could be given, but suffice it to say that while I encourage the reader to test this facet of the technique on their own in order to see if it works, for me it has become a standard and reliable rule.

Areas For Further Research

There are many other facets and interpretive nuances of this technique that I have discovered from personal practice, but for the purposes of this book, the general overview of the technique provided here is sufficient, and I will end my treatment of it here.

Over the past ten years, much research has been undertaken on the technique by a few individuals, and although many amazing things have been found, on some level I feel as if we have only scratched the surface. There are still many tantalizing avenues of research that have yet to be fully worked out. For example, one question that naturally arises for many people is whether it is possible to release from other lots besides Spirit and Fortune. While Valens doesn't say anything about this as a possibility, the idea was intriguing enough to me that I began testing it out in November of 2005 using Paulus' version of the Lot of Eros, and I found that it actually works quite well. I regularly use it in order to time periods in a person's life with respect to love and relationships, using many of the same guidelines as above. I have found that when a person reaches an angle from Fortune in the Eros releasing, it will often coincide with a period of heightened importance and activity within the context of their love life. I've also seen some interesting possibilities with other lots, although for the most part I have left that topic for other people to study and explore.

The approach to zodiacal releasing that I have emphasized in this chapter has been very much focused on the signs themselves and not so much on the rulers of the signs. This is partially because I find the condition of the signs to be more relevant and useful in most instances, but I think that this is an area that deserves further research, and I know that others such as Schmidt have developed approaches that are much more oriented around the rulers. One observation that Schmidt made in connection with the rulers that I have found to be particularly useful is that when the sign that contains the ruler of Spirit is activated, there is often something about the native's life work that becomes more clear to them or begins to manifest at that time.[34] I have seen many examples of this in client and celebrity charts since 2009, to the point that it has become a regular principle of interpretation in my work. Other uses of the rulers of the activated signs are still a matter of personal research.

Zodiacal releasing is a very old technique, but it is still very new for contemporary astrologers who have only started to recover it in the past ten to twenty years. Only a handful of people in the world really know how to use it effectively at the present time, but that is sure to change. Indian astrologers have used similar techniques continuously for nearly 2000 years with their *dasha* systems, which are often structured in a very similar way in terms of the interaction between general periods and subperiods, and there are many areas in which contemporary practitioners of Hellenistic astrology could stand to learn a great deal from them as we revive the ancient time-lord systems.

At the same time, there are a number of ethical and philosophical issues that techniques like this raise simply by the fact that they are so effective, and that they can do things many astrologers didn't even know were possible. In some ways, contemporary modern astrology is unequipped to deal with some of the issues that techniques like zodiacal releasing raise, because its approach and capabilities are so foreign to anything that was available until very recently. Dealing with issues like this comes part and parcel with reviving the techniques of Hellenistic astrology. We are not simply recovering an ancient technical doctrine; there is an entire tradition of procedural application that goes along with it that has been dead for quite some time now. But suddenly we have started to breathe life into it again, and now we need to develop protocols for how to use and explain what it means. This chapter is just the start of the process of fully reviving this technique, and now I leave the next step in that process up to you.

---

[34] Personal communication, 2007. The observation is partially based on an interpretive principle that may be implied in Valens, *Anthology*, 4, 7: 14. The importance of the activation of the sign that contains the ruler of the Lot of Spirit was first noted by Schmidt and Black in their paper "Peak Times and Patterns in the Life of Dane Rudhyar," p. 39.

Conclusion

Hellenistic astrology is a vast subject, and while we have covered a lot of ground in this book, there is still much that I was not able to include. For example, due to space limitations I was not able to address certain techniques such as "spear-bearing" (*doruphoria*), or other important concepts such as the overall ruler of the chart, known as the Master of the Nativity (*oikodespotēs geneseōs*). Fortune willing, I hope to be able to address these topics in other works, although I am acutely aware that Firmicus Maternus said something similar in the *Mathesis* about intending to write a separate book on the Master of the Nativity. It is not known if he was able to fulfill that promise, since no traces of that work have survived.

There is still much work to be done in reconstructing and reviving Hellenistic astrology, and this overview is still just one relatively early step in that process. My hope is that this work will inspire others to take part in this effort by demonstrating the value and complexity of the ancient astrological traditions. There is a need for additional people that have specialist training in history, ancient languages, philosophy, and other fields to engage with this material in order to develop a clearer understanding of it. I would encourage those who have the means and the passion for this material to seek training in some of these specialty areas in a university setting, as this is the best way to learn the necessary skills to engage with the surviving textual tradition to the fullest extent.

Aside from textual analysis, there is also much work that still needs to be done in putting some of these techniques into practice, testing them out, and refining them. While some techniques may work straight out of the box, so to speak, there are many others that need to be adapted to modern times before they can be applied usefully in a contemporary context. I have tried to demonstrate some ways in which this can be done in my chart examples, although there are many other instances that still require discussion. Additionally, many of these techniques can do things that were not possible in modern astrology, and as a result of this there are many ethical and procedural considerations that need to be developed in order to establish proper guidelines for how to interpret a client's chart when using these techniques. In some instances, just because an astrologer can say something about a person's life doesn't necessarily mean that they should. At the same time, the astrologer wants to be able to be straightforward and honest about what is indicated in the chart, and there can be drawbacks to not being candid about what the astrology says as well. While many of the major astrological organizations have adopted ethics guidelines in recent decades, the nature and scope of the practice of Hellenistic astrology carries with it a special set of considerations that may require unique solutions.

The techniques also raise major philosophical questions about fate, free will, and the nature of the cosmos in general. One of the things I found most startling when I first started studying Hellenistic astrology was the efficacy of some of the techniques, and in particular the way that the time-lord systems could outline the entire narrative of a person's life from the moment they were born. For me personally, this led to a philosophical crisis for a year or two as I struggled to reorient my views on what astrology is capable of, as well as what that means for myself and others in terms of the extent to which our lives are predetermined. Ultimately, I ended up with a much more deterministic and Stoic philosophical position than anything that I would have even considered previously, and I think that it is fair to say that the astrologers of the Hellenistic tradition itself were generally much more deterministic than their counterparts have been in the twentieth and early twenty-first century. Still, what may be appropriate for me as an individual in terms of the philosophical views that I am more inclined to adopt may not be appropriate for everyone, and there was enough philosophical and religious diversity in the Hellenistic tradition to assure us that no one approach can claim supremacy over the entire tradition. It is not clear to what extent Hellenistic astrology had a unified philosophical program underlying its practice in the foundational period, or if instead it just represented a sort of tool or technology that was used by many different types of astrologers who held a variety of different philosophical and religious positions. I do think that it would be beneficial for those who engage with this material to explore some of the broader philosophical issues in order to create a more well-articulated conceptualization and philosophy of astrology in modern times, and this is one area where going back to the sources has already helped to clarify some major issues that were still murky in the twentieth century.

Ultimately the purpose of studying the ancient traditions of astrology is not necessarily to go back into the past and stay there. Instead, the goal should be to look back into the past, reconstruct and understand what the tradition was, and then bring some of the best parts forward into the future. While one could practice a form of astrology that only uses techniques that were employed in the Hellenistic tradition, and this would be a perfectly valid and effective approach to take, one should realize that the tradition has always been a living and growing entity, and that it is not and has never been static. This realization alone should be enough to counter the crude sort of fundamentalism that can sometimes develop whenever groups look back into the past and begin to idealize it. While a large part of the premise of this book is that there is something valuable to be gained by studying the works of the ancient astrologers, this should not be misunderstood to mean that Hellenistic astrology is some sort of panacea that will solve all of the shortcomings of contemporary astrological practice. There is still much work to be done in the future surrounding the conceptual, philosophical, and technical premises of astrology. Reconnecting astrologers with our history and tradition is one piece of that, and it has allowed us to recover much cumulative wisdom from centuries of astrological practice. What comes next is the merging of the contemporary and ancient traditions, and in that we will see the emergence of a synthesis that will mark a new epoch in the astrological tradition, in the same way that the confluence of the Mesopotamian and Egyptian astrological traditions was part of what led to the creation of Hellenistic astrology two thousand years ago. It is in this sense that I believe that by looking back into the past we can and will create a better astrology for the future.

Appendix: Charts and Birth Data

This table lists all of the birth charts used in this work, given in the order in which they appear in the book, as well as birth data for the charts of any public figures whose charts were used as examples. My source for most of the birth data for public figures was the astrological database called AstroDatabank, which is available online at www.astro.com/astro-databank/. Each of the entries below has source notes that include the rating for each piece of birth data according to the Rodden Rating system, which is used by AstroDatabank in order to identify the sources for birth times. In some instances, I give additional information about the specific sources used, as well as other related notes about the chart or data. The birth data for anonymous charts from my private files have been withheld for privacy and confidentiality reasons, although all of these charts would be rated as either AA or A data (i.e. from a birth certificate, or otherwise quoted directly from the source, usually from a birth record).

1. **J. Paul Getty:** December 15, 1892 at 8:45 AM in Minneapolis, Minnesota. Rodden Rating: B data, from a biography, which indicates he was born shortly before 9:00 AM.

2. **Prince Charles:** November 14, 1948 at 9:14 PM in Buckingham Palace, England. A data, announced in the news at the time of birth.

3. **Che Guevara:** May 14, 1928 at 03:05 AM in Rosario (Santa Fé), Argentina. AA data, from birth certificate, as well as from a biography.

4. **Franklin D. Roosevelt:** January 30, 1882 at 8:45 PM in Hyde Park, New York. AA data, quoted in a biography from his mother's diary.

5. **Christopher Reeve:** September 25, 1952 at 3:12 AM in Manhattan, New York. A data, from a letter written to an astrologer who inquired. Other reported times of 3:14 AM and 3:30 AM quoted to other astrologers give the same rising sign.

6. **Judy Blume:** February 12, 1938 at 9:59 PM in Elizabeth, New Jersey. AA data, from birth certificate.

7. **Richard Houck:** April 13, 1947 at 12:51 AM in Des Moines, Iowa. A data, quoted from him in a letter to an AstroDatabank editor.

8. **Carl Sagan:** November 9, 1934 at 5:05 PM in New York, New York. AA data, from birth certificate.

9. **Anonymous (Doctor):** private data.

10.   **Pope Benedict XVI, Joseph Ratzinger:** April 16, 1927 at 4:15 AM in Marktl, Germany. AA data, from birth certificate, with secondary confirmation from brother's biography.

11.   **William Rehnquist:** October 1, 1924 at 11:32 AM in Milwaukee, Wisconsin. AA data, from birth certificate.

12.   **T. S. Eliot:** September 26, 1888 at 7:45 AM in St. Louis, Missouri. AA data, quoted in a letter written by his father.

13.   **George Lucas:** May 14, 1944 at 5:40 AM in Modesto, California. AA data, from birth certificate. I use a slightly modified time of 5:41:35 AM.

14.   **Steve Wozniak:** August 11, 1950 at 9:45 AM in San Jose, California. AA data, quoted from a public announcement.

15.   **Angelina Jolie:** June 4, 1975 at 9:09 AM in Los Angeles, California. AA data, from birth certificate.

16.   **Paul Newman:** January 26, 1925 at 6:30 AM in Cleveland, Ohio. AA data, from birth certificate.

17.   **Ted Kennedy:** February 22, 1932 at 3:58 AM in Dorchester, Massachusetts. AA data, from a birth record.

18.   **Anonymous (Financial Anxieties):** private data.

19.   **Emperor Akihito:** December 23, 1933 at 6:39 AM in Tokyo, Japan. A data, from a newspaper article published shortly after the birth.

20.   **Queen Elizabeth II:** April 21, 1926 at 2:40 AM in London, England. AA data, from official announcement.

21.   **Prince William:** June 21, 1982 at 9:03 PM in Paddington, England. AA data, from birth record.

22.   **Prince Henry:** September 15, 1984 at 4:20 PM in Paddington, England. A data, from news report on the day of the birth.

23.   **Prince Andrea Casiraghi:** June 8, 1984 at 10:50 PM in Monte Carlo, Monaco. A data, from news report on the day of the birth. One report gives 10:52 PM.

24.   **Maurizio Gucci:** September 26, 1948 at 1:10 AM in Florence, Italy. AA data, from birth certificate.

25.   **Steve Wozniak:** see Chart 14.

26.   **Ted Kennedy:** see Chart 17.

27.   **Vincent van Gogh:** March 30, 1853 at 11:00 AM in Zundert, Netherlands. AA, from birth certificate.

28.   **Reinhold Ebertin:** February 16, 1901 at 4:45 AM in Görlitz, Germany. A data, from a quotation by him about his own chart.

29. **Anonymous (Ruler of Fourth in Ninth):** private data. AA data.

30. **Anonymous (Ruler of Fifth in Ninth):** private data. AA data.

31. **Anonymous (Ruler of Fifth in Eighth):** private data. AA data.

32. **Ernest Hemingway:** July 21, 1899 at 8:00 AM in Oak Park, Illinois. AA data, from an account written in his mother's scrapbook.

33. **Michel Foucault:** October 15, 1926 at 7:30 AM in Poitiers, France. AA data, from birth certificate.

34. **Johnny Carson:** October 23, 1925 at 7:15 AM in Corning, Iowa. AA data, evidently from a birth record, although a conflicting 11:47 PM exists.

35. **Steven Spielberg:** December 18, 1946 at 6:16 PM in Cincinnati, Ohio. AA data, from birth certificate.

36. **Adolf Hitler:** April 20, 1889 at 6:30 PM in Braunau, Austria. AA data, from birth record.

37. **Anonymous (Ruler of Seventh in Eleventh):** private data.

38. **Ernest Hemingway:** see Chart 32.

39. **Princess Diana:** July 1, 1961 at 7:45 PM in Sandringham, England. A data, evidently in a letter from Diana's mother, confirmed by Diana herself to her personal astrologer.

40. **Anonymous (Ruler of Fourth in Ninth):** private data.

41. **Anonymous (Doctor):** private data.

42. **Eleanor Roosevelt:** October 11, 1884 at 11:00 AM in New York, New York. AA data, from birth record.

43. **Tiger Woods:** December 30, 1975 at 10:50 PM in Long Beach, California. AA data, from birth certificate.

44. **Anonymous (Ruler of Eleventh in Eighth):** private data.

45. **John F. Kennedy Jr.:** November 25, 1960 at 12:22 AM in Washington, D.C. A data, from a news report shortly after the birth.

46. **George Lucas:** see Chart 13.

47. **Anonymous (Ruler of Third Maltreated):** private data.

48. **Steve Wozniak:** see Chart 14.

49. **Che Guevara:** see Chart 3.

50. **Anonymous (Doctor):** private data.

51.   **Philippe Pozzo di Borgo:** February 14, 1951 at 2:45 PM in Tunis, Tunisia.
AA data, from birth certificate.

52.   **Michael Patrick MacDonald:** March 9, 1966 at 8:35 AM in Boston, Massachusetts.
AA data, from birth certificate.

53.   **Tiger Woods:** see Chart 43.

54.   **Chris Farley:** February 15, 1964 at 3:34 PM in Madison, Wisconsin.
AA data, from birth certificate.

55.   **Robin Williams:** July 21, 1951 at 1:34 PM in Chicago, Illinois.
AA data, from birth certificate.

56.   **Anonymous (Ruler of Eleventh Maltreated):** private data.

57.   **Maya Angelou:** April 4, 1928 at 2:10 PM in Saint Louis, Missouri.
AA data, from birth record.

58.   **James Eagan Holmes:** December 13, 1987 at 9:04 PM in La Jolla, California.
AA data, from birth certificate.

59.   **Anonymous (Life Insurance from Father):** private data.

60.   **Martin Luther King Jr.:** January 15, 1929 at 12:00 PM (noon) in Atlanta, Georgia.
A data, reportedly from mother's memory. Also given as approximately noon in one
biography.

61.   **Albert Einstein:** March 14, 1879 at 11:30 AM in Ulm, German.
AA data, from birth certificate.

62.   **Robert F. Kennedy:** November 20, 1925 at 3:11 PM in Brookline, Massachusetts.
A data, reportedly quoted from Kennedy's office.

63.   **Andre Romelle Young (Dr. Dre):** February 18, 1965 at 10:56 AM in Los Angeles,
California.
AA data, from birth certificate.

64.   **Jacqueline Kennedy Onassis:** July 28, 1929 at 2:30 PM in Southampton, New York.
A data, reportedly given to astrologer Frances McEvoy through a mutual friend.

65.   **Valens Triplicity Example 1:** From Valens, *Anthology*, 2, 22: 1–9. Chart no. L 50 in
Neugebauer and van Hoesen, *Greek Horoscopes*, p. 81, dated by them to October 25, 50
CE, about 4:00 AM.

66.   **Valens Triplicity Example 2:** From Valens, *Anthology*, 2, 22: 13–16. Chart no. L 85 II
in Neugebauer and van Hoesen, *Greek Horoscopes*, p. 93f, dated by them to February 5,
85 CE, shortly before sunset.

67.   **Valens Triplicity Example 3:** From Valens, *Anthology*, 2, 22: 43–44. Chart no. L 109
in Neugebauer and van Hoesen, *Greek Horoscopes*, p. 104f, dated by them to June 2, 109
CE, about 8:00 AM.

68. **Dorotheus Triplicity Example 1:** From Dorotheus, *Carmen*, 1, 24: 1–4. Chart "octava" in Pingree's edition, which he dated to August 2, 43 CE, around 2:00 AM.

69. **Dorotheus Triplicity Example 2:** From Dorotheus, *Carmen*, 1, 24: 9–11. Chart "septima" in Pingree's edition, which he dated to April 2, 36 CE, around 8:00 PM.

70. **Napoleon Bonaparte:** August 15, 1769 at 11:30 AM in Ajaccio, France. A data, supposedly from family sources, although others give 11:00 AM, which also barely gives Scorpio rising. This is the one piece of data that I had the most uncertainty about in terms of the sources, so the example should be viewed with that in mind.

71. **Anonymous (Died in Infancy):** private data.

72. **Robert Downey Jr.:** April 4, 1965 at 1:10 PM in Manhattan, New York. A data, quoted from him.

73. **Kurt Cobain:** February 20, 1967 at 7:38 PM in Aberdeen, Washington. AA data, from birth certificate.

74. **Bill Clinton:** August 19, 1946 at 8:51 AM in Hope, Arkansas. A data, quoted from his mother, although a conflicting time of 7:30 AM also exists.

75. **Whitney Houston:** August 9, 1963 at 8:55 PM in Newark, New Jersey. AA data, from birth certificate.

76. **Hans Christian Andersen:** April 2, 1805 at 1:00 AM in Odense, Denmark. AA data, from church parish records.

77. **Lisa Marie Presley:** February 1, 1968 at 5:01 PM in Memphis, Tennessee. AA data, from a hospital record.

78. **Robert F. Kennedy:** see Chart 62.

79. **Anonymous (Reconciliation with Mother):** private data.

80. **Anonymous (Birth of Child):** private data.

81. **Michael J. Fox:** June 9, 1961 at 12:15 AM in Edmonton, Alberta. A data, reportedly quoted from him to an astrologer.

82. **Anonymous (Met Future Husband):** private data.

83. **Patrick Swayze:** August 18, 1952 at 8:10 AM in Houston, Texas. A data, reportedly quoted from him to an astrologer.

84. **Amanda Knox:** July 9, 1987 at 2:47 AM in Seattle, Washington. AA data, from birth certificate.

85. **Carl Sagan:** see Chart 8.

86. **Anthony Louis:** September 3, 1945 at 9:05 AM in Waterbury, Connecticut. AA data, from birth certificate.

87.   **Rudolf Hess:** April 26, 1894 at 10:00 AM in Alexandria, Egypt.
A data, reportedly given to Hess' astrologer.

88.   **Andre Romelle Young (Dr. Dre):** see Chart 63.

89.   **Robert F. Kennedy:** see Chart 62.

90.   **Lisa Marie Presley:** see Chart 77.

91.   **Steve Wozniak:** see Chart 14.

92.   **Anonymous (Relocated to Foreign Country):** private data.

93.   **Anonymous (House Fire):** private data.

94.   **Jonathan Brandis:** April 13, 1976 at 8:00 PM in Danbury, Connecticut.
A data, reportedly quoted by him.

95.   **George Lucas:** see Chart 13.

96.   **Anonymous (Partner's Suicide):** private data.

97.   **Charlie Sheen:** September 3, 1965 at 10:48 PM in New York, New York.
A data, reportedly quoted by him from his birth certificate. A slightly different 10:58
PM time is also reported, although the rising sign, Lot of Fortune, and Lot of Spirit
remain in the same signs.

98.   **Lisa Marie Presley:** see Chart 77.

99.   **Anonymous (Husband's Death):** private data.

100.   **Anonymous (Started Relationship):** private data.

101.   **Spirit in Libra Example:** see entry for chart 111 (Demetra George).

102.   **George W. Bush:** July 6, 1946 at 7:26 AM in New Haven, Connecticut.
AA data, from birth certificate.

103.   **Al Gore:** March 31, 1948 at 12:53 PM in Washington, District of Columbia.
AA data, from birth certificate.

104.   **George Lucas:** see Chart 13.

105.   **Steve Wozniak:** see Chart 14.

106.   **Chris Brennan:** November 1, 1984 at 1:28 PM in Aurora, Colorado.
AA data, from birth certificate.

107.   **Charlie Sheen:** see Chart 97.

108.   **Vanessa L. Williams:** March 18, 1963 at 11:28 AM in Millwood, New York.
AA data, from baby card published in her autobiography.

109. **Nicole Brown Simpson:** May 19, 1959 at 2:00 AM in Frankfurt am Main, Germany. AA data, from birth certificate.

110. **Anonymous (Car Accident):** private data.

111. **Demetra George:** July 25, 1946 at 6:22 AM CST in Chicago, Illinois. AA data, from birth certificate.

112. **George Lucas:** see Chart 13.

113. **Arnold Schwarzenegger:** July 30, 1947 at 4:10 AM in Graz, Austria. A data, reportedly quoted from him.

114. **Linda Goodman:** April 9, 1925 at 6:05 AM in Morgantown, West Virginia. AA data, from birth certificate.

115. **Bill Gates:** October 28, 1955 at 10:00 PM in Seattle, Washington. A data, quoted by him to an astrologer. A conflicting time of "shortly after 9:00 PM" is reported in one biography. Both times have the same rising sign and Lot of Fortune, although the Lot of Spirit is in Sagittarius in the 9:00 PM time and Capricorn in the 10:00 PM time. I prefer the 10:00 PM time due to the way the resulting zodiacal releasing from the Lot of Spirit periods fit his chronology better.

116. **Queen Elizabeth II:** see Chart 20.

117. **Emperor Hirohito:** April 29, 1901 at 10:10 PM in Tokyo, Japan. B data, apparently from reports in two history books. A 9:51 PM is also cited, supposedly from contemporary news reports, although the sources are not given, and the placement of the rising sign, Fortune, and Spirit are the same.

118. **Barack Obama:** August 4, 1961 at 7:24 PM in Honolulu, Hawaii. AA data, from birth certificate. I have some reservations about the sect of the chart because he was born just after sunset. I have treated it as a night chart in this book for the purpose of demonstrating zodiacal releasing, although in some ways the natal placements might make more sense if the chart was diurnal. At the time of publication this is a matter of ongoing research.

119. **Princess Diana:** see Chart 39.

120. **John Kerry:** December 11, 1943 at 8:03 AM in Fitzsimons, Colorado. A data, quoted from his mother for "sunrise," as well as his sister-in-law who reportedly obtained it from him directly. Later a conflicting time of between midnight and 1:00 AM was reportedly obtained from him at a rally through his wife, although this time is so vague and wildly inconsistent with the other two that I consider it to be spurious.

Timeline

Fifth Century BCE

- The oldest known Mesopotamian birth charts date to 410 BCE. The concept of natal astrology or genethlialogy was developed by this time.

Fourth Century BCE

- The Greek philosopher Plato dies c. 347 BC.
- Alexander the Great launches a war against the Persian Empire in 334 BCE.
- The city of Alexandria is founded in Egypt by Alexander shortly after 332 BCE.
- The Greek philosopher Aristotle dies c. 322 BC.
- The Ptolemaic dynasty is founded in Egypt in the late fourth century BCE; Ptolemy I and II began setting up the famous Museum and Library of Alexandria.

Third Century BCE

- Zeno of Citium founds the Stoic school of philosophy c. 300 BCE.
- BEROSSUS immigrates from Mesopotamia and sets up a school for astrology on the Greek island of Kos in the early third century BCE.

Second Century BCE

- Depictions of the zodiac begin appearing in Egyptian temples c. 200 BCE.
- A mechanical device for calculating planetary positions known as the Antikythera Mechanism is currently thought to have been constructed sometime around 200 BCE (Carman and Evans, "On the epoch of the Antikythera mechanism").
- The foundational texts attributed to HERMES TRISMEGISTUS, ASCLEPIUS, NECHEPSO, and PETOSIRIS are probably written around the late second or early first century BCE.

First Century BCE

- The last cuneiform and the first Greek birth charts appear around the middle of the first century BCE.
- Julius Caesar is assassinated in 44 BCE. The era of the Roman Empire begins, and Caesar's nephew Octavian becomes the first emperor, known as Augustus.
- Rome annexes Egypt and the Ptolemaic dynasty comes to an end with the death of Cleopatra in 30 BCE.

- **TIMAEUS** writes a text which cites Hermes Trismegistus on the topic of the advantageous places in the late first century BCE or early first century CE.

- **TEUCER OF BABYLON** writes a text that deals with the planets, the signs, and co-rising stars, either around the late first century BCE or early first century CE.

First Century CE

- **THRASYLLUS** becomes the personal astrologer of the Emperor Tiberius prior to 2 CE, and writes an astrological manual titled *The Tablet* (*Pinax*) sometime before his death in 36 CE.

- **MANILIUS** writes his *Astronomica* within a decade or so before or after the death of Augustus in 14 CE.

- **BALBILLUS**, who is likely Thrasyllus' son, takes over his father's position in the Roman imperial court. He served the emperors Claudius, Nero, and Vespasian.

- **CRITODEMUS** writes a work known as the *Vision* and another named *The Tablet* around the early first century.

- **ABRAHAM** has a work attributed to him that covers the lots and zodiacal releasing.

- **ZOROASTER** has a few astrological works attributed to him by the first century.

- **SERAPIO OF ALEXANDRIA** writes on inceptional astrology and other topics.

- **ANTIOCHUS OF ATHENS** writes a book of definitions of astrological concepts, probably around the second half of the first century CE.

- **DOROTHEUS OF SIDON** writes a five-book instructional poem on astrology around the last quarter of the first century.

- **ANUBIO** writes an instructional poem on astrology probably around the late first or early second century CE.

Second Century CE

- **MANETHO** writes his *Apotelesmatika* sometime in the early second century. He was born May 27/8, 80 CE. The text was expanded in later centuries.

- **MICHIGAN PAPYRUS** is written sometime around the second century.

- **YAVANEŚVARA** translates the original Greek text of the *Yavanajātaka* into Sanskrit in 149/150 CE, according to Pingree.

- **CLAUDIUS PTOLEMY** writes the *Tetrabiblos* around the mid-second century.

- **VETTIUS VALENS** writes a series of books which were compiled as his *Anthology* around the third quarter of the second century. Born February 8, 120 CE.

- ANTIGONUS OF NICAEA writes a work that included examples of eminent nativities, such as the Emperor Hadrian, sometime around the late second or early third century.

Third Century CE

- SPHUJIDHVAJA versifies the *Yavanajātaka* in 269/70 CE, according to Pingree.
- PORPHYRY OF TYRE writes an *Introduction* to Ptolemy's *Tetrabiblos* probably sometime during the late third century, largely drawing on Antiochus.

Fourth Century CE

- Emperor Constantine legalizes Christianity in the Roman Empire in 313 CE.
- Constantine transfers the capital of the Roman Empire from Rome to Byzantium in 330 AD. It becomes known as Constantinople (modern-day Istanbul, Turkey).
- FIRMICUS MATERNUS writes the *Mathesis* in the middle of the fourth century.
- PAULUS OF ALEXANDRIA writes his *Introduction* in the year 378.
- ANONYMOUS OF 379 writes a work on the fixed stars in Rome in the year 379.
- MAXIMUS writes *On Inceptions* sometime around the fourth or fifth century CE.
- Stricter edicts outlawing the practice of astrology in the Roman Empire are issued in 357, 409, and 425 CE.

Fifth Century CE

- HEPHAESTIO OF THEBES writes his *Apotelesmatika* in Egypt sometime in the early fifth century. He was born November 26, 380.
- The city of Rome is sacked by the Visigoths in the year 410.
- HYPATIA OF ALEXANDRIA is murdered by a Christian mob in the year 415.
- The Emperor of the Western Roman Empire, Romulus Augustulus, is deposed in 476 CE. This traditionally marks the end of the Western Roman Empire.

Sixth Century CE

- JULIAN OF LAODICEA writes a work on inceptional astrology around 500 CE.
- Justinian, the Emperor of the Eastern Roman (Byzantine) Empire, closes the philosophical schools in Athens by banning the teaching of "pagan" philosophy in the year 529 CE.
- In the mid-sixth century, astrology flourishes in the court of the Sassanian Persian king, Kusrō Anūshirwān.

- **OLYMPIODORUS THE YOUNGER** produces a commentary on Paulus's *Introduction* in Alexandria in the summer of 564 CE.

Seventh Century CE

- **RHETORIUS OF EGYPT** assembles his *Compendium* either in the early sixth or early seventh century CE. He is the last major Hellenistic astrologer.
- Egypt is invaded by the Islamic Empire in 639, and is no longer under the control of the Greek-speaking Eastern Roman (Byzantine) Empire. This essentially marks the end of the Hellenistic astrological tradition.

Eighth Century CE

- The Medieval astrological tradition begins in the latter part of the eighth century, and flourishes in Baghdad under the Abbasid Caliphate. Works by earlier astrologers such as Dorotheus, Valens, and Rhetorius are translated into Arabic.
- Astrologers such as Theophilus of Edessa, Māshā'allāh, and Sahl ibn Bishr write some of the foundational texts of the Medieval tradition in the late eighth and early ninth century.

GLOSSARY

This glossary provides definitions for some of the major technical terms used in this book. Where relevant, I will provide the original Greek terminology. In other instances I will simply define the terms and phrases used in this work regardless of whether they have a precise equivalent in the Hellenistic texts. This glossary builds on and is partially indebted to important work done in defining Hellenistic technical terms in works such as Neugebauer and van Hoesen, *Greek Horoscopes*, pp. 2–13, Schmidt and Hand, *Project Hindsight Companion to the Greek Track*, Bezza, "Per un lessico astrologico: glossario dei termini tecnici dell'*Isagoge* di Paolo d'Alessandria," and Schmidt, *Kepler College Sourcebook*, pp. 23–38. More extensive entries for many of these terms can be found on my websites.[1]

adherence: *kollēsis*. An applying bodily "conjunction" within three degrees for planets, or thirteen degrees for the Moon. The two planets are said to be in an "adherence" or "conjoining."

advantageous: *chrēmatistikos*. The advantageous places are typically defined either as (1) the places that are configured to the rising sign according to a sign-based aspect in a chart, or (2) the places that are located closer to the four angles and which are thus "busy." When a planet is not located in one of these places it is said to be "disadvantageous." See also the entries for "busy" and *chrēmatistikos*.

angle: *kentron*. Usually one of the four angular places: first, fourth, seventh, and tenth. Alternatively, the term sometimes refers to one of the four angular degrees: Hour-Marker/Ascendant, Midheaven, Descendant, and Imum Coeli (IC). The angles are also known as "pivots" or "centers."

application: *sunaphē*. When two planets are still in the process of forming or moving towards an exact degree-based aspect, as opposed to moving away from each other in a "separation" (*aporroia*). For the more restrictive use of the term *sunaphē*, see the entry for "engagement."

Ascendant: *Hōroskopos*. Either the degree of the ecliptic that intersects the eastern horizon, or the entire zodiacal sign rising over the eastern horizon in a given chart. Sometimes refers to the first place in general, or the first whole sign house. More commonly referred to as the "Hour-Marker" in the texts.

ascending node: *anabibazō*. The north node of the Moon.

---

[1] *The Astrology Dictionary* (www.theastrologydictionary.com) and *The Hellenistic Astrology Website* (www.hellenisticastrology.com).

assembly: *sunodos.* An applying bodily conjunction that is more than three degrees from exact but less than fifteen degrees.

aversion: *apostrophē.* Planets that are in signs that are not configured with each other through a recognized "aspect" are said to be in aversion, which means to be "turned away" from each other. This occurs when planets are in signs that correspond with what modern astrologers call the semi-sextile or inconjunct/quincunx. Planets that are in these signs cannot see each other, and thus are not able to form a relationship.

bad places: the four places that are in aversion to the rising sign, which are the second, sixth, eighth, and twelfth. The fact that they are unconnected with the rising sign often results in negative or difficult significations being attributed to these places.

benefic: *agathopoios.* A planet that promotes good things. Usually this refers to the planets Venus and Jupiter, the two benefics. In some texts other planets such as the Sun, Moon, or Mercury are also categorized as benefics, or can become functionally benefic depending on their condition or function in the chart.

bodily conjunction: When two planets are in a conjunction with each other either in the same sign or close to the same degree, so that the "bodies" of the two planets are in close physical proximity in the zodiac. The phrase is sometimes used to distinguish between a "figural conjunction," which is when two planets are forming an exact aspect such as a sextile, square, trine, or opposition, since the term *sunaphē* can mean both "application" or "conjunction."

bonification: from *agathunō.* Specific conditions whereby the benefic planets are capable of affirming or improving the significations of other planets.

bounds: *horia.* Uneven subdivisions of the zodiacal signs, which are each ruled by one of the planets. More commonly known as the "terms" in Renaissance astrology, or sometimes as "confines" or "boundaries." The most common set of bounds in the Hellenistic tradition is the Egyptian system, which only assigns bounds to five of the planets and excludes the Sun and Moon.

busy: see *chrēmatistikos.*

center: *kentron.* See angle.

Chaldean Order: An ordering or sequence of the planets from slowest to fastest: Saturn, Jupiter, Mars, Sun, Venus, Mercury, Moon. In the Hellenistic tradition this is usually called the "seven zone system" or the "order of the seven-zoned sphere," although Macrobius calls it "the Chaldean system," and later astrologers seemed to have followed this by referring to it as Chaldean order. In some modern discussions it is also called "Ptolemaic order."

chariot: *lampanē.* A planet is said to be in its chariot when it is in its domicile, exaltation, or bounds. Porphyry adds by triplicity as well. It is primarily mentioned in the texts as a mitigating condition for planets that are under the beams, so that they are protected from the harsh rays of the Sun.

chrēmatistikos: An important Greek technical term that has the dual meaning of "advantageous" and "busy." When it is used to refer to places that are advantageous for the native, it usually refers to the places that are configured to the rising sign, using the whole sign system. When a planet is not in one of these places it is said to be "disadvantageous" or "unadvantageous" (*achrēmatistos*). However, it is more commonly used to describe how active the planets are and whether they are "busy" or not, which is tied in to the concept of angularity. Planets that are closer to either an angular whole sign place or to the exact degrees of the angles are said to be busy, while planets that are in declining places are said to be not busy. Alternatively, the planets could also be called "energetic" versus "unenergetic," or "operative" versus "inoperative."

Co-Master of the Nativity: *sunoikodespotēs.* Or "Joint Master of the Nativity." Additional overall ruler of the nativity mentioned by some sources, in addition to the Master of the Nativity.

configuration: *schēmatismos.* When planets occupy geometrical intervals either by sign or by degree in accordance with one of the five recognized "configurations," they are able to form relationships. Configuration is the generic geometical term used to refer to what modern astrologers call an "aspect." The recognized configurations are the conjunction, sextile, square, trine, and opposition. See also the entry for "witnessing."

conjunction: When planets are either occupying the same zodiacal sign or are around the same degree of the zodiac. The sign-based version is more commonly referred to as "copresence."

containment: *perischesis.* When a planet is in a sign that is surrounded by the sign-based rays of another planet, with no other planets sending in an interposing sign-based ray to the sign of the planet that is being surrounded. This is the sign-based version of the concept of "enclosure."

contrary to the sect: *para tēn hairesin.* When a planet is placed in a chart that is opposite to its own preferred sect. This occurs when the diurnal planets (Sun, Jupiter, or Saturn) are placed in a night chart, or when the nocturnal planets (Moon, Venus, or Mars) are placed in a day chart. For example, Saturn in a night chart is said to be "contrary to the sect."

copresence: *sumparousia.* When two planets are present together in the same sign. What modern astrologers would call a sign-based conjunction.

counteraction: *antanalusis*. Defined in Antiochus as either (1) when a planet is in the domicile or exaltation of another planet that is contrary to its own sect; or, more commonly, (2) when a planet is well-situated in a chart but its domicile lord is poorly situated.

decan: *dekanos*. Ten-degree subdivisions of each of the signs of the zodiac into three parts, resulting in thirty-six subdivisions or decans. They are also sometimes referred to as the "faces."

decline: *apoklima*. One of the four declining places, which are the third, sixth, ninth, and twelfth. The declines precede the angles in the order of the angular triads. Equivalent to what modern astrologers call a "cadent" house.

depression: *tapeinōma*. The sign opposite to a planet's exaltation. More commonly known in modern astrology as a planet's "fall." The depression of the Sun is Libra, of the Moon is Scorpio, Mercury is Pisces, Venus is Virgo, Mars is Cancer, Jupiter is Capricorn, and Saturn is Aries.

Descendant. The degree of the ecliptic that intersects the western horizon, where the Sun and other planets set each day. This is the degree opposite to the Ascendant. More commonly known as the "setting" in the texts. See the entry for "setting (place)."

descending node: *katabibazō*. The south node of the Moon.

diameter: *diametros*. Standard term for the configuration or aspect known as the "opposition," which is when planets are in zodiacal signs that are opposite, or 180° apart.

disadvantageous: *achrēmatistos*. See entry for "advantageous."

domicile: *oikos*. A sign of the zodiac that acts as the home or dwelling place of a planet. For example, the Moon has its domicile in Cancer, the Sun in Leo, Mercury in Gemini and Virgo, Venus in Taurus and Libra, Mars in Aries and Scorpio, Jupiter in Pisces and Sagittarius, Saturn in Aquarius and Capricorn.

domicile lord: *oikodespotēs*. A planet is said to be the ruler, lord, or master of the zodiacal sign that is its domicile. It both carries out the duties of that sign when it is placed in other parts of the chart, and also has some say in the affairs of any planets placed in its domicile, through the guest-host relationship.

domination: *epidekateia*. A planet that is in the tenth sign relative to another planet is said to "dominate" that planet, or to be "upon the tenth." It can be either a positive or negative condition depending on whether a benefic or malefic is in the superior position. Domination is a particularly powerful form of "overcoming."

double-bodied: *disōma*. The quadruplicity of zodiacal signs that includes Gemini, Virgo, Sagittarius, and Pisces. Referred to in modern astrology as the four "mutable" signs. Can also be called "bicorporeal."

exchange: *enallassō.* Typically when two planets are in each other's domiciles, such as for example when Venus is in Gemini and Mercury is in Libra, the two would be exchanging signs or exchanging domiciles. Also sometimes said of planets that are exchanging bounds. This is essentially the Hellenistic precursor to the medieval and modern concept of mutual reception.

enclosure: *emperischesis.* Either (1) when the degree-based rays of two planets land on either side of a third planet, within seven degrees on each side, with no other planet sending in "intervening" rays within the seven degrees on each side, or (2) when two planets are in close bodily proximity to a third planet (conjunction), with one on each side, with no other planets sending in intervening rays in the interval between them. This is the degree-based version of the concept known as "containment." Equivalent to Medieval "besiegement."

energetic: see *chrēmatistikos.*

engagement: *sunaphē.* An applying configuration between two planets, within three degrees for planets or thirteen degrees for the Moon. The two planets are said to be "engaged." Alternatively, the term is sometimes used in a generic sense when two planets move towards each other in an "application," as opposed to moving away from each other in a "separation" (*aporroia*), without reference to any degree range. See also "application."

exaltation: *hupsōma.* Signs of the zodiac in which the planets are thought to be "raised up" in a positive sense, opposite to the signs in which they are said to be "depressed." The Sun has its exaltation in Aries, the Moon in Taurus, Saturn in Libra, Jupiter in Cancer, Mars in Capricorn, Venus in Pisces, and Mercury in Virgo.

face: *prosōpon.* See decan.

fixed (sign): *stereon.* The four fixed or solid zodiacal signs are Taurus, Leo, Scorpio, and Aquarius.

good places: The places that are configured to the rising sign or first place, which are generally seen as positive or supportive of the native. This includes the third, fourth, fifth, seventh, ninth, tenth, and eleventh places. See also "bad places."

hexagon: *hexagōnos.* A configuration or aspect that connects planets that are either three signs apart, or separated by sixty degrees. In this work we generally use the modern convention of referring to this configuration as a "sextile."

Hour-Marker: *Hōroskopos.* Either the degree of the Ascendant or the entire zodiacal sign rising over the eastern horizon in a given chart. Sometimes refers to the first place in general, or the first whole sign house. The degree-based version is known as the "Ascendant" in modern astrology.

house: the modern term for what the Hellenistic astrologers usually refer to as a "place" (*topos*). See the entry for "place."

hurling a ray: Usually an aspect cast by a planet backwards in zodiacal order. See "striking with a ray."

IC. Abbreviation for *Imum Coeli*.

Imum Coeli. Modern term used to refer to what in the Hellenistic tradition would either be the fourth whole sign place, or to the exact degree opposite to the degree of the Midheaven. See "subterraneous."

inception: *katarchē*. The symbolic beginning of an event or undertaking, in which an astrological chart is cast in order to determine the outcome. Usually used within the context of inceptional or electional astrology to refer to the commencement of the subject under consideration.

inceptional astrology: from *katarchē*. A branch of astrology that involves casting a chart for the moment that something begins in order to determine its quality and outcome. Includes what is referred to in later traditions as electional astrology.

intervention: *mesembolēsis*. When a planet intervenes either bodily or by sending in a ray that breaks up a containment or enclosure, or one that interferes in the completion of an adherence or engagement between two planets.

joy: *chara*. Each planet is said to have its joy in one of the twelve places. Mercury has its joy in the first place, the Moon in the third, Venus in the fifth, Mars in the sixth, the Sun in the ninth, Jupiter in the eleventh, and Saturn in the twelfth.

left: *euōnumos*. Refers to an aspect cast to the "left" side of a planet, which goes forward from the planet in zodiacal order. See entry for "right."

like-engirding: *homozōnia*. Signs that share the same domicile lord even though they are otherwise in aversion according to the standard aspects, such as Aries and Scorpio, Taurus and Libra, and Capricorn and Aquarius.

lord/lady: *kurios/kuria*. A planet is usually said to be the lord or lady of a sign when it rules that zodiacal sign according to the domicile assignments. In some instances, the term lord can be used more generally in order to refer to other forms of rulership as well, such as rulership by triplicity or bound.

Lord of the Nativity: *kurios geneseōs*. One of the important rulers of the nativity, although apparently not mentioned as frequently as the Master of the Nativity. See the entry for the Master of the Nativity.

lot: *klēros*. A mathematical point in a chart that is usually derived by measuring the distance between two planets or points and then measuring the same distance from the degree of the Ascendant. This acts as a sensitive point in the chart that imports additional significations into whatever zodiacal sign it falls.

luminary: *phōta.* The Sun and Moon are known as the two luminaries or lights.

malefic: *kakopoios.* A planet that promotes bad things. Usually this refers to the planets Mars and Saturn, the two malefics. In some texts, other planets can act as functional malefics when they do negative things.

maltreatment: *kakōsis.* Specific conditions whereby the malefic planets are capable of negating or corrupting the significations of other planets.

master: *despotēs.* A general term that is occasionally used to refer to the ruler or lord of a sign, especially the domicile lord.

Master of the Nativity: *oikodespotēs geneseōs.* Usually considered to be the overall ruler of the chart, and sometimes used in length of life calculations. It is usually one of the rulers of the Predominator. Porphyry and Iamblichus say that some use it to find the native's *daimōn* or guardian spirit (Iamblichus, *On the Mysteries*, 9: 3). See Porphyry, *Introduction*, 30, for more information.

MC. Abbreviation for *Medium Coeli*, which is Latin for "Midheaven."

Midheaven: *mesouranēma.* Usually refers to the tenth sign relative to the rising sign, or in other words the tenth place in the whole sign system. Sometimes it can also be used to refer to the degree of the meridian, which is the degree of the quadrant Midheaven, or to the nonagesimal, which is the degree of the equal house Midheaven.

monomoiria: *monomoiria.* A system for assigning planetary rulership to each individual degree of the zodiac. See Paulus, *Introduction*, 32.

movable (sign): *tropika.* The four movable zodiacal signs are Aries, Cancer, Libra, and Capricorn. Equivalent to the "cardinal" signs in modern astrology. More commonly translated as "tropical" signs. Sometimes the tropical signs are restricted to just Cancer and Capricorn in the texts.

mutual reception. When two planets are in each other's domiciles and ideally are configured to each other through one of the recognized aspects. See also "reception" and "exchange."

nativity: *genesis.* Commonly used to refer to the birth chart of the native, or sometimes to the native's entire life in a more general sense.

neighboring: *homorēsis.* Either (1) when two planets are in an applying bodily conjunction within three degrees (adherence) while also being in the bounds of the same planet, or (2) when two planets are in different signs of the zodiac and are in a sign-based configuration while being in the bounds of the same planet. Defined in Porphyry, *Introduction*, 22.

of the sect: *tēs haireseōs.* When a planet is in a chart that matches its preferred sect, it is said to be "of the sect" or "belonging to the sect." This occurs when the Sun, Jupiter, or Saturn are in a day chart, or when the Moon, Venus, or Mars are in a night chart.

operative: see *chrēmatistikos*.

opposition: *diametros*. A configuration or aspect that connects planets that are either seven signs apart, or are separated by 180 degrees. Usually referred to as the "diameter" configuration in the texts.

overcoming: *kathuperterēsis*. When two planets are configured, the planet that is earlier in the order of signs "overcomes," "prevails," or has "superiority" over the planet that is later in the order of signs. The earlier planet, which is said to be on the right side, is in the "superior" position over the planet on the left.

passing by: *parallagē*. Occurs when the ray of one planet "passes by" the body of another planet.

pivot: *kentron*. One of the four angular or pivotal places: first, fourth, seventh, and tenth. Sometimes refers to the angular degrees, such as the Hour-Marker, Midheaven, Descendant, and Imum Coeli. See also "angle."

place: *topos*. One of the twelve regions or sectors in a chart that are connected with the diurnal rotation of the planets. The places are numbered successively starting with the rising sign or Hour-Marker. Equivalent to what modern astrologers call a "house."

post-ascension: *epanaphora*. A place that rises up after an angular place: the second, fifth, eighth, and eleventh places. More commonly known as a "succedent" house in modern astrology. See also "succedent."

pre-ascension: *proanaphora*. Occasionally used to refer to the four declining places, since they ascend prior to the signs that currently occupy the angular places in a chart. See also "decline."

Predominator: *epikratētōr*. A well-situated planet that is capable of partially representing the life force of the native, especially in the length of life technique. Also plays a special role in determining the Master of the Nativity.

profection. Derived from the Latin term *profectio*, which was used in the Medieval period to describe the process of "advancing" a significator through the chart at a certain rate. We use it here within the context of techniques such as annual profections in order to describe the process of "departing" from the rising sign and "advancing" from the starting point at the rate of one sign per year. Can also be used to refer to other rates such as monthly and daily profections.

reception. Used here to describe what happens when one planet receives another into its domicile, especially when one planet is in the domicile of another and the two are configured through one of the recognized aspects.

releasing: *aphesis*. The process of selecting a significator in a natal chart and allowing it to move around the chart at a certain rate, thus "releasing" it from its fixed position.

right: *dexios*. Usually said in reference to configurations on the right or left side of a planet. Anything that is earlier in zodiacal order relative to a specific planet is said to be on the planet's right side, while anything that is later is on the left side.

running in the void: *kenodromia*. When the Moon does not complete an exact bodily conjunction or degree-based configuration with any other planets within the next thirty degrees, regardless of sign boundaries. The origin of the modern concept of "void of course."

scrutinize: *katopteuō*. A close degree-based configuration, as opposed to a sign-based one.

sect: *hairesis*. The distinction between day charts and night charts, as well as between a team of day planets and night planets. If a person was born during the day then the sect of the chart is diurnal, while if they were born at night the sect is nocturnal. The diurnal sect of planets is comprised of the Sun, Jupiter, and Saturn, while the nocturnal sect of planets consists of the Moon, Venus, and Mars. Mercury is neutral, and capable of joining either sect depending on its condition in the chart.

sect light. The luminary that is of the sect in favor in a given chart. This would be the Sun in a day chart, or the Moon in a night chart.

separation: *aporroia*. When a planet begins moving away from either an exact bodily conjunction or an exact configuration ("aspect"). Known as a "separating aspect" in modern astrology. This is the opposite of the condition known as application, which is when a conjunction or configuration is still forming.

setting (place): *dusis*. Typically refers to the seventh place, which is the seventh sign relative to the rising sign in the whole sign system. In some instances, it can refer to the actual degree that is opposite to the Hour-Marker/Ascendant, which is known in modern astrology as the degree of the Descendant. Not to be confused with the concept of "setting" under the beams of the Sun.

sextile: *hexagōnos*. A configuration or aspect that connects planets that are either three signs apart, or separated by sixty degrees. Usually referred to as the "hexagon" configuration in the texts.

sign: *zōidion*. One of the twelve signs of the zodiac, which are thirty-degree segments of the ecliptic.

spear-bearing: *doruphoria*. Three specific conditions whereby certain planets in the chart are said to act as "guardians," "bodyguards," or "spear-bearers" for other planets, particularly the luminaries. These conditions indicate eminence, and possibly serve a protective function in a nativity. I was unable to address the topic in this book, but see Porphyry, *Introduction*, 29, for more information, as well as Denningmann, *Die astrologische Lehre der Doryphorie.*

square: *tetragonōs.* A configuration or aspect that connects planets that are either four signs apart, or separated by ninety degrees. Usually referred to as the "tetragon" configuration in the texts.

striking with a ray: *aktinobolia.* Also known as "hurling a ray." Either (1) in reference to an aspect cast from a planet that goes backwards in the order of signs, which is to the right side of the planet, or (2) a degree-based aspect cast backwards in the order of signs so as to strike another planet with that ray. A three-degree "orb" may be implied for the second type, and an applying configuration that is about to be completed is probably the ideal scenario.

subterraneous (place): *hupogeion.* Typically refers to the fourth place, which is the fourth sign relative to the rising sign in the whole sign system. In some instances it can refer to the actual degree that is opposite to the degree of the Midheaven, which is known as the *Imum Coeli* or IC in modern astrology.

succedent: *epanaphora.* A place that rises up after an angular place. Commonly used to refer to the second, fifth, eighth, and eleventh places. Equivalent to a "succedent" house in modern astrology. Also sometimes translated more literally as "post-ascension."

terms: *horia.* See "bounds."

testimony: *epimarturia.* See entry for "witnessing."

time-lord: *chronokratōr.* A planet that has become activated in a person's chart for a certain period of time, according to one of several timing techniques.

transit: *epembasis.* When a planet in the sky passes over or passes through a certain part of the chart. Usually it is a measurement of where the planets will be in the future relative to where they were in the birth chart.

trine: *trigōnon.* One of the standard geometrical configurations or "aspects" between planets, when they are either five signs apart or have 120 degrees separating them. Also known as a "triangle" or "trigon."

triplicity: *trigōnon.* A grouping of three signs of the zodiac that share similar qualities. There are four sets of three "triplicities" in the zodiacal signs. According to some authors, each triplicity is associated with one of the four classical elements: fire, earth, air, water. The same Greek term is used to refer to the trine aspect, although the two are conceptually distinct.

tropical (sign): *tropika.* Sometimes used in the texts to refer to the two signs that contain the tropics, Cancer and Capricorn, although more commonly used to refer to all four of what are called the "movable" signs in this work: Aries, Cancer, Libra, and Capricorn. See "movable."

twelfth-part: *dōdekatemorion.* Sometimes used as a synonym for *zōidion* in order to refer to an entire sign of the zodiac, insomuch as it is a division of the ecliptic into twelve parts. In other instances it is used to refer to a subdivision of an individual sign of the zodiac into twelve smaller segments.

under the beams: *hupaugos.* When a planet is within fifteen degrees of an exact bodily conjunction with the Sun it is said to be under the beams of the Sun.

upon the tenth: *epidekateia.* To be upon the tenth sign relative to another planet, which is the same as being in a sign-based square on the right side. See entries for "domination" and "overcoming."

void of course: see "running in the void."

witnessing: *epimarturia.* The basic term for a configuration, or what modern astrologers call an "aspect." When planets are in signs that share an affinity they are able to "witness" each other. Also known as "testimony."

zōidion: The Greek term for a "sign" of the zodiac. The plural is *zōidia.*

ABBREVIATIONS

This table contains a list of abbreviations that I have used throughout this work, either to refer to specific astrological texts and authors, or for frequently cited reference works. I have adopted shortened naming conventions for most of the major astrological authors; the corresponding critical edition of the Greek or Latin text is usually the primary citation in the table below, followed by references to some of the different translations cited. The full entry for each citation is listed in the bibliography.

Anonymous of 379, *Fixed Stars*	Edited in CCAG 5, 1, pp. 194–212. Trans. Schmidt = Anonymous of 379, *The Treatise on the Bright Fixed Stars*, trans. Schmidt, ed. Hand.
Antiochus, *Summary*	Edited in CCAG 8, 3, pp. 111–119. Trans. George = Antiochus, *Summary*, trans. Demetra George, 2010, unpublished.
	Trans. Schmidt = Schmidt, *Definitions and Foundations*.
Anubio, *Carmen*	Anubio, *Carmen Astrologicum Elegiacum*, ed. Obbink.
BDAG	*A Greek-English Lexicon of the New Testament and Other Early Christian Literature*, ed. Danker et al.
CCAG	*Catalogus Codicum Astrologorum Graecorum*, ed. Cumont et al.
Corpus Hermeticum	Hermès Trismégiste, *Corpus Hermeticum*, ed. Nock and Festugière.
Dorotheus, *Carmen*	Dorotheus of Sidon, *Dorothei Sidonii Carmen Astrologicum*, ed. and trans. Pingree, 1976.
Dorotheus, *Excerpts*	Vaticanus Graecus 1056, ff. 238–41, edited in: *The Liber Aristotilis of Hugo of Santalla*, ed. Burnett and Pingree, pp. 204–214.
	Trans. Gramaglia = Dorotheus, *Excerpts*, trans. Eduardo Gramaglia, ed. and comm. Benjamin Dykes, 2013, unpublished. For a partial translation see Hephaistion of Thebes, *Apotelesmatics, Book III*, trans. Gramaglia, ed. Dykes, pp. 147–156. A complete version should be available in Ben's forthcoming translation of Dorotheus.

Firmicus, *Mathesis*	Firmicus Maternus, *Iulii Firmici Materni Matheseos libri VIII*, ed. Kroll, Skutsch, and Ziegler.
	Trans. Bram = Firmicus Maternus, *Ancient Astrology, Theory and Practice: Matheseos Libri VIII*, trans. Bram.
	Trans. Holden = Firmicus Maternus, *Mathesis*, trans. Holden.
Hephaestio, *Apotelesmatika*	Hephaestio of Thebes, *Hephaestionis Thebani apotelesmaticorum libri tres*, ed. Pingree.
	Book 1, trans. Schmidt = Hephaistio of Thebes, *Apotelesmatics, Book I*, trans. Schmidt, ed. Hand.
	Book 2, trans. Schmidt = Hephaistio of Thebes, *Apotelesmatics, Book II*, trans. Schmidt.
	Book 3, trans. Gramaglia = Hephaistion of Thebes, *Apotelesmatics, Book III: On Inceptions*, trans. Gramaglia, ed. Dykes.
Liber Hermetis	*Hermetis Trismegisti de triginta sex decanis*, ed. Feraboli.
	Trans. Zoller (chapters 1–24) = Hermes Trismegistus, *Liber Hermetis, Part I*, trans. Zoller, ed. Hand.
	Trans. Zoller (chapters 25–37) = Hermes Trismegistus, *Liber Hermetis, Part II*, trans. Zoller, ed. Hand.
LSJ	*A Greek-English Lexicon*, ed. Liddell, Scott, Jones et al.
Manetho, *Apotelesmatika*	Manetho, *The Apotelesmatika of Manetho*, ed. and trans. Lopilato.
Manilius, *Astronomica*	Manilius, *Astronomica*, ed. and trans. Goold.
Michigan Papyrus	"Michigan Papyrus 149: Astrological Treatise," ed. and trans. Robbins.
Olympiodorus, *Commentary*	Olympiodorus, *Heliodori, ut dicitur, In Paulum Alexandrinum commentarium*, ed. Boer.
	Trans. Greenbaum = Paulus Alexandrinus and Olympiodorus, *Late Classical Astrology: Paulus Alexandrinus and Olympiodorus*, trans. Greenbaum, ed. Hand.

Paulus, *Introduction*

Paulus of Alexandria, *Pauli Alexandrini Elementa Apotelesmatica*, ed. Boer.

Trans. Greenbaum = Paulus Alexandrinus and Olympiodorus, *Late Classical Astrology: Paulus Alexandrinus and Olympiodorus*, trans. Greenbaum, ed. Hand.

Trans. Schmidt = Paulus Alexandrinus, *Introductory Matters*, trans. Schmidt, ed. Hand.

Pingree, *Yavanajātaka*

The Yavanajātaka of Sphujidhvaja, ed. and trans. Pingree.

Porphyry, *Introduction*

Edited in CCAG 5, 4, pp. 187–228, ed. Weinstock.

Trans. George = Porphyry, *Introduction to the Tetrabiblos of Ptolemy*, trans. Demetra George, 2010, unpublished.

Trans. Holden = Porphyry the Philosopher, *Introduction to the Tetrabiblos*, trans. Holden.

Trans. Schmidt = Schmidt, *Definitions and Foundations*.

Ptolemy, *Tetrabiblos*

Ptolemy, *Claudii Ptolemaei opera quae exstant omnia*, vol. III, 1: *ΑΠΟΤΕΛΕΣΜΑΤΙΚΑ*, ed. Hübner.

Trans. Robbins = Ptolemy, *Tetrabiblos*, ed. and trans. Robbins.

Book 1, trans. Schmidt = Ptolemy, *Tetrabiblos, Book I*, trans. Schmidt, ed. Hand.

Book 3, trans. Schmidt = Ptolemy, *Tetrabiblos, Book III*, trans. Schmidt, ed. Hand.

Book 4, trans. Schmidt = Ptolemy, *Tetrabiblos, Book IV*, trans. Schmidt.

Rhetorius, *Compendium*

Following the chapter structure first established in Pingree, "Antiochus and Rhetorius," and used in: Rhetorius the Egyptian, *Astrological Compendium*, trans. Holden. Chapters 1–53 edited in CCAG 1, pp. 140–64. Chapters 54–98, 104, and 113–17 edited in CCAG 8, 4: pp. 115–224. The rest edited in Rhetorius, *Compendium Astrologicum*, ed. Pingree and Heilen, forthcoming.

Trans. Holden = Rhetorius, *Astrological Compendium*, trans. Holden.

Sahl, *Introduction*	Sahl ibn Bishr, *Introduction*, in: *Works of Sahl and Māshā'allāh*, trans. Dykes, pp. 1–50.
Serapio, *Definitions*	Edited in CCAG 8, 4, p. 225–232.
	Trans. Gramaglia = Serapion of Alexandria, *Paranomasiai or Definitions of the Configurations of the Stars*, trans. Gramaglia, 2013.
	Trans. Holden = Porphyry, *Introduction*, trans. Holden, pp. 61–70.
Schmidt, *Definitions and Foundations*	Schmidt (ed. and trans.), *Antiochus, with Porphyry, Rhetorius, Serapio, Thrasyllus, Antigonus et al., Definitions and Foundations.*
Thrasyllus, *Summary*	Edited in CCAG 8, 3, pp. 99–101.
	Trans. Schmidt = Schmidt, *Definitions and Foundations.*
Valens, *Anthology*	Valens, *Vettii Valentis Antiocheni anthologiarum libri novem*, ed. Pingree.
	Book 1, trans. Schmidt = Valens, *The Anthology, Book I*, trans. Schmidt, ed. Hand.
	Book 2, chapters 1–37, trans. Schmidt = Valens, *The Anthology, Book II, Part 1*, trans. Schmidt, ed. Hand.
	Book 2, chapters 38–41, and book 3, trans. Schmidt = Valens, *The Anthology, Book II (concl.) & Book III*, trans. Schmidt, ed. Hand.
	Book 4, trans. Schmidt = Valens, *The Anthology, Book IV*, trans. Schmidt, ed. Hand.
	Books 5–6, trans. Schmidt = Valens, *The Anthology, Books V & VI*, trans. Schmidt, ed. Hand.
	Book 7, trans. Schmidt = Valens, *The Anthology, Book VII*, trans. Schmidt.
	Trans. Riley = Valens, *Anthologies*, trans. Riley.

BIBLIOGRAPHY

Abū 'Ali al-Khayyāt, *The Judgement of Nativities*, trans. James Holden, American Federation of Astrologers, Tempe, AZ, 1988.

Abū Ma'shar, *The Abbreviation of the Introduction to Astrology*, ed. and trans. Charles Burnett, ARHAT Publications, 1994 (rev. ed. 1997).

Adamson, Peter, "Plotinus on Astrology," *Oxford Studies in Ancient Philosophy*, vol. 35 (2008), pp. 265–91.

Adler, Ada (ed.), *Suidae Lexicon*, Teubner, Stuttgart, 5 vols., 1928–1938.

Al-Biruni, *The Book of Instruction in the Elements of the Art of Astrology*, trans. R. Ramsay Wright, Luzac & Co., London, 1934.

Alcinous, *The Handbook of Platonism*, trans. John Dillon, Clarendon Press, Oxford, 1993.

Alexander of Aphrodisias, *On Fate*, trans. R. W. Sharples, Duckworth, London, 1983.

Algra, Keimpe et al. (eds.), *The Cambridge History of Hellenistic Philosophy*, Cambridge University Press, Cambridge, 1999.

Algra, Keimpe, "Stoic Theology," in: *The Cambridge Companion to the Stoics*, ed. Brad Inwood, Cambridge University Press, Cambridge, MA, 2003, pp. 153–78.

Allatios, Leo (ed.), *Procli Diadochi Paraphrasis in Ptolemaei libros IV. De siderum effectionibus*, Elzevir, Leiden, 1635.

Amand, David, *Fatalisme et liberté dans l'antiquité grecque. Recherches sur la survivance de l'argumentation morale antifataliste de Carnéade chez les philosophes grecs et les théologiens chrétiens des quatre premiers siècles*, Bibliothèque de L'Université, Lovain, 1945.

Anonymous of 379, *The Treatise on the Bright Fixed Stars*, trans. Robert Schmidt, ed. Robert Hand, The Golden Hind Press, Berkeley Springs, WV, 1993.

Antiochus of Athens, *The Thesaurus*, trans. Robert Schmidt, ed. Robert Hand, The Golden Hind Press, Berkeley Springs, WV, 1993. [Actually a translation of Rhetorius, *Compendium*, 1–53, with other scattered chapters.]

Antiochus, *Summary*, trans. Demetra George, 2010, unpublished.

Anubio, *Anubio. Carmen Astrologicum Elegiacum*, ed. Dirk Obbink, Teubner, Munich/Leipzig, 2006.

Anubio, *Anoubion. Poème Astrologique: Témoignages et Fragments*, ed. and trans. Paul Schubert, Les Belles Lettres, Paris, 2015.

Appleby, Derek, *Horary Astrology: The Art of Astrological Divination*, 1985 (repr. Astrology Classics, Bel Air, MD, 2005).

Aratus, *Phaenomena*, trans. Douglas Kidd, Cambridge Classical Texts and Commentaries 34, Cambridge University Press, Cambridge, 1997.

Aristotle, *The Complete Works of Aristotle*, 2 vols., ed. Jonathan Barnes, Princeton University Press, Princeton, NJ, 1984.

Augustine, *City of God Against the Pagans*, 7 vols., trans. McCracken, Green et al, Loeb Classical Library, Harvard University Press, Cambridge, MA, 1957–72.

Augustine, *City of God*, trans. Henry Bettenson, Penguin, London/New York, 1972 (rev. ed. 2003).

Aulus Gellius, *Attic Nights*, trans. J. C. Rolfe, vol. 3, Loeb Classical Library 212, Harvard University Press, Cambridge, MA, 1927 (rev. ed. 1967).

Baccani, Donata, *Oroscopi greci: documentazione papirologica*, Ricerca Papirologica 1, Sicania, Messina, 1992.

Bagnall, Roger S., et al, *Consuls of the later Roman Empire*, American Philological Association, Atlanta, GA, 1987.

Bagnall, Roger S., "Alexandria: Library of Dreams," *Proceedings of the American Philosophical Society*, vol. 146, no. 4 (2002), pp. 348–362.

Bagnall, Roger S., Kai Brodersen, Craige B. Champion, Andrew Erskine, and Sabine R. Huebner (eds.), *The Encyclopedia of Ancient History*, 13 vols., Wiley-Blackwell, Malden, MA, 2012.

Baigent, Michael, *From the Omens of Babylon: Astrology and Ancient Mesopotamia*, Penguin/Arkana, London, 1994.

Barnes, T. D., "Two Senators under Constantine," *The Journal of Roman Studies*, vol. 65 (1975), pp. 40–49.

Barnes, Jonathan, *Early Greek Philosophy*, Penguin, Harmondsworth/New York, 1987.

Barton, Tamsyn, *Ancient Astrology*, Routledge, London, 1994.

Beck, Roger, "Thus Spake Not Zarathustra: Zoroastrian Pseudepigrapha of the Greco-Roman World," in: *A History of Zoroastrianism. Vol. 3: Zoroastrianism under Macedonian and Roman Rule*, ed. Mary Boyce and Frantz Grenet, Brill, Leiden, pp. 491–565.

Beck, Roger, "The Mysteries of Mithras: A New Account of Their Genesis," *The Journal of Roman Studies*, vol. 88 (1998), pp. 115–128.

Beck, Roger, *A Brief History of Ancient Astrology*, Blackwell Publishing, Malden, MA, 2007.

Beck, Roger, *The Religion of the Mithras Cult in the Roman Empire: Mysteries of the Unconquered Sun*, Oxford University Press, Oxford, 2006

Belmonte, Juan Antonio, and A. César González-García, "Nemrud Dag," in: *Handbook of Archaeoastronomy and Ethnoastronomy*, ed. Ruggles, 2015, pp. 1659–68.

Bernard, Alain, "Theon of Alexandria," in: *The Encyclopedia of Ancient Natural Scientists*, ed. Keyser and Irby-Massie, 2008, pp. 793–295.

Bernard, Alain, "The Alexandrian School: Theon of Alexandria and Hypatia," in: *The Cambridge History of Philosophy in Late Antiquity*, ed. Gerson, 2010, vol. 2, pp. 697–710.

Betz, Hans Dieter (ed.), *The Greek Magical Papyri in Translation, Including the Demotic Spells*, University of Chicago Press, Chicago, 1986 (2nd ed. rev. 1992).

Bezza, Giuseppe, *Arcana Mundi: Antologia del pensiero astrologico antico*, 2 vols., Rizzoli, Milan, 1995.

Bezza, Giuseppe, "L'astrologia greca dopo Tolemeo: Retorio," in: *Homo Mathematicus: Actas del Congreso Internacional sobre Astrólogos Griegos y Romanos (Benalmádena, 8–10 de Octubre de 2001)*, ed. Aurelio Pérez Jiménez and Raúl Caballero, Charta Antiqua, Málaga, 2002.

Bezza, Giuseppe, "Per un lessico astrologico: glossario dei termini tecnici dell'*Isagoge* di Paolo d'Alessandria," *MHNH: Revista Internacional de Investigación sobre Magia y Astrología Antiguas*, vol. 5 (2005), pp. 277–305.

Bezza, Giuseppe, "The Development of an Astrological Term – from Greek *hairesis* to Arabic *hayyiz*," *Culture and Cosmos*, vol. 11, nos. 1–2 (2007), pp. 229–260.

Bidez, Joseph, and Franz Cumont, *Les Mages Hellénisés: Zoroastre Ostanès et Hystaspe d'après la tradition grecque*, 2 vols., Les Belles Letters, Paris, 1938.

Bobzien, Susanne, *Determinism and Freedom in Stoic Philosophy*, Clarendon Press, Oxford, 2001.

Bomhard, Anne-Sophie von, *The Egyptian Calendar: A Work for Eternity*, Periplus, London, 1999.

Bomhard, Anne-Sophie von, *The Naos of the Decades: From the Observation of the Sky to Mythology and Astrology*, trans. Ludwig von Bomhard, Oxford Centre for Maritime Archaeology, University of Oxford, 2008.

Bonatti, Guido, *The Book of Astronomy*, trans. Benjamin N. Dykes, 2 vols., Cazimi Press, Golden Valley, MN, 2007.

Bos, A. P., "Supplementary Notes on the 'De mundo,'" *Hermes*, vol. 119 (1991), pp. 312–33.

Bouché-Leclercq, Auguste, *L'Astrologie grecque*, Leroux, Paris, 1899.

Bouché-Leclercq, Auguste, *L'Astrologie grecque*, trans. Lester Ness, forthcoming.

Bowser, Kenneth, *An Introduction to Western Sidereal Astrology*, American Federation of Astrologers, Tempe, AZ, 2012.

Brack-Bernsen, Lis, and Hermann Hunger, "The Babylonian Zodiac: Speculations on its Invention and Significance," *Centaurus*, vol. 41 (1999), pp. 280–292.

Bremmer, Jan N., "Foolish Egyptians: Apion and Anoubion in the Pseudo-Clementines," in: *The Wisdom of Egypt: Jewish, Early Christian, and Gnostic Essays in Honour of Gerard P. Luttikhuizen*, ed. Anthony Hilhorst and George H. van Kooten, Brill, Leiden, 2005, pp. 311–329.

Brennan, Chris, "The Katarche of Horary," National Council for Geocosmic Research *Geocosmic Journal*, Summer 2007, pp. 23–33.

Brennan, Chris, "The Theoretical Rationale Underlying the Seven Hermetic Lots," *The Tradition Journal*, no. 2 (Spring 2009), pp. 16–27.

Brennan, Chris, "Hellenistic Astrology," NCGR *Research Journal*, vol. 1, no. 1 (Summer 2010), pp. 15–24.

Brennan, Chris, "An Introduction to Hellenistic Astrology, Part 1," *The Mountain Astrologer*, no. 161 (Feb./Mar. 2012), pp. 64–75.

Brennan, Chris, "An Introduction to Hellenistic Astrology, Part 2," *The Mountain Astrologer*, no. 163 (Jun./Jul. 2012), pp. 68–80.

Brennan, Chris, "The Planetary Joys and the Origins of the Significations of the Houses and Triplicities," *ISAR International Astrologer Journal*, vol. 42, no. 1 (Apr. 2013), pp. 27–42.

Brunet, Stephen, "The Date of the First Balbillea at Ephesos," *Zeitschrift für Papyrologie und Epigraphik*, vol. 117 (1997), pp. 137–138.

Bugh, Glenn (ed.), *The Cambridge Companion to the Hellenistic World*, Cambridge University Press, Cambridge, 2006.

Burnett, Archie (ed.), *The Letters of A. E. Housman*, 2 vols., Clarendon Press, Oxford, 2007.

Burnett, Charles, and David Pingree (eds.), *The Liber Aristotilis of Hugo of Santalla*, The Warburg Institute, London, 1997.

Burnett, Charles, and Dorian Giesler Greenbaum (eds.), *The Winding Courses of the Stars: Essays in Ancient Astrology, Culture and Cosmos*, vol. 11, nos. 1 and 2 (2007).

Burnett, Charles, "Astrological Translations in Byzantium," in: *Actes du Symposium international Le Livre. La Roumanie. L'Europe. 4ème édition, 20–23 septembre 2011, Tome III*, ed. Martin Hauser, Ioana Feodorov, Nicholas V. Sekunda, and Adrian George Dumitru, Editura Biblioteca Bucureștilor, Bucarest, 2012, pp. 178–83.

Bushkin, Henry, *Johnny Carson*, Houghton Mifflin Harcourt, Boston/New York, 2013.

Caballero Sánchez, Raúl, and Hilario Bautista Ruiz, "Una paráfrasis inédita de los Tesoros de Antíoco de Atenas: el epítome IIa. Edición crítica, traducción y notas," *MHNH: Revista Internacional de Investigación sobre Magia y Astrología Antiguas*, vol. 6 (2006), pp. 177–242.

Caballero Sánchez, Raúl, "Historia del texto del Comentario anónimo al Tetrabiblos de Tolomeo," *MHNH: Revista Internacional de Investigación sobre Magia y Astrología Antiguas*, vol. 13 (2013), pp. 77–198.

Caballero Sánchez, Raúl, "El Comentario anónimo al Tetrabiblos de Tolomeo. Edición crítica y traducción castellana de los escolios metodológicos del libro I," *MHNH: Revista Internacional de Investigación sobre Magia y Astrología Antiguas*, vol. 13 (2013), pp. 221–258.

Campion, Nicholas, "The Traditional Revival in Modern Astrology: A Preliminary History," *The Astrology Quarterly*, vol. 74, no. 1 (Winter 2003), pp. 28–38.

Campion, Nicholas, *A History of Western Astrology. Volume 1: The Ancient and Classical Worlds*, Bloomsbury, London/New York, 2008 (repr. 2012).

Campion, Nicholas, *A History of Western Astrology. Volume 2: The Medieval and Modern Worlds*, Continuum, London, 2009.

Campion, Nicholas, "More on the Transmission of the Babylonian Zodiac to Greece: The Case of the Nativity Omens and their Modern Legacy," *ARAM Periodical*, vol. 24 (2012), pp. 193–201.

Cancik, Hubert, and Helmuth Schneider (eds.), *Brill's New Pauly: Encyclopaedia of the Ancient World*, 22 vols., Brill, Leiden/Boston, 2002–2011.

Carman, Christián C., and James Evans, "On the epoch of the Antikythera mechanism and its eclipse predictor," *Archive for History of Exact Sciences*, vol. 68, no. 6 (2014), pp. 693–774.

Cassius Dio, *Dio's Roman History*, trans. Earnest Cary and Herbert Baldwin Foster, 9 vols., Loeb Classical Library, London/New York, 1914–1927.

Chaniotis, Angelos, "The Divinity of Hellenistic Rulers," in: *A Companion to the Hellenistic World*, ed. Erskine, 2003, pp. 431–445.

Charlesworth, James H., "Jewish Interest in Astrology during the Hellenistic and Roman Period," in: *Aufstieg und Niedergang der Römischen Welt* (ANRW), II.20.2, ed. W. Haase, de Gruyter, Berlin/New York, 1987, pp. 926–950.

Cole, Susan Guettel, "Greek Sanctions Against Sexual Assault," *Classical Philology*, vol. 79, no. 2 (April, 1984), pp. 97–113.

Copenhaver, Brian P. (trans.), *Hermetica*, Cambridge University Press, Cambridge, 1992.

Coppock, Austin, *36 Faces: The History, Astrology, and Magic of the Decans*, Three Hands Press, Richmond, CA, 2014.

Cornelius, Geoffrey, *The Moment of Astrology: Origins in Divination*, Penguin Arkana, London, 1994 (2nd rev. ed. Wessex Astrologer, Bournemouth, 2002).

Cicero, *On Old Age. On Friendship. On Divination*, trans. W. A. Falconer, Loeb Classical Library 154, Harvard University Press, Cambridge, MA, 1923.

Cicero, *On Divination, Book 1*, trans. David Wardle, Oxford University Press, Oxford, 2006.

Cichorius, Conrad, *Römische Studien*, Teubner, Leipzig/Berlin, 1922.

Cichorius, Conrad, "Der Astrologe Ti. Claudius Balbillus, Sohn des Thrasyllus," *Rheinisches Museum für Philologie*, vol. 76 (1927), pp. 102–105.

Clagett, Marshall, *Ancient Egyptian Science, Vol. 2: Calendars, Clocks, and Astronomy*, American Philosophical Society, Philadelphia, PA, 1995.

Cramer, Frederick H., *Astrology in Roman Law and Politics*, American Philosophical Society, Philadelphia, PA, 1954.

Cramer, Frederick H., "Review of Catalogus Codicum Astrologorum Graecorum," *Speculum*, vol. 29, no. 2, part 1 (Apr., 1954), Medieval Academy of America, pp. 257–264.

Cumont, Franz, et al (eds.), *Catalogus Codicum Astrologorum Graecorum*, 12 vols. in 20 parts, Lamertin, Brussels, 1898–1953.
— Vol. I, *Codices Florentinos*, ed. Boll, Cumont, Kroll, Olivieri, 1898.
— Vol. II, *Codices Venetos*, ed. Boll, Cumont, Kroll, Olivieri, 1900.
— Vol. III, *Codices Mediolaneses*, ed. Martini, Bassi, 1901.
— Vol. IV, *Codices Italicos praeter Florentinos, Venetos, Mediolanenses, Romanos*, ed. Bassi, Cumont, Martini, Olivieri, 1903.
— Vol. V, Part 1, *Codicum Romanorum*, ed. Cumont, Boll, 1904.
— Vol. V, Part 2, *Codicum Romanorum*, ed. Kroll, 1906.
— Vol. V, Part 3, *Codicum Romanorum*, ed. Heeg, 1910.
— Vol. V, Part 4, *Codicum Romanorum*, ed. Weinstock, Boer, 1940.
— Vol. VI, *Codices Vindobonenses*, ed. Kroll, 1903.
— Vol. VII, *Codices Germanicos*, ed. Boll, 1908.
— Vol. VIII, Part 1, *Codicum Parisinorum*, ed. Cumont, 1929.
— Vol. VIII, Part 2, *Codicum Parisinorum*, ed. Heeg, 1911.
— Vol. VIII, Part 3, *Codicum Parisinorum*, ed. Boudreaux, 1912.
— Vol. VIII, Part 4, *Codicum Parisinorum*, ed. Boudreaux, 1921.
— Vol. IX, Part 1, *Codices Britannicos*, ed. Weinstock, 1951.
— Vol. IX, Part 2, *Codices Britannicos*, ed. Weinstock, 1953.
— Vol. X, *Codices Athenienses*, ed. Delatte, 1924.
— Vol. XI, Part 1, *Codices Hispanienses*, ed. Zuretti, 1932.
— Vol. XI, Part 2, *Codices Hispanienses*, ed. Zuretti, 1934.
— Vol. XII, *Codices Rossicos*, ed. Sangin, 1936.

Cumont, Franz, *Astrology and Religion Among the Greeks and Romans*, Dover, New York, 1912 (repr. 1960).

Cumont, Franz, "Antiochus d'Athènes et Porphyre," in: *L'Annuaire de l'Institut de Philologie et d'Histoire Orientales* 2 (Mélanges Bidez), 1934, pp. 135–56.

Cumont, Franz, *L'Égypte des astrologues*, Fondation égyptologique reine Élisabeth, Brussels, 1937.

Dan, Joseph, "Three Phases in the History of the *Sefer Yezira*," *Frankfurter Judaistische Beiträge*, vol. 21 (1994), pp. 7–29.

Darrigol, Olivier, *A History of Optics: From Greek Antiquity to the Nineteenth Century*, Oxford University Press, Oxford, 2012.

Deakin, Michael, *Hypatia of Alexandria, Mathematician and Martyr*, Prometheus Books, Amherst, MA, 2007.

DeConick, April D., "From the Bowels of Hell to Draco: The Mysteries of the Peratics," in: *Mystery and Secrecy in the Nag Hammadi Collection and Other Ancient Literature: Ideas and Practices*, ed. Christian H. Bull, Liv Ingeborg Lied, and John D. Turner, Brill, Leiden/Boston, 2012, pp. 3–37.

Denningmann, Susanne, *Die astrologische Lehre der Doryphorie: Eine soziomorphe Metapher in der antiken Planetenastrologie*, De Gruyter, Berlin, 2005.

Denningmann, Susanne, "The Ambiguous Terms ἐῴα and ἑσπερία ἀνατολή, and ἐῴα and ἑσπερία δύσις," *Culture and Cosmos*, vol. 11, nos. 1 and 2 (2007), pp. 189–210.

Denzey, Nicola, "A New Star on the Horizon: Astral Christologies and Stellar Debates in Early Christian Discourse," in: *Prayer, Magic and the Stars in the Ancient and Late Antique World*, ed. Noegel, Walker, and Wheeler, 2003, pp. 207–21.

Denzey Lewis, Nicola, *Cosmology and Fate in Gnosticism and Graeco-Roman Antiquity: Under Pitiless Skies*, Nag Hammadi and Manichaean Studies 81, Brill, Leiden, 2013.

Denzey Lewis, Nicola, *Introduction to "Gnosticism": Ancient Voices, Christian Worlds*, Oxford University Press, Oxford/New York, 2013.

Dieleman, Jacco, "Stars and the Egyptian Priesthood in the Greco-Roman Period," in: *Prayer, Magic and the Stars in the Ancient and Late Antique World*, eds. Noegel, Walker, and Wheeler, 2003, pp. 137–53.

Dillon, John, *The Middle Platonists*, Cornell University Press, Ithaca, NY, 1977 (rev. ed. 1996).

Dillon, John, "Plotinus on Whether the Stars are Causes," in: *La science des cieux. Sages, mages, astrologues*, ed. Rika Gyselen, Bures-sur-Yvette (Res Orientales 12), 1999, pp. 87–92.

Dio Cassius, *Roman History*, trans. Earnest Cary and Herbert B. Foster, 9 vols., Loeb Classical Library, Harvard University Press, Cambridge, MA, 1914–1927.

Diodorus Siculus, *Library of History*, Books 1–2.34, trans. C. H. Oldfather, Loeb Classical Library 279, Harvard University Press, Cambridge, 1933.

Diogenes Laertius, *Lives of Eminent Philosophers*, trans. R. D. Hicks, 2 vols., Loeb Classical Library, Harvard University Press, Cambridge, MA, 1925 (rev. ed. 1931).

Dodge, Bayard (trans.), *The Fihrist of al-Nadim, A Tenth Century Survey of Muslim Culture*, 2 vols., Columbia University Press, New York, 1970.

Dorotheus of Sidon, *Dorothei Sidonii Carmen Astrologicum, Interpretationem arabicam in linguam anglicam versam una cum Dorothei fragmentis et graecis et latinis*, ed. and trans. David Pingree, Teubner, Leipzig, 1976.

Dorotheus of Sidon, *Carmen Astrologicum*, trans. David Pingree, Astrology Center of America, Abingdon, MD, 2005. [Republication of Pingree's 1976 English translation of Dorotheus, *Dorothei Sidonii Carmen Astrologicum*, without the Arabic text, and with an English translation of Pingree's original Latin introduction by Dorian Greenbaum.]

Dorotheus of Sidon, *Excerpts*, trans. Eduardo Gramaglia, ed. and comm. Benjamin Dykes, 2013, unpublished.

Dudley, John, *Aristotle's Concept of Chance: Accidents, Cause, Necessity, and Determinism*, State University of New York Press, Albany, 2012.

Duffett-Smith, Peter, *Practical Astronomy with Your Calculator*, Cambridge University Press, Cambridge, 3rd rev. ed. 1988.

Dykes, Benjamin N. (trans.), *Works of Sahl and Māshā'allāh*, Cazimi Press, Golden Valley, MN, 2008.

Dykes, Benjamin N. (trans. and ed.), *Persian Nativities, Volume I: Māshā'allāh and Abū 'Ali*, Cazimi Press, Minneapolis, MN, 2009.

Dykes, Benjamin N. (trans. and ed.), *Introductions to Traditional Astrology: Abu Ma'shar and al Qabisi*, Cazimi Press, Minneapolis, MN, 2010.

Dzielska, Maria, *Hypatia of Alexandria*, trans. F. Lyra, Harvard University Press, Cambridge, MA, 1995.

Edwards, Mark (trans.), *Neoplatonic Saints: The Lives of Plotinus and Proclus by Their Students*, Liverpool University Press, Liverpool, 2000.

Emilsson, Eyjólfur Kjalar, *Plotinus on Sense-Perception: A Philosophical Study*, Cambridge University Press, Cambridge, 1988.

Erskine, Andrew, "Culture and Power in Ptolemaic Egypt: The Museum and Library of Alexandria," *Greece and Rome*, vol. 42, no. 1 (Apr. 1995), pp. 38–48.

Erskine, Andrew (ed.), *A Companion to the Hellenistic World*, Blackwell, Oxford, 2003.

Evans, James, *The History and Practice of Ancient Astronomy*, Oxford University Press, Oxford/New York, 1998.

Evans, James, "The Astrologer's Apparatus: A Picture of Professional Practice in Greco-Roman Egypt," *Journal for the History of Astronomy*, vol. 35, part 1, no. 118 (2004), pp. 1–44.

Fagan, Cyril, *Zodiacs Old and New*, Llewellyn, Los Angeles, 1950.

Fagan, Cyril, *Astrological Origins*, Llewellyn, St. Paul, MN, 1971.

Feke, Jaqueline, *Ptolemy in Philosophical Context: A Study of the Relationships Between Physics, Mathematics, and Theology*, PhD diss., University of Toronto, 2009.

Feke, Jaqueline, and Alexander Jones, "Ptolemy," in: *The Cambridge History of Philosophy in Late Antiquity*, ed. Gerson2010, vol. 1, pp. 197–209.

Feraboli, Simonetta (ed.) *Hermetis Trismegisti de triginta sex decanis*, Hermes Latinus, vol. 4, part 1 = Corpus Christianorum, Continuatio Mediaevalis 144, Brepols, Turnhout, 1994.

Festugière, André-Jean, *La Révélation d'Hermès Trismégiste*, 4 vols., Lecoffre, Paris, 1944–1954.

Firmicus Maternus, *Iulii Firmici Materni Matheseos libri VIII*, ed. Wilhem Kroll, F. Skutsch, and K. Ziegler, 2 vols., Teubner, Leipzig, 1897–1913.

Firmicus Maternus, *The Error of the Pagan Religions*, trans. Clarence A. Forbes, Newman Press, New York, NY, 1970.

Firmicus Maternus, *Ancient Astrology, Theory and Practice: Matheseos Libri VIII*, trans. Jean Rhys Bram, Noyes Press, Park Ridge, NJ, 1975 (repr. Astrology Center of America, Abingdon, MD, 2005).

Firmicus Maternus, *Mathesis*, 3 vols., ed. and trans. Pierre Monat, Les Belles Lettres, Paris, 1992–1997.

Firmicus Maternus, Julius, *Mathesis*, trans. and ed. James H. Holden, American Federation of Astrologers, Tempe, AZ, 2011.

Forenbaher, Stašo, and Alexander Jones, "The Nakovana Zodiac: Fragments of an Astrologer's Board from an Illyrian-Hellenistic Cave Sanctuary," *Journal for the History of Astronomy*, vol. 42, no. 4 (Nov. 2011), pp. 425–438.

Fowden, Garth, *The Egyptian Hermes: A Historical Approach to the Late Pagan Mind*, Cambridge University Press, Cambridge, 1986.

Fox, Michael J., *Lucky Man: A Memoir*, Hyperion, New York, 2002.

Freudenthal, Gad, "The Astrologization of the Aristotelian Cosmos: Celestial Influences on the Sublunar World in Aristotle, Alexander of Aphrodisias, and Averroes," in: *New Perspectives on Aristotle's De Caelo*, ed. Alan Bowen and Christian Wildberg, Brill, Leiden/Boston, 2009, pp. 239–282.

Friedrich, Hans-Veit (ed.), *Thessalos von Tralles: griechisch und lateinisch*, Beiträge zur klassischen Philologie, 28, Meisenheim am Glan, 1968.

Gansten, Martin, "Balbillus and the Method of *aphesis*," *Greek, Roman, and Byzantine Studies*, vol. 52 (2012), pp. 587–602.

Geminos, *Geminos's Introduction to the Phenomena: A Translation and Study of a Hellenistic Survey of Astronomy*, trans. James Evans and J. Lennart Berggren, Princeton University Press, Princeton/Oxford, 2006.

George, Demetra, *The Foundation of the Astrological Art: The Opinion according to the Chaldeans*, translation of CCAG 5, 2, pp. 130–37, unpublished.

Gerson, Lloyd P. (ed.), *The Cambridge History of Philosophy in Late Antiquity*, 2 vols., Cambridge University Press, Cambridge, 2010.

Gillispie, Charles C. (ed.), *Dictionary of Scientific Biography*, 16 vols., Charles Scribner's Sons, New York, NY, 1970–1980.

Graham, Daniel W., *Aristotle's Two Systems*, Oxford University Press, Oxford, 1987.

Gramaglia, Eduardo, *Astrología Hermética: Recobrando el sistema helenístico*, Kier, Buenos Aires, 2006.

Green, Peter, *The Hellenistic Age: A Short History*, Modern Library, New York, 2007.

Green, Steven J., and Katharina Volk (eds.), *Forgotten Stars: Rediscovering Manilius' Astronomica*, Oxford University Press, Oxford/New York, 2011.

Green, Steven J., *Disclosure and Discretion in Roman Astrology: Manilius and his Augustan Contemporaries*, Oxford University Press, Oxford, 2014.

Greenbaum, Dorian Gieseler, "Calculating the Lots of Fortune and Daemon in Hellenistic Astrology," *Culture and Cosmos*, vol. 11, nos. 1 and 2 (2007), pp. 163–187.

Greenbaum, Dorian Gieseler, and Micah Ross, "The Role of Egypt in the Development of the Horoscope," in: *Egypt in Transition: Social and Religious Development of Egypt in the First Millennium BCE*, eds. Ladislav Bareš, Filip Coppens, and Květa Smoláriková, Czech Institute of Egyptology, Prague, 2010, pp. 146–182.

Grubbs, Judith Evans, and Tim Parkin (eds.), *The Oxford Handbook of Childhood and Education in the Classical World*, Oxford University Press, Oxford/New York, 2013.

Gutas, Dimitri, *Greek Thought, Arabic Culture: The Graeco-Arabic Translation Movement in Baghdad and Early 'Abbāsid Society (2nd–4th/8th–10th centuries)*, Routledge, London/New York, 1998.

Hahm, David E., *The Origins of Stoic Cosmology*, Ohio State University Press, Columbus, OH, 1977.

Hall, James, *The Sinister Side: How Left-Right Symbolism Shaped Western Art*, Oxford University Press, Oxford, 2008.

Hamilton, N. T., N. M. Swerdlow, and G. J. Toomer, "The Canobic Inscription: Ptolemy's Earliest Work" in: *From Ancient Omens to Statistical Mechanics: Essays on the Exact Sciences Presented to Asger Aaboe*, ed. J. L. Berggren and B. R. Goldstein, University Library, Copenhagen, 1987, pp. 55–73.

Hand, Robert, *Night & Day: Planetary Sect in Astrology*, ARHAT Publications, Reston, VA, 1995.

Hand, Robert, *Whole Sign Houses, the Oldest House System: An Ancient Method in Modern Application*, ARHAT Publications, Reston, VA, 2000.

Hand, Robert, "Signs as Houses (Places) in Ancient Astrology," *Culture and Cosmos*, vol. 11, nos. 1 and 2, 2007, pp. 135–162.

Hankinson, R. J., "Stoicism, Science and Divination," *Apeiron*, vol. 21, no. 2 (1988), pp. 123–160.

Harland, Philip A., "Journeys in Pursuit of Divine Wisdom: Thessalos and Other Seekers," in: *Travel and Religion in Antiquity*, ed. Philip A. Harland, Studies in Christianity and Judaism vol. 21, Wilfrid Laurier University Press, Waterloo, 2011, pp. 123–140.

Hatzimichali, Myrto, "Antiochus' biography," in: *The Philosophy of Antiochus*, ed. Sedley, 2012, pp. 9–30.

Hatzimichali, Myrto, "Ashes to Ashes? The Library of Alexandria after 48 BC," in: *Ancient Libraries*, eds. Jason König, Katerina Oikonomopoulou, and Greg Woolf, Cambridge University Press, Cambridge/New York, 2013, pp. 167–182.

Hayman, A. Peter (ed. and trans.), *Sefer Yesira: Edition, Translation and Text-Critical Commentary*, Mohr Siebeck, Tübingen, 2004.

Hegedus, Tim, *Early Christianity and Ancient Astrology*, Peter Lang, New York, 2007.

Heilen, Stephan, "The Emperor Hadrian in the Horoscopes of Antigonus of Nicaea," in: *Horoscopes and Public Spheres*, ed. Oestmann, Rutkin, and von Stuckrad, 2005, pp. 49–67.

Heilen, Stephan, "Ancient Scholars on the Horoscope of Rome," *Culture and Cosmos*, vol. 11, nos. 1 and 2 (2007), pp. 43–68.

Heilen, Stephan, "Problems in Translating Ancient Greek Astrological Texts," in: *Writings of Early Scholars in the Ancient Near East, Egypt, Rome, and Greece: Translating Ancient Scientific Texts*, ed. Annette Imhausen and Tanja Pommerening, De Gruyter, Berlin/New York, 2010, pp. 299–329.

Heilen, Stephan, "Anubio Reconsidered," *Aestimatio: Critical Reviews in the History of Science*, no. 7 (2010), pp. 127–192.

Heilen, Stephan, "Some metrical fragments from Nechepsos and Petosiris," in: *La poésie astrologique dans l'Antiquité. Textes réunis par Isabelle Boehm et Wolfgang Hübner. Actes du colloque organisé les 7 et 8 décembre 2007 par J.-H. Abry avec la collaboration d'I. Boehm*, Paris, 2011 (Collection du Centre d'Études et de Recherches sur l'Occident Romain CEROR. 38), pp. 23–93.

Heilen, Stephan, "Ptolemy's Doctrine of the Terms and its Reception," in: *Ptolemy in Perspective*, ed. Jones, 2010, pp. 45–93.

Heilen, Stephan, "Antigonos of Nicaea," in: *The Encyclopedia of Ancient History*, ed. Bagnall et al, 2012, pp. 464–465.

Heilen, Stephan, *Hadriani Genitura. Die astrologischen Fragmente des Antigonos von Nikaia*, 2 vols., De Gruyter, Berlin/Boston, 2015.

Hephaestio of Thebes, *Hephaestionis Thebani apotelesmaticorum libri tres*, ed. David Pingree, 2 vols., Teubner, Leipzig, 1973–74.

Hephaistio of Thebes, *Apotelesmatics, Book I*, trans. Robert Schmidt, ed. Robert Hand, The Golden Hind Press, Berkeley Springs, WV, 1994.

Hephaistio of Thebes, *Apotelesmatics, Book II*, trans. Robert H. Schmidt, The Golden Hind Press, Cumberland, MD, 1998.

Hephaistion of Thebes, *Apotelesmatics, Book III: On Inceptions*, trans. Eduardo J. Gramaglia, ed. Benjamin N. Dykes, Cazimi Press, Minneapolis, MN, 2013.

Hermann of Carinthia, *The Search of the Heart: Consultation Charts, Interpreting Thoughts, and Calculating Victors in Traditional Astrology*, trans. and ed. Benjamin N. Dykes, Cazimi Press, Minneapolis, MN, 2011.

Hermès Trismégiste, *Corpus Hermeticum*, ed. A. D. Nock and A. J. Festugière, 4 vols., Les Belles Lettres, Paris, 1946–54.

Hermes Trismegistus, *Liber Hermetis, Part I*, trans. Robert Zoller, ed. Robert Hand, The Golden Hind Press, Berkeley Springs, WV, 1993.

Hermes Trismegistus, *Liber Hermetis, Part II*, trans. Robert Zoller, ed. Robert Hand, The Golden Hind Press, Berkeley Springs, WV, 1993.

Holden, James Herschel, "Ancient House Division," American Federation of Astrologers *Journal of Research*, vol. 1, no. 1 (August 1982), Tempe, AZ, pp. 19–29.

Holden, James Herschel, "The Horoscope of Cronamon," *American Federation of Astrologers' Journal of Research*, vol. 5, no. 1 (1989), pp. 7–10.

Holden, James Herschel, "House Division II," American Federation of Astrologers *Journal of Research*, vol. 5, no. 2 (1989), pp. 33–51.

Holden, James Herschel, "The Classical Zodiac," American Federation of Astrologers *Journal of Research*, vol. 7, no. 2 (Summer 1995).

Holden, James H., "The Sign-House System of House Division," American Federation of Astrologers periodical *Today's Astrologer*, vol. 62, no. 12 (Nov. 11, 2000), pp. 400–403.

Holden, James H., *A History of Horoscopic Astrology*, American Federation of Astrologers, Tempe, AZ, 1996 (3rd rev. ed. 2013).

Holden, James Herschel, *Biographical Dictionary of Western Astrologers*, American Federation of Astrologers, Tempe, AZ, 2012.

Holden, Ralph William, *The Elements of House Division*, Camelot Press, Southhampton, 1977.

Houck, Richard, *The Astrology of Death*, Groundswell Press, Gaithersburg, MD, 1994.

Houlding, Deborah, *The Houses: Temples of the Sky*, Ascella, 1998 (2nd ed. rev. The Wessex Astrologer, Bournemouth, 2006).

Houlding, Deborah, "The Transmission of Ptolemy's Terms: An Historical Overview, Comparison and Interpretation," *Culture and Cosmos*, vol. 11, nos. 1–2 (2007), pp. 261–307.

Hübner, Wolfgang, "Manilio e Teucro di Babilonia," in: *Manilio fra poesia e scienza. Atti del convegno, Lecce, 14–16 maggio 1992*, ed. D. Liuzzi, Galatina, 1993, pp. 21–40.

Hübner, Wolfgang, *Raum, Zeit und soziales Rollenspiel der vier Kardinalpunkte in der antiken Katarchenhoroskopie*, K. G. Saur, Munich/Leipzig, 2003.

Hübner, Wolfgang, "Maximus," in *Brill's New Pauly: Encyclopaedia of the Ancient World*, ed. Cancik and Schneider, 2006.

Hübner, Wolfgang, "Timaeus," in *Brill's New Pauly: Encyclopaedia of the Ancient World*, ed. Cancik and Schneider, 2006.

Hübner, Wolfgang, "Sulla's horoscope? (Firm., Math. 6,31,1)," in: *Horoscopes and Public Spheres*, eds. Oestmann, Rutkin, and von Stuckrad, 2005, pp. 13–35.

Hübner, Wolfgang, *Manilius, Astronomica, Buch V, Sammlung wissenschaftlicher Commentare*, 2 vols., De Gruyter, Berlin/New York, 2010.

Hunger, Hermann (ed.), *Astrological Reports to Assyrian Kings*, State archives of Assyria 8, Helsinki University Press, Helsinki, 1992.

Hunger, Hermann, and David Pingree, *Astral Sciences in Mesopotamia*, Handbook of Oriental Studies: The Near and Middle East, vol. 44, Brill, Leiden/Boston, 1999.

Hypsicles, *Hypsikles: Die Aufgangszeiten der Gestirne*, ed. V. de Falco and M. Krause, Vandenhoeck & Ruprecht, Göttingen, 1966.

Iamblichus, *On the Pythagorean Way of Life*, trans. John Dillon and Jackson Hershbell, Society of Biblical Literature (Texts and Translations 29, Greco-Roman Religion Series 11), Atlanta, GA, 1991.

Iamblichus, *On the Mysteries*, trans. Emma C. Clarke, John M. Dillon, and Jackson P. Hershbell, Society of Biblical Literature, Atlanta, GA, 2003.

Ideler, Julius Ludwig, *Physici et Medici Graeci Minores*, 2 vols., Reimeri, Berlin, 1841.

Irby-Massie, Georgia L., and Paul T. Keyser, *Greek Science of the Hellenistic Era: A Sourcebook*, Routledge, London, 2002.

Jasnow, Richard Lewis, and Karl-Theodor Zauzich, *Conversations in the House of Life: A New Translation of the Ancient Egyptian Book of Thoth*, Harrassowitz Verlag, Wiesbaden, 2014.

John Lydus, *De Ostentis* = Ioannes Lydus, *On Celestial Signs (De Ostentis)*, ed. and trans. Anastasius C. Bandy, Edwin Mellen Press, Lewiston, NY, 2013.

John of Nikiu, *The Chronicle of John, Bishop of Nikiu*, trans. R. H. Charles, The Text and Translation Society, Oxford University Press, 1916.

John Philoponus, *Ioannes Philoponus, De usu astrolabii eiusque constructione / Über die Anwendung des Astrolabs und seine Anfertigung*, ed. Alfred Stückelberger, De Gruyter, Berlin, 2015.

Johnson, Aaron P., *Religion and Identity in Porphyry of Tyre: The Limits of Hellenism in Late Antiquity. Greek Culture in the Roman world*, Cambridge University Press, Cambridge/New York, 2013.

Jones, Alexander, "The Place of Astronomy in Roman Egypt," in: *The Sciences in Greco-Roman Society*, ed. T. D. Barnes, Edmonton (*Apeiron*, vol. 27, no. 4), 1994, pp. 25–51.

Jones, Alexander, *Astronomical Papyri from Oxyrhynchus*, 2 vols. bound in one, American Philosophical Society, Philadelphia, 1999.

Jones, Alexander, "Maximus," in: *The Encyclopedia of Ancient Natural Scientists*, ed. Keyser and Irby-Massie, 2008, p. 536.

Jones, Alexander, "Timaios," in: *The Encyclopedia of Ancient Natural Scientists*, ed. Keyser and Irby-Massie, 2008, p. 810.

Jones, Alexander (ed.), *Ptolemy in Perspective: Use and Criticism of His Work from Antiquity to the Nineteenth Century*, Archimedes vol. 23, Springer, Dordrecht/New York, 2010.

Jones, Alexander, "Ancient Rejection and Adoption of Ptolemy's Frame of Reference for Longitudes," in: *Ptolemy in Perspective*, ed. Jones, 2010, pp. 11–44.

Jones, Alexander, and John M. Steele, "A New Discovery of a Component of Greek Astrology in Babylonian Tablets: The 'Terms'," *ISAW Papers*, vol. 1, 2011 (http://dlib.nyu.edu/awdl/isaw/isaw-papers/1/).

Jones, Alexander, "Ptolemy (astronomer, mathematician)," in: *The Encyclopedia of Ancient History*, ed. Bagnall et al, 2012, pp. 5651–4.

Jones, Prudence, "Celestial and Terrestrial Orientation: The Origins of House Division in Ancient Cosmology," in: *History and Astrology: Clio and Urania Confer*, ed. Annabella Kitson, Unwin, London, 1989, pp. 27–46.

Juvenal, *The Satires*, trans. Niall Rudd, Oxford University Press, Oxford, 1991.

Juvenal and Persius, *Juvenal and Persius*, ed. and trans. Susanna Morton Braund, Loeb Classical Library 91, Harvard University Press, Cambridge, MA, 2004.

Karamanolis, George, "Porphurios of Tyre," in: *The Encyclopedia of Ancient Natural Scientists*, ed. Keyser and Irby-Massie, 2008, pp. 688–89.

Kelley, Nicole, *Knowledge and Religious Authority in the Pseudo-Clementines: Situating the Recognitions in Fourth Century Syria*, (Wissenschaftliche Untersuchungen zum Neuen Testament 2, Reihe 213), Mohr Siebeck, Tübingen, 2006.

Keyser, Paul T., and Georgia L. Irby-Massie (eds.), *The Encyclopedia of Ancient Natural Scientists*, Routledge, London/New York, 2008.

King, David A., "A Hellenistic Astrological Table Deemed Worthy of Being Penned in Gold Ink: The Arabic Tradition of Vettius Valens' Auxiliary Function for Finding the Length of Life," in: *Studies in the History of the Exact Sciences in Honour of David Pingree*, ed. Charles Burnett, Jan P. Hogendijk, Kim Plofker, and Michio Yano, Brill, Leiden/Boston, 2004, pp. 666–714.

Klein, Jacob, *Lectures and Essays*, ed. Robert Williamson and Elliot Zuckerman, St. John's College Press, Annapolis, MD, 1985.

Koch, Walter, "Ceionius Rufius Albinus," *Astrologische Rundschau*, vol. 23 (1931), pp. 177–183.

Koch-Westenholz, Ulla, *Mesopotamian Astrology: An Introduction to Babylonian and Assyrian Celestial Divination*, Carsten Niebuhr Institute of Near Eastern Studies, Museum Tusculanum Press, Copenhagen, 1995.

Koertge, Noretta (ed.), *New Dictionary of Scientific Biography*, 8 vols., Charles Scribner's Sons, New York, NY, 2007.

Komorowska, Joanna, "Philosophical Foundation of Vettius Valens' Astrological Creed," *Eos*, vol. 83 (1995), pp. 331–335.

Komorowska, Joanna, *Vettius Valens of Antioch: An Intellectual Monography*, Ksiegarnia Akademicka, Kraków, 2004.

Krappe, Alexander Haggerty, "Tiberius and Thrasyllus," *The American Journal of Philology*, vol. 48, no. 4 (1927), pp. 359–366.

Kühn, C. G. (ed.), *Galen Claudii Galeni opera omnia*, 20 vols., Cnobloch, Leipzig, 1821–1833.

Lawrence, Marilynn, "Hellenistic Astrology," *Internet Encyclopedia of Philosophy*, 2005: http://www.iep.utm.edu/astr-hel/

Lawrence, Marilynn, "Who Thought the Stars are Causes? The Astrological Doctrine Criticized by Plotinus," in: *Metaphysical Patterns in Neoplatonism*, ed. John Finamore and Robert Berchman, University Press of the South, 2007, pp. 17–31.

Lawrence Moore, Marilynn, "The Young Gods: The Stars and Planets in Platonic Treatment of Fate," in: *Perspectives sur le néoplatonisme*, eds. Martin Achard, Wayne Hankey, and Jean-Marc Narbonne, Les Presses de l'Université Laval, Quebec, 2009, pp. 95–109.

Lehoux, Daryn, "Tomorrow's News Today: Astrology, Fate, and the Way Out," *Representations*, vol. 95 (2006), pp. 105–122.

Lehoux, Daryn, "Review of A Brief History of Ancient Astrology by Roger Beck," *The Classical Review*, vol. 58, no. 1 (Jan. 2008), pp. 288–290.

Lewis, Charlton T., and Charles Short, *A Latin Dictionary*, Clarendon Press, Oxford, 1879.

Liddell, Henry George, Robert Scott, Henry Stuart Jones, Roderick McKenzie et al (eds.), *A Greek-English Lexicon*, Clarendon Press, Oxford, rev. ed. 1996.

Lilly, William, *Christian Astrology*, 1647 (repr. Ascella, London, 1999).

Londino, Lawrence J., *Tiger Woods: A Biography*, Greenwood Press, Westport, CT, 2010.

Long, Anthony A., "Astrology: Arguments Pro and Contra," in: *Science and Speculation: Studies in Hellenistic Theory and Practice*, ed. J. Barnes, J. Brunschwig, M. Burnyeat, and M. Schofield., Cambridge University Press and Editions de la Maison des Sciences de l'Homme, Paris,1982, pp. 165–92.

Long, A. A., and D. N. Sedley, *The Hellenistic Philosophers*, 2 vols., Cambridge University Press, Cambridge, 1987.

Long, Anthony A., "Ptolemy on the Criterion: An Epistemology for the Practising Scientist," in: *The Criterion of Truth: Essays Written in Honour of George Kerferd Together with a Text and Translation (with Annotations) of Ptolemy's on the Kriterion and Hegemonikon*, ed. Pamela M. Huby and Gordon C. Neal, Liverpool University Press, Liverpool, 1989, pp. 151–78.

Longrigg, James, "Elementary Physics in the Lyceum and Stoa," *Isis*, vol. 66, no. 2 (June, 1975), pp. 211–229.

Lorenz, Dona Marie, *Tools of Astrology: Houses*, Eomega Grove Press, Topanga, CA, 1973.

Lucian, *The Passing of Peregrinus. The Runaways. Toxaris or Friendship. The Dance. Lexiphanes. The Eunuch. Astrology. The Mistaken Critic. The Parliament of the Gods. The Tyrannicide. Disowned*, trans. A. M. Harmon, Loeb Classical Library 302, Harvard University Press, Cambridge, MA, 1936.

Ludwich, Arthurus (ed.), *Maximus et Ammonis carminum de actionum auspiciis reliquiae*, Teubner, Leipzig, 1877.

Macrobius, *Commentary on the Dream of Scipio*, trans. William Harris Stahl, Columbia University Press, New York, NY, 1952.

Magdalino, Paul, *L'Orthodoxie des astrologues: La science entre le dogme et la divination à Byzance (VIIe-XIVe siècle)*, Lethielleux, Paris, 2006.

Mak, Bill M., "The Date and Nature of Sphujidhvaja's *Yavanajātaka* Reconsidered in the Light of Some Newly Discovered Materials," *History of Science in South Asia*, vol. 1 (2013), pp. 1–20.

Mak, Bill M., "The Last Chapter of Sphujidhvaja's *Yavanajātaka* Critically Edited with Notes," *SCIAMVS: Sources and Commentaries in Exact Sciences*, vol. 14 (2013), pp. 59–148.

Manetho, *The Apotelesmatika of Manetho*, ed. and trans. Robert Lopilato, PhD diss., Brown University, Providence, RI, 1998.

Manilius, Marcus, *Astronomica*, ed. and trans. G. P. Goold, Loeb Classical Library 469, Harvard University Press, Cambridge, MA, 1977 (rev. ed. 1997).

Manilius, Marcus, *M. Manilii Astronomica*, ed. George P. Goold, Teubner, Leipzig, 1985 (rev. ed. 1998).

Manitius, Carolus (ed.), *Hipparchi in Arati et Eudoxi Phaenomena Commentariorum Libri*, Teubner, Leipzig, 1894.

McCambley, Casimir, "*Against Fate* by Gregory of Nyssa," *Greek Orthodox Theological Review*, vol. 37 (1992), pp. 320–32.

McLaughlin, Raoul, *Rome and the Distant East: Trade Routes to the Ancient Lands of Arabia, India and China*, Continuum, London/New York, 2010.

Melanchthon, Philip (ed.), *Procli Paraphrasis in quatuor Ptolemaei libros de siderum effectionibus*, Oporinus, Basel, 1554.

Meyer, Marvin (ed.), *The Nag Hammadi Scriptures: The International Edition*, HarperCollins, New York, 2007.

Migne, Jacques-Paul (ed.), *Patrologia Graeca*, 166 vols., Imprimerie Catholique, Paris, 1857–1866.

Momigliano, Arnaldo, "The Fault of the Greeks," *Daedalus*, vol. 104, no. 2 (1975), pp. 9–19.

Mommsen, Theodor, "Firmicus Maternus," *Hermes*, vol. 29, no. 3 (1894), pp. 468–472.

Monroe, M. Willis, "The Micro-Zodiac in Babylon and Uruk: Seleucid Zodiacal Astrology," in: in: *The Circulation of Astronomical Knowledge in the Ancient World*, ed. Steele, 2016, pp. 117–138.

Montelle, Clemency, "The *Anaphoricus* of Hypsicles of Alexandria," in: *The Circulation of Astronomical Knowledge in the Ancient World*, ed. Steele, 2016, pp. 287–315.

Montanari, Franco, *The Brill Dictionary of Ancient Greek*, ed. Madeleine Goh, Chad Schroeder, Gregory Nagy, and Leonard Muellner, Brill, Leiden/Boston, 2015.

Moyer, Ian S., *Egypt and the Limits of Hellenism*, Cambridge University Press, Cambridge, 2011.

Neugebauer, Otto, "Demotic Horoscopes," *Journal of the American Oriental Society*, vol. 63, no. 2. (Apr. – Jun., 1943), pp. 115–127.

Neugebauer, Otto, "The Early History of the Astrolabe. Studies in Ancient Astronomy IX," *Isis*, Vol. 40, No. 3 (Aug., 1949), pp. 240–256.

Neugebauer, Otto, "The Study of Wretched Subjects," *Isis*, vol. 42, no. 2 (June 1951), p. 111.

Neugebauer, Otto, "The Horoscope of Ceionius Rufius Albinus," *The American Journal of Philology*, vol. 74, no. 4, 1953, pp. 418–420.

Neugebauer, Otto, "The Chronology of Vettius Valens' Anthologiae," *Harvard Theological Review*, 47 (1954), pp. 65–67.

Neugebauer, Otto, and H. B. van Hoesen, *Greek Horoscopes*, American Philosophical Society, Philadelphia, PA, 1959.

Neugebauer, Otto, and H. B. van Hoesen, "Astrological Papyri and Ostraca: Bibliographical Notes," *Proceedings of the American Philosophical Society*, vol. 108, no. 2 (April 15, 1964), pp. 57–72.

Neugebauer, Otto, and Richard Parker, "Two Demotic Horoscopes," *The Journal of Egyptian Archaeology*, vol. 54 (1968), pp. 231–235.

Neugebauer, Otto, *The Exact Sciences in Antiquity*, Dover, New York (2nd rev. ed.), 1969.

Neugebauer, Otto, and Richard Anthony Parker, *Egyptian Astronomical Texts, Vol. 3: Decans, Planets, Constellations and Zodiacs*, Brown University Press, Providence, RI, 1969.

Neugebauer, Otto, *A History of Ancient Mathematical Astronomy*, 3 vols., Springer, Berlin, 1975.

Noegel, Scott, Joel Walker, and Brannon Wheeler (eds.), *Prayer, Magic and the Stars in the Ancient and Late Antique World*, Pennsylvania State University Press, University Park, PA, 2003.

Nonnos, *Dionysiaca*, trans. W. H. D. Rouse, 3 vols., Loeb Classical Library, Harvard University Press, Cambridge, 1940.

Noonan, George, *Classical Scientific Astrology*, American Federation of Astrologers, Tempe, AZ, 1984 (repr. 2005).

North, John David, *Horoscopes and History*, Warburg Institute, London, 1986.

Obbink, Dirk, "Anoubion, Elegiacs" in: *The Oxyrhynchus Papyri*, vol. 66, ed. N. Gonis et al, Nos. 4503–7, Egypt Exploration Society, London, 1999, 67–109.

Oestmann, Günther, H. D. Rutkin, and Kocku von Stuckrad (eds.), *Horoscopes and Public Spheres: Essays on the History of Astrology*, (Religion and Society 42), De Gruyter, Berlin/New York, 2005.

Oliver, Revilo P, "Thrasyllus in Tacitus (Ann. 6.21)," *Illinois Classical Studies*, vol. 5 (1980), pp. 130–148.

Olympiodorus, *Heliodori, ut dicitur, In Paulum Alexandrinum commentarium*, ed. Æ. Boer, Teubner, Leipzig, 1962.

Olympiodorus, *Olympiodori in Platonis Gorgiam commentaria*, ed. Leendert Gerrit Westerink, Teubner, Leipzig, 1970.

Olympiodorus, *Commentary on Plato's Gorgias*, trans. Robin Jackson, Kimon Lycos, and Harold Tarrant, Brill, Boston, MA, 1998.

Origen, *Philocalia*, trans. George Lewis, T. and T. Clark, Edinburgh, 1911.

Packman, Zola M., "Instructions for the Use of Planet Markers on a Horoscope Board," *Zeitschrift für Papyrologie und Epigraphik*, vol. 74 (1988), pp. 85–95.

Panaino, Antonio, "The Two Astrological Reports of the Kārnāmag ī Ardašīr ī Pābagān (III, 4-7; IV, 6-7)," *Die Sprache*, vol. 36, no. 2 (1994), pp. 181–96.

Panaino, Antonio, "Cosmologies and Astrology," in: *The Wiley Blackwell Companion to Zoroastrianism*, ed. Michael Stausberg, Yuhan Sohrab-Dinshaw Vevaina, and Anna Tessmann, Wiley, Chichester, 2015.

Paolo d'Alessandria, *Introduzione all'astrologia. Lineamenti introduttivi alla previsione astronomica*, trans. Giuseppe Bezza, Mimesis, Milan, 2000.

Papathanassiou, Maria, "Stephanos of Alexandria: A Famous Byzantine Scholar, Alchemist and Astrologer," in: *The Occult Sciences in Byzantium*, ed. Paul Magdalino and Maria Mavroudi, La Pomme d'Or, Geneva, 2006, pp. 163–203.

Papathanassiou, Maria, "Stephanus of Athens," in: *New Dictionary of Scientific Biography*, ed. Koertge, vol. 6, 2007, pp. 516–8.

Parker, Richard Anthony, *A Vienna Demotic Papyrus on Eclipse- and Lunar-Omina*, Brown University Press, Providence, 1959.

Parker, Richard, "A Horoscopic Text in Triplicate," in: *Grammata Demotika: Festschrift für Erich Lüddeckens zum 15. Juni 1983*, ed. Heinz-J. Thissen and Karl-Th. Zauzich, Gisela Zauzich Verlag, Würzburg, 1984, pp. 141–143.

Parpola, Simo, *Letters from Assyrian Scholars to the Kings Esarhaddon and Assurbanipal*, 2 vols., Alter Orient und Altes Testament 5/1–2, Butzon and Bercker, Kevelaer, 1970–1983.

Parsons, Peter, *City of the Sharp-Nosed Fish: Greek Lives in Roman Egypt*, Weidenfeld and Nicolson, London, 2007.

Paton, W. R. (trans.), *The Greek Anthology*, 5 vols., Loeb Classical Library, Cambrige University Press, Cambridge, 1916–1918.

Paulus of Alexandria, *Pauli Alexandrini Elementa Apotelesmatica*, ed. Æ Boer, Teubner, Leipzig, 1958.

Paulus Alexandrinus, *Introductory Matters*, trans. Robert Schmidt, ed. Robert Hand, The Golden Hind Press, Berkeley Springs, WV, 1993 (2nd ed. rev.).

Paulus Alexandrinus and Olympiodorus, *Late Classical Astrology: Paulus Alexandrinus and Olympiodorus, with the Scholia from Later Commentators*, trans. Dorian Gieseler Greenbaum, ed. Robert Hand, ARHAT, Reston, VA, 2001.

Paul of Alexandria, *Introduction to Astrology*, trans. James Herschel Holden, American Federation of Astrologers, Tempe, AZ, 2012.

Pedersen, Olaf, *A Survey of the Almagest: With Annotation and New Commentary by Alexander Jones*, Springer, New York, 2010.

Pérez Jiménez, Aurelio, "Pseudepígrafos de la astrología griega," in: *Mundus vult decipi: Estudios interdisciplinares sobre falsificación textual y literaria*, ed. Javier Martínez, Ediciones Clásicas, Madrid, 2012, pp. 271–284.

Pingree, David, "The Indian Iconography of the Decans and Horâs," *Journal of the Warburg and Courtauld Institutes*, vol. 26, no. 3/4 (1963), pp. 223–54.

Pingree, David, "The Astrological School of John Abramius," *Dumbarton Oaks Papers*, vol. 25 (1971), pp. 189–215.

Pingree, David, "Paul of Alexandria," in: *Dictionary of Scientific Biography*, ed. Gillispie, 1974, vol. 10, p. 419.

Pingree, David, "Petosiris," in: *Dictionary of Scientific Biography*, ed. Gillispie, 1974, vol. 10, pp. 547–9.

Pingree, David, "Astrology," in: *Dictionary of the History of Ideas*, ed. Weiner, vol. 1, 1974, pp. 118–126.

Pingree, David, "Antiochus and Rhetorius," *Classical Philology*, vol. 72, no. 3 (1977), pp. 203–23.

Pingree, David (ed. and trans.), *The Yavanajātaka of Sphujidhvaja*, 2 vols., Harvard Oriental Series 48, Cambridge, MA, 1978.

Pingree, David, "Review of Manilius, *Astronomica*, trans. G. P. Goold," *Phoenix*, Classical Association of Canada, vol. 34, no. 3 (Autumn, 1980), pp. 263–266.

Pingree, David, "Classical and Byzantine Astrology in Sassanian Persia," *Dumbarton Oaks Papers*, vol. 43 (1989), pp. 227–239.

Pingree, David, "The Teaching of the Almagest in Late Antiquity," *Apeiron*, vol. 27, no. 4 (Dec. 1994), pp. 75–98.

Pingree, David, *From Astral Omens to Astrology, from Babylon to Bīkāner*, Serie Orientale Roma 78, Istituto italiano per l'Africa e l'oriente, Rome, 1997.

Pingree, "Review of Tamsyn S. Barton, *Power and Knowledge: Astrology, Physiognomics, and Medicine under the Roman Empire*," *Bulletin of the History of Medicine*, vol. 71, no. 2 (1997), p. 331.

Pingree, David, "Māshā'allāh's (?) Arabic Translation of Dorotheus," in: *La science des cieux. Sages, mages, astrologues*, ed. Rika Gyselen, Bures-sur-Yvette (Res Orientales 12), 1999, pp. 191–209.

Pingree, David, "From Alexandria to Baghdad to Byzantium. The Transmission of Astrology," *International Journal of the Classical Tradition*, vol. 8, no. 1 (Summer 2001), pp. 3–37.

Plato, *Charmides, Alcibiades 1 and 2, Hipparchus, The Lovers, Theages, Minos, Epinomis.*, trans. W. R. M. Lamb, Loeb Classical Library, Harvard University Press, Cambridge, MA, 1927 (repr. 1979).

Plato, *Timaeus and Critias*, trans. Robin Waterfield, Oxford University Press, Oxford, 2008.

Pliny, *Natural History*, trans. Rackham, Jones, et al, 10 vols., Loeb Classical Library, Harvard University Press, Cambridge, MA, 1938–1983.

Plotinus, *The Enneads*, trans. A. H. Armstrong, 7 vols., Loeb Classical Library, Harvard University Press, Cambridge, MA, 1966–88.

Pollock, Dale, *Skywalking: The Life and Films of George Lucas*, Da Capo Press, New York, NY, rev. ed. 1999.

Porphyry, *Letter to Anebo = Porfirio. Lettera ad Anebo*, ed. A. R. Sodano, L'Arte Tipografica, Naples, 1958.

Porphyry, *On the Cave of the Nymphs*, trans. Robert Lamberton, Station Hill Press, Barrytown, NY, 1983.

Porphyry, *On the Life of Plotinus and the Arrangement of his Works*, in: *Neoplatonic Saints: The Lives of Plotinus and Proclus by their Students*, trans. Mark Edwards, Liverpool University Press, Liverpool, 2000.

Porphyry, *Porphyry Against the Christians*, trans. R. M. Berchman, Ancient Mediterranean and Medieval Texts and Contexts 1, Brill, Leiden, 2005.

Porphyry the Philosopher, *Introduction to the Tetrabiblos, and Serapio of Alexandria, Astrological Definitions*, trans. James Herschel Holden, American Federation of Astrologers, Tempe, AZ, 2009.

Porphyry, *Introduction to the Tetrabiblos of Ptolemy*, trans. Demetra George, unpublished.

Porphyry of Tyre, *An Introduction to the Tetrabiblos of Ptolemy*, trans. Andrea L. Gehrz, Moira Press, Portland, 2010.

Porphyry, *To Gaurus on How Embryos are Ensouled and On What is in Our Power*, trans. James Wilberding, Ancient Commentators on Aristotle, ed. Richard Sorabji, Bristol Classics Press, 2011.

Porphyry, *Porphyry's Commentary on Ptolemy's Harmonics: A Greek Text and Annotated Translation*, trans. Andrew Baker, Cambridge University Press, Cambridge, 2015.

Proclus, *Procli Diadochi in Platonis rem publicam commentarii*, ed. Wilhem Kroll, 2 vols., Teubner, Leipzig, 1899–1901.

Proclus, *Commentary on Plato's Timaeus, Volume V, Book 4: Proclus on Time and the Stars*, ed. and trans. Dirk Baltzly, Cambridge University Press, Cambridge, 2007.

Prokopios, *The Secret History, With Related Texts*, ed. and trans. Anthony Kaldellis, Hackett Publishing, Indianapolis, IN, 2010.

Pseudo-Clement, *Homilies*, edited in *Patrologia Graeca*, ed. Migne, vol. 2, Paris, 1857, cols. 57–468; translated in *The Ante-Nicene Fathers*, vol. 8, ed. A. Roberts and J. Dondaldson, New York, 1895, pp. 223–346.

Ptolemy, Claudius, *Ptolemy's Tetrabiblos, or Quadripartite: Being Four Books of the Influence of the Stars*, trans. J. M. Ashmand, Davis and Dickson, London, 1822.

Ptolemy, Claudius, *Tetrabiblos*, ed. and trans. F. E. Robbins, Loeb Classical Library, Harvard University Press, Cambridge, MA, 1940 (repr. 2001).

Ptolemy, Claudius, *Phases of the Fixed Stars*, trans. Robert Schmidt, ed. Robert Hand, The Golden Hind Press, Berkeley Springs, WV, 1993.

Ptolemy, Claudius, *Tetrabiblos, Book I*, trans. Robert Schmidt, ed. Robert Hand, The Golden Hind Press, Berkeley Springs, WV, 1994.

Ptolemy, Claudius, *Tetrabiblos, Book III*, trans. Robert Schmidt, ed. Robert Hand, The Golden Hind Press, Berkeley Springs, WV, 1996.

Ptolemy, Claudius, *Tetrabiblos, Book IV*, trans. Robert H. Schmidt, The Golden Hind Press, Cumberland, MD, 1998.

Ptolemy, Claudius, *Claudii Ptolemaei opera quae exstant omnia, vol. III, 1: ΑΠΟΤΕΛΕΣΜΑΤΙΚΑ, post F. Boll et Æ. Boer secundis curis*, ed. Wolfgang Hübner, Teubner, Stuttgart/Leipzig, 1998.

Ptolemy, Claudius, *Ptolemy's Almagest*, trans. G. J. Toomer, Princeton University Press, Princeton, NJ, 1998.

Ptolemy, Claudius, *Ptolemy's Tetrabiblos in the Translation of William of Moerbeke: Claudii Ptolemaei Liber Iudicialium*, ed. Gudrun Vuillemin-Diem and Carlos Steel, with the assistance of Pieter De Leemans, Ancient and Medieval Philosophy Series 1, 19, Leuven University Press, Leuven, 2015.

Quack, Joachim Friedrich, "Les Mages Égyptianisés? Remarks on Some Surprising Points in Supposedly Magusean Texts," *Journal of Near Eastern Studies*, vol. 65, no. 4 (2006), pp. 267–82.

Quack, Joachim Friedrich, "On the Concomitancy of the Seemingly Incommensurable, or Why Egyptian Astral Tradition Needs to be Analyzed within Its Cultural Context," in: *The Circulation of Astronomical Knowledge in the Ancient World*, ed. Steele, 2016, pp. 230–244.

Reed, Annette Yoshiko, "Abraham as Chaldean Scientist and Father of the Jews: Josephus, *Ant.* 1.154-168 and the Greco-Roman Discourse About Astronomy/Astrology," *Journal for the Study of Judaism in the Persian, Hellenistic and Roman Period*, vol. 35, no. 2 (2004), pp. 119–158.

Rhetorius the Egyptian, *Astrological Compendium Containing his Explanation and Narration of the Whole Art of Astrology*, trans. James H. Holden, American Federation of Astrologers, Tempe, AZ, 2009.

Rafaelli, Enrico G., *L'oroscopo del mondo: Il tema di nascita del mondo e del primo uomo secondo l'astrologia zoroastriana*, Mimesis, Milan, 2001.

Ricl, Marijana, "Neokoroi in the Greek World," *Belgrade Historical Review*, vol. 2, 2011, pp. 7–26.

Riess, Ernestus, "Nechepsonis et Petosiridis fragmenta magica," in: *Philologus*, suppl. 6 (1891–93), pp. 325–394.

Riggs, Christina, *The Oxford Handbook of Roman Egypt*, Oxford University Press, Oxford, 2012.

Riley, Mark, "Theoretical and Practical Astrology: Ptolemy and his Colleagues," *Transactions of the American Philological Association*, vol. 117 (1987), pp. 235–56.

Riley, Mark, *A Survey of Vettius Valens*, originally published online in 1996; last accessed August 2, 2016: http://www.csus.edu/indiv/r/rileymt/PDF_folder/VettiusValens.PDF

Robbins, Frank Egleston, "A New Astrological Treatise: Michigan Papyrus No. 1," *Classical Philology*, vol. 22, no. 1 (1927), pp. 1–45.

Robbins, Frank Egleston (ed. and trans.), "Michigan Papyrus 149: Astrological Treatise," in: *Michigan Papyri, Vol. III, Papyri in the University of Michigan Collection, Miscellaneous Papyri*, ed. John Garret Winter, University of Michigan Press, Ann Arbor, MI, 1936, pp. 62–117.

Rochberg-Halton, Francesca, "New Evidence for the History of Astrology," *Journal of Near Eastern Studies*, vol. 43, no. 2 (1984), pp. 115–140.

Rochberg-Halton, Francesca, "TCL 6 13: Mixed Traditions in Late Babylonian Astrology," *Zeitschrift für Assyriologie und Vorderasiatische Archäologie*, vol. 77, no. 2 (1987), pp. 207–228.

Rochberg-Halton, Francesca, "Elements of the Babylonian Contribution to Hellenistic Astrology," *Journal of the American Oriental Society*, vol. 108, no. 1 (1988), pp. 51–62.

Rochberg-Halton, Francesca, *Aspects of Babylonian Celestial Divination: The Lunar Eclipse Tablets of Enūma Anu Enlil*, Archiv für Orientforschung Beiheft 22, Ferdinand Berger und Söhne, Horn, Austria, 1988.

Rochberg-Halton, Francesca, "Benefic and Malefic Planets in Babylonian Astrology," in: *A Scientific Humanist: Studies in Memory of Abraham Sachs*, eds. Erle Leichty, Pamela Gerardi, Abraham Sachs, Maria deJ Ellis, University of Pennsylvania, Philadelphia, PA, 1988, pp. 319–324.

Rochberg, Francesca, *Babylonian Horoscopes*, Transactions of the American Philosophical Society, vol. 88, part 1, American Philosophical Society, Philadelphia, PA, 1998.

Rochberg, Francesca, "Heaven and Earth: Divine-Human Relations in Mesopotamian Celestial Divination," in: *Prayer, Magic, and the Stars in the Ancient and Late Antique World*, ed. Scott B. Noegel, Joel Walker, and Brannon M. Wheeler, Pennsylvania State University Press, University Park, PA, 2003, pp. 169–185.

Rochberg, Francesca, *The Heavenly Writing: Divination, Horoscopy, and Astronomy in Mesopotamian Culture*, Cambridge University Press, Cambridge, 2004.

Rochberg, Francesca, "Teukros of Egyptian Babylon," in: *The Encyclopedia of Ancient Natural Scientists*, ed. Keyser and Irby-Massie, 2008, p. 778.

Ross, Micah T., *Horoscopic Ostraca from Medînet Mâdi*, PhD diss., Brown University, 2006.

Ross, Micah, "A Survey of Demotic Astrological Texts," *Culture and Cosmos*, vol. 11, nos. 1 and 2 (2007), pp. 1–25.

Rudolf, Stefanie, "Propaganda for Astrology in Aramaic Literature," *Aramaic Studies*, vol. 12, no. 1 (2014), pp. 121–134.

Ruggles, Clive L. N. (ed.), *Handbook of Archaeoastronomy and Ethnoastronomy*, Springer, New York, 2015.

Rutkin, Darrel H., "Astrology," in: *The Cambridge History of Science, Volume 3: Early Modern Science*, ed. Katharine Park and Lorraine Daston, Cambridge University Press, Cambridge, 2006, pp. 541–561.

Ryholt, Kim, "New Light on the Legendary King Nechepsos of Egypt," *The Journal of Egyptian Archaeology*, vol. 97 (2011), pp. 61–72.

Sachs, Abraham, "Babylonian Horoscopes," *Journal of Cuneiform Studies*, vol. 6, no. 2 (1952), pp. 49–75.

Sachs, Abraham J. and Hermann Hunger, *Astronomical Diaries and Related Texts from Babylonia*, 6 vols., Österreichische Akademie der Wissenschaften, Vienna, 1988–2006.

Salaman, Clement, Dorine van Oyen, William D. Wharton, and Jean-Pierre Mahé (trans.), *The Way of Hermes: New Translations of the Corpus Hermeticum and the Definitions of Hermes Trismegistus to Asclepius*, Inner Traditions, Rochester, VT, 1999 (repr. 2004).

Saliba, George, *A History of Arabic Astronomy: Planetary Theories During the Golden Age of Islam*, New York University Press, New York, 1994.

Sandwell, Isabella, "Outlawing 'Magic' or Outlawing 'Religion'? Libanius and the Theodosian Code as Evidence for Legislation against 'Pagan' Practices," in: *The Spread of Christianity in the First Four Centuries: Essays in Explanation*, ed. W. V. Harris, Brill, Leiden, pp. 87–123.

Sallustius, *Concerning the Gods and the Universe*, trans. Arthur Darby Nock, 1926 (repr. Cambridge University Press, Cambridge, 2013).

Schmidt, Robert, and Robert Hand, *Project Hindsight Companion to the Greek Track*, The Golden Hind Press, Berkeley Springs, WV, 1994.

Schmidt, Robert (trans.), and Robert Hand (ed.), *Dorotheus, Orpheus, Anubio, and Pseudo-Valens. Teachings on Transits*, The Golden Hind Press, Berkeley Springs, WV, 1995.

Schmidt, Robert (trans.), and Robert Hand (ed.), *The Astrological Record of the Early Sages in Greek*, The Golden Hind Press, Berkeley Springs, WV, 1995.

Schmidt, Robert, "Facets of Fate: The Rationale Underlying the Hellenistic System of Houses," *The Mountain Astrologer*, no. 88 (Dec./Jan. 2000), pp. 83–126.

Schmidt, Robert H., *Kepler College Sourcebook of Hellenistic Astrological Texts*, Phaser Foundation, Cumberland, MD, 2005.

Schmidt, Robert H., and Ellen Black, "Peak Times and Patterns in the Life of Dane Rudhyar," National Council for Geocosmic Research *Geocosmic Journal*, Fall 2006, pp. 35–43.

Schmidt, Robert H. (ed. and trans.), *Antiochus, with Porphyry, Rhetorius, Serapio, Thrasyllus, Antigonus et al., Definitions and Foundations*, The Golden Hind Press, Cumberland, MD, 2009.

Schmidt, Robert H., *The So-Called 'Problem of House Division': Definitions of Greek Terms and New Translations of Key Passages*, PDF e-book companion to an audio lecture, Project Hindsight, Cumberland, MD, 2016.

Scott, Walter (ed. and trans.), *Hermetica: The Ancient Greek and Latin Writings which Contain Religious or Philosophic Teachings Ascribed to Hermes Trismegistus*, 4 vols., Oxford, 1924 (repr. Shambhala, Boston, 1993).

Sedley, David (ed.), *The Philosophy of Antiochus*, Cambridge University Press, Cambridge/New York, 2012.

Seneca, *Naturales Quaestiones*, trans. T. H. Corcoran, 2 vols., Loeb Classical Library, Harvard University Press, London/Cambridge, 1971–2.

Seneca, *Letters From a Stoic: Epistulae morales ad Lucilium*, trans. Robin Campbell, Penguin Classics, 1969 (repr. 2004).

Seneca, *Dialogues and Essays*, trans. John Davie, Oxford University Press, Oxford, 2007.

Seneca, Lucius Annaeus, *Anger, Mercy, Revenge. The Complete Works of Lucius Annaeus Seneca*, trans. Robert A. Kaster and Martha C. Nussbaum, University of Chicago Press, Chicago/London, 2010.

Serapion of Alexandria, *Paranomasiai or Definitions of the Configurations of the Stars*, trans. Eduardo J. Gramaglia, The Hellenistic Astrology Website, 2013, http://www.hellenisticastrology.com/translations/serapion-definitions.pdf

Seutonius, *Lives of the Caesars*, trans. Catharine Edwards, Oxford University Press, Oxford, 2000.

Sextus Empiricus, *Against the Professors*, trans. R. G. Bury, Loeb Classical Library 382, Harvard University Press, Cambridge, MA, 1949 (repr. 2000).

Sextus Empiricus, *Against the Physicists, Against the Ethicists*, trans. R. G. Bury, Loeb Classical Library 311, Harvard University Press, Cambridge, MA, 1949.

Sextus Empiricus, *Sesto Empirico: Contro gli astrologi*, ed. and trans. Emidio Spinelli, Centro Di Studio Del Pensiero Antico, Elenchus XXXII, Bibliopolis, Naples, 2000.

Sharples, Robert, "The Stoic Background to the Middle Platonist Discussion of Fate," in *Platonic Stoicism – Stoic Platonism*, ed. M. Bonazzi and C. Helmig, Leuven University Press, Leuven, 2007, pp. 169–188.

Shipley, Graham, *The Greek World After Alexander, 323–30 B.C.*, Routledge, London, 2000.

Sidoli, Nathan, and Berggren, J. L., "The Arabic version of Ptolemy's *Planisphere* or *Flattening the Surface of the Sphere*: Text, Translation, Commentary," *SCIAMVS: Sources and Commentaries in Exact Sciences*, vol. 8 (2007), pp. 37–139.

Smith, A. Mark, "Ptolemy and the Foundations of Ancient Mathematical Optics: A Source Based Guided Study," *Transactions of the American Philosophical Society*, vol. 89, no. 3 (1999), pp. 1–172.

Spiegelberg, Wilhelm, "Die ägyptische Namen und Zeichen der Tierkreisbilder in demotischer Schrift," *Zeitschrift für ägyptische Sprache und Altertumskunde*, vol. 48, pp. 145–151.

Steele, J. M., "Greek influence on Babylonian astronomy?," *Mediterranean Archaeology and Archaeometry*, vol. 6, no. 3 (2006), pp. 153–160.

Steele, J. M., "A Late Babylonian Compendium of Calendrical and Stellar Astrology," *Journal of Cuneiform Studies*, vol. 67 (2015), pp. 187–215.

Steele, John M., *The Circulation of Astronomical Knowledge in the Ancient World*, Brill, Leiden/Boston, 2016.

Struck, Peter T., "A World Full of Signs: Understanding Divination in Ancient Stoicism," in: *Seeing with Different Eyes: Essays on Astrology and Divination*, ed. Patrick Curry and Angela Voss, Cambridge Scholars Press, Newcastle, 2008, pp. 3–20.

Struck, Peter T., "Hermetic writings," in: *The Encyclopedia of Ancient History*, ed. Bagnall et al, 2012, pp. 3161–3.

Swartz, Michael D., "Ancient Jewish Mysticism," in: *Jewish Mysticism and Kabbalah: New Insights and Scholarship*, ed. Frederick E. Greenspahn, New York University Press, New York, 2011.

Swerdlow, Noel M. (ed.), *Ancient Astronomy and Celestial Divination*, MIT Press, Cambridge, MA, 1999.

Tacitus, *The Annals of Imperial Rome*, trans. Michael Grant, Penguin Books, London, 1956 (rev. ed. 1989).

Tarán, Leonardo, *Academica: Plato, Philip of Opus, and the pseudo-Platonic Epinomis*, American Philosophical Society, Philadelphia, 1975.

Tarrant, Harold, *Thrasyllan Platonism*, Cornell University Press, Ithaca, NY, 1993.

Tester, Jim, *A History of Western Astrology*, The Boydell Press, Woodbrige, 1987.

Thayer, Joseph Henry, *Thayer's Greek-English Lexicon of the New Testament*, National Foundation of Christian Education, Marshallton, DE, 1889.

Thomann, Johannes, "Square Horoscope Diagrams in Middle Eastern Astrology and Chinese Cosmological Diagrams: Were These Designs Transmitted Through the Silk Road?," in: *The Journey of Maps and Images on the Silk Road*, ed. Philippe Forêt and Andreas Kaplony, Brill, Leiden, 2008, pp. 97–117.

Thorndike, Lynn, "A Roman Astrologer as a Historical Source: Julius Firmicus Maternus," *Classical Philology*, vol. 8, no. 4, (Oct. 1913), pp. 415–435.

Thorndike, Lynn, *A History of Magic and Experimental Science*, 8 vols., Columbia University Press, New York, 1923–58.

Timaios of Locri, *On the Nature of the World and the Soul*, trans. Thomas H. Tobin, Society of Biblical Literature (Texts and Translations 26, Graeco-Roman Religion Series 8), Scholars Press, Chico, CA, 1985.

Toomer, G. J., "Hipparchus," in: *Dictionary of Scientific Biography*, ed. Gillispie, vol. 15, 1978, pp. 207–24.

Unterman, Alan (ed. and trans.), *The Kabbalistic Tradition: An Anthology of Jewish Mysticism*, Penguin Classics, London/New York, 2008.

Valens, Vettius, *Vettii Valentis Anthologiarum Libri*, ed. Wilhem Kroll, Weidman, Berlin, 1908.

Valens, Vettius, *Vettius Valens d'Antioche, Anthologies, Livre I: etablissement, traduction et commentaire*, ed. and trans. Joëlle-Frédérique Bara, Brill, Leiden/New York, 1989.

Valens, Vettius, *Vettii Valentis Antiocheni anthologiarum libri novem*, ed. David Pingree, Teubner, Leipzig, 1986.

Valens, Vettius, *The Anthology, Book I*, trans. Robert Schmidt, ed. Robert Hand, The Golden Hind Press, Berkeley Springs, WV, 1993.

Valens, Vettius, *The Anthology*, Book I, Part 1, trans. Robert Schmidt, ed. Robert Hand, The Golden Hind Press, Berkeley Springs, WV, 1994.

Valens, Vettius, *The Anthology, Book II (concl.), & Book III*, trans. Robert Schmidt, ed. Robert Hand, The Golden Hind Press, Berkeley Springs, WV, 1994.

Valens, Vettius, *The Anthology, Book IV*, trans. Robert Schmidt, ed. Robert Hand, The Golden Hind Press, Berkeley Springs, WV, 1996.

Valens, Vettius, *The Anthology, Book V & VI*, trans. Robert Schmidt, ed. Robert Hand, The Golden Hind Press, Cumberland, MD, 1997.

Valens, Vettius, *The Anthology, Book VII*, trans. Robert Schmidt, The PHASER Foundation, Cumberland, MD, 2001.

Valens, Vettius, *Blütensträuße*, trans. Otto Schönberger und Eberhard Knobloch, Subsidia Classica, 7, Scripta Mercaturae Verlag, St. Katharinen, 2004.

Valens, Vettius, *Anthology, Book 1*, trans. James Herschel Holden, American Federation of Astrologers, Tempe, AZ, 1994 (rev. ed. 2009), privately circulated.

Valens, Vettius, *Anthologies*, trans. Mark T. Riley, originally released online in December 2010; last accessed August 2, 2016. http://www.csus.edu/indiv/r/rileymt/Vettius%20Valens%20entire.pdf

Valerius Maximus, *Memorable Deeds and Sayings, Book 1*, ed. and trans. David Wardle, Clarendon Press, Oxford, 1998.

Van der Horst, Pieter Willem, *Chaeremon: Egyptian Priest and Stoic Philosopher. The fragments collected and translated with explanatory notes*, Brill, Leiden/New York, 1987.

Van der Sluijs, Marinus Anthony, "A Possible Babylonian Precursor to the Theory of *Ecpyrōsis*," *Culture and Cosmos*, vol. 9, no. 2 (2005), pp. 1–19.

Varro, *On the Latin Language*, trans. Roland G. Kent, vol. 1, Loeb Classical Library 333, Harvard University Press, Cambridge, MA, 1938.

Vasunia, Phiroze (trans.), *Zarathushtra and the Religion of Ancient Iran: The Greek and Latin Sources in Translation*, The K. R. Cama Oriental Institute, Mumbai, 2007.

Verbrugghe, Gerald, and John M. Wickersham, *Berossos, and Manetho, Introduced and Translated: Native Traditions in Ancient Mesopotamia and Egypt*, University of Michigan Press, Ann Arbor, MI, 1996.

Vitruvius, *On Architecture, Volume II: Books 6-10*, trans. F. Granger, Loeb Classical Library 280, Harvard University Press, Cambridge, MA, 1934.

Volk, Katharina, "Review of *A Brief History of Ancient Astrology* by Roger Beck," *Aestimatio*, vol. 3 (2006), pp. 162–165.

Volk, Katharina, *Manilius and his Intellectual Background*, Oxford University Press, Oxford/New York, 2009.

Warren, James, *Presocratics: Natural Philosophers Before Socrates*, University of California Press, Berkeley/Los Angeles, 2007.

Waterfield, Robin, "The Evidence for Astrology in Classical Greece," *Culture and Cosmos*, vol. 3, no. 2 (1999), pp. 3–15.

Wiener, Philip P. (ed.), *Dictionary of the History of Ideas: Studies of Selected Pivotal Ideas*, 4 vols., Charles Scribner's Sons, New York, 1973.

Wee, John Z., "Discovery of the Zodiac Man in Cuneiform," *Journal of Cuneiform Studies*, vol. 67 (2015), pp. 217–33.

Wee, John Z., "Virtual Moons over Babylonia: The Calendar Text System, Its Micro-Zodiac of 13, and the Making of Medical Zodiology," in: *The Circulation of Astronomical Knowledge in the Ancient World*, ed. Steele, 2016, pp. 139–229.

Weinstock, Stefan, "C. Fonteius Capito and the 'Libri Tagetici'," *Papers of the British School at Rome*, vol. 18 (1950), pp. 44–49.

Westerink, L. G., "Ein astrologisches Kolleg aus dem Jahre 564," *Byzantinische Zeitschrift*, vol. 64 (1971), pp. 6–21.

Williams, Clemency, "Some Details on the Transmission of Astral Omens in Antiquity," in: *From the Banks of the Euphrates: Studies in Honor of Alice Louise Slotsky*, ed. Micah Ross, Eisenbrauns, Winona Lake, IN, 2008, pp. 295–318.

Williams, Craig A., *Roman Homosexuality: Ideologies of Masculinity in Classical Antiquity*, Oxford University Press, New York, NY, 1999.

Wilson, Malcolm, and Demetra George, "Anonymi, *De Decubitu*: Contexts of Rationality," *Museion*, series III, vol. 6, no. 3 (2006), pp. 439–52.

Winkler, Andreas, "On the Astrological Papyri from the Tebtunis Temple Library," in: *Actes du IXe Congrès International des Études Démotiques; Paris, 31 août–3 septembre 2005*, ed. Ghislaine Widmer and Didier Devauchelle, Bibliothèque d'étude 147, Cairo, 2009, pp. 361–375.

Winkler, Andreas, *Looking at the Future: Divination and Astrology in Ancient Egypt*, PhD diss., Uppsala University, 2011.

Winkler, Andreas, "Some Astrologers and Their Handbooks in Demotic Egyptian," in: *The Circulation of Astronomical Knowledge in the Ancient World*, ed. Steele, 2016, pp. 245–286.

Wolf, Hieronymus (ed.), *Claudii Ptolemaei Quadripartitum enarrator ignoti nominis, quem tamen Proclum fuisse quidam existimant; PWorphyrii philosophi introductio in Ptolemaei opus de effectibus astrorum; Hermetis philosophi de revolutionibus nativitatum libri duo incerto interprete*, Basel, 1559.

Young, Gary K., *Rome's Eastern Trade: International Commerce and Imperial Policy, 31 BC–AD 305*, Routledge, London/New York, 2001.

Zoller, Robert, *The Lost Key to Prediction: The Arabic Parts in Astrology*, Inner Traditions, New York, NY, 1980.

Zosimos of Panopolis, *On the Letter Omega*, ed. and trans. Howard M. Jackson, Society of Biblical Literature (Texts and Translations 14; Graeco-Roman Religion 5), 1978.

Index

CPSIA information can be obtained
at www.ICGtesting.com
Printed in the USA
LVHW101557010920
664635LV00001B/50